HUMAN
MEMORY

Cognitive Psychology Program

Senior Consulting Editor
James S. Nairne (Purdue University)
Consulting Editors
Martin Conway (University of Leeds, UK)
Stephan Lewandowsky (University of Western Australia, AUS)
Elizabeth F. Loftus (University of California at Irvine, USA)
Mark McDaniel (Washington University in St. Louis, USA)
Hal Pashler (University of California at San Diego, USA)

SAGE Publications is pleased to announce a new, international program of titles in cognitive psychology—both textbook and reference—brought together by a team of consultant editors led by James S. Nairne, the *SAGE Cognitive Psychology Program*. Featuring books written or edited by world-leading scholars (or younger academics "on the rise") and infused with the latest research in the field, the program is intended to be a self-contained, comprehensive resource that meets all the educational needs of a cognitive psychology program including and beyond the introductory level.

The aim of the *SAGE Cognitive Psychology Program* is to offer both breadth and depth. Student textbooks are written by leading and experienced scholars in a style that is carefully crafted to be stimulating, engaging, and accessible. They are scholarly, comprehensive, and up-to-date, and boast the appropriate pedagogical devices and supplements—thus making them appropriate for building courses around at a variety of levels. Reference works, including Handbooks and Encyclopedias, survey the landscape with an even broader sweep and should become benchmark volumes for years to come.

Existing and forthcoming titles:

- **Handbook of Cognition** (Koen Lamberts, *Warwick*; Rob Goldstone, *Indiana University*)
- **Cognitive Psychology, Second Edition** (Ronald Kellogg, *St. Louis University*)
- **Fundamentals of Cognitive Psychology** [in development] (Ronald Kellogg, *St. Louis University*)
- **Cognitive Psychology & Metacognition** [in development] (John Dunlosky, *Kent State University*; Janet Metcalfe, *Columbia University*)
- **Attention: Theory & Practice** (Addie Johnson, *University of Groningen*; Robert Proctor, *Purdue University*)
- **Culture & Cognition: Implications for Theory & Method** (Norbert Ross, *Vanderbilt University*)
- **Rational Choice in an Uncertain World: The Psychology of Judgment & Decision Making** (Reid Hastie, *University of Chicago*; Robyn Dawes, *Carnegie Mellon*)
- **Handbook of Understanding & Measuring Intelligence** (Oliver Wilhelm, *Humboldt-University, Berlin*; Randall Engle, *Georgia Tech*)
- **Cognitive Science: An Introduction to the Study of Mind** (Jay Friedenberg; Gordon Silverman, both of *Manhattan College*)
- **Handbook of Implicit Cognition & Addiction** (Reinout Wiers, *Universiteit Maastricht*; Alan W. Stacy, *University of Southern California*)
- **Human Memory: Structures & Images** (Mary Howes, *SUNY-Oneonta*)
- **Prospective Memory** (Mark McDaniel, *Washington University*; Gil Einstein, *Furman University*)
- **Cognitive Modeling** [in development] (Jerome R. Busemeyer, *Indiana University*; Adele Diederich, *International University Bremen*)
- **Handbook of Cognitive Aging: Interdisciplinary Perspectives** [in development] (Scott M. Hofer, *Pennsylvania State University*; Duane F. Alwin, *University of Michigan*)

HUMAN MEMORY

STRUCTURES AND IMAGES

MARY B. HOWES
STATE UNIVERSITY OF NEW YORK, ONEONTA

SAGE Publications
Thousand Oaks ▪ London ▪ New Delhi

For information:

Sage Publications, Inc.
2455 Teller Road
Thousand Oaks, California 91320
E-mail: order@sagepub.com

Sage Publications Ltd.
1 Oliver's Yard
55 City Road
London EC1Y 1SP
United Kingdom

Sage Publications India Pvt. Ltd.
B-42, Panchsheel Enclave
Post Box 4109
New Delhi 110 017 India

Printed in the United States of America

Library of Congress Cataloging-in-Publication Data

Howes, Mary B.
Human memory: Structures and images/Mary B. Howes.
      p. cm.
Includes bibliographical references and index.
ISBN 1-4129-1629-1 or 978-1-4129-1629-5 (pbk.)
   1. Memory—Research. I. Title.
BF371.H74 2007
153.1′2—dc22   2006020697

This book is printed on acid-free paper.

06   07   08   09   10   10   9   8   7   6   5   4   3   2   1

Acquisitions Editor:	Cheri Dellelo
Editorial Assistant:	Anna Mesick
Associate Editor:	Deya Saoud
Production Editor:	Libby Larson
Copy Editor:	QuADs
Typesetter:	C&M Digitals (P) Ltd.
Proofreader:	Caryne Brown
Indexer:	Jeanne Busemeyer
Cover Designer:	Glenn Vogel

#70251122

Brief Contents

Contents

How to Use This Book

C hapters 1 to 9, combined with Chapter 11, provide a basic or core course in the field of human memory. Chapter 3 can be omitted without undermining this structure. The remaining chapters (10, and 12 to 16) are "modular" chapters, which can be added to the core sequence as the instructor chooses. It is recommended that a brief overview of Chapters 12 and 13 be included in the core sequence, if these chapters are not covered in their entirety.

Within the structure described above, the core sequence covers the traditional field of research into memory. There is a slightly more extended sequence that can be followed to provide deeper understanding of research based on constructivist principles. The sequence includes Chapters 8 and 9 (in the core group) and also Chapter 10. These three together cover the most important tenets of the model. Chapter 14 also fits within this sequence, although no new explanatory ideas are introduced.

Two additional chapters are available online. At www.sagepub.com, go to *Human Memory* in our online catalog, and click on "Additional Resources" to view these chapters. The first provides a brief introduction to computer functioning, with emphasis on how computers represent information and different types of computer simulation of memory. The second covers a range of computer models of long-term memory, expanding on material introduced briefly in Chapter 7.

Some of the material in the book is starred. This reflects more advanced or extended content, in each chapter. As such, it is not part of the core sequence. It is intended for honors courses, for graduate courses, and also to be included when the instructor wishes to move more deeply into a specific area within an undergraduate course. It would have provided a neater organization if it had been possible to place all the starred content at the end of each chapter. This approach was not taken, however, since the starred material often related directly to passages placed within the body of the text.

Organization of the Book

The book is organized partly on a temporal basis and partly on the basis of subject matter. The temporal basis reflects the fact that early discoveries are placed toward the beginning of the book.

Chapter 1 provides an introduction to theories concerning human memory. The material is presented on the basis of the historical models in which the relevant ideas first emerged. The final material in the chapter involves methodology.

Chapter 2 describes the early verbal learning tradition. It focuses on two areas that provide foundational material. The first involves the associative model of memory, as developed by Ebbinghaus. The second reflects interference effects and consolidation theory.

Chapters 3 to 5 are subject-matter based. They cover sensory, short-term and working memory, with Chapters 3 and 4 moving from earlier to later research.

Chapter 6 introduces long-term memory. It begins with the issue of transfer of information from short-term to long-term store and with the associated debate concerning multiple or single memory models. The focus of the chapter after that is on cueing and featural models of memory. This material provides the foundations of knowledge of the tradition providing cue-dependent models of memory.

Chapter 7 continues coverage of long-term memory. Here the focus is primarily on current associative models, with some additional coverage of recent work in the cueing tradition. The two approaches are compared. Research into false memory for words is also included here due to its association with other forms of word-based experimental research.

Chapter 8 introduces the constructivist theory of memory in modern form, followed by a brief overview of a range of different types of research based on constructivist principles.

Chapter 9 introduces research and current theory in the area of altered memories. The focus is on changes that occur within the context of an otherwise essentially accurate recollection. Part I centers on laboratory research. Part II centers on work in the area of eyewitness testimony and the influence of emotion on memory.

Chapter 10 introduces research based on the assumption of higher-order structures operating to support the memory function, in a variety of ways. This material is based primarily on research into prose recall, including work in the area of computer simulation. This is a modular chapter.

Chapter 11 covers research into autobiographical memory. It is one of the ten core chapters.

Chapters 12 to 16 are modular chapters. The content is organized strictly on the basis of subject matter, and is indicated by the title of the chapter (memory for images, implicit memory, traumatic memory, disorders of memory, and neuroscience).

Chapter 17 is an afterword in which various themes, emerging from the earlier chapters, are briefly discussed. The chapter attempts to highlight some of the critical issues relating to the study of memory today.

Preface

Certain issues tend to recur in any serious examination of memory. Why can I recall some facts and some episodes, but not others? If you ask me where I live, I can tell you. No effort is needed in regaining the information, and it will return quickly. But if you ask me to describe the garden of a friend that I visited 10 years ago, I cannot. What then constitutes the difference between the information concerning my home and my friend's garden?

Across the past decades several new, critical insights have been developed within the present field. It was once believed that the material we store in our heads and call "memory" fell into roughly two classes: There was the content that you could remember and the content that you could not remember.

It is now understood that the nature of your thoughts, at the moment when you try to recall a given episode, can make a difference concerning your success or failure in recollection. What is activated in thought makes contact with the vast store of memory and influences the representations in that store. That is, we may be unable to recall a given episode when certain ideas or perceptions are present in awareness, and yet recall that same episode when different ideas are present. How this can occur is no longer considered mysterious.

Psychologists are divided, however, between two ways of interpreting these findings. According to one view, the relationship between currently activated thought and stored memory content will wholly determine whether the target memory is recalled. According to another, while this relationship plays a critical role in the events involved in remembering, it does not fully determine success or failure in recollection.

A second intriguing aspect of human recall involves the fact that memories can change. If you want to determine how well you have remembered a given body of information, a direct approach might be to measure the *quantity* of material. There is, again, the quantity of information that you can recall and the quantity that you cannot recall. But it is understood today that the situation is a good deal more complex. You may remember a body of content that is generally correct, but contains errors. Should the errors be considered the same as failure to recall anything? What if the errors are close to the original information, although not exact? Or you may recall wholly inaccurate information. Memories can change. This leads to yet another question. Why and how—and perhaps when—do memories alter?

The following is an example taken from a personal memory. I had gone to visit a town where I had lived for 5 years during my childhood.

I got off the bus on what was known as the High Street. The view, along the road, as the bus moved off, did not look right. It was familiar, but uneasily wrong somehow. I looked at the other way: That view was wrong, too. I then realized that the difficulty came from the big clock tower beside which I was standing. It was on the wrong side of the street. As I sat on the bus, I had seen the tower in memory. It stood next to a movie house, which was itself set back in a paved, open area. I was not surprised to find that the movie house had gone, although the paved area remained. But I was quite startled to find that I had moved the clock tower from one side of the street to the other. It had never stood by the movie house. The reason that the road had looked so wrong, both to the left and the right, was that, standing beside the clock tower, I had expected to see to my right the view that really lay to my left and vice versa. I thought I was on the opposite side of the street.

I have no original memory (that is, formed when I looked at the real scene) in which the clock tower stood beside the movie house: since it never did. My mind had transported that large object and placed it in another location. Nor was I mistaking one memory for another. I had had no commerce with other clock towers on a High Street. I had altered the original images, and it took quite an unpleasant collision with reality to discover this.

After I had walked around the town for a while, my knowledge of the area came back more and more clearly. I was now amazed that I could have forgotten the location of that tower. I had known it so well: And apparently, I still did. But how could my memory then have been weak and error-prone an hour ago, and yet strong now?

The present book addresses these issues, among others.

Acknowledgments

I wish to thank Jim Brace Thompson, Margo Crouppen, Cheri Dellelo, Karen Ehrmann, Deya Saoud, Linda Gray, and Libby Larson for their help in the editing and preparation of this book. Additional thanks go to Tammi Holtslander and Dana Haywood for their patient work in entering references.

Sage Publications thanks the following reviewers for their contributions to this book:

Harriett Amster
University of Texas at Arlington

Jeff Bowers
University of Bristol

Michael Dougherty
University of Maryland

David Gerkens
California State University,
    Fullerton

Robert Heredia
Texas A&M International University

Robert H. Logie
University of Edinburgh

James S. Nairne
Purdue University

David Pearson
University of Aberdeen

Kerri L. Pickel
Ball State University

T. Lee Ryan
University of Arizona

Bennett L. Schwartz
Florida International University

Harvey Shulman
Ohio State University

CHAPTER 1

Memory

Historical and Current Perspectives

Overview

1. Four historical traditions have shaped theories of human memory—namely, the Aristotelian (classic), rationalist, empiricist, and constructivist models.

2. The operation of computers has provided a fifth, recent model of human cognition and memory. According to this view, representations (concepts) consist of symbols.

3. The models outlined above have produced specific traditions of research. Empiricist thought led to the verbal learning tradition, founded by Ebbinghaus. A computer model, also influenced by empiricist tenets, led to the information-processing tradition. Researchers influenced by constructivism have focused on the issue of changes in memory and also on the role played by higher-order structures in memory.

4. Methodologies used in research into memory include experimentation, observational work, computer simulations, mathematical models, and neuroimaging.

Learning Objectives

1. Knowledge of the five major theories of cognition and memory and the fact that such theory shapes the nature of research. Theory determines what is researched and often the interpretation of the data.

2. Knowledge of the roots of current research traditions in the theories noted above.

3. Knowledge of the methodologies used to study memory.

There have been four great historical traditions concerning the nature of human thought. Each has influenced the way in which we understand memory. The recent development of computers has provided yet a fifth approach, which is now gradually taking shape in the form of theoretical models.

One issue concerning memory involves the nature of any content that we may recall. For instance, suppose I ask you to think of the concept DOG. You must retrieve this concept from memory. Then I might ask, What is the concept that you are now experiencing? What is it like? If you examine the material that is now in your awareness, you are likely to find an image of a dog. Is the dog concept, then, an image, and are memories in general, images? Perhaps. But suppose I then ask, Is a dog a living thing? The answer to this question cannot be found in the image, and yet I imagine that you will answer it easily. Does this mean that concepts consist of both images and some other kind of information? And if so, what is "the other kind"?

The theories described below all address this question, among others. But they are important for other reasons. The theories that we hold concerning memory directly shape research conducted into memory. They also play a major role in the interpretation of data. It is therefore of critical importance to understand the ideas that have framed the research covered in the present book. What follows is a brief description of some of the major issues.

1. The Classic Model: Aristotle

The Greek philosopher Aristotle (384–323 BCE) examined the question of memory in a brief treatise, translated into Latin as *De Memoria et Reminiscentia,* and later into English (Aristotle, 1941). It is strange to consider this, but almost all the principles concerning memory developed by European philosophers and later adopted by psychologists were first stated in this small body of writing.

Aristotle did not achieve such a level of sophistication working alone. He was the inheritor of an already well-developed history of philosophical examination, including examination of the nature of ideas, of memory, and of the role of *function* in both. His teacher, Plato (427–347 BCE) was engaged in all of these areas and developed metaphors concerning human recall. One was that memory could be likened to a piece of wax, on which impressions (the memories) could be made. In some people the wax was soft and would take the impressions well; in others it was harder and would imprint less readily and not retain the traces as long.

Aristotle not only thought in similar terms to some extent but also introduced ideas that far transcend any form of wax model. First, he noted that memory *moves.* When you remember one thing, you do not then sit with a freeze-frame picture of the thing. The content changes, and you either remember something else or think of something else.

This movement, Aristotle suggested, is not random. It obeys laws or rules. For instance, the thought or recollection of a given thing "A" will lead to the thought or recollection of another thing "G" if the two are similar to one another. On meeting a stranger, you might suddenly think of your cousin because the stranger looks like your cousin. Other such principles, according to the philosopher, included *opposition, contiguity*, and *causal properties.*

Contiguity involves a situation in which two things occur (or exist) together. If you constantly experience tables and chairs together, the thought of *table* will tend to activate the thought of *chair*—an outcome now known to occur when we free-associate. Perhaps the most surprising intuition here, however, involved the notion that causal relations guide memory.

If you see or think of an event, and that event will necessarily or generally lead to a certain outcome, you tend to think of (recall) that outcome—whether it occurs in front of your eyes or not. One of the most influential approaches to memory today includes this principle as a fundamental constituent of the model (Schank, 1982).

Aristotle wrote that memory frequently involves a kind of search. Here, you begin with one thought and may trace a path, based on the principles described above and no doubt other principles, between your starting point and the target memory. "One act of recollection," he wrote, "leads to another," in regular order (Aristotle, 1961, p. 612).

Aristotle also noted that when we recall memories, we experience images or "presentations." But underneath these presentations lies something else, which might be described as abstract meaning. When I think of a dog, I not only see an image but am also aware of what a dog is, including the fact that it is a living thing. One of the major questions facing researchers (in the field of memory) today concerns the nature of this meaning content. How is it expressed? What is it?

Aristotle thought that *all* memory content involves presentations. This may be true. However, Sir Francis Galton (1879), much later, explored the issue of memory in a somewhat different way. He found that some individuals are high imagizers and see images when they think of entities or remember events. Others are low imagizers and generate little or no imagery when they think and recall. There's probably a range of levels in between. Imagine your breakfast table as it was this morning. Do you see the objects on it? Or do you just "know" what was there? Or do you see a kind of schema or general image? Aristotle saw such things vividly—and always saw them. He appears to have been a high imagizer.

1.1. Meanings

Another of the great classic philosophers, Socrates (469–388 BCE) noted that we consider many things to be exemplars of the same idea, although they may not look or sound alike. And other things that do look or sound alike are not considered to represent the same concept. A worm and a crocodile bear little physical resemblance to one another, but we consider them to "be" the same thing in that both are animals. In contrast, an egg and a ping-pong ball look quite similar and certainly share many sensory features in common, but we consider them to be exemplars of different concepts. What then provides the basis for conceptual membership? Apparently, not appearance or feature similarity.

Some classic scholars believe that Aristotle answered this question (Randall, 1960). It is not clear that Aristotle intended to frame the issue in exactly the way that has been attributed to him, but his work can be read as expressing the following critical idea.

It may be that the nature or meaning of a thing is expressed in human cognition on the basis of the actions or *functions* that it can perform. For instance, the meaning of the concept "chair" reflects an object designed to allow a human being to sit down (with back support). Anything that possesses this function is a chair, regardless of what it looks like. The material of which it is made is also irrelevant. Thus, when I think of "chair," I will not only see an image of a chair but also know what it is. The latter property involves the function described above.

By the same logic, a thing is an eye if it is structured in such a way as to provide sight (a function). Appearance, again, does not matter. The structure that provides sight to a fly looks altogether different from the structure that provides sight to a horse or a human. But they are all eyes, since all perform the same function. According to the Aristotelian view, the function that determines the meaning of a thing depends on it having an organization that would normally provide that function. For instance, a blind eye is still an eye because it is designed to provide sight. The fact that it has been damaged and so cannot actually perform that function, does not matter. The human mind identifies "potential function," in addition to actual function.

The classic or Aristotelian view of meaning, described above, is supported today by philosophers within the neoclassic tradition. They have also extended the theory in several critical ways. Aristotle thought that there was one fundamentally important function that determined the nature of a thing. He called this its "form." The form of an eye, for instance, would be the function of sight. This property wholly determines conceptual membership. That is, if a thing has a structure that provides sight, it is an eye and not a tree, a dog, or a table. Neoclassic philosophers agree with this claim, although the word used to designate it is now "core." They believe, however, that the meaning of a thing does not only involve the core. Instead, the meaning of any given concept involves both the core and all other functions that members of the concept could perform (a chair could be used to prop open a door, for instance). The concept also includes general, nonfunctional information (chairs are found in houses) and, of course, perceptual information (Putnam, 1975b). Perceptual information reflects how a thing looks or sounds and any other relevant sensory properties.

A final claim made by Aristotle that has considerable resonance in the field of memory today, is that human concepts operate in a hierarchy. Lower-level representations (an alternative word for "concept") all have a meaning of their own. But they also include the meanings of all the conceptual classes directly above them in the hierarchy. Thus, a poodle is a dog, a mammal, a vertebrate, and a living thing. The poodle will inherit the core function of each of the classes above it. To put this somewhat differently, the meaning of "poodle" includes the meaning of mammal, vertebrate, and so on.

An example of the Aristotelian view of hierarchical concepts is provided in Figure 1.1.

2. Empiricism

John Locke (1632–1704) is generally identified as the founder of the empiricist tradition. In Locke's day it was believed that ideas are innate. That is, we are born

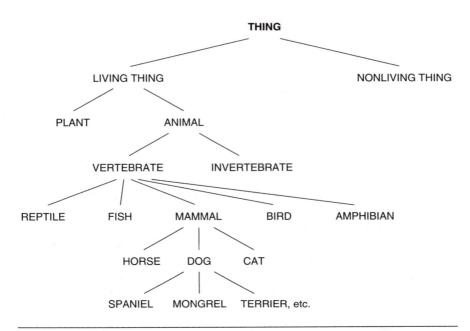

Figure 1.1   An Example of Hierarchical Format in Human Concepts

NOTE: One set of nested classes (THING to SPANIEL) is shown.

knowing what a dog, a cow, or the moon, is. The knowledge itself would be awakened or triggered in the child when a child first saw an example of the concept. Thus, the concept *dog* would be triggered when an individual saw a dog (or heard about a dog) for the first time.

Locke (1690/1956) rejected the innateness hypothesis. Obviously, he argued, we do not possess innate ideas. This would be like supposing you could know what oysters taste like if you had never tasted an oyster.

The philosopher suggested that we acquire our ideas through perceptual experience. The child see, hears, tastes, and so forth. Concepts are built of sense impressions. A sense impression is a unitary perception of some kind of, say, redness or roundness or a straight line, or a musical note. Our minds receive sense impressions and put them together into more complex unities (complex ideas). Conceptual representations are complex ideas. Thus, an idea can be described as an image—a kind of combination of sensory units.

Critical to the present theory, there is no direct, abstract knowledge in human thought or memory. All ideas and all mental content consist of copies of impressions received directly through the senses.

The model included the concept of an abstraction function, however. A child will see many trees, and the child's mind will abstract out those sensory properties they all hold in common. These properties, combined, will constitute her idea, *tree*. This entity may be quite complex; it should probably not be equated with a straightforward picture of an average tree.

Locke described the mind as a *tabula rasa*, a blank slate, at birth. The mind writes on the slate on the basis of experience. All *representation* (a formal word for "idea") is therefore, in one form or another, a copy of something derived through the senses.

The mind is nonetheless capable of deploying active mental processes, such as comparing objects, identifying relational properties, employing logical thought, and so on.

The philosopher assumed that mental content—ideas, thoughts, and memories—are built from an addition of units. The ultimate units were sense impressions, which could not be further reduced. A thought or a memory should be understood as the *additive sum of its parts*. Given this position, understanding a high-level form of cognition, such as a memory, depended on understanding the parts of the memory. The correct methodology would thus be to break the object of study down into its ultimate components. Thus, Locke advocated *reductionism* and the study of units as the correct methodological approach within this context.

Locke, as well as other empiricist philosophers, notably David Hume, believed that a fundamental principle in the organization of human thought and human memory was that of *environmental contiguity*. That is, if two things, maybe a knife and a fork, repeatedly occurred together in your experience—in the environment—they would become associated together in your memory. In time, thinking of (recalling) "knife" would lead you to think of (recall) "fork."

Hume (1739/1965) wrote that thought depends on at least three major principles: resemblance (similarity), cause and effect, and contiguity of either time or place.

The empiricists believed that memories were a copy of earlier sensory experience. But David Hume noted that memories are not usually as clear as the original perceptual experience. If you once saw a house and an apple orchard, your memory would include the same images but in weaker form, and some might have faded entirely. Thus, memory is here a copy of direct perception. It follows that normal memories are also accurate memories. If you see an apple, it is usually because an apple is there. Hume (1739/1965) described this point as follows:

> Memory preserves the original form in which its objects were presented, and that wherever we depart from it in recollecting anything, it proceeds from some defect or imperfection in that faculty. (bk. 1, sect I)

Hume is saying here that memory content accurately copies the original event. Change and distortion do not occur, unless the memory function is not working as it should. This view has been strongly defended in the modern era, and the issue of whether memory content does or does not actually change remains controversial.

3. Rationalism

Rationalism involves the view that ideas are innate and that mental processes are the most reliable source of accurate knowledge concerning the world.

The French philosopher René Descartes is generally considered the father of European rationalism. Descartes was taught as a young man that a human idea involves the picture or image of some external object. Thus, one's idea *tree* was a mental image of a tree. Also, ideas were acquired wholly through direct experience with the world; they were copies of things seen and heard.

The philosopher rejected both these claims. He noted that we possess abstract concepts, such as the concept of time, extension, hope, selfhood, infinity, and so on. These ideas cannot be represented in sensory form and so cannot be duplicates of things experienced through the senses. Since they cannot be provided through sensory experience, Descartes reasoned, they must be innate.

Descartes's second argument was a good deal more complex. When we think of an object that is not abstract, such as a table, there nonetheless (he believed) exist abstract ideas embedded within the imagery of the concept. For instance, we understand the surface of the table as having *extension* through space. You can see a line reflecting the edge of the tabletop in sensory experience. But you cannot see extension as such. In the same way, we think of a table as having density. You can feel muscle pressure when you push against a table, but you do not feel density as such. The latter is an abstract concept.

There has been debate from Descartes's time until the present over this particular argument. Can such concepts as extension and density be directly expressed as sensory experience or not? And if not, where and how do we acquire such concepts?

4. Constructivism

Aristotle had noted that memory takes sensory form but that its images carry abstract information with or beneath them. Locke dealt with this issue, whose implications he appeared to see quite clearly, by suggesting that abstract ideas are in fact represented by imagery, although imagery whose nature we do not understand or cannot see directly. Descartes took the opposite position: that abstract notions are clearly not images and cannot be reduced even to "strange" images. But this led him to the position that the true nature of human thought involves innate representations, since the crucial elements could not be sensory.

Immanuel Kant (1724–1804) developed a possible solution to the issue outlined above. Rationalists believed in pure knowledge, provided from inside the mind. Empiricists claimed that all knowledge is given through sensory experience: None derives from "inside" our cognition. Kant began his philosophical life as a rationalist but also read and was impressed by the writings of David Hume. He concluded that both traditions were wrong in major part, although also partially correct.

Kant (1781/1965) suggested that there are no full-blown ideas provided genetically within us. In other words, there are no innate ideas, such as the idea of a table or a rabbit. And yet some aspect of human representation *is* biologically provided.

This constituent involved ways of potential understanding, which could be brought into play when sensory experience was encountered. In modern terms, some form of interpretive capacity was involved. This capacity, in its various manifestations, was innate. But it did not consist of knowledge as we know it, such as knowledge of the nature of trees or the moon. It was rather a way of making sense of the perceptual experience arriving through our eyes and ears. This involved bringing abstract ways of thinking to bear in the interpretation of such experience.

Kant identified a range of such interpretive capacities. When we experience the world, we understand it in terms of a space, in which there are objects. We also understand events as occurring in time. This tendency to conceptualize the external universe in terms of both space and time is innate. Many other such "categories" (ways of thinking) also exist. They include notions such as unity and plurality, existence, causality, reality, and negation. Each of these implies subsidiary others. Involved in causality, for instance, are the concepts of force, action, and so on. It is important to note that these ways of thinking are not conscious. The child is not aware of them when concepts are first developed. They are unconscious processing capacities.

The ideas developed by Kant could be roughly translated into modern terms as follows. A child who has experience with apples will come to develop a concept of "what apples are." The knowledge is not innate. The child has developed it through dealing with actual apples. He has come to understand (earlier) that there are individual objects in the world, with individual properties. The capacity to think of sensory experience in terms of objects (things with boundaries and particular properties) is innate. If it did not exist, the sensory flux arriving at eyes and ears would never be organized into individual stimuli. He will learn the properties of apples, such as the ability to roll, to be thrown, to be eaten. All of these properties involve innate abstract forms of comprehension, coming into play as the child interacted with apples. For instance, the idea of eating could not be developed unless one had the abstract mental capacity to understand things in terms of containment: One thing can be contained inside another. The result of all this mental construction is a concept.

One important implication for memory of Kant's model is that experience is interpreted or *constructed*. This means that our cognition is not simply a copy of perception, of reality coming directly from outside. What we know is largely generated from the way that we can think. Thus, the interpretation of events or stimuli at even higher levels is likely to occur and likely to play a critical role in all forms of mental life, including memory.

Kant used the term *schema* to refer to a function that maps the two constituents of our knowledge of the world (the abstract capacities to understand and sensory experience) to one another. Psychologists sympathetic to the notion of constructivism, which entails the belief that memory content is an interpretation of incoming stimuli (rather than a copy of such stimuli) have tended to adopt the term, although it has now been applied in such diverse ways that the constructivist implication has, in some cases, been diluted.

4.1. Concluding Note

The material described above has involved fundamental or central positions concerning the nature of human memory. A wide variety of theories have been developed around each of these models. For instance, the famous empiricist psychologist Edward B. Titchener believed that memory content consisted of images. However, he had found on the basis of introspection that his own memory images were not literal, if weak, copies of the original perception, as claimed by Hume, but were for the most part altered from the original.

5. Computer Models

The development of computers led naturally to a model of human cognition based on computer functioning.

A computer stores and manipulates information. It is clear that these are also functions of the human mind. We know how computers achieve such functions, and thus the computer offers a model that has the advantage of being fully understood.

In traditional programs (*symbolic AI*, standing for symbolic artificial intelligence), computers operate by means of symbols. When the machine is in a certain state (that is, its electronic switches are either on or off in a certain pattern), this state can be used to represent numbers. The numbers in turn can be used to represent symbols, which can stand for whatever content the programmer wishes them to stand for. If the program needs to represent HOUSE, for instance, then the symbol *88* could stand for HOUSE. There is also a program as such, with an executive function that directs how the symbols will be manipulated. These manipulations parallel activities that might occur in thought. For instance, the program might direct the computer to activate the symbol *2*, then activate the symbol *3*, and add them (a manipulation). The outcome will be the symbol *5*. Early computer models of human cognition thus posited that ideas consist of symbols, which are states of the brain, and that there exist in humans various programs that manipulate the symbols. One such activity is the activity that we call thought (Putnam, 1960, 1975a, 1975b).

A symbol is defined in this context as a representational element that does not in any way resemble the thing that it represents. For instance, I might ask you to accept the symbol ^^^^^ as meaning CAT. If you do accept this suggestion, then you would treat ^^^^^ as indicating the cat concept, although the marks clearly do not look like, act like, or have any intrinsic relation with actual cats. Words are also symbols. CAT does not look or act like a real cat either. (The older word for this concept was "sign." It was probably a better designation than "symbol," since "symbol" is used within the clinical and literary traditions to mean precisely an entity that does in some fashion resemble the thing that it designates.)

Today, the field is divided between individuals who believe that a computer model is an accurate and adequate theory of human cognition (Dennett, 1991) and those who believe that it is not (Searle, 1984). The approach raises a number of intricate questions and issues. For instance, if the concept CAT is in fact a symbol, then how does it derive its particular meaning? Roughly, why does it represent CAT and not HAM SANDWICH? Proponents of a hard-line computer model have found arguments to explain how a symbol can denote meaning, while critics of the model feel that these arguments don't work. The second major issue within this context involves consciousness. It is generally agreed that computers do not possess awareness, while humans do. This raises the question of whether an entity that is not aware, or has no mind, can be an adequate model of human cognition. Again, opinion is divided on this issue.

There is another form of computer functioning known as connectionism or artificial neural networks (ANNs). Here information is represented as a pattern of activity moving among units. It is generally said that no symbols are involved. And there are no programs; the activity is preset to move in certain ways, rather than being directed by outside "rules." Another critical property is that the same units are used to represent different patterns, just as (very roughly) the same letters can be used to represent different words (DOOR and ROPE use several of the same letters.) Traditional symbolic AI is known not to function in the way that the human brain functions, while neural nets come much closer.

Within psychology, a moderate approach has been taken within this context. The dominant cognitive school today is called *information-processing psychology* and claims only that human cognition (including memory) involves active processing on the part of the brain and that much of this processing is unconscious. It is thus a model based to some extent on computer functioning, as implied by its name. The claims of information-processing psychology are so mild, however, that it could be argued that most individuals in modern Western culture would say that they are obviously true.

6. The Study of Memory

6.1. Research Within the Empiricist Tradition

The fundamental empiricist view with regard to memory is that (1) memory content consists of images (complex sensory information); (2) certain principles operate to connect these images together, with *contiguity* being one such principle; (3) memory content is accurate content; and (4) memories consist of units added together. An appropriate methodology for understanding memory is thus to identify the units from which a memory is built; when these are understood, the memory as a whole will be understood.

The first research conducted into memory operated wholly within the empiricist tradition. Hermann Ebbinghaus, working in the 19th century, examined human recall of nonsense syllables such as HYF or WAZ. He considered each such item to be a pure unit of memory, which became associated with other units on the basis of contiguity. His research, which laid the foundations for the study of memory on a scientific basis, is described in Chapter 2.

A school known as the verbal learning tradition grew out of Ebbinghaus's research. Here researchers continued to study human recall of language items, although by the 20th century the research focused on memory for words. The first clear demonstration of a factor that causes forgetting was achieved by researchers within this school. Progress was also made concerning the issue of the "codes" that express human memories. The model directing this work remained within the empiricist tradition, although John McGeoch, probably the most famous researcher of that era, began to doubt that word meanings did in fact involve images (Chapter 2).

Information-processing psychology also had its roots in empiricist thought but tended to be eclectic in its approach to theory. Research focused on what occurs when we encounter a stimulus, such as a word, and enter it into memory. It was found that our cognition establishes a series of different codes to represent the stimulus. These codes change very quickly from one to another in a predictable sequence. This led to the hypothesis that different memory stores were involved. Later researchers challenged the multistore view, however. Another issue today concerns whether different memory functions are handled by different memory systems. For instance, if I recall a picture, are the processes and the codes involved dependent on a memory that is a distinct domain from what would is involved when I recall the content, say, of a novel? Do we really have many "memories," or just one? (Chapters 3–7 and 13).

It has also been found that information can be retained in memory—in some form—even when we cannot recall it. The unavailable information may nonetheless influence our behavior. We may feel an emotional response, for instance, and yet be unable to identify why we feel as we do (Chapter 13).

There has also been a fairly recent development concerning the nature of abstract meanings. According to this view, meanings may be represented in *propositional form* in our thought and in our memories. This notion developed first within philosophy on the basis of the fact that we may know what something looks like but not know "what it is." Suppose I come from a culture in which chairs do not exist. I might see a chair repeatedly, perhaps in my new room, such that I could draw it from memory. But if I were asked for my concept of the object, my sense of what it was, I would be unable to reply. The idea was developed within the positivist philosophical tradition that the meaning of the object might be a *verbal statement*, such as, "A chair is an object in which you can sit." This was seen as a series of words, which are elements that can be seen or heard (they are sensory). Psychologists, considering this approach in the 1970s, speculated that there may be structures in our thought that have essentially the same organization as language. These might represent, "A chair is an object in which you can sit," not as words but as symbols, formed by the brain, that included both the concepts and the relevant grammatical functions that connect the concepts together in a statement or proposition. This view is today the dominant theory concerning the nature of abstract meaning codes. Meaning codes may be propositions (Chapter 7).

Probably the most influential development in memory research across the past half century, however, involves the notion of *cues*. If I am consciously thinking, say, about houses, this information will make contact with house representations in my memory. The idea "houses," in my awareness at the moment, is a cue. It has been found that success in recall depends in major part on the relationship between the operating cues and the target memory content. It is not the case that you can either recall a memory because it is adequately strong or cannot recall it because it is weak. Success can depend on what you are thinking at the time you make the attempt at recall. Some psychologists believe that this relationship completely determines whether (any) memory will be recalled. Others think that cues are only one determining factor. This debate reflects one of the most important issues in the field of memory research today (Chapters 6 and 7).

6.2. Research and Ideas Within the Rationalist Tradition

Rationalist thought has produced little research into human memory and so will be mentioned only briefly here. An influential modern philosopher has noted that the meaning inherent in concepts, even simple concepts, involves such an astonishing degree of complexity and precision that this large body of information could not simply be picked up (learned, acquired) on the basis of experience. The implication is of some form of innate knowledge (Fodor, 1975).

A related issue concerns the symbols that are hypothesized to operate in propositions. Why does one symbol "mean" ROSE and another symbol "mean" TABLE? Given that symbols have no internal structure or nature, what provides individual meanings of this kind? This is a thorny issue, particularly if it is assumed that representations consist only of symbols (and not of some other constituent that might provide meanings.) One solution is to posit that the meaning of the symbols is innate.

6.3. Research and the Aristotelian/ Constructivist Tradition

The work of Jean Piaget, founder of the Genevan school of psychology, is probably the best-known example of the present tradition.

Piaget believed that when we encounter a stimulus, we construct its meaning and enter that meaning code into memory (along with the relevant perceptual information). The concepts in long-term memory (LTM) used to provide the meaning constituent he termed *schemas*. According to the present view, a memory will be strong (easily retrieved) or weak, depending above all other factors on the nature of the schemas used to construct that memory. Some of these background schemas are strongly interrelated or integrated in LTM. These provide memory strength. Others are more weakly connected together and so can "maintain" only weak memories. While rehearsal will of course play a role, the nature of the background schemas was viewed by Piaget as the most critical factor of all (Chapter 8). No claims exactly corresponding to this model have been made within mainstream psychology, although the work of Roger Schank comes close (Chapter 10).

The Piagetian view of meaning codes is Aristotelian (and Kantian) in nature. Piaget held that the meaning of an entity reflected a code that specified all the actions that the object could perform (in any context) and also its perceptual properties and its shape. Here, the meaning of a spoon, for instance, is a code specifying an object, again of a certain shape, that can convey food or a small amount of liquid, to the mouth. Piaget's research in the field of developmental psychology involved a highly detailed model of how the relevant schemas are built within the individual child from the time of birth to the time of what might be called adult representation.

Of particular interest, Piaget believed that these codes for actions were not symbolic in nature. That is, the notion of carrying food in a convex area (as in a spoon) was not understood as being represented in propositional form—as a string of wordlike elements. Instead, it involved an *analog code*. In general, an analog code is a code that directly corresponds to the thing that it represents. Both visual experience and memory images are now widely believed to involve a code of this kind (Chapter 12). For instance, if the edge of Table A is longer than the edge of Table B and you look at them both, the lines representing Table A will be directly longer, in the percepts that you see, than the lines representing Table B. This can be contrasted with a symbolic description, in which it is stated "A is longer than B." Thus, the Piagetian view is that we possess analog codes directly expressing motion and action, just as we possess analog codes for visual experience.

Piaget believed that these "action codes" were first developed in infancy on the basis of the child acting on the world: that is, pushing, pulling, or moving objects and discovering what the objects could do. An alternative theory is that the child learns about activity not primarily through doing but through watching. According to this view, the child watches the actions of objects and other people and begins to build representation on the basis of what she or he sees.

Theory based on these assumptions has developed from the work of cognitive linguists (Johnson, 1987; Langacke, 1987; Talmy, 1983). Johnson (1987), for instance, has urged that much of our abstract thinking is metaphorical, in the sense that it has its basis in the actions of our bodies: in what they do and how they interact with the world. He calls the relevant image structures "schemata" and emphasizes that they are indeed analog, and not propositional, representations.

J. M. Mandler (1988, 1992) discovered that infants at 4 months of age discriminate between animate and inanimate objects. This is such a sophisticated discrimination (implying concepts corresponding to "living" and "nonliving" in very young babies) that Mandler speculated as to whether the findings would imply rationalism. Four months appears a very early age to have learned the difference between animate and inanimate things or indeed even to be thinking about such issues. Mandler concluded, however, that the phenomenon can be explained on the basis of the infant's perception of objects in the world.

Specifically, it was suggested that the animacy notion is built from several more fundamental elements of meaning. These elements reflect the way in which objects move. Some things only move if they are pushed or pulled, while others initiate actions by themselves. The infant notices this difference. Also, animate objects often move in an irregular way, changing direction or stopping and starting. Nonliving things tend to move smoothly in the same direction, as, for instance, in the case of a toy car that has been pushed. From these building blocks, the infant develops an early discrimination between animate and inanimate objects. In support of the present view, it has been established that infants do indeed pay particular attention to motion and to self-motion even more than general motion.

According to Mandler's model, meaning codes are built from elements that reflect types of movement. These elements are ultimately put together to form concepts. Again, the codes are posited to be analog and not symbolic. Another critical point is that the resulting image schema (concept) is not itself a perceptual representation: That is, it is not a direct copy of what was originally seen. It is instead an abstract cognitive entity derived from what was seen or "redescribed." This stage provides the poorly understood transition from perceptual experience to abstract, semantic representation.

Activity models overcome the problem of why some concepts "mean" one thing, rather than another. Different concepts have a different internal structure; the constituents for the concept "spoon" are not the same as the constituents for the concept "table."

6.4. Alterations in Memory and Higher-Order Structures

According to the empiricist view, memories are copies of perceptual experience and as such are almost always accurate. Any distortion of the original content would imply that some form of pathology or dysfunction was involved.

The constructivist tradition implies the opposite. Here it is assumed that sensory input is interpreted. That is, when we live through an event, it is our understanding of the event that forms the most fundamental memory code.

Understanding of this kind draws on background knowledge, which becomes part of the memory. It is also believed, within this context, that when there are gaps in a given memory, the gaps can be filled in on the basis of background knowledge. Suppose I know that the buses in a certain town are painted blue and I am trying to remember a visit to that particular town that occurred 5 years ago. I may recall an event in which I saw the bus (that I hoped to enter) turning a corner. I may then recall the color of the bus as blue, not because the original memory codes are available but due to an unconscious inference based on my background knowledge. Constructivists believe that inferred content of this kind cannot be distinguished from the "original codes." Inferred material could, however, be incorrect. It may be that the particular bus sent to pick me up was yellow.

The extent to which memories can change is currently a subject of great interest and a focus of ongoing research (Chapters 8, 9, and 14). The debate today, however, does not involve whether the content of a memory as experienced may change. Everyone agrees that this can happen. The debate today centers on whether or not the unconscious codes representing the memory may change. A related issue, however, concerns the *extent* of possible change at the level of awareness. Roughly, it is possible that entire memories can be generated from background knowledge, including beliefs. Or is such reconstruction confined only to individual elements within a "real" memory?

According to constructivist thought, background knowledge plays a critical role in memory. It is widely believed within this tradition that memory content (involving events) has a hierarchical structure. It is also believed that the higher levels in this organization provide strength to the memory as a whole. Research into the issue has been conducted since the 1970s (Chapters 8 and 10).

7. Methodology and Research Traditions

A large number of methodologies are used today in the study of memory.

The best known among these is the experiment, in which an independent variable is manipulated and its influence on a dependent variable measured. For instance, a researcher wishing to know whether time of day influences learning might conduct an experiment in which participants are tested for the learning of identical material across different periods of the day. In an approach of this kind, all variables that might influence learning, other than time of day, need to be equated across conditions. A variable that is not so equated is labeled a *confounding variable*. For instance, the intake of food might affect learning, such that a session directly following lunch might reflect this factor rather than time of day.

There have been two dominant lines of experimental research into memory: the verbal learning tradition and information-processing psychology. The former involves the study of the learning and retention of language materials, usually individual words in the form of lists. The latter reflects a psychological tradition in which it is assumed that the brain actively processes information, both in the forming and the retrieving of memories and across all other cognitive functions.

Another methodological approach to the study of memory involves *observation*. Here, no variable is manipulated, but a given function is described. This approach has been adopted in the study of autobiographical memories, including earliest memories. Here the recalled content may be classified into different kinds (verbal, imagistic, abstract, numeric, basic, or generalized) in addition to being quantified.

An advantage of the experimental approach is that it can operate within a predictive framework. Thus, it may be predicted that if Hypothesis A is true, then the data should reflect significantly higher scores under, say, Condition 1 than Condition 2 or 3, whereas if Hypothesis B is true, then the scores should be higher under Condition 3. A major goal of a predictive methodology of this kind is to eliminate subjective bias (a biased interpretation of the data), since the outcome is not known prior to the study. A second advantage is that experimental results are capable of being replicated. Reliability, measured by replication, is viewed as the most fundamental means of ensuring that information gained in the course of scientific research is accurate information.

A major advantage of the observational approach is that it can reveal facts or relations of which the researcher had been previously unaware. It is not always possible to predict the nature even of conscious psychological functions. Observational data are also capable of being replicated.

Today, computers are widely used to study mnemonic functions. As described above, the term *artificial intelligence* (AI) refers to cognitive tasks that are performed by computers in an effective ("intelligent") manner; the processes involved here may be of any kind. In contrast, a model that attempts to perform a given cognitive function in the way that a human would perform it is known as a *computer simulation*. The most common approach in computer simulations is to identify the specific forms of processing that occur when a human performs such a function and to copy these into a computer program. For instance, if it is assumed that in memory a conscious representation enters the memory store on the basis of a matching process, involving specific features of the representation, then this series of events would be modeled in the program. The same would occur for all subsequent processing involved in the recall of the target memory.

Computer simulations do not generally involve prediction. Their success can be measured, however, in other ways. With complex functions (such as prose comprehension and recall), one criterion is simply success in performing the function

(Pylyshyn, 1984). If some critical step or steps had been omitted or misunderstood, then the program would be at risk of failure. The more complex the function, the more difficult it becomes to model it at all. Second, the pattern of errors made by a simulation can be measured against the pattern of errors made by human subjects performing the same task. If the two are similar, this is an indication that the program appears to be functioning in the way that a human would function. Relative ease or slowness, or success and failure, of handling task components can also be measured against human performance.

Computer simulations are considered to have the virtue of being explicit. At a theoretical level, it might be possible to say, "The conscious element is matched somehow to information in memory store." But a program cannot operate in this fashion. Every processing step must be specified exactly, or the program will not run.

Simulations also have to be efficient. A program that could learn a paragraph of prose but required an entire day to do so would not look like a good model of human learning. There is therefore a requirement on the programmer that the functions be performed well, rather than simply performed. This means that the organization of information within the program should be optimal. (This is the case because the organization present in human memory, whatever it may prove to be in the end, is highly efficient.)

Computer simulations can also embody complex, or what might be called high-powered, models of memory. They are not restricted to simple functions.

Yet another modern approach in the field of memory research involves the use of mathematical models. Here a function (such as recall) is described in terms of mathematical formulas and equations. For instance, it might be assumed that a conscious representation has a certain mathematical probability of matching an element in memory store and that this event will vary depending on the number of elements in the store (in a way that can be mathematically described). A mathematical simulation of the events is then run and the outcome (how many or what elements are recalled) noted. The approach is validated by seeing the extent to which the math model outcomes match actual human data. It is generally expected that the match should be very precise.

There are also some disadvantages to mathematical models. One is that they tend to be restricted to simple forms of learning, and these are often further simplified to make the formulas workable. A second difficulty is that the same outcome (the human data outcome) can often be achieved in multiple different ways: for instance, by placing different weights on the variables in an equation. It is also the case that different mathematical models can predict the same outcome. The approach is nonetheless useful in that it can point to relations and possibilities that had not been envisioned before, and it can identify incorrect assumptions within a model.

The most recent approach to the study of memory involves the use of *neuroimaging techniques*. Here it is possible to identify locations in the brain that become active when a given psychological task is performed and also to identify specific patterns of neural response. This is achieved through a variety of techniques, including electroencephalograms (EEGs), positron emission tomography (PET) scans, and functional magnetic resonance imaging (fMRI), among others.

Research involving disorders in memory related to physical damage is described in Chapter 15 and research centering on neuroimaging, in Chapter 16.

It was believed at one time that scientific data should require no interpretation. They should "speak for themselves." But it has become increasingly clear that only the simplest kinds of knowledge can be derived by simply looking at data. If we are to understand human recall and recognition, the use of theory and knowledge derived from theory is no less important than skill in running experiments or creating computer simulations. This is so for several reasons. Theory will direct the kind of research that is performed. Equally important, an understanding of theoretical issues will provide the most competent interpretation of the empirical outcome.

Also, a failure to understand the ideas that inform a history of research can lead to the belief that certain assumptions are obviously true, when this may not be the case at all.

Summary

There are four major historical models of human cognition and memory. According to the Aristotelian view, the process of recall moves from one constituent to another on the basis of laws or principles. These include contiguity, similarity, and causality. Meanings are based on representations of function.

According to the rationalist view, we possess abstract concepts. Since these cannot be derived through the senses, they must be innate. In contrast, empiricists believe that all representation, and all memory content, is built from elements of sensory experience acquired after birth. There are no abstract components.

According to the constructivist view, concepts and so the content of memories do include abstract content. But concepts are not innate. We have a biological capacity to interpret sensory experience in various ways. This interpretation provides abstract understanding. Memories for events are the result of the individual's understanding or interpretation of the event. As such, they are not always accurate. There is a further implication in the model that forgotten information could be inferred. This can also lead to alterations from the original codes.

A more recent theory of the nature of human cognition and memory is based on the computer. Traditional computer programs involve the manipulation of symbols under the control of a program (symbolic AI). According to a computer model, human concepts are symbols and memories are formed when these are manipulated, again under the control of a program.

A different type of approach to computer simulations, known as connectionism, involves programs in which computer functions very roughly mimic the activities of human (or other) brains. Here the units that perform the processing are associated together at varying degrees of strength. There is no external program running them.

The theories described above have provided differing frames for research into memory. These include the verbal learning tradition founded on empiricist views

CHAPTER 2

Mainstream Foundations

The Associative Model of Memory

Overview

1. The verbal learning tradition, involving the learning of word lists or nonsense syllables, was founded by Ebbinghaus. Methodologies include free recall, order recall, and paired-associate recall.

2. Forgetting occurs when new information is entered into memory. This is known as interference. Interference occurs when the memory content has been weakly learned.

3. Two opposed explanations have been offered for interference effects. According to interference theory, new material blocks old so that the old cannot be recalled and vice versa. According to consolidation theory, the brain is limited in the amount of information it can fix into memory sequentially. New material may overtax this capacity.

4. When we memorize word items, the primary code that expresses or stands for the items in memory is a semantic code. "Semantic" is a term that denotes "meaning."

5. When we deploy two sequential memory tasks that use the same code (visual and visual or semantic and semantic) the level of interference increases. This is called *similarity-based interference.*

Learning Objectives

1. Understanding of the Ebbinghausian associative model of memory.

2. Knowledge of research methods used in the study of consonant-vowel-consonants (CVCs) or words.

3. Knowledge of the nature of interference effects and the theories related to them.

4. Knowledge of the primary code employed when we memorize words and of similarity-based interference within this context.

T he present chapter introduces the associative model of memory and the nature of interference effects in human recall. Both the theory and the research context were established early; however, they continue to influence the field today.

The material primarily reflects work in the verbal learning tradition.

1. Ebbinghaus: Origins of the Associative Model

1.1. Methodology and Research

Cognitive psychologists in the 19th century had been criticized for their failure to generate reliable research data. Without such data, it was widely believed that psychology could not claim the status of a science. Yet a successful methodology had in fact been developed by the German researcher Hermann Ebbinghaus, working outside the dominant academic framework, before the 1880s.

Ebbinghaus believed that the major difficulty facing a scientist who wished to produce reliable data on human memory involved the complexity of the subject. There are a huge number of variables that may influence our cognition. If I enter a life episode into memory, my interest in the event, my feelings concerning it, my knowledge relevant to it, the colors presented to me, the imagery present—all these factors and a hundred others might influence my subsequent recall. The problem for an experimenter, then, lay in finding some way to standardize the content entered into memory. You can hardly run a good study if the material in one experimental condition is easier to retain than the material in the next experimental condition. As in all experiments, the material has to be equated across conditions.

Ebbinghaus's solution to the difficulty was to work with content that was extremely simple. He chose nonsense syllables, consisting of CVC combinations, such as HUF or WIS. Since this material carried no meaning, it could not, he reasoned, provide a situation in which the material in one experimental condition might be of more interest or provoke more emotion, or more imagery, and so on, than in any other. Twenty nonsense syllables learned under Condition 1 should provide exactly the same ease or difficulty as 20 nonsense syllables learned under Condition 2. Given this equality, an independent variable could be manipulated in such a fashion as to obtain reliable data.

In the course of his work in the field of human memory, Ebbinghaus served as his one, and only, subject. Yet his findings have stood the test of time extremely well. They include a range of parameters relevant to the learning of lists of verbal elements. He used a single method of learning: that of repetition (rehearsal). He repeated the critical items until the first test when he could recall them perfectly (or sometimes, the second test that provided perfect recall). He required that the items be retained in their original order.

Ebbinghaus examined a number of questions concerning human memory that would be likely to occur to any interested researcher and some that were not so obvious. If there is twice as much material in Set B as in Set A, does it take twice as long, more than twice as long, or less than twice as long to learn B? Is forgetting a steady process occurring over time or does it show different slopes after learning?

He found that learning twice the amount of material takes more than twice the amount of work. And forgetting is not a linear function. Ebbinghaus used a "savings method" to assess how much information was lost over time. He would learn a list and then at a later point relearn it. The second learning would take less time than the first. The amount of time thus saved between learning of the first day and learning of the second was an indication of how much had been retained in memory.

Ebbinghaus also discovered that forgetting occurred very quickly after learning, with 50% of the loss typically occurring in the first hour. The loss of items continued, although less sharply, up to 24 hours. After that point the curve leveled (there was little forgetting).

The relevant forgetting curve is shown in Figure 2.1 on the next page.

CVCs are particularly difficult to retain in memory. When other forms of material are used, such as words or sentences, forgetting tends to be less steep over time. However, the slope of Ebbinghaus's curve holds across a very large range of materials. Under most conditions (of weak learning), forgetting occurs most sharply following the acquisition of the content and then shows the same kind of leveling pattern as obtained with his data.

The time of day influences recall. Ebbinghaus recalled material better in the morning than in the evening. But of more immediate theoretical importance, he was concerned with events that are not directly available to verbal report. If a list had been learned and then completely forgotten (that is, if the researcher could no longer remember even one target CVC), was it the case that nothing remained in memory at all relevant to that list, or might the brain be in some fashion different because of the earlier learning?

Ebbinghaus found that after a list had been wholly forgotten, based on behavioral evidence, he could relearn it in fewer trials than had been required for the original learning. That is, something was indeed different in his brain because of the earlier learning.

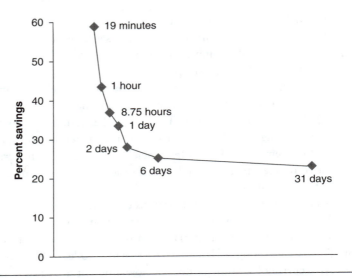

Figure 2.1   Ebbinghaus's Forgetting Curve for Consonant-Vowel-Consonants (CVCs), Based on the Savings Method

SOURCE: From Ebbinghaus (1913/1964).

NOTE: The *x*-axis shows the passage of time. There is dramatic loss by 19 minutes and more than 50% loss by an hour. Loss continues steeply for 2 days and then begins to level out.

1.2. The Ebbinghausian Model of Memory

Ebbinghaus was an empiricist and hard-line, in that he supported the views originated by John Locke. Three fundamental empiricist principles were incorporated into his model of memory. He believed that (1) memory representations (the CVCs used in his own research or any other form of memory content) were images; (2) when two such elements occurred together in experience they would become linked or associated together in memory, on the basis of the principle of contiguity; and (3) the properties of a psychological system can be identified through the study of *units of the system*. That is, higher-level functions will be the same as basic-level functions.

Given these assumptions, Ebbinghaus reasoned as follows. When he rehearsed a list of CVCs, each unit would occur together in his experience with the next unit. They would thus become associated together. At each rehearsal or repetition, the association would become stronger. At the end of a session the structure of memory might be something as follows:

List 1–HIF–GOS–WYL–CAS–ZUB, etc.

On his thinking of List 1 (because he wished to recall it) Ebbinghaus assumed that the List 1 representation would be present in awareness. The system could then "pull" the first item, HIF, also into awareness, along the thread or connection between List 1 and HIF, and so on along the series.

The model of recall described above implies the following. The attempt begins with a certain representation; if it is possible to move from that representation, along associative links, to the target, the target can be recalled. To put this another way, if the target can be *reached*, it can be recalled. There are modern associative models that endorse this view, although now what is assumed is that the target is first contacted in long-term memory (via associative connections) and then returned to awareness. That is, the search process moves from consciousness into long-term memory before the target is actually recalled.

1.2.1. Remote Links

Ebbinghaus also examined the question of whether the contiguity principle operates at a distance, as well as between directly contiguous items. That is, in a list such as HYS-GOL-WYF-MIN, do associative links form between HYS and WYF or HYS and MIN, as well as between adjacent items? In a series of careful experiments, Ebbinghaus found that these "remote" links do exist. They become weaker, the further the two items are from one another in the list. But perhaps the most surprising discovery was of backward links. These appear to be very weak but nonetheless real. If the items on an already memorized list are presented again but in reverse order (last to first), the newly formed list is easier to learn than a control list.

2. The Verbal Learning Tradition

Due to the success of Ebbinghaus's approach, an identical methodology was pursued across the opening decades of the 20th century. Psychologists studied human recall of CVCs and later language items in general. In doing this, they established a school known as the verbal learning tradition. When it became clear that not all CVCs are in fact equally easy to learn, researchers turned to the study of the learning and retention of words.

It was found that words high in imagery (I value), concreteness (c value), frequency of occurrence in language (f value), and something called m (for "meaning") value were all easier to learn than words low in these same properties (Kucera & Francis, 1967; Noble, 1952; Thorndike & Lorge, 1944). The m value of a word involved the number of items that were permanently associated with it in memory. For instance, a word like DOG has many permanent associations for most individuals (ANIMAL, BONE, BARK, etc.), while a word like GURNEY has few.

The influence of m value and frequency could be explained within the classic Ebbinghausian model. A word that possesses many associations with other words should be easy to recall due to the fact that multiple ways of "reaching" it would be present in the system; if any one of its many associates were activated, it would be activated. By the same logic, items that have occurred frequently in the experience of the individual should have become associated with a wide range of other items, on a contiguity basis, again providing multiple opportunities for their activation. But the effects of concreteness and imagery were more problematic. Why should it be easier to find an associative pathway to a word that could be imaged, than a word that could not?

The issue is examined again in Chapter 12.

3. List Learning and Serial Recall Curves

Various methods of testing were developed across the early decades of the 20th century. *Free recall* involves an approach in which any recalled item is scored as correct if it had been present on the original list. *Order recall* (used by Ebbinghaus) requires that items be reported in their original order. A third method, *paired-associate learning*, proved particularly useful for the studying the effects of multiple lists on memory. In this approach, items are presented in pairs, such as HOUSE-APPLE. During the test, the first item is presented and the task of the subject is to report the second, associated item.

When two lists are learned in succession, a paired-associate approach can be used to manipulate different levels of similarity among the items. Thus, a first list of the structure A-B (HOUSE-APPLE) might be followed by a list of the structure A-C (HOUSE-TRAIN.) It was found that different list structures produced reliable effects on memory. For instance, A-B, A-C is harder to learn than A-B, C-D (Underwood, 1983, chap. 9). Table 2.1 shows various patterns of similarity-based interference in the paired-associate paradigm.

When lists of individual words are learned, the probability of recalling an item is related to its position on the original list (Glanzer & Cunitz, 1966; Murdock, 1962; Postman & Phillips, 1965). Typically, items near the beginning of a list are well retained and items from the middle of the list are relatively poorly retained. Items at the end of a list show a different pattern depending on the method of test. Under free recall, the last items tend to be retained even more strongly than the first. Under order recall, this does not occur. These differences in recall based on position in the list are known as *serial position effects*. Figure 2.2 shows typical retention curves under free and order recall. The level of recall at each position represents the average recall of a group of subjects, for each item on the curve.

Table 2.1   Paradigms for the Learning of Two Paired-Associate Lists

	List 1	List 2	Description
I	A-B	C-D	Basic control list
II	A-B	A-C	Different responses to the same stimuli
III	A-B	C-B	Same responses with new stimuli
IV	A-B	A-Br	Stimuli and responses are re-paired

NOTE: These were known as *transfer designs*, in that researchers wished to discover how the learning of the first pair would transfer to the learning of the second pair. The control condition was the easiest to learn since each associative link was unique. The most difficult learning involved the same stimuli and responses but with re-pairings (A-B, A-Br).

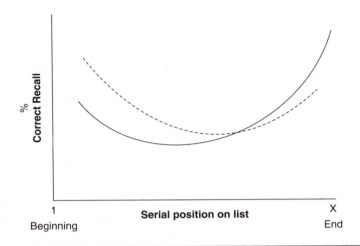

Figure 2.2   Serial Position Curves for Free and Serial Recall

NOTE: Free recall shows a marked recency effect and only a small primacy effect. Serial recall shows a marked primacy effect and only a small recency effect.

Although the overall shape of the serial position curve remains the same across different list lengths, the precise shape changes. For instance, in free recall, shorter lists show a shorter "low-recall" span in the middle of the list, while in longer lists that span is relatively extended. Figure 2.3 illustrates this change.

Serial recall patterns are highly reliable. The advantage at the beginning of lists is called a *primacy effect*, while the advantage at the end of a list is called a *recency effect*. The causes of both have been intensively investigated.

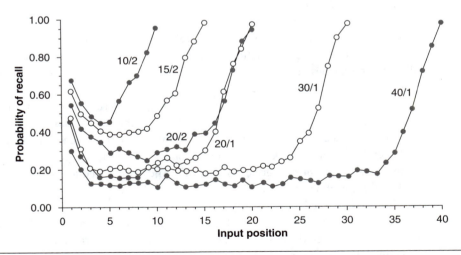

Figure 2.3   Free-Recall Curves for Lists of 10, 15, 20, 30, or 40 Items Presented at Rates of Two or One Item Per Second

SOURCE: From Murdock, B. B., Jr. "The serial position effect in free recall," in *Journal of Experimental Psychology*, *962*, 64, copyright © 1962, American Psychological Association. Reprinted with permission.

Primacy effects, recency effects, and what mechanism enables us to recall items in the correct order, are all topics of current research. Ebbinghaus had assumed that order recall depends on links formed between items on a list. This possibility has been explored across recent decades, under the title of *chaining models*. The data on the whole do not appear to support the notion that order memory is provided by links formed between specific word items. Other approaches have been explored. One, *ordinal theory*, posits that the order of items is established on the basis of relational properties among the items (Estes, 1972; Shiffrin & Cook, 1978). For instance, the first item in a series might possess the highest level of strength, the second item, the next highest level of strength, and so on. A third approach, *positional theory*, favors the view that each unit is associated with a structure indicating position, with one for the first position, one for the second, and so on (Burgess & Hitch, 1999; Henson, 1998). The data suggest that there may in fact be a hierarchy of such structures, from general descriptions "toward the beginning of the list," to more precise descriptions, with the general level providing a stronger code than the more specific. Another approach has centered on the notion of distinctiveness. According to this view, distinctive items are more likely to be recalled, and this property could differ depending on serial order position (Neath, 1993a; Neath & Crowder, 1996).

These various approaches have succeeded in explaining some aspects of serial position curves relevant to order recall, but none has been able to explain the entire set of known properties. Thus, although it appeared at one time that it would not be difficult to develop explanations for the effects found in word list learning, it is now apparent that this is not the case. The phenomena are wonderfully lawful. They are not, however, simple.

4. Interference Theory

At the turn of the 20th century it was generally believed that forgetting was due to a decay factor. Although the nature of decay was conceptualized in different ways, all such approaches assumed that memories were lost spontaneously over time. They simply decayed out of the system.

In 1932, John McGeoch, a researcher within the verbal learning tradition, launched a major attack on decay theory. He argued that the facts of daily life did not support a decay hypothesis. If decay explained forgetting, then a memory that had been lost at moment X in time could not be recovered later; if it had decayed from the system, it must be gone permanently. And yet it is frequently the case that we forget information or skills, only to recall them later.

McGeoch claimed that all forgetting was in fact due to *interference effects*. Material stored in memory would remain in memory and available, until other material entered the system. The new material caused the phenomenon of forgetting. If nothing interfered with memory A, memory A would not be lost. Roughly, forgetting memory content A is due to the entry into the system of new memory content B.

4.1. Interference Effects: Basic Findings

McGeoch and his colleagues launched an extensive program of research during the 1930s and 1940s in support of his claim. Their standard methodology could be described as follows. A group of subjects, the experimental group (E), learned a list of random words, List 1. Directly after learning List 1, they learned a second list, List 2. A control group learned only List 1. During the time that the experimental subjects were memorizing a second list, the control performed an activity that did not involve learning. (McGeoch required the control subjects to read jokes during this period.) Both groups were then given a test of List 1.

The control subjects retained significantly more than the experimental subjects. The work of the latter group in entering List 2 into memory had interfered with their ability to retain List 1. This type of memory loss was labeled *retroactive interference* since it worked backward. Later-learned material had disrupted the retention of earlier-learned material.

In an alternative paradigm, experimental subjects learned two lists in succession, as before. The control subjects learned only List 2. Then both were tested on List 2. The control subjects retained significantly more than the experimental subjects. This was perhaps a more startling finding. Having learned a list earlier disrupted the experimental group's ability to retain a currently learned list. The effect became known as proactive interference, because the effect worked forward in time.

The experimental paradigm used by McGeoch is shown in Table 2.2.

McGeoch had clearly demonstrated that interference does operate in human memory. He had also shown a straightforward but critical pattern in recall.

Memory task 1 + Memory task 2 → More forgetting

Memory task 1 + Nonmemory task → Less forgetting

Table 2.2   Design of Experimental Demonstration of Retroactive and Proactive Interference (RI and PI, respectively)

Retroactive Interference Paradigm

EXPERIMENTAL GROUP	CONTROL GROUP
Learn List 1	Learn List 1
Learn List 2	Read jokes
Test on List 1	Test on List 1

Proactive Interference Paradigm

EXPERIMENTAL GROUP	CONTROL GROUP
Learn List 1	Read jokes
Learn List 2	Learn List 2
Test on List 2	Test on List 2

NOTE: More forgetting occurs in the experimental groups under both conditions. RI on List 1 is caused by learning List 2; PI on List 2 is caused by having previously learned List 1.

The discovery that the more content is entered into memory, the more we forget, might at first seem a little disturbing. However, it is important to note that interference effects operate for weak memory content only. Material that is solidly learned does not suffer interference (McGeoch, 1932). This is true for random word items and also—critically—for general knowledge. Nobody is at risk for forgetting that Paris is the capital of France, no matter how much information he or she learns concerning France in the years to come. It is also the case that interference occurs when two sets of information are learned successively with no break in between. Under most conditions, a list of word items learned on Monday will not suffer (measurable) interference from a second list learned on Tuesday. The same is true for study sessions involving meaningful material.

4.2. Memory Codes and Similarity-Based Interference

Memory content can be expressed in different codes. This is true of information in general. The word CAT conveys certain information to an English reader. Here the input is linguistic/visual. The same content could be conveyed by a picture of a cat, which is clearly a different "code." Or if I knew Morse, the same content could be conveyed by a series of dots and dashes. In the same way, information in human cognition appears to be represented in some format or vehicle.

This raises questions concerning the nature of the codes deployed in human memory. The empiricist position had been that all such codes consist of (for the most part, visual or auditory) images. Ebbinghaus had believed this, as did McGeoch at the beginning of his career. Both researchers, however, were disposed to finding data that might support (or refute) their theories, and McGeoch therefore researched the question of the codes used when we learn and recall verbal items.

When material is learned, it enters a store known as long-term memory (LTM). For reasons to be explained later, LTM is widely defined as content that can be retained for longer than about 45 seconds. The upper boundary of LTM is permanent retention.

Thus, the research question centered on the code used when we memorize words and so enter them into long-term store.

McGeoch reasoned that since Memory Set 1 + Memory Set 2 produces interference, this relationship must also be true for codes. That is, if information were entered into LTM on the basis of a visual-pictorial code, then subsequent information based on a visual-pictorial code should produce a higher level of interference than would be the case for nonvisual information. (This assumption was confirmed experimentally by Brooks [1968].)

McGeoch generated word lists that were characterized by visual similarity (they looked alike), auditory similarity (they sounded alike), or semantic similarity (the words were alike in meaning). He found no effect on recall of any kind with lists high in visual or auditory similarity. In contrast, semantically similar lists influenced recall in several ways. They tended to enhance free recall and impair order recall. (A semantically similar list might, for instance, be a series of names of vehicles: CAR, TRAIN, BICYCLE, etc.)

McGeoch concluded that the code used to store words in LTM is a *semantic code*. When we memorize items, it is the *meaning* of the words that is being represented in some fashion. (Later research uncovered the fact that other codes, such as a visual representation of visually presented words, also operate. However, they were so weak compared to the semantic that they produced no measurable influence on the earlier data.)

Interference effects due to similarity of code are known, quite reasonably, as *similarity-based interference*. Thus, the impairment of performance when lists of semantically similar items are tested for order recall involves similarity interference reflecting the underlying semantic code. Similarity-based interference is a phenomenon that occurs throughout human memory.

McGeoch had concluded (correctly) that the code deployed by the system when we memorize words is a semantic code. However, the model that he originally endorsed had claimed that all codes in human cognition involve images. One of the difficulties for competitors with this position is that they appeared unable to offer an alternative. If a memory representation was not after all an image, what was it? McGeoch faced the same dilemma. He concluded that semantic codes clearly existed but that no model capable of explaining their nature was available.

4.3. Response Competition * * * * *

McGeoch generated a theoretical explanation of why memorizing two lists produces greater forgetting than the learning of one list. The theory was called *response competition*.

According to this view, items are learned when they become associated to one another, as claimed by Ebbinghaus. The items also become associated, however, with their spatial position on the list. If the series PIN-HAT-BOY were memorized, for instance, PIN would be associated with the first spatial position on the list, HAT with the second, and so on. The physical position #2 would thus operate as an eliciting stimulus for the response HAT. But if two lists were learned in succession, Position #2, present on both lists, would become associated with two different items. Perhaps the items in Position #2 on the second list would be STONE.

A subject attempting to recall List 1 might have formed only a weak link between PIN and HAT. At recall the link might fail to play through. At this point the system might depend on the link between position stimuli and list items. The correct position, #2, has been associated with both HAT and STONE. The two items would compete to emerge as the response or memory, and only one could in fact emerge. If the link between Position #2 and STONE was the stronger of the two, STONE, an incorrect response, would emerge. This would result in lower accurate recall scores when two lists were learned, as compared to one list.

In the decades that followed McGeoch's work, his response competition theory of memory was tested extensively. It emerged that although response competition does occur in some cases, most errors in recall do not involve substitutions from the "wrong" list (Melton & Irwin, 1940).

Two final claims made by McGeoch were deeply influential across the following decades. He believed that once an association was formed between items or between other stimuli and items, it was a permanent association. It would neither strengthen nor weaken over time. In other words, memories were never lost. They simply became incapable of retrieval under certain conditions.

He also believed that a memory is established across the period of time when an individual consciously works to form the memory. Once that time is over, there will be no further change relevant to memory strength.

5. Consolidation Theory

An alternative explanation of interference effects had been advanced by Muller and Pilzecker (1900). They assumed that the memory system operates actively to store and retain material. According to this view, when a list of words is memorized, the system deploys biochemical activities to encode Word 1. This activity continues when the individual is no longer consciously dealing with Word 1 but has moved on to Words 2, 3, 4, and so on. The same situation occurs across lists. When a learner has finished working on List 1 (rehearsing, associating items, etc.) and moves on to the conscious work involved in learning List 2, activities relevant to retaining List 1 are still occurring within the system.

As a result, the learning of two lists in succession tends to overtax the processing capacity of LTM. While List 2 is being learned, the biochemical functions involved in memory are still engaged in consolidating List 1. The capacity to code and so recall both lists is therefore weakened, compared with a situation where only one list is memorized. In the case of a single list, once the work of conscious memorization is completed the system can consolidate that single list without a drain on capacity caused by other, simultaneous "work" demands. Note how this assumption differs from McGeoch's position that the work of learning is completed when conscious learning is completed. The implication of McGeoch's view is that entry into LTM occurs at a specific point in time and is then achieved once and for all. The consolidation view implies that such "entry" may not be the product of a single moment or period but may extend over time.

A second prediction of consolidation theory is that in many cases the system will not be able to maintain information, coded in LTM, over time. Such maintenance requires an ongoing drain on capacity. Thus, in many cases, codes will weaken to the point where the relevant information cannot be retrieved, even under the most optimal conditions for recall.

6. The Classic Associative Tradition * * * * *

6.1. Data Relevant to the Associative Model

Under the original model proposed by Ebbinghaus, items presented next to one another on a list should generally be recalled together (a contiguity effect). It was established later, however, that under conditions of free recall, there is routinely an alteration of the original order of items on the list. Here extra-experimental contiguity plays a role. For instance, items such as DESK/BOOK are likely to be recalled together, even if they were not presented together on the original list. Also, a word list that contains many high-associate items of this kind can be learned more easily than a list that does not (Deese, 1961; Jenkins & Russell, 1952). Items that are similar in meaning also tend to be reported together, with superordinate classes being particularly effective in leading to recall of a subordinate class (Bousfield, 1951, 1953). The opposite is not the case. That is, BIRD will reliably activate SPARROW but SPARROW will not reliably activate BIRD. The findings were interpreted as implying some form of hierarchical organization of concepts.

Tulving (1966) suggested that when people learn lists of word items, they change the order of items based on conscious organizational principles, which he termed *subjective organization* (SO), such as similarity of meaning. Here the critical idea was that the way an individual processes a list, based on personal knowledge, may play as large a role as unconscious automatic principles such as environmental contiguity, reflecting, for instance, items appearing together on a to-be-learned list.

Recently, however, evidence has been gathered in support of the claim that items presented together or close together in a list frequently are reported together in a free-recall test (Kahana, 1996; Schwartz, Howard, Jing, & Kahana, 2005). This effect is now widely viewed as reflecting temporal information: that is, items that were encountered close together in time. It is also widely (although not universally) seen as involving conscious awareness of the temporal information, rather than an automatic/unconscious function.

In summary, tests of free recall produce reports in which items presented together or close together on a list are frequently recalled together, although other factors are also clearly operating. These other factors, such as extra-experimental contiguity or similarity of meaning, operate to change the original order of the items. Also, when the order of recall is changed on a first test, the new order normally persists over subsequent tests.

When a higher-order cue, reflecting a category, is offered, a subject can typically recall about five associated items. This is the case even if the cue can be assumed to have hundreds of items associated with it in memory (Battig & Montague, 1969; Slamecka, 1968, 1969). It appears that reporting an item from a given category tends to block items from the same category. This effect, and others like it, later became known as *output interference*. Output interference is now believed to be centrally implicated in some types of forgetting.

6.2. The Classic Associative Model of Memory

Based on the data outlined above, a model of memory was developed throughout the 1960s and 1970s. It is sometimes labeled as the *classic associative model*.

Within this context, it was assumed that associations form between list items and other list items, between the items and the name of the list (for example, List One or List from Monday), and between list items and perceptual information in the environment where the list was learned. Serial position stimuli were also assumed to play a role.

Another critical assumption was that any given word item possesses permanent associations with other items in memory. Thus, CAT may be associated with WHISKERS, MEOW, MILK, TIGER, or even DOG. And each of these items will have additional associates in long-term store. This principle was cited as explaining the appearance of new items on a list at the time of recall. (New items are generally the source of many and even most errors.) Thus, an individual might fail to recall CAT and instead recall TIGER. Here the association is apparent. In many cases, however, it is not. Perhaps the individual will incorrectly recall CHAIR. This could occur because of a strong association between CAT and CHAIR in LTM, perhaps because the subject owns a cat that habitually sleeps in a certain prominent chair in her house.

The strength of associations among all the items differs. Also, the number of associations that any given item has with others will differ. This was assumed to play the critical role in memory strength. To add to the variability in which Item X might produce Item Y in memory, some items could be associated together (via other items) redundantly: that is, have many indirect links joining them.

The model assumed that memories were retrieved on an associative basis. It followed that if a given item had multiple links with other items, there would be more ways of "reaching" it. In each case, the system begins at a certain point, say X, and traces associative paths through all the elements associated with X above a threshold strength. If any one of these paths is directly or ultimately linked to the target, the target memory will be activated.

In summary, recall involves reaching or locating a target. The more paths available to reach the target, the better the probability of recall. The influence of this early model will be seen in later chapters examining current research into the retrieval of information from memory.

7. Interference Theory (1940s–1980s) * * * * *

Forgetting due to interference effects was studied extensively across the decades following McGeoch's work. It was found that certain highly consistent patterns emerge following the learning of two or more lists.

When two lists are learned in succession and tested immediately after learning, retroactive interference (RI) is greater than proactive interference (PI).Thus, the second list will be retained more strongly than the first. However, over time the first list gains in strength, relative to the second, until the two functions cross. In addition to the relative strengths of the two lists, if List 1 is tested over time, there is some absolute recovery of responses. Items that could not be recalled under immediate testing may be recalled after a delay, such that recall can be slightly stronger after a retention interval than under immediate testing (Underwood, 1948). The improvement continues for about an hour and a half after the end of learning (which is the end of List 2 learning), and then recall steadily declines again (Koppenaal, 1963).

If more practice occurs on the second list of two lists learned in succession, there is greater RI. Such interference increases steadily as the second list is practiced from 5, to 10 or 20 times. However, the effect does not continue to increase beyond 20 trials. Whatever causes the interference has a ceiling, that ceiling being almost precisely 20 trials on the second list, beyond which the effect no longer operates. (Melton & Irwin, 1940; Underwood, 1945)

The tendency for items from the nontarget list to intrude on recall of the target list shows a different profile from overall interference effects. If the second list is rehearsed repeatedly, intrusion errors increase up to about 5 or 10 rehearsals. Then they diminish. As they diminish, RI effects continue to increase. And finally, a delay between learning Lists 1 and 2 eliminates interference effects.

At one time it was believed widely that interference theory could explain these and other phenomena involved in forgetting. However, predictions based on the theory were frequently disconfirmed. When this occurred, attempts were made to modify the theoretical position by introducing multiple possible assumptions (for example, that a given list was inhibited when another list was learned, that inhibited list items underwent extinction, etc.).

Many researchers continued to believe that interference involved some form of item blocking. Others began to hypothesize that the learning of a second list operated to cause "unlearning" of the first (Hintzman, 1972; Melton & Irwin, 1940). According to this position, interference involved the weakening of earlier traces. Others held that both response competition and unlearning must be involved (Postman & Underwood, 1973). The fundamental opposition between a blocking, no-memory-weakening assumption, and a memory-weakening assumption has remained a topic of debate up to the present (Curran & Hintzman, 1997; Jacoby, Begg, & Toth, 1997).

Underwood came to believe (on the basis of data apparently supporting this position) that almost all forgetting was due to PI, not RI. The PI came not only from previous items on a target list but also from other lists learned in the past. This view was held within the field for many years. But disconfirming evidence, often produced by Underwood himself, steadily mounted (Underwood & Ekstrand, 1967; Underwood & Postman, 1960). It is now widely believed that most forgetting is not due to PI from material learned in the past.

It became increasingly clear that interference theory, even when repeatedly modified, could not explain the empirical findings (Tulving & Madigan, 1970). Underwood (1983) agreed. What remains is a body of data that shows extremely lawful patterns of forgetting over time but that as yet has found no adequate theoretical explanation. Learning two sets of information one after the other produces large and predictable, negative, effects on recall. (This is the case unless the two sets are logically interrelated in some way.) Also, when coding formats are identical across Set A and Set B, the outcome of interference is particularly severe. Wixted (2004), noting the failure of interference theory in spite of the many years it which it dominated the field, has suggested that the consolidation hypothesis should be examined again.

Interference theory has failed to explain why forgetting of this particular kind occurs. But the *facts* concerning interference have proved an invaluable research tool. They can be used to determine the nature of the codes operating in human recall and much more. Interference phenomena will be cited repeatedly across the present book.

Summary

Ebbinghaus was the first researcher to succeed in developing data concerning memory that could be replicated. He used nonsense syllables (CVCs), which he learned through rehearsal. It was his belief that the CVCs were represented as images in memory and became linked together on the basis of the principle of contiguity.

Ebbinghaus's successful research led to the development of the verbal learning tradition. Working within this tradition, McGeoch demonstrated that forgetting occurs when new material is entered into LTM directly following the learning of earlier material. Interference effects operate only when the material has been fairly weakly coded. Under interference theory, the material that cannot be recalled has not been lost from the system but is being blocked. Under consolidation theory, the system performs ongoing work over time to fix newly learned material into memory and the learning of two lists of items sequentially will overtax the capacity of the system to achieve this. Therefore, more forgetting occurs when two lists are learned than when one is learned.

Similarity-based interference occurs when the two bodies of material are similar in code. Such interference is greater than the interference found when the codes are not notably similar. The code that McGeoch found showing similarity-based interference following list learning was a semantic (meaning) code.

According to the classic associative tradition, word items are interassociated in LTM. Whether an item can be recalled depends on whether it can be "reached" from the given starting point, along associative links.

Many decades of research have been devoted since the 1930s to interference theory. The theory has not stood up well, and some researchers believe that consolidation theory should be reconsidered.

Discussion

Certain basic discoveries concerning human memory were introduced above. Some of the early theorizing has exerted a considerable influence within the cognitive field. Ebbinghaus reported, for instance, that material that appears to have been wholly forgotten does in fact leave some trace in the system. This appears to have led to widespread support for the permanent memory (no memory weakening) hypothesis: the view that any information entered into long-term store remains permanently in that store, at its original strength. McGeoch was also an influential supporter of the theory.

Current research into implicit recall, however, has shown that changes in the system, due to earlier learning, should not always be equated with the retention of a full-blown "ordinary" memory.

Such content may be more weakly coded or less integrated than ordinary memory content. Across the period of research described here, three major theories of forgetting were developed. These were decay, interference and consolidation (or failure of consolidation). A fourth (discrimination failure) will be introduced in Chapter 4. These remain the primary contenders for the explanation of forgetting today. (Of course, they need not be mutually exclusive.)

In Chapters 3 and 4, the issue of memory codes and of forgetting is examined again. This research centers on events occurring directly after a verbal stimulus is encountered and before the entry of its representation into long-term store.

CHAPTER 3

Sensory Memory

Overview

1. The information-processing tradition is a school of cognitive psychology based on the claim that the brain actively processes information, usually in stages.

2. Early research posited three memory stores: sensory, short-term memory (STM), and long-term memory (LTM). Sensory memory codes for the physical properties of a stimulus, such as shape or sound. It is preconscious and preattentional.

3. Although only about four items can be reported following a very brief display of an array of items, most or all are entered into sensory memory. It is widely believed that the items are also identified preconsciously.

4. It appears that the system can only maintain items in a condition such that they can be attended and entered into awareness for about a second. Items are lost through decay.

5. Masking involves a phenomenon in which a second stimulus, projected over an earlier stimulus in sensory memory, makes it impossible to recall the first stimulus.

6. Sensory memory for auditory stimuli appears to last about 4 seconds and perhaps longer.

Learning Objectives

1. Knowledge of the tenets of information-processing psychology, including the concept of stages of processing.

2. Knowledge of the codes involved in sensory memory: coding type, length of life, how forgetting occurs.

3. Knowledge of the issue concerning the unconscious identification of stimuli.

The verbal learning tradition described in the previous chapter was based on the view that memories involve images. The model's origins lay in the empiricist philosophy developed in Europe during and after the 18th century. From roughly the 1950s, an information-processing school of psychology began to emerge in the United States and Great Britain. It was predicated on the view that the brain actively processes information.

1. Information-Processing Psychology

The older tradition had assumed that images were received through the senses and stored in memory. This implied a relatively passive role on the part of the memory function. In contrast, information-processing psychology is loosely founded on a computer model, in the sense that computers store and manipulate information, and the present school holds that the human brain also stores and manipulates information. Thus, the formation of a memory involves "work" on the part of the system, and the same is true when a memory is recovered.

The information-processing tradition posited that what is involved is a sequence of processing activities; some information cannot be handled until other information has been established. For instance, it would not be possible to identify the nature of a visual stimulus before some data had been coded concerning its shape; if you encounter a chair, you cannot tell that it is in fact a chair until the system has determined what the object looks like. This information will be generated before the chair is seen consciously. Psychologists were therefore interested in determining the various *steps* or *stages* involved when we enter content into memory.

Another critical tenet within the present tradition involves the view that, as in the example given above, much of the processing relevant to memory occurs at an unconscious level. It is only the end products of such activity that enter awareness; and, in some cases, no representation enters awareness.

Information-processing psychology assumes that memories can be expressed in different codes, as was established within the early verbal learning tradition. Thus, the content that we recall is not restricted here to images (although images are present in many memories) but also includes abstract semantic representation.

1.1. The Stages Model

Research performed during the 1950s and 1960s in the field of information processing indicated that when verbal stimuli (such as words) are encountered, a code reflecting those stimuli is established in the system. The nature of that code changes across time. Three major types of code change were identified. They occurred quickly, in less than a minute after the encounter with the stimulus.

It was assumed that each of the three dominant codes reflected a specific and distinct memory store. It was further assumed that the representation of the external stimulus was entered into the first store, then (if attended) moved to the second, and finally (if further processing occurred) to the third. This view was formulated as a specific model of memory, called the *stages* or *modal model* (Atkinson & Shiffrin, 1968). The stages model as such and later theoretical developments are described in further detail in Chapter 6.

Across the decades that followed the discovery of swift "recoding" activities in verbal memory, intensive research was performed to examine the properties of each of the hypothesized memory stores. The first was called *sensory memory*, the second, *verbal short-term memory* (verbal STM) and the third, *long-term memory* (LTM). The properties of the first of these stores, as established by more than 50 years of research, are described below.

2. Sensory Memory

When a stimulus is first encountered, it is entered into sensory memory. This involves the retention of a literal copy of the stimulus. That is, if a chair is present, sensory memory codes for the shape of the object, its size, its color, and its location in space. If a sound is encountered, the physical properties of the sound, such as its loudness, tone, pitch, and location in space, are held in sensory store. The relevant code is therefore termed a *physical*, and sometimes a *structural*, code.

Sensory memory is essentially preconscious. As it was first researched, it also appeared to be preidentification or *precategorical*. That is, no code reflecting the meaning of the stimulus was found at this level. If a chair was encountered, the shape and location of the chair would be stored. In contrast, no information reflecting the meaning of the stimulus (the fact that it was, in fact, a chair) was assumed to be present prior to the time when the stimulus was actively attended (Crowder & Morton, 1969).

Entry of material into sensory store does not depend on attention. Stimuli within the visual or auditory field (whether attended or not) automatically enter the system at this level. Such entry appears to occur in parallel. That is, whatever stimuli are present enter at the same time, rather than sequentially. Information is lost from sensory memory through decay. Material vanishes from the system whether new material is entered or not.

Neisser (1967) labeled sensory memory for visual stimuli as *iconic store*, with a visual array being called the *icon*. Auditory sensory memory was called the *echoic store*. These terms are now widely used within the field.

2.1. Research Into Sensory Memory: The First Years

In 1859, Sir William Hamilton was curious to know how much information can be perceived or apprehended at a single glance. He studied the question by throwing marbles onto the ground and trying to instantly judge their number. He found that he was able to estimate the presence of up to six and sometimes seven marbles accurately. A larger number could not be accurately judged, unless they formed simple groups of twos or threes. Our ability to establish information in the briefest of glances became known as the *span of apprehension*. The estimates of this span varied slightly from researcher to researcher.

Later interest focused on more complex stimuli that could be identified for meaning (as against simple number of items present). Sperling (1960, 1967) examined the question under experimentally controlled conditions. He presented his participants with a screen typically showing three rows of four letters each. The items might be physically present for 50 milliseconds (1 millisecond, or ms, is 1/1000 of a second). Under the standard *whole report* condition participants were then asked to report as many of the items in the array as possible. They were typically able to identify four and sometimes five items.

When the participants named these items, the screen was dark. They were recalling the material from sensory memory. The (on average) four-item report occurred across different exposure times, ranging from 15 to 500 ms.

Participants in the studies often claimed, however, that they had registered more than four items but were unable to name them. Sperling (who had apparently a strong intuition concerning the reason for this difficulty) therefore developed a *partial report procedure*. Under partial report, an array of items was presented briefly as before. Immediately following presentation, the participants heard a high, medium, or low tone. The high tone signaled report of the top line of items only; the medium tone signaled the middle row, and the low tone signaled the bottom row. (It is important to note that the items were no longer physically present when the tone was heard.) Under these conditions about three out of four possible items were reported from each line. This necessarily meant that all three lines had been coded in sensory store.

An example of the arrays used by Sperling is shown in Figure 3.1.

In a second series of experiments using partial report, Sperling delayed the onset of the signal tone for periods ranging to a second. He found that recall declined as the delay increased.

Under what might be called standard lighting conditions, participants were able to report only one or occasionally two items if the signal was delayed by 500 ms. The data clearly indicated that the icon had decayed substantially within half a

Figure 3.1   An Example of the Type of Stimuli Used by Sperling in His Experiments

second. By a second, almost all the iconic information was lost. Figure 3.2 shows the number of items that Sperling estimated to be present in sensory store across varied intervals of time.

In fact, lighting conditions affect the length of life of the trace in sensory store. Sperling (1963) also showed that when the field against which the items would be presented was dark and the postexposure field was also dark, the decay of the items was slower. Partial report continued to be superior to whole report across delays of several seconds. That is, the trace appeared to endure for several seconds, rather than 1 second only.

The earlier findings still needed to be explained. Why could the participants recall items from any of the three lines under partial report, thus clearly demonstrating that material from all three lines was present in sensory memory and yet only recall a total of four items under conditions of whole report?

A theory developed in the 1960s suggested that the explanation lay in the time required to identify the items. (It was such a logically tidy explanation that it became widely endorsed. It was not, as things turned out, accurate but remains helpful in any attempt to conceptualize sensory memory.) To recall an item from the visual array, the participant had to first identify the item. You clearly cannot report that a given item is an "H" if you have not identified it as an H. But sensory memory holds only patterns; there are no codes for meaning. It was therefore concluded that in order to report each item, the participant would have to attend to its "pattern" in sensory memory and identify it. *Identification* is a term used for the function that ascribes meaning to a stimulus. Thus, to establish the fact that a given

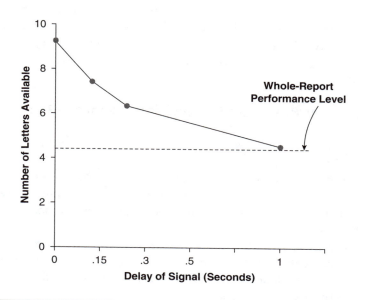

Figure 3.2   Estimated Number of Letters Available Across Delays Extending to 1 Second Under Conditions of Partial Report

SOURCE: From Sperling, G., "The information available in brief visual presentations," in *Psychological Monographs, 74,* copyright © 1960, American Psychological Association. Reprinted with permission.

item was, in fact, an H, its identity would have to be established. (Some researchers assume that identity here can be equated with the *name* of the stimulus only. And the names of stimuli are clearly established when identity is established. However, the position taken here is that letter identity is more than a name. For instance, if you recall the item "H," you are aware that you are naming a letter.) Once the item was identified, it would be entered into the next higher memory store: And of course it could be reported.

But it was widely believed in the 1960s that the work of identification is performed serially and thus requires time to complete. And Sperling had shown that the icon has largely decayed by 500 ms after presentation. The critical question could thus be framed as follows: How many items can be identified during a period of 500 ms, or perhaps slightly longer, before the icon decays?

If identification requires time, the following sequence of events could be assumed. Under whole report, a participant would attend to the first item, identify it and report it. These events would take perhaps 200 or 250 ms. The identification and report of the second, third, and fourth items would each require the same interval of 200 to 250 ms. By the time the participant had identified and reported the last of the four items, from 800 ms to a second would have passed. When the subject's attention moved to the next item, that item would already have decayed from the store. It could thus not be reported.

The interpretation outlined above was based on the belief that the identification process requires time and is performed serially. But there was evidence to suggest that both of these claims were incorrect. Baxt (1871) had performed work indicating that a hundred items could be "read off," that is, identified, in 1 second! The brain is a relatively slow serial processor and could not achieve identification at the speed required on the basis of serial processing. It is, however, a formidable parallel processor (Franklin, 1995). Thus, a hundred items a second could perhaps be handled through parallel processing.

2.2. Later Research: Preconscious Identification

We can identify an item that is presented for no longer than 1 ms (Coltheart, 1977). This fact is perhaps the clearest of all demonstrations of the existence of sensory store. One millisecond is an extremely brief period of time, far too short to sustain identification. But the stimulus is entered into sensory store even under conditions of a 1 ms exposure and held long enough in that store for identification to be possible.

As described above, it was widely believed after the 1960s that the reason we cannot continue this impressive performance and recall, say, 10 items after a 10 ms exposure is that the sensory code decays before we can attend and serially identify more than about four stimuli.

However, several studies in the 1970s and 1980s reported data that were compatible with Baxt's claim that in fact identification of stimuli occurs very quickly after presentation (Coltheart, 1977; Merikle, 1980). Merikle presented an array of letters and numbers to his participants under conditions of partial report. However, the partial report did not involve spatial location. It involved category membership. Thus, participants were instructed on some trials to report only the letters (not the numbers) in the array. On other trials they were instructed to report the numbers only, ignoring the letters

According to the model described above, these instructions should not have improved performance. Suppose the following array was presented:

H 6 3 A

7 G B 1

K 8 W 2

If the instructions were to report only letters, a participant would attend to the first item and report it; he or she would then need to attend to the second item and identify it in order to determine whether it was a letter or a number. The participant would then need to perform a similar act of identification of the next item and identify and report the fourth item. By this time (based on the assumption that identification takes time) the icon would have decayed. In fact, however, roughly four letters were reported on each trial. The participants were performing in the same manner as had occurred under partial report conditions for spatial location.

It is now widely believed that when items enter sensory memory, they are first expressed in a physical code (as assumed by the earlier models) but that further coding, which establishes the identity of the items, takes place very quickly and in parallel. These events occur at a preconscious level and—critically—prior to the deployment of attention. The coding is automatic.

Attention *is* required, however, to enter the items into awareness. The bottleneck in recall occurs at this point. The system stores the physical information present in the icon (its size, its shape, etc.), and information reflecting the identity of verbal items, for a period of perhaps slightly less than a second (under average viewing conditions). Throughout that period, attended material can be entered into awareness. But this preattentional information apparently begins to decay almost at once and is significantly degraded after 500 ms. As a result, by the time about four items have been reported, the remaining information is no longer available.

Due to the fact that identification occurs soon after the presentation of the stimulus, some researchers have concluded that the *original* physical code is of even shorter duration than suggested here, being rewritten almost immediately into new coding formats. One of these is a semantic code. The other involves a representation of the physical properties of the stimulus in a more flexible form. By "more flexible" is meant a code that can be used in ongoing processing (Coltheart, 1983; Cowan, 1995). It is likely that the original sensory code (defined as the visual pattern or sound information first established when a stimulus is encountered) cannot be used in ongoing processing. It may involve instead a fundamental holding function: That is, stimuli information is maintained in sensory store until further processing can take place (Loftus & Irwin, 1998). According to the present view, a good deal of processing occurs between sensory memory, as originally conceptualized, and the entry of information into the next store, labeled short-term memory.

There is now a body of data that supports the hypothesis of a preconscious stage of stimulus identification. When experimental participants display errors in reporting material after very brief exposures (such that the stimuli are entered into store before they have been attended), the errors made reflect phonemic similarity: For instance, a T might be reported instead of a B but an O would not. This implies processing beyond the simple retention of sounds because the memory function is apparently reconstructing information. That is, if the second phoneme of the input T has been retained but not the first, the system has generated another letter possessing the second phoneme. Also, Loftus and Irwin (1998) found that different tasks tapping sensory memory did not all correlate with one another; some tasks were drawing on the original stage of "true" sensory store and some on the stage of further preconscious processing.

2.2.1. Location Information

Some intriguing research in the 1980s suggested that the content that becomes unavailable to the system after a second (following very brief exposure) is not identity information but rather location information.

Mewhort and Leppman (1985) presented a row of letters to their participants for 50 ms. They then asked whether a target letter, such as P, had been present in the array. The participants were able to respond correctly as the interval after presentation increased beyond a second. That is, performance did not deteriorate between immediate recall and a second's delay, as it had in Sperling's experiments. When the researchers asked for recall of the *location* of a specific item in the row, however, performance deteriorated as the interval between presentation and test increased. After 500 ms, only a single item could be reported. An experiment also varying requests for item or for location recall was conducted using Sperling's original methodology (Yeomans & Irwin, 1985). The findings were the same. Item recall could extend beyond a second after presentation. In contrast, recall of an item's location was significantly impaired by 500 ms.

The earlier studies, which involved reporting items from some starting point and moving from location to location, had all required some spatial information. However, it should be noted that in studies that require item report based on location, the individual must be able both to use codes reflecting identification and location. Location alone would amount to no more than the report that there was *some* item at the beginning or middle of an array. This more complex information appears to become unavailable under standard conditions after about a second. (The point is that if there was some way of testing for location alone, this content might also last beyond a second; it may be that the combination of identity and location information cannot be established or maintained after a period of a second following presentation of the stimulus.)

It is widely believed today that sensory memory (as against the subsequent analytic/preconscious processing) involves a persistence in the neural activity created in response to the external stimulus. Nairne (2003) has suggested that this stage should therefore not be considered memory as such but that only the later, more flexible processing stages should be so considered. However, since content in sensory store is retained when the stimulus is no longer physically present, the alternative view that this is indeed a memory store can also be taken.

2.3. The Bottleneck

As described above, visual sensory store is unable to maintain content (in a condition available for conscious entry) for a period longer than about a second. Given that the system can apparently identify an item in one thousandth of a second, why should there be such a major limitation in its holding capacity?

The limitation may simply be a question of time; or it may be the quantity of information, in that a large amount of information may put more strain on the relevant capacity. Or the problem could involve output interference.

It is also possible that there is a stage of additional processing prior to the entry of material into awareness that requires time and/or functional capacity to achieve, such that only about four items can be processed in this fashion before the code becomes degraded to the point where it cannot be used. For instance, it is known that visual stimuli are coded across different areas of the brain: one area for shape and color, another for size and location, and yet another for the identification of the stimulus.

The dissociatively coded information has to be reunited into a single stimulus before that stimulus is entered into awareness. This reuniting or "binding" of the information requires attention (Treisman, 1998; Wheeler & Treisman, 2002). It is possible that the bottleneck in sensory memory reflects the need to perform the complex processing involved in connecting the relevant codes (for shape, meaning, etc.) back together. The processing may drain the capacity of the system to maintain information in sensory store or may simply take time so that only a few items can be organized and retrieved within a second, assuming that the system can only hold the relevant content for about a second.

Regardless of the explanation for the bottleneck in processing, when (still available) content in sensory memory is attended, it will enter the next higher memory stage: STM. Recall based on this type of memory is covered in the following chapter.

3. Masking

It was described above that information is lost from sensory memory on the basis of decay. A second factor, known as masking, also influences recall from iconic store.

During the 1960s, various procedures were developed to test for the recall of individual items in sensory memory. For instance, in one approach, an array of items would be shown on a screen, the screen would go dark and a bar marker would occur just beneath the location where a given (target) item had been. The subjects' task was to report the item. Subjects could typically do this. They sometimes, however, misreported an item that was physically close to the target. Here the spatial code had not been maintained at sufficient strength for the subject to identify the "right" target.

In an attempt to overcome this difficulty, researchers tried a new approach in which an entire circle was projected onto the darkened screen. The circle surrounded the area where the target item had been. This was expected to minimize spatial errors. Instead, subjects could not recall the target item even under conditions of immediate testing. It was as if the circle had erased the item from sensory store (Averbach & Coriell, 1961).

The effect became known as *masking*. If a new stimulus is coded in the same spatial location as an earlier stimulus, it appears to erase the first. The timing between the two presentations needs to be exact.

3.1. Sensory Memory: A Peripheral or a Central Process?

When we see a stimulus, we can form an afterimage. This is an effect of chemical changes on the retina. If you stare at a light, the afterimage will be the same shape but dark. If you stare at a red pattern and then look at a blank screen, you may see an afterimage—the same pattern—but it will appear green. Afterimages are complementary: Red produces green, blue produces yellow, and so on. Sakitt (1976) and Sakitt and Long (1979) suggested that sensory memory may be no more than a kind of afterimage, based on physical processes in the retina. But if the icon is an afterimage, experimental participants should report the items from iconic store as the complementary colors of the stimulus. This does not occur (Banks & Barber, 1977).

It has emerged, however, that two forms of masking operate in sensory memory (Turvey, 1973). The first involves brightness masking, in which a light of greater intensity than the stimulus is presented just after the stimulus. The second is pattern masking, in which a random pattern of lines is projected across the spatial location of the stimulus, also immediately after the presentation of the stimulus. Brightness masking is effective only when both the light and the stimulus are presented to the same eye. It is thus a peripheral effect operating at the retina. Pattern masking is effective even when the mask and the stimulus are presented to different eyes. This means that the effect is central: That is, it occurs in the brain after the point at which information from the two eyes becomes integrated. Unlike brightness masking, intensity has no influence on the effectiveness of pattern masking.

Thus it appears that sensory memory involves a continuum of processes, beginning at the retina, close to the status of an afterimage and continuing to a central level.

3.2. Unconscious Processing for Meaning

Marcel (1983) suggested that masking an item does *not* cause the item to be erased from sensory memory or from the system in general. He presented his participants with a series of words. The presentation was auditory. Some of the words, such as JAM, were ambiguous. The participants faced a screen. At the moment of the auditory presentation of an ambiguous item, a word was projected onto the screen and immediately masked. As a result, participants were not conscious of seeing any word on the screen. As JAM was heard, half the participants were presented with the word STRAWBERRY on the screen, the other half with the word TRAFFIC. Remember that the screen appeared blank; participants did not consciously see these items.

In a subsequent recognition test, individuals who had been presented with the masked item STRAWBERRY tended to recognize JAM when presented as a food item but not when presented as the kind of jam you encounter on a road. Subjects who had been exposed to TRAFFIC on the screen showed the opposite tendency.

The masked item had influenced the semantic interpretation of the attended words. Thus, in some fashion, or to some degree at least, the meaning of the masked item had been established within the system. This occurred although the participants in the study had no awareness of seeing that word.

One interpretation of the findings would be that the masked item was fully processed for meaning. That is, it was identified. If it is assumed that such identification would require time (more time than had elapsed by the time of the presentation of the mask), then the data also implied that a mask does not erase (masked) content from the system.

At the least, the Marcel study indicated that stimuli may be identified for meaning (again, to some degree or in some fashion) even though they are not perceived consciously.

There is in fact a long history of research supporting the hypothesis of unconscious identification. This tradition has usually centered on one of two approaches. In the first, stimuli are presented in so degraded a fashion that the participant cannot consciously identify them. Yet, as in the Marcel study cited above, the "unreadable" stimuli may influence the interpretation of other items. In the second, unattended stimuli may be shown to have the same effect. (An unattended stimulus does not normally enter awareness, except perhaps as a blur.)

Sidis (1898) showed his participants cards marked with a letter or a number. The cards were presented at such a distance that the participants could not see the letter or number except as an unreadable blob. When they were asked, however, to guess as to the nature of the item, they reported on whether it was a letter or a number and the identity of the letter or number at a higher than chance level.

Later studies established that a range of simple stimuli can be identified even when they are not consciously experienced. These include oriented lines, geometric shapes, word meanings, and emotions expressed in faces (Baker, 1937; Cheesman & Merikle, 1986; Esteves, Dimberg, & Öhman, 1994; Merikle & Daneman, 2000; Merikle & Joordens, 1997). Mack and Rock (1998) required their participants to look at a fixation point on a screen. A cross was then shown in one quadrant of the screen. The task was to determine which arm of the cross was longer. On Trial 3, a cross was again presented in one quadrant, with the same requirement, but now a word was also presented in the center of the display. Sixty percent of the participants did not notice the presence of the word. But when they were later told that a word had been on the screen (a fact that surprised them) and shown five word items and asked to choose, by guessing, the one that had been presented, 47% of the group selected the correct item.

3.3. Determining Conscious
Versus Unconscious Processing * * * * *

Two methods have emerged for determining whether an individual has become conscious or was previously conscious, of a given stimulus. The first method is to ask the participant. This is considered a "subjective" approach. An alternative, "objective" method is to present an item and mask the item. Participants are then required to decide whether a stimulus had or had not been present. If they cannot answer the question——if they cannot discriminate between trials when a stimulus is present or when it is not present——it is decided that no conscious awareness has occurred. Psychologists have tended to trust the objective approach more than the subjective, although of course both depend ultimately on introspection. It is also the case, as Merikle, Smilek, and Eastwood (2001) noted, that the first is the more valid measure since a determination of whether an item had or had not been present could depend on unconsciously processed information, as well as on conscious experience.

Another approach to the attempt to distinguish between information that has been consciously experienced and information that has not is to determine whether a dissociation occurs in the effect of the stimulus on behavior. That is, it is possible that an item that enters awareness may have a different influence on a behavioral response, as compared to the same item if it has not entered awareness.

One such dissociation might involve the following. It appears likely that material present in awareness can be used within the context of conscious decisions: But unconscious material may be intractable within this context. Debner and Jacoby (1994) tested this possibility by the use of word items that were followed by a mask, with the onset of the mask being either at 50 ms or at 150 ms. The 150 ms delay could be expected not to fully eliminate the word items, such that they would possibly enter awareness to some extent. In contrast, the 50 ms delay should have fully eliminated any conscious experience of the items. One of the masked items was the word "frigid."

Participants were then presented with word stems that corresponded to the masked word items. They were told to complete the stem in any fashion that they wished, except that they should not use the item presented earlier on a screen (which they may or may not have seen.) Thus, if "fri-" were presented as the stem, they could say, "Friday" or "frisky," but not "frigid."

Participants who had been exposed to the 150 ms delay mask were able to comply with the instructions to some significant extent. That is, they avoided completing the stem, in the present example, as "frigid." Participants exposed to the 50 ms delay were unable to comply. They tended to complete the stem precisely as "frigid." Thus, the 150 ms participants appeared to have consciously seen the masked item, at least to some degree, and were thus able to avoid using it in the stem completion task. The 50 ms participants, who had not consciously seen the item, were unable to determine that they should not report it. However, since the item had been activated, there was a tendency for it to be used in the stem-completion task. Smith and Merikle (1999) and Jacoby and Whitehouse (1989) reported similar results. It thus appears that another form of dissociation exists between consciously and unconsciously identified items. The former can be bound up in a conscious decision process, while the latter cannot. That is, unconsciously processed information proved resistant to being used in a consciously directed decision process.

There thus exists an extended body of data in support of the claim that content may be processed for meaning, and be present in memory, even though no representation of that content finds expression in awareness. A further examination of data of this kind is provided in Chapter 14.

4. Output Interference

There is evidence for a phenomenon in sensory memory known as *output interference*. Recalling an item from sensory store makes it relatively difficult to recall other items (Dick, 1971; Neath, 1998, p. 37). The reasons for the effect are at present unknown.

Output interference means that under standard experimental conditions, as participants attempt to recall items from a given line in an array or from a given category, some of the loss of the other items appears to be due to output interference rather than simply the passage of time. Thus, if a single item is to be recalled, performance is superior after a given interval (say 3/4 of a second) when compared to the recall, after the same interval, of a third item. Equally, however, if more than a second passes before the attempt is made to recall any item, recall will fail. Thus, both factors (output interference and some negative effect of the passage of time) appear to operate in sensory memory.

5. Echoic Memory

As described above, we have the capacity to retain sounds in a sensory store. The information held in auditory sensory store or echoic memory includes loudness, rhythm, frequency, spatial location, and (in the case of a voice) tone and pitch.

It has proved methodologically difficult to identify the length of life of sounds in echoic store. Elements in a visual array do not appear to produce interference effects within the array, but this is not the case for multiple sounds at different locations. Thus, exact analogs of Sperling's work have been difficult to achieve. It seems clear, however, that echoic store has a longer life than the icon. (Most people have had the experience of registering that someone just spoke and of being able to "play back" the words from echoic store. A sentence such as, "What did I just say?" can be recovered in this fashion, although the relevant coding extends for more than a second.) Darwin, Turvey, and Crowder (1972), using sounds presented at three different locations, estimated echoic store as enduring for about 4 seconds. Glucksberg and Cowan (1970) required their participants to attend to material being presented to one ear, while unattended or ignored information was presented to the other ear. Control of attention of this kind is possible, and participants do not typically retain any information concerning the meaning of the items on the ignored channel, while it remains ignored (Moray, 1959). At a given signal, they were asked to switch attention to the other ear and determine whether a digit had just been presented on that channel. They were able to report (to some extent) digits presented up to 4 seconds before the signal, with performance leveling at about 5 seconds. Information had thus been retained in echoic memory over a period of 4 to 5 seconds. The trace appeared to deteriorate rapidly, however, across that interval. Figure 3.3 shows the percentage of digits recalled as a function of the delay between the presentation of the digit and the signal.

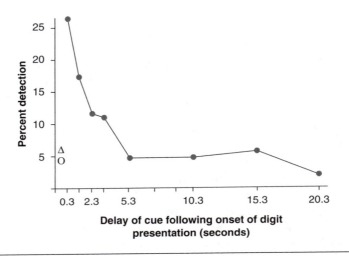

Figure 3.3   Probability of Reporting a Digit Presented on the Unattended Ear as a Function of the Delay Between Digit and Cue

SOURCE: From Glucksberg, S., & Cowan, G. N., Jr., "Memory for non-attended auditory material," *Cognitive Psychology 1*, copyright © 1970. Reprinted with permission of Elsevier.

In the Glucksberg and Cowan (1970) study, auditory information was constantly received on the unattended channel. This may have produced interference with the target digit. If the target is followed by silence, the echoic trace continues longer, perhaps for as long as 20 seconds (Cowan, Lichty, & Grove, 1988).

There is widespread agreement in the field that echoic memory, like iconic memory, includes at least two stages or components, one peripheral and one (or several) central. Estimates of the duration of these stages differ to some extent, ranging from 150 to 350 ms for the peripheral and from 2 to 20 seconds for the central (Cowan, 1995; Deatherage & Evans, 1969; Efron, 1970a, 1970b).

Summary

Information-processing psychology assumes that the brain actively processes information. Entry of material into memory and retrieval from memory involves such active processing. The processing typically occurs in stages.

Three dominant memory codes were identified within this tradition. They were posited to reflect three different memory stores: sensory, short-term memory, and long-term memory. Sensory store involves a physical (also called structural) code that represents the physical properties of the stimulus, such as shape, size, color, spatial location, or sound properties. Information is entered in parallel. It is lost through decay.

When an array of items is presented for fractions of a second, they enter sensory memory. Only about four items can be recalled. But a much larger number, probably the entire array, is in fact coded. It is also believed by many researchers today that items in the array are identified, in parallel, at a preconscious level.

The "bottleneck" in sensory memory involves the fact that although many items are coded, following a very brief exposure, only four or five can be reported. The system appears unable to maintain the relevant information for longer than a second. About four items can be reported across that second; the rest have then decayed or become unavailable for conscious entry. The 1 second limitation on recall appears to center on the ability to recall the position of the items and not their identity.

When an item enters sensory memory, it can be masked. This involves projecting a second item over the physical area of the first. Masking produces a situation in which the first item cannot enter awareness and thus cannot be recalled, although it may influence the interpretation of other, attended items.

When items are recalled from sensory store, this creates output interference. Output interference means that it becomes more difficult to recall the remaining items.

Sensory memory for auditory stimuli (echoic memory) lasts for about 4 seconds and in the absence of interference may last for as long as 20 seconds.

Discussion

Research into the iconic and echoic stores has established that decay does operate in human memory. Decay here implies the loss of information when no further information is encountered. The findings cannot, however, be extrapolated to other systems. Sensory store has unique properties, such that it is not possible to generalize from this level of processing to STM or LTM.

Interference, however, a function known to operate in LTM, has been demonstrated in echoic store. It does not appear to operate in the icon.

Decay was once conceptualized (within the context of sensory memory) as the total loss of information from store, like the erasure of chalk from a blackboard. There is evidence now that an item may be incapable of being recalled, although some code or codes reflecting its properties may be present in the system. Marcel's masked icons showed this quite clearly. Thus, "decay" may be better conceptualized as sometimes involving a state in which information can no longer be retrieved into consciousness. This does not of course imply that final decay or the total loss of any form of information will not occur over longer periods of time. It is hard to imagine that the masked item STRAWBERRY would persist as an isolated semantic item in the brain across decades. It would certainly serve no function if it did persist.

Although the evidence for unconscious semantic coding (of input stimuli) has been disputed, it remains fairly compelling. It should be noted, though, that these events may be different in several ways from the meaning codes that we experience in awareness. For instance, if a word item, ROSE, is present in the visual field but not attended, it is possible that it may activate related meaning codes (FLOWER, etc.), thus indicating a clear role of semantic information. But the brain may not establish the fact that this meaning code was generated by a stimulus written on a board and located in the left hand area of the visual field. That is, the established ROSE meaning code may be dissociated from all other information. In contrast, attended content enters awareness, and here meaning codes become embodied in the stimuli that gave rise to them. In other words, an attended stimulus produces a representation in which the shape of the stimulus, its size, its spatial location and its meaning are all present, and integrated. This may not occur, even at an unconscious level, with unattended stimuli.

It is also possible that the semantic code generated by an unattended or masked stimulus may not be capable of "unpacking" the full body of potential information that becomes readily available when a meaningful item is attended and capable of being consciously perceived.

When researchers first examined sensory memory and discovered the presence of the physical/structural code, they assumed that a distinctive code meant a distinct memory store. Now the picture has emerged as vastly more complex. The function we term *iconic memory* alone involves an entire continuum of processes, beginning at a peripheral level (barely a step beyond the afterimage) but quickly moving to a central locus and deploying several forms of physical code (shape, size, color, patterning, and location information) and in all likelihood the products of an identification process as well. At least four different sites in the brain are involved in these functions.

The fact that a continuum of processing occurs within "sensory memory" raises the question of whether memory in general may show the same pattern. Perhaps there are not three definite stores that can be distinguished from one another almost as clearly as boxes, but rather an overlapping series of processing events that occur over time. The issue is examined in further detail in Chapter 6.

At the least, however, it would be difficult for anyone to absorb the data now established concerning the iconic and echoic stores and deny the fundamental claim of information-processing psychology: that human cognition involves dynamic processing activities, many of which occur at an unconscious level. A student once asked me how we could ever prove this. The data are either an astonishingly coherent fantasy or the point has been proved.

CHAPTER 4

Verbal Short-Term Memory

1. Verbal short-term memory (STM) involves recall of verbal items presented only once. In the case of random items, an average of just under seven items can be retained (the length of a telephone number). This is called the memory span. Items can be retained under optimal conditions for about 45 seconds. The primary code is phonemic, with a weaker semantic component.

2. Theories concerning loss of items from verbal STM include the assumption of decay (that they decay out of the system over time), interference, and discrimination failure.

3. Longer words usually produce a shorter memory span (the *word-length effect*). This appears to be because certain kinds of vowel are difficult to maintain in STM and longer words are more likely to have vowels of this kind.

4. When many trials are involved in a test of short-term recall, items on the first trial can generally be retained perfectly. Also, if the semantic class of the items is changed on a given trial, recall again returns to a high level.

5. Various models of short-term recall have been developed. These include models positing decay, interference, or discrimination failure as the explanation for loss of items from STM. Some involve the view that items are strongly coded (high activity) when first encountered and lose this high level of activity over time. An alternative view is that the items do not differ in strength as such over time but may suffer from interference.

Learning Objectives

1. Knowledge of the properties of verbal STM, including the memory span, coding format, length of life, and reasons for loss of information from STM. Also, understanding of chunking and the word-length effect.

2. Knowledge of the major theoretical positions concerning forgetting from STM.

W hen verbal information is encountered it is entered into sensory memory. If content in sensory memory is then attended, it will be entered into verbal short-term memory and into consciousness.

STM is widely understood as the memory function that retains stimuli when they are first encountered and attended. If the stimuli are random verbal items, the average number that can be retained is about seven, with some individuals being able to report only five and others as many as nine items (Miller, 1956). The number of units that an individual can report after encountering them once is known as the *memory span*. The memory span reflects the number of input stimuli that can be successfully recalled on 50% of the relevant trials.

The following pages introduce our established knowledge concerning the nature of STM for linguistic items. This material is followed by an examination of forgetting from short-term store. More recent research into variables that influence this form of memory comprises the third section of the chapter. Finally, some theoretical models of short-term recall are briefly overviewed.

1. General Properties of Verbal Short-Term Memory

A good way to understand the nature of verbal STM is to consider what happens when you hear a telephone number. It consists of seven items. You can usually repeat it back if you begin to do this quickly. If on the other hand you even briefly turn your attention to other things, you will find that you have failed to retain the number. The function used here is defined as verbal STM.

Given the speed of forgetting in verbal STM, as with the telephone number not repeated immediately, and the limited capacity of roughly seven items, it is generally believed to be a memory store or a function of both small capacity and short life.

STM can be partly identified with conscious awareness. As described above, when a stimulus is attended, a representation of the stimulus enters awareness. In the case of a longer series, such as a telephone number, introspection reveals that as you are hearing the last several digits of the number, you are no longer immediately conscious of the first several digits. You can play them back, however, in most cases quite reliably, once you reach the last item in the series. Thus, some researchers believe that STM should be conceptualized as consisting of whatever is held in immediate awareness (the "focus of attention") and a second holding capacity, which appears to be in the wings of awareness, although not immediately present to awareness (Cowan, 1988, 2000).

As described above, STM can hold an average of seven independent units. These reflect any material that is in fact identified psychologically as a verbal unit: one word, one letter, one number, or one (familiar) syllable. Thus, the letter C operates as a unit within STM, as does the word CAT, even though CAT consists of both C and other letters. Due to this property of the system, the word *chunk* was developed to signify a unit in verbal STM (Miller, 1956). Figure 4.1 shows the recall function for three words and three letters across periods ranging from immediate recall to a delay of 18 seconds. Note that the recall levels are identical for both types of material.

The fewer the items in the system, the longer they can be retained. One or two chunks can be retained without conscious rehearsal longer than four or five chunks (Brown, 1958). By the time the memory span is reached and about seven items are being held, the individual will begin to forget them immediately. Again, the telephone number example comes to mind.

In the case of just a few items, a frequent estimate of the length of time that they can be held in STM (without rehearsal) is 30 seconds. However, data have been reported for a retention period of up to 45 seconds (Reitman, 1971, 1974). This was achieved by eliminating, as far as possible, all sources of interference during the retention interval, through the use of demanding visual tasks imposed following the presentation of the target items and the time of the test. A visual task should produce no similarity-based retroactive interference (RI) on the target items and, if difficult and speeded, should also prevent rehearsal.

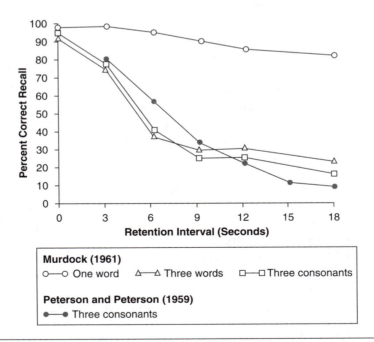

Figure 4.1   Recall of Items as a Function of Time, in the Presence of a Verbal Distractor Task

SOURCE: From Melton, A. W., "Implications of short-term," *Journal of Memory and Language, 2,* copyright © 1963. Reprinted with permission of Elsevier.

Verbal STM is characterized by a rehearsal loop. We can reactivate items at will, playing them through the loop. If you want to retain that telephone number as you walk down a long hall, you can simply repeat the number. So long as the string is within the memory span, this can be achieved effortlessly. No system other than verbal STM appears to possess a function of this kind. Items in sensory memory cannot be "replayed." The same is true of images in STM and abstract content.

A final and critical point: Any attended verbal item enters STM automatically. If verbal items are presented and attended, it is not possible to ignore any of them and so not enter that item or those items into store (Wickelgren, 1964) This is the case whether the individual hears an item, speaks it himself or herself aloud or silently, or even if the item is lip-read (Spoehr & Corin, 1978). It appears possible that if a participant even thinks of a verbal item, it will also enter STM. It is therefore not wise to present a list of items followed by the instruction, "Now write everything down!" The problem here is that the four words of the instruction will also enter verbal STM.

2. Codes in Verbal Short-Term Memory

Both item and order codes are established in verbal STM. The item specifies the nature of the individual chunk (the word or letter, etc.) and the order its position on the list. Order codes are weaker than item codes (Wickelgren, 1965a). That is, you will typically begin to recall items in the wrong order at a point where you can still name all of them correctly.

Further evidence for order codes involves the fact that when an item in a list is recalled in the wrong position, it tends nonetheless to be close in the series to the correct position (Healy, 1974), and in the case of multiple trial studies, items recalled from the wrong trial tend to be reported in the correct position (Henson, 1999).

It should be noted that there are order codes within as well as between items. The different syllables of a word must be retained in the correct order, and the phonemes within each syllable must also be retained in the correct order. These internal order codes appear to be stronger, however, than those that maintain an item's position in a sequence of items.

Conrad (1964), working with the recall of letters from STM, reported that when his subjects made errors, the errors tended to be letters that *sounded like* the original item. For instance, "D" might be recalled as "B" but not as "F." The data indicated that the code used in verbal STM was based on sound. When you enter a chunk into short-term store, you are coding the way that the chunk sounds. The term *phonemic code* is widely used within this context. A phoneme is a unit of language sound, such as /t/, /a/, /p/, etc.

Conrad found that even when the items were presented visually, the pattern of errors was the same. The visual stimuli had been recoded into a phonemic format. It was later established that codes other than the phonemic do operate in verbal STM, but they are so much weaker that it took some years to discover them. There is also a semantic code, with the strength relationship between the semantic and phonemic forms within the memory span estimated at 1:9 (Shulman, 1972). And predictably, when items are presented in a visual modality there is a (relatively weak) visual code.

Research prior to the 1990s failed to identify any influence of variables such as imagery, concreteness, or frequency on short-term recall. Since these factors were known to affect long-term memory (LTM) (for instance, high-imagery words are easier to learn than low-imagery words), the data appeared to support the view that STM and LTM reflect two different stores. However, current research has shown that imagery, concreteness, and frequency do influence the memory span, although the effect is small (Neath, 1997; Roodenrys & Quinlan, 2000; Turner, Henry, & Smith, 2000). It has also been found that a series of word items leads to a longer memory span than a series of nonwords (Walker & Hulme, 1999). With the exception of imagery, these variables all appear to reflect the semantic-code component involved in short-term recall.

2.1. Similarity-Based Interference in STM

As described in Chapter 2, it was established by the 1940s that *semantic similarity* impairs order recall for word items from LTM (a similarity-based interference effect). Phonemic similarity did not measurably influence long-term recall. In contrast, Baddeley and Dale (1966) reported that semantic similarity had no influence on verbal short-term recall, while Baddeley (1966) found a significant but small effect. Under average presentation conditions, however, the memory span for semantically similar item is the same as the span for semantically different items.

Marked similarity-based interference does operate in the memory span, but the basis of the interference is phonemic, not semantic, similarity (Kintsch & Buschke, 1969). This makes intuitive sense when one considers that the primary code in LTM, when words are memorized, is a semantic code, while the primary code in STM is phonemic. Consider the following lists, under auditory presentation. Short-term recall should be the same for each.

List 1.   train, cat, boy, light, dragon, pencil, pot.   (Control)

List 2.   train, car, bike, ship, wagon, hotrod, van.   (High semantic similarity)

In contrast, the higher the phonemic similarity in a string of items presented for short-term recall, the shorter the memory span (Wickelgren, 1966). Compare the difficulty level involved in repeating the following lists, after a single presentation of each:

List 1.   dog, boy, sun, pin, top, light, man   (Control)

List 2.   cat, hit, hat, shut, nut, mat, shop   (High phonemic similarity)

List 2, with its high phonemic similarity, is considerably harder. In attempting to repeat it, you may find yourself producing nonwords or words not on the list.

In the case of material under the memory span, where recall can be tested over time, it has been established that the negative effect of phonemic similarity is of very short duration.

Under conditions of immediate recall, the effect of phonemic similarity operates as described above. But after a delay of a few seconds, high- and low-phonemic similarity items are retained at the same level. The reason for this phenomenon (the dissipation of similarity effects across very short periods) has not been established.

2.2. Chunking, Grouping, and Higher-Order Rhythmic Patterns

The memory span can be increased by a technique known as "chunking." Since we can retain an average of seven chunks in STM, the span can be increased if more information is entered into each chunk. Thus, the sequence 1, 0, 1, 1, 0, 2, 1, 0, 1, 1, 0, 2 involves twelve chunks, which far exceed the memory span. But if you recode the series into 101, 102, 101, 102, it becomes four chunks and is easily retained. In fact, Ericsson and Chase (1982) worked with a graduate student who was a track runner. The student developed a code for rechunking individual numbers on the basis of known track scores and other aspects of the sport. After training he could repeat back as many as 80 unrelated items following a single presentation.

A second influence on the memory span involves any form of rhythm or higher-order sound structure. If items are spoken in a rhythmic way, such as dividing the first three from the last four units as in a telephone number, it becomes easier to retain the entire string. There is also a facilitation effect for the last number in each group (Frankish, 1985; Ryan, 1969). Also, strings tend to be retained in the rhythms in which they were originally presented, even when this pattern violates meaning codes.

Rhythm also plays a major role in interference effects. If seven random items of the same length are presented, followed by five more items of the same length, there will be massive interference. If, in contrast, the seven items are followed by a syntactic string, such as, "Ok, go ahead and recall," there will be interference from this sentence, but its effects will be far less.

3. Word Length

The memory span generally shortens as words become longer (Baddeley, Thomson, & Buchanan, 1975). A representation of the relation between the length of words in a target list and the memory span for the list is shown in Figure 4.2.

Longer words take a relatively long time to pronounce or articulate. A number of researchers have found a strict linear relationship between the time taken to articulate a string of items and the memory span (Hulme, Thomson, Muir, & Lawrence, 1984; Nicolson, 1981). That is, the longer the time taken to speak the items, the shorter the memory span. This relationship, known as the *time-based word-length effect*, is shown in Figure 4.3.

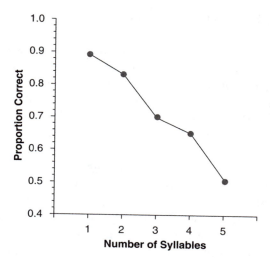

Figure 4.2   The Relationship Between the Number of Syllables in a Word and
                   Memory Span

SOURCE: From Baddeley, A. D., Thomson, N., & Buchanan, M., "Word length and the structure
of short-term memory," in *Journal of Memory and Language, 14* (6), copyright © 1975. Reprinted
with permission of Elsevier.

NOTE: The more syllables, the shorter the span.

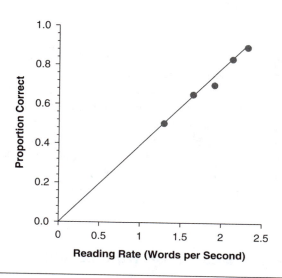

Figure 4.3   The Relationship Between Articulation (Reading) Rate and Short-Term
                   Recall

SOURCE: From Baddeley, A. D., Thomson, N., & Buchanan, M., "Word length and the structure of
short-term memory," in *Journal of Memory and Language, 14* (6), copyright © 1975. Reprinted with
permission.

At first a large body of data appeared to support the effect. Ellis and Hennely (1980), testing Welsh children for digit span in Welsh and English children for digit span in English, found that the latter group consistently showed a larger memory span. When Welsh bilingual children were tested in both Welsh and English, however, the same child would typically show a longer span in English than in Welsh. The Welsh vowels take longer to pronounce.

The findings can be interpreted in terms of decay. When items take longer to pronounce, there is more time for them to decay out of STM by the time the series has been spoken aloud (Baddeley et al., 1975; Schweikert & Boruff, 1986).

Later research, however, indicated that in some cases strings of items that took longer to pronounce produced a superior memory span as compared to items that took less time to pronounce (Caplan, Rochon, & Waters, 1992) or equal amounts of time (Lovatt, Avons, & Masterson, 2000). This finding is difficult to explain in terms of decay. An alternative view would be that, in the case of word length, the increased number of phonemic constituents within a word may tax the capacity of the memory function to hold the material over time (Lovatt & Avons, 2001). There could be several reasons for this. Since long words consist of a larger number of phonemic segments, the requirement on the system to hold each in "the right place" would be more demanding (Neath & Nairne, 1995). Also, the internal *complexity* of the vowels in a string may play a major role (Caplan et al., 1992; Service, 1998). Some vowels can be more complex and again place more drain on the capacity of the system. This could explain why some short strings are in fact more difficult to retain than (some) long strings. Thus, both vowel complexity and the number of segments within a word may influence the memory span.

Hulme, Surprenant, Bireta, Stuart, and Neath (2004) found that when long and short words are presented alternately (for example, STOAT, HIPPOPOTAMUS) in the same list, STM recall operates at as high a level as would normally obtain in a short-word-only list.

The authors explained this finding on the basis of a distinctiveness factor. The items had been scored as correct only if they were reported in the correct order. It might be easier to retrieve items in the correct order when highly discriminable (long and short) words were next to one another in the original list.

An alternative view would be that rhythmic factors play a role in supporting verbal STM, in the sense that specific structures coding for this property would suffer less interference if the same structure (for example, one for single-syllable items only) was not used repeatedly across the list and so overtaxed.

The data on recall of items from lists in which word length is varied are shown in Figure 4.4.

3.1. Summary of Findings on Word Length

The number of chunks involved in a test series plays a critical role in memory span; a series of nine short words will be harder to retain than a series of six longer words. However, when the number of chunks is equated, some types of word produce a shorter memory span than others. Usually (although not invariably) this

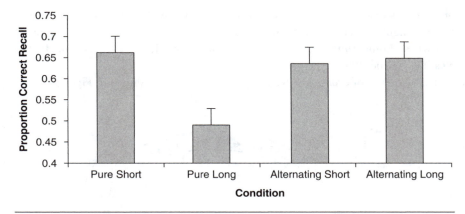

Figure 4.4   Mean Proportion of Words Recalled in the Correct Position as a
Function of Word Length and Type of List (words uniform in length or
alternating in length)

SOURCE: From Hulme, C., Surprenant, A., Tamra, B., Stuart, G. & Neath, I., "Abolishing the
word-length effect," in *Journal of Experimental Psychology: Learning, Memory, and Cognition,*
30, copyright © 2004, American Psychological Association. Reprinted with permission.

is true of longer rather than shorter words. This outcome may be due to greater
complexity in the codes of some word strings (either vowels that are harder to
maintain or more drain on order codes within word segments) or some other
factor. Alternating long and short items eliminate the negative effect of the long
words. This may be a function of improved distinctiveness.

4. The Events That Occur When Information Enters Verbal STM

Early models of memory assumed that verbal stimuli first entered sensory store.
Attended items would then move on to STM and possibly later to LTM in a simple
linear manner.

Today it is assumed that material in sensory memory first makes contact with
the corresponding information in LTM when possible. That is, if the phonemes
present in the word CAT were established in sensory store, they would contact the
CAT representation in LTM. This event would establish that the input was a single
unit: one chunk. Phonemic information, word-length information, and probably
semantic information would be established. This information would next be
entered into STM and maintained there for some limited period of time.

According to some theories, higher-order descriptions of the input would also
be established through processing that depended on LTM information and then
entered into STM. For instance, the system might establish that the string consisted
of all single-syllable nouns or of words of mixed length and so on. It also appears
likely that at the time of recall the items still present in STM, which may now be
degraded, may make another contact with LTM. This could lead to reconstruction

of (some) degraded items. For instance, if the phonemes C-T are still available, the system might contact the CAT item and reconstruct "cat" at the time of recall (Brown & Hulme, 1995; Hulme, Roodenrys, Brown, & Mercer, 1995; Nairne, 1990a; Neath & Nairne, 1995).

The sequence of events involved in short-term recall is shown in Figure 4.5.

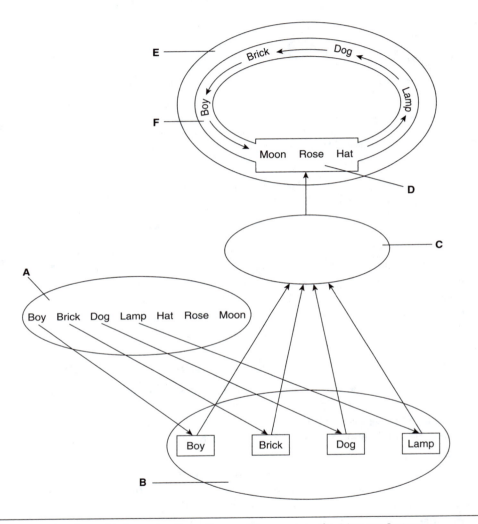

Figure 4.5   The Flow of Information From Sensory Memory Into the Memory System as Conceptualized in Some Modern Theories

NOTE: Here the items Boy, Brick, Dog, Lamp, Hat, Rose, and Moon have been input. They are held in sensory memory (A). This input makes contact with representations in long-term memory (B). BOY makes contact with the phonemes corresponding to the word, with a structure coding for BOY as a word item and with the relevant semantic information (the item's meaning). The same occurs for all the items. The input is organized for input into short-term memory, including order codes (level C). The figure shows the stage of processing as the last item in the sequence is entered into short-term memory. It is entered at the focus of attention, that is, in immediate awareness (box D). About three items can be held in the focus of attention. HAT and ROSE are still in the focus. The earlier-presented items have moved from the focus but are still in short-term memory (E) and also in the rehearsal loop (F), which will make it easy for them to be reentered into D if the individual wishes to do this.

5. Forgetting in Verbal Short-Term Memory

By the time of recall, some material has often been lost from STM. And, as described above, some items appear to have been reconstructed. For instance, the original input item in a string might have been COT. But a participant in an experiment will often then report "cat." Here the item has been incorrectly reconstructed. In further support of the reconstruction hypothesis, it is rare for a nonword, such as "bose" to be recalled.

Research into LTM had established four possible reasons for forgetting by the 1970s. These were (1) decay, (2) interference, (3) discrimination failure, and (4) consolidation failure.

5.1. The Case for Decay

A common approach to a decay model of STM forgetting is to posit that when items are attended they become strongly activated. Quite simply, if you attend to a verbal string such as HORSE, SUN, BOY, LIGHT, DOG, CART, these items develop a strong level of activation over a brief period of time. The activation fades automatically across time. Thus, you can recall the items across a brief period and then they become unavailable. The spontaneous weakening can be characterized as decay.

Cowan (1988, 1995) noted that when an item is first in a state of high activation in STM and is later forgotten, the state of the item has clearly changed. For interference alone to be responsible for such loss, it would have to be assumed that there is some mechanism to keep an activated item in a permanent state of activation (unless it suffers interference). Such a mechanism, Cowan noted, appears unlikely.

In support of the decay assumption, Conrad (1967) found that when experimental participants were required to recall a series of items at the slow rate of 2 seconds per item, retention was lower than under conditions in which the same item was spoken more quickly. The potential for interference was clearly the same but the longer retention interval under the first condition did impair recall. Cowan (1995) reported the same findings.

5.2. The Case for Interference

In reading the following material, please note that retroactive interference (RI) means interference due to material entered into LTM after a target item or items. Proactive interference (PI) means interference due to material entered into LTM before a target item or items.

Memory span data provide support for an interference interpretation of forgetting. Three items can be recalled without error. If 10 items are presented, the series cannot be retained. The most straightforward explanation is that the 7 extra items entering STM produce interference.

It takes longer to present and report 10 items than 3 items. Thus, the argument could be made that the effect is due to decay. The 10-item string would be subject to a longer period in which items might decay. However, under conditions in which an attempt is made to eliminate further verbal input to the system, and also to eliminate rehearsal, short-term recall without errors has been shown to extend to 45 seconds (Reitman, 1974). In these studies, only a few items had to be retained. There was therefore little intrastring interference. Thus, the elimination of new input items leads to the capacity to retain items over periods far longer than 2 or 3 seconds, with apparently no loss from decay. These cases make a strong case for RI.

Another possibility is that output interference, rather than RI, produces forgetting in STM. (Output interference involves the forgetting of material in a given set when other material is recalled from that set.) Perhaps reporting the items creates marked interference, such that the eighth item typically cannot be recalled because seven earlier items have been retrieved and spoken. Waugh and Norman (1965) examined this possibility by the use of a *probe procedure*. They presented lists of 16 digits to their subjects. The last digit was a probe. Participants were instructed to report the item that had followed the probe in the critical list. Thus, a series might be as follows:

$$8, \ 3, \ 0, \ 2, \ 9, \ 7, \ 4, \ 1, \ 5, \ 6, \ 2, \ 3, \ 9, \ 7, \ 8, \ 6$$

The participants' task would be to report item 2. Across trials, the authors varied the number of items that occurred after the target item and before the probe. In the present example there were five items presented after the target. They found that more items presented after the target, the lower the recall. By 12 items, recall was no longer possible. However, subjects had to report only the target item or the item they thought was the target. Thus, output interference could not have been the cause of forgetting when more, rather than fewer, items followed the target. The effect was due to RI. A second critical finding was that proactive interference (PI) did not appear to be operating.

The study did support the position that output interference operates in immediate recall, however. Participants could handle a much longer string, when tested with a probe procedure, than is possible when the whole set of items is reported. Only the increased forgetting found as the number of items between the target and probe increased was due to RI.

It appears likely that output interference is also the cause of the word-length effect (Nairne, 2002a). This claim reflects the finding that a probe procedure reduces or fully eliminates the disadvantage suffered by lists of long words (Avon, Wright, & Palmer, 1994; Henry, 1991).

Peterson and Peterson (1959) hoped to determine how long a pure (neither rehearsed nor elaborated) trace could be retained in STM. They used a design (now identified as the Brown-Peterson design) in which there were repeated trials. Three critical (to be recalled) letters were presented on each trial, followed by a distractor task. For this task, participants heard a number and had been instructed to count backwards, rapidly, out loud, by threes, from this number. The object of the distractor task was to prevent rehearsal. Clearly, if the participants had rehearsed the critical items, they could retain them for any length of time. Recall was then tested over different retention intervals, ranging from 3 to 18 seconds.

Forgetting occurred rapidly. After a delay of 3 seconds, participants retained only 80%, on average, of the critical items. After a delay of 18 seconds, only 12% of the items were retained.

The forgetting rate in this and in a study conducted by Murdock (1961) was shown in Figure 4.1. Box 4.1 shows the Brown-Peterson experimental design.

Box 4.1   The Brown-Peterson Design

Target Letters

TRIAL 1:   C, H, Y + DISTRACTOR TASK   -------->   Test

TRIAL 2:   G, Z, R + DISTRACTOR TASK   -------->   Test

TRIAL 3:   W, K, F + DISTRACTOR TASK   -------->   Test

TRIAL 4:   B, G, L + DISTRACTOR TASK   -------->   Test

The number of trials can vary. Fifteen or twenty trials would frequently be conducted.

Length of distractor task varies. Lengths of 3, 6, 9, 12, 15, and 18 seconds were used in the original study.

Distractor task: Counting backwards from a given number, by threes. If "97" is the given number, participant says 94, 91, 88, 85, etc., out loud, as fast as possible.

At the signal for test, the participant attempts to recall the three target letters.

Peterson and Peterson interpreted their findings in terms of rapid decay. They thought that no RI was involved because the counting task was not (as they believed) a memory task.

However, as described above, any attended verbal material enters verbal STM, whether it is the intention of the individuals to remember it or not. As the participants in the study generated and spoke words during the distractor task (saying, for instance, "One hundred, ninety-seven, ninety-four," etc.), all of these items would have entered STM, thus causing considerable RI.

5.3. The Case for Discrimination

According to a *discrimination hypothesis*, it can occur that traces stored in memory are similar to one another, such that the retrieval function cannot discriminate the target trace from nontargets. As a result, there may be failure to recall. By the same logic, if target versus nontarget traces are highly discriminable in some fashion, the targets should be recalled.

Interference effects due to the entry of new material into STM can be explained by the assumption that, after such entry, target material cannot be distinguished from the newly entered nontarget material and so recall fails.

The dominant explanation for the discriminability effect today involves the concept of *cues* (Nairne, 1990a, 1990b, 1991, 2001, 2002a). Cues are representations that contact information in LTM, such that, in some cases, retrieval will occur. They are generally seen as conscious representations. Roughly if I think TREE, in awareness, the TREE representation can be understood as a cue. It will contact tree representations stored in LTM, on a matching basis.

Contact implies only access into the memory system; it does not necessarily imply retrieval. If, however, the cues correspond adequately to a unique body of memory content, then retrieval (under most theoretical models) will follow.

The role of discrimination in recall from STM can be described as follows. Suppose a string of target items is presented, followed by some additional verbal material. For instance:

A. GULL HOUSE TREE LIGHT ROSE BOY
LAMP: IS IT RAINING OUTSIDE?

In contrast, suppose the same items are presented, followed by four additional items, to produce the string:

B. GULL HOUSE TREE LIGHT ROSE BOY LAMP:
CHAIR DOG SAND GAME.

If it is assumed that the participant knows that the target items are random nouns, then this knowledge will operate as a cue. The attempt will be made to contact random nouns. Given this requirement, the question about rain, which has syntactic structure, will not be selected for retrieval. In the case of String B, however, the specification "random nouns" will not discriminate between the first items and the added items since all correspond to the specification.

A situation in which cues match with many items and cannot distinguish between a given target and the other nontarget matches has been described by Watkins and Watkins (1975) and by Nairne (2002a, 2002b) as *cue overload*.

We are all familiar with situations in which spatial properties operate as cues. On a test, for instance, you may recall that the information you wish to recall was at the top of the right-hand page in your notes. This may help you recall the information. Today it is widely believed that temporal factors operate in the same way. We may code the passage of time as we encounter target material and use these time tags as a powerful aid in recall (Brown & Chader, 2001; Nairne, 2002a).

Turvey, Brick, and Osborn (1970) conducted an experiment similar to the Brown-Peterson study described above. In the Brown-Peterson study, however, the varied retention intervals had been randomly mixed. That is, a retention interval of 3 seconds might be followed on the next trial by a retention interval of 18 seconds and so on. In the Turvey et al. study, these retention intervals were blocked. That is, an entire block of 5-second delay trials would be followed by an entire block of 10-second delay trials and so on. The researchers found equal retention regardless of the length of the retention interval.

A possible explanation for these findings has been offered on the basis of *temporal cues*. According to the present hypothesis, temporal cues involve the attempt to discriminate between the last two sets of target information. One is further back in time than the other, and the desired set is closer. The judgment appears to be made on the basis of a very crude comparison of times, in which "further back" and "closer" cannot always be determined. Critically, the function is relational rather than absolute. For instance, if set A is the target and set B the last but one target, then, given that both are "back" in time at the moment of attempted recall, the relatively *further* back in time B, compared with the distance back in time of A, the better the chances of the temporal cues succeeding and providing recall.

In Turvey et al.'s (1970) study, the relative time ratios in the blocked trials were always the same: 1:2. For instance, if the interval in a given block was 5 seconds, then the target would have been presented 5 seconds earlier and the last from target, 10 seconds earlier. If the interval in a given block was 10 seconds, then the target would have been presented 10 seconds earlier and the last from target, 20 seconds earlier. In every case, again, the recall function would be dealing with a relative difference in time of 1:2. As a result, no condition was easier or harder than any other.

In all cases, participants finished a set of blocked trials with a special trial, which involved a 15-second delay. Now participants who had just been tested following a 5-second delay would have a discrimination of 25:20 seconds (much worse than 1:2), while participants who had been tested under the 20-second delay condition faced a discrimination of 15:35 seconds (better than 1:2). This first group should perform worse than the others, and the second group should perform better. This did in fact occur.

5.4. Conclusions

The case for RI in verbal STM is extremely strong. New material entered into STM produces forgetting even in memory span tests. This outcome cannot be explained by discrimination failure since participants are required to report all the items. They do not have to discriminate targets from nontargets. Probe tests have provided further support for interference.

Equally, there is no evidence to suggest that decay does not operate in verbal STM, although its effects may be slower than those of interference and thus often overridden by this factor. Under conditions in which an attempt is made to eliminate all sources of interference, material is nonetheless "lost" after 45 seconds. This could of course be due to a decay factor.

Current data also support a discrimination factor, particularly with regard to the match between cues and content in verbal STM. The Turvey et al. study described above remains difficult to interpret, however. It implies that, in some situations, temporal cues are more important than any other factor, including RI, a claim that does not appear to be supported by the full range of empirical findings. Also, in a Brown-Peterson design, participants usually report some items on each trial. They do not simply fail to report any items (as can occur in cases of cue overload). If the critical factor was a failure to discriminate between the last trial and the last but one, it might be expected that incorrect recall would reflect the last but one trial, which is not what typically occurs. Thus, the interpretation of the study remains problematic.

6. Factors That Eliminate or Diminish Forgetting in Verbal STM

Keppel and Underwood (1962) discovered that there is typically no forgetting of the items presented in the first trial of a Brown-Peterson design. In this study, three items were presented on each trial as shown in Figure 4.6.

The researchers thought at first that forgetting must therefore be caused by PI. The first-trial items would not suffer from such interference, and the second- and third-trial items might not suffer greatly. As described in Chapter 2, however, this position was later abandoned.

The reason for the high levels of recall on the first trials in the Brown-Peterson study has not been established. Cowan (1995), however, suggested that it may be possible for the memory function to enter a few random items directly into LTM.

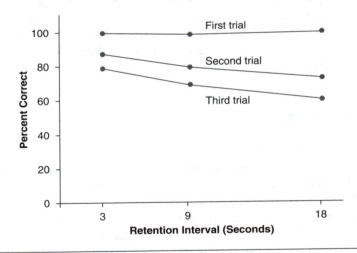

Figure 4.6   Data Indicating Perfect Recall of First-Trial Items in the Brown-Peterson Design and Strong Recall of Second- and Third-Trial Items

SOURCE: From Keppel, G. & Underwood, B. J., "Proactive inhibition in short-term retention of single items," in *Journal of Verbal Learning & Verbal Behavior, 1*(3), copyright © 1962. Reprinted with permission of Elsevier.

NOTE: For a comparison with recall across later trials, see the three-word and three-consonant recall functions shown in Figure 4.1. Single item trials show the same pattern as first-trial recall for multiple (for example, three) items.

After the first items, it could be assumed that this can no longer be achieved, and so the coding format begins to depend on a primarily phonemic representation that can be established more quickly. This coding format would be subject to RI based on phonemic similarity and/or decay, thus showing the usual patterns of STM recall.

Wickens, Born, and Allen (1963) conducted a study using the Brown-Peterson design, in which the semantic class of items was changed after a short series of trials. Thus, consonants were used as target items for several trials and then the target items would change to numbers. On the first trial when the numbers were presented, recall returned to an almost perfect level. The effect was called *release from proactive inhibition* and has been replicated using animal names that were changed to plant names and shifts from auditory to visual presentation (Loess, 1968). The same effect has also been found in LTM, when target material is altered from one subject to another (Dempster, 1985; Gunter, Berry, & Clifford, 1981).

Today a number of explanations can be advanced for the "release" effect. For instance, it could be explained either on the basis of discrimination theory or on the basis of consolidation theory.

7. Cues and Verbal Short-Term Memory

At one time it was believed that cues did not operate in verbal STM. There is now evidence to the contrary. Tehan and Humphreys (1996, 1998), for instance, presented a series of items in a "block." In some cases an item in the first block shared semantic properties with an item in the second block as in the following:

JAIL SILK ORANGE PEACH	Block 1
PAGE LEAP CARROT WITCH	Block 2

ORANGE and CARROT share a number of properties. Both can be taken as nutrients, they are the same color, and both can be drunk in the form of a juice. When *vegetable* was presented at recall as a cue for the item CARROT, there was no interference from the similar item in the previous block. An orange is not a vegetable. If, however, the cue *type of juice* was presented, there was similarity-based interference. The study clearly demonstrated that items are not simply read out of short-term store, as on a conveyor belt, but that operating cues can influence which items will return to awareness.

8. Research Into Manipulations That Influence Short-Term Recall * * * * *

Baddeley and his colleagues, and later other researchers, have conducted an extensive program of research into a range of variables that are either known to influence STM or believed likely to influence STM. They are described in the present section.

8.1. Modality and Suffix Effects

When a string of random items is reported from verbal STM, the last several items are recalled better than earlier items. The final element in the string is particularly advantaged. This occurs in all known forms of presentation, with the exception of visual presentation. This has remained a puzzling outcome since the last items are advantaged even when the series has been lip-read (Campbell & Dodd, 1980). The phenomenon is known as the *modality effect* (Corballis, 1966; LeCompte, 1992; Nairne & Walters, 1983). Why visual items fail to show the effect is not currently understood.

Figure 4.7 shows serial recall under conditions of auditory and visual presentation.

If an irrelevant (not to be recalled) linguistic item is added to the end of a string presented for short-term recall, the memory span is impaired. As described above, any attended verbal item enters STM (Crowder & Morton, 1969). Nonspeech sounds, however, such as a buzzer, do not generally reduce the memory span. Figure 4.8 shows the serial recall of a series of nine items, followed either by an irrelevant word or by the sound of a buzzer.

Later research established that the suffix language sound must be a vowel. Consonants have no negative effect (Darwin & Baddeley, 1974). It is also necessary for the subject to perceive the suffix as an element of language, as against a nonlanguage sound. Ayres, Jonides, Reitman, Egan, and Howard (1979) presented the suffix "wa," which subjects understood to be either a spoken nonsense syllable or as a musical note. The physical noise was identical in both cases. A suffix effect

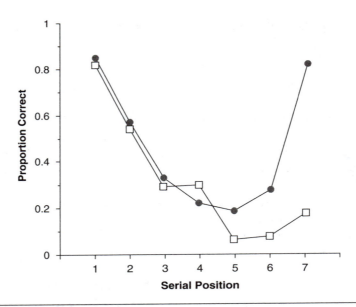

Figure 4.7   The Modality Effect

SOURCE: From Conrad, R. & Hull, A. J., "Input modality & the serial position curve in short-term memory," in *Journal of Memory and Language*, 10, copyright © 1968. Reprinted with permission of Psychonomic Society, Inc.

NOTE: In short-term recall, the final items are advantaged over earlier items. The exception to this occurs in visual presentation, in which the final items are not advantaged.

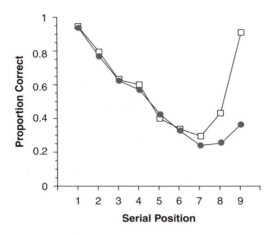

Figure 4.8   The Suffix Effect

SOURCE: From Crowder R. G. in James Kavanagh & Ignatius Mattingly, *Language by Ear and by Eye: The Relationships between Speech and Reading,* copyright © 1972. Reprinted with permission of the MIT Press.

NOTE: The line marked with white dots shows memory span recall when the list is followed by the sound of a buzzer. The black-dot line shows recall when the list is followed by a spoken word.

occurred only when the item was understood as spoken language. Neath, Surprenant, and Crowder (1993) demonstrated the same effect for the sound "baa," which the subjects were primed to believe was either the word "baa" or an actual animal sound. There was a suffix effect only in the former case. Figure 4.9 shows the patterns of immediate recall when participants believe that the last item that they hear is either a spoken word or an animal sound.

It is thus clear that interpretive structures come into play to determine the constituents of a series of items in STM.

8.2. Irrelevant Speech and Articulatory Suppression

When participants attend to a series of visually presented items while other, irrelevant language sounds are present, the irrelevant sounds disrupt short-term recall of the attended material (Colle & Welch, 1976). Instrumental music produces some interference but less than that produced by language sounds. Noise that is neither verbal nor musical produces no interference. When the irrelevant words and the target words are phonemically similar, some studies have shown increased interference (Cole, 1980; Salame & Baddeley, 1987), while some have not (Jones & Macken, 1995).

If experimental participants are required to articulate a word or nonsense syllable while hearing and recalling material presented for short-term retention, the memory span is shortened. The effect is known as *articulatory suppression.* A typical approach to articulatory suppression is to have subjects say "the, the, the" or any other easily repeated item. ("Cola, cola, cola" has also been used.)

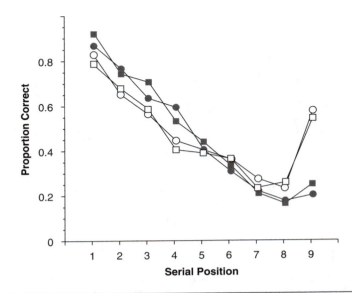

Figure 4.9 Different Patterns of Recall When Participants Believe a Final Item Is Either an Animal Noise or a Word

SOURCE: From Neath, I., Surprenant, A. M. & Crowder, R. G., "The context dependent stimulus suffix effect," in *Journal of Experimental Psychology: Learning, Memory, and Cognition, 19,* copyright © 1993, American Psychological Society. Reprinted with permission.

NOTE: The same sound was used in all cases. Circles indicate that the sound was made by a person. Squares indicate that the sound was made by an animal.

When strings of phonemically similar or dissimilar items are presented in an auditory mode, under conditions of articulatory suppression, the span is further impaired for the phonemically similar list. This would imply that the auditory stimulus is capable of being coded in phonemic form in spite of interference with the coding function created by the articulation task.

When critical material is presented visually, in concert with articulatory suppression, phonemic similarity no longer impairs the span. It is also no longer the case that the largest number of errors in recall reflects phonemic similarity with the target. Thus, the code appears here to be either nonphonemic or to involve a weaker phonemic component than usual. Yet visual similarity errors do not occur either, suggesting that the primary code is not, as might be expected, visual (Murray, 1967). Under these conditions, fewer items are recalled (about two thirds of a presented sequence) than would obtain in the absence of articulatory suppression.

Articulatory suppression also eliminates the word-length effect (Longoni, Richardson, & Aiello, 1993).

9. Models of Verbal Short-Term Memory * * * * *

Currently, there exist many theoretical interpretations of immediate recall. Some posit that forgetting is due to decay (Baddeley 2002; Schweikert & Boruff, 1986; Stiglerr,

Lee, & Stevenson, 1986), some cite both interference and decay (Brown & Hulme, 1995; Lovatt et al., 2000; Service, 1998; Turner, 2000), and some others, interference only (Nairne, 1990a, 1990b; Neath & Nairne, 1995). An example of each of these approaches is described below.

9.1. The Trace Decay/Rehearsal Model

Probably the best-known theory of STM is Baddeley's (1976, 1986, 1992a, 1992b, 1994, 2002) model of the phonological loop.

According to this approach, attended verbal items are established in a *phonological loop* in STM. They can be held in the loop for only a brief time, of about 2 seconds. After 2 seconds they will begin to decay. Decay can be offset, however, if the items are picked up by the *articulatory control process* (ACP). This process refreshes (reestablishes) items in the loop.

It is conceptualized as being a form of covert rehearsal. The items decay at a set rate over time. If an item has decayed before it can be picked up by the ACP, it will be lost. An assumption of the model is that the covert rehearsal process operates at essentially the same speed as an overt articulation or at the least that the two are strongly correlated.

A wide range of data concerning STM can be explained by the trace decay/rehearsal (TDR) model. For instance, an auditory item could be expected to enter the phonological loop directly, while a visual item would need to be recoded for such entry (the modality effect). An extra item on a string would extend the period for decay (the suffix effect), irrelevant speech sounds would automatically find their way into the phonological loop and so disrupt recall of targets (the irrelevant speech effect), and articulatory suppression would tie up the ACP so that it could not function as well as usual to pick up items that had decayed, thus again impairing short-term recall. Also, series of longer words should impair the span more than series of shorter words (the word-length effect), and there should be a relationship between rate of articulation and memory span. This last relationship would occur because the faster the items could be spoken, the sooner the ACP could pick up early items that had begun to decay and refresh them through rehearsal.

A weakness of the model may be its assumption that loss of items from STM is due solely to decay. As described above, Lovatt et al. (2000) found that in some cases a series of short items can be retained better than a series of long items. Also, phonemically similar lists do not take longer to articulate than phonemically dissimilar lists, but the forgetting rate is higher with the similar items (Schweikert, Guentert, & Hersberger, 1990).

Another claim that does not appear to have held up well under investigation is that the trace decays within 2 seconds, such that longer retention intervals are provided by the covert rehearsal. Cowan (1995, chap. 3), favoring a decay hypothesis, has noted that the process of decay may in fact extend considerably beyond 2 seconds. In other words, it may be the case that items can be held in STM for much longer periods, in the absence of any form of rehearsal.

9.2. An Activity/Strength Model of STM: Assumption of Both Interference and Decay

A second approach to STM is to assume that just-encountered items are strongly activated and that this activation decreases naturally over time (a decay hypothesis) but that other variables also influence short-term retention. Such variables could include both interference and reconstruction at the time of recall.

According to the Brown and Hulme (1995) model, when items have several syllables, each will be coded with its own level of strength (activity level) in STM. Decay would thus be expected to operate differentially across the segments. In any given word, a weaker segment would be likely to decay faster than a stronger segment. Also, long words would be more likely to suffer decay, given that there would be more segments within a long word and thus a greater probability of decay for some segment. This would of course provide a weaker memory function for a series of long words.

This liability would be offset to some degree in the present model, however, by reconstructive processes occurring at the time of retrieval. If the traces of a given word item were HIPPOP—MUS, that item would be easily matched with *hippopotamus* as a known word in LTM and so reconstructed. If the trace of a short item was –AT, it would be unlikely to find any match. This is the case because a match that can provide retrieval needs to be specific. A trace that corresponds with many word items could not be reconstructed.

The present approach differs from the TDR model in that it assumed (1) decay need not be conceptualized as occurring within 2 seconds and (2) no covert rehearsal process was operating.

The authors had found earlier that different types of material were recalled at different levels in STM (Hulme, Maughan, & Brown, 1991). Meaningful items were recalled best and then familiar phonemic sets, with meaningless and unfamiliar items being recalled at the lowest level. A "familiar phonemic set" involved foreign words whose meaning was not known but that had been rehearsed until the sound of the words was familiar. All three types of material showed the same linear relationship between the speed of articulation of the participant and the participant's memory span.

It was posited that meaningful words were recalled best because of reconstructive processes at the time of retrieval and that this was also true of familiar sound sets.

The authors ran a series of computer simulations, incorporating the assumptions of the model and using the three types of material described above. In the first simulation, it was assumed that only decay was operating to impair recall. The resulting memory function corresponded to that found with human participants. There was a linear relationship between articulation rate and memory span, with different intercepts (lowest level of recall) for the three types of stimuli. The data were also of interest because the linear relationship between articulation and span was found in the absence of a covert rehearsal factor, indicating that the linear

(a)

(b)

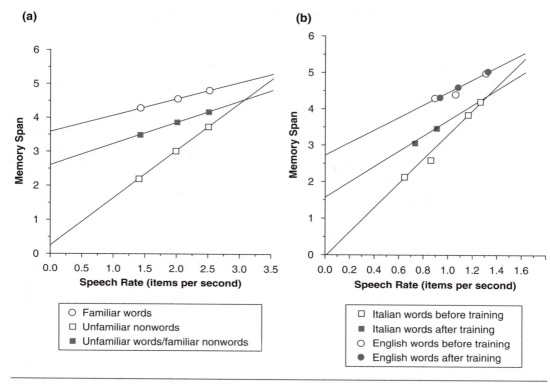

Figure 4.10   Comparison of Serial Recall Curves for Human Participants and the Corresponding Serial Recall Curves Produced by the Brown and Hulme (1995) Computer Simulation

SOURCE: From Brown, G. D. A., & Hulme, C., "Modeling item length effects in memory span: No rehearsal needed?" in *Journal of Memory and Language, 34*(5), copyright © 1995. Reprinted with permission of Elsevier.

relationship need not be explained by this factor. Figures showing the human and computer simulation results are shown in Figure 4.10 above.

The authors also ran a simulation modeling loss of information through interference only, with no decay factor. They posited that any new item entering STM would interfere with other items in the system, whether it was phonemically or semantically similar to those items or not. The results from the simulation again showed a linear relationship between articulation rate and memory span and the three different intercept levels. The outcome fit the human data slightly less well, however, than had been the case under the "decay only" simulation.

In conclusion, the present study showed that the relationship between articulation rate and memory span need not depend on covert rehearsal. The findings also imply that material does not necessarily decay from STM in 2 seconds. A model positing segment-by-segment loss of information, either through decay or through interference, and with the loss being counterbalanced by some reconstruction at the time of recall, matches the human data well.

9.3. A Feature/Cueing Model of Immediate Recall

Activity/strength models posit that attended material is highly activated for a short period but that the activity diminishes quickly over time. If the activity of a target item has become too low, it will not be possible to recall the item from STM.

An alternative view centers on the role of cues in immediate recall. Nairne (1988, 1990a), for instance, posited that recently encountered verbal items do not possess variable levels of activity. They can, however, be degraded through interference effects. At the time of attempted immediate recall, success will depend on the extent to which the operating cues match the (often degraded) target items. Decay was not posited to operate in this model.

Nairne used the terms *primary memory* and *secondary memory*, first introduced by William James (1890), to denote the critical functions within this context. James had suggested that experiences that have just been encountered remain in the "rearward portion" of awareness; they are still in a way present. This state constitutes primary memory. For instance, if you have just heard a string of six words, the last few words will be placed in the focus of awareness, while the first items will have entered primary memory. Secondary memory, in contrast, reflects material stored at an unconscious level, corresponding to the concept of LTM.

According to the present model, when a series of verbal items are encountered, the items may be coded into primary memory. A certain level of probability is associated with this event, for each item. General information concerning the items is also coded. For instance, it might be established that the input consists of a string of random, single-syllable words, spoken in a certain kind of voice and, roughly, the time when they were encountered. This latter information establishes a particular search set in secondary memory. A search set is a set of content, delimited from other content in secondary store, that will be drawn on at the time of recall. For instance, if the input series consists of digits ranging from 1 to 9, then the search set established would be "digits 1 to 9." If the input items are single-syllable nouns, then items of this kind would constitute the search set in secondary memory. The material entering primary memory and the search set in secondary memory are established at the same time (as the items are coded).

A series of items would not enter primary memory in a kind of vacuum, set apart from other aspects of ongoing cognition. Whatever is being attended, including immediate thought content, will also be represented.

Each input item involves a complex, multiattribute trace, which could be conceptualized as a complex of features. It is known that short-term recall shows different properties depending on whether the input stimuli have been presented auditorily or visually. As a result, the model includes both *modality-dependent* and *modality-independent* features. The former reflect the physical, sensory properties of the input stimuli: that is, how the input sounded or how it looked (loudness, rhythm, pitch, visual outline, etc.) and also information concerning context (perhaps how the apparatus looked or the surrounding room). In contrast, modality-independent features reflect nonsensory codes used by the memory function, such as the representation of the input as a phonemic string and some other properties, such as the representation of word units as units and possibly semantic content (aspects of the meaning of the items) and factors such as time duration.

Items are expressed as vectors, that is, strings of features. Each feature can have a value of either +1 or −1, with 0 representing the absence of a feature. Interference operates exclusively across adjacent items. Thus, if items B and C follow one another, feature #5 of item B has a value of +1, and feature #5 of item C also has a value of +1, then #5 in B will be overwritten. Modality-dependent features can only be overwritten by other modality-dependent features, and the same is true of those that are modality independent. Since items are susceptible to interference both from their own modality-independent features and from those being generated on the basis of ongoing cognition within the system (internal thoughts), they are likely to suffer more interference than modality-dependent features. As a result, it is the latter that are likely to prove more critical to successful recall. Overwriting involves the removal of that feature from primary memory. Thus, as new material is input to the system, the primary memory traces will be degraded.

Suppose a nine-item string of digits has been encoded. By the time the string is entered, there will be extensive degradation of the traces present in primary memory. More general information, however, such as the representation that the input consisted of digits will be present.

At the time of recall, the information in primary memory makes contact, if possible, with the information in the secondary memory search set (in the present example, with the representation of the names of digits, stored in secondary memory). In other words, the information in primary memory can be seen as cues. If an adequate match is found between one of the degraded traces in primary memory and a representation in the search set, the system will regenerate the whole target item and recall it. This event is described as a process of *redintegration*. For instance, if the primary memory trace THR— was present, it could be expected to contact the word item THREE and the full word item would be recalled.

It is important to note that the degraded traces themselves do not enter awareness. The individual would be aware of recalling "Three" and not of a fragment of the word only, nor of the reconstructive process that had generated the word.

It is not enough in the present model for an item in primary memory to correspond to an item in the search set for recall to be achieved. This is the case because of the factor of *cue overload*. If a primary memory item corresponds to many representations in secondary memory, it is likely that none of them will be retrieved (Nairne, 1991).

The present approach has been embodied in computer simulations by Neath and Nairne (1995), Nairne (1990a, 1990b, 1991), and Nairne and Kelley (1999). It is capable of explaining a wide range of immediate-recall phenomena, including primacy, recency, modality, and suffix effects and those of articulatory suppression. For instance, recency is explained because the final item in a series may be followed by some form of verbal thought, but this will not possess modality-dependent characteristics and thus the last item will suffer interference only from modality-independent characteristics, while earlier items in the series will be degraded by both. If the input was visual, visual codes do not translate into the kind of modality-dependent features that are registered in verbal STM, and so the final item recency advantage will not be present for visually presented items. And the presence of a verbal suffix removes the auditory recency effect since it can overwrite the last item in the series on the basis of both modality-dependent and modality-independent features.

Summary

Verbal STM reflects the ability to recall language items after a single presentation. Roughly seven random items can be recalled on average, with a range of plus and minus two. The number of items that can be recalled is known as the *memory span*. Items are represented in a primarily phonemic code, with a small semantic component. Rhythmic factors are also coded. Length of life under optimal conditions is about 45 seconds. The fewer the items in the system, the longer they can be retained.

Any item in STM is known as a chunk. Items can be reorganized into larger chunks (single units that carry more information). This increases the memory span.

Strings of long words are retained less well than strings of short words (the word-length effect). This appears to be due to the fact that certain vowels are hard to retain in STM and longer strings tend to have more such vowels. The first item in a series of trials is usually retained perfectly. The reasons for this are disputed. If the semantic class of the item is changed on a given trial, it again tends to be well recalled (release from PI).

Theories differ as to whether content is lost from verbal STM through decay, interference, and/or discrimination failure.

According to Baddeley's model of STM, items are held in a phonemic loop for about 2 seconds, after which they decay. If they can be reactivated prior to decay, they are retained; if not, they are forgotten. The reactivation is achieved through an articulatory control process, which involves a form of covert rehearsal.

According to Brown and Hulme's strength theory, items are originally strongly coded—highly activated—when they are first attended and lose activation over time. They are also subject to interference. At the time of recall, items can sometimes be reconstructed from remaining, partial codes. Items take longer than 2 seconds to decay.

According to Nairne's featural model, verbal items consist of features that do not differ in coding strength over time. However, they are subject to interference from later-occurring verbal items. The critical factor in recall involves whether the operating cues adequately match the still-remaining item features held in memory.

Discussion

We forget a series of random verbal items very quickly, unless they are rehearsed. This outcome is due to interference, discrimination failure, decay, or some combination of these factors. Interference is generally seen in short-term recall as involving actual loss and/or degradation of the items, as against a blocking effect. (In a memory span task, for instance, there does not appear to be any obvious factor that would produce blocking.) Discrimination failure is sometimes viewed as a form of interference since it depends on the entry of nontarget information into the system. Output interference has been shown to operate but does not appear to be the factor that causes the heaviest loss of information in tests of immediate memory.

Each of the causal factors named above are supported by some researchers as playing either the only or the dominant role in forgetting from STM. The evidence in support of each factor is quite good, and it may well emerge in the end that they all play some part.

A central issue within the present area involves whether STM items may be more strongly or more weakly coded. Under one model, if you have just attended to some verbal items, they will be highly activated in STM. They can thus be "played out" until the level of activation decreases below some threshold level. At this latter point, they will no longer be available. This is a decay model but one that can easily include interference effects. According to the interference view, the system has a limited capacity to maintain the activation of a string of items, such that the entry of others into STM will disrupt the original targets.

It has been shown recently that these events are not as simple, however, as originally imagined. Under the first formulations, items would simply appear in STM and become capable of being reported, like objects being moved on a conveyor belt. Now it has been shown that cues influence short-term recall. The cues frequently appear to consist of general descriptions of the target material, established during encoding. For example, they might consist of the information: "a string of single-syllable nouns."

Given the role of cues in short-term recall, two theoretical positions remain. Items in STM may have different levels of strength, such that some strings are easy to recall, as originally assumed. Weaker items (those that had perhaps lost a little strength through decay) might require appropriate cues, if they are to be recalled at all. The alternative view is that there is no variability in item strength and that successful recall depends entirely on the extent to which the cues can contact the traces in short-term store. According to this latter view, while there may be no variability in strength, variability may nonetheless exist in terms of the completeness of the items. If phonemes have been lost through interference, recall may not occur even in the presence of many appropriate cues.

Another major development within this field involves the concept of *reconstruction* or *redintegration*, occurring in STM at the time of recall. Instead of items being "played out" again in a simple fashion from store, the evidence appears clear that more complex processing occurs, in which the STM traces are actively matched with LTM traces, where possible, and the reconstruction of a degraded item may occur.

There is also some implication in this recent research that cues may not always be elements represented at the level of awareness. For instance, the system might

CHAPTER 5

Working Memory

Overview

1. Working memory (WM) is the function that holds material in awareness or at the fringes of awareness.

2. WM is of limited capacity. There is disagreement as to whether there are independent subdomains of capacity (domain-specific WM) or there is one general capacity (domain-general WM).

3. Baddeley established that running items through the rehearsal loop in short-term memory (STM) impairs performance on other tasks only minimally. Verbal STM appears to be a domain-specific function. Also, visual and verbal codes appear not to draw on the same capacity.

4. There exists a range of different theoretical models of WM. According to some, there are special structures or buffers that hold content in WM. A second model posits that any highly activated information in long-term memory (LTM) is also in WM (and there are no special structures for WM).

5. There are also capacity, cueing, and attention-based models of WM. Capacity models assume that storage and information-processing activities draw on the same pool of capacity within any given domain. Cueing models posit that WM is of strictly limited capacity but that new material is continuously retrieved into WM from LTM. Attentional models posit that WM capacity is a function of attentional capacity, which differs from individual to individual.

Learning Objectives

1. Knowledge of working memory as representing awareness and material on the fringes of awareness, and knowledge of the limitations of WM capacity.

2. Knowledge of the codes that produce no or little interference with content in WM.

3. Knowledge of structural, high-activation, capacity, cueing, and attentional models of WM.

nformation held within the sphere of our cognition can be in one of two general states. It can be stored in long-term memory (LTM) and not represented at any given moment in awareness. Or it can be represented in awareness. Content held in verbal short-term store is content that appears ready to enter awareness, as when we hear a list of random items and begin to repeat them, or content that is already in awareness. It thus falls essentially into the second state of the two described above. From the early days of research into verbal STM it was of course understood that content other than verbal items can be held in or close to awareness. Also, it appeared likely that an important function of short-term store would be that of holding material while that material underwent further processing (Atkinson & Shiffrin, 1968; Hunter, 1957). The function of maintaining information close to or in awareness, and in such a way that additional processing would operate on that material, became known as *working memory* (WM).

While some psychologists apply the term working memory only to information received from the outside world, most view this system as reflecting whatever you are perceiving or thinking about at the moment (Cowan, 1997; Meyer & Kieras, 1997). For instance, when planning to cook dinner, a person might maintain considerations of what is in the fridge, the kind of meal he or she likes to eat, the available pots and pans, and a defective back burner on the stove, all in WM.

Since the construct of WM developed out of the notion of verbal STM, the original models of WM inherited some of the properties of STM. For instance, it was assumed that WM must be of quite sharply limited capacity. The system might be capable of holding, for instance, about seven items along with the processes needed to operate on those items. Some, although not all, current models make the same assumption.

1. Attention and Working Memory

The concept of WM is closely linked to that of attention. Most researchers believe that when material is attended, it could be described as being "in" WM. The same is true of material that was attended a moment previously.

The term *focus of attention* is often used within this context. The focus of attention reflects those items of which the individual is clearly aware, at any given moment. Thus, it is widely believed that WM consists of the following: (1) activated content that is not currently the focus of attention and (2) activated content that is currently the focus of attention (Cowan, 1993, 1995; McElree, 2001). For instance, if I am reading a novel and the current paragraph involves a quarrel between two individuals, that information will be in the focus of my attention; my knowledge that they married only a week before, against their parents' wishes, is also activated in WM but not as the immediate focus. Such models assume in fact that memory is tripartite, consisting of the two forms of activated content described above and also of content in LTM (Cowan, 1995; Dosher, McElree, & Hood, 1989; Nairne, 1996). Note that LTM content is held in the system but is inactivated or passive. It is not involved in ongoing cognition.

There are capacity limits on attention and thus also on WM. We can only attend to a single channel of (new) information at a time. For instance, it is not possible to read one story while simultaneously listening to another and follow the content of both (Mowbray, 1953). This is another way of saying that at any given moment we can only hold a single channel of information active in WM.

The second limitation on WM involves the quantity of information—now related to a single channel—that can be maintained in WM, and how long the information can be maintained across time. Here, questions of interest center on (1) the reasons for the limitation, (2) the amount of content that can in fact be held at any given moment, (3) the amount of content that can be held across time, and (4) whether there exist differences in holding capacity across different domains of content.

2. The Emergence of the Concept of Working Memory From Short-Term Memory: STM Maintenance of Verbal Items Combined With a Separate Cognitive Task

Given that verbal STM appears to be a part or aspect of general WM, researchers in the 1970s wished to determine whether other cognitive tasks (not involving verbal STM recall) would interfere with such recall. This issue reflects the question of whether there is all-purpose WM that can be turned to either one form of task or another and in which capacity it is shared across tasks or whether functions such as recalling verbal items operate independently of other cognitive tasks and so do not draw on a shared processing capacity.

The issue outlined above can take many forms but is widely characterized as the question of whether WM is *unified* or *domain general* (that is, general purpose) or *domain specific*. The former term implies that the same limited capacity is shared across different kinds of task, while the latter implies that the capacity is specific to particular kinds of tasks. Within the present context this would mean that if WM is unified, performing nonverbal memory tasks would draw on the same resources as verbal memory tasks and so cause mutual interference. If WM is domain specific, then nonverbal recall tasks would not interfere with verbal recall since it would draw on a separate pool of resources.

Baddeley (1986), Baddeley and Hitch (1976), and Hitch (1978) addressed this question in a series of experiments. They required that their participants (1) hear and repeat a series of verbal items, repeating them continuously across the retention interval (a verbal STM task); and (2) perform a separate cognitive task while repeating the short-term items.

A total of 0, 3, 6, or 8 items were presented for short-term store across different conditions. Thus, a participant would hear perhaps three random items and then repeat them (play them through the rehearsal loop) while performing a given cognitive task. The cognitive tasks included (1) reasoning, (2) memorization of other items, (3) arithmetic work, and (4) prose comprehension.

In general, the findings were that maintaining items in short-term store could produce a small impairment in the work of performing other cognitive tasks but nothing close to the impairment that would be expected if both functions were drawing on a shared WM capacity.

It was clear from these data that maintaining items in short-term store, or at least playing the items through the rehearsal loop, does not draw on the same capacity that is involved in the performance of general cognitive work. Eight items generally exceed the memory span. Had an all-purpose system been involved, there should have been no capacity left to perform the interpolated task. Yet the two functions did not operate wholly independently since some impairment was found when six or more short-term items were rehearsed. Some general WM constituent may be required, for instance, to initiate and then maintain the operation of rehearsal, but not to hold the verbal items as such. However, the source of the limited interference that occurs under these conditions remains unidentified.

3. Models of Working Memory: Structural Assumptions

3.1. Baddeley and Hitch: The Original Working Memory Model

One way of viewing WM is to posit that content in WM is maintained in certain special structures or *buffers*. Content maintained in these structures is either made available to awareness or is held in a state of immediate readiness to enter awareness. Baddeley (1986, 1992a, 1992b, 1994, 2002) and Baddeley and Hitch (1974) developed a model of this kind, which was also the first and most influential model of WM.

The authors examined WM for random verbal items (as in traditional verbal STM tasks) and also for visual information. They posited that WM included at least two special buffers, the *phonological loop* and the *visuospatial sketchpad* and also a *central executive*. The executive controlled activities within the system. For instance, it might initiate an imagery technique in an attempt to memorize a list of items. The other two components were described as *slave systems*, under the control of the executive. Their function was to hold (maintain) the information being processed. They constituted the structural component of WM. The buffers were specialized to retain different types of information. The phonological loop coded for language sound content (as in the case of verbal items) and the visual sketchpad for visual/spatial content.

The *phonological loop* and *articulatory control process*, together, comprised the functions traditionally identified as verbal STM (understood now as a part of the larger function of WM). Baddeley's model of verbal STM was described in Chapter 4.

It consisted of the two components noted above. It was posited that the phonological loop could only hold information for about 2 seconds; following 2 seconds, the information would be lost through decay if it was not reinstated by the articulatory control process. As described earlier, however, the data have not on the whole supported the view that verbal STM traces decay in 2 seconds.

Under the present model, when items are presented visually, they do not have automatic access to the phonological loop. Here, the same articulatory control processes code the visual material into phonemic form and enter the phonemic representation into the phonological loop.

3.2. Working Memory: The Experimental Data

Many predictions based on the original WM model were confirmed in subsequent research (Baddeley, Lewis, & Vallar, 1984; Estes, 1974, 1986; Levy, 1971; Longoni, Richardson, & Aiello, 1993; Murray, 1968; Peterson & Johnson, 1971). The assumption of the relative independence of the slave systems from the influence of other, general cognitive, functions, for instance, has fared well. The first of the slave systems, the phonological loop, is assumed to code selectively for language sound information. The second, the visuospatial sketchpad, is geared to retain visual and spatial information across brief periods of time. It could be characterized as visual STM.

A number of experiments have supported the model's claim that there exist separate phonemic and visual-spatial buffers, specialized to retain these different kinds of information in WM. Tasks that require the use of a verbal code have now been shown not to interfere with visual content stored in WM and the opposite is also true: Visual tasks produce little interference in the retention of phonemic content (Baddeley, 1986, 1992a, 1992b; Logie, Gilhooly, & Wynn, 1994; Smith & Jonides, 1994). The methodological approach in these studies generally involved a dual task procedure. That is, participants would be exposed to information to be held in WM followed by the requirement that they perform a cognitive task (whose code might or might not correspond to the code of the WM content).

Further support for the reality of independent buffer systems has come from studies of cognitive development in children (Hitch, 1990). This is the case because children show different patterns of increasing competence in verbal and visual skills. A given individual, for instance, might begin to move ahead in the verbal domain while showing no change in visual ability.

Structural models of WM have also been developed in the form of computer simulations (Schneider & Detweiler, 1987; Schneider & Shiffrin, 1977). The Schneider et al. approach involved a hybrid connectionist/symbolic model of associative learning in which WM played the critical role. Here it was assumed that there are multiple buffers for different types of information, such as, for instance, individual phonemes and, at a higher level, buffers for combinations of phonemes into syllables and additional buffers for syllables combined into words. The program was successful in modeling the processing that occurs as individuals move from the state of novice to that of an experienced participant in a learning study.

3.3. Neuroimaging

Neuroimaging techniques are capable of identifying increases in the flow of blood to various structures within the brain. The increase in blood flow is believed to reflect an increase of neural activity (above baseline activity). As a result, it is possible to identify which areas of the brain become selectively more active as the brain performs various tasks. Using positron emission tomography (PET), Jonides et al. (1993), Smith and Jonides (1994), and Awh et al. (1996) examined the loci of increased activation within the brain when experimental participants recalled letters, the spatial location of dots, or "objects" (simple pattern pictures).

Smith and Jonides (1997) replicated and extended these findings. The experimental task involved first the presentation of a cross that participants were asked to fixate. Then came the test stimuli (four uppercase letters, three dots, or two object patterns) followed by a 3-second delay. A recognition test involved the presentation of a lowercase letter, a circle, or an object pattern. The task of the participants was to determine whether the letter had been present in the test stimuli, whether the circle enclosed a spatial area where a dot had been present or whether the object pattern had been presented among the test stimuli. The materials used in the study are shown in Figure 5.1. The first was a verbal task, the second a spatial task, and the third a visual-pattern task.

The results were that the different tasks activated markedly different areas of the brain. This meant that WM for verbal items such as letters, for spatial information, and for visual-pattern (object) information all involve separate structures. They do not draw on the same neural substrates or presumably a "shared capacity." Thus the neuroimaging data fitted well with the experimental findings described above. The Smith and Jonides (1997) study also found that the functions of maintaining verbal items in WM and rehearsing those items again activate separate areas of the brain. And there was evidence that executive functions draw on yet another, frontal-lobe, region. The areas of increased brain activity reflecting the maintenance of verbal, spatial, or pattern object material in WM are shown in Figure 5.2.

3.4. Status of the Original Working Memory Model

Assumptions developed within the context of the original WM model include the following. WM consists of the following three components: (1) a maintenance or storage component, which "holds" the activated information; (2) a processing component (the capacity to perform processing activities on the information being maintained), and (3) a central executive, which directs the processing activities. It is posited that there are specialized buffers for different kinds of content (such as phonemic, visual, spatial, etc.). Baddeley (1986, 1992a, 1992b, 1994, 2002), Baddeley and Andrade (1994), and Logie (1995) have revised the original model in several ways. It is posited, for instance, that there are a larger number of specialized constituents than were originally identified. According to this view, there are subcomponents to both the phonological store and the visuospatial sketchpad. For instance, the sketchpad appears to involve specialized (domain-specific) processing

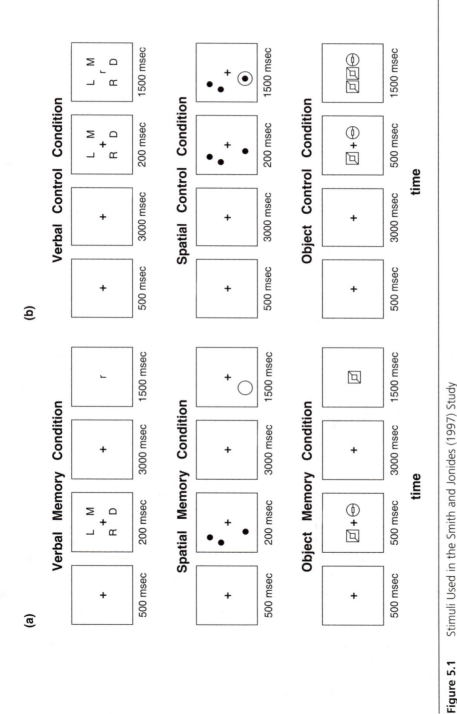

Figure 5.1   Stimuli Used in the Smith and Jonides (1997) Study

SOURCE: From Smith, E.E. & Jonides, J. "Working memory: A view from neuro-imaging," in *Cognitive Psychology*, 33(1), copyright © 1997. Reprinted with permission of Elsevier.

NOTE: The experimental conditions are shown in the blocks to the left (a). The recognition test stimulus is in the fourth square from the left. In each case, the correct answer is given in these examples and so does not have to be recognized from memory.

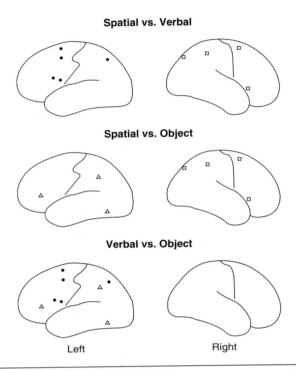

Figure 5.2 Activations in Various Regions of the Brain in the Smith and Jonides (1997) Study

SOURCE: From Smith, E. E. & Jonides, J. "Working memory: A view from neuro-imaging," in *Cognitive Psychology, 33*(1), copyright © 1997. Reprinted with permission of Elsevier.

NOTE: The squares (shown on right) indicate location of responses in the spatial task. Only the right hemisphere showed activation. The dots show responses to the verbal, letter identification task. These are left-hemisphere responses. The triangles show responses to the object (pattern) identification task. These again occurred in the left hemisphere but in different locations from those involving letter responses.

capacities for visual shape information and separate (domain-specific) capacities for spatial information. An additional revision of the model involves the belief that the central executive is probably not a single function either. Instead, there may be a variety of executive functions depending on the specific type of attentional control process (Baddeley, 1992a, 1992b; Baddeley & Logie, 1999). For instance, the work of shifting attention may be controlled by processes other than the processes involved in the work of managing more than one task.

As described above, under Baddeley's interpretation of storage or maintenance in WM, special buffers (or functions) are involved. When material is in WM, it is in a particular "state." An alternative view, described in Section 5 below, is that WM involves highly activated content present in LTM. Here, the difference between content being in WM and not being in WM reflects solely the degree of activation of the content. In support of the "special state" view, Baddeley and Andrade (2000) cited a range of neuroimaging studies that showed activation in various parts of the brain that occurs when material is maintained in WM but that do not appear to be involved in LTM storage.

4. Capacity Theories of Working Memory

4.1. Reading and Operation Spans

Research within the context of WM has led to the conclusion that when we try to understand some body of content or reason about a problem, what is involved is more than simply knowing how to think effectively. The relevant content must be maintained, available for the process of thought to act on it. This issue in fact defines the role of WM—the maintenance of content, while cognitive activities are performed on or with that content.

Memory span, as described in Chapter 4 (the ability to repeat a string of random items after hearing them once), does not appear to be a good measure of WM. For instance, it shows only a weak correlation with tasks such as prose comprehension. Attempts have therefore been made to develop a more appropriate test. Within this context, Daneman and Carpenter (1980) required their participants to read a series of sentences and process them for meaning. They were then tested for comprehension of the material and were also required to recall the last word of each sentence. The test began with two sentences and was expanded to a steadily larger number if the participant had succeeded in retaining the last word items on the previous trial. The approach was called the *reading span task* (RST). Reading span was found to correlate with prose comprehension and is generally accepted as a valid tool for measuring the capacity of (one form of) WM. An individual who can retain five final word items is considered to have a larger WM capacity for language than an individual who can only retain three final word items. In support of this position, Daneman and Merikle (1997), after reviewing 77 published studies, found the RST predicted reading comprehension more effectively than either word span or digit span as used in traditional tests of STM.

Other, analogous forms of measurement have been developed. In a test of operation span, participants are required to perform a simple arithmetic manipulation on a string of numbers and retain the answer. In some cases, a word is included in the string and subjects are required to retain that word rather than the solution to the problem. For instance, a string might be as follows:

$$(6 - 1) \times 2 = \underline{\hspace{2cm}} \text{ trees.}$$

The item to be held in WM for this string would be either *10* or *trees*. Operation span also correlates significantly with prose comprehension. Miyake (2001) noted that span tasks of this kind are somewhat unnatural in that the processing requirement is often unrelated to the storage requirement, while in everyday cognition this is not the case. However, at present more ecological measures have not been developed.

As evaluated by reading and operation span tasks, the capacity of WM has been found to vary from individual to individual and also with age (Daneman & Carpenter, 1980; Gick, Craik, & Morris, 1988; Hasher & Zacks, 1988). WM also shows a general increase across childhood. Within the domain of prose comprehension, the WM function has been found to increase to the age of 20, while somewhat different methodological procedures suggest increase until early middle age, followed by decline (Chiappe, Hasher, & Siegel, 2000).

Children and adults with reading difficulties are characterized by a severely limited WM for prose content (Siegel, 1994; Swanson, 1994). This relationship has been found not only for English-speaking subjects but also across a wide range of other languages, including Italian (DeBeni, Palladino, Pazzaglia, & Cornoldi, 1998), Portuguese (Da Fontoura & Siegel, 1995), and Chinese (So & Siegel, 1997).

In contrast to the individuals described above, persons who are experts or well learned in a given cognitive area can display a pattern of very large WM capacity (in that area only). For instance, master chess players can recall or maintain a great number of patterns or organizations among pieces on a chessboard (Chase & Ericsson, 1981, 1982).

4.2. Just and Carpenter's Capacity Model

It is clear that there are limitations on working memory. One way of viewing this is to assume some processing or functioning resource that is itself limited, such that only a certain amount of "work" can be handled by the system across a given span of time. A position of this kind involves a *capacity model* of WM.

Under a capacity model, the demands placed on the capacity will determine how well WM can function. A task that is more demanding will require more of the underlying resource. Equally, individuals with a relatively limited WM capacity in a certain domain would be likely to find a given task harder to perform than individuals with a larger WM capacity. Some children are able to understand prose passages better than other children. Just and Carpenter (1992) suggested that the most fundamental reason for these differences does indeed reflect the capacity of WM.

A second issue concerns how the function of maintaining content in WM relates to the function of processing that content (deriving new information from it, comparing information, reaching conclusions, and so on). The two functions might be independent, drawing on different "pools" of capacity, or they might draw on a single underlying resource.

When an individual reads a prose passage, an extended body of content must be held available for the work of ongoing comprehension. For instance, the system must extract the meaning of individual phrases and hold this content available until each can be integrated with the others. Such higher-order representations must then be integrated with the meaning of the passage as a whole, including content reflecting the general situation reflected by the passage (Glanzer, Fischer, & Dorfman, 1984; Kintsch, 1988; Kintsch & Van Dijk, 1978). This reflects a widely held view that one function of WM is to retain the intermediate steps, or *partial products*, involved in many higher cognitive activities until they can be assimilated into the higher-level content. Information also needs to be maintained across extended bodies of new input. If I am reading a novel and learn on page one that it is set in the Brazilian jungle, I may need to maintain this fact in WM in order to understand events described some pages later in the story.

Just and Carpenter (1992) posited that the limited capacity of WM is in fact shared (within any given domain) between the two major functions: that of processing and of storage. Thus, if an individual reads a prose passage, he or she must maintain (store) the information, identify relations between various facts in the story, and draw inferences from it (the processing component). According to the present model, the more the capacity required for processing, the less it will be available for storage/maintenance and vice versa.

Some researchers believe that the processing involved in understanding prose may be modular, in the sense of the term described by Fodor (1983). According to this view, there are specialized subsystems in cognitive processing that do not interact with one another, or with any aspect of the system, until the processing in each has been completed. For instance, Ferreira and Clifton (1986) found that pragmatic (semantic) information, available to their participants, did not help them interpret an ambiguous verb. This meant that semantic information was not interacting with syntactic processing. An ambiguous sentence is shown below,

1. The defendant examined by the lawyer shocked the jury.

As the reader encounters "examined," the word could either reflect an active verb (that is, the defendant examined something) or a passive verb, as was the case here (the defendant was examined by someone). Participants typically slow their reading at this point. Presumably they are registering the not yet resolved ambiguity.

A similar unambiguous sentence is,

2. The evidence examined by the lawyer shocked the jury.

Since "evidence" is not capable of examining anything, the only interpretation here is that the verb must be passive: The evidence is being examined by someone. However, Ferreira and Clifton (1986) found that participants slow in their reading at "examined" in these unambiguous sentences, just as in the ambiguous form. This indicated that the meaning of the preceding noun, which includes information as to whether this entity could or could not actively examine something, was not feeding into the syntactic interpretation of the subsequent verb. In other words, semantic and syntactic processing here appeared to be modular (in Fodor's sense)—noninteractive before the completion of the processing in each domain.

Just and Carpenter (1992) replicated this study but divided their participants into high-capacity and low-capacity readers, as previously indicated by the RST. The low-capacity readers showed the same pattern as had been found in the earlier study: They slowed at "examined" for both ambiguous and unambiguous sentences. But the high-capacity readers slowed only in the ambiguous sentences; there was no slowing of pace when they read the unambiguous sentence.

The findings clearly supported the view that, for readers with good comprehension skills only, the product of semantic processing has fed into the syntactic component. They were thus able to see that the verb had to be passive and their reading was not slowed. But why should this difference between good and poor readers have occurred?

This outcome is predicted by the Just and Carpenter capacity model. It can be explained as follows. An *interaction* of information between two areas of processing (here, semantic and syntactic) requires processing capacity. For readers of relatively limited capacity, there may be only enough to handle each subdomain but not the additional capacity needed to provide an interaction between subdomains. As a result, semantic information does not affect the processing of syntactic information at this level. For good readers, possessed of a larger WM processing capacity, there is enough capacity to provide the needed interaction between the two subdomains.

In summary, the present approach, as a comprehensive processing model, assumes that there is a limited pool of processing resources and that attentional limitation is due to this factor. This raises the question of whether there is a general, all-purpose WM that operates across all domains or types of cognition (that would be drawn on, for instance, for both prose comprehension and mathematical operations). The authors concluded that this was not the case. Instead, there are domain-specific resources.

The Just and Carpenter model thus assumes that (1) attentional limitation is due to processing/WM maintenance capacity limitation, (2) there exist subdomains of capacity, (3) within each subdomain capacity is shared between processing and maintenance functions, and (4) differences in competence reflect individual differences in the quantity of processing capacity within that domain.

4.2.1. Computer Models of Language Processing: The CC Reader, 3CAPS, and 4CAPS

The authors also developed a computer simulation as a test of the model, which was partly a production system and partly connectionist (see **Web Chapter 2**). The program was thus able to provide symbolic functions, which enable certain forms of complex, high-level processing and also the strength of connectionist nets (nets can absorb mistakes in a way that strictly symbolic systems cannot). The program was later developed as 3CAPS and 4CAPs, with 4CAPS involving an attempt to model findings, relevant to WM, based on neuroimaging (Just, Carpenter, Keller, Eddy, & Thulborn, 1996; Just, Carpenter, & Varma, 1999; Just & Varma, 2002).

4.2.2. Neuroimaging Research and Location of Function

The 4CAPs neuroimaging research involved, in part, identifying those areas of increased brain activity found when images were rotated mentally. The data indicated that it is probably incorrect to imagine that a particular function (or even a constituent only of a function) is handled in a specific location within the brain. Different areas may cooperate in performing cognitive tasks. For instance, parietal and inferior temporal lobes appear to work conjointly, coming into play variably depending on the nature of the cognitive activity and probably on other, related factors (Carpenter, Just, Keller, Eddy, & Thulborn, 1999). It is possible that sites within the brain are capable of performing various functions and that it is the particular neural patterns established within these sites that reflect a given task (such as image rotation). According to this view, the sites themselves are not critical.

The data also suggest that it may be incorrect to think of a task of a given kind as operating in and of itself within the brain. Instead, whatever is the total—or general—psychological state of the individual may be critical in providing the relevant activation. As a result, what might appear to be an identical requirement (such as image rotation) may not in fact be identical, in terms of neural activation, from one day to the next. Given the profoundly interactive nature of these events, some researchers have begun to question whether a computational model is in fact a valid approach to human cognition (at least in domains of the present kind). In summary, it is possible that a radically different theoretical approach to the nature and activities of the human brain is beginning to emerge within this context.

5. Working Memory as Strongly Activated Content

Some theories, such as Baddeley's model described above, assume that there are particular structures involved in maintaining information in WM. An alternative position holds that content in WM is in fact highly activated LTM content. Here it is posited that when information become activated above a certain level, it becomes automatically available to awareness. Models of this type have been developed by Anderson (1983a, 1983b), Cowan (1995, 1999, 2001), Just and Carpenter (1992), and Just et al. (1999).

Cowan (1995, 1999) described a model of WM in which it was assumed that WM includes two critical components: (1) LTM content that is strongly activated and so in the focus of attention and (2) LTM content that is activated beyond baseline although not in the focus of attention. The former would be present in awareness; the latter would be easily entered into awareness. WM content is therefore content held in "an unusually accessible state" (Cowan, 1999, p. 62).

A further claim is that if there is a pointer in WM to some content in LTM, then that content can also be considered as part of WM (Cowan, 1995; Ericsson & Delaney, 1999).

Cowan also emphasizes the view that the same encoding, maintenance, and retrieval processes are likely to operate across different forms of memory content, for instance, visual and phonemic content. As a result, even though there may be little interference across the different coding types, it would be a mistake to view such functions as wholly separate or unrelated.

6. Working Memory in Adaptive Control of Thought (ACT)

A model that conceptualizes WM as a strongly activated subset of LTM is Anderson's ACT* and ACT-R, a computer simulation of human cognition (Anderson, 1983a, 1983b, 1993; Anderson, Budiu, & Reder, 2001).

In the ACT model, a current goal or goals play a major role in WM. For instance, if you wish to remember the content of a film seen last week, your goal would of course be to retrieve the film's content. This requirement, established in awareness, provides cues that enter LTM on a matching basis (they would match with your coded memory of the film) and increase the activation level of that content. If the increased activation is great enough, the content will thus be retrieved (entered into WM).

The model is also a capacity model, as defined above: A model assuming that limitation in WM is due to a limited processing capacity rather than limitation in buffers or structures. This capacity differs in supply across individuals and also is understood to be fixed within a single individual, across tasks.

The claim for a fixed WM capacity across tasks might appear to contradict empirical findings that have established major differences in WM performance across different domains: That is, the same individual may display a large WM capacity in the area of prose comprehension and a small working capacity in the area of arithmetic calculation or vice versa. Findings of this kind led Shah and Miyake (1996), among many others, to conclude that there are separate WM systems across domains. Lovett, Reder, and Lebiere (1999) explained the apparent discrepancy between these findings and the ACT model of WM as involving possibly different strategies employed by individuals as they perform tasks. That is, the processing strategy used in one domain may be more effective than the strategy used in another. A second possible explanation involves the concept of different levels of activation in the nodes (representations) embodying information in LTM. Thus, an individual with LTM nodes functioning at a high level of activation within one domain may appear to have a stronger WM in that domain than in another, where the node activation level may be lower. According to the present view, the processing capacity, however, is the same across these—and all—domains. Levels of interference within the memory content may also differ from one type of content to another.

The ACT model of cognition is described in further detail in **Web Chapter 2**.

7. Loss of Information From Working Memory: Ongoing Research * * * * *

According to a capacity model, WM's performance will depend on the demands (that is, the difficulty) of the task. The more demanding either the storage or processing requirements, the poorer the outcome.

Towse and Hitch (1995) and Towse, Hitch, and Hutton (1998, 2000) suggested that difficulty did not in fact influence WM performance. They suggested instead that information decays out of WM and that this factor alone determines how well or how long content can be held in the system. Thus, if individuals can perform the processing task quickly, they will perform better (completing the task before the relevant items have decayed). The authors manipulated the difficulty and the duration of counting-span tasks and found that duration appeared to be the critical variable.

Barrouillet and Camos (2001) and Barrouillet, Bernardin, and Camos (2004) reported, however, that the critical factor was not difficulty as normally defined (the complexity of an operational task, etc.) but difficulty defined as the number of times information had to be generated (that is, retrieved from LTM). A large number of very simple retrievals (such as adding one or two to a given number) produced severe decrement in WM performance. This factor had more influence than the passage of time as such. Time did make a difference in that, all other factors being equal, longer periods of maintenance produced a lower function than short periods of maintenance. The authors attributed this to a decay factor. However, the load of work was the more critical variable. And, of particular importance, workload and time showed an interaction. WM capacity reflected the amount of work to be performed divided by the amount of time available to perform that work. Thus, having to retrieve five items in 3 seconds produced a greater drain on WM capacity than having to retrieve five items in 6 seconds. (Here, the retention function would be lower when the time for which content had to be held in WM was shorter.) The authors attributed these data to the fact that when information is being retrieved from LTM, the full attentional process is caught by this work. That is, there is no ability on the part of the system to simultaneously rehearse or reestablish (retrieve again) the target items. Thus, the longer attention is devoted to other processing tasks (other than reestablishing the targets), the weaker the ability to retain the targets will be.

The findings described above are compatible with earlier research suggesting that it is the entry of material into awareness (its retrieval from LTM) that produces the greatest drain on attention. *Manipulating content in WM, even in the course of a cognitively intricate task, may produce less of a drain on the system than acts of simple retrieval (adding 1 to a given digit).*

Thus, Barouillet et al.'s (2004) research supported a capacity theory. However, time was included as yet another variable that does in and of itself produce an influence on WM. It emerged that the demands of the task (here, the high demands of constant retrievals) proved more of a drain on WM resources than did time (maintenance of target items over short periods of time) Barouillet identified his interpretation of the data as a *time-based resource-sharing model*. Here it was assumed that the "resource sharing" involved the attentional process, which, at any given moment, could be devoted either to processing or to a maintenance function but not to both at once.

In a further examination of the issue of loss of information from WM and the question of independence versus resource sharing, Bayliss, Jarrold, Gunn, and Baddeley (2003) examined verbal and visuospatial tasks performed by both adults and children. Factor analysis was used to identify shared resources. Their findings were of domain-specific storage and of a separate, domain-general processing capacity. That is, maintenance of information within one domain (such as linguistic content) drew on one resource, which was not shared with maintenance of other kinds of information, and the same was true of visuospatial content. However, processing capacity appeared to be shared across all domains.

The present findings thus failed to support a resource-sharing model of WM, in which the storage/maintenance and the processing of information draw on a single pool of functioning capacity. Duff and Logie (2001) reported similar findings of maintenance and processing functions operating independently.

8. A Cueing Model of Working Memory * * * * *

The previous sections in this chapter introduced the view that WM involves content held in a particular state of readiness for ongoing (and conscious) processing. Some models, such as Baddeley's, see this as involving special structures separate from LTM. Others, reflecting the activation hypothesis, claim that the state of readiness is supplied by high levels of LTM activation. Both approaches assume, however, that WM reflects a body of highly available content. For instance, if I am reading a novel, my understanding of the content of the novel will be maintained in WM as I read.

A number of researchers have pointed out that traditional views of both STM and WM reflect too small a capacity for almost any form of natural cognitive work. If at any given moment in time I could maintain the information from only two sentences from a novel, I would not understand the novel.

This consideration has led some researchers to assume that the content of WM is in fact considerably larger than originally believed. A third approach, however, rejects the position that an extended body of content is maintained in a highly accessible state at any given moment in time.

According to this third position, WM is in fact of quite limited capacity. But there is a kind of continuous or ongoing retrieval of new information from LTM into awareness. Information is thus constantly being retrieved and then dropped. This activity supplies (over time) an extended body of information of the kind necessary to perform most cognitive tasks.

The LTM content is retrieved on the basis of *cues*. A cue is a representation in awareness that is capable of retrieving other representations from LTM on a matching basis. That is, if I am currently thinking about the concept *tree*, this concept will operate as a cue to retrieve tree content memories or other tree-based information from LTM. It follows that the functioning of WM reflects the efficiency of the cues available in STM (Schneider & Detweiler, 1987; Shiffrin & Schneider, 1997).

Ericsson and Kintsch (1995) suggested that the critical variable in supplying an extended body of content into WM is *the organization of the target (LTM) material.* According to this view, an individual with a large body of knowledge relevant to content X would be able to (1) organize this knowledge in an effective, generally hierarchical manner; and (2) develop highly efficient cues that could retrieve components of content X, as these were needed. For instance, facts concerning a prose passage could be speedily retrieved from LTM and used in ongoing processing. This speed of retrieval might appear to imply a large-capacity WM.

The model posited that special *retrieval structures* can be developed in WM. These provide the relevant cues. Various short-term buffers were also hypothesized. These would hold the products of current processing activities. The authors characterized the STM function that stored cues as *ST-WM* (short-term component of working memory) and the information available for retrieval on this basis from long-term store as *LT-WM* (long-term component of working memory).

The model built on the fact that the memory span can be extended by means of chunking (see Chapter 4, Section 2.3) and also on data reflecting "expert memory." Chase and Simon (1973) had shown that chess masters can retain the pattern of chess pieces on a board after a single exposure. It was also found that medical experts could recall incidental new information after a medical review and analysis better than medical students. Ericsson (1985) has provided a review of similar studies.

Ericsson and Kintsch (1995) suggested that the difference between expert and novice recall depends on the organization of the content in LTM and that parallel events occur in general retrieval from LTM. That is, an effective organization provides effective retrieval cues (corresponding to cues that retrieve large chunks of information). According to this view, good organization provides what has traditionally been considered a large-capacity WM, while poor organization (and so poor cues) provides a small-capacity WM.

The authors noted that a superior memory function is domain specific and also depends on the amount of relevant information already stored in LTM. That is, individuals with a large body of knowledge within a given domain show an enhanced memory function for new knowledge in that domain compared with individuals without the same extended background knowledge. Numerous studies have also shown that memory for and comprehension of texts are influenced by the amount of relevant knowledge possessed by the reader rather than intelligence quotient (IQ) or general reading ability (Ericsson & Kintsch, 1995, p. 222).

9. Working Memory as Attentional Capacity * * * * *

According to a quite different approach to the issue of limitation in WM, it is posited that each of us possesses a particular amount of *attentional capacity* (Conway, Kane, & Engle, 2003; Engle, Cantor, & Carullo, 1992; Engle, Kane, & Tuholski, 1999; Kane, 2001; Kane & Engle, 2003; Roberts, Hager, & Heron, 1994). This capacity is shared across all cognitive domains and is conceptualized as varying from individual to individual.

The role of this attentional factor is to maintain goals (such as the task in hand), control the processing of information in the system, and resist interference.

The authors suggest that a hierarchical system is involved in WM. Attentional capacity operates at the dominant level and controls storage functions that can be understood as similar or identical to the slave systems described by Baddeley. It is assumed that there is relatively little individual variation in the slave systems. In other words, storage is not an important function in terms of drain on WM capacity. The limitations in WM reflect, instead, the attentional capacity factor. The same is true of individual or age-related differences in WM.

In the area of research into cognitive functioning, a distinction has existed for many years between general (*g-factor*) intelligence and domain-specific (*s-factor*) intelligence (Spearman, 1927). The general factor reflects a kind of all-purpose capacity that can be deployed in any cognitive task. The s-factor involves capacities or skills that vary from one cognitive area to another.

Engle et al. (1999) reported that measures of WM (the RST, etc.) have been found to correlate highly with a wide range of natural cognitive tasks (MacDonald, Just, & Carpenter, 1992; Engle, Carullo, & Collins, 1991). They believe that this is because WM reflects the capacity for controlled processing, which must operate across domains. According to this view, attentional capacity provides the g-factor aspect of intelligence and accounts for most of the individual and age-related variability in WM. In support of this claim, the authors found that after variability in complex tasks due to a traditional verbal STM function (the phonemic slave system) was factored out, the remaining variance (which was attributed to the controlled-attention factor) did correlate highly with tests of g-factor intelligence.

Engle and his colleagues believe that the source of the attentional capacity involves the prefrontal cortex (PFC) of the brain. Damage to the PFC in humans is associated with extreme difficulty in performing tasks that require vigilance, an attentional function, and with marked susceptibility to proactive interference. In contrast, healthy individuals show increased activity in the dorsolateral and anterior PFC under conditions of high, but not of low, interference. The increased activity can be interpreted as a controlled attentional process blocking the potentially interfering material.

In conclusion, the present models suggest that differences in WM capacity are due to differences in the strength of attentional processing, which operates at the same level across all domains of knowledge. The maintenance of information content would not affect this type of function. Domain-specific coding of information does exist, as indicated by the operation of memory buffers such as the slave systems but is seen here as not actually reflecting WM.

10. The Genevan View * * * * *

Piaget (1926a, 1926b, 1950, 1952) developed a theory concerning *the span of attention*, which corresponds to "working memory" as the latter term is used today.

The Genevan (Piagetian) view was that all material maintained in awareness (all attended material) is supported in that state (in WM) by the background, LTM structures used to construct (encode) that material. For instance, if I am thinking now of my garden, the garden schemas in LTM (the garden concept) support my ability to maintain this thought within the span of my attention.

According to this view (which differs markedly from mainstream assumptions), the structures (schemas) in LTM that provide representation and thought show different degrees of integration with one another. Schemas that are highly integrated will provide strong support for content in WM. Structures that are weakly or minimally integrated (in LTM) will not. Thus, our ability to maintain content in an activated state depends on the *nature of the underlying functions that have constructed the content.* If they are "strong," then an extended body of information can be maintained in WM with relative ease.

Here, working memory can differ between individuals and also from one domain to another within the same individual. This is the case because the LTM schemas will be more highly integrated in some domains than others due to both biological and experiential factors. The more the structures of a given kind have been exercised and developed, the stronger they will be.

Verbal STM has a limited capacity because random word items have almost no integration with other material. If a task shifts from random items to maintaining the content of, for instance, a story, a large number of highly integrated LTM schemas will come into play and the individual will be able to maintain an extended body of information in the activated state known as WM. Experts can show impressive performance in their own domains for the same reason.

The capacity of WM in children increases over time, this increase being due both to biological/developmental factors and to the "use" of the relevant structures.

A model of the present kind implies that apparently complex content is often easier to maintain in WM than simple content. The hardest material to maintain is, again, random units and these would also be the hardest to retrieve into "the span of attention." (Note that this position is compatible with the data on very simple activities, such as adding one to a random number, described in the work of Barouillet in Section 7 above.)

Piaget and his colleagues conducted extensive research into reasoning in both children and adolescents. Limitations in reasoning were reported as being due to limitations in WM capacity—specifically limitations on the capacity to maintain the information in WM that was needed for the task. For instance, problems in physics, posed to adolescent individuals, required that a set of abstract facts be maintained simultaneously, if the problem were to be solved. All such facts had to be held at the same time because it was necessary to coordinate them to find the solution to the given problem. Failures reflected a situation in which some of the needed content was "held" but other content failed to be maintained simultaneously. According to this view, limitations in WM are limitations on the capacity to maintain content, with the processing aspect playing only a minor role.

The Genevan model does not endorse the view that WM involves highly activated LTM content (the activation hypothesis) as such. Piaget and Inhelder (1973) discussed this possibility but rejected it on the basis of the following argument. In the context of natural episodes, it is necessary to maintain relational information, which exists only within the context of the specific episode. For instance, if I see a rose in a huge green vase with sunlight falling across it, this specific combination of ROSE, HUGE, GREEN, and SUNLIGHT is not simply those representations in a high state of activation in LTM but those representations expressed in a unique relationship with one another. The relationship did not preexist in LTM and indeed may never be experienced again. There must therefore be some processing "arena" in which such content is coded, and this is in fact the span of attention or what is now called WM. A similar argument has been made more recently by Potter (1993).

11. Inhibition of Unwanted Material in Working Memory * * * * *

The most common view of WM limitation, as described in the sections above, involves the construct of some limitation on capacity: the view that, for one reason or another, some individuals possess a greater holding and processing capacity in WM than others.

An alternative view is that the capacity of WM is the same across individuals and across different periods of the life span. However, the ability to block out interference differs. If an individual is able to inhibit or control the negative effects of potentially interfering material, then his or her WM capacity will be large, and the opposite will also be the case, if that individual's system is weak at controlling interference (Hasher, Zacks, & May, 1999; Lustig, Hasher, & May, 2001; Waters & Caplan, 1996; Zacks & Hasher, 1994).

The role of proactive interference (PI) in reducing WM span has been amply demonstrated (Chiappe et al., 2000; Conway & Engle, 1994; Dempster & Cooney, 1982). May, Hasher, and Kane (1999), for instance, varied the amount of potential PI (such as similarity-based interference) within a span task and found that as PI decreased, the span increased. Lustig et al. (2001) demonstrated that under standard conditions of presentation, experimental participants with high spans achieve superior prose recall scores compared with low-span subjects. But when PI materials designed to minimize PI were used, high- and low-span individuals achieved the same prose recall scores.

12. Domain-Specific Versus General-Capacity Working Memory

As indicated across the sections above, there is disagreement today concerning the domain-specific aspects of WM. According to one view, the function is indeed fundamentally different across domains. According to another position, there is an underlying general capacity, with the apparent specialization reflecting other non-WM variables.

There appears to be evidence for both domain-specific and general-capacity functions. Shah and Miyake (1996) demonstrated, for instance, that measures of spatial WM do not correlate with verbal ability and that measures of verbal WM do not correlate with spatial ability. In each case, the WM function does correlate with the corresponding cognitive area (reading span with prose comprehension, etc.) Hitch, Towse, and Hutton (2001) reported both shared and domain-specific factors between measures of verbal and quantitative WM and prose comprehension. If it is assumed that WM within a particular area and cognitive ability in that area are related, then there is a great deal of evidence in support of domain-specific WM since there is a large body of data indicating domain-specific cognitive abilities. These may be quite fine grained. For instance, in language, development, comprehension, and production (the ability to talk) develop on the basis of different time schedules (Bates,

Bretherton, & Snyder, 1988). It has also been established in the mainstream as well as the Genevan tradition that if a given individual shows a very strong WM function in one domain, it cannot be predicted that he or she will be strong in another.

There is also a considerable body of data supporting the hypothesis of a general factor in WM, that is, a factor that would operate equally across all domains. It has been found that verbal and numerical WM spans are equally good predictors of general attainment in adults, and numerous measures of WM have been found to correlate highly with general ability (Kyllonen & Christal, 1990).

A view that appears widely accepted today is that both domain-free and domain-specific processes operate in WM.

13. Working Memory and Phenomenological Experience

Baddeley and Andrade (2000) hypothesized that conscious representation, such as the vividness of experienced imagery, should be related to the amount of processing capacity available in WM. Greater processing capacity should lead to a richer, more vivid experienced image.

The researchers presented novel images to their participants. The images were either visual or auditory. The visual consisted of shapes that varied in their relative positions and spacing, and the auditory of musical notes, as shown in Figure 5.3.

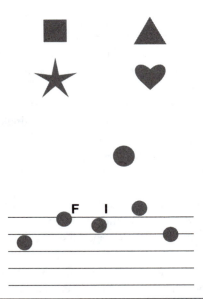

Figure 5.3   Examples of Visual and Auditory Stimuli Presented in the Baddeley and Andrade (2000) Study

SOURCE: From Baddeley, A. D. & Andrade, J., "Working memory and the vividness of imagery," in *Journal of Experimental Psychology: General, 29*(1), copyright © 2000, American Psychological Association. Reprinted with permission.

Under the experimental conditions, participants were required to perform a cognitive task after exposure to the target stimuli. One task involved counting repeatedly from 1 to 10 and the other involved tapping in a spatial pattern that had been learned earlier. The counting task was already known to interfere with phonemic recall and the tapping task was known to interfere with visuospatial recall. Under the control condition, there was no requirement of a secondary cognitive task.

The participants were required to attempt to form and maintain a representation of the target image stimuli, while performing the (counting or tapping) secondary task. They then reported on the vividness of the experienced images. They were also tested on their ability to recognize the image stimuli.

Visual and auditory stimuli were rated at similar levels of vividness. There was a significant effect of condition, in that the vividness of the maintained images was rated as significantly higher under the control than under either of the experimental conditions. There was also a highly significant interaction effect. The tapping task produced lower ratings of visual images than of auditory images (a rating of 5.57 vs. 7.27), while the counting task produced significantly lower ratings of auditory than of visual images (5.33 vs. 7.54).

The experiments described above thus provided support for the view that WM capacity plays a role in phenomenological experience. Tasks in WM that required either visuospatial or phonemic coding were shown to selectively affect the vividness of visual or auditory images.

Summary

WM involves the function that holds content in or close to awareness. When material is attended, it is in WM. If it is consciously experienced, it is within the focus of attention.

WM appears to involve a single channel (the attended channel) and is of limited capacity. There is disagreement as to whether there is a single general pool of capacity or whether this differs across different domains. The empirical data show marked differences across domain, but some researchers think that this is due to the operation of "slave systems," which differ across such domains, rather than to variation in WM capacity as such.

Nonverbal STM cognitive tasks produce little or no interference with material in verbal STM, and verbal codes show little interference with visual codes in STM.

Some models posit that WM involves special structures or buffers. Others believe that whenever content is activated above a certain level, it is present in WM. Another issue involves whether the capacity of WM is shared across storage and activity functions within a given domain in WM. WM frequently appears to hold a large body of information (as when we read a novel, for instance), but according to cueing models WM is of sharply limited capacity and seems larger because material is constantly being retrieved from LTM and entered into WM from which it is quickly lost. Attentional theories of WM posit that WM capacity can be seen as attentional capacity, which is general in nature (does not differ across domains), although it does differ with age and from individual to individual. Some psychologists think that WM capacity is simply a function of how much interference is operating in the system. According to the Piagetian view, conceptual structures (schemas) in LTM directly support content in WM, such that if the LTM structures are strong (strongly integrated), a large body of information can be maintained simultaneously, while if the LTM structures are weak, only a limited amount of information can be maintained.

Discussion

Based on the work described above, it appears that WM is indeed a limited-capacity system. Capacity here involves the degree to which a pool or pools of resources may be drawn on by the particular requirements of a task.

There remains uncertainty as to whether maintenance and processing do in fact draw on a single capacity (within a given domain) or on separate pools of resource. On the whole, the data appear to support the view of separate resources, but the issue has not been resolved as yet.

In contrast, the existence of *domain-specific interference* in WM has been solidly established. There also appears to be agreement that individuals may show strong performance in one domain but not in others. That is, an individual might have a good WM for prose comprehension but not for mathematical reasoning and so on (Shah & Miyake, 1996). The reasons for this are contested, however. Engle et al. (1999), for instance, suggest that WM reflects a general capacity, shared across domains, and that the differences in performance are due to variability in "slave systems." Anderson et al. (2001) take a similar view, according to which certain types of content may have high levels of background activation in LTM, making them easier to "hold" in WM. (It is not clear, however, why this should not be considered to imply a strong WM function.)

An important issue that has emerged from the research into WM is that there is no direct or intuitive relationship between the complexity of material and the ease with which it can be held in WM. The direct assumption would be that simple material would be easy to maintain and complex material, difficult. However, the data suggest that the opposite may be the case. Within this context, for instance, Barrouillet et al. (2004) found that adding a one or a two to a number in WM caused very heavy drain on capacity.

The capacity of WM remains a focus of disagreement. Given the issue outlined above, concerning complexity, it is possible that an extended body of complex material can be maintained in WM more easily than a small body of simple material. The traditional WM span was measured as a list of random words or numbers. This very "simple" content is clearly difficult to maintain, providing a memory span of about seven items. Yet we appear able to hold the entire major content of a story in WM as we read the story. Two notable positions have been taken on this issue. According to Kintsch, WM is of very limited capacity and material is held "active" on the basis of the continuous retrieval of information from LTM. In contrast, according to Piaget, the type of content involved determines the capacity of WM, with random items (having minimal LTM support) providing a very small capacity and meaningful material (having relatively extended LTM support), a large capacity. According to this view, we really are capable of holding the content of a story in an activated state as we read the story.

Research in this area appears to be on the threshold of a range of discoveries that will play a major role in our understanding of memory. These include the relations between awareness and ongoing thought and the passive (although perhaps not so passive) long-term store.

CHAPTER 6

Encoding and Retrieval in Long-Term Memory

Foundations

Overview

1. Early research within the information-processing tradition identified three dominant codes in memory—namely, physical, phonemic, and semantic. These were assumed to reflect three different memory systems and many studies supported the three-store view.

2. The single-store model of memory posits that there is in fact only one, general-purpose memory system. According to the levels of processing model, as more processing occurs, different memory codes will be generated.

3. Three techniques have been identified for the entry of random word items into long-term memory (LTM). These are rehearsal, association forming, and image forming.

4. Cues are defined as representations present in awareness. They enter LTM on a matching basis. According to cue-dependent models of recall, cues wholly determine whether a memory will be successfully recalled or not. There are situations in which material can be recalled, although it cannot be recognized. According to the encoding specificity model, this occurs because the cues in certain recall tests match better with the target memory content than the cues present in some recognition tests.

5. Single-stage models of retrieval posit that cues contact information in memory and if there is a sufficient level of contact, which is also distinctive

contact, the memory will be recalled. Two-stage models posit that first material is contacted in memory and also generated from LTM, and then there is a second-stage decision process.

6. Recognition shows some properties in common with recall and some properties that are different. According to the dual process theory of recognition, there are two functions involved—namely, familiarity and "recollection."

7. According to signal detection theory, items that have recently been encountered have a higher familiarity or activation level than items that have not been recently encountered. An item is recognized if its familiarity value is sufficiently high.

Learning Objectives

1. Knowledge of the distinction between three- and single-store models of memory.

2. An understanding of the nature of cues and cue-dependent theories of recall.

3. Understanding of the hypothesis of encoding specificity.

4. Understanding of single and dual stage models of recall and recognition.

5. Understanding of the concepts of episodic, semantic, and procedural memory.

Long-term memory (LTM) has been defined within experimental psychology as involving retention for any period longer than 45 seconds to retention for life. According to this view, the 45-second lower limit reflects the operation of short-term memory (STM).

Some psychologists feel that the span of time defined above is too long to be identified as a single memory store. Instead, it should be understood as involving several distinct stages. In the present chapter, however, the data reflect content that has been retained in memory, without a more detailed breakdown into time-related functions. The issue is examined again in Chapter 17.

1. Memory Stores

1.1. Multiple- and Single-Store Models of Human Memory

The research described in Chapters 3 and 4 originated in the belief that there exist three distinct memory stores: sensory, STM, and LTM. In the 1960s, several approaches of this kind were developed (Glanzer & Cunitz, 1966; Waugh &

Norman, 1965). The most famous of them, however, is probably the Atkinson and Shiffrin (1968) model.

The model assumed that when verbal material was attended in sensory memory, it would be entered into verbal short-term store. This store possessed an average of seven "slots," and each chunk of input would be held in a single slot. The material might then be entered into long-term store by the deployment of special strategies, under the conscious control of the subject. These strategies included rehearsal, image forming, and association forming.

An important theoretical aspect of the present model was that two components of mnemonic functioning should be identified. The first involved the capacity for storage, such as the various slots for items in STM. The second involved *control processes*. These were the strategies used by the individual to process the STM content. For instance, a subject might decide to rehearse the material. The distinction between these two functions has been maintained in almost all later theories.

An additional assumption of the Atkinson and Shiffrin model was that as long as an item was held in STM, its representation would strengthen in LTM. That is, the two functions were not independent. Support for this view had been provided by Hebb (1961), who presented his subjects with a series of digit strings somewhat above the memory span, for short-term recall. The subjects were not aware that the same sequence was in fact being presented repeatedly—once in every three trials. The probability of recalling this sequence increased across trials, showing clear evidence that the information had entered, and was gradually strengthening in, long-term store.

The Atkinson and Shiffrin model is shown in Figure 6.1.

In the 1960s and 1970s, a great deal of evidence was gathered in support of the concept of separate memory stores. The codes appeared different, the length of life in each store was markedly different, and a range of variables seemed at that time to influence long-term, but not short-term, recall. However, as research continued, it was found that visual, phonemic, and semantic codes all operate in STM as well as LTM. And it emerged that variables such as frequency, concreteness, and imagery, once thought not to influence STM, did in fact influence that system (Engle, Nations, & Cantor, 1990; Roodenrys & Quinlan, 2000).

When a long list of items is presented and tested under conditions of immediate free recall, the last items are often recalled first, and recalled almost perfectly. A plausible explanation for this phenomenon is that the items are being reported directly out of STM. Glanzer and Cunitz (1966) showed that if a delay is imposed prior to the test (such that the last items would no longer be in short-term store), the previous advantage in recall for these items vanishes. The delay was achieved by presenting subjects with a distractor task, so that they would not be able to rehearse the items during the retention interval. Figure 6.2 shows a typical serial position curve when items are learned and tested under conditions of immediate free recall and when a delay of either 10 or 30 seconds is imposed following the final item.

Bjork and Whitten (1974), however, demonstrated a recency effect in free recall under a continuous distractor (CD) paradigm. Here, a distractor task follows the presentation of every item on the list, including the final item, such that the final item should no longer be present in STM.

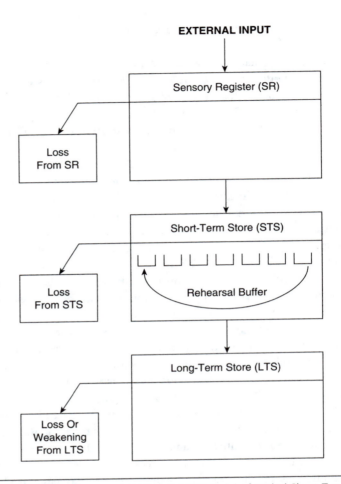

EXTERNAL INPUT

Figure 6.1   The Atkinson and Shiffrin (1968) Model of Verbal Short-Term Store

SOURCE: From Atkinson, R. C., & Shiffkin, R. M., "Human memory: A proposed system and its control processes," in K. W. Spence & J.T. Spence (Eds.), *The Psychology of Learning and Motivation: Advances in Research and Theory,* vol. 2, copyright © 1968. Reprinted with permission of Elsevier.

NOTE: Stimuli enter a sensory register and, if attended, into short-term store. They are held in a variable number of slots and can be reentered into short-term memory (STM) on the basis of rehearsal. Material may be simultaneously in STM and LTM (long-term memory).

Figure 6.3 shows recall under conditions of immediate testing, delayed testing, and the CD paradigm.

The evidence for separate memory stores now appeared far less clear-cut than had been the case earlier. There remained some support for the modal memory view, however. In a condition known as the amnesic syndrome, individuals who have suffered certain forms of brain damage display intact short-term recall and deeply impaired long-term recall (Milner, 1971). People suffering from the amnesic syndrome can form no new long-term memories. For instance, if an amnesic meets someone, he or she will retain a memory of this episode for only a few minutes. Data of this kind support the hypothesis of distinct memory stores underlying short- and long-term recall.

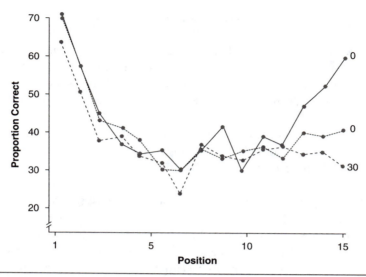

Figure 6.2   The Serial Position Curve Under Immediate Free Recall (No Distraction) and the Serial Position Curve When There Is a Delay of 10 or 30 Seconds Following Learning

SOURCE: From Glancer, M., & Cunitz, A. R., "Two storage mechanisms in free recall," in *Journal of Memory and Language,* 5, copyright © 1966. Reprinted with permission of Elsevier.

NOTE: Under the delay condition, participants perform a distractor task after the last to-be-learned item has been presented. As a result, the STM trace is not available by the time the test begins.

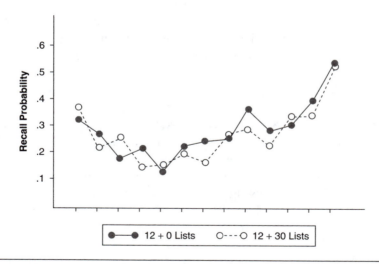

Figure 6.3   Immediate Free Recall Under Standard Conditions, Shown by the Line With Black Dots, and Free Recall Under Conditions in Which a 30-Second Distractor Task Was Performed Following the Presentation of Each Item

SOURCE: From Bjork, R. A., & Whitten, W. B. "Recency-sensitive retrieval processes in long term free recall," in *Cognitive Psychology,* 6(2), copyright © 1974. Reprinted with permission of Elsevier.

NOTE: There is a recency effect even though the final item was not recalled until 30 seconds had passed.

1.2. The Levels of Processing Model

By the 1970s, it had become clear that the available evidence did not definitively support, or refute, either the multiple- or a single-store model of human memory. Against this background, a number of single-store models were developed, of which Craik and Lockhart's (1972) *levels of processing* approach is probably the best known.

Craik and Lockhart suggested that that it would not be correct to imagine information being moved out of one distinct store (STM) and into another distinct store (LTM). Instead, it was proposed that information entering memory is processed along a continuum. In the case of a word item, a small amount of processing would generate a weak, physical code. More processing could lead to an acoustic or articulatory (phonemic) code, and more again to the semantic level. These stages of processing had traditionally been associated with sensory, short-term, and long-term verbal memory. The shift in theory here, however, involved the view that distinct stores were not involved. All forms of code were established within a single memory store.

Once the semantic level was achieved, some information (such as highly familiar, meaningful stimuli) would be compatible with existing cognitive structures and so would be established faster than less familiar stimuli. They would also be retained longer. In addition, at this level elaboration of the material could occur. That is, content might be associated with other content or with imagery, and so on. This would reflect a deep level of coding. (The nature of elaborative processing is described in Section 3 below.)

Craik and Lockhart thus wrote of processing from a shallow to a deep level. The deeper the level, the longer the code would be retained. Thus codes relating to word items could be described as follows:

Structural   A shallow level of processing. The physical properties of the word stimulus, such as its length, shape, or sound, would be established.

Phonemic   A slightly deeper level of processing. The shape of the word or its physical sound would be coded in terms of known phonemic properties.

Semantic   A deeper level of processing. The meaning of the stimuli would be established: That is, a semantic code would come into play. This could lead to association with other material based on semantic relations: a very deep level of encoding.

The authors also posited that memory codes were a by-product of cognitive activities: that is, of the fashion in which the material was being analyzed. According to this view, there is no specific memory function. As the cognitive system analyzes material, a code reflecting the nature of the material is established and can be recalled (in some cases) from memory. The type of analysis will determine the nature and the longevity of the resulting memory traces.

1.2.1. Research Into Levels of Processing

A range of studies provided support for the claim that the "deeper" the code, the more likely it becomes that an individual will recall some target information. It was also shown that strong recall could be achieved without the active intention to memorize the material, a phenomenon known as *incidental learning* (Bellezza, Cheesman, & Reddy, 1977; Fisk & Schneider, 1984; Hyde & Jenkins, 1969). There was also some evidence that supported the notion of a continuum of analyses (as against material being moved at a specific point from one store to another). Baddeley (1990, chap. 3), for instance, reported that slower presentation of word items results in a more evident semantic code being established within the time frame normally associated with STM.

Other studies failed to support a straightforward level of processing claim. Slamecka and Graf (1978) required their participants to think of a word that rhymed with a target item, such that a correct response to FLOWER would be POWER. In a second condition, they presented these already established rhyming words to other participants, with the instruction that they should study the pair for later recall. The first task required phonemic analysis and the second should have elicited semantic analysis. Recall was significantly higher under the first (phonemic) condition than under the second (semantic) condition.

This outcome is known as the *generation effect*. When individuals produce items themselves from LTM, they retain these items better than under conditions in which the same material is presented to them "from outside." And here, type of code did not determine strong recall in the fashion predicted by the levels of processing model. Some other variable appears to be at work.

It has also been demonstrated that success in recall depends on the relationship between the encoding and the kind of test that is applied. For instance, if the test requires memory for phonemic information, it appears unlikely that semantic coding would produce better performance than phonemic coding. A number of studies have demonstrated that phonemic coding can be more effective than semantic coding for a test of phonemic recall (Kolers, 1978; Morris, Bransford, & Franks, 1977; Stein, 1978). The notion that the code must be relevant to the demands made during testing has been described as *transfer appropriate processing*. (The work at encoding must transfer appropriately to the test.)

It is not clear, however, that data such as this undermine the original claim that a semantic code, in general, will endure longer than a phonemic code. It has also been shown that semantic coding can in some cases provide superior *phonemic* recall. For instance, if a surname such as BUTCHER is to be learned, participants recall the material better if they think of the concept *butcher* and translate this into phonemic form at the time of the test, than if they simply repeat the name on a phonemic basis.

1.3. Multiple- Versus Single-Store Models: Conclusions

Opinion remains divided among researchers concerning whether human memory is in fact multiple- or single-store.

In support of a single-store assumption, there appears to be good evidence that STM cannot be identified with a particular kind of code (that is, the phonemic). Also, if an item has been attended, the data suggest that what follows is a continuum of analyses, rather than a definite act of transfer from one store to another.

In support of a multistore assumption, however, it is clear that recently presented (and attended) items can always be recalled; they show a different pattern from other material. Also, the amnesic syndrome provides evidence for the selective impairment of LTM, with STM left intact. Under a formulation such as levels of processing, it is difficult to see how material within a single system, which is simply being recycled within that system, should be impervious to damage, when all other functions are not impervious.

It remains possible, however, that content entering memory moves through a continuum of processing, but that the various stages of the continuum involve underlying processing structures that are qualitatively different from one another.

2. Spread of Encoding Versus Meaningfulness

Craik and Lockhart had suggested that one reason for the effectiveness of semantic codes is that they can be readily elaborated (connected with other information). If I think of the meaning CAT, I can associate this quickly with memories of particular cats, for instance. In contrast, phonemic information, such as the sound /c/ leads to no particular or organized associations. Numerous studies have shown that elaboration, or *spread of encoding*, provides superior recall of target material (Craik & Jacoby, 1975; Craik & Tulving, 1975).

Some researchers believe, however, that the amount or quantity of processing of target information is not the most critical factor in providing strong recall (as held by the levels of processing model) and also that spread of encoding does not achieve its results simply because a target body of content has been linked to another body of content. Instead, it is believed that the extent to which the material achieves meaningfulness or "makes sense" is the critical factor. According to this view, when two bodies of content are linked together, this often leads to a greater degree of logical integration within the material. In other words, the content becomes more coherent or meaningful, and this is the real cause of any improvement in memory that may result.

Bransford and Johnson (1972) presented their participants with sentences that were either coherent/meaningful or not coherent/meaningful. An example of the sentences is shown below. Under a third condition, a cue word was provided that changed an apparently meaningless sentence into a meaningful form.

Type 1. COHERENT.

The apple was sour because it had not ripened.

Type 2. INCOHERENT.

The note was sour because the cloth ripped.

Type 3. CUES.

Bagpipes.

The note was sour because the cloth ripped.

The participants spent more time studying Type 2 sentences than Types 1 or 3 and yet showed weaker recall of Type 2 than of the other forms. Here, there was a greater degree of effort expended to process Type 2, and yet a weaker memory function was observed. The findings therefore showed that the *amount of processing* is not critical in some forms of learning.

The present study demonstrated that when memory content is meaningful (makes sense) the memory function is markedly heightened. Thus, a critical factor in determining our ability to recall information centers on whether that information does or does not carry higher-order meaning. Higher-order meaning reflects information derived from entire statements taken as a whole as against the meaning of individual words.

3. Strategies for the Entry of Information Into, and Retrieval From, Long-Term Memory

A great deal of research has been conducted concerning how random items coded in STM can be learned: that is, entered into LTM.

Two major techniques have been established. One is rehearsal. This approach is highly reliable; if an item is repeated enough, it will be learned. The second technique involves *elaboration* of the material, a term that covers two different strategies: (1) *association forming* and (2) *image forming*.

In association forming, the target material (say, the first word on a list) is connected with other items or other material. This can be achieved either by forming associations among the items themselves or by associating them with information external to the critical list. For instance, if you were asked to learn the items HAT, DUCK, ROSE, PIN, MOON, BOY, and so on, it would be possible to associate them together by forming a sentence in which they all participate, such as, The BOY saw a DUCK PIN a ROSE on its HAT on the MOON. Here the items have been connected with one another in such a way as to provide crude higher-order meaning. Letters can be memorized in the same way. Further associative techniques include *acronyms* and *acrostics*. Acronyms involve using the first letters of the target items to form a word. A well-known example would be the word HOMES to represent the names of the Great Lakes (Huron, Ontario, Michigan, Erie, Superior).

An acrostic involves a sentence or phrase in which again the first letter of each word provides the first letter of each target item (or the item as a whole). Random letters can be recalled in this fashion. RNSF, for instance, could be retained through the phrase, Registered Nurse, San Francisco. And the colors of the spectrum have often been learned through the sentence, Richard of York Gave Battle In Vain (red, orange, yellow, green, blue, indigo, violet).

Mnemonics can involve danger, though. I recall describing the Richard of York acrostic in the form "Richard of York fought . . ." and was momentarily baffled to recall the color beginning with F.

The third major technique for learning random words involves *image forming*.

Here, the approach involves forming mental images of the critical items. The images need to be interrelated. Thus, an image of a duck with a rose in its hat would be an effective strategy, while forming three separate pictures, of the duck, the rose, and the hat, would not be effective.

An image strategy can be used to provide effective order recall. In one such technique, images are imagined in pairs. For the present list, the first pair would involve HAT and DUCK. You might imagine a duck sitting in a hat. The second pair could involve the DUCK image again but now with the associated image of a ROSE. A duck smelling a rose would be appropriate. The next pair would involve ROSE and PIN, and so on. At recall, the subject simply runs through the image pictures, ignoring the duplications, that is, moving from HAT to DUCK to ROSE to PIN. The items will be maintained in this fashion in the correct order (and can even be recalled backwards quite easily). Examples of these image pairs are shown in Box 6.1.

Both associative and image techniques require a short period of time to achieve the relevant statement, story, or series of images. But they are more effective than rehearsal, under conditions in which there is sufficient time to form the elaborations. That is, they result in quicker learning and longer periods of retention. In contrast, due to the risk of losing some items while others are being elaborated, rehearsal is more effective when there is no time to elaborate the material. If you hear a phone number only once, you need to rehearse the series in order to retain it. If you stop to associate the beginning of the string, you will probably fail to retain the final items and vice versa. In short, rehearsal is the best strategy for material at or near the memory span that will be presented only once.

Image techniques of the kind described here are routinely offered in books on the commercial market that claim to provide ways of dramatically improving one's memory. They work but only for random, unrelated verbal items. They have little relevance to meaningful material of the kind needed, for instance, to master a new subject matter or remember a book or a film.

There are some memory techniques that do have real-world application, however. Gruneberg (1992) developed an approach called the *linkword language system*. Its object is to help in the memorization of foreign language vocabulary, and the trick is to take a foreign word, find an English word or phrase that sounds like it, and relate the latter to the translation of the word in English. You are then instructed to imagine the situation that has been created. For instance, the French word for tablecloth is "nappe." This would lead to the following mnemonic:

Imagine having a NAP on a TABLECLOTH.

And the French word for cat is "chat," leading to:

Imagine having a CHAT with your CAT.

Box 6.1   An Illustration of an Imagery Mnemonic

NOTE: The items to be recalled are HAT, DUCK, ROSE, and PIN. Order recall can be established because one item is duplicated across sequential image pairs. If it has already been recalled, it should not be recalled again.

This technique has proved effective, beyond the results achieved through straightforward repetition of the material.

The most famous of all mnemonic strategies, however, is probably the *method of loci*, developed for the use of orators in Greek and Roman cultures. The great advantage of this approach is that it can be used with meaningful content, no less than random words. It involves taking each word or fact to be recalled and symbolizing it in some fashion. The symbol must be concrete, something that you can see. You might, for instance, represent the information "High-frequency words are better recalled than low-frequency words" by visualizing a crammed basket of objects shaped like words being carried by a smiling elephant (for retention), while a mostly empty basket is left behind.

You next imagine walking into a well-known location, such as your house. You place the first set of images against a given wall, perhaps the first wall to your right, and visualize the result. You then continue to walk through the house, placing the symbolic images against its walls in a definite sequence. At the time of test, you again move through the house, retrieving the images.

This technique is useful for essay writing since you are unlikely to miss any given set of content in your organized walk through the house. Also, the material can be rehearsed anywhere (sitting on a bus, etc.) and the technique is less boring than straightforward rehearsal.

The techniques described above centered on efficient ways of entering material into memory. There are also effective strategies for recalling material that has already been encoded, particularly within the context of actual events. Geiselman, Fisher, MacKinnon, and Holland (1985, 1986), for instance, developed an approach known as the *cognitive interview*. Here, in addition to a standard attempt to recall the target memory, four retrieval methods are recommended. These include directions to (1) report even material that seems unimportant; (2) mentally recreate the context/environment in which the episode occurred, to the last possible detail and also remember the emotions experienced at the time of the episode; (3) recall the events in many different orders, for instance, beginning at the beginning and then moving through to the end, then beginning in the middle of the episode and moving forward again, then starting at the end and moving backwards; and (4) report the event not only from one's own perspective but also from that of other individuals present. Additional prompts are supplied for various aspects of the event. For instance, when trying to recall a given person, try to establish whether the person's appearance, speech, and so on reminds you of anyone and, if so, of whom. The cognitive interview has proved extremely effective in increasing the amount of accurate information recalled, without leading to a corresponding increase in false recall (Koehnken, Milne, Memon, & Bull, 1994). In all, the approach produces better results than are achieved through hypnosis.

4. Retrieval of Information From Long-Term Memory: Cues

If I want to recall a certain memory, I may succeed. Yet I have an enormous amount of information stored in LTM. This raises the question of how it is possible to "find" the right content.

It is believed that we in fact achieve this through the operation of *cues*. Cues are generally defined as any representation that is present in awareness: a thought, a single idea, a perceptual image or images, an emotion, or even a physiological state, such as feeling tired. Cues make contact with material in LTM on a matching basis. That is, if I am thinking HOUSE consciously, HOUSE is a cue that will contact house representations in LTM.

When cues contact material in LTM, this is known as *access*. Access does not imply that the contacted material will be recalled. The term *retrieval* is used for the actual event of recollection.

Some researchers believe that not all content in awareness operates as cues (Tulving, 1983, p. 169). If I walk into a room, I might see a lamp and a table. If I have no interest in these objects, they will not trigger memories. Thus, it is possible that they did not act as cues.

Other researchers believe that all conscious representations operate as cues. This implies that access is an automatic process, not one related to the intentions or interests of the individual. According to the present hypothesis, if I see a table in which I have no interest, this will contact table representations in memory, but the resulting low-level activation in LTM will be overridden by stronger activations and will not produce any form of retrieval (Kintsch, 1974, 1998, chap. 1). The stronger activations involve content that is of interest and that is therefore attended.

The most important cues, with regard to remembering, involve descriptions or *specifications* of a desired memory (Norman & Bobrow, 1979, p. 109). Thus, the thought, "What did I eat for dinner last night?" involves the direct specification of a memory and in most cases would result in the memory being retrieved.

4.1. The Cue-Dependent Theory of Forgetting

In the past, recollection was generally conceptualized as involving either strong memories that could always be recalled or very weak, or perhaps lost, memories that could not be recalled. Some were seen as borderline, such that they might be retrieved only with a degree of effort.

Today, it is understood that there is a critical interaction between cues and memory content at the time of retrieval. In some cases, the presence of "good" cues will make it possible to recall a memory that could otherwise not be recalled.

Tulving (1974, 1983) and Watkins and Tulving (1975) advanced the claim that all successful recall is in fact due to the presence of good cues. According to this view, memory content does not differ in "strength" in LTM. In other words, no set of memory content differs in its potential to be recalled. When cues are available that overlap extensively with a target memory, successful recall will follow. (The exception to this outcome involves the phenomenon of *cue overload*, in which a cue or cues match with multiple memory sets. When there is a failure of distinctive matching of this kind, it is believed that recall will generally not occur.) The belief that cues entirely determine success or failure in recall is known as the *cue-dependent theory of forgetting*.

In support of the cue-dependent hypothesis, Tulving and Psotka (1971) required their participants to learn six consecutive lists of words. A test was given after each list had been learned (here called Test 1), a major test of all six lists (Test 2), and finally a cued-recall test (Test 3).

Under cued recall, a cue was given that was the superordinate class of the target item whenever an item had failed to be recalled spontaneously. Thus, if the target was JACKET, the cue "clothing" would be given or if the target was ORANGE, the cue would be "fruit."

There was massive retroactive interference under Test 2, with the first list suffering the highest level of forgetting. Under Test 3, however, when the cues were provided, recall returned to as high a level as under Test 1 (immediate testing of each list).The authors interpreted their data as implying that the impairment of recall produced by retroactive interference did not involve either weakening or loss of the original memory traces. The traces were still present in their original form. But they had become inaccessible, because of the loss of appropriate cues. The presentation of new lists for learning had changed the cues present in the retrieval environment. When good cues were presented, the recall function was as high as had been the case when there was no retroactive interference. An assumption made here was that subjects had been able to generate the higher-order category cues themselves under immediate testing but that these cues had become unavailable over time.

4.2. Distinctiveness and Temporal Cues

From the 1970s on, many researchers noted the critical function played by *distinctiveness* in memory content. Material that can be clearly differentiated from other material in LTM will be better recalled and better recognized than nondistinctive content.

The effect is particularly strong in the case of recognition memory. For instance, if a series of pictures shows items of furniture and among this series there are just two pictures depicting ships, then the ship pictures will later be recognized more reliably than any of the furniture pictures. The images that are different appear to stand out in memory.

An explanation of this effect has been provided in terms of cues. According to this position, where many LTM items are of the same type, cues may fail due to the factor of cue overload. That is, they may fail to be able to distinguish between a target item and other competing items of the same kind (Nairne, 1990a; Neath & Nairne, 1995). Thus, the well-known influence of distinctiveness in improving memory performance may depend on the operation of cues.

Murdock (1960) introduced the idea that material in LTM may include temporal information, reflecting when that material had been encountered. A further suggestion was that temporal information might provide content that could be matched by cues. Thus, an individual might attempt to recall "the material that I saw last," or "the material that I saw first," and so on.

Murdock also urged that this temporal information could possess a property similar to that found in perception. For instance, if you look back at a line of telephone poles, the poles nearest to you are more distinctly seen than those further away. The present argument involved the view that the same phenomenon holds for temporal coding. Information that has been recently encountered possesses the same clarity—is distinct in the way that obtains for an object that is spatially close. And information remote in time lacks that clarity, just as remote telephone poles would tend to blur.

The idea of temporal-code "blurring" is important because it provides an explanation of why remote memories tend to be weak memories. Among researchers who believe that cues fully determine success or failure in recall, it has been difficult to explain why memories established far in the past are, for the most part, hard to remember. According to the theory, good cues should work as well for these long past recollections as for just-formed recollections. The present hypothesis—that there is a parallel between the perception of distant objects and the capacity to "read" temporal information on remote memories—provides a tentative explanation for the fact that we tend to forget over time.

5. Separate Memory Stores for Different Kinds of Information

5.1. Episodic and Semantic Memory

In 1972, Tulving described an idea that had been considered by some earlier researchers, but not developed. It was the idea that memory for life events, and memory for general information, may involve two different systems. Tulving labeled the first of these *episodic memory* and the second, *semantic memory.*

When we recall episodes from our lives, several distinct properties emerge in the memories.

First, there is a central time factor. We locate the relevant scene in the past, either vaguely or precisely. This does not occur when we note, for instance, that two and two make four. There is also spatial/perceptual information; we remember at least to some extent how things looked or sounded. And there is a bedrock awareness of self. This episode was one that the individual himself or herself lived through, such that this is central to the quality of the recollection.

In contrast, our general store of information, semantic memory, is not located in the past. It has no temporal associations. Memories of this kind consist of factual information (whether true or false). Two and two is four. Paris is the capital of France. Such knowledge is often experienced in a fully abstract way. At least, it can be experienced by many individuals without accompanying images. In other words, it does not carry intrinsic perceptual information. And it has no inherent relation to the self. Our conceptual knowledge, as well as general knowledge, is also a part of semantic memory. I know what tables are. This knowledge is not located in the past, is largely abstract, and has no relation to me as an individual.

Support for the distinction between episodic and semantic memories has now emerged from several areas of research and clinical investigation. There are data from neuroimaging suggesting that different physical areas of the brain become more fully activated when semantic and episodic memories are recalled (see Chapter 17). Also, a typical symptom of the amnesic syndrome, a condition produced by damage to the brain, is that the individual is grossly impaired in recalling episodes from his or her life (usually for a distinct period of time stretching into the past), while semantic memory remains intact.

If two distinct systems do exist, it is also clear that they interact. We learn new information as we live through life episodes, and the information may be stored in semantic memory. Even more critical, the meanings of everything that we see and hear around us are supplied from conceptual/semantic memory.

Most researchers today include a third type of memory store known as *procedural memory*. Procedural memory involves knowledge of how to perform actions (Anderson, 1983a; Squire, 1992a, 1992b). The actions may be either motoric (riding a bike) or cognitive (performing addition).

5.2. Processing Models Versus Multisystem Models

In conformity with the ideas outlined above, some researchers today have come to believe that there exist many different memory systems, specialized to generate different kinds of information.

The opposing view, the processing model, is that memory involves a single "store." In other words, episodic information, perceptual information, and abstract information are all generated by a unified general-purpose system. The different types of content simply reflect different processing operations performed by the brain (Anderson, 1983a, 1993; Crowder, 1976). This is in fact the fashion in which digital computers operate.

Adherents of the single-system model do not dispute the claim that memory involves different kinds of codes. The dispute is over the issue of whether such codes are developed by separate memory systems, which specialize in particular coding formats.

According to the multisystem model (MSM), different areas of an organic brain are precisely specialized to perform different cognitive functions. In other words, there is not one single memory system, but many. This approach is clearly more biological in orientation than the processing view, reflecting not only the issue of location of function but also the fact that there are many different kinds of neurons within the brain. These may differ because they underlie different cognitive functions (Moscovitch, 1992; Nadel, 1992, 1994; Schacter, 1990b, 1992; Schacter & Tulving, 1994; Squire, Knowlton, & Musen, 1993).

The present issue has been difficult to resolve, because the brain is geared to move information from site to site, apparently with great ease. For instance, the act of memorizing a single word will engage multiple different loci within the brain and, as described earlier, several different coding formats. Since these are processes geared to a single final outcome, however, should they be considered to represent different memory systems, as against stages of processes (or even a continuum of different processes, handled by different underlying neural structures) within the same system? Due to considerations of this kind, some advocates of the MSM view nonetheless do not consider sensory, verbal STM, and verbal LTM to be different systems (Nadel, 1994).

A difficulty facing researchers within this field involves deciding just where the boundaries lie between real, nonidentical memory systems. Squire (1992b) advocated a global distinction between *declarative memory* and *nondeclarative memory*. Declarative memory involves content that can be retrieved into awareness. It thus includes both semantic and episodic memory. Nondeclarative memory involves processing events that cannot be expressed in awareness. Each of these divides into several subsystems.

There is also an extended debate today concerning the criteria that should be used to define a memory system. Schacter and Tulving (1994), for instance, suggested that different systems should also involve distinct cognitive functions, operate according to different laws, and show variable emergence in terms of phylogeny. For instance, many animals, such as rats or pigeons, show capacities similar to those found in human nondeclarative but not declarative memory.

In addition to the large global distinction outlined above, researchers have been finding increasing evidence of specialized substructures. For instance, varying kinds of visual information appear to reflect different areas of activation within the brain (Cooper & Lang, 1996). Data of this kind provide a further challenge to theory, since they clearly make the task of identifying independent systems more difficult. Psychologists wish to carve memory and its true joints; but these are not always easy to identify.

6. Encoding Specificity

Tulving (1983, chap. 1) noted that when a word is memorized, the primary code established in LTM is not a copy of the appearance of the word. That is, if the word is ROSE, the memory is not constituted simply of R-O-S-E. Instead, it is the meaning of the item that is coded. Further it is not the entire meaning of the concept that is established as this particular memory but a subset only of that meaning. The particular subset depends on context.

These ideas had been developed as Tulving and his colleagues found repeatedly that, when word lists are learned, the particular conditions of encoding influence the nature of the resulting memory. What is stored appears to differ, depending on what is thought about, relevant to the material, at the time of encoding.

Tulving therefore assumed that when a word is memorized as part of a list, a new body of information is established in LTM. This information will be a subset of the word's full conceptual meaning. For clarity's sake, this content will be called the "new memory" here. Any cues that matched with the new memory should be effective in providing recall. However, since only a subset of the full concept had been coded, not all or any cues relevant to that concept would be effective. Tulving labeled the assumption that different information is coded across different contexts (for a physically identical stimulus) as the *encoding specificity* assumption.

An important aspect of the model is the belief that once a new memory is formed, no further contact is maintained between it (the new memory) and the full conceptual representation in LTM. This view will be described here as the *divorce hypothesis*.

The encoding specificity model predicts that there are situations in which recall may be possible when recognition is not possible, as described below.

6.1. Success in Recall When Recognition Fails

As every student knows, it is usually much easier to recognize something than to simply recall it.

Tulving endorses a feature model of meaning. According to this view, a concept consists of a large set of features and a new memory consists of a subset only of those features. Which feature subset is entered into the new memory depends on context, including both the physical context in which the events occur, and whatever is present in the thoughts of the individual memorizing the word list at the time the new memory is formed. The second factor plays the larger role. Tulving and Thomson (1973) presented paired-associate words for learning in which the stimulus terms were weak associates of the target items.

A strong associate of a word is a response that most people make when asked for free associations to that word (for example, Pen → Ink), while a weak associate of a word is an item that is only reported occasionally in a free-association test to that word (for example, Blue → Plum). In the Tulving and Thomson study, one such pair was spider-BIRD. Spider is a weak associate of BIRD. In paired-associate learning, the first of the two items is presented at the time of the recall test and the participant's task is to recall the target (the second word) from memory. Thus, the test here would be

$$\text{spider} \underline{\hspace{2cm}} ?$$

The paired-associate learning constituted Stage 1 of the experiment.

In Stage 2 of the experiment, participants were presented with words that were strong associates of the target and asked to think of items that they associated with these new words. A strong associate of the target item "bird" is EAGLE. Here, a participant who was asked to free-associate to EAGLE might produce the items "wings, talons, soars, majestic, bird, cliffs." Participants were next asked to identify any of these generated words that corresponded to the targets that had been learned in the first session. It was thus a recognition test.

The success rate in the recognition task was 24%. That is, about 24% of the participants recognized BIRD (or some other target item) as having been present on the original paired-associate list. Note that BIRD here had just been generated as an associate to EAGLE.

In Stage 3 of the experiment, participants were given the original stimulus items as cues and asked to recall the targets. For instance, a participant would be presented with the cue "spider" in the attempt to elicit recall of BIRD. The success rate here was 63%.

Participants had thus been more successful in recalling the target items, in the context of a cue, than they had been at recognizing the items, in the context of the item itself. Tulving and Thomson explained this outcome as follows. When "bird" is encountered within the context of the cue "spider," a subset of bird features is selected and entered into the new memory. This subset would generally reflect the kind of medium-sized bird that eats insects such as spiders—often dark, crowlike animals.

When participants were given the item "eagle," and free-associated to eagle, they often generated the item "bird." But now they were thinking of "bird" within the context of eagle, and the subset of bird features was likely to reflect a large, majestic, cliff-dwelling animal. This set of features did not match with the set of features that had been deployed in Stage 1 to represent "bird." As a result, the cue BIRD generally did not make contact with the new memory BIRD formed in Stage 1 and recognition failed.

When, however, the cue "spider" was provided, this item either corresponded directly to, or was likely to evoke, the features present in the new memory for the item BIRD coded in Stage 1. As a result, when the cue was provided, participants were able to recall "bird" even though they had just failed to recognize the word in the recognition test.

Under this view, both recognition and recall involve an identical process. The process centers on the operating cues matching with the memory content. The nonintuitive aspect of the model reflects the fact that BIRD may not correspond to BIRD in a recognition test (since the subset of features in the two representations may be different).

Replications of the recall without recognition effect have been provided across a range of experimental situations (Dong, 1972; Fisher & Craik, 1977; Roediger & Adelson, 1980). Not all researchers interpret the effect as involving the matching of *features* between cues and memory content. Some believe that memories are accessed through higher-order levels of content, such that, in the present example, "bird" in Tulving and Thomson's Stage 1 might be coded as a "type of bird that eats spiders," complete with an imagined bird of that kind. This would again be a different memory set from one developed within the context of eagles, but it would be organized, hierarchical information, rather than a set of features.

6.2. The Divorce Hypothesis Versus the Classic Associative Hypothesis

Tulving's position differs from that of classic associative theory (described in Chapter 2) on several points. According to the classic associative model, all word items are interassociated in LTM either closely or remotely. When a word is memorized, its representation in LTM is tagged. For instance, if BIRD is an item on a target list, the BIRD representation in LTM might be tagged as "Present on List X." No independent new memory is formed. In other words, there is no divorce between the newly learned words and other words or concepts in LTM.

Under the classic associative view, a strong associate of a target item should generally be an effective cue. Under the divorce hypothesis, on the other hand, a strong associate of a target will not be effective unless it was actively thought about at the time of learning.

The data on this question have not been conclusive. There is clear evidence that content actively thought about at the time of learning constitutes good cues. But there are also findings supporting the position that items probably not thought of during learning, but that are strong associates of the target, can be effective cues. Some researchers believe that "thoughts during encoding" and strong permanent associates, activated at the time of the test, can both operate to determine successful recall (Nelson & McEvoy, 2002).

A third position is also possible. According to Piaget and Inhelder (1973), a separate complex of information (the new memory) is created when a set of new

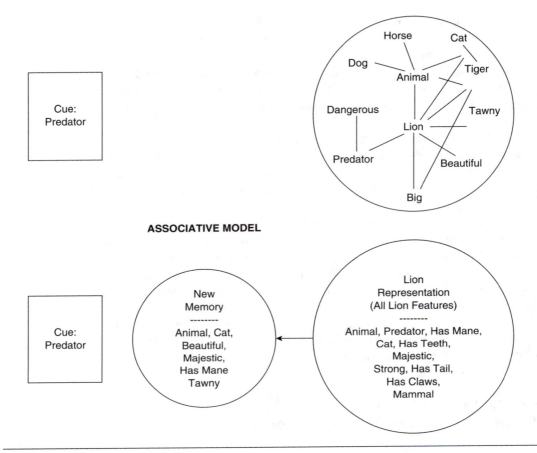

ASSOCIATIVE MODEL

Figure 6.4   Two Conceptualizations of the Way in Which Access Occurs

NOTE: A subject has seen a lion at the zoo and considered it beautiful and majestic. A memory is formed of this event. According to the classic associative view, elements are interrelated permanently within the system. Since LION and PREDATOR are associated, PREDATOR may serve as an effective cue for LION.

According to encoding specificity theory, a new memory is generated by the system at the time of encoding. It includes the meaning constituents "beautiful" and "majestic," along with others, as the code for LION. This new memory operates independently of all other information in LTM. If the subject did not conceptualize the lion as a predator when the memory was formed, the item "predator" is not present in the new memory and cannot operate as a successful cue.

material is learned (or an episode lived through). But the new memory remains in contact with the concepts from which it was developed in LTM and with LTM content in general. This third model is briefly introduced in Chapter 8.

The encoding specificity model and the classic associative model of list learning are shown in Figure 6.4.

7. Single- and Two-Stage Models of Retrieval

According to a single-stage model of retrieval, success in recall depends on the relations that hold between the operating cues and the target memory content. If the cues match with the content, if there is a large degree of overlap and if the match is unique (that is, the content has elements that make it distinctive from other content in LTM), then recall will be successful. When this situation occurs, retrieval will automatically follow.

The hypothesis described above reflects the single-stage model of retrieval. According to the single-stage view, recall, and recognition involve the same processing events.

A second theory of retrieval involves a two-stage model. This view was developed when psychologists found that certain variables influence recall and recognition differently. Given these findings, some researchers assumed that different processes must be involved in the recognition of stimuli, as against the recall of stimuli, and various two-stage models were developed. These are known as *generate-recognize* models since they posit a stage involving LTM access, followed by item generation and a stage involving item recognition. The term *generation* is used because it is believed here that the memory function uses strategies to recall targets that do not immediately return when specified (by the operating cues). This involves a memory search. For instance, if asked, "What insect name ends with *r*?" an individual might generate a list of insect names (bee, ant, spider, etc.) The second stage, item recognition, involves a judgment as to whether any candidate fits the specification (Anderson & Bower, 1972; Bahrick, 1970, 1979; Jacoby, Bishara, Hessels, & Toth, 2005; Kintsch, 1970, 1974).

In the case of list learning, Stage 1 involves an attempt to generate items that had been on the target list, Stage 2 involves determining whether each such generated item was or was not in fact on the list. According to some models, this is achieved by means of time and place "tags." For instance, suppose an individual is trying to recall a target list learned that morning. He or she might remember that there were the names of several small birds in the list and so generate some small bird names. The next step would be to check each bird name to see if the information "learned this morning" or "learned in Room 110" (time and place tags) was associated with it. This checking function involves the decision or recognition phase of the process.

According to the two-stage model, recall is more difficult than recognition because it involves both the access/generation component and the recognition component. Failure could occur at either stage. In contrast, it was assumed that in a recognition test the first (access) stage would always succeed, because the test item would simply have to match with itself in LTM. If the test item was HUMMING-BIRD, it would only be necessary for the item to match with HUMMINGBIRD as stored in LTM and determine whether it was associated with the information that this item had been encountered or learned at a certain time. It was assumed that the access stage would be automatic, and unlikely to fail. Failure could occur at the decision stage if the information associated with HUMMINGBIRD in LTM was weakly or inadequately coded.

Tulving's demonstration of successful recall in the absence of successful recognition failed to support one of the original assumptions of the two-stage model—that items have a unified representation in LTM. By "unified representation" is meant that HUMMINGBIRD would always be coded in the same way, so that a recognition test would invariably provide successful contact with a target item stored in LTM. The data do not refute the notion of a two-stage process as such. They clearly do imply, however, that in a word recognition test, access is not always automatic.

It should also be noted that two-stage models do not posit that generation and decision always occur in recall. Sometimes the cues specify the memory exactly and no other content need be generated. As Tulving (1983) noted, if you are asked the name of your wife, you do not proceed to generate a list of women's names and select among them! It is only in memories that require a search process that two stages are involved.

Today it is increasingly understood that complex evaluative processes can come into play during retrieval. For instance, if I am asked whether I saw a pavement in a certain village, and I know that there is an ordinance in that village to the effect that there must be places for pedestrian use throughout the area, this knowledge could increase the likelihood that I will retrieve some (true) recollection of a pavement. This consideration appears to support a two-stage model in that the information about the village ordinance could be used in the evaluation of a pavement image thrown up by the first-stage generation process. The argument might be made, however, that the background information itself operates as a cue—that the information "There was a pavement" may be a different and stronger cue than the question "Was there a pavement?"

8. Recognition Memory

Recall and recognition memory are affected in the same way by a range of variables. For instance, the organization of the material affects both (Mandler, Pearlstone, & Koopman, 1969) and the same is true of repetition effects. It is also the case that some variables influence the two forms of memory differently.

High-frequency words are recalled better than low-frequency words. Low-frequency words, on the other hand, are generally recognized better than high-frequency words (Deese, 1961; Gregg, 1976). Word frequency is defined as the number of times a word is likely to be encountered within prose material (newspapers, books) per million words.

There is a phenomenon in recognition memory called the *mirror effect*. Some words appear to be easy to remember; they are recognized well, and experimental participants can also identify that a word of this kind was *not* present on a critical list. Other words are hard to recognize or to identify as not being present on the critical list (Brown, Lewis, & Monk, 1977). Low-frequency words tend to be the ones that are easily recognized and high-frequency words tend to be the ones that are difficult to recognize (Rao & Proctor, 1984). In fact, a range of variables that enhance recall tend to weaken recognition memory. These include high concreteness, meaningfulness, and imagery. All three show a mirror effect, as does presentation rate (Ratcliff, Sheu, & Gronlund, 1992). In contrast, high-frequency words are more easily *recalled* than low-frequency words.

Another striking difference between recall and recognition involves a difference between deliberate versus incidental recall. (Incidental recall reflects what is retained following exposure to some information but with no active attempt being made to learn the information.) Under standard conditions, recognition performance is always higher than recall. Recall, however, is higher under deliberate learning conditions as against incidental learning conditions, while recognition is higher under incidental, as against deliberate, learning conditions. Figure 6.5 shows the interaction between deliberate and incidental learning and test type.

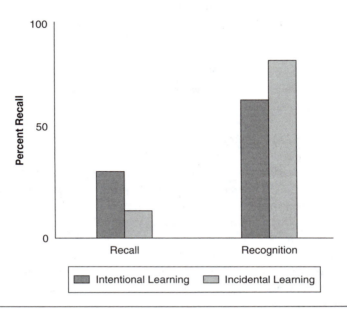

Figure 6.5   Recall and Recognition Scores Under Intentional and Incidental Learning

NOTE: Recall is better under intentional than incidental learning, but recognition is better under incidental than under intentional learning. When recall and recognition are compared with one another under standard testing conditions, recognition is always better than recall.

8.1. Familiarity and Recollection

From the 1970s on, a number of researchers have suggested that there may be two distinct processes involved in recognizing a stimulus (Atkinson & Juola, 1973; Mandler, 1980; Yonelinas, 2002). The first is *familiarity* and the second is *recollection*.

Familiarity is involved when you encounter something and sense that you have seen it before. You might glimpse a woman on the street and feel that you have indeed seen her before but not recall where or when. The sense of familiarity can be either strong or weak, with a range of strengths in between.

Recollection involves recalling the context in which some person or information was encountered in the past. Here, you may remember that you met the woman at a dinner party a year ago at Mark James's house. Although there may be some variability in the strength of this memory, the contextual information is usually simply present, if it is recalled at all. That is, it does not possess the range of strengths associated with familiarity.

Familiarity appears to be established more quickly than recollection and is believed to reflect an earlier stage of processing. The original concept of familiarity was that when we encounter a stimulus, such as a tree in the front garden, the corresponding structure in LTM (our concept of the tree in the front garden) becomes activated above baseline and continues activated over a period of time. If we see the tree again soon after, the high level of activation of that structure will provide an easy, indeed automatic, sense of familiarity.

When researchers first examined these concepts, it was generally believed that the system might first establish a sense of familiarity and so recognize the stimulus, with no need to move on to the stage of recollection. Recollection was seen as involving a search process, which would be deployed only if familiarity failed. Mandler (1980) broke with that view, however, positing that both processes begin to operate at the same time and in fact work independently of one another.

Atkinson, Juola, and Mandler all thought of familiarity as involving perceptual information. That is, the structure being activated would reflect the physical appearance of the tree. Jacoby (1992) rejected this assumption, noting that familiarity can occur on a semantic as well as a perceptual basis. That is, knowledge of having seen a tree might be activated, as against knowledge of what the tree looked like. Jacoby believes that familiarity may not always be established but that when this does occur, you recognize the stimulus automatically. In contrast, he assumes that recollection involves an analytic, consciously controlled process.

Yonelinas, in contrast, emphasizes the view that familiarity and recollection provide different kinds of information. For instance, recognizing relations (associations) among elements as against recognizing isolated elements as such, requires the process of recollection.

Extensive research has been performed to see whether familiarity and recollection really do reflect different processes. A number of empirical dissociations have been established concerning them. As described above, judgments based on familiarity can be achieved more quickly than judgments based on recollection. If less, or more, time is given to a recognition task, the pattern of responses change. With a shorter period for response, stimuli that were not presented earlier but are similar to the real target stimuli, tend to be "recognized"; with more time, this tendency to mistake similar stimuli for the targets diminishes (Arndt & Reder, 2003). But perhaps the most compelling evidence involves the fact that different areas of the brain appear to become activated, when familiarity and recollection are in play (Curran, 2000; Rugg & Yonelinas, 2003). It is also the case that some amnesic individuals can recognize that certain stimuli are familiar, but cannot establish any context for the stimuli (Yonelinas, 2002).

8.2. Recognition and Context

Recognition tests were traditionally understood to tap only memory for the target stimulus itself, with associated context information (such as other critical stimuli encountered during the learning session) assumed to play no role (Murdock, 1974). It has recently been demonstrated, however, that associated factors can influence recognition. Schwartz, Howard, Jing, and Kahana (2005), for instance, showed that if Pictures X and Y are presented next to one another during the learning session, then Picture Y is more likely to be recognized if it is tested directly following the test for Picture X than when it does not follow X in the testing session. In general, the smaller the lag (spacing) between two items during the learning session, the more likely that the second stimulus will be recognized.

The effect is found only for stimuli that participants appear to remember clearly and to which they indicate a high or fair degree of certainty concerning their response. This finding is compatible with the view that low-confidence responses reflect familiarity only, without context information being involved.

Many models of recognition today cite the role of context. According to this view, when we recognize a stimulus (on the basis of recollection), we activate or retrieve information originally associated with the stimulus. This could be time and place information or general associative information. Such content can be used to aid in the recognition of subsequent test stimuli which occur close in time and identically in place (Dennis & Humphreys, 2001; Howard, 2004; Howard & Kahana, 2002).

9. Signal Detection Theory

Signal detection theory was originally applied to the issue of auditory stimulus perception. The critical question centered on how we may hear or fail to hear a signal encountered against a noisy background. It was assumed that we would either hear a soft stimulus or fail to hear it. This would imply some absolute criterion: If the signal was stronger (louder) than the criterion level, we would hear it, and if the signal was below criterion, we would not hear it.

This assumption proved incorrect. Within our cognition there is always some form of background "noise": Neurons fire, whether a stimulus is present or not. In some cases, the random firing of neurons may produce a stronger signal than the neural response to an external but weak stimulus. There is therefore no absolute threshold or cutoff point at which a stimulus can be registered as present.

The same appears to be true in the case of recognition memory. When we try to determine whether a given item has just been encountered, some match must be sought in memory between that target item and item representations present in LTM. But there is no absolute distinction between recently encountered item codes in memory and other item codes. Nontarget representations may appear to have the same properties as target representations, and this is the "noise" factor in recognition.

Suppose a target list of items, List X, has been presented and is followed by a recognition test. In signal detection theory, an item that actually was on List X is labeled as OLD, while a foil item that was not on List X is labeled as NEW. It is assumed that OLD items will have a higher familiarity count than NEW items. There may be some sense of familiarity associated with NEW items, though, due to the background activation in the system.

If the familiarity-level distribution of all the OLD items was plotted, most OLDs would appear quite familiar, some less so, and some might seem very familiar. There would thus be a normal distribution of the familiarity level. Equally, if a familiarity-level chart were made of the NEW items, most would appear not very familiar, some would appear definitely unfamiliar, and some (at the top end of the distribution) would appear a little familiar. Again, a distribution could be plotted. The most familiar seeming of the NEW items should overlap in level with the least familiar of the OLD items. Due to this fact, some NEW items (those at the high end of the familiarity distribution) could be mistaken for OLDs. Equally, in some cases an OLD item would be tested and might have such a low familiarity value that it fell toward the bottom of the OLD distribution and was thus misidentified as a NEW item. Familiarity distributions of OLD and NEW items are shown in Figure 6.6.

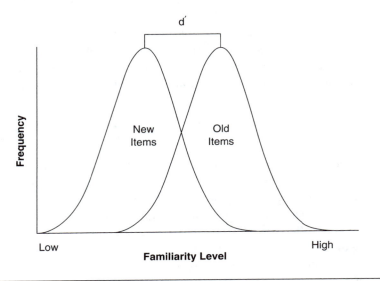

Figure 6.6   Familiarity Distributions for OLD and NEW Items

NOTE: OLD items were heard recently and have a higher average familiarity value. All items have some level of familiarity. The two distributions overlap so that an OLD item falling in this area may be not be accepted as OLD or a NEW item may be mistaken for an OLD (a false alarm). The frequency count shows the proportion of items that are experienced at a given level of familiarity.

There are four possible outcomes in an old-new test of recognition memory: An OLD item might be correctly identified as old (a hit) or an OLD item might be mistaken for a NEW item (a miss). Equally, a NEW item might be correctly identified as NEW or it might be incorrectly identified as an OLD (a false alarm).

Each of the familiarity distributions has an average score. The difference between the average familiarity of OLD and NEW items is described as d′ (d prime). Where items are easy to recognize, d′ will be large. That is, the distributions will be so far apart on the plane reflecting familiarity that there will be almost no overlap between them. Equally, if items are difficult to recognize correctly, d′ will be small: There will be considerable overlap between the two distributions.

Another factor that operates here involves the criterion chosen by a participant in determining whether he will identify an item as OLD. This is termed *response bias*. If an individual is offered $10 for every correct reply and only a $1 penalty when he misses at item, a good strategy would be to respond OLD to almost every item. If, however, the reward for a hit is equaled by the penalty for a miss, a good strategy would be to simply attempt to determine the familiarity value as accurately as possible, perhaps by setting the criterion in the area where the OLD and NEW distributions overlap. The subjective experience across these two situations would of course be the same, but the actual response pattern would differ.

It is widely assumed that recognizing an item or other stimulus may operate in the fashion described above. That is, recognition may involve a judgment of familiarity in which a range of familiarity levels must be assessed against background noise in the system.

Summary

The three-store or modal model posits that memory consists of three distinct stores: sensory, short term, and long term. The single-memory model posits that there is only one memory store. According to the well-known levels of processing view, different quantities of processing will produce different coding formats within the same system. These have different lengths of life.

Rehearsal, association forming, and image forming were examined as means of entering random items into long-term store. Other techniques include the linkword language system and the method of loci.

A cue is any element present in awareness. It will match with elements corresponding to itself in LTM and so provide access into LTM. According to the cue-dependent theory of forgetting, success in recall is completely dependent on the cues present at the time of the attempt at recall. If they overlap sufficiently with the target memory and do not overlap with a number of other memories, the target will be recalled.

It has been found that within certain word contexts target items can be recalled but not recognized. One explanatory theory is that each target memory consists of a subset of all the features present in the relevant concept. If the cues match the particular subset, the item will be recalled or recognized. In the cued recall test used to demonstrate this phenomenon, the cue word elicits features similar to those in the memory. A critical finding within this area is that the semantic information coded to represent a word is not always identical across contexts.

Single-stage models posit that cue memory overlap (when the cues do not also overlap with other nontarget memories) provides successful recall. Two-stage models of retrieval posit that first there is access and generation of candidate material, followed by a decision process concerning whether the material is in fact the target.

Recognition memory involves properties that often differ from those involved in recall. It has also been hypothesized that recognition may be achieved in two different ways involving different processing structures. One reflects familiarity and the other recollection.

Signal detection models posit that when word items have been recently encountered, their familiarity (or activity) level increases. However, all items have a background level of familiarity. The distribution of familiarity values for target items will be different from that of nonpresented items, but there will be some overlap between the highest levels of the nonpresented and the lowest levels of the presented. This leads to some errors in the recognition process.

Discussion

Probably the most important discovery of recent years concerning human memory is the realization that success in remembering can depend on the cues operating at the time of attempted recall. The precise nature of the matching remains to be identified. The quantity of the match appears to play a major role, but other factors, such as the extent to which the matched content is unique or distinctive, are also critical.

Many researchers today have taken the position that the match between cues and memory content is the sole determining factor with regard to successful recall. Others believe that this is not the case. This opposition is probably one of the most central issues to be found in the field of memory research today.

Several other major questions have not been resolved as of the present. These include the older issue of whether three separate systems handle memory formation in the case of verbal items or whether there is a single system. A related but distinct opposition of views concerns whether different kinds of material and types of memory function also involve separate, specialized systems or whether this is not the case. Finally, the relationship between the content of a new memory and the corresponding background LTM (conceptual) representations remains an area of disagreement among researchers. In this final area, the answer has extensive implications for how human memory operates.

CHAPTER 7

Long-Term Memory

Ongoing Research

Overview

1. Network, spreading-activation models posit that activation spreads from representation to representation along links. Success in recall depends on the level of activation of the memory content.

2. Connectionist computer simulations of semantic memory are spreading-activation models. They show properties of generalization and inference.

3. Anderson's ACT* and ACT-R are spreading-activation, symbolic artificial intelligence (AI) computer simulations. Cues increase the activation level of the content that they access.

4. Propositional models of memory posit that semantic representation possesses an organization similar to the organization of human language. ACT includes propositional codes.

5. Global memory/compound cue models assume that successful recall depends on the relationship between cues in working memory and long-term memory (LTM) content. Cues contact material in LTM and retrieve that material. The newly retrieved material may then be used to contact LTM again.

6. Nonpresented words are sometimes recalled as if they had been presented. This occurs when many words on a target list are associatively related with the same, nonpresented word. People may even recall their sensory properties and be certain that these words had in fact been on a target list.

7. Context effects involve the possibility that incidental conditions present at learning might enhance recall if they are present again at the time of test. Such matches include physical context, physiological state, and emotional state. The effects are generally small but significant.

8. Output interference operates in LTM.

Learning Objectives

1. Knowledge of the assumptions of spreading-activation models and knowledge of the assumptions of compound-cue/global memory models and of the research associated with each.

2. Knowledge of the theory of propositional representation of semantic (meaning based) information.

3. Knowledge of research and theory related to false memory for words.

The original associative model of memory was introduced in Chapter 1. Chapter 6 covered an alternative approach, a feature model. The following pages describe current associative models of various kinds with the research that they have generated. There is also further discussion of research based on featural assumptions and assumptions of cue-dependent recall.

1. Spreading-Activation Models

1.1. Collins and Quillian's Semantic Network

Today many associative theorists conceptualize memory as a huge net of associated representations. As with the early models, if Representation X is strongly associated with Representation Y, the activation of X will lead to the activation of Y. In network models, cues make contact with information in LTM on a matching basis. That is, the cue HOUSE will contact house representations. Activation will then spread outward through the net from the contacted representations to others associated with them in LTM. Thus, *house* encountered as an isolated word should contact the house concept, from which activation should spread out through the net to content associated with the idea of a house (to memories associated with *house*). The activation spreads through the network automatically and spreads in LTM itself, outside of consciousness. Some of the activated information may then be retrieved and become a conscious memory.

The term *representation* was used above to designate information stored in LTM (such as a house representation). Many researchers prefer a more neutral word, such as *node* or *unit*. Figure 7.1 shows a schematic representation of part of an LTM net.

Most current spreading-activation models trace their origins, in one way or another, to an approach first developed by Collins and Quillian (1969, 1972). These researchers introduced the notion that links may vary in kind and also that they may, in and of themselves, provide information. For instance, in addition to the familiar contiguity principle, Collins and Quillian posited the existence of *similarity links* and *identity links*. I once saw a white cockatoo in a shop and this caused me to remember another white cockatoo, one I had encountered as a child. This involved the operation of an identity link (white cockatoo → white cockatoo). An example of a similarity link could involve my seeing a young woman who reminded me of my niece due to a similarity in appearance between them. I would not only recall my niece but also notice the relation between her and this new person (this latter information being provided by the link itself). Today, as will be seen below, associative theorists assume the existence of yet other, often quite abstract, links in human memory.

Collins and Quillian were among the first researchers to suggest that LTM may operate as a network structure. They also suggested that related sets of information would be stored physically close together. The particular model that they developed involved LTM for semantic representations; specifically, representations of concepts. However, the same ideas were believed to be relevant to episodic memories (memories of events).

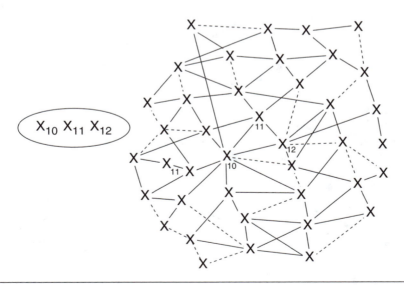

Figure 7.1   An Example of a Small Portion of a Network of Representations in Long-Term Memory (LTM)

NOTE: The smaller circle to the left denotes working memory, with three cues shown as operating. The cues will contact their corresponding representations in LTM.

The Collins and Quillian model for conceptual structure involving a part of the network that represents concepts of animals is shown in Figure 7.2. The researchers assumed that information stored "close" to the point of entry to the network could be retrieved more quickly than information stored remotely from that point. (The point of entry involves representations corresponding to the operating cues.) Thus, the question, "Is a canary a bird?" would result in the cues "canary" and "bird" contacting the nodes for *canary* and *bird* in the LTM network. Activation would then spread outward from these nodes along the relevant links. If an intersection was found between the activations leading from the two items, the correct answer would be determined to be "Yes."

The model predicted that a question such as "Is a canary a bird?" would be answered more quickly than a question such as, "Is a canary an animal?" because the spreading activation would have further to travel for the second question before an intersection was found. This reflected the premise of the model that the more closely related two sets of information were, the physically closer they would be stored in the net.

The first research findings supported this hypothesis, but later research did not. It was found, for instance, that participants respond more quickly to "Is a bird an animal?" than to, "Is a bird a vertebrate?" although "*vertebrate*" should be below "*animal*" in the nested hierarchy of concepts and so closer to "*bird*." It appeared that familiarity with the relation between two concepts (a frequency factor, reflecting how often two concepts had been activated together) played as great or greater a role than spatial distance.

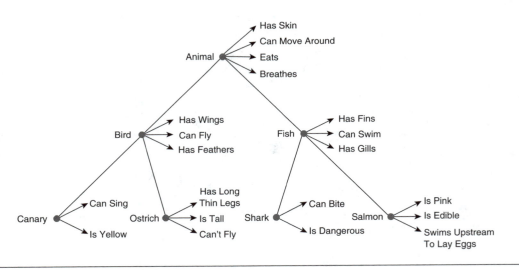

Figure 7.2   Collins and Quillian's Network Model of Semantic Memory

SOURCE: From Collins, A. M., & Quillian, M. R., "Retrieval time from semantic memory," in *Journal of Memory and Language, 8*(2), copyright © 1972. Reprinted with permission of Elsevier.

NOTE: Representations operate in a hierarchy. Those with closely related meanings are located physically close to one another within the network. Properties of the representations are stored with the representations.

The *spatial hypothesis* (the view that conceptually related and/or similar material is stored physically close together in LTM) was therefore abandoned and a new generation of spreading-activation models emerged.

1.1.1. Spread of Activation Based on Link Strength

Current associative models assume that activation spreads through the net based on link strength only. If two representations are strongly linked, then the activation of one will lead to the (strong) activation of the other. If two representations are only weakly linked, then there will be little spread of activation from one to the other. There is no spatial property in this kind of net. That is, constituents within it are never close to or far apart from one another.

The first *nonspatial models* assumed that a stronger link would lead to faster contact although recent empirical work does not appear to support this assumption. It appears rather that strong links provide high levels of activation. That is, if A and D are strongly associated, A will provide strongly increased activation levels in D but will not activate D faster than other representations.

1.2. Connectionist Models

As described in Chapter 1, a good deal of recent research has centered on computer simulations that (very roughly) correspond to the operation of neurons. These are known as *connectionist* or *artificial neural net* models. They involve the assumption of spreading activation, again through a large net of interassociated units.

Researchers within this tradition have developed nonspatial models of human memory, including semantic (conceptual) memory (Hinton, 1989; McClelland, McNaughton, & O'Reilly, 1994; Rumelhart, 1990; Rumelhart & Todd, 1993). These share many of the assumptions of the original Collins and Quillian approach. For instance, it is assumed that semantic memory possesses hierarchical organization.

In connectionist models, the information within the net is coded in the form of *distributed representations*. In distributed representation, the coded meaning is expressed through the activation of many units within the net, playing through in a pattern. Some of the units involved in Pattern A will also come into use in Pattern B, in which a different "meaning" is represented. The more similar the meaning representations, however, the greater the extent to which the same units will be involved.

It should be noted that the present hierarchical organization does not mean that concepts are most strongly related to concepts directly above or below them in the hierarchy. It means only that the relevant organization is in fact present. For instance, if you ask me whether a fish is a vertebrate, I can retrieve the hierarchical relation in which "fish" is indeed a subset of "vertebrate." But if you simply say, "fish" to me, I am likely to think of "water" rather than "vertebrate." The implication is that there is a *stronger* link between these concepts than between "fish" and "vertebrate," such that "water" becomes the dominant (free) response.

Researchers have found that networks of the present kind generate new material that has not been presented to them from "outside." Suppose a given net again

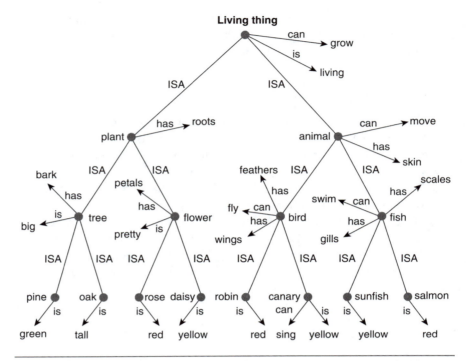

Figure 7.3   A Semantic Network of the Kind Used in Recent Connectionist Research Into Semantic Memory

SOURCE: From Rumelhart, D. E. & Todd, P. M., "Learning and representations," in D. E. Meyer & S. Kornblum (Eds.), *Attention and Performance XIV,* copyright © 1993. Reprinted with permission of the MIT Press.

represents animal concepts. One unit, say, again, FISH, will be associatively connected to a body of information specifying the properties of fishes (fish have scales, fish can swim, etc.). Now suppose that the statements, "Sammy is a fish" and "Sammy is silver" are input. This new content will be established and added to the net. If the next input involves a statement that has not been completed, the net will be capable of supplying the missing information. For instance, if "Sammy can_____ " is offered, the program can determine that a correct final word would be *swim.* The associative connections have run from Sammy to "*fish*" to the properties of fishes. The network will also determine that fishes can be silver. By the same logic, if it receives the input, "A guppy is a fish," it can determine that guppies swim, have fins, lay eggs, and so on. The critical point is that the neural nets spontaneously generate new content, as many researchers believe also occurs in human representation.

Figure 7.3 shows a portion of a connectionist model of semantic representation.

1.3. ACT* and ACT-R

Computer simulations of memory have also been extensively developed within the symbolic AI tradition (see Chapter 1). Of these, the series of models by

Anderson, labeled as ACTE, ACT*, and ACT-R, is probably the best known. (ACT stands for adaptive control of thought.) ACT has been used in major part to examine variables related to forgetting.

In spreading-activation models, it is assumed that all information stored in LTM has a background level of activation. This is the activation level present before cues come into operation. The activation or activity level of different sets of information content differs from one another; some may possess a high background level and some a low background level with all degrees in between. The activation level reflects how strongly the information is coded in LTM. Content that you know very well, such as your name, has a very high background activity level on a permanent basis. Content that you do not know well, such as, perhaps, a chapter in a book studied a year ago, will have a low background activity level.

Neurons in the brain are constantly active. Researchers within the present tradition assume that this fact relates to the hypothesis of background activity level in spreading-activation models.

In Anderson's ACT simulations, when cues contact a body of information in LTM, they increase the activation level of that content, say Content X. The increased activity also spreads out along links leading from Content X to other bodies of content associated with X in LTM. The stronger the link between X and other information, the more that information will show an increase in activation.

Content can only be recalled if it possesses an activation level above a certain threshold. Thus, two factors play a critical role here in determining successful recall. One is the background activity level of the target. If that activity level is high, any cue that adequately specifies "what is wanted" will serve to retrieve that content. If the background activity is low, then the content is only likely to be retrieved if the cues are "good" cues, and probably if there are multiple good cues. A good cue will match with the target content and increase its activation level. The increase may be enough to provide retrieval. In the case of content with a very low background activity level, however, even a large number of "good" cues will fail to retrieve it. This is the case in the present model because cues are not able to make the match with very weak content. (Other models could posit that the failure is not due to the inability of cues to match weak LTM content but the fact that even the increased activation provided by the cues does not reach the threshold level needed for retrieval.)

As described in Chapter 6, we tend to forget information over time. The present model explains this in terms of activation levels. If material is coded at only a moderate level of strength and is not reactivated again, its background activation level will decrease over time.

When cues contact the LTM network, the activation spreads through the net for a limited period of time and then dies back. Thus, there is an increased window of opportunity for recalling "weak" content but the window closes quite soon.

In all forms of the ACT model, it follows from the description above that cues do not necessarily need to overlap extensively or uniquely with target content. If the target has a high activation level, it is capable of being retrieved even by a cue that shows minimal overlap with it.

The various forms of ACT were instantiated in a type of computer program known as a *production system*. In ACT*'s production system, deliberate acts of recall begin with a goal. For instance, someone might be asked, "Was there a chase sequence in the film *Charade?*"

The first attempt would be simply to match the memory specification "Chase sequence in *Charade,*" present in working memory, with content in LTM. If no immediate match was found, a *production rule* would be called up to apply some form of search. There might, for instance, be a production rule corresponding to "When you want to recall an event in a book or film," followed by a directive for what actions to take.

The first production rule called up in this fashion might correspond to "retrieve the opening scene of the film." This can be an effective strategy in recalling a weak memory since information appears to be linked on a temporal basis in LTM. The opening scene might therefore activate later information, which could be retrieved. One critical point of the present approach is that it does not simply use whatever cue material happens to be present in working memory. It utilizes strategies in the attempt to recall a target.

The ACT model has changed to some extent over the years. In the first version, ACTE, it was posited that variations in memory strength depended solely on the strength of the relevant links. The representations themselves played no role. (Ebbinghaus had also endorsed this position). Anderson (1981), however, conducted some research to examine whether it was possible to learn new information about a well-known or famous person more easily than new information about a new, "unknown" person. It emerged that new information is better retained when it is in fact associated with a well-known person. Anderson examined several theories that might account for this phenomenon and found that the data did not support the theoretical constructs provided by the current ACTE model. The hypothesis supported by the data was that some representations are stronger than others. Strong representations mean that the links leading to or from them are also relatively strong. That is, new, associated material can be retained more easily, and associations leading to other material also tend to be strong (relative to other representations, with factors such as rehearsal held constant). This situation was built into the later, ACT* and ACT-R, models (Anderson, 1993, 2005; Gunzelmann & Anderson, 2001).

1.4. Construction Integration Theory

A second well-known spreading-activation model was developed by Walter Kintsch. The current approach, known as construction integration (CI) theory, focuses on the representation of prose material in LTM (Kintsch, 1988, 1992a, 1992b, 1998; Kintsch & Mross, 1985; Kintsch & Van Dijk, 1978; Kintsch & Welsh, 1991).

1.5. Further Properties of Memory Networks

According to current network models of memory, such net structures are not uniform across all areas. For instance, in any given area of LTM, the number of links among nodes will vary. Also, in the case of an individual representation, the extent to which that representation is associated with others (the number of links leading to or from it) will vary. This is known as the property of *connectivity*. Nelson, Zhang, and McKinney (2001) established that the higher the connectivity of an individual word item—the more it was associatively connected with other word items in LTM—the more easily it could be recalled or recognized.

Further, differences in connectivity can exist between entire, extended bodies of information.

It is believed within the present tradition that there exist *mediated links* among word items. Here, two words that are not directly associated may become so through the medium of a third word. For instance, BLUE may activate CLOUD, via the link to SKY (BLUE → SKY → CLOUD).

Another form of connection involves the concept of *shared associates*. Here, two word items are both linked with a third item. For instance, BREAKFAST and DINNER should both be linked to EAT and the two items SALT and PEPPER with SPICE (or CONDIMENT).

Mediated links, in that an item such as BLUE will facilitate the identification of CLOUD, have been reported by Balota and Lorch (1986), Bennett and McEvoy (1999), and P. McNamara (1992). Nelson, McKinney, and McEvoy (2003) found similar effects of facilitation in the case of shared associates.

1.6. Spreading Activation and Time * * * * *

The early spreading-activation models (Anderson, 1973; Collins & Loftus, 1975; Collins & Quillian, 1969; Dell, 1986) had assumed that activation spreading from node to node through a network would require time, perhaps 50 to 100 milliseconds (ms) per link. It was also assumed that the level of activation would decrease with each link traversed.

Wickelgren (1976) had reported data suggesting a much faster time for the spread of activation, closer to 1 ms per link. In a study also examining the speed with which target items can be retrieved, Ratcliff and McKoon (1981) used words to prime other material. They found a different effect depending on whether the prime word was closer to or more remote from the target in the structure of the text. Strikingly, however, the effect *began* with each of the target items at about the same time. In other words, it did not take the system longer to reach or contact the more weakly associated word than the more directly associated word. The difference was that the priming effect built to a greater extent with the latter than the former. Also, it did require time for the effect to build.

These findings clearly raised questions concerning how the idea of spread of activation can be conceptualized. It may be that contact from Structure A leading to any other structure, say Structure G or H, is achieved so quickly that there is no functional difference in the time between them even if G is a strong associate of A and H is a weak associate of A.

1.7. Activation at a Distance* * * * *

Memory is strengthened in the case of word items that have many associates in LTM. Collins and Loftus (1975), in an early spreading-activation approach, hypothesized that this occurs because the activation feeds back from the associates into the target. Thus, if A and B are connected and A is contacted by cues, activation will spread to B and some of this activation will feed back into A.

Nelson, McEvoy, and Pointer (2003) used a cue-target procedure to examine the effects of connectivity, resonance, and strength of cue-target association in LTM. As described above, connectivity involves the extent to which a target is connected with others items in long-term store ("dog" has many connections, "gurney" has few). A resonant link is the kind of link that leads back to a given item from one of its associates, as posited by Collins and Loftus. For instance, SKY activates BLUE and if activation then spreads back to SKY, this "backward" activation reflects a resonant link.

The authors found that all three variables increased the probability of correct recall. Most striking, however, was the discovery that the effects of connectivity were unrelated to the presence of resonant links. In other words, a high level of connectivity aided recall even in the absence of any identified links leading back from the associate words to the targets! Figure 7.4 shows levels of recall in relation to cue-target strength, connectivity, and resonance.

The phenomenon was labeled action at a distance. The authors suggested that what is critical in this context is a synchrony of action across all the related elements rather than spreading activation.

A second possibility is of course that associated items invariably (or often) possess backward links. This would fit with the early Ebbinghausian finding that when a string of consonant-vowel-consonants (CVCs) is learned, not only are the expected strong forward links established but so are weak backward links. (Remote links, as between A and C in an A-B-C series, are also established). Link strength and the existence or nonexistence of links between word items were established in this study on the basis of free-association data. Thus, the findings raise the question of whether free-association data do in fact validly establish all the links that may exist between items. It is possible that the resonance links here were too weak to be generated on this basis or possessed some other characteristic that made them unlikely to be generated.

2. Propositional Coding:
The Representation of Semantic Content

When an episodic memory (the memory of a past event) is examined, it is possible to find two kinds of material present (Anderson, 1983a; Kosslyn, 1994; Piaget & Inhelder, 1973; Shepard & Cooper, 1982). One involves imagery. You may recall, for instance, how a certain house looked as you first saw it, the appearance of a friend at the door, and so on.

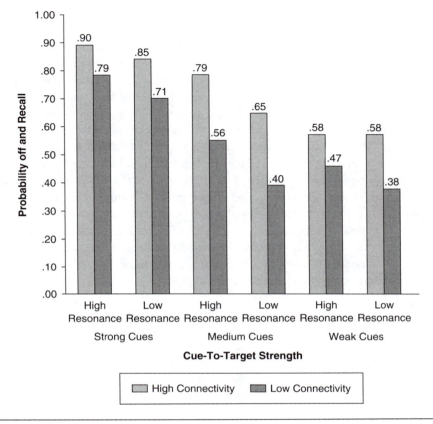

Figure 7.4   Levels of Recall Reflecting Cue-Target Strength, Connectivity, and Resonance

SOURCE: From Nelson, D. L., McEvoy, C. L., & Pointer, L., "Spreading activation or spooky action at a distance?" in *Journal of Experimental Psychology: Learning, Memory, and Cognition 29,* copyright © 2003, American Psychological Association. Reprinted with permission.

NOTE: Note the strong influence of connectivity even when there are no resonance links.

The second form of information is abstract. You may recall that you were anticipating that the visit would be pleasant, and that you thought well of your friend. This involves semantic content, a phenomenon for which there appeared to be no adequate model as of the early 1970s.

According to one theoretical approach, memory content must have internal organization. (The same argument would be made for human thought in general.) Imagine that you hiked yesterday in new boots to a mountain cabin. The memory is obviously not a collection of disorganized representations such as WALK, PATH, CABIN, PUSH, BOOT, NEW, FLOWER, SWOLLEN, WOOD, WET, JAMMED, MOUNTAIN, and so on. Instead, these elements of the memory would be connected together on the basis of certain logical relations. In the hiking episode, you recall yourself as the active agent (the person who hiked), and there would be a directional element (you hiked to a cabin) and the location of the actions, as well as the objects acted on (*at* the cabin, you pushed *on* the door). There would also be many representations of causal relations.

These relational elements are expressed in human language in the form of grammar. The grammar specifies how the "ideas" connect together. It thus seemed possible that human thought and memory content may possess the same kind of organization as human language. It was further suggested that the units of this mental language could be understood as *propositions*. A proposition can be roughly defined as the expression of a complete fact that cannot be divided into two smaller facts, as in "The man saw the dog," "The sky was blue," or "The boy painted a picture" (Anderson, 1976; Kintsch, 1974; Kintsch & Van Dijk, 1978; Minsky, 1975).

In propositional structure, there are representations ("man," "dog," etc.) and grammatical relations that connect them together. Basic or atomic (unitary) propositions can be connected to form complex propositions that contain many facts. As a result, propositional representation is capable of expressing both simple semantic information and also complex semantic information, such as the notion that you are looking forward to a visit or think well of a certain individual. Essentially, it is a vehicle that can represent abstract meanings.

According to most current models, propositional thought is expressed in the form of symbols within the human brain. Thus, there would be a symbol for "*boy*" and for "*painted*" and "*picture*," in the memory content "*The boy painted a picture.*" There would also be symbols representing the grammatical functions relating these concepts together. Critically, the relevant symbols are not words. Most psychologists today also believe that this symbolic coding format is different in kind from the codes that represent perceptual information.

2.1. Models of Propositional Notation

There are two major structures used in human languages. In the first (Type A), an entity performs some action. The action may be directed to an object. (The dog chased the cow.) The second (Type B) structure involves a situation in which an entity is described or characterized in some way, as in "The rose was red." Here, the rose does nothing, but it is described.

These two forms of organization are also present in propositional models of thought and memory. The structure of propositions can be expressed in a number of different notations. The best known of these today is probably Anderson's (1983a, 1983b) approach. Here, each proposition was represented by a node. Arrows extended from the node, pointing to representations. The arrows or "links" were labeled with the labels reflecting the relevant grammatical function.

For example, in a Type A statement there is an active agent, an activity performed and a thing acted on. These aspects of the situation are expressed in language by the grammar. Suppose the statement is again, "The dog chased the cow." In the notation, an *agent label* is present on the link leading to DOG, a *relation label* on the link leading to CHASED, and an *object label* on the link leading to COW.

In a Type B statement, a subject label leads to the entity that is to be characterized or described and a relation link to the description. Thus, "The cow was brown" would involve a *subject link* pointing to COW and a *relation link* pointing to IS BROWN.

Figure 7.5 shows these two propositions separately and combined into a single complex proposition. The latter provides the information, "The dog chased the brown cow" (information corresponding to two simple propositions: (1) The dog chased the cow and (2) The cow was brown).

Other meanings, of the kind expressed in grammar, can be supplied in the same way. Thus, a *recipient link* indicates an entity that has *received* some thing (or abstraction). A *location link* indicates where the primary action of the proposition (expressed by the relation link) occurred. A diagram of the proposition "John gave Ann the book in the library" is shown in Figure 7.6.

The recipient and location links are "special links" in that although they supply information they are not considered to involve additional propositions. Instead, they constitute an addition to the basic proposition "John gave a book." Links indicating time and the use of a tool or instrument in a given action (an instrument link) are also conceptualized here as special links.

The representations can be written in any order. Their relations are fully established by the links. Links always lead out from a propositional node. That is, representations are never directly connected to one another. When the same concept is involved in different propositions, only one representation of the concept is written, and two arrows lead to that representation. This is the case because the underlying meaning involves the same entity in both propositions.

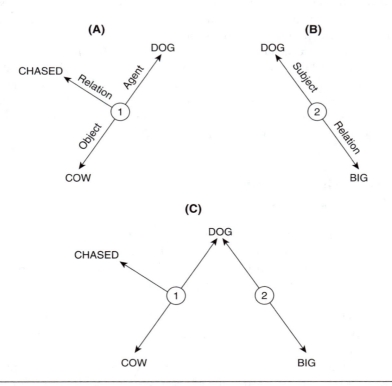

Figure 7.5   A Diagram of Propositional Representations

NOTE: A = Representation of "The dog chased the cow." B = Representation of "The dog was big." C = The two propositions related together.

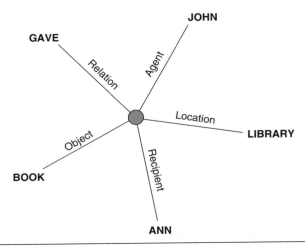

Figure 7.6   A Propositional Diagram Showing "John gave Ann the book in the library"

Relatively complex facts implying particular relations among the constituents of a thought can also be modeled. Thus, THE DOG CHASED THE COW BECAUSE HE SAW IT RUN would be expressed as an entire grammatical subject-proposition related to an entire object-proposition on the basis of the relation BECAUSE. This set of interrelated propositions is shown in Figure 7.7.

Propositional information is also assumed, within this tradition, to provide the meanings of individual concepts. Thus the *dog* concept, when activated or "unpacked" would include content such as the following: A dog is an animal that has been domesticated for a long period of time; they are identified as belonging to the canine biological line; they often live with families as pets; and so on. This content would again be associated with perceptual information.

2.2. Does Human Memory Possess Propositional Structure?

Research has been conducted to determine whether memory content actually does assume the propositional structure postulated by these models. For instance, Barshi (1997) presented verbal instructions to his participants that differed in the number of propositions or in the number of words. If in a given sentence the number of words was held constant, but the number of propositions was doubled from two to four, errors in recall increased from 3% to 52%. If in a given sentence the number of propositions was held constant and the number of words doubled, there was no effect on recall.

Other studies have consistently shown that representations that are close together in the propositional structure of a text, although not in the surface wording, prime one another more strongly than words that are close together in the text

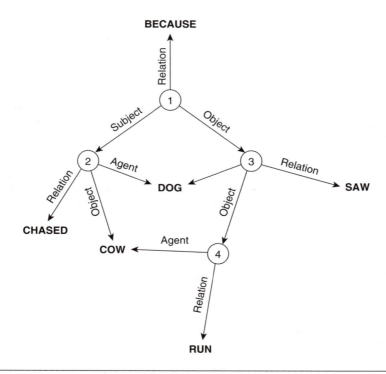

Figure 7.7   A Propositional Network Showing, "The dog chased the cow because he saw it run"

NOTE: Here, a whole proposition (Proposition 2) is the subject of the higher-order or complex proposition (Proposition 1) and another proposition (Proposition 3) is the object. Also, Proposition 4 is the object of Proposition 3.

but not in the underlying propositional structure (Graesser, Millis, & Zwaan, 1997; Wanner, 1975).

It has also been found that items within atomic propositions cue other items within the same atomic proposition significantly faster than items that only co-occur in the complex, overarching propositional structure, even though the absolute difference in response time is small (Kintsch, 1998, p. 71).

3. Secondary Cues, Recursive Processing, and Ecphory

The models described above assumed the spreading of activation within LTM, from the point at which cues entered the system. An alternative view posits that spreading activation does not occur but rather that the critical process involves new information entering working memory from LTM, on a changing basis, due to the operation of cues.

Tulving (1983) suggested that when new content is retrieved from LTM, that new content can operate as a cue: here, a secondary cue. The secondary cue may enter LTM again, possibly activating a different memory set. Thus, a kind of recursive process could be established, with new material constantly entering awareness, as the relevant cues change. For instance, you might be trying to recall the name of your third-grade teacher and fail. A moment later a memory of her face may return (newly retrieved information). Following this, you may recall her name. Her face had operated as a secondary cue and entered LTM again, this time contacting a feature set that contained both the face and the name.

Ecphory, another concept introduced by Tulving, involves the notion that recall involves an active interaction between cues and memory content. Within this tradition, memory content consists of sets of features (not of associated representations). Ecphory occurs when the cues and memory content interact and the product of this interaction is retrieved. The product could in fact be changed from the original information. For instance, rehearsal may have occurred, leading to change. Or the cues themselves may supply new information that is entered into the memory set.

4. Cyclical Retrieval/Global Memory Models

Gillund and Shiffrin (1984) and Raaijmakers and Shiffrin (1981) introduced a computer model of word list learning called SAM (search of associative memory). An approach of the present kind is often officially called an *episodic trace model.*

In SAM, cues in short-term memory (STM) make contact with information, called "images," in LTM. All the available cues operate together to achieve this contact. Each cue has a certain associative strength with the content of images in LTM. Thus, the entire set of cues will make contact with all the content in LTM. The image in LTM that is most strongly activated by this contact will be selected for retrieval. It is critical to note that the activation of any given image depends on the degree of associative strength between all the cues and all the images in LTM, occurring simultaneously. Then the most strongly activated image will be selected. When it has been retrieved, the system will access long-term store again, and attempt to select and retrieve another image. Models of this kind are called *global memory models.* They are global because the selection of an item for retrieval depends on contact between the cues and *all* the relevant material in LTM, not just on contact between cues and that item.

A cue item always has a fairly strong associative relation with its corresponding representation in LTM (although the exact strength will vary). Thus, if the word *dog* was present in STM and an image including DOG was coded in LTM, this "dog" cue would show a strong associative relation with the LTM image. If the item "bone" were present in STM, this would also provide a quite strong association value with the DOG constituent. Items that do not already possess strong interassociations will also become associated if they are rehearsed together in STM. So if "dog" and "chair" had been rehearsed together when the list was learned, an associative relation would have formed between them, and the cue "chair" would also contact the DOG constituent in LTM. In summary, cues in STM would possess varying association values with the target images in LTM, and if the sum total of the association values was high enough, a target image or images would be recovered. "High enough" here means that the total association values was higher than the total association values for any other image.

In the SAM model, material once stored in LTM does not decay or suffer interference. Success in both recall and recognition depends entirely on whether "good" cues operate or do not operate.

When an attempt is made to recall a given word list, the available cues will contact information in LTM. At the beginning these are usually context cues: representation of the context in which the list was learned. In human cognition, such cues would correspond to "The list I learned two hours ago" or "The list I learned in Room 110." These cues may recover an image that had been stored in LTM. The newly retrieved information can then operate as a secondary cue, working in conjunction with the original context cues, to make contact with other information in LTM. When this additional information is retrieved, it may contact yet other information in LTM. A cyclical process is thus established. The critical events here thus depend on the cycle of retrieval from LTM into STM. In SAM, there is in fact a small factor that involves associative connections within LTM itself, but it plays a very minor role.

SAM in the form of a computer simulation has provided data closely resembling the patterns of human recall and recognition and can also handle the phenomenon of successful recall when recognition has failed. This is the case because contact with information in LTM depends heavily on context cues. Thus, the context "list learned this morning + stimulus cue SPIDER" may have a stronger association value with a stored word item BIRD than the word *bird* has with the stored item BIRD.

Other global memory models include Hintzman's MINERVA (1984, 1988) and Murdock's TODAM (1982). SAM is described in further detail in **Web Chapter 2**.

4.1. Compound Cue Models

The approach to retrieval provided by SAM led to the development of *compound cue* models of memory (Dosher & Rosedale, 1989; McKoon & Ratcliff, 1992a; Ratcliff & McKoon, 1992).

In SAM, retrieved information operates as secondary cues, along with the original context cues. Compound cue models posit that a similar event can occur when items are presented for identification. It was established in the 1970s that when two semantically related words are presented together, the second word is identified faster than usual. For instance, if the series *nurse, doctor* is presented, DOCTOR will be identified faster than when *bread, doctor* is presented (Meyer & Schvaneveldt, 1971). The effect is known as *semantic priming*. The word that produces the priming effect (sometimes called the prime) is here *nurse*, while the target is *doctor*.

Priming effects also operate if the two words are presented one after the other, with only a short time interval between them.

According to compound cue models of identification, the word items *nurse* and *doctor* operate together as a compound cue to contact the DOCTOR concept in LTM. The word item *doctor* will be strongly associated with the DOCTOR concept representation; in addition, the word *nurse* will have a fairly strong association with the DOCTOR concept. The two working together will access the target quickly. In contrast, the words *doctor* and *bread* will be less effective when paired together since *bread* would have only a minimal association with DOCTOR.

What is involved here is the activation of a conceptual representation, stored in LTM, that will provide meaning to the stimulus. This event is described as the *identification* of the stimulus. Compound cue models typically posit no form of associative spreading activation in LTM. All recall and identification are a function of the relations between the operating compound cues and the target LTM content.

5. Priming and Spreading-Activation Models

Associative network (spreading-activation) models explain priming as follows. When a word such as *nurse* is presented, it will make contact with the NURSE concept or node (a more neutral term) in LTM. The NURSE concept will supply meaning to the stimulus.

Concepts or nodes in LTM are interconnected in an extended net. Any given concept node is strongly linked to others that are similar to it in meaning. Links based on contiguity are also probably present. Thus, if the NURSE concept becomes activated, activation will spread along links in LTM to other, related concepts, such as DOCTOR, HOSPITAL, and so on. These constituents thus become partly activated, or primed. If the DOCTOR constituent has been primed, and the word stimulus *doctor* is then presented, the DOCTOR constituent will come into play faster than usual. It will reach threshold and so provide identification of the stimulus at greater speed than would otherwise have been the case.

A more detailed description of spreading-activation models of priming is also provided in Chapter 14.

5.1. Spreading-Activation Versus Compound Cue Models of Priming: Empirical Research * * * * *

Attempts to provide empirical evidence in support of one or the other of the two models have proved inconclusive.

One body of research has focused on *sequence effects*. Ratcliff and McKoon (1995) noted that if a nonword, as against a word, is included as a prime (a cue), this should slow responses to a target (under a compound cue model). This is the case because a nonword (for example, PLAME) has only a very low association value with the target (perhaps a value of 0.1), while even an unrelated word, say TABLE, for the target CAT, has a stronger value (perhaps 0.2). This nonword inhibition effect does normally occur (P. McNamara, 1992, 1994; T. P. McNamara, 1992; Ratcliff & McKoon, 1995). That is, CAT will be identified faster when it follows TABLE as compared with a condition in which it follows PLAME. According to Ratcliff and McKoon, spreading-activation models cannot explain the nonword inhibition effect since they have no mechanism to produce influences derived from nonwords on word items.

Current spreading-activation models, however, include an inhibition component (P. McNamara, 1992). Here, the activation of certain nodes will decrease the activation of other, specific nodes. This is a standard component of both general spreading activation and connectionist models, it having been known for many years that both excitatory and inhibitory processes play a role in neural functioning (Pavlov, 1927/1960).

In the present case, it is believed within the spreading-activation tradition that the presentation of any word produces a mild priming effect on all words in LTM and that a nonword produces a mild inhibitory effect on all words in LTM. Thus, a spreading-activation model would predict that the presence of a nonword as a prime would slow responses to the target word.

5.2. Mediators and Priming * * * * *

Under spreading-activation theory, it is possible for a word, A, to prime another word, B, even though they are not directly associated. As described above, the effect is known as *mediated priming*. Thus, TRAIN might prime its strong associate TRACK, and TRACK might prime its strong associate RUNNER. The result would be that the presentation of TRAIN would produce speeded identification of RUNNER. This is known as a two-link series of associations (Train → Track, Track → Runner). These priming events are assumed to occur in LTM at an unconscious level.

In contrast, compound cue theory assumes that all priming effects are due to an association between a cue, or cues, in working memory and content in LTM. In other words, all associative relations are direct relations. In the case of what might appear to be priming between two unrelated word items, it is suggested within this tradition that words may have a very large number of direct associations, which we cannot identify at a conscious level. In other words, if TRAIN primes RUNNER, then there is in fact a direct association between them.

T. P. McNamara (1992) suggested that examining free associations would provide a way of determining the direct associations possessed by any given word. Unfortunately, there are different ways of measuring free associations. A target item, such as TRAIN, may be presented, with the requirement that participants respond with the first word that comes to mind (the *single response method*). A second approach is to present the target word and allow participants to continue to respond across a period of time with all the word items that then come to mind (*the continuous production method*). The first approach shows no associations between items such as TRAIN and RUNNER, while under the second approach participants may in fact produce "runner" as one of their responses. The issue thus remains at present unresolved.

6. False Memory for Word Items

It has been established that memory content can change over time and also that material not present during encoding may be "recalled" (or recognized) at a later time. The present section deals with this phenomenon within the context of word learning.

Underwood (1965) found that if a to-be-learned list contained several associates of another word, not present on the list, that other word was often later recalled. For instance, the presence of "crown," "queen," and "royal" could lead to the false recollection of "king."

Underwood explained this in terms of an *implicit associative response* (IAR). That is, activation would spread in LTM from "crown" to its associate "king," from "queen" to its associate "king," and so on and so activate "king" to the point where it was mistakenly recalled.

In a variation of this procedure, Deese (1959) had presented his participants with a list of words, all of which were associated with the same item. For instance, "nap, slumber, night, bed" would all be associated with the word *sleep*. "Sleep" itself, the lure item, was not present on the list. When participants were later tested for recognition of the items, they frequently recognized the lure as having been on the target list.

Roediger and McDermott (1995) replicated this effect using an approach now known as the Deese-Roediger-McDermott (DRM) method. They found that participants tended to be as confident of their recall or recognition of lures as of genuine target items. The authors had included a strong admonition against guessing: Participants had been instructed to report an item only if they definitely remembered or recognized it. The material used by the researchers and its relationship to the lure item is shown in Figure 7.8.

Payne, Elie, Blackwell, and Neuschatz (1996) explored the parameters of the false-item recall, finding recall of target (real) items to operate at 60%, with recall of lures at 45%. There were strong primacy and recency effects in the list recall, with the middle portion of the list being recalled at only 52%. This level was not significantly different from the recall of the lures.

Recognition of target items declined more quickly across a retention interval than did recognition of lures. Requiring that the participants perform a mathematical task after list study also reduced the number of list items recalled significantly more than the number of lure items recalled. The "false memory" effect thus appeared to be more resistant to loss or change over time than veridical memory content.

6.1. Remember/Know Judgments

Tulving (1985a) had suggested that it is possible to distinguish between two different kinds of memories. The first involves "Remembered" content, in which we recall an episode in the form of an actual memory. That is, we recall experiencing the relevant episode. At the moment I recall that I read a news item involving India over lunch. I can recall where I sat, what was on the table and the nature of the article. This is a "Remember" memory.

In the alternative form, a "Know" memory, the individual possesses some fact or item of information. I know, for instance, that the city of Albany is situated to the northeast of my own town. But I do not remember where or how I acquired that information. Nor is it associated with any episodic content, no "memory" in the usual sense. In the same way, I know that Paris is the capital of France.

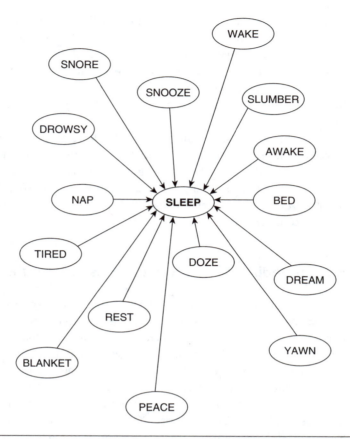

Figure 7.8   An Illustration of the Type of Material Used in Studies Demonstrating False Memory for Words

SOURCE: From Roediger, H. L., Balota, D. A. & Watson, J. M. "Spreading activation and arousal of false memories," in H. L. Roediger III, J. S. Nairne, I. Neath and A. M. Surprenant (Eds.), *The Nature of Remembering,* copyright © 2001, American Psychological Association. Reprinted with permission.

NOTE: All the items here are associated with the lure word *sleep*.

Roediger and McDermott (1995) hypothesized that the Remember/Know distinction might be capable of separating true from false memory content. Perhaps experimental participants would have a sense of remembering only in the case of real memories.

In the study described above, the authors led their participants to recall certain items (such as "sleep") that they had either recalled or recognized as being on the list. The participants indicated that they "Remembered" the lure items, as against reporting that they simply "Knew" or believed that the item had been on the list, at as high a rate as they remembered the actual list items (the targets).

Roediger and McDermott (1995) also required their participants to perform a mathematical task after list learning. The effect of this was to reduce Remember responses to a greater extent for targets than for lures.

In another experiment, two individuals read parts of the target list to the participants during list learning. When a participant later recalled a given item, he was asked whether he could remember which of the two presenters had spoken the item. Participants were again warned not to guess but only to indicate a presenter on the basis of an actual memory of that individual speaking the word. The participants identified a presenter for 87% of the lure items that they believed they had recalled. The impression of an actual memory was so strong that some refused to believe that the lure items had not been on the list, even when the tape was replayed to them.

In other studies, participants have claimed to remember where a lure item was placed on the list and whether the lure items were presented in a visual or an auditory mode (Read, 1996). The authors found an equal level of confidence was given to real target and to lure items. The highest possible level of confidence was directed to 60% of the lures. Payne et al. (1996, 1997) and Read (1996) reported similar, high levels of confidence for lures.

6.2. Spreading Activation and False Memories

The demonstration of priming effects, possibly based on spreading activation, described in Section 5 involved semantic memory. Semantic memory is defined as that aspect of LTM that stores general, abstract information, such as the fact that water is composed of hydrogen and oxygen or that a cow eats grass. Conceptual representations, and their internal organization, also reflect semantic memory. Thus, the finding that TREE may prime VEIN would reflect the semantic store.

In contrast, when an individual recalls a list of word items, it is generally believed that this involves episodic memory: our memory for events (see Chapter 6). We have recalled that we learned a certain item on a certain list.

Roediger, Balota, and Watson (2001) raised the question of whether the false memories for word items, described above, could be attributed to spreading activation. If spreading activation was involved, priming effects should occur in both semantic and episodic memory.

Although most of the findings relevant to priming have centered on semantic codes, Balota and Duchek (1989) reported a priming effect found when individuals recalled a prose passage. That is, the same phenomenon appeared to be operating in episodic memory.

Roediger et al. (2001) urged that spreading activation implies associative links that can act in concert. That is, there can be multiple links leading to a certain item—for instance, B-A, F-A, and R-A, within the system. If B alone is activated, there should be some associative activation of A. If both B and F are activated, the level of associative input to A should be greater, and greater again, if B, F, and R are all activated together. Roughly, the associative input to A should summate. The authors thus focused on the question of whether summation effects would be found in the DRM paradigm.

A second theoretical aspect concerning spreading activation is that spreading activation itself is believed to be automatic. In other words, the individual does not decide that activation should spread among associated elements; this simply happens. Thus, one aspect of SA should not require the operation of attention or even of awareness. (Attention is likely to have an effect on other aspects of the relevant processing. For instance, attended elements may produce a higher activation response. Also, as demonstrated by Neely (1977), when participants are aware of the prime-target relation, this establishes expectancies, which can increase a priming effect. However, the event of SA itself is believed to be automatic.) A second question thus concerned whether DRM effects would be found in the absence of awareness of the relevant associative connections.

Robinson and Roediger (1997) presented lists of 3, 6, 9, 12, or 15 items in a DRM design. That is, each of the items was related to the lure word. If associative activation of the lure summated, then more false memories should occur with the longer lists. The findings were of weaker recall as the lists grew longer (participants recalled a smaller percentage of the total items) but that false memory of the lure increased.

Figure 7.9 shows the relationship between the number of associates of the lure present in the to-be-learned lists and the outcome of a false memory.

In the standard DRM design, items are presented at a fairly slow rate, and there is enough time for it to be theoretically possible that participants could notice the relationship between the items and the lure. Given this fact, it is not clear that the false-memory effect is due to an automatic process; it could be due to conscious, attention-driven processing.

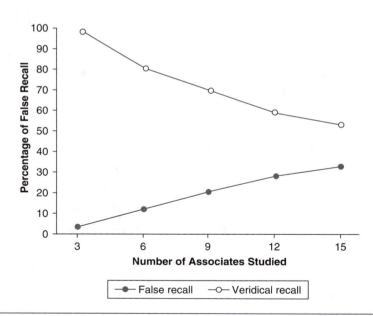

Figure 7.9   The Relationship Between the Number of Lure-Associated Items Studied and Recall of the Lure

SOURCE: From Roediger, H. L., Balota, D. A. & Watson, J. M. "Spreading activation and arousal of false memories," in H. L. Roediger III, J.S. Nairne, I. Neath and A. M. Surprenant (Eds.), *The Nature of Remembering,* copyright © 2001, American Psychological Association. Reprinted with permission.

NOTE: The larger the number of associates studied, the greater the percentage of false (lure) recall. In contrast, as the studied lists grew longer, recall of items on the list declined.

To control for this latter possibility, Roediger, Balota, and Robinson (2000) presented 15-item DRM lists at very fast rates, at 20, 80, 160, and 320 milliseconds (ms) per word. At the fastest rate, all 15 words were presented in less than a second. Here, probably no more than one or two of the list words themselves would have entered awareness, and there would clearly have been no time to look for possible relations with other words. Recall of both the words and the lures increased as the presentation rate slowed. Interestingly, the probability of word recall and lure recall were strikingly similar (of item recall 0.1, 0.22, 0.28, and 0.31 across the four presentation rates and of false recall 0.1, 0.25, 0.31, and 0.33). These findings were compatible with the view that associative activation of the lure increased as the exposure time of the target items increased, and the effect did not require conscious awareness.

At slow presentation rates, a different pattern emerges. Toglia, Neuschatz, and Goodwin (1999) and Gallo and Roediger (2002) found a negative relation between accurate item recall and false recall under presentation conditions in which participants had relatively extended time in which to study the items. Roediger et al. (2001) explained these findings as implying that, with fast presentation rates, the system must rely on a simple and automatic measure such as level of activation to retrieve target items. When more time is given, the information can be processed more deeply, in such a way as to involve factors other than activation. For instance, information such as "NIGHT was present on this list" may be explicitly established. The lure items would lack this kind of tagging.

Figure 7.10 shows the relationship between presentation rate and the probability of false recall.

Roediger et al. (2001) concluded that the data at present support a spreading-activation explanation of false memory for word items, although various related issues remain to be explored.

6.3. Fuzzy Trace Theory and False Memory for Words * * * * *

A somewhat different interpretation of the findings on false word memory was provided by Brainerd, Wright, Reyna, and Mojardin (2001), Brainerd and Reyna (1998), and Reyna and Brainerd (1995a, 1995b) within the context of a model labeled as *fuzzy trace theory* (FTT).

According to FTT, items are coded in memory in two forms: verbatim and gist. Recall and recognition can be based on either of these codes, which coexist in LTM.

Verbatim content is in most cases forgotten more quickly than gist. The verbatim involves a literal copy of the surface characteristics of the input words (their sound, appearance, etc.). It is therefore always veridical. Gist memory in the present model is not a representation of meaning that could be seen to closely correspond to the most direct or same-level meaning code of the items. Instead, it is a rough, simplified, or general representation of the input. Thus, REST, DOZE, or SNOOZE might actually be *coded* as meaning "sleep." As a result, the individual would recognize or recall "sleep" in a subsequent test.

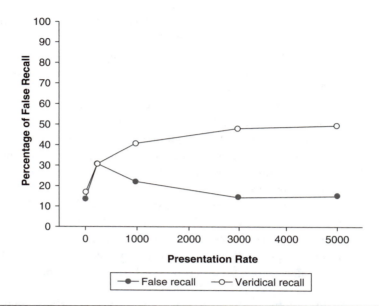

Figure 7.10   Relationship Between Presentation Rate and the Likelihood of Recalling a Lure

SOURCE: From Roediger, H. L., Balota, D. A. & Watson, J. M. "Spreading activation and arousal of false memories," in H. L. Roediger III, J. S. Nairne, I. Neath and A. M. Surprenant (Eds.), *The Nature of Remembering*, copyright © 2001, American Psychological Association. Reprinted with permission.

NOTE: At fast presentation rates (less than 500 ms per word), there are more cases of lure item recall. With slower presentation rates, where more specific information may be established, lure recall diminishes. Also, at slower rates, accurate recall of the list items increases.

Since gist codes endure longer than verbatim codes, an extended retention interval should result in more forgetting of the real targets (coded in both verbatim and gist form) but relatively slow forgetting of the lures (coded only in gist form). This was the outcome of the Payne et al. (1996) study described in Section 6.

Thus, Underwood's IAR theory and Roediger's spreading-activation theory posit that false word memory is due to associative processes that strongly activate a non-target item in the course of list learning and of retrieval. The item is therefore retrieved at the time of test and may appear highly plausible to the subject: That is, it may appear as clearly a real memory. In contrast, FTT theory suggests that the false item is actively coded at the time of learning, such that when it is retrieved, it is in some sense the recollection of the original information.

The theories are not mutually exclusive. Both associative and active coding may be involved in the development of false word memories.

7. Context and Memory

7.1. Context-, Mood-, and State-Dependent Recall

Under associative theory, superior recall could be predicted under conditions in which learning and testing take place in the same location. Suppose the location is a given room. Participants will see the objects in that room in contiguity with the appearance of the target words on the list and also in their thoughts. The two should become associated together. At the time of test, if the same objects are physically present, they would be expected to access their own representations in LTM. These representations are now associated in LTM with the target words and therefore should increase the activation of those words.

The same outcome could be predicted under an encoding-specificity theory. As participants learn the list, they should notice the appearance of the room to some extent, and so the appearance of the room would be entered into the new memory. Being present in the same room should therefore provide cues that directly correspond to the new-memory content.

These hypothesized events are shown in Figures 7.11a and 7.11b.

Smith (1979) found that subjects could recall a list of random items better if they were learned and tested in the same room, as against being learned in one room and tested in another. It also emerged that recall was facilitated if participants merely thought about the room in which they had learned the items (without physically being present in that room).

A large number of studies have been performed to further examine the effect of context on learning. The results have been mixed. In some cases, a context-dependent facilitation was found (Godden & Baddeley, 1975; Smith, Glenberg, & Bjork, 1978);

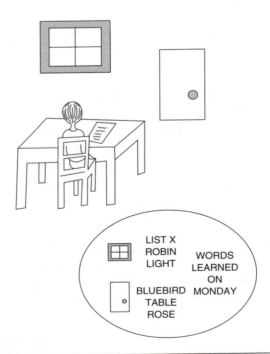

Figure 7.11a   Illustration of Learning a List of Items in a Room With a Window and a Door in the Participant's Field of Vision

NOTE: The circled figure to the right shows the resultant memory of the target list, List X, in long-term memory.

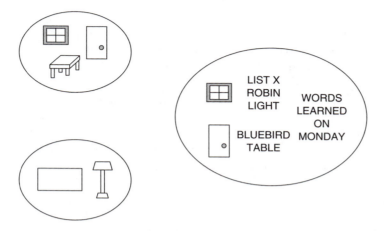

Figure 7.11b   Illustration of What Participants May See in the Original Room (Top)
or a New Room Featuring a Floor Lamp (Bottom)

NOTE: To the right is the memory of the list in LTM. Cues from the first room will access this
memory on a matching basis. Cues from the second room will not match with the memory.
A cue operating for all participants would be "Recall List X."

in other cases, there was no effect (Saufley, Otaka, & Bavaresco, 1985; Smith, Vela,
& Williamson, 1988). When effects are found, they tend to be small, although
significant.

Effects on retrieval due to mood and physiological state (mood- and state-
dependent recall) have also been examined. For instance, if an individual is in a particular mood when learning, the feeling of that mood (occurring together with the
list items) should become associated with those items in LTM. The same logic holds
for a physiological state, such as fatigue, illness, the effect of drugs, alcohol, and so on.

Goodwin, Powell, Bremer, Hoine, and Stern (1969) examined individuals who
had been either drunk (Group A) or sober (Group B) when some given learning
occurred. Half of both the groups, A and B, were tested when they were drunk or
when they were sober. There was a state-dependent effect; individuals who had
been drunk when they learned recalled the information better if they were drunk,
as against sober, when tested, and less surprisingly, individuals who had been sober
at learning performed worse when they were drunk during the test compared with
individuals who were again sober. The good news was that a sober-sober combination provided the highest recall of all conditions. The effects were only found, however, in tests of recall (not of recognition).

Bower (1981) used hypnotic techniques to induce a happy or a melancholy state
of mind in his participants during list learning. The participants were tested when
in the same mood as at learning, or a different mood, and there was higher recall
when the two matched. Bower found, however, that there is little evidence for
mood-dependent effects for content with higher-order meaning, such as prose passages. And other researchers, working with random items, have found only a small,

or no, effect of either state- or mood-dependent recall (Bower & Mayer, 1985; Gage & Safer, 1985; Wetzler, 1985). It has also emerged that mood-dependent recall operates only under certain conditions, as follows: (1) when two lists are learned in succession but not when a single list has been learned or (2) when a very strong level of affect is present (Blaney, 1986; Ellis & Ashbrook, 1991).

With regard to some of the successful findings of mood-dependent recall, as reported by Bower (1981), there may also be some methodological problems. McConkey (1991), for instance, noted that the procedures used to induce a hypnotic state may in some cases influence recall, such that a positive finding may be due to these procedures rather than to the induced mood.

It is known that environmental context effects (a form of incidental learning) play a very large role in both human infant and animal recall (Boller, Grabelle, & Rovee-Collier, 1995; Richardson, Riccio, & Axiotis, 1986). The research described above has demonstrated that this is not the case with adult human recall, where deliberate learning tends to be far more effective than incidental learning. The implication appears to be that automatic associative processes play a more dominant role in the first two groups than in the third.

7.2. Mood Congruence

When an individual is a marked emotional state, he or she is more likely to recall memories characterized by the same emotion than other memories. The effect appears to be particularly strong for happy moods but also operates for anxiety or depression (Nasby & Yando, 1982).

The phenomenon described above is different from mood-dependent recall because it does not appear to reflect differences in successful access. Both pleasant and unpleasant memories may be available, but the individual selects one type or the other. The same thing occurs (quite markedly) at encoding. During a given episode, an individual who is feeling depressed may focus on negative aspects of the episode and give more attention to their encoding in memory (Blaney, 1986; Singer & Salovey, 1988). In contrast to the findings on mood-dependent recall, mood-congruent recall is a fairly reliable effect.

Most of the traditional research into mood and memory has focused on "negative mood" and "positive mood." Laird (1991) noted that there are many different kinds of negative emotion, such that a significant outcome may not be found if two different kinds of negative affect are involved. In other words, the cueing function may be as precise within the context of emotions as it appears to be within the context of general information. The researchers found that an induced happy mood elicited a majority of happy memories, while an induced angry mood elicited memories of anger or disgust but not other negative memories, such as apprehension or sadness. An induced feeling of sadness, however, did not provide the retrieval of sad memories. The parameters of these intriguing findings remain to be explored.

Research into mood congruent memory typically involves the recollection of an episode that carries emotional valence in and of itself. That is, the emotion is part of the memory. In the mood-dependent studies, the induced mood has no relevance to the target itself, perhaps a list of word items; it is simply present, somewhat arbitrarily, when the list is learned. This could of course provide a major difference, in that mood congruence involves cues that match the *internal* structure of the relevant episode.

8. Output Interference in Long-Term Memory

Output interference operates in LTM as well as STM (Roediger, 1974, 1978; Rundus, 1980). Roediger (1978) found that when participants reported words from a nontarget list before an attempt to report words from the target list, their ability to recall the target items was impaired.

If participants rehearse certain words, Set X, on a list, more extensively than they rehearse other words, Set Y, they generally recall Set X items first and may fail to remember Set Y items at all (Anderson & Green, 2001; Anderson & Neely, 1996). The failure to recall Set Y items appears to be due to output interference, stemming from Set X. The effects of output interference, however, are brief, extending only for a few minutes after the recall test (Smith & Vela, 1991).

Summary

Spreading-activation models posit memory units connected by associative links, in what can be imagined as a huge net. Cues provide access to the net, and then activation spreads from the representations corresponding to the cues, say Representations M and L, to other representations associated with M and L.

Early spreading-activation models assumed that the representations were organized on a spatial basis. Current models are nonspatial. They posit that the critical factor is the strength of the association between the units.

There has been extensive work with connectionist models in the area of semantic/conceptual representation. Models of this kind can generalize information and can infer new information.

ACT and ACT* are associative, spreading-activation models based on symbolic AI. ACT shows properties similar to human recall across a range of memory tasks. In this model, as representations strengthen, so do the links leading to and from them. Here, the level of background activation of memory content is critical. Content with strong background activation can be recalled. However, cues entering the net increase the activation level of the content that they access. As a result, a weak memory may be recalled if good cues are available.

Propositional models concern how abstract, semantic information is coded. They posit a language-like structure, with representations (corresponding to words) and grammatical functions linking the representations together. The entities that embody this coding are assumed to be symbols. Perceptual information involves a qualitatively different code.

Cyclical retrieval/global memory models assume that cues contact information in LTM, and that nontarget content, which has been contacted by the cues, may return to working memory and so provide further access to LTM. A memory search thus involves a cyclical sequence of events, in which new content repeatedly enters working memory and then may activate additional content in LTM, possibly leading to the target. Successful recall and recognition depend entirely on the relationship between the cues and the target memory content.

It has been found that when many words on a target list are associated with another, "lure" (nonpresented) word, that word is often recalled. The word may appear to the participant to be "remembered" clearly, even with sensory content.

Context-, state-, and mood-dependent effects have been found to operate in adult participants but very weakly. There is a more reliable effect of mood congruence. Output interference has been established in LTM.

Discussion

Several different, major, theoretical positions have emerged in the course of research into LTM. The first involves semantic codes. According to one tradition, these consist of unitary features gathered into collections or sets. According to a second tradition, semantic information has propositional structure. Research focused on the recall of individual words (as in word lists) has tended to support the featural view, while research involving memory for prose content generally supports propositional models.

A second important division involves the issue of whether all retrieval involves direct content between cues in working memory and content in LTM or whether spreading activation occurs within LTM itself. Attempts to resolve the question empirically have not been successful. The research is ongoing, however, and there can be little doubt that an answer will be found in the near future.

Probably the most important issue, among the various diverging currents of theory that have emerged in recent years, involves the opposition between activity theorists and those who posit that the relations between cues and memory content fully determine whether an attempt at recall will succeed. Either the internal nature of a memory is critical in determining whether the memory can be recalled, or this is not the case.

Some researchers who support the cue-dependent view also support the permanent memory hypothesis (the view that information entered into LTM is never weakened or lost). Others do not. In the latter case, it is assumed that some information may be lost from LTM through decay or interference. But whatever remains does not differ in the "strength" with which it is coded.

Current research in the area of forgetting cites the same factors as were identified in the 1970s. Decay remains a possibility, and interference effects have been clearly established. Some researchers interpret interference in terms of a weakening or impairment of the relevant codes (a view associated with consolidation theory); others see the effect as due to a blocking phenomenon or as the result of difficulty in discriminating target material. The first group generally reflects the "activity" view of memory, in which memory content differs in strength and the second group, cue-dependent theory, in which the relationship between the cues and memory content exclusively determines recall.

CHAPTER 8

The Constructivist Model of Memory

Overview

1. According to the empiricist or copier tradition, the memory of an event reflects what was seen and heard during the event (perceptual information). In contrast, constructivist theory assumes that the primary code in memory involves the individual's *understanding* of the event.

2. According to constructivist theory, memory content is supplied by relevant background knowledge as well as by a representation of the sights or sounds present during the target episode.

3. Gaps in the original memory can be filled in at the time of recall on the basis of inference. As a result, memories can change.

4. Sir Frederick Bartlett emphasized the role of higher-order *schemas* in memory. The term *schema* is used within the present tradition to denote an interpretive structure.

5. According to Jean Piaget, memory strength also depends on the background integration of schemas present in long-term memory (LTM).

6. M. Minsky assumed that concepts are schemas, which consist of frames geared to encode certain specific kinds of information. McClelland and Rumelhart have shown how schemas can be instantiated in neural nets and also how such nets spontaneously infer information. R. Schank has developed a detailed model of higher-order knowledge structures.

7. Experienced memories can change. Nonconstructivists believe that the underlying memory codes do not change, while constructivists believe that they do change.

Learning Objectives

1. Knowledge of the constructivist model of memory, including the implications for memory, when it is assumed that the primary code involves understanding of an event or other material. Knowledge of why this model assumes that memory content can change and of the concept of a schema.

2. Knowledge of the role of higher-order structures in memory, under constructivist theory.

There exist two major theoretical traditions concerning the nature of human memory. The older, which can be traced to empiricist thought, assumes that an episodic memory is a copy of the stimuli encountered during the relevant episode, and that interpretation of the input can be seen as separate from the memory itself. It is also assumed that memory sets do not interact within long-term memory (LTM) to produce new content.

The more recent, constructivist tradition, holds that episodic memory content is a fundamentally interpretive event, drawing extensively on background knowledge at the time that the memory is formed. It is further assumed that background knowledge comes into play again at the time of recall. This belief carries the implication that a given memory set relevant to an episode can interact with other memory sets, at the time of recall, to produce new (altered) memory content.

1. Constructivism: Basic Tenets

Within the empiricist tradition, memories are conceptualized as images. More precisely, they are believed to be copies of percepts. If I enter my room and notice a chair, then a representation of the chair percept will be stored in LTM. It will constitute my memory of the object.

Across entire episodes, a range of objects and people will be coded. Memory may here be viewed as roughly similar to a stored film. It differs from a film, however, in that not all the details of an original scene will be held. If an individual fails to notice a blue vase on a table, then no vase image will be coded into memory.

According to the empiricist model, then, our recollections of any given episode consist of codes reflecting what we saw and heard during the episode. It follows that the content held in LTM will normally be accurate content. This is the case because perception is for the most part reliable. If I see a table or a person, it is generally because the table or person is in fact there.

This view of human recall framed the work of Ebbinghaus and McGeoch, among many others. Research examining the parameters of word learning and forgetting and the first models of memory were all developed within an empiricist framework.

During the 1930s, however, two researchers suggested an alternative model of human (although not animal) memory. One was the English psychologist Sir Frederick Bartlett, and the other was the Swiss developmentalist and biologist Jean Piaget. The new approach became known as *constructivism*.

According to the constructivist view, the primary code in human memory does not reflect perceptual information. It is instead a semantic code. In other words, it is a representation of meaning. When I recall seeing a chair, I recall not only what the object looked like (although I do retain this content too) but also what it was: its nature. And the meaning code plays the more critical role in memory.

Taking this position to its logical conclusion, an individual's memory for a given episode reflects his or her understanding of the episode.

Semantic codes can operate in a hierarchy. And in the case of human memory (according to the constructivist view) this hierarchical property is of fundamental importance. Thus, one's understanding of an event includes not only a meaning representation for individual objects or people but also a generalized level that might be described as "the nature of the event as a whole."

Suppose I attend a wedding. I will see various objects and people directly. There will be guests, flowers, a white cake, the bride in her long dress. I will code the meaning of these individual things and also their appearance. But a higher-level semantic understanding of the event will also be generated. I will understand that I have just watched a ceremony: one familiar and accepted in the present culture. I will know the implications of the ceremony, including those of a social contract. Above this level of knowledge, there will be the broader frame of the significance of weddings as such.

According to the constructivist model, this general and "background" knowledge forms a fundamental part of the memory. In other words, it is not something added to the memory but rather is part of the memory fabric as such. It is in fact as bedrock a component as the tables, chairs, or people that I see directly.

As this line of theory was developed, the high-level or generalized information in fact plays a more critical role than most objects and people encountered during the target episode. This is the case because the high-level information integrates the memory content (in ways to be described below) and also directly provides memory strength.

Thus, the older view of memory for a given episode saw it as constituted of the specific events that occurred during the episode itself: a representation of the things seen and heard across that span of time. The memory was therefore bounded. Its content was confined to the stimuli/events experienced at the time of encoding. In contrast, the constructivist model of memory assumes a function that is not bounded. If an individual lives through a given episode, the events of the episode will be interpreted. As described above, this effort at understanding may draw on any relevant body of information already stored in LTM. There is no specific boundary to the memory content. Within this context it can be said that memory content is "interactive." Information reflecting the immediate stimuli and motions of the target scene interacts with background information to provide the final memory content (Bartlett, 1932; Conway, 1997; Graesser, Singer, & Trabasso, 1994;

Kihlstrom, 1998; Kintsch & Van Dijk, 1978; Neisser, 1967; Reiser, 1986; Rumelhart, 1980; Schachter, 1995; Schank, 1982, 1999).

A final difference between nonconstructivist and constructivist views of memory centers on the events that occur at the time of recall. Within the former line, the content coded and stored at an unconscious level is the same information that may be entered later into awareness as an actual memory. At recall, the content is moved from an unconscious to a conscious level. No other cognitive events occur.

In contrast, the constructivist view could be described as follows. At the time of recall, the memory function attempts to reconstruct the target memory. It will draw on the body of content coded at the time of the original event and also on any additional, relevant information stored in LTM. In short, a comprehensive interpretive act occurs when the information is retrieved, just as had occurred when the information was originally coded.

Either of two activities may come into play at the time of memory reconstruction. Within this tradition is it believed that some elements of memory content may weaken over time. If this does occur, and the original material is too weak to be generated, then the system may infer it. This act of inference occurs at an unconscious level, and its products are subjectively indistinguishable from originally coded content. That is, the inferred material appears to be a memory or a component of a memory.

Perhaps I always wear my brown coat when it snows. If I am asked (for some reason) to recall what I wore on February 12th, and if I know that there was a snowstorm that morning, I may recall wearing the brown coat. But this recollection may not reflect an original code (one formed at the time.) It could be an unconscious inference. The sense that I wore that coat may "feel" like a memory, however.

It is also possible that at the time of retrieval some nontarget information might be entered into the memory, due to its having been mistaken for a component of the target episode.

In the example given above it was suggested that knowledge of the nature of weddings would form an integral part of an episodic memory of a particular wedding. It follows that information derived from LTM is indistinguishable in memory from information directly perceived during the event, such as the appearance of a table. One is not more clear or more valid than the other. In the same way, it is assumed that even memory images are supported by "background" perceptual knowledge. If I briefly see a house while walking past it, I may be able to recall an image of the house quite clearly. But this image will probably have been drawn in major part from my long-term knowledge of what houses in general look like. In other words, I did not memorize the details of the original house, although the memory image is complete and without gaps. If the object had been something entirely unknown to me, I would not be able to remember it with anything like the same clarity.

According to the present view, information supplied from LTM is simply a part of the memory: of equal status with content that has been coded as a direct copy of the object seen. For instance, the house might have a crenellated pattern along the edge of the roof, which I notice and actively code into memory, while I may give little attention to the shape of the roof, which is a standard shape. Later I may be able to recall both the crenellated pattern and the shape of the roof behind it; but the latter has been derived from my long-established knowledge of roof shapes. I did not memorize it as I walked past. Again, it follows that inferred content in memory is not qualitatively different from directly "copied" content. As a result, if an incorrect inference were made, there would be no way to distinguish the false content from other, valid content.

In summary, the constructivist tradition assumes a dynamic memory function that operates to understand events and that at the time of recall attempts to regenerate the original episode using all relevant information available to it. At recall, new material could in some cases be coded into the memory. For instance, if at the time of attempted recall (perhaps on May 8th) my memory function infers that I wore a black coat on February 12th, then a black-coat code will be entered into the memory stored in LTM. (To be more precise, at the time of recall, the memory function establishes a complex of information in LTM, representing what I recall of February 12th. The black coat will be present in that complex, such that the memory has changed from the original. Also, the information that I actually recall will reflect that complex. Earlier information, possibly coding for a brown coat, may also be present in LTM. The issue is explained in further detail in Chapter 9.)

Nonconstructivist researchers, on the other hand, assume that if a brown coat was coded into memory on February 12th, the code reflecting that particular day can never change. If the memory that truly represents February 12th is recalled, it will include a brown coat. If I recall a black coat, it is either because I am guessing (not remembering) or because I have retrieved the wrong memory.

2. Bartlett

In 1932, the English psychologist Sir Frederick Bartlett published a book, *Remembering*, in which he introduced the ideas outlined above.

Ebbinghaus, an empiricist, had assumed that memory should be studied on the basis of a reductionist technique. Reductionism within this context means reducing memory content to basic units. Memory strength could be measured by the quantity of units retained, across different conditions. It was Ebbinghaus's assumption that the laws that held for memory units would hold equally for more complex material.

Bartlett argued that it was inappropriate and unrealistic to attempt to measure human memory in terms of units. He suggested that there is in fact no such thing as a unit in human understanding and recall: no such thing as a "single response" to a stimulus item. For instance, if I encounter the nonsense syllable QOG I may automatically activate Queequog, Moby Dick, and also cog. I am not registering and storing an isolated unit.

Bartlett also believed that we code memory content on the basis of higher-order schemas, or higher-order comprehension of the nature of an event. For instance, as described above, when attending a wedding we conceptualize the actions around us within the frame of what is likely to happen at weddings. According to the Bartlettian view, these higher-order structures play several vital roles in the memory function. If this is the case, then the study of random word units, where no higher-order constituents are present, will fail to reveal some of the most important causal variables in human recall.

According to the present tradition, a memory does not involve the copying of specific stimuli but rather a complex mass of constructed information. This content goes beyond the immediate images presented to eyes and ears, to a more generalized level. This generally involves abstract content. For instance, in watching a film we are likely to determine that it is a war story or a romance or a fantasy, and this information will guide the way in which we interpret the events unfolding on the screen.

Bartlett used the Kantian term *schema* (pl. schemas or schemata) for the structures that perform the work of interpretation: at every level. A schema may be seen roughly as an interpretive structure (a structure that establishes meaning or understanding or sometimes motor organization). The higher-order schemas (supplying generalized context information) operated to provide at least two critical functions. The first of these was memory strength. If all the details or facts of an episode fit the higher-order schema that had been generated to understand that episode, the details would be supported. The result would be a body of strongly retained memory content. If the details did not fit the higher-order schema, they would soon be forgotten.

A corollary of this aspect of human recall, according to the present model, was that if the details could not be fitted to the higher-order interpretation, an attempt would be made to make them fit. This could result in distortion of the original content.

The second major function of the higher-order context was that of content integration. If all the information being entered into LTM fit the relevant context, it would appear integrated, in the sense of all the material "belonging together."

A critical point urged by Bartlett was that we expect the world to be meaningful: to make sense. If some body of content does not appear to have this property, we try to reinterpret the content and infuse some coherence into it. This can further influence memory since, as described above, the "effort after meaning" can sometimes change the original material. Material will not appear to make sense if it fails to fit the higher-order frame that has been established. In some circumstances, however, as will be shown below, attempting to change the material to make it fit the established context can result in alteration of the original content.

Bartlett researched these claims by the use of various materials such as stories, descriptions, and pictures. In some cases, he included a confusing passage in the target story. His prediction was that recall of this passage would be both weak and particularly subject to distortion, as the reader struggled to make sense of it. His most famous story (an adaptation of an American Indian folk tale, translated by Franz Boas) is shown below.

"The War of the Ghosts"

One night two young men from Egulac went down the river to hunt for seals, and while they were there it became foggy and calm. Then they heard war cries, and they thought, "Maybe this is a war party." They escaped to the shore and hid behind a log. Now canoes came up and they heard the noise of paddles, and saw one canoe coming up to them. There were five men in the canoe, and they said, "What do you think? We wish to take you along. We are going up river to make war on the people."

One of the young men said, "I have no arrows." "Arrows are in the canoe," they said. "I will not go along. I might be killed. My relatives do not know where I have gone. But you," he said, turning to the other, "may go with them."

So one of the young men went, but the other returned home. And the warriors went on up the river to a town on the other side of Kalama. The people came down to the water and they began to fight, and many were killed. But presently the young man heard one of the warriors say, "Quick, let us go home; that Indian has been hit." Now he thought, "Oh, they are ghosts." He did not feel sick, but they said he had been shot.

So the canoes went back to Egulac, and the young man went ashore to his house, and made a fire. And he told everybody and said: "Behold, I accompanied the ghosts, and we went to fight. Many of our fellows were killed, and many of those who attacked us were killed. They said I was hit, and I did not feel sick." He told it all, and then he became quiet. When the sun rose he fell down. Something black came out of his mouth. His face became contorted. The people jumped up and cried.

He was dead.

The following content was reported in Bartlett's study by Participant H, 20 hours after hearing the story. "Two men from Egulac went fishing."

According to the present model, H recalled the men as fishing (when in fact they had gone to hunt seals) because the story established that these were American Indians, engaged in some activity on a river. The original code had not been sufficiently strong for retrieval, and the system had inferred fishing. This would be a plausible inference since Europeans do not tend to think of American Indians as seal hunters.

Another common change in the memory protocols involved the hiding place of the young men when they fled to shore. It had been a log. Some of the participants in the experiment (whom Bartlett called "observers") recalled a boulder or a tree. This can again be seen as a reasonable inference, if an attempt is being made to reconstruct something large enough to hide behind, at the edge of a river, in Indian territory.

Bartlett found that his observers generally recalled the first two thirds of the story, and its end, accurately and in some detail. In contrast, the battle scene was poorly recalled and often changed from the original.

The battle scene does not make sense. Many on both sides were killed, and yet the warriors decide to go home when they note that someone has been hit. It is not clear who the ghosts are, nor is it clear what the young man suddenly sees or hears that makes him realize that "they" (whoever they are) are ghosts. As a result, recall of this component tended to be both weak and distorted in the effort to make the content sensible. Bartlett believed that many of his observers had taken "The War of the Ghosts" for an adventure story, thus making "adventure story" the higher-order schema for the passage as a whole. But the events of the battle scene do not fit the expectations generated by an adventure story.

Bartlett suggested that higher-order schemas operate like doors. If you deploy an adventure story schema, you have walked through one door. Elements that do not fit your interpretation, although presumably understood as isolated statements, are quickly forgotten.

A number of other critical points were developed within this context. According to Bartlett, events usually have "connections" that are often not stated in the text but are supplied by the reader. The effort after meaningfulness appears to be related to this finding of connections. Under the wrong higher-order schema, the reader may be looking for connections that cannot operate because the schema does not include or permit them.

A second claim outlined, although not pursued, in 1932 was that emotion influences memory. Bartlett's position was that emotional material is coded in a stronger fashion than neutral material. (The effect was unrelated to cue matching.) Thus he noted that of the four men in his original experiment who recalled the excuse of the arrows, all of them reversed the original order of the excuses, reporting first the "I might be killed" objection or the individuals' family might be worried, and only second that he had no arrows. The participants in the study were young men at Cambridge during World War I (1914–1918); all were likely to be engaged in that conflict in the immediate future.

Bartlett's position concerning the representation used in memory was that both semantic and perceptual codes are generated. These differ in nature from one another: The codes are different.

In general, the semantic outlasts the perceptual. It does so because it can benefit from the hierarchical structure described above, while perceptual representations exist "in and of themselves" and do not participate in hierarchical relations.

Bartlett further believed that information in the system often weakens across time, to a point where it is no longer maintained in any form: That is, it is forgotten. He thus rejected the permanent memory hypothesis that had been endorsed by McGeoch and many other researchers.

A summary of Bartlett's model is shown in Box 6.1 on page 113.

3. Piaget: The Genevan View

Jean Piaget's lifework was the development of a constructivist model of human cognition (Piaget, 1926a, 1926b, 1950, 1951, 1952, 1954, 1969, 1972, 1976, 1977). Memory is discussed throughout his work, although he did not publish a book devoted solely to this topic until the 1970s (Piaget & Inhelder, 1973).

Piaget endorsed Bartlett's assumptions concerning memory but extended them in several ways. Both authors assume that memory involves an interpretive event and that schemas perform the work of interpretation. Roughly, if I see a table, I understand what it is because I possess a table schema stored in LTM. The table schema provides information concerning the nature of the object. In the same way, if I inter-pret a given event as a political rally, it is because I possess an organized body of knowledge—a higher-order schema—specifying the nature of political rallies.

In Piaget's model, schemas are also implicated in cognitive abilities. If I can add numbers, for instance, this reflects an organized body of knowledge concerning the procedures involved in addition.

Piaget believed that schemas possess a background organization of their own in LTM. They are interrelated; some are tightly integrated with other sets of schemas, while some possess only a loose integration of this kind. The nature of the back-ground schemas is critical in the Piagetian (Genevan) model to memory strength. *A memory that has been constructed on the basis of strongly integrated schemas will be a strong memory*. In the same way, a memory constructed on the basis of weakly integrated schemas will be a weak memory.

For instance, some schemas do not lend themselves to a high level of integration with other schemas. Most sensory properties would be of this kind. Consider color. Suppose a year ago I saw a man in a yellow shirt. The shirt happened to be yellow but could equally well have been white or blue or green. There are no constraints on the memory to help me recall the color, which I may forget quickly.

Now suppose a year ago I saw a fire and firemen working on it. This memory will be supported by many schemas that interrelate with other schemas. For instance, there are temporal factors, causal factors, psychological factors, and background knowledge. The former will support my recollection of the order in which the events occurred and the causal will supply outcomes of the actions that I saw, which should also integrate with the time factors. In addition, my background knowledge of firemen should "fit" everything that I saw and connect with many other knowl-edge structures, such as my knowledge of social norms concerning people who guard our society, and so on. This large complex of interrelated, often higher-order, schemas will underlie the memory. Perhaps I will recall 50 facts about the episode, although I only experienced it once. In contrast, if someone presented me with 50 unrelated words, just once, I could not recall them even immediately, let alone a year after the event! The difference is that the schema underlying each word would have no relation with any of the other schemas, for the other words.

As with Bartlett's claim, this view implies a very important variable underlying the strength of a memory, at least as "strong" as that of rehearsal. Also, this factor is not the same as conscious elaboration. It comes into play automatically and is not under the individual's control.

A second important aspect of Piaget's theory involves coding formats. At the level of theory, it might be possible for the coding or structure of information at an unconscious level to be the same as the coding or form of conscious representation. Or the two might be qualitatively different. Within the Kantian tradition, they are different. Piaget also endorsed this view. According to the Genevan model, a schema is a type of code that can only be unconscious; it is not capable of being expressed in the forms available to conscious representation (Piaget & Inhelder, 1973). This is because a schema involves a complex, diverse body of information. At the level of awareness, we cannot represent a single (singular) entity that is complex in the way that a schema is complex. Conscious representation is singular and linear. For instance, I can picture a tree from one perspective but cannot in imagination "see" the tree from all sides at once. In contrast, the perceptual tree schema includes all this information within itself. Equally, if I activate the concept TREE, it will be expressed in awareness as a word, or as a picture, or perhaps simply as a sense that I know what a tree is. In fact, my concept TREE includes a large body of information. But I am unable to express all this information at one time in awareness. Instead, I experience a kind of symbol (such as the word *tree*) that represents or stands for the meaning of the concept. In contrast, the meaning itself is coded at an unconscious level. This is the tree schema.

There is a major debate in the field of memory today concerning whether there exist different memory systems, with different codes. However, the emphasis in the mainstream field has been on different systems related to different kinds of information. In contrast, the Genevan view, expressed above, posits what might be called a bedrock distinction between conscious and unconscious representation.

Piaget labeled the singular, simple representations that we experience in awareness as *signifiers*. A signifier can be a word or an image. In the case of images, the image may be direct (an image of a chair to represent the idea CHAIR) or, particularly in a child's early cognition, and in dreams, symbolic (an image of a tiger to represent anger). The term *significate* was used for the schemas that provide meaning to a signifier. And in the case of a memory, the term *memory significate* designated the complex of schemas used to construct the memory. At the time of recall, under the present model, the system would reconstruct the memory, drawing on both the original memory significate and also on any other relevant information. If new, and perhaps inaccurate, information was entered into the final memory significate (the one established at the time of recall), then the experienced memory would be changed from the original event, and the underlying memory significate would also be different from the one that had been formed originally. A final term of the present model involved the entities in the outside world that are represented in our cognition: For instance, the signifier "chair" represents actual chairs in the world. The external (nonmental) chair was labeled as the *thing signified*.

It should be noted that in the present model all abstract content in a memory is constructed. Most memories contain a very large body of abstract content. This content is usually accurate, particularly at its higher, more critical, levels. Although a memory function that is constructive *can* (and does) lead to changes and alterations in recall, this is not the point or purpose of reconstructive memory. A memory function of this kind is capable of moving beyond perceptual imagery; and this is the source of its being so effective in dealing with the world.

4. Constructivism in Mainstream Psychology

In an influential text, Neisser (1967) noted that it is incorrect to assume that memories are stored in LTM and later simply moved again into awareness (retrieved). Instead, at the time of recall the memory function uses some of the originally coded information but may also infer additional content (for instance, , to fill in gaps or weaknesses in the original codes). And critically, it is the reconstructed memory that is entered into awareness. This remains the cornerstone position of constructivism today. Chapter 9 introduces two models of how the relevant events may unfold.

Constructivist ideas have found various forms of expression in the mainstream field. Work with neural network models has emphasized how information can naturally be inferred at the time of recall and how the state of the system, at recall, is necessarily different from the state of the system during encoding. The artificial neural networks of this tradition are based on the functioning of units, which might at first appear contrary in spirit to the notion of schemas, including higher-order schemas, which is fundamental to the constructivist tradition. McClelland and Rumelhart (1986, vol. 2, chap. 1), however, showed how emergent, higher-order properties, identified as schemas, can emerge from the operation of connectionist networks.

Minsky (1975) outlined a model of conceptual representation, labeled *schema theory*. Here it was posited that a concept can be understood as a schema. This involves a structure designed to "pick up" only certain kinds of information from the environment, with a strong internal organization.

A number of researchers have developed models of higher-order structures against which information entering memory can be matched. The structures work to support (strengthen) the relevant content in LTM. Such structures range from models of story organization, to more generalized forms that can handle everyday episodic events (Bobrow & Norman, 1975; Mandler & Johnson, 1977; Rumelhart, 1977, 1980; Schank, 1982, 1999; Schank & Abelson, 1977).

A final area of extensive research has involved the issue of changed memories. Here, models positing direct retrieval have been pitted against models that assume an active process of reconstruction at the time of recall (Bekerian & Bowers, 1983; Belli, 1989; Conway, 1996; Loftus, 1979a, 1997; Loftus, Feldman, & Dashiell, 1995; McCloskey & Zaragoza, 1985). As described earlier, a major area of dispute today centers on whether the underlying codes in LTM have changed when there is change in the experienced memory.

Chapter 10 is devoted to research focusing on higher-order knowledge structures of various kinds. Chapter 9 covers research into change in a memory that is otherwise accurate. Chapter 14 includes coverage of wholly false episodic memories.

Summary

Empiricist or copier theories of memory assume that memories of events are copies of what has been seen or heard during the event. This being the case, memories should be accurate depictions of the original episode.

Constructivists believe that the primary code in memory involves understanding. The understanding is achieved through interpretive structures called *schemas*. An understanding of an event involves a large component of abstract, nonsensory information.

Bartlett rejected the empiricist view that memory could be studied on the basis of units. He held that no memory content was an isolated unit but that all such contacts interact. He advocated a constructivist model of memory with emphasis on higher-order schemas. We establish higher-order interpretations of an event as we live through it. When the details of the event fit the higher-order structure, there is a significant increase in memory strength. Also, if events do not fit the higher-order structure, they appear not to make sense. A critical implication of Bartlett's model is that there exists another source of memory strength in addition to rehearsal or elaborating activities. This factor comes into play when information fits the currently operating higher-order schemas. Perceptual information is also retained in memory. It is simply not the primary memory code.

According to Piaget, schemas differ in their background, mutual integration in LTM. Strongly integrated schemas provide significant memory strength. This claim provides a second "new" factor related to the strength of a memory.

Piaget also distinguished between representations that we experience in awareness ("signifiers") and the complex of information in LTM that generates the signifiers (the significate). These are qualitatively different kinds. Significates consist of interrelated schemas. Schemas cannot enter awareness.

Various researchers have developed models reflecting constructivist ideas. These range from neural net simulations of memory, through models of conceptual representation, to a range of theories concerning higher-order structures. The assumption of changed memories based on active reconstructive processing at the time of recall has also led to a wide range of research, some in short-term and some (the lion's share) in long-term memory.

CHAPTER 9

Memory Change: Alteration in the Components of a Memory

1. Researchers have shown that misleading information, provided after a memory has been formed, can alter the memory. Nonconstructivists believe that the underlying memory codes in long-term memory (LTM) have not altered. Instead, a nontarget memory has been selected and mistaken for the target. Constructivists believe that processing activity occurs at retrieval, in which information in LTM is drawn on to generate the recalled memory and that when the experienced memory changes it is because the LTM codes, formed at retrieval, have also changed.

2. Research into eyewitness testimony has shown that objects suggested to have been present during an episode may be recalled as actually having been in the episode. Eyewitness identification of individuals who have committed a crime is often inaccurate. Human memory for unfamiliar faces is markedly poor. Research into lineup procedures has indicated that sequential lineups work better than traditional, simultaneous forms.

3. The effects of strong emotion on memory, including eyewitness reports, have been found to differ across situations. In some cases, memory is enhanced; in some cases, it is impaired.

Learning Objectives

1. Knowledge of the empirical data concerning memory change and of the opposed theoretical positions concerning such change.

2. Knowledge of the findings concerning inaccuracy in eyewitness testimony and knowledge of research relating to the improvement of eyewitness identification.

3. Knowledge of the influence of emotion on eyewitness recollection.

T he present chapter covers changes that may occur in memories. It involves change in only one or a few aspects of an otherwise accurate recollection. Memories that are false as such, in that they involve an event that did not actually occur, are covered in Chapter 14. Chapter 8 should be read as a foundation for the present material.

In most real-life situations, there is a body of information that is weakly coded in long-term memory (LTM). Any natural episode includes a large amount of casually attended events and trivial detail. This is the case because there is far more potential content in a single episode than can be attended.

Because changes in memory appeared most likely to occur in the case of weakly coded material, the first research in this area centered on natural episodes, often shown on videotape or in the form of slides.

PART I: RESEARCH AND THEORY

1. Postevent Information and Memory Change

1.1. Change in the Recollection of Perceived Content

During the 1970s and 1980s, Elizabeth Loftus and her colleagues conducted a program of research into the nature of changed memories. Loftus's claim was that she could take a weak memory and alter it by direct manipulation, such that the nature of the changes could be predicted.

Loftus and Palmer (1974) presented their experimental participants with a film showing a traffic accident. Participants were then asked a series of questions about the film. Under Condition A, one question was phrased as, "How fast were the cars going when they hit one another?" Under Condition B, the statement read, "How fast were the cars going when they smashed into one another?"

A week later the participants returned for the second stage of the experiment. They were again asked a series of questions. One such question centered on whether they had seen broken glass during the crash. There had in fact been no broken glass. Of individuals exposed to the verb "hit," 7/50 incorrectly recalled broken glass. In contrast, in the "smashed into" condition, 16 /50 recalled seeing broken glass.

A critical point concerning this research is that it demonstrated the influence of information, relevant to a target memory, acquired after the memory was originally coded. Information received after a memory has been formed is termed *postevent information.*

In a further study on memory change, Loftus, Miller, and Burns (1978) showed their participants two variations in a set of slides. One featured a STOP sign (Condition 1) and the other a YIELD sign (Condition 2.) After seeing the slides, participants were asked a series of questions. For participants who had seen a yield sign, a misleading question was, "Did another car pass the red Datsun while it was stopped at the stop sign?" with "yield" substituted in the question for those who had seen a stop sign.

The participants then engaged in a 20-minute filler activity, followed by a test. The test consisted of a series of 15 pairs of slides and the requirement that the participants pick the slide they had actually seen.

Of the nonmisled participants, 75% correctly identified the sign. Of the misled participants, 41% correctly identified the sign.

In later experiments, the retention interval was varied from immediate recall to 1 day, 2 days, or 1 week. The placement of the misleading information was also varied, between immediately following the slides and just before the test.

The greatest alteration in recall was found under delay conditions, in which the misinformation was presented just before the test. Here the original memory had weakened, while the misinformation benefited from a recency effect. Figure 9.1 shows correct recall on the part of participants who were exposed to the misleading questions immediately or following a delay.

The experiments described above involved change induced in memory content after no more than a single exposure to misleading information. A range of studies have replicated this effect under varying conditions (Ackil & Zaragoza, 1995; Belli, Lindsay, Gales, & McCarthy, 1994; Ceci, Ross, & Toglia, 1987b; Lampinen & Smith, 1995; Lindsay, 1990; Zaragoza & Lane, 1994).

1.2. Compromise Memories

The Loftus et al. (1978) study described above involved target objects that were not mutually compatible. A participant in the study could not believe that she had seen a STOP-YIELD sign, and unreal objects of this kind are not retrieved or reconstructed as actual memories. But what might happen if the original item and the inaccurate, suggested item could both have been correct, in terms of life experience or of memory content?

Loftus (1977) showed a series of slides again involving a traffic accident. A green Datsun passed the scene of the accident in the background. In a series of questions asked after the video had been shown, participants in the misled condition were asked, "Did the blue Datsun that passed the scene of the accident have a luggage rack?" After a further week's delay, the participants were asked to identify the color

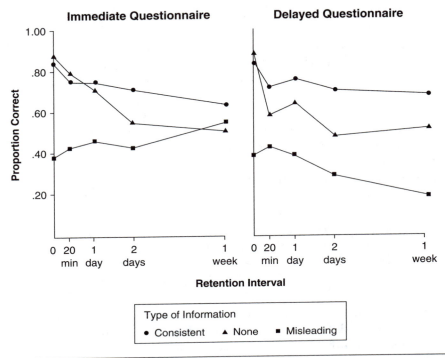

Figure 9.1   Correct Recall When the Misleading Questionnaire Was Given Directly After Participants had Viewed the Slides and Recall When It Was Presented After a Delay

SOURCE: From Loftus, E. F., Miller, D.G., & Burns, H. J., "Semantic integration of verbal information into a visual memory," in *Journal of Experimental Psychology: Human Learning and Memory 4*(1), copyright © 1978, American Psychological Association. Reprinted with permission.

of the car that had passed the accident, using a color wheel. Of the individuals in the misled condition, some picked a blue color, and some a green. Most interesting of all, however, was a group of individuals who selected a mixed blue-green color from the wheel. In the nonmisled condition, the majority of the participants who could identify the car's color remembered it correctly.

The recollection of a blue-green car was labeled as a *compromise memory*. For the compromise subjects, the system had apparently retained the information (1) the car was green (almost certainly visually coded) or (2) the car was blue (probably coded as abstract information). Both items were used in the later reconstruction of the memory.

Continuing research has demonstrated that memory change can be achieved across a wide range of situations, including altered memory for actions (Goff & Roediger, 1998), for content of films (Allen & Lindsay, 1998; Lindsay & Johnson, 1989), and for staged events (Eisen & Carlson, 1998).

1.3. Variables That Influence Memory Change

When experimental participants can be led to recall incorrect information, it is likely that the original memory was weak. Greene, Flynn, and Loftus (1982) examined whether strongly coded memories could be changed in the same way. The findings were that they could not.

The researchers had also discovered that if a given item of misleading information was blatantly unlikely, then it did not provide memory change. Even more striking, the presence of such an unlikely suggestion led to the participants' resisting the influence of other, more reasonable, items in the same experiment. Dodd and Bradshaw (1980) reported a similar effect when they warned their participants that an individual might intend to mislead them.

Greene et al. believed that a warning against misleading information might be effective only if it was delivered immediately before the misleading information, but not if it was delivered after. The hypothesis was confirmed. However, the effect of a warning was found to be relatively small, even under optimal placement conditions. Misleading information produced somewhat less memory change when subjects were warned that postevent input might not be reliable. But the target memories were still altered to some extent.

1.4. Memory Change in Natural Contexts

Alterations in memory have also been established in nonlaboratory settings. Wright, Self, and Justice (2000) showed their participants a videotaped crime. The participants later recalled the episode first individually and then after talking about the episode with another participant (who had seen the same video). When tested again, the participants showed some alterations in memory, due to the influence of the earlier-held discussion.

Niedzwienska (2003) tested 60 individuals on their recollections of two major events in their lives: (1) a final examination taken by Polish students before they leave school and (2) a ball, The Hundred Days Ball, which is thrown before the examination. Participants were tested a year after these events. The experimental group was then exposed to suggested, incorrect details concerning the examination and ball and also to a guided imagery technique in which they were asked simply to imagine the original events as now described to them. Four months later, their memories were tested again. Now, the experimental group included elements of the suggested, misleading content in their new memories. There was not a high level of changed content, but it appeared to be a standard outcome. Twenty-nine out of 30 recollections showed changed material.

2. Nonconstructivist Theories of Memory Change

One nonconstructivist view of memory change is that participants who do not recall the target content, simply make guesses. If they have been exposed to misleading information, they pick that information as the content of their guess (Zaragoza & McCloskey, 1989).

It has been suggested that individuals who don't recall the target may have a particular reason for selecting a given response. This is known as *response bias*. One form of response bias involves *demand characteristics*. Here, it is assumed that participants believe that they know what the experimenter wants them to say. The claim has even been made that individuals who do recall the correct target but think the experimenter wants them to pick something else, may pick the nontarget item (Orne, 1973)!

The second nonconstructivist explanation of memory change involves a situation in which a nontarget memory is mistaken for the target and recalled as the target. Here, both memories are real. When the nontarget is retrieved, nothing is changed in LTM. This event is known as *source misattribution* (Johnson, Hashtroudi, & Lindsay, 1993).

The situation described above involves the assumption both of source misattribution and of incorrect content retrieval. Bekerian and Bowers (1983) suggested that misleading postevent information may in fact block (or "preclude") the earlier, target information, thus leading to a tendency for the misleading item to be recalled more often than would otherwise be expected.

3. Constructivist Models of Memory Change

3.1. The Replacement Hypothesis

According to the *replacement hypothesis*, when an individual recalls, for instance, a YIELD sign, although what had actually been seen was a STOP sign, the YIELD sign information replaces the STOP sign information in LTM. Both the conscious memory and the unconscious LTM codes have changed. This event will occur, however, only under two conditions: (1) when the changed information has actually been recalled and (2) when the two items are logically contradictory. By "logically contradictory" is meant that the object had to be either one or the other and could not be both, such as a stop-yield sign (Loftus & Loftus, 1980).

3.2. The Multiple-Trace Hypothesis

The *multiple-trace hypothesis* is the view endorsed by most constructivist researchers today. Here, it is assumed that at the time of recall, the memory function establishes a new complex of information on the basis of which the given memory will be recalled. In establishing this complex, the function may draw on any relevant information present in LTM. In the case of an experiment in which misleading information has been suggested, the codes for the original event will be used when the new complex (in Piagetian terms, the new memory significate) is established. Other relevant information may also be entered into the new significate.

When material is first coded in LTM, the system establishes time and place information, sometimes referred to as an *episodic tag*. For instance, if I have just seen the film *Gandhi*, the episodic tag information concerning the film would be something like, "seen today, Monday, in South Side Cinema." There is evidence that time-and-place information is lost more quickly than general content information, however. As a result, I may later recall the film, but not where or when I saw it.

In the case of experimental research into altered memories, codes relating to the relevant objects may still be available in LTM, when episodic-tag information is not. If an individual saw a STOP sign, for instance, and was misled by information suggesting a YIELD sign, the resulting LTM codes would be: There was a stop sign, and There was a yield sign (lacking the information "that I saw in the video," or "that I heard about in the experimental session"). In the act of reconstruction, the memory function must then choose between the two candidates. Here, a correct STOP sign might be chosen, or an incorrect YIELD sign might be chosen. Whichever item is in fact selected, it will be entered into the new memory significate. By "new memory significate" is meant the significate formed at the time the material is recalled.

It is not known on what basis the selection of an uncertain item is achieved. In the present example, the incorrect YIELD information should benefit from a recency effect, and be slightly stronger, since it was encountered after the STOP sign information. The STOP item, however, may include a little perceptual information. Both of these factors are known to influence recall. Equally, the selection may be random or based on some other form of interaction of content within LTM.

A critical point concerning the multiple trace model is that at the time of recall, if the wrong item is selected, the experienced memory will have changed from the original event, and the codes in LTM will also have changed. This is because the new memory significate, created at the time of recall, not only includes much of the original scene but now also includes a YIELD sign that was not present in the original.

Constructivists agree that source misattribution is often (although not always) the basis of a changed memory. However, when this occurs, the incorrect information is again entered into the new memory significate and thus change has occurred in LTM itself. A second cause of changed memories is simply inferred information, not reflecting an alternative, "real" episode.

In the present model, the *original* complex of codes in LTM, formed during the event, is not changed at the time of recall. That is, an incorrect yield sign item does not replace the correct stop sign item in this original significate. The change occurs only in the new significate, established at the time of recall. However, researchers who support some form of consolidation theory would assume that the earlier memory significates (those reflecting the target event and those reflecting the later session in which misleading information was given) would only be maintained as long as the system had the capacity to maintain them. The last significate, created at the time of recall, may be the one most likely to be conserved.

Figure 9.2 shows the source misattribution/direct retrieval, replacement, and multiple-trace models.

4. Research Data Relating to Nonconstructivist and Constructivist Models

4.1. The Nonimpairment Hypothesis

McCloskey and Zaragoza (1985) suggested that many subjects simply guess at the time of testing, since they do not recall the target item. Misled subjects would

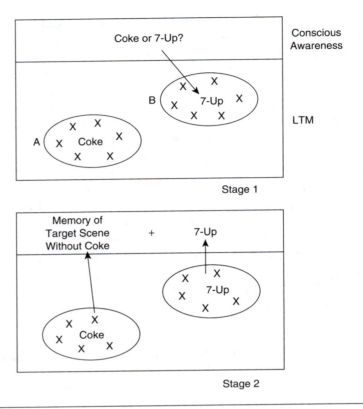

Figure 9.2a Effect of Misleading Postevent Information Under the Direct Retrieval Hypothesis

NOTE: Stage 1. Two episodic memories have been formed, one involving the Coke seen on a desk in the original slides and one involving a postevent session in which it was suggested that 7-Up had been seen in the slides. A recognition test is given in which the participants must decide between Coke and 7-Up. The cues contact the most recent memory first and so make contact with the 7-Up item.

Stage 2. The 7-Up item, having been contacted first, is retrieved. The retrieval blocks or inhibits access to the Coke item in the older memory. The memory consists of the desk and other elements seen in the slides, plus the belief that a can of 7-Up had been on the desk. The 7-Up is not "seen" on the desk in the memory, since it was not in fact on the desk.

be likely to guess the misleading item. However, according to the present view, the original memory, as coded in LTM, has not been affected in any way whatever. It is still coded at its original strength. This is the *nonimpairment* hypothesis.

In support of their guessing hypothesis, McCloskey and Zaragoza introduced a new procedure known as the *modified test*. In this approach, participants are misled in the usual way. In one study, the target was a wrench, and the misleading item a hammer. At the time of test, however, the participants were exposed to a forced-choice recognition test between the original target and a novel item, a screwdriver, which had not been seen during the experiment.

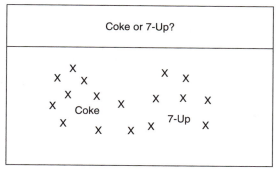

Stage 1

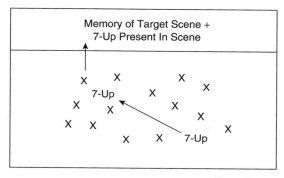

Stage 2

Figure 9.2b   The Replacement Model.

NOTE: Stage 1. The memories of the target episode and the episode in which misleading information was given are both coded in long-term memory (LTM). Although there is episodic-tag information at first, specifying which content belongs to the slides and which to the experimental session, this information is lost, or becomes unusable, with the passage of time.

Stage 2. At the time of test, cues contact the target memory, involving a room with a desk and a can of Coke. They also contact the record of the later session in which it was suggested that there was a can of 7-Up on the desk in the target episode. The memory function now has the information that the object on the desk (one object) was a can of Coke and was a can of 7-Up. The memory function will not accept logical impossibilities in the episode that will be reconstructed. One of the two items is therefore selected, and the other overridden. Here, the 7-Up item is selected, and the Coke item is overridden. This model assumes active reconstruction of the target memory at the time of recall.

Stage 3. The experienced memory includes the target scene, but with a can of 7-Up on the desk. When this version of the target event is generated as a memory, the 7-Up item replaces the Coke item in LTM. Both the experienced memory and the LTM codes have changed from the original.

The authors reasoned that true memory for the target would be at about a 30% level in both the misled and nonmisled groups. But now misled participants who did not recall the wrench, but who recalled hearing about a hammer, could not guess a hammer. They would then simply guess 50-50 between the two options, with about half the group (35%) choosing the target and half choosing the misleading item. This should lead to roughly 65% correct report of the target.

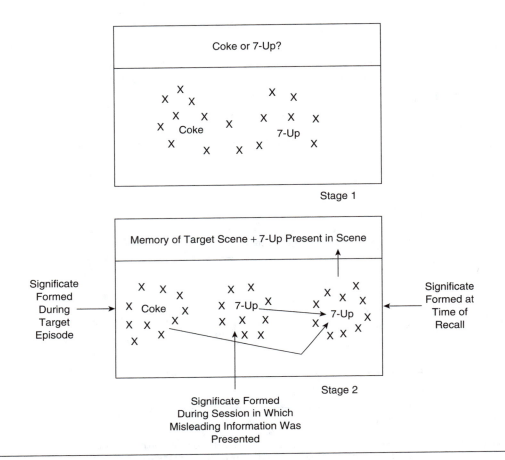

Figure 9.2c The Multiple Trace Model

Stage 1. The memories of the target episode and the episode in which misleading information was given are again both coded in LTM.

Stage 2. At the time of recall, the memory function develops—a new complex of information (a third memory significate) that will serve to generate the material entered into awareness. The original target episode is drawn on, to be part of this complex. Any additional relevant information may also be drawn on. The memory function again finds contradictory information in LTM, and will not accept contradictions in the memory significate. The 7-Up item is selected to be part of the new complex, and the Coke item is not selected. The 7-Up item is entered into the memory significate. The two bodies of earlier information (the target episode as first coded, and the session involving misinformation as first coded) remain in LTM. Both the experienced memory and the codes present in LTM have again changed. The system may not have the capacity to maintain all this information in LTM, and some of it may fail over time to be conserved. But there is no act of replacement.

The nonmisled participants would be in the same position. Thirty percent of them would recall the wrench, and 70% would guess. The 70% would guess 50-50 between the two options, also leading to a roughly 65% correct report of the target wrench.

The findings were as predicted. That is, there was an equal level of correct answers on the part of the misled and the nonmisled groups.

Zaragoza and McCloskey had shown that when the misleading item is not a possible candidate for response at the time of the test, misled participants recall the target item as well as nonmisled participants recall it. In another striking demonstration, the researchers showed slides in which a can of Coke was present on a desk and later suggested that the item had been a can of peanuts. In a recall test, participants were told, "The keys to the desk drawer were next to a soft drink can." And then, "What brand of soft drink was it?" Here, the conditions of testing again eliminated the misleading item (a can of peanuts). Again, misled participants recalled the target at as high a level as nonmisled participants.

The researchers' conclusion was that the target information was "there" in LTM, unchanged and unweakened by the misleading information.

4.2. The Impairment Hypothesis

One of the problems involved in the attempt to resolve the present issue empirically is that different theories provide different interpretations of the data.

Under the multiple-trace model, for instance, it would be expected that the elimination of the misleading information at the time of test would provide a high level of recall of the target information. Under this view, at the time of recall the memory function must select a candidate (relevant to the target item) to enter into the new memory significate. Under the tests described above, the available information would be: ———— It was a can of Coke: It was a can of peanuts: It was a soft drink can. ———— Given this weighting, the system would normally select the Coke. (Or, under a less rule-directed, associative approach, such as those embodied in connectionist nets, the greater level of activity would flow to the Coke item.) It is important to note that this involves preconscious processing events, engaged in generating a memory. The system is not "guessing" the Coke can. It is entering this object into the actual memory significate, and of course also into the memory as experienced.

In an earlier study, Loftus (1979a, chap. 6) had tested the replacement theory on the basis of a second-guess technique. Here, misled participants recalled what they believed they had seen in the original slides. They were then invited to make a guess at a second item.

Participants did not then report the other item. For instance, if subjects had mistakenly first recalled the foil, they did not, with their second-guess option, recall the target. This outcome is not consistent with a guessing hypothesis. If participants were guessing between two "available" items and were given a second choice, they would presumably then guess the second item.

Some research evidence now suggests that two factors, both of which can be identified as impairment, operate in studies that involve misleading information. The first of these is of course the alteration of the original memory (as may occur in the final memory significate relevant to the target episode). The second involves a possible, slight weakening of the codes formed at the time of the original event (the first memory significate).

Belli (1989) used a modified test in which the test items were presented singly. That is, the target (Coke) item was presented alone, such that participants were asked to respond either that it was the target or that it was not the target. And the novel (Sunkist) item was presented alone. By using this procedure, Belli was able to identify those individuals who did not recall the Coke but did recall the misleading item, since they would reject both the Coke and the Sunkist. Belli found not only that source misattribution (recalling the misleading item) was indeed operating but that in addition to this form of misrecall, participants under the misled condition could not remember the target item as well as participants under the nonmisled condition.

The data thus indicated that misleading information impairs the individual's ability to recall the target trace, *in addition to the effect of source misattribution.* That is, even among those individuals who do not report the misleading item, there is a slightly reduced chance of recalling the target.

Lindsay (1990) used a procedure known as the logic of opposition to further examine the question of target memory impairment. Participants were shown slides that included a target item. One of two misled groups was exposed to the misleading information in the usual way. This was the low discriminability group. A second misled group was also exposed to misleading information, but here the misleading content was introduced only minutes before the test. This was the high discriminability condition. All misled participants were told that the information provided in the second, misleading, session was inaccurate.

Under the high discriminability condition, participants' recall of the information presented in the misleading session, accompanied by a warning against this information, was strong, due to a recency effect. It was relatively easy *not* to mistake it for the target information. Many participants made no such error (that is, they did not report the incorrect, suggested item as the target item). But even among these individuals, correct memory for the original target was significantly lower than occurred under the control condition. Brainerd and Reyna (1988a) and Chandler (1991, 1992) reported similar data.

Eaken, Shreiber, and Sergeant-Marshall (2003) extended the research involved in strongly coded warnings by inducing their participants to actively think of the wrong item. In this study participants were warned, at the time of the test, that the information they had read (in the misleading-information session) was incorrect. They were also given a hint as to what that misleading information had been. The participants were thus thinking about, or focusing on, the wrong nontarget content.

The procedure resulted in a significant impairment in the ability to recall the target information. Participants did not report the incorrect item (which was not surprising, since they had just been warned against it), but the outcome was to make recall of the target lower than under conditions in which no such warning (and hint) are given.

This outcome can be characterized as some from of interference. Its source is not currently understood. It could be due to a blocking effect, as would be posited under classic interference theory. It could also be the result of some inability of the system to maintain two codes relating to a given item at the same level of strength as would be the case for a single code. This second interpretation reflects consolidation theory.

5. Is Incorrect Information Incorporated Into the Experienced Memory?

According to either a guessing or an incorrect retrieval interpretation of changed memories, incorrect memory content should not be experienced as being embedded in, or clearly a part of, the target episode. It should instead be content that the individual simply believes was present in the memory (Zaragoza, McCloskey, & Jamis, 1987). In contrast, under a constructivist view, the changed content would precisely be embedded in the memory.

The early research into this question suggested that participants did not recall misleading content as being embedded in the original memory (Lindsay & Johnson, 1989; Zaragoza & Koshminder, 1989). Later approaches, however, did find this to be the case (Zaragoza & Lane, 1994). Answering misleading questions appeared more likely to produce the embedded quality than simply reading misleading content. In many cases, participants not only recalled that the incorrect content had been present in the postexperimental (misleading) session but also recalled it as being in the original, target scene or passage.

Loftus, Feldman, and Dashiell (1995) showed a series of slides, followed, under the misled condition, by misleading information presented in a prose passage. Fifty-one percent of the misled participants recalled the target correctly. Loftus then asked those individuals in the misled condition who had not recalled correctly to describe the reasons for their response (that they had guessed, that they recalled reading about this material, and so on). Thirty-two percent of this group recalled the material as having been seen in the slides.

Of the 32% who traced their memory to the slides, 15% reported explicitly that they had seen it, and 17% reported that they recalled it from the slides. Forty-three percent of the participants recalled reading about this material (source misattribution from the misleading session), and 12% said they had guessed. Various other responses, such as the claim that the material seemed familiar, were given by a small number of the participants

6. Source Monitoring

Johnson and Raye (1981) suggested that it might be possible to distinguish between the phenomenological experience of true memory content and the experience of imagined or fantasized content. They hypothesized that real memories, as against imagined events, should possess more of the following characteristics:

1. Perceptual information

2. Information concerning context (time, place)

3. Semantic detail

4. Emotional content

Their hypothesis was supported.

Discriminating real from imagined happenings is not the same, however, as discriminating real from changed memories. In the case of deliberately imagined events, the information is developed at a conscious level. But changed or false memories, like real memories, are developed at an unconscious level. Further research was needed to see whether the same discrimination could be made between the two different forms of memory content.

The term *source monitoring* was developed for the attempt to distinguish between real and false memory content (Hashtroudi, Johnson, & Chrosniak, 1989; Johnson & Foley, 1984; Johnson et al., 1993; Lindsay & Johnson, 1991). It was again hypothesized that real memories would possess more of the four properties listed above than would false memories.

The researchers suggested that we can also deploy cognitive judgment in assessing memory content. If we appear to recall Jane as being critical of a friend but know that Jane never deploys a critical attitude, we may reject this content as a real memory.

A range of studies have now been conducted to determine whether it is in fact possible to distinguish between real and nonoriginal, generated memory content. It has been found that when a large number of studies are analyzed, the results often support a source monitoring hypothesis. That is, there may be more perceptual content, or semantic detail, across the studies as a whole in the case of real memories. Unfortunately, however, it is also the case that false memories can be characterized by vivid perceptual content, detail, or strong emotion. It has emerged that although groups of memories can be distinguished with regard to whether the content is real or false, individual memories cannot (Holmes, Waters, & Rajaram, 1998; Payne, Neuschatz, Lampinen, & Lynn, 1997; Roediger & McDermott, 1995; Schooler, Gerhard, & Loftus, 1986). Commonsense intuitions that changed material would necessarily appear weak, nonsensory, or at least in some way different from original memory content, have not been supported.

A related issue concerns the properties in a memory that incline people to believe that the memory reflects an actual event. Perceptual content has been shown to have this effect (Johnson, Raye, Foley, & Foley, 1981). It has also been found that when experimental participants are asked to imagine a given episode, they are more likely at a later time to believe the episode actually occurred, than if they had not attempted earlier to imagine it (Garry & Polaschek, 2000).

A further intriguing discovery has been that the strength of a memory may play an even greater role than perceptual qualities, when participants are trying to determine whether the memory is real or imagined (Hoffman, 1997). If a memory appears "stronger," it is more likely to be accepted as real.

In summary, although real memories may on average be characterized by more perceptual properties and more semantic detail than false memories, it is not possible to determine whether any individual episode in fact reflects an event that actually occurred. This is particularly the case in that remote memories, even when real, usually lack the detail of more recent memories. Also, false recollections can include clear perceptual content and may appear to be vivid.

PART II: EYEWITNESS TESTIMONY

If weak memories are subject to distortion, then there are clearly some troubling implications concerning testimony given by individuals who have witnessed a crime. Such events are likely to unfold quickly, to be confusing, and to alarm the witness. All these variables might tend to produce a weak original memory code. In addition, extended intervals of time may occur before the memory content is reported in the course of an investigation or trial, a situation likely to produce weak memory content, vulnerable to change.

A final concern is that police investigations frequently involve the repeated questioning of eyewitnesses, and there is reason to believe that repeated suggestions may have a greater influence on memory than a suggestion made only once (Wells & Olson, 2003).

1. Inference and Suggestion in Eyewitness Recollection

Loftus (1979a) reported a study performed by her graduate students. Two women and a man staged a robbery at a railway station. The women went for a cup of coffee, leaving a paper bag on a platform seat. The young man—their confederate—arrived and took the bag. The women on returning claimed loudly that they had been robbed; they said that their tape recorder had been stolen from the bag. They next took the names and addresses of individuals present on the platform. These people were later contacted by a presumed insurance agent. The witnesses' recollection of the supposed thief was often inaccurate. Even more striking, a number of them recalled seeing the tape recorder and some were able to describe it. There had in fact been no tape recorder in the bag. Similar data have been reported by Schooler, Clark, and Loftus (1988) and by Schooler et al. (1986).

The study described above involved a direct attempt to mislead the witnesses. There was suggestive postevent information. The question thus emerges as to whether eyewitness testimony is likely to be inaccurate in the absence of any confusing or misleading input.

Buckhout (1974) staged an attack on a professor at a college campus. The attack occurred in the open, with many potential witnesses present. The professor, although aware of the study, did not know which individual was going to attack him. The eyewitness descriptions of the attacker were low in accuracy. Worse, when the real attacker was shown in a lineup with other individuals, including one student who had been present at the scene of the attack (but had nothing to do with the attack), 25% of the witnesses selected the student as the attacker. Even more sobering in terms of witness credibility, the professor himself selected this same man.

There now exists an extensive body of literature supporting the claim that eyewitness testimony is often inaccurate. Testimony can be inaccurate even when the individual is sure that he or she can recall the event clearly (Tversky & Tuchin, 1989). The primary area of weakness appears to be that of correctly recognizing individuals who were seen engaged in criminal activity. It has been reported that mistaken eyewitness identification is in fact the single most common cause of innocent people being convicted of a crime.

1.2. Eyewitness Recollection of Events Not Involving Crime

In 1904, the German psychologist William Stern decided to examine the memory function for events that were given minimal attention (Stern, 1904/1982). He arranged for a collaborator, a Mr. Lippman, to come into a room where he was conducting a seminar. Mr. Lippman gave Stern an envelope, asked if he could examine some books, went to the bookcase, and left.

Eight days later the students were asked to recall the event. They typically recalled a good deal of information. But the information was often distorted. Under free recall, 25% of the content of the students' protocols was inaccurate. When they were asked a list of specific questions, as much as 50% of the content was inaccurate. Mr. Lippman's brown hair was recalled as black or blonde, his light brown hat became black, his gray jacket transmuted to blue or brown (across different protocols). Nobody remembered the color of either the jacket or the hat correctly. Three individuals recalled a full beard (he had a small pointed beard and moustache), two, a moustache alone, and two made him clean shaven. Only one person recalled that he had taken a book with him, also reporting that he had asked Stern if he might do this. Mr. Lippman had asked if he might look at the books, but not if he could take one with him.

In conclusion, it could be said that the basic facts of the episode were recalled correctly (an individual entered, spoke with the professor, left). But details, particularly perceptual details, showed a high level of distortion.

In 1992, an El Al plane left Schiphol Airport in Amsterdam, The Netherlands, and two of the plane's engines failed. The plane crashed into an 11-story apartment building. Forty-three people were killed.

Crombag, Wagenaar, and von Koppen (1996) described the results of an investigation of the local residents' memories concerning the tragedy. They had been interviewed 10 months after the event. They were asked, among other questions, "Did you see the televised film of the moment the plane hit the apartment building?" Fifty percent of the respondents replied that this was the case. In a follow-up study, two thirds of the respondents replied that this was the case. Many recalled details concerning what they had seen, such as the speed of the plane and whether it had been on fire when it crashed.

In fact no film had been made of the moment when the crash occurred. The events seen on television involved what happened after this moment, when television cameras arrived on the scene. (Note that the extended period of ten or more months would have made this a weak memory.)

2. Memory for Faces

It has been clearly established that we are poor at recognizing unfamiliar faces (Wells, 1993). This is in fact a difficult visual task, since the most central attributes of faces (eyes, mouth, etc.) are common to all.

When a new face is seen, we register external features, such as hair and face outline. These are not highly distinctive properties. Then, as a face is encountered on several occasions, we code more about the internal features such as eyes, nose, and mouth (Bonner & Burton, 2003).

There is neuropsychological evidence that different processing events occur in the recognition of familiar and unfamiliar faces.

It has been found that we are poor at identifying faces from pictures, and even at matching the face of someone who is physically present to a picture, as is needed, for instance, in checking images on credit cards. Kemp, Towell, and Pike (1997) found that when the individual was similar in appearance to the pictured face, fewer than 40% of these individuals were challenged. Henderson, Bruce, and Burton (2001) found, again, very poor recognition from typical TV camera images and a level of only 64% correct when the images, unlike the typical video camera product, were clear and distinct.

These data reflect unfamiliar faces, such as might be seen during the commission of a crime. The outcome is markedly different with familiar faces, where recognition tends to be good, even when the images are poor. Limited familiarity with a face appears to help in identification if clear images are involved, but may not be effective with poor-quality images. In general, women tend to be more accurate as witnesses than men.

The data described above involved the identification of individuals of the same race as the eyewitness. Identification of individuals of other races tends to be significantly worse, across all racial groups, an effect known as the ORB, or own race bias (Meissner & Brigham, 2001; Shapiro & Penrod, 1986). This phenomenon has notably bad implications for the criminal justice system, in which members of one race may be involved in identifying members of another (Doyle, 2001). No relation has been found between racial attitudes and the ORB, however. As described above, most facial recognition is holistic of type and is now known to involve an area of the brain labeled as the FFA, or *fusiform face area* (Tanaka & Farah, 1993; Tong, Nakayama, Moscovitch, Weinrib, & Kanwisher, 2000). It appears that holistic analysis is more effective in coding for faces, under conditions of limited exposure, than focusing on individual features as such. Also, we apply a different form of processing (more global, more spatial) to faces than to objects (Maurer, Le Grand, & Mondloch, 2002). Yet the data suggest that identification of individuals of other races may not involve the usual kind of holistic processing but focuses more on individual features (Rhodes, Brake, Tan, & Taylor, 1989; Tanaka, Kiefer, & Bukach, 2004). The features that draw attention appear to be those that provide clues to racial identity (Levin, 2000; Maclin & Malpass, 2003). Also, identification of an individual as belonging to another race is achieved very quickly, faster even than gender identification (Ito & Urland, 2003). It has been found that there is less FFA engagement in cross-race than same-race identification, an outcome that supports the hypothesis of less global processing (Golby, Gabrieli, Chiao, & Eberhardt, 2001). In summary, cross-race identification appears to focus on features related to race, which are analyzed very quickly but do not provide good individuation of the face from other faces at a later point in time.

It has been suggested that positive affect tends to widen the scope of processing, shifting it toward a more global, as against local, approach (Fredrickson & Branagan, 2005). Johnson and Fredrickson (2005) examined this hypothesis by means of inducing joyous, fear-based, or neutral emotions in their participants, either prior to exposure to test faces or prior to a recognition test of the faces. The emotions were induced through watching a comic or horrific video. In conformity with the theoretical prediction, same-race bias was completely eliminated under the "joy" condition, while persisting in the other two conditions.

3. Eyewitnesses and Investigative Procedures

3.1. Eyewitnesses' Characteristics and Memory Accuracy

Psychologists have been concerned to determine whether any personal characteristics of eyewitnesses may be linked to accurate testimony. Very few correlations have in fact been found. Occupation does not predict accuracy (Ainsworth, 1981), nor does intelligence (Brown, Lewis, & Monk, 1977), with the possible exception of individuals at the lowest end of the scale (Wells & Olson, 2003). A wide range of personality characteristics have been found to show no relation to the reliability of eyewitnesses' reports. Young children and the elderly do worse in lineup identification in which the culprit is not present (that is, they are more likely to pick an innocent person from the lineup). But if the culprit is present, these groups perform as well as others (Pozzulo & Lindsay, 1998).

Individuals who are high self-monitors perform less well than low self-monitors in lineup identification (Hosch & Platz, 1984). A high self-monitor is someone who adapts his or her behavior to cues for what is socially appropriate. Individuals who are high in chronic anxiety perform better than the average person. Individuals who are field independent perform worse. Field-independent individuals are people who tend to differentiate parts of a visual field from the whole.

3.2. Eyewitness Confidence and Performance

It is known that jurors place more weight on the testimony of individuals who appear confident than on those who do not (Cutler, Penrod, & Stuve, 1988; Wells, Lindsay, & Ferguson, 1979). A 1972 decision of the Supreme Court suggested that jurors should use confidence as a measure of the probable reliability of their testimony.

Research into the issue has found little support for this position, however. Most studies have found that the relationship is weak (Daffenbacher, 1980; Sporer, Penrod, Read, & Cutler, 1995). Among individuals who do make an identification, a correlation across studies between confidence and accuracy has been estimated at 0.37 (Sporer et al., 1995). But the correlation decreases under a variety of conditions, one of which involves a situation in which the witness has been given confirming input, perhaps at the time of a lineup. This greatly enhances confidence whether the identification was accurate or not. And it appears that this kind of feedback often is given by the detective conducting the lineup procedure (Wells & Olson, 2003).

Witnesses who supply a detailed description of a suspect are not more accurate in identification than witnesses who supply a minimal description (Daffenbacher, 1991; Wells, 1985). In some cases, a negative relation has been found between the extent of verbal description and accurate identification (Geiselman, Schroppel, Tubridy, Kinishi, & Rodriguez, 2000). It has also been established that lay observers, such as jurors, are not good at estimating witness accuracy; they tend to "overbelieve" the witness.

However, one strong predictor of accuracy is speed. Accurate judgments are usually made quickly (Dunning & Perretta, 2002). Of responses made within 10 to 12 seconds, 90% have been found to be accurate.

3.3. Type of Lineup

Not surprisingly, the type of lineup has been found to notably influence eyewitness accuracy. When "fillers" (nonsuspect people participating in the lineup) do not in general resemble the culprit, witnesses tend to identify an innocent individual who does bear at least some resemblance. Trying to devise an optimal form of lineup, however, has proved difficult. If fillers are chosen deliberately to be similar to the suspect, this can produce an effect where the suspect is picked from the lineup simply because he represents a central tendency for the group as a whole! (Wells & Olson, 2003). In the traditional lineup, where all individuals are shown together, witnesses are at risk for picking the person who most appears to resemble the culprit. The suspect may not be the culprit but may resemble him or her. Sequential lineup, in which each individual is presented alone, overcomes this difficulty and indeed has been found to reduce errors by 50% (Steblay, Dysart, Fulero, & Lindsay, 2001). But they are also somewhat less likely than traditional lineups to produce any form of identification (including accurate identifications).

3.4. Conclusion

Abundant evidence has been developed in support of the view that eyewitness testimony can be unreliable. When DNA testing became available within this context in the 1990s, more than a hundred convicted individuals were shown to have been innocent. Of these, most (more than 75%) had been convicted on the basis of eyewitness testimony (Loftus, 2004; Scheck & Kinicki, 2000; Wells & Bradfield, 1998). The figures are the more troubling in that the present cases, involving individuals who could be DNA tested, reflect no more than a small subset of people who have been convicted of crime. There is undoubtedly a very large group of individuals in prison today who are the innocent victims of mistaken eyewitness identification.

4. Emotion and Eyewitness Testimony

It appeared a plausible assumption that eyewitness memory might be subject to error because the experience of seeing a crime would involve intense emotion, possibly of a kind capable of disrupting recall. According to the Yerkes-Dodson law (Yerkes & Dodson, 1908), developed on the basis of animal studies, memory improves as arousal in the subject increases, up to a certain point. Once a very high level of arousal is reached, the recall function deteriorates, decreasing as arousal increases. The shape of the curve for memory is thus described as an inverted U.

Researchers from the 1970s to the present have explored the relationship between emotion and memory. If the Yerkes-Dodson law can be applied to affect in humans, then very intense affect might serve to weaken the memory function.

4.1. Emotion and Memory

Studies in this area have produced conflicting results. Some indicate that strong emotion impairs memory, while others suggest a facilitating effect.

Baddeley (1972) simulated an emergency during the course of which servicemen, who believed the emergency to be real, were issued detailed instructions. They had greater difficulty in remembering the instructions than was the case with a control group.

Kramer, Buckhout, Fox, and Widman (1991) reported that experimental participants recalled traumatic surgery slides more poorly than nontraumatic slides. Kuehn (1974), analyzing police reports, found that the victims of markedly violent crimes, such as rape or assault, recalled fewer details concerning the attacker than did victims of milder crimes, such as robberies.

But other studies reported that emotion enhanced recall. Yuille and Tollestrup (1992) found that witnesses to murder showed a strong memory function, including the accurate recall of trivial details. An alternative approach has been to compare the memories of victims of crimes with the memories of bystanders. It appears reasonable to assume that the victim will experience a stronger level of emotion than an eyewitness. Some studies have found superior recall for victims (Christianson & Hubinette, 1993; Hosch & Bothwell, 1990), while others have found no difference. But even the latter studies fail to support the hypothesis that strong emotion impairs memory.

It has been suggested that a strongly emotional event may draw attention to the central or important elements of the event, and so facilitate memory for such elements, while draining attention from noncritical details. The view is known as the *Easterbrook hypothesis*. According to the Easterbrook model, strong emotion has the effect of narrowing the range of cues deployed when we attend to an event (the cue-utilization hypothesis). As a result, recall of general or irrelevant detail declines. If these assumptions are correct, the strength of a memory would of course appear different when only central information was measured, as against a condition in which all information was measured.

Loftus and Burns (1982) presented their participants with two versions of a film depicting a bank robbery. In one, the traumatic version, a boy is abruptly shot in the face. The nontraumatic version of the film was identical except that the shooting did not occur. Participants in the nontraumatic version recalled more detail from the beginning of the film. In particular, they were able to identify the number on the boy's jersey, seen immediately before the shooting, significantly better than participants who viewed the traumatic version (58% accuracy vs. 28% accuracy). The recognition level in the traumatic group was in fact very poor, since they were shown four possible numbers, such that a chance level would have been 25%. The study indicated that a traumatic event, even when viewed on film, can seriously impair recollection of stimuli seen just before the event.

The Easterbrook hypothesis also predicts that if a weapon is involved in a crime, it is likely to draw the attention of eyewitnesses, so that they may be weak in recalling other details (the *weapon focus hypothesis*). Empirical support for this position has been reported by Loftus, Loftus, and Messo (1987) and Maass and Kohnken (1989), among others.

The role of emotion is further complicated by data suggesting that emotion differs in its effect on memory across time. Typically, an emotional item or event is better recalled after a delay, as compared to a nonemotional item or event. It has also been found that emotionally negative word items are recognized more slowly than neutral items under immediate testing, but that the effect reverses after a week's retention interval (Kleinsmith & Kaplan, 1963, 1964).

Recent research has attempted to identify the interactions between emotion, the centrality or noncentrality of the relevant information, and time. Burke, Heuer, and Reisberg (1992), for instance, found that for emotional as against neutral content: (1) central (important) information was retained equally well under immediate testing, (2) central information was retained at a significantly higher level under delayed testing, (3) trivial information was retained more poorly under delayed testing, but (4) trivial information that was related to the important information, although of no importance in and of itself, was also retained significantly better under the delay condition. This kind of content, called "central details," might involve, for instance, the color of an important protagonist's coat.

4.2. Anxiety and Misleading Information

A range of models concerning the effect of anxiety on memory have been developed. According to one view, a state of anxiety will draw on the available processing capacity for a cognitive task, thus reducing competence. Empirical support for this outcome has been provided by Gudjonsson, (1988) and Wolfradt and Meyer

(1998). An alternative view is that anxiety will lead the individual to process information with more care and rigor, out of fear of making mistakes (Eysenck & Calvo, 1992). Clearly, both positions could be right, depending on the degree of anxiety involved. This form of emotion is likely to follow the inverted U that has been found for arousal as such.

Ridley and Clifford (2004) conducted a study in which some participants were misled, concerning the kidnapping of a baby seen on video, and some participants were not misled. A state of "anxiety" was induced in half of the participants under each condition, prior to viewing the video, prior to the misleading session, or prior to test. The anxiety-producing manipulation involved telling the participants that their performance would be filmed and evaluated by a mock jury. It should be noted that this procedure is likely to produce a state of increased caution and rigor in the way in which participants approach the issues involved in memory. It might not, in many participants, actually invoke anxiety, so much as increased attention.

The results were that nonmisled participants recalled the incidents in the video equally well under conditions of high and low anxiety. Misled participants, however, performed better under all the high-anxiety conditions (anxiety at encoding, at the time of being misled, and at test). The authors reviewed several possible explanations for this outcome, including complex demand characteristics, but were inclined to support the view that the anxiety condition produced more rigorous processing at the time of retrieval. For instance, low-anxiety participants may have been inclined to accept the version of the video that was most easily accessed, which would often have been the misleading information , since that information was the last presented. In contrast, high-anxiety participants may have worked harder to evaluate the origin of contradictory information.

The difference between the high- and low-anxiety groups was small, but significant. The authors noted that a small difference of this kind would be expected, since many variables must operate to influence correct responses. One would be simply the strength of the memory function; some participants only would have a clear recollection of the original video (Jaschinski & Wentura, 2002). A further intriguing finding mentioned by the authors was that high levels of chronic, or trait, anxiety in a participant were later found to correlate with accepting misinformation, while temporarily induced anxiety (state anxiety) correlated, as found here, with the tendency to reject misinformation. This could relate to the level of experienced anxiety, just as the level of arousal has different effects on memory in general.

4.3. Emotion and Context Reinstatement

A technique known as the cognitive interview, described in Chapter 6, Section 3, has been used with some success to improve eyewitness memories of a crime. In the cognitive interview, eyewitnesses are asked to return to their memories of the target episode and recall it in different ways.

Brown (2003) examined the effects of reinstating the context (context reinstatement or CR) of an episode, as in the cognitive interview, under either a neutral condition or one of enhanced arousal. Previous studies had suggested that CR is not effective when emotional episodes are involved (Ready, Bothwell, & Brigham, 1997), while the approach improves memory in the case of nonemotional events (Smith & Vela, 1992).

Brown reported that CR enhanced recognition in the case of nonarousing events, but not, when overall data were involved, in the case of arousing events. It seemed that, in accordance with the Easterbrook hypothesis, participants did not code strongly for peripheral—and thus, context—details in the arousing condition. Here, CR even *diminished* recognition rates for peripheral information. For the target emotional incident itself (which was only a small component of the overall materials), CR produced a very mild enhancement.

The findings thus supported the view that an emotional event does draw processing capacity from peripheral information to central information. As a result, CR techniques tend to be relatively ineffective for emotional events, since they depend essentially on background information associated with the target episodes, rather than on the central events themselves. In the case of neutral episodes, however, CR appears quite effective.

Summary

Researchers have shown that misleading postevent information can alter a reported memory. Nonconstructivists believe that the effect is due either to incorrect guessing or to source misattribution: mistaking a nontarget memory for the target (incorrect retrieval). According to an influential constructivist view, a complex of information is formed in LTM at the time of retrieval. This complex generates the experienced memory, and when the memory changes it is because the information in this complex has changed from the original codes. The original codes, however, are not altered (the multiple memory hypothesis).

Recent research has shown that not only can misleading information alter a memory, substituting for the original content in some cases, but it appears to also slightly weaken the original memory codes.

It has been found that when an item in a memory changes from the original, participants often recall that item as being embedded in the original memory.

Source monitoring involves the attempt to distinguish between a "true" and a changed memory. No method has been found for making a reliable distinction in the case of individual memories.

When misleading suggestions are made to individuals concerning objects or events related to an episode, they may later recall these elements as having been actually present. This can occur in natural situations as well as in the laboratory. Eyewitness recall is quite unreliable, human memory for unfamiliar faces being markedly weak. There are few indicators that can distinguish a good from a poor witness. It has been found that sequential lineups produce a higher level of accurate identification than occurs with traditional lineups in which many individuals are presented simultaneously.

Strong emotion has been found to influence memory, including eyewitness accounts, variably. In some cases, memory is enhanced, and in some, it is impaired.

The difference may be due to the level of intensity and anxiety involved in the emotion. In crime situations, attention appears to shift more to central details, at the expense of peripheral details. The Easterbrook hypothesis involves the view that when a weapon is present, attention will be drawn heavily to the weapon, again at the expense of recall of other details. The influence of emotion is often greatest after a delay.

Discussion

The reality of memory change has now been clearly demonstrated. The critical area of disagreement today centers on whether there is change at the level of the unconscious codes in LTM relevant to the memory. In spite of several decades of research into the question, the issue has not been resolved. Support for a guessing hypothesis has not been strong, but both a source misattribution/mistaken retrieval interpretation and the assumption that the memory system reconstructs the original memory at the time of recall (creating a new memory significate at that time) are compatible with the available data. Either (but not both) could be the correct explanation of memory change. A theoretical argument against the incorrect-retrieval hypothesis, however, involves the fact that often very precise "new" information is fitted into the target memory, with nothing of the surrounding, nontarget memory accompanying it. If cues have simply contacted the nontarget memory, more of that content might be expected to be retrieved.

The fact that there is no litmus test for invalid memories is clearly an important finding with relevance to daily life. Such memory content may in some cases even be vivid and appear "strong." Related to this issue, it has become clear that eyewitness testimony can be unreliable, and equally clear that there has been and continues to be profound miscarriage of justice because of this phenomenon.

The data on emotion and memory appear at times to be contradictory. However, human beings experience a range of different emotions. It might therefore be naive to assume that this factor would have a single influence on memory. There appears to be support for the view that sudden, shocking affect can disrupt recall, while strong (or even extremely strong) but nondisruptive emotion may have the opposite effect. For instance, individuals who are victims of a crime or who witness a crime, but remain calm, may experience a strong memory function at a later time.

This chapter has focused on memory change. It may be worth emphasizing that most memories that appear strong are essentially accurate, particularly at the more generalized level. If you remember catching a bus this morning, you can be pretty sure that you did catch the bus. Recollection of a similar episode 10 years in the past, however, may be less reliable.

CHAPTER 10

Long-Term Memory

Higher-Order Structures

Overview

1. Research has indicated that participants do infer material when they read prose passages and that they code the inferred material as part of the memory.

2. Bransford demonstrated that when we read a prose passage that is not meaningful (does not make sense), recall of the passage is poor. If a cue is given that makes the material comprehensible, recall significantly improves.

3. Mental models are four-dimensional conceptualizations of events read about, heard about, or recalled. Readers of prose passages appear to keep track of spatial context, the passage of time, causal relations, and other properties present in texts.

4. Schank developed a model of higher-order structures, identified as knowledge structures, used in daily life. One such structure is a script. A script specifies the events that occur in highly familiar situations, such as eating in a restaurant. Schank also identified the roles in recall of causal chains and knowledge concerning human goals.

5. W. Kintsch's model of prose comprehension includes three levels: text base, propositional, and situation model.

6. Research into memory for prose (prose discourse) has supplied extensive support for the view that causal relations play a critical role in providing memory strength. Researchers have also attempted to determine exactly what kinds of inferences are generated when we read prose.

Learning Objectives

1. Knowledge of models of higher-order structure and the role that these play in recall.

2. Knowledge of Schank's model of knowledge structures.

3. Knowledge of Kintsch's model of prose comprehension.

4. Knowledge of research involving memory for prose material, including knowledge of the debate over inferences and the type of inferences that have been shown to operate in prose recall.

According to Bartlett's constructivist model of memory, described in Chapter 8, content that has meaning is better retained in memory than random or nonmeaningful content. Also, and critically, meaningfulness is provided when information can fit a higher-order schema or structure (or more exactly, a set of structures).

Since the 1970s, a number of theories have been developed concerning the nature of the higher-order constituents. A common term used today within this context is *knowledge structure*. Knowledge structures are generally assumed to provide understanding of an event, prose passage, or other material. There has also been emphasis in current research on the role of these elements in providing information that may not be directly seen or heard during an episode or that may not be directly stated in a body of text.

Research in this area has involved the use of various forms of spoken—or, more commonly, written—language (discourse) materials, such as narrative or expository texts. The term *inference* is generally used when the system generates new content: that is, content not present in the original passage or event. The present chapter examines research into inferential processes in memory as well as models of higher-order structures. The final pages cover current experimental research into the cognitive events that occur when we read and understand prose.

1. Inferences

Early research into the nature of inferences focused on whether inferred material does in fact become part of a given memory. An alternative possibility would be that original mnemonic content and inferred content both exist but can be distinguished from one another.

Sulin and Dooling (1974) presented their subjects with prose passages in which the characters were identified by different names, across conditions. One such passage read as follows:

Carol Harris was a problem child from birth. She was wild, stubborn and violent. By the time Carol turned eight, she was still unmanageable. Her parents were very concerned about her mental health. There was no good institution for her problem in her state.

In the alternative condition, the name Helen Keller was substituted for Carol Harris. A week after reading the passage, subjects were given a recognition test. Critical sentences in the test included, "She was deaf, dumb, and blind." This datum had not been present in the passage. Fifty percent of the Helen Keller subjects nonetheless "recognized" the sentence as having been in the passage.

An area of dispute within the field of memory research focused in the 1970s on whether inferences were developed only at the time of recall (to fill in gaps in the memory) or whether information was also inferred from background knowledge at the time of encoding. Thorndyke (1977) presented a prose passage to his subjects, designed such that it would be necessary to construct inferences if the passage was to be comprehended. Subjects read the material repeatedly and were tested after each reading. If inferences are generated the time of retrieval only to fill gaps in the memory content, then inferred material should decrease as the memory function grows stronger. If, on the other hand, inferences are generated at the time of encoding (as a means of making sense of the material), inferred content should not decrease over time. Thorndyke found that inferred material in fact increased slightly as the memory function strengthened.

2. Spatial Contexts

According to the model described above, background knowledge is often deployed when we attempt to understand prose. It has been claimed that an important component of such knowledge reflects the generation of a *spatial context for the actions or events described* (Bransford & Johnson, 1973; de Vega, 1995; Gernsbacher, Goldsmith, & Robertson, 1992; Haenggi, Kintsch, & Gernsbacher, 1995). Bransford and Johnson (1972) presented the following material to their participants:

If the balloons popped the sound wouldn't be able to carry since everything would be too far away from the correct floor. A closed window would also prevent the sound from carrying, since most buildings tend to be well insulated. Since the whole operation depends on the steady flow of electricity, a break in the middle of the wire would also cause problems. Of course, the fellow could shout, but the human voice is not loud enough to carry that far. An additional problem is that the string could break on the instrument. Then there would be no accompaniment to the message. It is clear that the best situation would involve less distance. Then there would be fewer potential problems. With face to face contact, the least number of things could go wrong. (p. 719)

The participants were asked to recall the passage, under the following conditions:

1. No context 1: In this condition, the subject heard the passage once.

2. No context 2: Here the passage was heard twice.

3. Context before: In this condition a picture was shown before the passage was read. The picture showed the situation that was the basis for the prose passage; that is, it provided a spatial context.

4. Context after: The passage was read once, and the picture was shown after the reading.

5. Jumbled context: A picture was shown that included the same stimuli as the context picture, but rearranged so that the correct spatial relations between the people and objects in the passage were not portrayed.

The Context and Jumbled Context pictures are shown in Figures 10.1 and 10.2, respectively.

Recall was significantly higher under Condition 3 (context before) than all other conditions. The other conditions, including Condition 2 (context after), produced markedly weak recall and no significant difference was found among them.

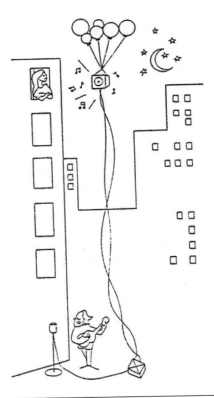

Figure 10.1   The Correct Context Picture

SOURCE: From Bransford, J. D. & Johnson, M. K., "Contextual prerequisites for understanding," in *Journal of Memory and Language*, *11*, copyright © 1972. Reprinted with permission of Elsevier.

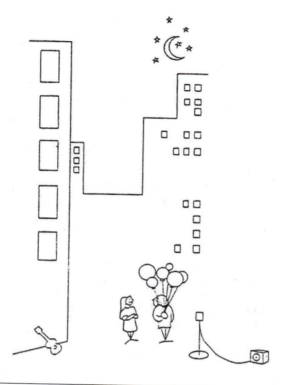

Figure 10.2   The Jumbled Context Picture

SOURCE: From Bransford, J. D. & Johnson, M. K., "Contextual prerequisites for understanding,"
in *Journal of Memory and Language, 11,* copyright © 1972. Reprinted with permission of Elsevier.

The picture had made it possible for the subjects to understand the prose passage. If the picture was presented before the passage, that general understanding
could be brought to bear in the generation of relatively strong codes. It appeared
that the Context After condition did not help the participants because they had
been unable to hold the details of the passage long enough to reinterpret them
when they finally saw the context picture.

The picture had provided a spatial context. This showed how the elements in the
passage related to one another. As a result, when a part of the scene was described or
discussed the subject could "see" (understand) the referents for the words in the passage, and how the named person or object related to the other named person or
object. For instance, the line "if the string broke the sound would not carry, because
everything would be too far away from the correct floor" could be understood, given
the context picture, because the reader would know that "the string" referred to the
string holding the speaker up in the air, that "the sound" referred to the sound from
the speaker, and that the breaking of the string would result in the speaker falling to
the ground, thus taking it away from the floor of the building where the woman sat
listening. Seeing these referents and relationships provided the property of meaningfulness. And because the passage had become meaningful, recall was strengthened.

The Jumbled Context condition had been included to control for a cueing explanation of the data. It could have been argued that it was the sight of the objects and people in the picture, not the provision of meaningfulness to the passage as a whole, that enhanced recall under the Context Before condition.

Note that this research was informed by a theory concerning meaningfulness. According to the theory, a passage appears coherent when we can see how all the relations and interactions among the elements described in the passage could physically occur in three-dimensional space.

Not all researchers have accepted a context interpretation of the present data, however. Alba and Hasher (1983), for instance, argued that the picture simply provided a different way of interpreting the meaning of the words and provided local connections between the sentences of the text. According to this view, the subjects did not construct a three-dimensional context, and map interactions occurring within that context, when they saw the picture under Condition 3.

3. Context Effects: A Theory of Spatial Relations, Motions, and Constraints

Bransford and McCarrell (1974) described a theoretical model of the functions that are in play when a prose passage makes sense—appears meaningful—as against the passage being incoherent. It was this model that informed the balloons passage study.

The authors noted that words are generally rejected as the units of meaning in a prose passage. That is, the meaning of a text is not the sum total of all its individual word meanings. The same is true of sentences. Instead, as we read a passage, we establish a context in which the events are seen to unfold. This context is often a four-dimensional scene. As the content of each sentence is established, it is fit into the developing scene.

There is a theory of meaning according to which meaning codes are representations of the relations and motions that can occur between objects and people. The authors suggested that a model of this kind is appropriate both for real-life events and for the understanding of written passages. Suppose an individual encounters a long metal stick with two prongs at one end. If he has never seen anything like this before, it will carry no meaning for him. He could stare at the object and examine it, but still not know "what it was." (Note that an image does not appear to provide a sense of meaning.) But if he then saw someone take the stick, spear a marshmallow on it and toast the marshmallow over a fire, the stick would acquire meaning. It would now be understood as an instrument for cooking food over an open flame.

According to the present argument, the meaning of a thing is a code specifying what it can do: that is, the actions and relations with other things of which it is capable. Some of the "doing" may be passive. For instance, a large tree may provide shade.

However, objects and people are not typically restricted to the performance of a single activity. Most objects can move in many ways and can interact with other objects in many ways. It follows that, of a thing's possible actions and relations, only a subset will be involved in any specific situation. A toasting fork could be used to prop open a window or dig a hole or hold down papers. But typically, only one of these possible actions will be involved in a single context.

Given these considerations, when we read a prose passage, we will identify the constituents (things, people) in the passage and their interactions with one another. For each constituent we would generally know the actions that it is capable of performing. For instance, I know the activities (active or passive) that could be expected of kettles and chairs; I also know the activities that are not possible for kettles and chairs. If a possible activity is described in a prose passage, then the passage to that extent appears meaningful. If, on the other hand, I read, "The three-legged chair woke up and made breakfast," I will feel that the material is incoherent.

Context now plays a critical role. The described movements of an object are possible if they constitute a subset of the whole repertoire of that object. But certain objects (and relations) are possible in one context, but not in another. Tom is capable of tapping someone on the shoulder. But if Tom and Jane are separated by the width of a garden, it will not make sense to claim that Tom actually did tap Jane on the shoulder.

According to the present model, then, a prose passage will appear meaningful if

1. the actions and relations of the constituents described in the passage are possible for them in general,

2. A and B interact, this specific interaction is possible, and

3. the interactions and relation are possible within the specific context established by the passage.

The last point is the final constraint placed on meaning.

Of course, if all these criteria are met (as in the balloons passage) but the reader cannot see *how* all these interactions, and situations, relate to one another, then the passage will not appear meaningful.

3.1. Standard Prose Passages:
The Generation of Spatial Context

In the passage described above, it was not possible for most readers to generate a frame that would make the passage coherent, without additional information (the picture). In the case of most prose passages, however, the relevant context can be established as the material is read. It can usually be established quickly.

According to the present tradition, the context may provide (through inference) additional information. This information will normally be entered into the memory.

Bransford, Barclay, and Franks (1972) presented the following two versions of a very short story to their participants, across different experimental conditions.

Version A: A beaver hit a log that a turtle was sitting on and the log flipped over from the shock. The turtle was very surprised by the event.

Version B: A beaver hit a log that a turtle was sitting beside and the log flipped over from the shock. The turtle was very surprised by the event.

A recognition test included the sentence: A BEAVER HIT THE LOG AND KNOCKED THE TURTLE INTO THE WATER. Individuals who had been exposed to Version A generally claimed that they had heard this statement in the original passage. Individuals exposed to Version B claimed that they had not heard this statement. The participants in the experiment had clearly established a physical scene, in which the implied spatial relations between the turtle, beaver, and log were all tracked.

4. Mental Models

Johnson-Laird (1980) suggested that when we read or hear about a given episode, we establish a *mental model* concerning it. This is a representation of the general situation implied by the episode. It would include spatial and temporal factors, as well as other relevant content. We then trace the unfolding events within that framework.

Bransford's work, as described above, provided an example of one major aspect of a mental model: the spatial context. A large number of studies have subsequently supported the claim that we establish spatial contexts for new information, where possible, and that the information that can be inferred from such contexts may be entered into the subsequent memory (Glenberg, Meyer, & Lindem, 1987; Haenggi et al., 1995; O'Brien & Albrecht, 1992; Rinck, Williams, Bower, & Becker, 1996).

Researchers in this area have provided additional data concerning factors such as causal relations, and the goals and the emotions of individuals described as they live through a given episode (Morrow, 1994; Zwaan & Radvansky, 1998; Zwaan, Radvansky, & Witten, 2002). The implications of these variables appear to be mapped, as we read or hear about an event. Another important aspect of a mental or situation model involves temporal information.

Anderson, Garrod, and Sanford (1983) presented their participants with two versions of a story, involving "Jenny," who went to the movies. A projectionist was mentioned. Later in the story, it was stated that 7 hours later the film was forgotten, because a certain individual was fast asleep. Under one condition, the referent to that individual was "she," and under another, it was "he." Participants reading "he" hesitated at this pronoun, while participants reading "she" did not. They had tracked time across the story. Seven hours later, when Jenny would no longer be at the movie house, the referent "he" (which referred back to the projectionist) no longer made sense. But this could only have been understood if the passage of time had been tracked, along with the possible locations of the characters across time.

Other studies have supported the claim that we map the passage of time when we read of both fictional and nonfictional events. In particular, it has been found that if a temporal context is established and then at some later time incompatible information is presented (that does not fit the implications of the original temporal context), participants again read the content that doesn't fit more slowly and recall it less well than they recall compatible information (Bestgen & Vonk, 1995; Ohtsuka & Brewer, 1992; Rinck, Haehnel, & Becker, 2001; Zwaan, 1996).

5. Story Schemas

Rumelhart (1975, 1977, 1980) found that traditional folk stories have an underlying, invariant organization. He identified this as a *story schema* or *story grammar*. The grammar (learned on the basis of experience with folk stories) specified the kind of events that are present in a simple story and the fashion in which they are related. Such stories begin with a setting component (time and place), the introduction of a character or characters, followed by an episode component, in which something happens, and so on.

A range of studies later showed that material that fits with the relevant story schema structure is well recalled, while material that violates the schema (such as events occurring out of the usual order) is poorly recalled (Black & Bower, 1979; J. M. Mandler, 1979, 1982, 1984; Mandler & De Forest, 1979; Omanson, 1982; Trabasso & Sperry, 1985). In addition, when a schema constituent was removed from a story subjects tended to infer it and also recall it as having been present in the story (Glenn, 1978; Whaley, 1981).

Not all researchers agree that a story schema was operating to provide these effects, however. It has been argued that the same outcome can be provided by associations present among individual words in the relevant prose passages (Alba & Hasher, 1983; Weaver & Dickinson, 1982).

6. Schank's Model of Knowledge Structures: Goal-Based Theory

The first data reflecting story schemas were generated within the context of rigidly organized stories. Most prose material does not, however, reflect a highly rigid or stereotyped structure. There was thus clearly a need for models that could be applied to nonstandardized material and in 1977 Schank and Abelson published a theory that met this requirement.

Their approach centered on the role (in human understanding) played by our knowledge of goals and of causal relations.

The first Schank and Abelson model included a higher-order constituent known as a *script*. A script involves relatively standardized information.

6.1. Scripts

A script is a higher-order structure, one that codes information concerning stereotyped events, such as what happens when we visit a restaurant or a doctor's office. Scripts are developed after extended experience with the target event.

A script provides the following:

1. Understanding of the event

2. Memory strength

3. The capacity to infer relevant information

We begin to build a body of knowledge concerning these events across childhood. After a good deal of experience, we typically develop a script in which nonrepeated elements have been dropped and only constantly repeated elements are retained. The script consists of a series of typical events, objects, and people. In the case of the restaurant script, the events would involve entering the restaurant, sitting down, ordering, eating, paying, and leaving. The people, or "actors" involved, would be waiters, waitresses, other customers, and a cashier, and the objects—the "props"—would be tables, chairs, a menu, and so on.

As we live through an episode in which we visit a restaurant, the events that actually occur are mapped against the events specified in the script. If the two match (which they generally do), we feel that the event is making sense. The fitting of the events that occurred onto the script also heightens the relevant memory function.

Scripts provide the possibility of inferring forgotten material. If I fail to strongly encode the fact that a menu was present during a restaurant episode, I can easily infer this information later on the basis of my restaurant script. I will therefore recall the menu. As claimed originally by Bartlett, this reconstructive work may occur either at a conscious or at an unconscious level. That is, in some cases I may infer information but not be aware of the act of inference. Thus, my memory of a visit to a restaurant will typically consist of the activation of original codes, established as I lived through the episode and information provided by my restaurant script.

It is likely that the memory function is strengthened by this form of operation, in that the individual does not have to code for each important fact concerning a visit to a restaurant. Many of the facts are already coded. Only nonstandard, or irregular, content has to be established across the actual episode.

When an individual encounters some new but recurring fact about restaurants (for example, many fast food chains require that you pay before eating), the script is modified to include both the old and the new information, with a pointer indicating a change in the original pattern.

The authors assumed in 1977 that each script existed as a body of knowledge that was stored as a unit in long-term memory (LTM). This assumption—of a single body of information, stored as a unit—was later rejected (Schank, 1982, 1999).

6.2. Experimental Research Into Scripts

According to the script concept, we may recall chairs or a menu present during a restaurant episode not because these items were strongly coded in memory, but because the information is being inferred from the restaurant script.

Bower, Black, and Turner (1979) examined this possibility by asking their participants to wait for a period of time in a professor's office. The participants were later tested for their memory of objects seen in the room. The majority recalled seeing books, although no book had been present.

Scripts also play a role in identification. When we expect to see a given object, we identify it (establish its nature or identity) more quickly than would otherwise be the case. It also appears that we perform less processing than would otherwise be the case. For instance, a general awareness of the shape of the object may be enough for identification. It follows that we probably deploy relatively little processing when we identify objects specified by a script. If I see a table in a restaurant, I should be able to register it as a table on the basis of its rough outline, and without deploying much attention.

If the ideas described above are true, we should recall the presence of script-defined objects quite well, but their details poorly. However, if something occurs that violates the script, we will probably pay close attention to it and form a detailed and strong memory. If the waitress wears ski goggles, this will probably stick in your mind for some while.

These predictions have all been confirmed experimentally (Friedman, 1979; Graesser, Gordon, & Sawyer, 1979; Mandler & Goodman, 1982). We recall the existence of script-based items well, over short or long periods, but their details poorly. We recall unusual and striking elements well over short periods, and in detail.

Stories that involve script information have also been used to examine the properties of altered memories.

As described in Chapter 9, not all memory content is accurate, and it has proved impossible, up to the present time, to develop a method for reliably determining whether some constituent of a memory is valid (it reflects the original event) or invalid. Lampinen, Faries, Neuschatz, and Toglia (2000) conducted a study in which they attempted to determine (1) whether scripts can generate false memories and (2) whether it might be possible to distinguish between inaccurate and accurate memory content by the use of special techniques.

The authors presented their participants with script-based stories. A later recognition test examined their memory for the original facts and for plausible (script-based) facts that had not been present in the story. If a participant recognized a given fact, she was asked whether she "remembered" it as part of the story or simply "knew" that it had been present in the story. The remember/know distinction was originally developed by Tulving (1985b). The former involves having an actual recollection of reading the information; the latter involves the belief that the target fact was present, although you have no personal memory of reading it. The authors thought that only accurate material might produce a Remember response.

There were significantly more Remember judgments for original items than for items not present in the text. But there were also Remember judgments for items that had not been in the text. There was no difference in experiential detail (recall of perceptual, emotional, verbal, and thought-based details) between items that had really been in the story and items that hadn't. And of the incorrect judgments, about 50% were reported as Remembered.

It thus emerged that scripts can produce false memory content that is subjectively indistinguishable from accurate content.

6.3. Causal Chains

In their 1977 book, Schank and Abelson noted that we often understand prose material on the basis of additional information, supplied from our own memories (from LTM) and not by the text itself. For example, we can understand Paragraph A below, by drawing on our restaurant script. But Paragraph B appears odd. This is because we have no body of information stored in LTM that could serve to link the sentences together.

Paragraph A: John went to a restaurant. He asked the waitress for coq au vin. He paid the check and left.

Paragraph B: John went to the park. He asked the midget for a mouse. He picked up the box and left.

But not all events draw on a highly stereotyped situation, such as a visit to a restaurant. The authors concluded that we have other, higher-order structures that are deployed in the work of understanding events as they unfold around us, and also events described in prose.

After examining the inferences that readers make in the work of following a story, they concluded that one of the major variables within this context was the mapping of *causal relations*.

As events occur through time, they relate to one another in a *causal chain*. The chain is never broken. The authors posited that we have structures in our cognition that code for possible or lawful causal relations. As events unfold around us, they are mapped onto these structures. If there is a correspondence between the real-world event and the lawful relation, as specified by the causal knowledge structures, then we feel that what has happened makes sense.

In addition to noting possible causal relations, the knowledge structures specify (1) the possible (lawful) antecedents for any given event and (2) the possible (lawful) outcomes for any given event.

It might be objected that there are too many potential actions and outcomes in the world for it to be possible for human cognition to specify them all. In short, there could not be knowledge structures adequate to so complex a task. How could we possibly code all possible outcomes of every action?

The authors suggested that this is achieved on the basis of certain "primitive" actions that they called "ACTs." An ACT describes (at a very general level) a class of motions. There are a limited number of ACTs specified in human cognition. In the 1977 model, 11 such ACTs were posited. All possible motions could be subsumed under one (or more) of the 11 ACTs.

The causal knowledge structures specified the following for each ACT: (1) the conditions that must be in place if the ACT is to occur (the necessary preconditions) and (2) the possible outcomes of the ACT.

As a result, the preconditions and outcomes of any action could be established, since all "smaller" actions would nest under a given ACT, and share in the preconditions and outcomes of that ACT.

For instance, there is an ACT called a PROPEL. It involves applying force to an entity. A PROPEL is involved when we push, pull, shift, tug, or move an object (among many other possible verbs). If any of these actions occurs, the system identifies it as a PROPEL.

The necessary preconditions for a PROPEL are (1) there must be an agent embodying the force and an object acted on and (2) the agent embodying the force must be in physical contact with the object (directly or through some medium). The lawful outcomes of a PROPEL are the following: (1) The PROPEL can leave the object motionless, (2) it can cause the object to move in the line of the exerted force, and (3) the object may cause another PROPEL.

Suppose I want to make some tea. I enter the kitchen and see the kettle on the far side of the room. Before I can grasp the kettle, however, it sails across the room by itself and settles tidily onto one of the burners on the stove. An event like this would disturb me. I would immediately be aware that there had been a violation of causal relations. For a PROPEL to have a movement outcome, the force (here, myself) must be in physical contact (directly or indirectly) with the object of the PROPEL, and in the present example no such physical contact occurred. Luckily, such events are rare to nonexistent in everyday life.

In contrast, if, as I entered the kitchen, a pan fell on the kettle, knocking it from the stove onto a counter and causing it to hit against a glass, breaking the glass, all this would conform to the lawful outcomes of a PROPEL. In this fashion specific, widely diverse events (lifting, falling, hitting, smashing) can all be mapped onto a higher-level knowledge structure. We are not required to specify thousands of possible causal relations, but only which specific motions are examples of one of the 11 ACTs. (It is also possible for a motion to reflect a combination of different ACTs.)

The 11 ACTs are described in Table 10.1.

6.3.1. Causal Chains as Higher-Order Structures

Causal chains perform the functions of higher-order structures, as described in Chapter 8, Section 1. These include the following:

1. The function of understanding: If events map onto the knowledge structure, we have understood the event.

2. Support for memory: If events map onto the knowledge structure, the corresponding memory is strengthened.

3. The provision of inferred material: The knowledge structure often codes for information not directly experienced during the event.

4. The provision of the ability to anticipate the kind of action/interaction that is likely to occur next, at any given moment in time: If we have exerted a PROPEL, we know at a general level what is going to happen next. This makes it possible to plan.

Table 10.1   The 11 ACTs of Conceptual Dependency Theory.

1. ATRANS	The transfer of an abstract relationship such as possession, ownership or control. (To give, to buy, to take).
2. PTRANS	The transfer of the physical location of an entity. (To go, to put).
3. PROPEL	The application of physical force to an object. (To push, pull, throw kick).
4. MOVE	The movement of a limb, head, or other body part by an animal. (To move, e.g., foot, to wave, to kick).
5. GRASP	The grasping of an object by an actor. (To hold, grab, let go, throw).
6. INGEST	To take any substance into the body (of an animal). (To eat, drink, smoke, breathe).
7. EXPEL	To expel substance from the body. (To spit, sweat, cry).
8. MTRANS	The transfer of mental information (To see, tell, remember, forget, learn).
9. MBUILD	The construction by an animal of new information. (Decide, conclude, imagine, consider).
10. SPEAK	Action of producing sounds by animal. (To say, to play music, purr).
11. ATTEND	Action of attending, or focusing, a sense organ on a stimulus. (To attend, listen, see).

The fourth claim made here is new and reflects an idea that has become increasingly central in the field of cognitive science. It involves the ability to predict "what will happen next," of course at a highly generalized level. Franklin (1995, chap. 11) has suggested that this may be the most important question asked by higher organisms, as well as by certain robots now developed in the field of artificial intelligence. If you cannot predict, you cannot deal with danger until it is upon you, and you won't know where your food is.

6.4. Memory Organization Packages (MOPs)

In their 1977 model, Schank and Abelson offered a second critical hypothesis concerning the nature of human memory. They suggested that much of the work of coding information in LTM depends *on the human capacity to understand goals.*

This claim also related to the issue of causality. Most events are caused by physical forces of one kind or another. The pavement becomes wet because a cloudburst pelted it with rain. But another form of causality lies behind many physical events. This is human, or psychological, causality. If a pair of cutting shears closes around the stem of a plant, they will cut the stem. The outcome will be an object in two pieces. The shears caused this outcome. But they moved only because a human wanted the stem to be cut. Thus, many events in the world, and most events in the social world, have as their primary cause a human goal or motivation.

The authors suggested that our cognition is specialized to understand events on the basis of human goals. We develop structures that code for goals. In association with these, a body of knowledge is established, in each of us, concerning the actions that can achieve any particular goal. Suppose I know that Jane is broke. I will assume that she probably therefore needs to get some money in order to eat and have a place to live. These are likely to be her goals. I may then hear that Jane went yesterday and applied for a secretarial job at a certain office. This behavior will map onto my knowledge of the actions that people perform when they need money. The information will therefore make sense to me; her behavior will be understood. Schank used the term *memory organization packages* (MOPs) to denote the bodies of information that specify what we must do to achieve a given goal.

There are usually alternative ways of achieving a goal. Also, the relevant actions often occur in a definite sequence (or they wouldn't be effective). The situation could be described as follows:

GOAL X → Actions A, B, C (in that order)

Or Actions G, H, I
Or Actions J, K.

Which set of actions is likely to result from the presence of Goal X will depend on context. The relevant context information is also coded.

When we see events unfolding in the world, we look (unconsciously) for the goals associated with such events. When we match the events with the goals, we feel that we have understood the target episode. Also—and very critical—once we have established the presence of certain goals, *we can anticipate the actions that will follow, before they occur.*

All this is achieved because the critical relations are represented at an extremely general level, as in the case of the ACTs. Specific events are subsumed under these general relations.

Thus, the Schank and Abelson model posited that memory codes involve our understanding of an event (or other material). Understanding an event means *matching its details against higher-order structures already established in memory.* One group of these structures concerned causal relations. Another reflected our knowledge of human goals and the behaviors likely to achieve such goals.

There is now an extended body of data in support of the claim that goals and causal relations play a critical role in human memory (Bloom, Fletcher, van den Broek, Reitz, & Shapiro, 1990; Noordman & Vonk, 1998; van den Broek, Linzie,

Fletcher, & Marsolek, 2000). It has also been shown that readers will infer characters' goals and that these inferred goals become part of their memory of the target passage (Albrecht & O'Brien, 1993; Rinck et al., 2001; Seifert, Robertson, & Black, 1985).

6.5. MOPs, Thematic Organization Packets (TOPs), and Hierarchical Structure * * * * *

There are three kinds of MOPs in Schank's model. The type of MOP described above was a *physical MOP*, which provides information concerning the actions that must be performed to achieve a particular goal. Schank (1982, 1999) described MOPs as possessing hierarchical structure. A high level of the hierarchy would involve a quite abstract description. For instance, for the "going on a trip" MOP, the highest level would involve the knowledge that one has to plan for a trip, get some kind of resources, make arrangements, prepare to travel, and travel. At lower levels, the information becomes more and more specific, until, at the lowest point in the hierarchy, there will be detailed knowledge concerning, for instance, what you must do if you wish to go from one city to another.

There is in fact a yet higher level (for the MOP trip) than the one described above. This involves extremely abstract knowledge concerning the kind of activities required for any activity of this general kind.

The other two forms of organizing structure are *societal and personal MOPs*. The societal MOP specifies the abstract human conventions usually in play when we perform actions. For instance, buying a ticket for a plane trip involves a social contract. Personal MOPs reflect events organized by our personal goals. My intention in flying on a plane might be to visit relatives. All three types of MOP are typically active in the work of constructing the meaning of an event.

The personal MOPs described above appear fairly simple. But according to the present model there exist in our cognition more complex, high-level structures that reflect our knowledge of human goals as such. These are called thematic organization packets (TOPs).

A *TOP* is an organized set of knowledge concerning events driven by a particular kind of goal. The TOP includes both the relevant events and the motivations that led to these events. We know a good deal about general themes that operate in human motivation: themes related to love, ambition, aggression, and so on. TOPs include this level of highly abstract knowledge. A TOP needs to operate at a generalized or abstract level, since the events associated with it can be extremely diverse.

One TOP identified by Schank involves the motivation for power or gain, combined with willingness to exploit others to achieve its ends. Schank labeled this structure as *possession goal: evil intent* (PG:EI). As adults, we may encounter many concepts that would activate this TOP. For instance, the term "imperialism" implies PG:EI motivation. But note that the TOP concept is far more generalized than the concept of imperialism. That is, it can subsume not only the imperialistic situation but many others as well.

This property of high-level generalization in TOPs has provided us with the ability to move, in thought, from one context to another that *may be wholly different in its specific content.* Schank (1982) noted that you might hear of a slumlord who has begun to buy decrepit buildings and who has told the authorities that he will stop this unacceptable behavior if he is allowed to buy just one more building. In fact, the slumlord does not intend to stop. This might remind you of the Munich Conference in 1938. The two events share no actors or locations or specific episodes in common. But at Munich, Hitler resisted attempts to stop his acts of invasion in a fashion similar to the arguments of the slumlord. You have unconsciously noted the Possession Goal: Evil Intent similarity between the two markedly different situations.

TOPs thus provide almost unlimited flexibility for the movement of thought and of memory content. Clearly, a slumlord and a military fanatic share little in common in terms of their specific actions and the worlds in which they live. MOPs do not provide this form of flexibility, since they are quite context bound. They involve the achievement of specific, particular goals, as against the broad spectrum that could result from the ambition to have power or to do good in life, and so on.

It has been established for many years that identity and similarity links function in human memory (see Chapter 7). But in the past these were conceptualized as operating at the level of individual representations. Seeing one parrot may produce the memory of having seen another parrot at some earlier time. This relationship, however, would in most cases produce only a rather disorganized form of thinking (or memory). That is, the movement from one concrete object to a second, similar or identical, object: parrot to parrot, table to table. Schank's assumption of TOPs changes this. The model opens the possibility of thought moving on an identity basis at a very high level—of the kind that might be expected to produce effective cognition.

The present goal-directed model of human understanding and memory has been embodied in a series of computer programs. One of these, *script applier mechanism* (SAM), "reads" and "understands" prose material and can answer questions concerning what it has read. Its answers show an analog of comprehension of the material; they are the kind of answers a person would give.

Although the examples given above have involved fairly stereotyped situations, the present model is designed to handle any normal or standard life episode. It is not restricted to dealing with scripts.

6.6. Revision of the Script Concept * * * * *

In the original script concept, a script consisted of a unified body of information. This information was stored as a unit in LTM. Thus, there would be a restaurant script that, as a single body of content, specified what occurs when we visit a restaurant.

The difficulty with this view was that scripts show interference effects across one another. For instance, a memory of sitting in a dentist's waiting room may be confused with a memory of sitting in a doctor's waiting room. If the two involve different information sets, as posited by the original model, this kind of interference should not happen.

Schank concluded that the constituents of memories all exist independently. The constituents are scenes. When a memory is constructed (or retrieved), this occurs top-down. There will be a high-level MOP that will point to the appropriate scenes. The high-level MOPs typically subsume a good deal of lower-level information. Thus, there is probably an M-PROFESSIONAL HEALTH CARE that would subsume (1) M-VISIT-TO-A-DOCTOR and (2) M-VISIT-TO-A-DENTIST. Perhaps in (1) the MOP would order the Scenes C, D, F, and H and construct those events as the memory. And perhaps in (2) the MOP would order Scenes A, D, F, and M. Here, there would be the use of the same two scenes (D, the waiting-room scene, and F) in different memories. An individual might recall Scene D. However, the system might then move "up," as would usually be the case, to the relevant superordinate structure, but take the wrong associative path and construct, at retrieval, the waiting room as being present during a visit to the doctor—when it was in fact present during a visit to the dentist.

The approach to memory outlined here implies the notion that in forming a memory the system draws on certain element representations and binds them together in a unique order. This order does constitute the nature of the memory as it is first encoded, *but that order need not be permanently fixed.* New relations can be established at the time of recall. This assumption has been labeled as *constructionist*, although the term may be a little confusing, since more is implied here than the basic assumptions of traditional constructivism. For instance, a researcher working in the Bartlettian frame might assume that information in memory consists of a body of content that is established as a set during encoding, although inferred data might later be added to this body (particularly to fill in gaps due to forgetting). This would not, however, imply that memory is profoundly dissociative in nature. A dissociative hypothesis means that memory consists of units of representation that can be flexibly ordered, or "broken apart" and constructed in a new order, as posited by Schank. Perhaps serious models of constructivist memory have always carried this implication, but it appears possible to conceptualize the function as an interpretive and a dynamic process, without necessarily assuming recombinatorial representational elements.

7. Kintsch's Model of Prose Comprehension

Kintsch and Van Dijk (1978) suggested that prose comprehension involves three major coding types or levels. The first is the *surface code*. This consists of the actual words and syntactic relations present in the text itself. The second level, known as the *text base*, reflects the information generated from the text in propositional form, along with a small number of inferences needed to provide local text coherence. For instance, if two sentences read, "John saw that the window was jammed shut. He pushed at it hard," the reader would infer that John pushed the window hard because this is a means of making jammed windows open. The third level of prose comprehension involves the *situation model*, which provides background knowledge that may be needed to interpret an event. For instance, if John washes the window and is then given money by the house owner, an adult witnessing these events would understand that people are often paid for doing work, this being a common kind of social contract.

Data supporting the hypothesis of three levels of comprehension have been reported by Fletcher (1994), Glenberg and Langston (1992), Graesser, Singer, and Trabasso (1994), and Kintsch, Welsch, Schmalhofer, and Zimny (1990), among others.

Not all researchers agree that three distinct levels of coding operate when we read and understand prose material, however. For instance, it has been claimed that there is no propositional component (Gernsbacher & Robertson, 1992; Perfetti & Britt, 1995) and that the data on forgetting can be explained without an assumption of distinct surface, propositional and situation model codes.

8. Inferences, the Situation Model, and Knowledge Structures: Ongoing Research * * * * *

Research into memory for written materials (often called prose discourse) today ranges across almost all forms of such material, from the earlier folktales through literary stories (Dixon, Harrison, & Taylor, 1993) to short, artificially constructed texts, discourses on history and science (Chi, de Leeuw, Chiu, & LaVancher, 1994; Kintsch, 1994; Perfetti, Britt, & Georgi, 1995; Voss & Silfies, 1996), and computer simulations (Britton & Graesser, 1996; Golden & Rumelhart, 1993).

An extended body of data has been collected concerning causal relations in prose recall. In the work based on story grammars, described in Section 5 above, it was consistently found that causal relations produce a stronger memory function than other forms of association (Black & Bower, 1980; Mandler & Johnson, 1977). It has also been found that reading speed is influenced by causal relations within the body of the text (Graesser et al., 1994; Omanson, 1982).

A variety of other classes of inferred material have been identified. In some cases, two statements can be related to one another if the reader retrieves some explanatory fact from LTM.

Haviland and Clark (1974) named these *bridging inferences*. Suppose you read, "Joe poured water on the fire. The fire went out." A bridging inference would reflect your knowledge that water puts out fire (Singer, 1993). When text material can be supported by an inferred bridging inference, it is again read more quickly than under conditions in which a bridging inference cannot be made.

Table 10.2 provides a list of the inferences that have been hypothesized to operate when we attempt to understand prose material. It should be noted that the majority of discourse psychologists reject the view that all these inferences are routinely generated.

9. What Inferences Are Generated in Natural Text Comprehension?

There are two major, and opposed, views concerning the kind of inferences that are generated when we read text. According to one position, inferences are generated in

Table 10.2   Inferences Assumed to Operate in the Construction of Prose Material (or Daily Events)

GOALS
(Goals/Intentions of others)

ACTIONS TO ACHIEVE GOALS

CAUSAL RELATIONS
(Preconditions and outcomes)

SPATIAL CONTEXT

TEMPORAL CONTEXT

WHAT PEOPLE KNOW

STATIC PROPERTIES
(Properties of known objects,
e.g. giraffe has long neck)

almost all cases only to provide *local text coherence*. Local text coherence involves relating the content of several consecutive statements together. Here it is believed that working memory can hold only a few propositions.

The alternative position involves the construct of *global text coherence*. Here it is posited that the reader generates an understanding of the material as a whole, such that statements that are widely separated in the text can nonetheless be related to one another, on the basis of inferred connections. For instance, if it was noted on page 1 in a story that Character X was an heiress, and on page 10 she is described as taking a job as a dishwasher, the reader might be surprised.

Graesser, Millis, and Zwaan (1997) described three major theories concerning the nature of inferences constructed when we read story material. What is involved here reflects inferences that are generated automatically as we read, without any special—problem-solving—effort to do so.

According to the first, *promiscuous theory*, all possible inferences are coded. The second, a *constructionist model*, posits that a range of particular inferences are routinely generated, although others would only be produced under special conditions: that is, when the reader had some particular goal of understanding or read with unusual concentration (Graesser et al., 1994). Both these models posit global text coherence. According to the third, *minimalist theory*, as described by McKoon and Ratcliff (1992b), only two kinds of inference are constructed as we read texts under standard conditions: (1) inferences required for local coherence and (2) inferences that are easy to generate, because they involve highly familiar information. Global inferences are not constructed. According to this view, the extended background information implied by the mental model or the situation model hypotheses is not inferred under standard conditions. It would be claimed here, for instance, that we do not construct a spatial scene in which to place the events of a story. If a text cannot be understood on the basis of local coherence, the system may then attempt to move to the global level. But this will be achieved only if the needed inferences are easy to generate, in that they reflect highly familiar information.

9.1. Research Into Local Versus Global Coherence

Huitema, Dopkins, Klin, and Myers (1993) tested the hypothesis advanced under the constructionist model, to the effect that if a goal is established and a character then, even considerably later in the story, performs some action that is incompatible with the goal, readers will notice the discrepancy. This means that the earlier-stated goal has been seen in relation with the inconsistent action. The data supported this conclusion. Others researchers suggested that inferred goals would be likely to operate in the same way (Sanford & Garrod, 1998; Zwaan, 1999). Poynor and Morris (2003) examined what would occur when a goal was either implied (but not explicitly stated), or explicitly stated early in a prose passage, and a character later acted in a way that was inconsistent with the goal. They found that readers spent more time on the inconsistent action both when the goal had been implicitly stated and when it had not. The readers had clearly inferred the goal under the latter condition and maintained this information as they read the passage (an outcome implying global coherence). Explicitly stated or implicitly implied goals were retained equally well in memory, but the inconsistent actions were recalled better overall than were the consistent actions.

9.2. Kinds of Inferences Generated in the Course of Story Comprehension and Recall

When researchers attempt to determine the type of inferences generated during text comprehension, a common approach involves presenting material that might or might not have been inferred, on the basis of earlier reading. If there is speeded reading of that target material, it is assumed that the relevant inference had been made.

Using this and other approaches, Chafe (1994) and Graesser, Baggett, and Williams (1996) have reported data supporting the view that background context is constructed.

Concerning the issue of what kind of information is entered into the memory content, Keysar (1994, 1996) found that participants track (1) who said what, (2) who knows what, and (3) the intentions of speakers. Also, the intentions of speakers are inferred and retained better than the intentions of those individuals being addressed.

Graesser et al. (1997) attempted to determine which, of the full range of all imaginable inferences, may in fact be generated when we read prose. The constructionist model claims that the following three types of inference are in fact routinely generated: (1) inferences needed to make the material comprehensible, (2) inferences that explain why events occur (causal inferences), and (3) inferences that establish integration of the material at both the global and local levels.

The authors concluded that some, but not all, of the full range of possible inferences are in fact generated. However, those three listed above as reflecting the constructionist model are in fact generated. A range of studies have supported this conclusion (Magliano, Baggett, Johnson, & Graesser, 1993; Millis & Graesser, 1994; Trabasso & Magliano, 1996).

Thus, the hypothesis that a situation (otherwise called *mental*) model is constructed when we read prose, and that global coherence is established, has received extensive support. Minimalist theorists, however, urge that the inferences described above may not be generated at the time of encoding, as a means of understanding a prose passage, but only during retrieval, as a means of filling in gaps in the memory content. It has also been suggested that the sets of information that were originally separated in the text may be retrieved into working memory together, at a later time, such that relations established between these sets reflect local rather than global coherence (Albrecht & O'Brien, 1993; Myers, O'Brien, Albrecht, & Mason, 1994; O'Brien, Albrecht, Hakala, & Rizzella, 1995).

Summary

It has been established that inferences are made when prose material is read. These may occur at encoding, or at retrieval.

A wide range of higher-order processing structures have been identified. One involves the ability to create a three-dimensional context in which the events described in prose are positioned. If the individual can identify how all the described actions could occur within that context, the passage is better retained in memory and appears to make sense. Bransford demonstrated that incomprehensible prose passages are poorly retained.

A mental model involves a four-dimensional context established in our cognition when we read prose, or encounter information in some other form. It is four dimensional in that it includes time, as well as three spatial dimensions.

Data have been gathered supporting the claim that we track the passage of time, as implied by the events in a prose passage, when we read prose.

Higher-order structures specifying the way events will unfold in certain traditional types of story have been shown to exist. R. Schank posited that higher-order knowledge structures also operate when we live through daily events or read nonstereotyped stories. One of these involves causal chains: tracking cause and effect relations in an unfolding event. These relations should fit the preexisting knowledge structures relating to causality, in LTM. Other knowledge structures involve goals. MOPs are bodies of organized information in LTM that specify how specific goals (such as going to a given destination) can be achieved. TOPs are abstract bodies of information involving human motivation at a more general level, such as the motivation to power. TOPs indicate the kind of actions that occur when individuals possess such motivation. Their information is not context bound. Scripts are a specific form of knowledge structure specifying how events unfold in highly familiar situations, such as eating in a restaurant.

Schank endorses the view that memories are actively generated at the time of retrieval: That is, new codes are put together which provide the retrieved memory.

Kintsch has developed a model of prose comprehension that involves three levels: text base, propositional, and situational. Text base involves the surface structure of the prose, the propositional level involves connected propositional information derived from that structure, and the situation model level involves the inclusion of background knowledge.

Research into memory for prose, labeled as *prose discourse*, has established that causal relations do play a central role in memory strength. There has been extensive research to examine the types of inferences derived when we read prose. A central issue concerns whether only local inferences are generated, to tie several sentences together, or whether "global" inferences are generated that may connect widely separated statements together. The data appear generally to support the latter view.

Discussion

The present chapter provided an overview of a range of theories in which it was assumed that higher-order or background processing structures play a fundamental role in memory. Such structures are believed, within the present tradition, to provide information critical to the understanding of memory content. They are also assumed to come into play when content is inferred.

A widespread belief, within this context, is that higher-order structures supply memory strength. When information fits such structures, it is supported. Across the majority of models that endorse the notion of higher-order processing structures, it is also believed that such structures play a role no less effective than rehearsal. This is an important claim, in that earlier research focused on rehearsal and elaboration as the most fundamental mechanisms providing stronger recall.

The present tradition also differs from an older approach, in which it is posited that associations among basic-level representations (as against more generalized, or background, knowledge) fully determine the content of material that is recalled. This is essentially the debate that underlies the opposition between local-coherence and global-coherence models.

Most researchers who posit the role of higher-order structures in memory also believe that these structures provide the ability to predict events, at a generalized level, and so to act effectively in the world. According to this view, it is less critical to know the "features" (a round shape, the possession of legs, etc.) of things in the world, than to know how things in the world act.

Finally, Schank's recent model of memory involves the view that memory content is actively reconstructed at the time of retrieval. This places him within the multiple-memory-trace tradition described in the previous chapter.

CHAPTER 11

Autobiographical Memory

Overview

1. We do not recall the first years of our lives, a phenomenon known as infantile or childhood amnesia. Fragment, isolated memories begin to appear at around the age of 3 and narrative, ongoing autobiographical memory at 5 or 6 years.

2. Current theories concerning childhood amnesia include a weakness in coding assumption, a cueing assumption (according to which adult thought cues do not match infantile thought structure), and theories of social interaction, according to which children learn to form memories due to contact with adults who model this function.

3. From later childhood, through adulthood, memory has hierarchical structure. This ranges downward from general themes, to extended periods of life, to particular episodes, to details of such episodes. In general, the higher levels are recalled better than the lower ones.

4. In recalling hard-to-retrieve memories, we appear to use both temporal order and hierarchical structure. In the latter strategy, a more generalized event is used to access a target memory.

5. We are poor at recognizing plausible but false autobiographical memories as being false.

6. Events involving (nontraumatic) negative affect are forgotten more quickly than positive events.

7. Flashbulb memories are memories formed following unexpected events of major importance to the individual. They retain trivial contextual details across time. There is disagreement concerning whether these recollections involve an unusual memory function or inferential reconstruction that may not be accurate.

Learning Objectives

1. Knowledge of the nature of childhood amnesia and theories concerning it. Knowledge of the nature of fragment memories.

2. Knowledge of the hierarchical structure of autobiographical memory and of how this and temporal factors can aid in retrieving memories.

3. Knowledge of factors that influence autobiographical recall, such as goals and emotions, and knowledge of "shared" memories and the reminiscence bump.

4. Knowledge of the nature of flashbulb memories and the controversy concerning them.

T he experience that we generally think of as "memory" involves recollection of the past. When I recall walking up a range of stone steps, I think of the event as a memory. Material of this kind provides the content of the present chapter. More specifically, it involves recall of the facts and happenings of one's life.

The term *episodic memory* refers to recollection of actual happenings. But we may also remember abstract information concerning our past. For instance, I may recall that I was hired at a law firm during my graduate days, but not "see" any event related to that hiring. I just know that it happened. This is part of my autobiographical, but not my episodic, memory.

Autobiographical memory also draws on semantic memory—that is, representational or conceptual knowledge. Suppose I recall seeing a certain house. I may see the house in my mind, and thus episodic memory is clearly involved. But I also know "what it is"; I am drawing on my house concept as I recall that individual house.

We are amnesic (as adults) for the first years of our lives. The following pages first describe research relating to this stretch of time, through the period of "fragment recall" to that of mature recollection. Some unusual forms of autobiographical memory are also covered.

PART I: THE FIRST YEARS OF LIFE

1. First Recollections

Freud used the term *infantile amnesia* for the lack of memories that characterizes the first years of human life, but since the effect extends long past infancy, some researchers prefer the term *childhood amnesia* (Nelson, 1989).

Although the first years are not recalled, many people can remember a few brief episodes dating from their third or fourth year. These are labeled *fragment memories*, because they usually involve a brief scene that lacks any extended temporal or spatial context. The individual does not remember what happened before, or after, the little scene, which has been described as resembling a lighted stage on which the curtain lifts for a moment and then drops again (Salaman, 1970). Also, there is no sense of ongoing autobiographical life in which the scene is embedded.

The first fragment memories date on average from the age of three and a half, with females tending to recall episodes from a slightly earlier age than males (Dudycha & Dudycha, 1933; Waldfogel, 1948). A few individuals report recollections that they believe date from the first year of life; others have no memory until the age of 8 or even older.

Certain events appear more likely to provide enduring recollections than others. Goodman, Rudy, Bottoms, and Aman (1990) found that experimental participants often recall painful medical experiences dating to the second year of life. Sheingold and Tenney (1982), examining adults' memories for the birth of a sibling when they were children, found a steep offset of childhood amnesia at the age of three and a half (conforming to the usual date) but also reported that 2/22 individuals recalled the sibling birth although they had been only 2 years of age at the time of this event.

Pursuing the possibility that certain kinds of episode may be relatively likely to produce memories dating from a very young age, Usher and Neisser (1993) examined adults' recollection of an emergency room visit, a sibling birth, the death of a grandparent, and an episode in which the family moved to a new house. The participants had been 1 to 5 years of age at the time of the original event. Roughly half the participants from the 2-year-old group recalled both the hospital experience (the largest number) and the sibling birth experience. There was a yet higher count of recall from the 3-, 4-, and 5-year age groups for these two events, as well as cases of recall concerning the other episodes (grandparent's death and family move). It thus appears that the date of the first fragment memory is in part a function of the type of life episodes experienced by the individual, some being more likely to produce a permanent record than others.

First memories usually contain little information. They tend to be fragments, as described above, characterized by imagery and the presence of emotion (Robinson, 1977). Around the age of 5 or 6 years, memory begins to take on a narrative aspect. At this time the individual recalls an ongoing sequence of events, the background of his or her life, in which any given memory episode is now embedded.

2. Causes of Childhood Amnesia

Organized cognition is present in human infants by at least the end of the first year (Mandler & McDonough, 1993; Rovee-Collier & Boller, 1995). That is, the child understands a good deal of what is occurring around her. This raises the question of why we do not, as adults, remember many events dating from before the fourth year.

It could be that we do not form episodic memories during infancy and early toddlerhood. Or it could be that such memories are formed but are weakly coded, and the codes fail to endure across time. A third possibility reflects the view that there is some fundamental qualitative difference between cognition in the first years of life and later years. Due to this difference, cues in adult thought might be unable to contact infantile memories; the adult and infantile codes might not match well enough.

Freud offered two accounts of childhood amnesia. One involved the claim that our earliest memories are repressed. The second Freudian hypothesis was that the infant memory system is immature and therefore lacks the capacity to routinely form permanent recollections (Freud, 1963). The psychoanalyst had noticed that early memories tend to be imagistic and fragmentary. Content of this kind might suffer from two disadvantages. It would, again, be inherently weak, and it might also be difficult to understand within the context of adult cognition.

Freud's theory of memory was constructive in nature. He assumed that we retain certain elements of a memory that need to be understood or interpreted at the time of recall. Within this context, he noted that some infantile memories include odd information, in that an adult type of cognition appears involved—or at least cognition too advanced for a young child. He believed that this was due to reconstructive processes working on the original memory content. Roughly, it was due to the adult attempting (unconsciously) to interpret the original material of the memory.

2.1. Memories in Infancy and Early Childhood

Even young infants form recognition memories. This fact was established across a series of experiments conducted by Rovee-Collier and her associates. Rovee-Collier (1999), Rovee-Collier, Griesler, and Early (1985), and Rovee-Collier, Hartshorn, and DiRubbo (1999) taught infants to kick when they saw a certain target mobile suspended over their cribs. Younger infants required a longer training period to achieve this response. They also forgot more quickly. Thus, 2-month-old subjects could retain the response for 1 or 2 days, while infants of 6 months could remember across a period of 2 weeks. From 2 months to 2 years, the children's ability to retain a learned response to a target stimulus emerged as a linearly increasing function of age (Hartshorn et al., 1998). The growth of recognition memory with age is shown in Figure 11.1.

There is thus clear evidence that infants form recognition memories. Autobiographical memory is understood, however, as the ability to *recall* past objects or events. Recall is defined as the ability to remember some past content when no corresponding stimulus is present.

Carver and Bauer (1999) determined that infants can copy actions that they have seen a model perform at an earlier time (delayed imitation). This implies some form of recall of the earlier actions and also of their sequence in time. Delayed imitation was present in 45% of a group of infants aged 9 months, tested after 1 month. Bauer, Wenner, Dropik, and Wewerka (2000) and Bauer (2002a, 2002b) found a similar pattern to that involved in recognition memory: The older the infant, the longer the memory could be retained. Here, tests ranged across retention intervals from 1 to 12 months.

By the age of 2 years, children can recall episodes from their own past experience (Fivush & Haden, 2003; Nelson & Fivush, 2000; Sachs, 1983). In some cases, the memories may date back as far as 12 months (Howe, 1994; Simcock & Hayne, 2002).

Pillemer (1992) examined the memories of 3.5- and 4.5-year-old children concerning the evacuation of a preschool due to a possible fire hazard: Some popcorn had burned in the kitchen. Fifty-four percent of the younger children claimed,

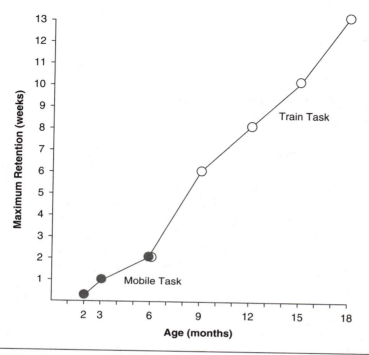

Figure 11.1   Recognition of Stimuli Shown by Infants From 2 to 18 Months of Age

SOURCE: From Collier, Rovee, "The development of infant memory," in *Current Directions in Psychological Science*, 8(3), copyright © 1999. Reprinted with permission of Blackwell.

incorrectly, that they had been outside when they heard the fire alarm. They also showed a poor grasp of causality related to the event and of temporal factors. The older children performed better on all these measures. The author interpreted these data as suggesting that the weak memory function of young children may be due, in part, to the absence of the relevant higher-order structuring abilities.

2.2. Childhood Amnesia and Changing Cognitive Structure

As described above, some researchers believe that childhood amnesia is due to major qualitative changes in cognitive structure that occurs between the first years of life and later years (Neisser, 1962; C. A. Nelson, 1995; Pillemer & White, 1989; Schactel, 1947; White & Pillemer, 1979). According to this position, two distinct memory systems are involved between infancy and early toddlerhood, and the later preschool years. Due to this factor, later cognition fails to match well with infantile cognition, and cues for remote episodes may be ineffective.

Pillemer and White (1989) noted differences in style found in the memories of 2-year-olds, as recorded by psychologists, compared with the memories of even 3- or 4-year-olds. The former group tends to show a very loose organization in the memory content.

It is widely believed within the present tradition that language may play a large or the fundamental role in the shift from primitive to mature cognition (Pillemer & White, 1989).

2.3. A Social Interaction Theory of Childhood Amnesia

K. Nelson (1993, 1995) noted that a distinction should be made between *episodic memory*, *generic event memory*, and *autobiographical memory*. An episodic memory involves an event that has only occurred once. Generic event memory involves happenings that are repeated. In a child's life, these would include eating breakfast, playing in a certain room, visiting with a relative, and so on. These repeat episodes tend to be quite strong, with 3-year-olds showing good retention across periods ranging to several years (Nelson, 1978; Nelson & Gruendel, 1981). Nelson suggested that the first true autobiographical memories that children form, as they begin to establish a personal history, tend to involve generic events.

Nelson (1993) offered the further claim that true autobiographical memory is made possible through children learning to talk about their experiences, with an adult as model. The adult, often the child's mother, will discuss and explain past events, offering a high-level narrative structure that the child can then learn and use in structuring his or her own memories (a social interaction hypothesis). The capacity requires the presence of language and social learning (Nelson, 1993, p. 13). A similar position has been advocated by Fivush and Nelson (2004) and Gergen (2000), and a review of the data on this form of "structuring" has been provided by Nelson and Fivush (2000).

Within a somewhat different context, Nelson has also noted that discussing an event (as in early child-adult discussions) may serve as a reinstatement of the original code. The evidence concerning this possibility, however, remains ambiguous. Hudson (1990) found that the memories retained by her daughter after a period of years were not the particular episodes that they had discussed. Young children often attend to aspects of an event that would not be considered important by an adult and would thus rarely lead to discussion.

A somewhat related model of childhood amnesia involves the view that an individual cannot form autobiographical memories until he or she possesses a self-concept. Clearly, personal memories involve the self. There is disagreement among researchers concerning the point in development at which this awareness emerges, with some placing it at the end of the first year (Neisser, 1988) and some closer to the end of the second year (Howe & Courage, 1997). It is also possible, however, that there may be a primitive sense of this kind that co-occurs with awareness.

2.4. Cues and Children's Recall of Earlier Events

Children of 12 or 18 months are clearly limited in their verbal skills, and it appears likely that they can remember more than they can tell. Given these facts, researchers have examined the possibility that a child might be able to report a preverbal memory, once he or she begins to talk. At first it appeared that this was not possible: Asking the young subjects about the memory, or showing them pictures, was not effective. Bauer et al. (2004) found, however, that (1) if the original event had been repeated and (2) if contextual cues were employed, 2-year-olds were able to recall and report events that had occurred when they were 13 and 16 months of age. The contextual cues involved recreating the situation inn which the target event had unfolded.

2.5. Infantile Amnesia and Language

It was once widely believed that ideas or thought "were" internalized language. This meant that there could be no representation or memories until the child could talk (or at least understand speech). Current research has shown that in fact ideation is present well before language ability and even that some representation of abstract concepts emerges in the first year of life (Bauer, 1995; Eimas & Quinn, 1994; J. M. Mandler, 1992). The implication of these findings is that the memory function, at least for fragment memories, is not dependent on language.

3. Fragment Memories: Why Even Fragments During the Period of General Amnesia?

Since we cannot recall most of the episodes from the first years of life, some explanation is needed of why some particular memories do endure. The most commonly cited factors here are rehearsal and emotion. It may be that fragment memories have been talked about or thought about more than others. With regard to emotion, Freud believed that this variable could greatly strengthen memory. He claimed that fragment memories in fact reflected traumatic episodes. The trauma was not assumed necessarily to involve events; in most cases, it centered on the feelings and cognition present in the child at that particular time. It has been found that most fragment memories do involve distinct affect (although some do not). The affect, however, may be either positive or negative. Freud explained this phenomenon as involving the distortion that the child's mind had imposed on the recollections, to hide their traumatic nature. According to this view, positive and bland memories are invariably distorted, to hide their original nature.

Some current researchers believe that strong affect is indeed the explanation of the strength of fragment memories but that the affect can be either positive or negative (White & Pillemer, 1979).

3.1. Affect and Distortion in Early Memories

Early research within the clinical tradition attempted to determine whether first memories were in fact characterized by less emotion than recollections formed in adulthood (due to the divorce of the threatening underlying trauma from the memory content). But this assumption was not supported; as noted above, first memories are generally characterized by definite emotion.

In contrast, the existence of distortion in some early memories has been solidly documented. Probably the most famous example involves an episode reported by Piaget (1951). He had for many years recalled an infantile experience in which a man had tried to kidnap him, the baby Piaget, in Paris. He recalled the nurse fighting the villain off and the scratches that she had received on her face during the encounter. When he was 15, however, the nurse admitted to his family that the incident had never occurred.

The novelist Esther Salaman described a fragment memory in which she was standing at a window in her home, watching some women run by in the street below. She heard her mother say, "The revolutionaries." She had recalled an alarming scene from the 1905 revolution. But the room that she saw in the memory was not part of the house where she had lived in 1905. It belonged to a second house, similar in location and appearance to the first. Current research, however, has supported the view that many fragment memories are not distorted. Howes, Siegel, and Brown (1993) compared their students' first recollections with an independent report of the event given by a parent or parents. In those cases where a parent could identify the target memory, the recollections of the participants were found to be accurate in the overwhelming majority of cases. Only 13% involved any form of distortion. Positive episodes were confirmed at as high a level as negative episodes. In addition, it was found that a few recollections that the participants remembered as emotionally neutral had in fact involved strong emotion, including strong positive emotion, at the time they were formed (as described by the parent). This was of interest, since the "emotion hypothesis" concerning fragment memories appears contraindicated by the fact that such memories sometimes are recalled as nonemotional. These data suggested that the emotion may simply have been forgotten, just as details of an event can be forgotten.

A striking aspect of fragment recollections is that they are drawn from a period of almost complete amnesia and are thus clearly very strong memories. Yet they can include inaccurate details. The implication appears to be that even very strongly coded content, which is for the most part veridical, is not immune from inferential reconstruction. In other words, a memory may be "real," without being accurate in every detail.

My favorite example of this phenomenon, taken from the 1993 study cited above, involves a participant who recalled, as the earliest memory of her life, looking at a floor. The floor showed a pattern of white, orange, and green squares. This constituted the entire memory. (Many of the fragment recollections were of this, very brief, kind.)

The mother was asked whether her child might have formed an early memory of a floor with colored squares. The mother said that the kitchen floor at one of their homes had indeed consisted of colored squares. The colors were white and green. There had been no orange component. The family had moved from the house when the participant turned three. The floor had not been a subject of family conversation.

The available data thus do not support the hypothesis of "motivated" and routine distortions in early memories. Such changes as are present appear more likely to be due to the work of inference or source amnesia (or both).

3.2. Borrowed Memories

It can occur that an individual remembers a given episode, with himself or herself as the protagonist, while another individual recalls exactly the same episode, with himself or herself as the protagonist. Sheen, Kemp, and Rubin (2001) reported that this was a particularly common event among twins, with 65% to 75% of twin pairs reporting at least one disputed memory, while this occurred in only 8% of sibling memories. Ikier, Tekcan, Guelguez, and Kuentay (2003), investigating the same phenomenon, found that borrowed memories were more common among identical than among fraternal twins and more common among fraternal twins than among siblings. Further critical findings were that this kind of recollection tended to date to young ages, with 35% from under the age of 5, tended to have low reported frequencies of being talked about, and tended to involve low levels of detail and of imagery. (The latter two qualities may be because the memories are remote, however, rather than because they are borrowed. For half the participants, of course, the memories were their own.)

PART II: AFTER THE FIRST YEARS

1. The Nature of Autobiographical Memory

When we recall personal memories, we normally *see* the target episode. I recall leaving my house about an hour ago, and the appearance of the trees and the wet grass of the garden form a central part of the recollection. This kind of experience contrasts with my knowledge that Paris is the capital of France, which involves a wholly abstract code. Due to the spatial and sensory qualities of autobiographical memories, it was common at one time, among both philosophers and psychologists, to believe that such memories were tied to a perceptual code (Brockelman, 1975). According to this view, personal histories involved the representation of visual, auditory, and spatial information, while our general knowledge was represented in abstract, propositional form.

It is understood today, however, that episodic memories involve a great deal of abstract information. If we see a table, we are aware not only of how it looks but also of what it is (a table), and we are also aware of the higher-order nature of autobiographical events, such as the fact that a given episode may involve a job interview, a religious ceremony, and so on. We may also remember our thoughts across a life episode (Brewer, 1999). Thus, personal memories are by no means coded exclusively on a perceptual basis. They are, rather, characterized by the presence of perceptual information.

1.1. Methods of Research

Galton (1879) devised a method of testing the contents of his mind by writing a list of items, such as "boat" or "house," and attempting to observe his thoughts concerning each item.

Crovitz and Shiffman (1974) used the same approach as a means of tapping memories, rather than thoughts. Thus, on reading "boat" the participant would attempt to recall a personal memory involving a boat. Later researchers extended this cueing method to include not only objects but also events, actions, and moods.

A second approach involves the requirement that a particular, targeted episode be recalled. This can involve the use of either questionnaires or free recall. And finally, a diary method is the procedure of recording episodic events across a period of time and later testing one's memory of the events.

1.2. General Properties of Episodic Recollections

The bulk of content in an autobiographical memory that is spontaneously reported tends to be accurate, at least in the case of recent memories, although inaccuracies also occur (Brewer, 1988). When questions are asked concerning a given episode, recollection is often less accurate. And remote memories can be subject to major changes in content.

Several variables strengthen episodic memory. Emotional events tend to be well recalled (Rubin & Kozin, 1984; Smith, 1952; White, 1982), as do unusual or unique episodes and episodes of a kind that would be expected not to occur (Linton, 1979).

Some events unfold only once; others are repeated. In the latter case, it appears that a generalized description is formed in long-term memory (LTM) (Linton, 1986; Nelson, 1993; Wagenaar, 1986). The generalized description includes the standard aspects of the memory. These are coded at some strength. For instance, if one has taken many examinations, a memory will be formed that includes what always happens at examinations. But when this occurs there is a tendency for the individual details to be forgotten. In contrast, the details of unique events are retained relatively well. If you have taken only one examination in your life, you may recall that the window was open and that the person in the front row dropped a book.

Generalized memories, however, tend to be retained over long periods of time, showing superior recall to most individual memories.

The reason why we lose details from repeated memories is not known. The effect is sometimes called *mushing*, in that the lower-level elements might seem to have mushed together. But in fact there is no evidence for some form of combining, particularly in that details (by their very nature) don't combine.

2. Hierarchical Structure in Autobiographical Memory

Many authors have reported that autobiographical memory involves a hierarchical structure (Barsalou, 1988; Brown, Shevell, & Rips, 1986; Conway, 1992, 1999;

Conway & Bekerian, 1987; Linton, 1975; Neisser, 1986; Schooler & Hermann, 1992). According to this view, personal memories are subsumed under what might be called categories. Some of these are high in the hierarchy; they will have subcategories nested beneath them, and each of these will have more restricted subcategories positioned yet lower in the hierarchy.

Linton (1975, 1979, 1986) reported a structure of this kind at which the highest level was identified as *mood tone*. Memories have a particular complex of emotion attached to them. This property was placed at the top of Linton's hierarchy because all her personal memories possessed mood tone. At the next level Linton placed *themes*. Themes involve a major area of concern that runs through one's life. Examples would be a *work theme* (all memories reflecting aspects of professional work) or *relations with loved ones*. Many memories, occurring at disparate times, would be subsumed under each theme. The model also posited *subthemes*, these being smaller aspects of theme material.

Beneath subthemes Linton placed *extendures*. Extendures involve periods of life of a certain kind. There exists within extendures some significant persistent orientation (Linton, 1986, p. 57). Examples would be "The time that I was married," "The time when I worked for Company X," and so on. Extendures involve periods of time that can occur either sequentially or be broken into different times, and they would typically involve many episodes. The extendure as a whole, however, has a beginning at a certain time and an end at a certain time. Note that this is not the case with themes.

Beneath extendures were *episodes*. These involved specific events, such as going on a hike or throwing a dinner party. The next level down involved *elements*, or features of an event. For instance, during a given hike the party might have lost its way. The final level of the hierarchy consisted of *details*: the specific information that clothe memories, such as color of leaves on a tree or the way a puddle splashed. Details would often involve perceptual information.

An important property of hierarchies of this kind is that a subcategory can be described as being part of the categories above it. Thus, seeing a particular leaf (a *detail*) was part of the *element* of going down a certain trail on a hike. The act of going down the trail was part of the hiking *episode*, and that in turn would be part of some period of life, an *extendure*, such as "The time I worked for Company X."

Figure 11.2 shows Linton's hierarchy of memory types.

Other psychologists have described similar models of hierarchical organization in personal memories. The model developed by Anderson and Conway (1993) and by Conway (1995), shown in Figure 11.3, corresponds closely to the Linton model.

Although in general the highest levels of the hierarchy are recalled best, the researchers noted that there can be exceptions to this general rule. Sometimes information relatively low in the hierarchy will be well retained, even when other and "higher" content is forgotten. Information of this kind was labeled as a *strong element*. One participant in a study examining personal memories, for instance, remembered the episode of "Dancing With Angela" with particular clarity.

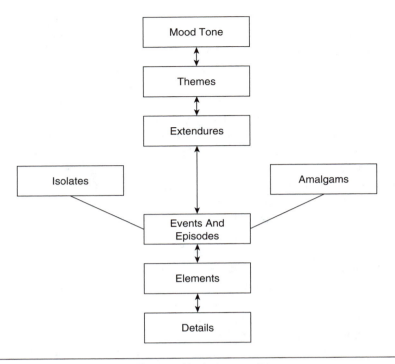

Figure 11.2 Linton's Hierarchy of Autobiographical Memory Content

NOTE: Isolates are events that do not relate in a logical fashion to the episodes in one's life. Amalgams are episodes that become connected in memory even though they, too, show no logical relation. They are usually connected simply on a temporal basis—because they occurred close together in time.

SOURCE: From Linton, M., "Ways of searching and the contents of memory," in D. C Rubin (Ed.), *Autobiographical Memory,* copyright © 1986. Reprinted with permission of Cambridge University Press.

2.1. Hierarchies Within an Event * * * * *

Neisser (1986) examined the hierarchical structure of memory within the context of individual actions. Each such action can be seen as operating at the bottom (or close to the bottom) of a hierarchy.

While writing the 1986 article, Neisser touched a T on the keyboard. The act of touching the T would nest under the act of *typing*, which would nest under that of *writing an article*, and that under *writing a series of articles* to be published by a given editor. It would thus be possible to describe this event from the lowest level—how the T-key looked—to the level of an *episode* and an *extendure*, given that this form of activity made up part of the author's life. At the highest levels, it could be part of a *writing/professional* work theme. The point is that all the information mentioned here would be coded as the memory of this single event. Critical to the present view of memory, the lower-level elements would be forgotten almost at once, while the episode itself might be retained for some while, and the higher level, of having written articles, for a very long time. Thus any given act of memory

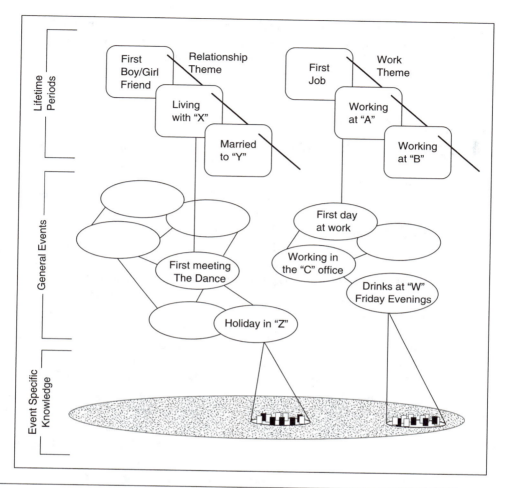

Figure 11.3   Conway's Hierarchy of Memory Content

would reflect only some of the originally coded levels (with the fact that a T had been pressed at a particular time and a range of other lower-rank information, being forgotten).

Neisser (1986, p. 75) further suggested that these levels are all represented in memory, leaving more or less independent traces behind. Again, the high-level or generalized information will be retained most strongly across time. Repeated information will also be retained (and may be mistaken for a single event).

A further important point involves the way in which memory moves. Traditionally, researchers have tended to think of such movement in terms of associations among relatively low-level elements, such as stimuli (for example, one word being associated in memory with another) or, at a somewhat higher level, among events. But according to the present model, the most powerful associations would be mediated through the high-level cognitive structures, not the details.

Neisser also advocated a multiple-trace view of memory. The multiple levels of the hierarchy would coexist for a while, as would different bodies of content related to the same episode, even if the retrieved memory for that episode, and the LTM codes associated with it, changed.

3. Access and Retrieval in Autobiographical Memory

In many cases when a memory is specified, the content returns at once. This may be because it is material placed high in the autobiographical hierarchy, or has been rehearsed, or is of particular emotional interest. Recency will also provide a strong recall function.

Suppose I am asked whether I have ever seen any pink-colored rocks. If I had in fact encountered such objects a few days earlier, I am likely to recall the fact with no effort. Short of this, however, I would probably have to search my memory.

It is believed that autobiographical memory possesses a high level of organization and that we use this organization when we perform a memory search. In fact, memory appears to have many different forms of internal organization. Two major forms include the hierarchical structure, described above, and temporal structure. We appear to code for events based on the temporal order in which they occur.

If I do not instantly recall whether I have ever seen pink-colored rocks, I might try to imagine a superordinate category, under which the target memory might be stored. For instance, I might reason that the only place I would be likely to encounter pink rocks would be on a beach, and so specify my "Holidays Taken at the Ocean" memories and see if any of these would provide a beach with the target objects. This would reflect a strategy using the property of hierarchical organization.

Why does it work? Higher-level information is generally strongly coded and so potentially available. Once it is activated, it will lead to other, associated information, increasing the probability that the latter can be retrieved. For instance, you might be asked to recall events related to May 12th and at first have no such memories at all. But if you then recollect that you went to dinner at Sam Smith's, a wealth of details may follow. Sam Smith (a restaurant) provided a reasonably high-level entry into LTM, associated with many more specific details.

Linton (1975) reported success in recalling memories through the use of the strategy described above (entry at a high level in the hierarchy) and also through temporal strategies. Beginning at the beginning of an event, and moving through it, could lead to more detailed recollection than just trying to recall the event as such. Backward temporal organization was also helpful.

3.1. Strategies for Retrieval Involving Constraints, or No Constraints

Anderson and Conway (1993) examined their participant's memories, requiring that the searches be performed on the basis of free recall, forward-, or backward-order recall, or recall based on centrality. "Centrality" involved beginning with the most important or interesting component, then moving to the next most interesting component, and so on.

Small changes in the task produced somewhat different patterns of data. When the cue specified any personal memory within the last 10 years (with 10 seconds for recall), a free recall approach worked best, followed by forward-order recall. When the task was to recall a memory in response to a noun (for example, "memory involving a tree"), forward-order worked best, followed by free recall, interest value, and backward recall, in that order.

In the case of personal memories, the order in which content was recalled varied relatively little between free recall and forward-order instructions. Under free recall, about 50% of the content was generated in its original temporal sequence. Participants were using not only a temporal strategy but also some other approach, which may have focused on selecting strongly coded elements of the memory quickly and easily, thus providing an edge over the "temporal-only" approach.

In contrast to the study described above, Reiser, Black, and Kalamarides (1986) tested their participants without specifying any strategy to be used in recall. Here, the participants reported the strategies that they were using as they recalled the target material. They were asked to remember the following: an event, a mental state, a combination of event/mental state, or an activity that ended in failure. For example, the questions included (1) Do you recall having your hair cut? (2) Do you recall ever feeling impatient? (3) Do you recall ever feeling cold during an examination? (4) Could you ever not pay for an item while shopping?

During a search, participants used the hierarchical order strategy. Strikingly, when they identified the higher-level constituent for the beginning stages of the memory search, they always chose activities (events), and never states. For instance, when asked if they had ever been cold at an examination, they would first search their memories for times when they had taken an examination (the activity) and then try to determine if they had felt cold during any such event. They did not attempt to recall feeling cold and then "see" whether this had occurred during an examination. Other strategies were also used. For instance, causality was deployed on occasion as the starting point for the search. If a participant was trying to think of a particular kind of episode, he or she might first imagine what events would produce the target situation. Temporal organization was also used.

It thus appears that the hierarchical organization of autobiographical content is based largely on activity codes. The researchers interpreted these data as indicating the existence of multiple knowledge structures that supply a rich matrix of information and that can lead to a target memory, given the interassociations within these sets. They also endorsed a constructivist model of memory, positing that memories are reconstructed at the time of attempted recall.

4. Accuracy and Distortion in Adult Recall

As described above, information placed at a high or generalized level in episodic memory is retained longest and is least likely to include errors. By the same logic, it is generally the lowest elements (Conway's Event Specific Knowledge (ESP) or Linton's details) that are forgotten first and are also most subject to being changed in memory.

The form of testing also influences the likelihood of accurate recall. Memories reported under conditions of free recall are least likely to contain errors. When questions are posed, and memory content is weak, errors reliably emerge (Christiansen, 1989; Neisser & Harsch, 1992). As a general rule, the more pressure exerted on the individual to recall, the more risk of changed memory content.

In contrast, as might be expected, strongly coded information does not suffer distortion when the individual is exposed to questions or to misleading information (Loftus, Altman, & Geballe, 1975; Loftus & Hoffman, 1989).

As described in Chapter 9, personal memories are not always accurate. They can change due to source misattribution and (according to some models) due to the presence of inferred but invalid content. The weaker the original memory content, the more likely this is to occur. It is also reasonable to assume that much of our autobiographical memories do reflect weak content. We form continuous personal memories, including a very large body of information. It is unlikely that all this vast store of content would be strongly coded.

Concerning the issue of weak autobiographical content outlined above, Conway, Collins, Gathercole, and Anderson (1996) examined the ability of the first two authors to distinguish between true and false memories on the basis of recognition. These authors kept a diary of certain events that had occurred in their lives. They also created false diary entries in which one component of an otherwise true episode was altered or an entire false event was constructed. Another experimenter created a series of wholly false events. All were made to be plausible. Seven months later, the authors examined this set of memories, attempting to distinguish the true from the false.

Recognition of true events was very strong (95% accurate). However, there was a high false-recognition rate of the changed and completely fabricated memories, 50% false recognition for the changed and 23% for the fabricated.

The authors explained the high count of false memories on the basis of a similarity effect. All the memories had been constructed in such a way as to fit with the background knowledge and other relevant aspects of the participants' lives. In the case of the changed memories, most of the information of course conformed to a real event, and this was enough to convince the authors that the entire episode was true. In the case of the fabricated memories, the background and general information all fitted the author-participants' knowledge of their own histories, and apparently this strong match, even though the specific event had not happened, also (in roughly a quarter of the cases) provided a sense of the episode reflecting an actual event.

It is clear from the data outlined above that the memory function depends strongly on background knowledge when evaluating material that may or may not be a real memory. This does not, however, appear to be the only variable involved in accepting information in this fashion, since some false but wholly plausible memories are not accepted. There is some other factor at work. What this factor may be is difficult to conceptualize, but it may simply be memory strength, as such, or some kind of effective personal autobiographical stamp, such as "I saw this; I lived through this."

4.1. Observer Memories

Henri and Henri (1898), studying children's memories, found that the children would at times see themselves in the recalled episode from "the outside" (as if they were external observers of the scene). Nigro and Neisser (1983), examining the same issue, found that adults sometimes recalled an episode from their own viewpoint (that is, remembering what they saw or heard from the perspective in which they had originally seen or heard it), and sometimes, as with the children, they recalled an episode as if viewing it from outside. The authors called the first form of recollection a *field memory* and the second, an *observer memory*. Recent recollections were more likely to be of the field type, and more remote recollections, of the observer type. Robinson and Swanson (1993) further reported that the cues deployed when an individual is trying to recall a given episode can influence the likelihood of retrieving either a field- or observer-type recollection.

Since we cannot see ourselves from a different vantage point when we form a memory, the existence of this kind of recall implies the ability to generate details that were not part of the original code. In other words, the changed memories are constructed at the time of recall.

5. Goals, Perspective, and Meaning * * * * *

It is widely believed today that motivation, goals, emotion, and background knowledge and interests play a central role in determining the particular information that will be retrieved, for any given body of memory content (Bartlett, 1932; Blaney, 1986; Robinson, 1999). Today, the term *perspective* is used for this combination of variables.

Goals determine the selection of what will be attended within an episode. They also determine which components of already coded material in LTM will later be remembered. It has been found that when individuals are interested in, or mentally focused on, some particular aspect of a memory, different information is retrieved from the same memory set (Anderson & Pitchert, 1978). The potential information available when we encode and when we recall an episodic memory is extremely large, and selection must occur within this body of content. The same episode can be interpreted in many ways. It has been found that a given episode can even be constructed differently, across different occasions, by the same person (Robinson, 1999).

One major factor that can provide variable interpretation of an event centers on the inferred goals of the participants in a memory. Although the specific events are usually not open to interpretation, the reasons for their occurrence are. Within this context Robinson (1999) noted, "People can agree about referential details, but disagree about what they mean" (p. 207).

I can easily infer why Jane put a full kettle on the stove and tea leaves into a teapot. It was to make tea. But I may also know that Jane does not like tea. Her actions now need to be explained. The explanation will probably reflect what this scene is really about. And, clearly, there are multiple possible explanations, and these might differ from person to person.

Williams (1992) described the case of a woman who had previously recalled an event but whose memory of the event changed after she had learned some unpleasant information. Apparently, the newly acquired knowledge altered her understanding of the earlier event and thus changed the content of the memory.

Holmberg and Holmes (2001) examined recollections on the part of married couples of their past conversations with one another. Their memories were examined early in the period of the relationship and again after a delay. Those individuals whose marriages were stable remembered the conversations in essentially the same way. In contrast, the memory content of the couples whose marriages were not going well tended to show change. The shift was toward recollection of more negative content in the exchanges than had been recalled previously.

The perspective assumption thus posits that emotional frame may lead to the increased likelihood of retrieval of some aspects of a memory over others and to reinterpretation of memory content. The same appears to be true of goals and general attitudes maintained in the present.

6. Positive and Negative Affect in Episodic Memory

When individuals are asked to rate their mood across daily living, all groups, with the exception of those living in extreme poverty or social isolation, report more happy than unhappy mood overall (Diener & Diener, 1996; Lykken & Tellegen, 1996). This is true even of individuals suffering from physical or mental handicaps.

A parallel finding is that when experimental participants choose memories to report, they retrieve a higher incidence of positive than negative memories, and this outcome holds across a wide variety of testing conditions (Suedfeld & Eich, 1995; Thompson, Skowronski, Larsen, & Betz, 1996).

It is generally known that the strength of emotion associated with a particular episode tends to fade across time, just as memory content fades. A more striking discovery, however, is that negative emotion (except for very strong, traumatic emotion) fades more quickly and to a greater extent than positive emotion (Cason, 1932; Walker, Skowronski, & Thompson, 2003; Walker, Vogl, & Thompson, 1997). This outcome is identified as *fading affect bias*. In an interesting corollary to the phenomenon, Holmes (1970) found that although the affect associated with negative events fades to a greater extent than affect associated with positive events, the level of content recall of the two forms of memory, across time, is the same.

It is widely believed that the fading of negative emotions involves a healthy coping mechanism (Walker et al., 2003). This view is supported by the finding that mildly or severely depressed individuals do not show the usual pattern. Here, negative rather than positive memories are more likely to be retrieved when the participant is free to select episodes for recall, and the negative affect does not decrease as rapidly across time as occurs with nondepressed individuals (Abramson, Metalsku, & Alloy, 1989; Seidlitz, Wyer, & Diener, 1997).

The decline of affect over time in nondepressed participants, and also in mildly depressed participants, is shown in Figure 11.4.

6.1. The Reminiscence Bump

When people are asked to report memories from their past, without any restriction as to which memory should be recalled, individuals more than 50 years of age tend to remember events ranging from their middle teens to the middle or late 20s (Conway & Haque, 1999; Jansari & Parkin, 1996; Rubin, Wetzler, & Nebes, 1986). This stretch of autobiographical time has therefore been identified as involving a recollection or *reminiscence bump.*

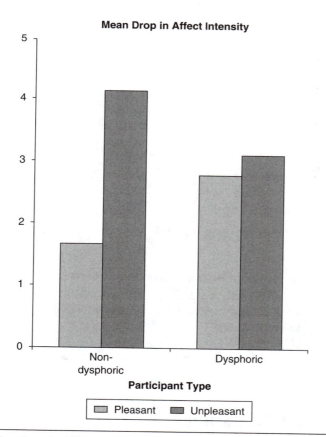

Figure 11.4   Drop in Affect Intensity Across Time for Pleasant and Unpleasant Memories, on the Part of Nondepressed (Nondysphoric) and Mildly Depressed (Dysphoric) Individuals

SOURCE: From Walker, W. R., Skowronski, J. J., & Thompson, C. P., "Life is pleasant and memory keeps it that way," in *Review of General Psychology,* 7(2), copyright © 2003, American Psychological Association. Reprinted with permission.

A number of theories have been developed to explain this effect. Berntsen and Rubin (2002) found that most of the memories from this period were happy memories. "Important" recollections also tend to center here. This period of time may simply be one of particular emotional vividness, implying the usual influence of strong emotion on memory. Berntsen and Rubin (2004) have invoked an alternative view, however, according to which the period is one in which the individual experiences may important cultural life scripts (going to college, marriage, etc.) and that these scripts may enhance recollection.

In contrast to the standard findings, Rubin and Berntsen (2003) reported that when participants are asked to report negative memories, there is no recollection bump, but instead the incidence of negative memories increases with age. These three forms of recall (happy, important, sad) are shown in Figure 11.5.

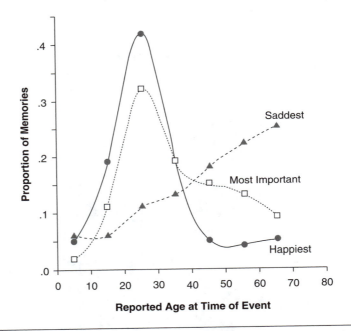

Figure 11.5   Recall of Happy, Important, and Sad Memories by Individuals Aged 40 Years or Older

SOURCE: From Rubin, D. C. & Berntsen, D., "Life scripts help to maintain autobiographical memories of highly positive, but not highly negative events," in *Memory & Cognition, 31*(1), copyright © 2003. Reprinted with permission of Psychonomic Society.

PART III: FLASHBULB MEMORIES

1. The Nature of Flashbulb Memories

Colgrove (1899) described a study in which 179 individuals were asked to recall their memories concerning the death of President Lincoln, 33 years earlier.

Typical examples from two respondents (aged 76 and 79, respectively) were, "I was standing by the stove getting dinner; my husband came in and told me," and, "I was setting out a rose bush by the door. My husband came in the yard and told me."

In 1977, Brown and Kulik conducted a similar study for unexpected and shocking news. They interviewed 40 African Americans and 40 Caucasian Americans concerning their memories of hearing of the assassination of various prominent figures, including President Kennedy, and also their memories for personal shocks.

The authors predicted that a special memory function would come into play under these circumstances. It would not only involve the retention of the critical news, as would be expected but also heightened (in the sense of long-lasting and also detailed) memory for context. Context included recall of (1) place (where the individual was when he or she heard about the news, (2) ongoing event (what the individual had been doing), (3) informant, (4) affect in others, (5) own affect, and (6) aftermath. Brown and Kulik described this nonstandard recall as a flashbulb memory. They suggested that a special neural mechanism is probably activated when individuals live through highly emotional events. The effect may be somewhat like a flashbulb going off, in that the mechanism "indiscriminately" catches information about the immediate context.

All but one participant showed flashbulb effects for the time when they heard of Kennedy's death. Other memories also provided flashbulb effects. These indicated a role played by the emotional importance of the event to the individual. For instance, more African American participants displayed a flashbulb memory for the time when they heard of Martin Luther King's death than did Caucasian Americans.

There was support for earlier claims to the effect that highly trivial, perceptual details are or can be retained in flashbulb memories. A colleague of Brown's remembered walking up some steps at his college, as he was told of Kennedy's death. He could still recall the feeling of the steps under his feet, 13 years after the event.

Although the term *flashbulb memory* was coined in 1977, Brown and Kulik rejected the view that the function was in all ways camera-like. It was so, in that it was indiscriminate. Unlike ordinary recall, the effect did not favor important information over unimportant information. But it was not camera-like in that it also indiscriminately picked up some details, while failing to retain others. The second author, for instance, recalled his teacher crying in his homeroom immediately after hearing the news; but the teacher's hairstyle and dress were both missing from the memory.

Nor is associated, detailed semantic information, concerning the critical event, retained over the years. Brown recalls that he was on the telephone and received the news over the phone. He later returned to his work, but no longer recalled, in 1977, what that work had been.

Brown and Kulik examined the effects of rehearsal and consequentiality on the forming of flashbulb memories. Consequentiality was defined as the extent to which the participant felt that the event might have some impact on his or her own life. Both variables were found to correlate with flashbulb memories. Later studies have failed to consistently replicate the association between rehearsal and consequentiality and flashbulb recall. Pillemer (1984) found no relation between them, while Conway, Anderson, and Larson (1994) did find a relation. The only property that appeared to be invariably present across episodes involving flashbulb effects was characterized by Rubin and Kozin (1984) as "personal importance."

1.1. Flashbulb Memories and Reconstruction

Neisser (1982, chap. 4) noted that no evidence had been gathered concerning whether the flashbulb memories reported by Brown and Kulik were accurate. The implication would appear to be that if a special neural mechanism comes into play at such times and if it is flashbulb-like, then the retained content would be veridical. Neisser suggested that an alternative way of viewing flashbulb recall could involve the following. In the case of highly emotional events, the memory system may tend to work on the material to an unusual degree. The original episode is likely to be discussed and also activated in thought. The result could be an unusual level of inferential reconstruction, rather than heightened, veridical recall.

Neisser (1982, chap. 4) described a personal memory that he had retained from adolescence to middle life. He had been listening to a baseball game on the radio, and the game was interrupted with news of the Japanese attack on Pearl Harbor. He had been 13 years old. He recalled running upstairs to tell his mother. The memory seemed clear. Much later, however, it occurred to him that nobody broadcasts baseball games in December.

In an intriguing footnote to this flawed memory, however, Thompson and Cowan (1986) reported an interview heard on the National Public Radio Morning Report on December 6, 1985. Red Barber was being interviewed on the subject of the Army-Navy game. Barber noted that it was ironic that the game was to be played on the anniversary of the bombing of Pearl Harbor. He also noted that on the same day, years ago, he had been covering a game between the Giants and the Dodgers, these being in that year the names of two football teams. He had heard about the bombing at half time.

Neisser's recollection, then, was possibly accurate in almost all details and had endured for a very long time. It was not, however, an example of purely veridical memory, since a small inference, likely to have been based on LTM retention of the names of the teams, had been generated; this concerned the type of game being broadcast.

Within the context of the accuracy question, a large number of studies were conducted in which participants were questioned directly following some public disaster and then questioned again some extended period of time (usually between 6 months and 3 years) later (Bohannon, 1988; Christianson & Engelberg, 1999; Lee & Brown, 2003; Neisser & Harsch, 1992; Schmolck, Buffalo, & Squire, 2000; Wright, 1993). In the majority of these studies, a memory was scored as being a flashbulb memory if the participants recalled information from a given number of Brown and Kulik's context categories. As described above, the categories involved where the participants were when they heard the news, who told them of the news, and so on. The studies typically found a mixture of accurate and changed recall after the period of delay. Also, the changes were of the kind that might be expected if the participants were inferring, as against actually remembering, the original content. It was therefore widely concluded that flashbulb memories did not involve any unusual mechanism.

Questions were later raised, however, concerning whether the memories tested should have been classified as flashbulb memories at all. Although many involved hearing of public disasters, this is a common occurrence today. It is not clear that the fact of a disaster would be sufficient to provide the very strong emotional impact associated with the first identification of flashbulb recall. Wright and Gaskell (1995) noted that these events may well have been of flashbulb caliber for only a small, unknown subset of the individuals who heard about them. A further difficulty centered on the practice of classifying a memory as flashbulb recall if various aspects of the context had been recalled. Since this classification occurred on the first interview, shortly after the target event, a standard memory function would be expected to retain context information. The remarkable thing about the first demonstrations of this possibly special form of recall was that these trivial aspects of context were retained after 13 or 17 years.

Larson (1992) noted that interpretation of any flashbulb research is not possible in the absence of reliable information concerning how long individuals normally retain "unimportant" context information. Yet no such standards had been established. Larson tested his own retention of news items and autobiographical events. He found that recall of context information was at roughly chance level within 2 months. Predictably, the semantic content of the nature of the events or news lasted much longer.

In another study of the *Challenger* disaster, Bohannon and Symons (1992) separated participants who reported higher levels of distress over the event from participants reporting relatively low levels of distress. They examined their participants' recall shortly after the study and again after 3 years. Those who had reported higher levels of distress showed significantly better recall of context information than the nondistress group, and recall was often high. Location, for instance, was recalled correctly by 93% of the high distress participants, but only by 18% of the others. Perhaps most striking, however, was that the high-distress individuals recalled the context events over time at a higher level than they recalled the semantic content (reversing the normal pattern of adult episodic recall).

Also of some interest, recall was most accurate on the part of the high-distress participants who had *not* rehearsed the event or had rehearsed it to a limited extent. Within the same group, low-accuracy scores were provided by individuals who had more extensively rehearsed the episode.

Er (2003) examined the recollections of individuals who had been caught in the devastating Marmara earthquake in 1999 and compared these with memories of individuals who had not been victims of the quake. Both groups reported feeling very strong emotion concerning the event. Er tested for context memory and for general semantic recollection, both following the episode and after a delay of a year. Victims of the quake showed almost perfect memory for the context details, with "where" showing 100% correspondence and the other categories scoring close to that figure. The participants who had heard about the event showed a significantly weaker memory function in each category. The data are shown in Figure 11.6.

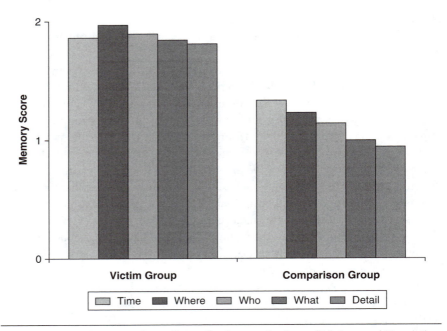

Figure 11.6 Context and Detail Recollection on the Part of Victims and Nonvictims of the Marmara Earthquake

SOURCE: From Er, N., "A new flashbulb memory model applied to the Marmara earthquake," in *Applied Cognitive Psychology, 17*(5), copyright © 2003. Reprinted with permission of John Wiley & Sons, Limited.

In the present study, participants in both groups had rehearsed the event frequently. However, rehearsal alone did not provide perfect recall following a year's delay. The author attributed the effect not to "personal importance," the variable most often cited in earlier flashbulb studies, but to emotional impact. Her claim is that personal importance may produce a strong emotional reaction, but it is the emotion as such that provides flashbulb recall.

Other studies involving political events (reported as having a powerful emotional impact) have again indicated context recall extending across very long periods. Tekcan and Peynircioglu (2002), for instance, tested recall, on the part of Turkish subjects, of news of the death of Ataturk, the founder of the Turkish republic, 55 years after the event. Seventy-two percent of the participants who had been 6 years or age or older at the time recalled details about informant, location, activity, and others present.

1.2. 9/11 and Flashbulb Memory

One of the striking aspects of the research into flashbulb memory is that very long-term recall for trivial, contextual information is often present, while no study has reported a parallel increase (above that found in other contexts) concerning the details of the event itself. Thus, recall for aspects of setting, normally forgotten after about 2 months (based on Larsen's estimate) may be retained for 14, 33, or even 55 years, while there is no spectacular increase in semantic recall of the happening that produced the flashbulb outcome.

Given this background, Tekcan, Ece, Gulgoz, and Er (2003) suggested that when flashbulb recall is involved, context memory (also termed *autobiographical* memory) is coded differently from event memory (compared with control nonflashbulb conditions for both). That is, the effect impacts primarily on context recall. Tracing the two forms of memory for the events of 9/11 after a year, the authors found that event accuracy and quantity declined more or less linearly, while context memory declined very little. Smith et al. (2003) reported similar findings: a decline in event recall after a 6-month delay, with a slight increase in context recall (possibly due to inferential reconstruction).

Summary

Human beings are generally amnesic for the first years of their lives. Various theories have been advanced to explain this phenomenon. The first memories that can be recalled in adult life are "fragment" memories, with no extended context. Freud posited both that the earliest memories were repressed and that they were inherently weak. Current theories include the view that first memories may be inherently weak or that infantile thought may be structured differently from later thought, rendering cues ineffective. It has also been suggested that autobiographical recollection (a form more advanced than the fragment type) is dependent on the exposure of the child to adult models. Various unusual forms of autobiographical memory have been identified. In some cases, two individuals may recall the same memory as being their own, when the memory must in fact belong to only one of them.

Later childhood and adult memory have hierarchical structure. Material at the higher levels is well recalled, while material at lower levels is often forgotten and can also become altered with the passage of time. The hierarchical structure has been shown to aid in recall since the activation of the stronger, higher-level content can lead to the activation and retrieval of lower-level content. A second factor that aids in autobiographical recall is time. We appear to code for events on a temporal basis.

It has been found that when episodic-memory events appear highly plausible, we are at risk for "recognizing" them as having occurred, even when they have not.

"Observer" memories are recalled as if the individual were watching his memory from outside. A phenomenon known as *perspective* also plays a major role in determining the nature of memory content. This involves goals and beliefs and feelings, which may lead to the retrieval of different information relating to an identical episode.

When older adults are asked to recall episodic memories at random, they tend to recall memories from their late teens to their 20s. This is known as the reminiscence bump.

Flashbulb recall involves the very long-term recollection of trivial context information following the news of some unexpected, highly emotional event. There is dispute as to whether this is valid recollection or an outcome of inferential reconstruction.

Discussion

Concerning episodic recall from the first years of life, the hypothesis that infants and toddlers may not form memories has been clearly proved to be inaccurate. Thus, today the explanation for infantile amnesia lies between the assumption of a weak mnemonic capacity (that cannot endure across long periods of time) and of qualitatively different forms of representation, as compared with adult representation, such that cues are ineffective. Both views may be correct.

With regard to the endurance of fragment memories, the theoretical interpretations fall between that of rehearsal, as the primary cause, and of emotion, as the primary cause. Here, it is assumed that the fragment memories are not weak memories and that their availability or strength is due to rehearsal, emotion, or both. A cueing interpretation is rarely cited within this context. Such an approach would have to assume that there is something about early fragment memories that corresponds to adult (as against infantile) thought. The content of the memories does not appear to support this position. Related to the same argument, the fact of fragment memories—the fact of their existence—weighs somewhat against a general cueing hypothesis as an explanation for early-childhood amnesia. Such memories appear to have been created on the basis of the normal forms of representation for a 3- or 4-year-old child, and yet they have been retained permanently.

Research into autobiographical memory has emphasized the importance of hierarchical organization in human episodic recall. Such hierarchies appear to determine memory strength in several ways. While rehearsal was emphasized in the verbal learning literature as the principal means of strengthening memory, high-level structures emerge in the present field as playing an equally important role.

Recollection is generally considered strong if it is accurate. It is also considered strong if it has endured across a period of time when most memories have been forgotten. An important question here appears to be whether a recollection can be considered a strong memory if it is not fully accurate. Fragment memories endure for life and, of course, date from a time when almost all episodic content cannot be remembered at all. And although the majority of such memories appear, on the basis of current research, to be accurate, they are not always so. You may remember a green, white, and orange floor, last seen when you were 2 years old. But the floor may really have been only white and green. Within this context, probably most people would conclude that what is involved is essentially "a real memory."

The same issue emerges within the context of flashbulb effects. Their critical property appears to be that they produce context memories of extraordinarily long duration. This does not mean that the memories are completely accurate. It appears likely that no remote memories can lay claim to perfect accuracy. The original assumption of some form of unusual memory process, however, appears to be supported by the available data. Context information is trivial information; it is not normally retained for 13, 17, or 35 years. Yet if this content had simply been inferred, it would be reasonable to expect a high level of inferred content concerning the critical event itself. But this outcome has not been found.

CHAPTER 12

Memory for Images

Overview

1. Human recognition of images (scenes, etc.) is strong. However, it appears that this high level of recognition is achieved on the basis of identifying the general contours of the scene or picture, and that it does not include identifying more trivial detail. Human recall of detail therefore tends to be weak and, often, changed from the original image.

2. At one time, there was a controversy concerning whether images were coded as propositional descriptions or in the form of a direct, analog image code. The latter view has generally prevailed.

3. In support of the analog view, it appears that when geometric images are rotated mentally, the rotation takes longer when the corresponding object would have to be moved for a longer time through physical space.

4. For the same visual stimulus, shape and location/size information are believed to be processed in different areas of the brain. The two sets of information are then "bound" back together.

5. Many of the processing structures involved in perception appear to come into play when mental images are formed.

6. Eidetic individuals can maintain a visual picture in memory across periods of minutes and "see" it on a screen as if it were present.

7. Hypermnesia is the improvement in memory for stimuli across time, with repeated testing. The effect occurs reliably for pictures, but not for words.

Learning Objectives

1. Knowledge of the general properties of human recall and recognition of visual images.

2. Knowledge of evidence supporting the analog view of imagery.

3. Knowledge of the sites within the brain involved in processing shape and location information.

4. Knowledge of the relationship between mental images and perceptual processing.

The present chapter covers research into memory for visual images, both those that reflect perceptual information stored in long-term memory (LTM) (as when we see a tree and later recall its appearance) and imagery generated from LTM, as when we imagine a tree that we have never in fact seen. The former kind of imagery is described as a memory image and the latter may be described as a mental image.

1. The Strength of Visual Memory

In the early years of research within the verbal learning tradition, it was found that words whose referents can be easily visualized are remembered better than words representing abstract, nonvisualizable concepts. Thus, DOG or WINDOW is recalled more readily than EFFORT or PLAN.

Paivio (1969, 1971, 1991) offered a *dual coding hypothesis* to explain these findings. According to the dual coding position, when an item that can be easily visualized is learned, two representations are stored in LTM. The first reflects a verbal representation of the word, and the second an image of the object that the word denotes. Paivio (1991) suggested that the two coding formats involve different processing structures, operating on different knowledge structures, and that these functions are probably located in different areas of the brain. At the time of attempted recall, the subject thus has two associative routes by which the target can be reached, as against only one. The dual coding hypothesis was compatible with the view that successful recall involves finding an associative path between the relevant cues and the target memory (see Chapter 2, Section 5.2). The cues in a word list recall test, when the individual was trying to remember List X, would correspond to the representation "List X" and perhaps some additional contextual information. If two potential paths, rather than one, are available, associating these cues with the memory representation, there should be a higher probability of retrieving the target item.

However, something more than finding adequate ways of accessing targets may be involved in the recollection of visual images. Human recognition memory for image-stimuli is generally very strong. In a demonstration of this fact, Shepard (1967) presented his experimental participants with 612 pictures. They examined these stimuli at a self-paced rate. Later, there was a recognition test, in which the participants were shown one original picture and one foil (a new picture) in pairs and were asked to identify the original. The first test occurred 2 hours after the last presentation session, and recognition memory performance for the 612 pictures was virtually perfect. A week later, correct recognition was still operating at 88%.

Standing (1973) presented 10,000 pictures to his experimental participants. The work of presenting the material required 5 days. A recognition test followed in which targets and foils were presented in pairs, as in Shepard's (1967) study. From the resulting data, Standing calculated that his participants had on average retained 6,600 pictures! Testing had occurred directly at the end of the 5-day period. The pictures had been presented only once.

In another experiment, Standing exposed his participants (across different conditions) to 1,000 ordinary pictures, 1,000 words, or 1,000 "vivid" pictures (reflecting a striking situation of some kind). A recognition test was conducted 2 days later. The participants were able to recognize 615 words, 770 ordinary pictures, and 880 vivid pictures.

These data appear to support the hypothesis of image codes (for individual pictures or word items) providing better capacity to determine whether a stimulus had been encountered in the past, rather than an alternative paths to access hypothesis, since vivid pictures should not have an advantage under the second interpretation. It is always possible, however, that the effect of imagery on word recall and the superior recall of pictures as compared with words have different causes.

2. The Weakness of Visual Memory

2.1. Image Recognition

The tests of recognition memory described above did not require much more than the establishment of the global appearance of objects in pictures and their relations to one another. Here, human performance is quite impressive. Recognition memory for internal details (and some other properties of the image) tends to be weaker.

Nickerson and Adams (1979) showed their participants a series of pictures depicting a penny. All but one of the pictures was inaccurate. The participants' task was to recognize the correct drawing. This required that the specific internal details of an actual penny be distinguished. The majority of individuals failed to pick the right drawing.

Critically, we do not need to memorize the specific details of a penny in order to recognize one in daily life. Even so, the test involved a highly familiar object, seen and handled on hundreds of occasions. The pictures used in the recognition test are shown in Figure 12.1a.

2.2. Image Recall

When we perceive stimuli, the resulting conscious experience is extremely detailed. If we are looking, for instance, at a deer standing near a fence, we will perceive the shape, size, and physical location of the deer, the fence and all other stimuli within the field of our attention. In addition, we see a manifold of specific visual detail, reflecting patterning, textures, shadows, and line contours internal to the global contour, brightness, movement, and color. This information, and a good deal more than this, is developed in the stimulus-encoding stage of perception and is at some point in the sequence of ongoing processing connected together into the unified percept. A percept is an organized image that is experienced in awareness. (The preceding description assumes that the individual can see normally.)

Visual LTM does not operate like this. We typically retain only a small portion of the information available in the percept, and while perception is generally veridical, long-term visual memory is subject to distortion.

Nickerson, in the study described above, also required his participants to draw a penny from memory. A sample of the resulting drawings is shown in Figure 12.1b.

Although the subject here was simple and familiar, many distortions occurred in the drawings (particularly distortions in figure orientation).

In the case of complex visual stimuli with which the individual is not highly familiar (such as objects viewed in the course of a natural episode), image recall is characterized by a selective process. Certain kinds of information in the image are more likely to be retained than other kinds. It appears that content that would be

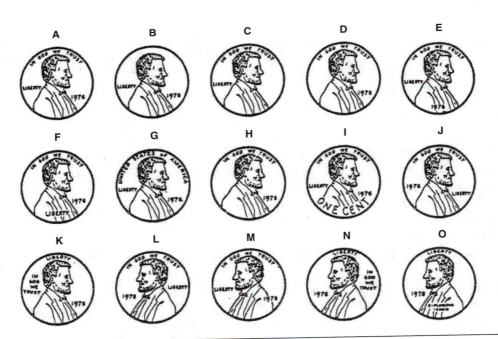

Figure 12.1a   A Sample of the Stimuli Used in the Nickerson and Adams (1979) Recognition Study

SOURCE: From Nickerson, R. A. & Adams, M. J., "Long-term memory for a common object," in *Cognitive Psychology, 11,* copyright © 1979. Reprinted with permission of Elsevier.

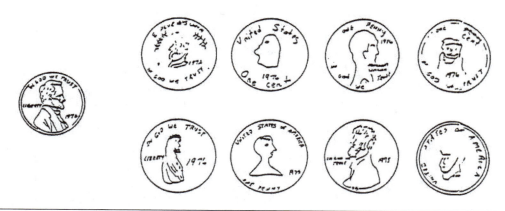

Figure 12.1b   A Sample of the Memory Drawings From the Nickerson and Adams (1979) Recall Study

SOURCE: From Nickerson, R. A. & Adams, M. J., "Long-term memory for a common object," in *Cognitive Psychology, 11,* copyright © 1979. Reprinted with permission of Elsevier.

NOTE: An accurate picture of a penny is shown to the left.

described as important or meaningful is retained, while unimportant details are likely to be forgotten. In the example used above of a deer, for instance, the deer will be recalled visually, while a large blob of shadow falling across the fence and the ground (as large as the deer and with enclosed contours) is not likely to be present in the corresponding memory image. (In contrast, if the picture is drawn when physically present, both important and unimportant details are normally included.)

Memory images can show both changes in small details (lettering in the wrong place) and also changes in the global contours of the original. For instance, the way in which the individual conceptualizes the object can significantly alter the corresponding memory image. (This may be because the memory is being supported by background knowledge concerning what "objects of that kind" generally look like.) Figure 12.2 shows a series of ambiguous objects that were provided with different word labels (and so activated different concepts) when shown to the experimental participants (Carmichael, Hogan, & Walter, 1932).

The memory images were altered from the original to more closely approximate the fashion in which the participants had conceptualized them.

In spite of the biasing influence of word labels, it is easier to retain an image in memory if you can identify the stimulus than if you cannot. Figure 12.3 shows four pictures and a series of corresponding memory drawings. Of the originals, two in the set show objects that can be identified (a horse, men in spacesuits) and two show unidentifiable objects. The participants had studied the pictures for 20 seconds and drawn their copy from memory either immediately after or twenty seconds after the study period.

The memory drawings show a global similarity to the original pictures. But they are obviously unlike photographs. They are characterized by the omission of details that were present, the insertion of details that were not present, distortion of outlines, changes in spatial relations between objects, misrecall of the number of objects, and (a common pattern) changes in the spatial orientation of the object drawn.

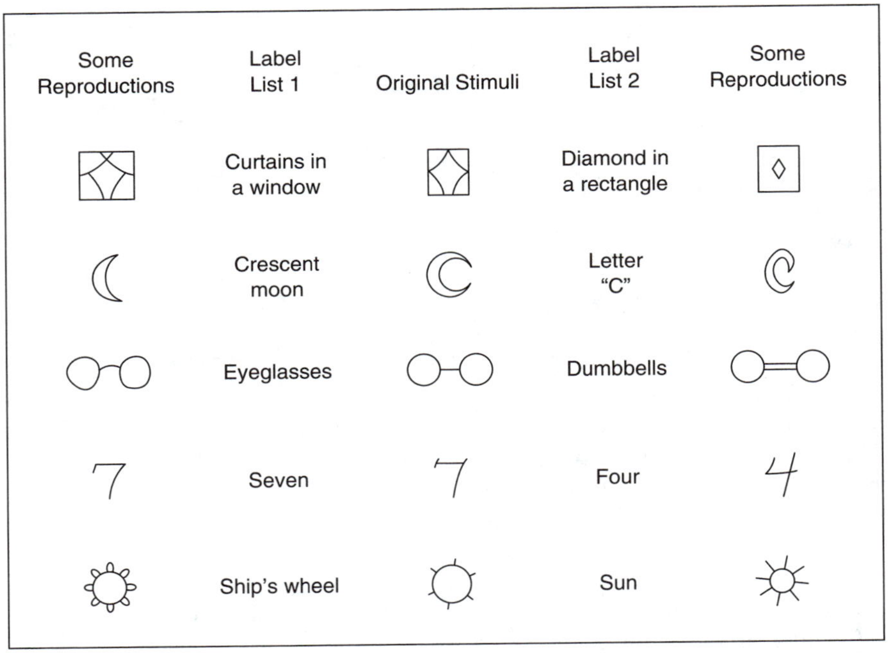

Some Reproductions	Label List 1	Original Stimuli	Label List 2	Some Reproductions
	Curtains in a window		Diamond in a rectangle	
	Crescent moon		Letter "C"	
	Eyeglasses		Dumbbells	
	Seven		Four	
	Ship's wheel		Sun	

Figure 12.2   The Stimuli and Memory Drawings Used in the Carmichael, Hogan, and Walter (1932) Study

Global outline recall is much superior to internal detail recall, which is often missing from the memory images. The memory drawings of the identifiable objects (in the present example, a horse and two men in spacesuits) were all recognizable. In the case of the unidentifiable objects, some pictures were so poorly recalled after 20 seconds that they could not have been matched with the original model.

There is great variation between individuals in the ability to recall visual material. Here, some participants drew quite accurate pictures from memory, while others showed high levels of inaccuracy even under immediate testing. All could draw the images more or less correctly if they copied from a physically present model.

2.3. Different Aspects of a Memory Image: Dissociable Coding

When we perceive visual stimuli, certain kinds of information enter awareness before other kinds of information. Global contours are made available very quickly; internal details are established somewhat later (Glass & Holyoak, 1986, chap. 4). Under conditions of brief exposure, an individual may be aware of the overall shape of an object, but not of its subsidiary parts or features. Also, the location of an object is established more quickly than its shape (Anderson, 1983a, chap. 2), color

Figure 12.3a   Memory and Copy Drawings of Two Identifiable and Two Unidentifiable Pictures

NOTE: In each set, the top left-hand picture is the original. The top right-hand picture is a drawing of the original made when it was physically present (a copy drawing). Pictures in the second row of each set are memory drawings, made after a 20-second study of the original picture and a retention interval, also of 20 seconds. Both copy and memory drawings provided by undergraduate students at SUNY, Oneonta. Memory drawings do not tend to be fully accurate, or in some cases identifiable, even after very brief retention intervals.

information is established earlier than most other visual content, and properties of color and of shape are processed in different areas of the cortex (Spence, Wong, Rusan, & Rastegar, 2006). Clearly, subcomponents of the visual processing system operate to some extent independently of one another.

Visual memory shows many properties similar to those of perception under conditions of brief exposure. As described earlier, global information is remembered better than detail in memory images, and there is dissociation between memories for different aspects of an image: One aspect may be retained, while another is not retained. These include such features as orientation, size, color, spatial location, and so on.

3. The Debate Over Coding

There is no definite agreement at the present time concerning the nature of semantic (meaning) codes in human cognition. According to one dominant theory, however, such codes are propositional (see Chapter 7).

A proposition is a language-like string. For instance, "Nobody likes bad food" is a proposition. According to the present theory, cognitive processes can establish symbols inside our heads corresponding to "nobody," "likes," "bad," and "food." Other symbols indicate the grammatical relations that connect these words together. This complex provides the thought (the meaning content) corresponding to the verbal expression.

A *symbol*, as the term is used today, means an arbitrary representation of meaning. A symbol is arbitrary in that it does not resemble the thing that it represents. The word *rose*, for instance, does not look or smell like a rose. Words are symbols. A neural state (a particular pattern of neurons firing) could also be a symbol: perhaps the symbol for the concept *rose*. Adherents of a propositional model of representation assume that the symbols involved are not words, coded in our heads, but probably states of the brain.

When models of this kind were first introduced into psychology, many researchers, particularly in the field of artificial intelligence (AI), believed that all memory codes must be propositional in nature (Anderson & Bower, 1973; Dennett, 1969; Pylyshyn, 1973; Reid, 1974). This included the codes involved in memory images. The assumption was that we do not represent visual material in a direct visual-spatial format (as images or pictures) but instead in the form of a symbolic/propositional description. An implication of the present hypothesis is that not only would the abstract content relevant to a holiday be coded in propositional form but so would the visual memory images retained from the holiday. The two codes would be identical.

According to the present, imagery as propositional, view, if I remember seeing the horse image shown in Figure 12.3, the codes at an unconscious level would be something like, "The drawing shows the head and neck of a horse, with the neck projecting down toward some water. The horse image begins on the right-hand side of the frame; its top is located distance p downward from the top of the picture, and the front of the head is located at distance q from the right-hand frame," and so on. The description could operate at a less or a more detailed level in terms of specifying the exact length and spatial relations of the pictured contours.

The propositional information would later be translated into the visual-spatial images that we experience in awareness. These images are analog representations. An analog code represents some entity in a form that shows a direct correspondence to that entity. A map is an analog code because distances on the map correspond one-to-one with distances in the external world described by the map.

A picture is also an analog code, to the extent that it shows similarity to the thing represented: A picture of a cat preserves many of the physical dimensions of the cat. Percepts show the same analog property.

Pylyshyn (1973) argued that the LTM image codes must be propositional, since memory images are not photograph-like. As shown above, they include distortions, omissions, and intrusions. Such changes could be explained if it was assumed that the system had generated a description of the original stimulus, which might often be too general to provide a precise image copy. For instance, if the description had merely included "the head and neck of a horse, leaning toward water," then the memory image might show a total left-right reversal. The present approach would also explain why important information is retained in memory images, while trivial information is generally not retained. The description would focus on the critical constituents—not, for instance, the alignment of the horse's mane.

Pylyshyn argued further that the conscious experience of imagery (which, as described above, involves an analog and not a propositional code) is not a valid token of the processing functions of human cognition. Such functions are all based on a propositional format. According to this (symbolic-functionalist) position, awareness does not reflect the underlying nature of our cognition. It is instead a side effect of the "real" functions, characterized as an epiphenomenon.

Other researchers believed that the codes involved in visual imagery and visual memories are analog of type, not only in awareness but also in the underlying levels of processing (Kaufman & Richards, 1969; Kosslyn, 1980, 2006; Kosslyn & Pomeranz, 1977; Piaget & Inhelder, 1971). These individuals did not dispute the claim that a memory image is not like a photograph. It was understood that such images tend to omit information that was originally present and can also show distortions and various forms of reorganization. However, the argument within the propositional camp was that because a camera records visual information, and does so in a strictly mechanical fashion, if a human were coding for visual-spatial information as such, the human must also perform this activity in a strictly mechanical fashion. In addition, since the camera has the capacity to code everything that is physically present, so would the human brain (if it were deploying a visual-spatial code). According to this argument, if mechanical, "copier" coding is not found in human image recall, then the code used must be something other than visual-spatial. The alternative view was that visual-spatial codes can be interpretive, no less than propositional codes. They are interpretive in the sense that there is a processing function involved. This function is of limited capacity. In other words, it does not work in any sense like a camera, even though both the cognitive function and the camera do in the end provide visual-spatial images. The visual-spatial coding involved in the recall of pictures will come into play most strongly when attention is given to a stimulus and not operate when no attention is given. Thus, if the observer attends to a deer in a picture but not to a shadow, the result will be a memory image of the deer and not the shadow. More important elements receive more attention. Also, since the function is of limited capacity, much of the information present in the stimulus will not be retained.

Both neuroimaging and experimental research have provided data that are relevant to the symbolic code versus analog code debate. The work is described in Sections 4 and 5.

4. Propositional Versus Analog Codes in Visual Images: Experimental Research

Kosslyn, Ball, and Reiser (1978) presented the map of an imaginary island to their experimental participants. The participants memorized the map, including various objects (wishing well, etc.) shown on it. They were then asked to focus in memory on a certain object on the map, perhaps the well, and imagine a black speck moving from that object to another, designated object, perhaps the tree. They were to indicate when the speck arrived at the second object. The map of the island is shown in Figure 12.4.

If the memory representation of the map was spatial (that is, reflected an analog code), the participants would mentally "move" the speck across a larger area for objects that were relatively distant from one another and a smaller one if they were not distant. Responses should be slower for the former task than the latter.

If the code for the map was propositional, it would not be possible to mentally move an imagined black speck across a mental map, and response times should not vary as a function of the distance between the two named objects. Thus, the information, "X is 30 centimeters from Y" can be read as quickly as, "X is 3 centimeters from Y."

Figure 12.4　The Map of an Imaginary Island

SOURCE: From Kosslyn, S. M., Ball, T. M., & Reiser, B. J., "Visual images preserve metric spatial information: Evidence from studies of image scanning," in *Journal of Experimental Psychology: Human Perception and Performance, 4,* copyright © 2003, American Psychological Association. Reprinted with permission.

NOTE: Participants memorized the picture, and later were directed to imagine a black spot at a given location, such as the hut, and then to imagine the spot moving across the island to another location, such as the tree.

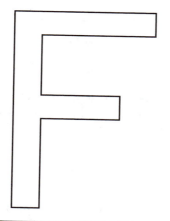

Figure 12.5   An F Shape, as Used in Brooks's Study

NOTE: Tracing each corner from the bottom left, which corners are or are not on the extreme top or bottom of the figure? Participants responded either verbally or by pointing. There was superior performance when they responded verbally, since maintaining the F in memory was a visual task.

The findings were that a one-to-one relationship obtained between the distance on the map between objects and the response time for the participants in imagining the path between them. That is, the longer the distance on the map, the slower the response times. The hypothesis of an analog code for images of maps was thus supported.

Brooks (1968) presented his participants with two tasks, one verbal and one visual-spatial. The verbal task involved hearing sentences ("A bird in the hand is worth two in the bush") and indicating whether each word in the sentence was or was not a noun. The visual task involved remembering a large letter F, which had been presented earlier, and tracing an imaginary path around the F determining whether each corner of the letter was on the extreme top or extreme bottom position on the F. (That is, beginning at the bottom left corner, answers would be: yes, yes, yes, no, no, no, no, no, no, no, yes.)

There were two ways of giving the answer to each task. One was verbal; the other involved pointing to a complex visual array of Ys and Ns (for the answer "yes" and "no," respectively) and thus required visual processing. The letter used in the visual task is shown in Figure 12.5.

The logic of the study was that if different codes were being used for the verbal (semantic) and the imagery task, then there would be less interference under the condition in which the task was in one code and the means of response in another. If the codes were the same, however, then the modality of response should make no difference to the memory performance.

This reasoning was based on long-established knowledge concerning similarity-based interference (see Chapter 2).

The relation can be shown as follows:

Task using Code X + Task using Code X → greater interference

Task using Code X + Task using Code Y → less interference

The participants' performance was superior when the task code and the code used to report their answers varied. The study thus supported the hypothesis that verbal and visual information reflect different codes.

4.1. Rotation Studies

Perhaps the most famous of all the studies involving the question of analog versus nonanalog codes in visual memory, however, involved a long series of experiments conducted by Roger Shepard and his colleagues (Cooper & Shepard, 1973, 1975; Metzler & Shepard, 1971, 1974; Shepard & Cooper, 1982/1986; Shepard & Metzler, 1971). Shepard had become interested in our ability to rotate images of three-dimensional objects in our minds. This kind of movement in the mind has been involved in many famous acts of discovery, including, for instance, Watson and Crick's identification of the structure of DNA. Human beings can achieve mental transformations of objects, such as rotation, in the form of imagery. But does this ability involve an analog code for the space and the objects moving in it or some form of symbolic code?

It is clear that humans can transform and move mental images, which for many individuals is a common experience in daily life. Shepard (1986) added an interesting footnote within this context, however. He had seen a German shepherd jump through a narrow space in the wall in pursuit of a large stick. The dog returned at top speed with the object in its mouth. Shepard imagined that an accident was about to occur as the animal rushed back to the space in the wall, since there would not be room for the stick as well as the other shepherd to pass through it. At the last moment the dog turned its head 90 degrees and went smoothly, complete with stick, through the aperture.

Shepard and Metzler (1971) designed a series of pictures depicting geometrical objects. The objects were shown to the experimental participants in pairs. In some cases, the two objects were the same shape, although this was not apparent because they were presented at different orientations. In some cases, they were not the same. The task of the participants was to decide whether or not the two shapes were congruent. In about half the trials, the two did match, and in about half they did not.

A sample of the objects used in these experiments is shown in Figure 12.6.

Across different conditions, the pairs of objects were shown at different degrees of separation from one another. Thus, one pair might be separated by 20 degrees, and another pair by 80 degrees. This meant that if one of the objects was rotated mentally, to see if it would "fit" the other, the distance traveled would be greater for the 80 degrees of separation and less for the 20 degrees of separation. Thus, if an analog code was being used, it should take longer to identify a match (in those cases where a match did exist) for a pair separated by 80 degrees of separation, as against 20 degrees.

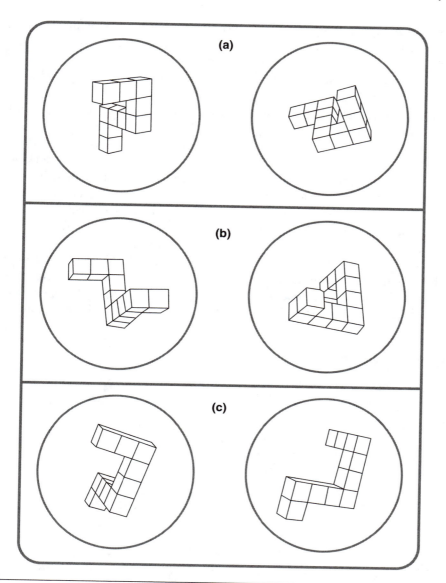

Figure 12.6   A Sample of the Objects Used in the Shepard and Metzler Studies

SOURCE: From Shepard, R. N. & Cooper, L., *Mental Images and Their Transformations,* copyright © 1982. Reprinted with permission of the MIT Press.

If, however, a nonanalog (propositional) code was being used to perform the task, the amount of rotation needed to make one object fit the other would not affect the response. The system would simply describe each object and then see if the descriptions were the same. Response times should be the same for pairs characterized by many or relatively few degrees of separation.

The findings were that the amount of cognitive space through which one object had to be rotated to fit the other was directly related to the amount of time required for a response. The greater the distance of rotation, the slower the response. The match was so good that distance and response times fell on a straight line. The findings are shown in Figure 12.7.

The findings thus supported the hypothesis that an analog code is used when we rotate memory images.

A second variable that was manipulated in this study involved the plane in which the pairs were rotated. In one set they were rotated in the picture plane. That is, the second of the matching objects was a picture of the first after it had been rotated clockwise "in" the picture. (If the top of the object had been pulled along in a clockwise direction, with the rest following, this would produce the second drawing of the pair.)

In a second set, the object was rotated "in depth": That is, as if it were rotating out of the paper toward the observer, top leading and bottom following.

These two planes involved an important difference between the images, since in the case of a physical picture plane rotation a viewer would see no change in the shape of the object. That is, the projection of the retina would retain the original shape. In the case of a depth rotation, however, the object would appear quite different as it rotated; there would be large changes in the projection on the retina. If all these changes were maintained in a rotated memory image, it should require

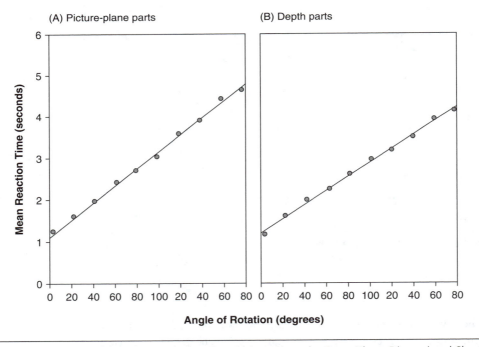

Figure 12.7   Mean Time to Determine That Two Objects Have the Same Three-Dimensional Shape, as a Function of the Angular Difference in Their Portrayed Orientations, Plotted Separately for Pairs Differing by a Rotation in Depth (Squares) and by a Rotation in the Picture Plane (Circles)

SOURCE: From Shepard, R. N. & Cooper, L., *Mental Images and Their Transformations,* copyright © 1982. Reprinted with permission of the MIT Press.

a larger amount of time to imagine the rotation of an image in depth, than in the picture plane.

The findings were that it did not require more time to rotate images in depth, as against the picture plane. It appears that a detailed representation of all the changes that are seen perceptually when an image rotates in depth are not coded when this act is performed mentally. A somewhat schematic representation is apparently maintained, but this image does appear to be moved through "mental space."

4.2. Challenges to the Analog Code Hypothesis

Although the data provided by scanning and rotation studies of the kind described above conformed to the predictions of an analog coding assumption, supporters of the propositional view were able to describe different modes of functioning (of a propositional model) that could also account for the empirical findings. For instance, it could be assumed that if an object is 10 inches distant from another object, the memory description does not correspond to the statement, "X is 10 inches from Y." Instead, each half inch could be specified separately, with the requirement that the cognitive function move through each statement concerning distance. The description might be closer to, "X is one-half inch from Y," plus (1) "X is another half inch from Y," plus (2) "X is another half inch from Y," and so on. Greater distances would thus provide a slower response time!

Anderson (1978) noted that it is possible to explain any data that are consonant with an analog/structural code for an object, by assuming some kind of processing (of an abstract propositional representation) that would result in the same outcome. It thus appeared difficult to resolve the issue on an empirical basis.

Critics of the analog position also attacked the research on methodological grounds. Pylyshyn (1981) suggested that asking people to scan visual objects may lead them to respond as they think should occur when visual images are scanned. In an attempt to mimic these events, they may wait longer than needed before responding in the case of widely separated objects. The data were thus explained as reflecting "task demands."

A related view was advanced by Intons-Peterson (1983), who suggested that experimental participants may be able to predict the "correct" result in an experiment and attempt to please the experimenter by producing what is assumed to be this response.

These arguments were countered, however, by studies in which conditions were such that the participants would be unable to predict scanning times and yet again showed a pattern of slower responses when the target objects were spatially distant from one another (Finke & Pinker, 1982; Reed, Hock, & Lockhead, 1983). With regard to pleasing the experimenter, Jolicoeur and Kosslyn (1985) misled their researchers, such that the researchers themselves expected (and presumably wanted) a certain outcome. But experimental participants did not generate data that fitted the "desired" results. The data remained unchanged. For instance, tasks that would require greater scanning times (even if researchers indicated that they should require shorter scanning times) led to slower responses.

5. Neuroimaging Studies

If visual memories are coded propositionally, then there would be no reason to expect abstract/semantic information to be handled at different sites from visual information within the brain. Also, if all information is coded propositionally, there will be equally little reason to expect different constituents of a visual stimulus to be handled at different sites. This is the case because all would be represented in the same way.

Neuroimaging studies, however, have shown differences in location of processing both for different aspects of a single stimulus (such as its size or shape) and for visual as against semantic information.

5.1. Neuroimaging and Visual Stimuli

The most consistent finding from neuroimaging research within this context is that when we see objects, their shape and size are processed at nonidentical sites within the brain. The information first receives some early processing in the occipital lobes (the site of the primary and secondary visual cortex). Kohler, Shitij, Moscovitch, Winocur, and Houle (1995) used positron emission tomography (PET) imaging to establish those areas of the brain that show increased activation when the shape of an object is identified and when the location of an object is identified. The analysis of shape produced increased activation in both hemispheres in the occipitotemporal cortex, while location analysis produced increased activation, in the right hemisphere only, of the occipitoparietal cortex. These regions are sometimes labeled as the ventral and dorsal systems, respectively.

Researchers working with monkeys had earlier found a similar pattern, suggesting that visual information involves two distinct, specialized paths—namely, the ventral and the dorsal. The former appeared to code for shape, color, and texture information, and the latter for size and spatial location (Ungerleider & Mishkin, 1982). The two paths as established on the basis of animal studies are shown in Chapter 16, Figure 16.5. It should be noted, however, that although the brain appears to respond to a visual stimulus by increased activity in nonidentical areas of the cortex for size and shape information, these areas are not always the same. Some studies have reported increases in activity in the parietal lobes (the dorsal system) for shape (Cohen, Kosslyn, & Breiter, 1996; Smith & Taylor, 1995). Thus the same task, or what appears to be the same task, does not always activate identical areas of the cortex. The reason for this variability is one of the more challenging questions facing researchers in the field of neuroimaging today.

5.2. Neuroimaging in Visual and Nonvisual Tasks

Extensive neuroimaging work has also been performed to determine the locus of processing of visual information concerning a given stimulus, such as shape or location, as compared with the processing involved in nonvisual tasks, such as the identification of a stimulus (establishing a meaning code, such as the information that the object is a chair). Different sites are involved for these two functions, both at encoding and at retrieval (Cabeza et al., 1997; Nyberg et al., 1996; Rugg, Fletcher, Frith, Frackowiak, & Dolan, 1997).

Similar data have been established across a range of studies. Roland and Frieberg (1985), for instance, required their participants to perform mental arithmetic, recall a musical jingle, or imagine walking through their neighborhoods. There was increased activity in the visual cortex for the last (a visual imagery) task, but not for the other two. Kounios and Holcomb (1994) also reported a difference in the locations of increased activity in the brain when their participants learned either abstract (semantic) or high-imagery words.

5.3. Neuroimaging and Rotation * * * * *

A number of neuroimaging studies have reported that the parietal lobes show increased activation when participants perform tasks involving mental rotation (Alivisatos & Petrides, 1997; Cohen et al., 1996; Peronnet & Farah, 1989; Smith & Taylor, 1995). In addition to these findings, Carpenter, Just, Keller, Eddy, and Thulborn (1999) demonstrated that as the rotation angle increased (as the image had to be moved further) so did activation in the parietal area (in the left and right intraparietal sulcal region). The data thus implied a relationship between increases in the demands posed by the task and increases in brain activity.

Just, Carpenter, Maguire, Diwadkar, and McMains (2001), using functional magnetic resonance imaging (fMRI), required their participants to imagine an alarm clock and to rotate the clock memory image in their minds based on various instructions. (The participants had become familiar with the clock prior to the study). The required activities involved both picture plane and in-depth rotations. There was a further requirement in some conditions that the rotation be imagined as centered first on one axis through the clock and then on another.

The authors assumed that a number of brain sites in addition to the parietal might become activated during this task. These included the dorsolateral prefrontal cortex (DLPFC), possibly involved in executive functions such as establishing goals, and the inferior frontal gyrus (IFG), possibly involved in verbal activities related to task monitoring or responding to instructions.

The parietal areas showed increased activity in both hemispheres during the task, with large additional increases for the harder rotations (two axes or involving greater distance). There were no differences when the picture plane and in-depth rotations were compared. The DLPFC showed a significant increase in activity reflecting the two versus one axis rotation task, but it showed an effect of path length only in the right hemisphere. The IFG also showed more activation under the two axes task and an effect of path length, but in this case for the left hemisphere only. The authors explained this as possibly involving more verbal self-generated instructions under the more difficult task.

Three participants performed mental rotations under conditions that duplicated the original Shepard and Metzler task, described in Section 4.1 above, in which a visual stimulus of the to-be-rotated object was presented. The question of interest here was whether the parietal engagement would be similar between the rotation task for a physically present visual stimulus and the rotation task for a memory image. This should occur if the parietal engagement involved the work of rotation rather than the reception of the stimulus or the generation of a memory image. A close correspondence was found between the activated areas in the two tasks.

The authors hypothesized that visual images are originally constructed in three-dimensional form, but that they are likely to be collapsed to a two-dimensional form at the beginning of a rotation activity and then rotated segment by segment. If this does occur, the image would have to be collapsed only once in the case of the single axis task, but in the case of the dual axes requirement the image would need to be reconstituted in three dimensions after each segment rotation and then collapsed again prior to the next rotation. This would explain the marked difference in activity level between the two tasks. Other studies have indicated that three-dimensional rotations can be performed, but that they are difficult and prone to error (Diwadkar, Carpenter, & Just, 2000). Thus, if the activity can be handled on a two-dimensional basis, the system may favor this approach.

The present study indicated that increases in task demand lead to increases in brain activity and also that the relative activity of a region can shift as a function of the exact nature of the task. Carpenter, Just, and Reichle (2000) noted that this pattern of variable activity operates across the two hemispheres, such that a given task may increase left-hemisphere activation in one context, but increase right-hemisphere activation within another context. Although clinical cases and split-brain research have appeared to indicate that a given cognitive function may be handled by one of the two hemispheres only, the neuroimaging data suggest that this is not the case.

6. Perception and Memory Images: Deployment of the Same Neural Structures

Evidence was described above in support of the view that nonvisual (including semantic) and visual imagery processing involve different codes and are processed at different locations in the brain. If it is assumed that memory and mental images do involve a visual-spatial code (the code that clearly operates in perception), then the opposite relation might be anticipated between visual images and perception: the possibility that the two functions are handled, at least to some extent, by the same processing structures.

Perky (1910) required subjects to visualize objects while certain pictures (of other stimuli) were simultaneously presented. She found that the imagery task made the work of identifying the perceptual stimuli difficult.

The argument could be made, however, that the difficulty encountered in the Perky experiment was due to the participants having to perform any two tasks simultaneously (as against two tasks drawing on the same processing structures). Segal and Fusella (1970) controlled for this possibility and found that the interference was specific to the requirement of generating imagery while engaging in perceptual identification.

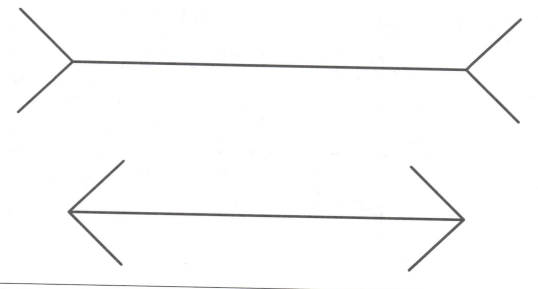

Figure 12.8   Stimuli Illustrating Visual Illusions

NOTE: Inward-angled arrows at the end of a line will make it appear shorter than a line of equal length bounded by outward-angled arrows. The effect is obtained both in perception and in memory images.

The McCullough effect occurs in perception when individuals stare at black bars against a red or green background. If the bars are next presented against a white background, a faint afterimage occurs of the complementary color. That is, if the background was red, the afterimage will be green. Finke and Schmidt (1977) found that the same outcome can be achieved on the basis of simply imaging black-on-red or black-on-green bars.

It is also the case that imagery can produce many of the visual illusions that obtain when certain misleading perceptual stimuli are viewed. For instance, when experimental participants form mental images of two equal lines and add arrows at the end of the lines as shown in Figure 12.8, the second image appears subjectively to be shorter than the first. An identical effect occurs in perception, with lines that are objectively of equal length.

Further material in support of the partial identity between perceptual and imaging structures has been gathered from clinical studies. For instance, individuals who suffer from *parapagnosia* (a condition in which people are unable to recognize faces) are also unable to imagine faces. The same is true of colors, in that subjects who lose the ability to perceive colors can also no longer form mental or memory images of them (Beauvois & Saillant, 1985).

Perhaps the most compelling evidence, however, comes from the use of cerebral imaging techniques. It has been found that there is increased electrical activity in the occipital areas of the brain when individuals are engaged in either perceptual tasks or memory-image-forming tasks. There is also an increased flow of blood to the same area (Farah, Peronnet, Gonan, & Girard, 1988).

7. Kosslyn's Theory of Image Generation

Psychologists now possess a detailed body of knowledge concerning the locations in the brain in which visual processing is performed. Visual information received from the world is passed along multiple routes "downstream" into the brain. There appear to be some 55 specialized areas devoted to this function. A simplified map of these areas is shown in Figure 12.9.

Kosslyn (1994, 2005) offered a theory of the nature of mental and memory images based on a program of experimental research into visual processing and also on the extensive use of brain-imaging techniques. Kosslyn noted the striking fact that there are almost as many neural connections in the brain moving upstream as downstream: That is, just as there are multiple pathways to carry information from

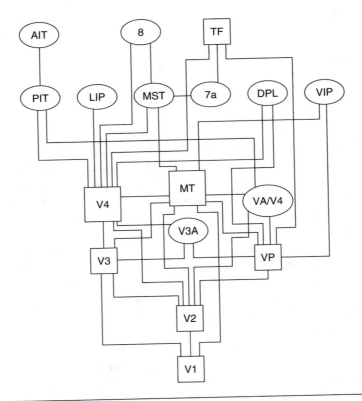

Figure 12.9   Van Essen and Maunsell's (1983) Diagram of Areas Within the Visual Cortex

SOURCE: From Van Essen, D. C. & Maunsell, J. H., "Hierarchical organization and functional streams in the visual cortex," in *Trends in Neuroscience* 6(9), copyright © 1983. Reprinted with kind permission of Springer Science and Business Media.

NOTE: There are six major layers. V1 is the first layer, receiving information from the environment. Connections go both from V1 deeper into the system, "downstream," and from areas within the system back to V1 or other areas close to V1, "upstream." The areas on the left reflect the ventral pathway; areas on the right reflect the dorsal pathway.

the eyes and retina toward the higher visual centers, there are multiple pathways originating in the higher centers and carrying information back toward the "lower-level" areas of the visual cortex.

Kosslyn suggested that this top-down information is used to effect visual priming. It has been established for many years that identification of stimuli is strongly influenced by top-down processes (Reed, 1996, chap. 2). Expectation is one such variable. If an individual expects, for instance, to see a car within a certain context (such as a street), a car stimulus will be identified faster than would be the case when no such expectation existed. The identification will also be highly efficient; if only a small part of the car is visible—not enough to identify it if a car had not been anticipated—identification will nonetheless occur.

According to Kosslyn's model, the cognitive system, having generated an expectation of, say, a car, activates its knowledge of the appearance of cars and uses this to guide the search of the visual array. According to the present view, the system actively "picks out" from the visual scene those aspects of stimuli that it expects to find. In doing this, the system must send information from the higher centers—concerning what cars look like—down to the lower processing centers that are analyzing the incoming visual stimuli.

Kosslyn noted that we clearly possess visual information (a perceptual schema) that specifies what objects look like. This information is stored in LTM. This follows inescapably from our everyday performance within the context of identification. If I did not already know what cars or tables or owls look like, I could not recognize any of these things when I encountered them.

According to the present model, perceptual schemas are also utilized when we imagine images or when we recall imagery. Suppose an individual imagines the appearance of a house that she has never seen. She will draw on the high-level knowledge concerning what houses look like. However, this knowledge needs to be unpacked or expressed, in visual-spatial format. For this to occur, the system must send the information to (at least some of) the lower-level areas, whose task is also to perform stimulus encoding in the case of external visual stimuli. These assumptions would explain why the data indicate that imagery and perception share many of the same processing structures (Ganis, Thompson, & Kosslyn, 2005; Kosslyn, Thompson, & Sukel, 2005).

The same would occur in the case of memory images: visual memories of objects that have in fact been seen. Here, the actual line contours coded when the object was seen would work together with the background knowledge. The latter could fill in gaps in the original line contour coding. Again, the actual expression of the recalled image would depend on structures also used during perception.

Although images and perception are thus similar in many ways, Kosslyn notes that the two forms of representation also differ. Images are extremely transient: That is, they are difficult to maintain. This is also true of perceptual information when the exposure is brief; but in most cases the stimuli that give rise to perceptions remain available (to the eyes or ears) across an extended period, making it possible to maintain the corresponding percept quite easily. Images can also be manipulated at will, which is of course not true of normal perception.

An intriguing implication of the present model is that the potential for imagery in human cognition is in fact varied and in a sense strong. Since perceptual knowledge, as represented in perceptual schemas, must be available for all known objects, our ability to generate imagery should be no less extensive than our ability to interpret visual and auditory information arriving from the world.

7.1. Other Aspects of Visual Reconstruction: Visual Images as Possessing Two Components

Piaget and Inhelder (1971) examined the nature of both static and moving visual memory images in children. They found that such images were always hybrid in nature. One constituent involved a rough memory copy of the actual lines seen in the original stimuli. The other involved the participant's understanding of the nature of the image, particularly in the case of moving images. For instance, an older child, visualizing, for instance, a flow of water from one container to another, would "see" an image of the water actually flowing—a component of the liquid moving from point to point in space—even though this movement is not visible in actual perception. This tendency to include abstract comprehension in memory images increased with age, such that the adolescent (and, by extrapolation, an adult) would be likely to include more content of this kind in visual memory than the young child. Piaget cited this effect in explaining why, in recollection, we sometimes "see" ourselves from the outside, perhaps walking across a room, although this could not reflect the original perceptual experience.

Thus, it appears that we not only fill in visual memories with information from perceptual structures that represent objects as they can in fact be seen, but we also fill in abstract comprehensions, somehow embedding them in the experienced visual images.

8. Eidetic Imagery

Some individuals can retain a detailed visual image in memory after viewing the original only once and for periods as short as 30 seconds. The material is retained almost as if it were physically present. This form of retention is known as *eidetic imagery*. An eidetic image will last on average from a minute to a minute and a half and under some conditions for as long as 5 minutes (Woodworth, 1938).

Eidetikers (people who can form such images) are most common in the preadolescent population. It has been estimated that about 8% of children possess eidetic ability (Crowder, 1992; Gray & Gummerman, 1975; Haber & Haber, 1964; Haber, 1979). Its incidence appears to diminish from adolescence on, although there are many case records of eidetic adults (Coltheart & Glick, 1974; Stromeyer & Psotka, 1970).

Eidetic imagery is not photograph-like in that it may not preserve all details of the original scene (as they would be represented in perception). It is nonetheless highly detailed, down to the level of trivial constituents of the presented image.

Eidetikers are likely, however, to lose content if that content does not make sense to them. The function shows additional parallels to "ordinary" memory in that inferred content may appear in the remembered images. One college-age eidetic individual, for instance, was shown a complex street scene including a fire engine. When she later recalled the picture (looking at a blank piece of cardboard and "seeing" the picture on it), the image included a dog running beside the fire engine, although none had been present in the original scene (Siegel, personal communication, 2004).

9. Hypermnesia

Ballard (1913) found that his participants frequently recalled picture material better on a second than on a first test, although the to-be-remembered (TBR) material had not been presented a second time. The same effect emerged for the recollection of poetry. Later researchers replicated Ballard's findings under a variety of testing conditions (Erdelyi & Becker, 1974; Roediger & Payne, 1982; Roediger & Thorpe, 1978). Erdelyi and Becker labeled the effect *hypermnesia*.

The first interpretation of hypermnesia had been that some materials, such as pictures, may spontaneously strengthen in memory even in the absence of a second exposure to the material. This view became less tenable when it was found that exposure to the material followed by a delayed (and no immediate) test did not appear to produce superior recall as compared with a control, immediate test plus second test, condition (Ammons & Irion, 1954).

Researchers hypothesized that hypermnesia might be due to the act of testing as such, a position supported by the widely held belief that an act of retrieval functions as an additional rehearsal. Haber and Erdelyi (1967) required their participants to study a set of pictures and a set of words. They were tested after 30 seconds and again after a 15-minute interval. There was hypermnesia for the picture stimuli but not for the word stimuli. If the effect was simply one of extra rehearsal, it should have operated for both types of material.

Roediger and Payne (1982) nonetheless continued to examine the possible role of test reactivation in hypermnesia. They varied the number of tests and also the retention interval between tests. Thus, there could be three tests in a set interval of time, or only two tests, or one test. They found that hypermnesia depended on repeated testing, not on the length of the retention interval. Three tests across a relatively short interval produced as much hypermnesia as three tests separated by a long retention interval; and a long retention interval without additional tests did not produce hypermnesia.

It was thus clear that the effect was associated with repeated testing, rather than the image memory code spontaneously changing and strengthening across time.

Roediger and Payne established in the end that the critical factor was the length of time across which participants attempted to recall the target materials. That is, three tests of time X each would produce hypermnesia (in the case of imaged materials). Equally, a single test extending three times longer than X produced an equivalent degree of hypermnesia. The causal variable was the time spent by subjects in an active attempt to retrieve the stimuli.

Roediger & Thorpe (1978) examined recall of pictures and words, using three free-recall tests. They found hypermnesia for both types of material.

Most studies had failed to demonstrate hypermnesia for words, and it was widely believed by the 1980s that the effect depended on the type of material (usually images), interacting in some fashion with repeated testing. An alternative view was that hypermnesia was a function not of material type but of the degree of learning achieved before the first test. This view became known as the *cumulative recall hypothesis*. Pictures are more easily and quickly learned than words. Thus the argument could be made that hypermnesic effects for pictures is a function not of the image codes themselves but of the higher level of learning prior to the first test.

This possibility was examined by achieving equivalent levels of learning of word and picture stimuli, followed by repeated testing (Payne, 1987). Picture recall still showed significantly more hypermnesia than word recall.

In summary, improvement in overall recall levels without reexposure to the target material can occur when a repeated testing measure is used. The higher the original degree of learning, the greater the hypermnesic effect is likely to be. Also, the more tests and/or the longer the time in which subjects are actively attempting to recall the items, the greater the effect. Hypermnesia can occur for either picture or word stimuli, but is far greater in the case of pictures. Some improvement of visual memory with repeated testing is the normal outcome (while this does not always obtain with words). Thus it appears that there is some property possessed by visual/pictorial codes that interacts with repeated testing in such a way as to considerably strengthen memory. An alternative possibility, noted by Payne (1987) is that testing might produce equivalent results with pictorial and nonpictorial stimuli, in terms of strengthening the level of new-element recall, but pictorial stimuli may suffer from less forgetting of already-remembered material.

Little research has been conducted on the effects of repeated testing for natural materials, such as memory for stories or autobiographical content. The possibility thus remains that the standard hypermnesic outcome for pictures is a function of the complex internal structure involved in an image. If this is the case, then other forms of information displaying high internal organization may also produce hypermnesia under conditions of repeated testing. At an anecdotal level, I have on several occasions been told by students that they were astonished to find how much information returned to them after they repeatedly tried to recall a weak episodic memory (as part of a classroom project). In the words of one individual, "I began to see things. Then I remembered."

Repeated efforts to recall had again demonstrated hypermnesia (first) for images.

Summary

The dual coding hypothesis involves the view that "imageable" words are better recalled than abstract words because they are represented as both a visual and a separate linguistic code, and thus they provide two channels of access to the target information, as against only one.

Human recognition performance is extremely strong, but appears to be based on recognition of general contours, not of more trivial detail. Human recall of images tends to be poor, with many details omitted or changed from the original. An identifiable image is recalled better than an unidentifiable image.

When recalling images, we tend to recall important content, not unimportant content. This led some researchers to posit that image coding involves a propositional description of the material, focusing on important aspects. The alternative view is that there is a direct or analog visual-spatial code that comes into play with visual stimuli, although it may be accompanied by abstract meaning representations. This second view has been generally supported empirically.

It has been established that verbal and visual information are represented in different codes. In support of the analog view, it has been shown that when geometric images are rotated mentally, rotations require more time when they correspond to a rotation that would also take more time if it were performed on a physical object. There appears to be a mental space in which mental objects are "moved" spatially.

When image stimuli are processed, properties such as shape are handled in a different physical region of the brain from size and location properties.

When mental images are generated, some of the processing structures used in perception come into operation. There are also nonperceptual processes involved.

Individuals who are eidetic can hold a visual scene in memory and project it onto a screen as if they were looking at a physically present stimulus. However, inferred content can appear in the projected picture.

Hypermnesia involves the improvement of images in memory across time, following repeated testing. The critical factor is the amount of time across which the individual is trying to recall the image. The effect is not found reliably for verbal material.

Discussion

A good deal of evidence has been gathered indicating that imagery enhances the recall of individual words and that visual images produce a stronger recognition function than do words. That is, if a picture of a rose and the word *rose* are measured against one another, recognition for the picture will be better.

Paivio's explanation of the superior recall of high-imagery words is that two paths of possible access become available. This view conforms to the hypothesis that material is easier to recall if it enjoys multiple paths of access.

The strong recognition of pictures, as against words, however, is difficult to explain on the basis of superior access. Some researchers believe that access is automatic in the case of recognition tasks (Anderson & Bower, 1972; Kintsch, 1970). Other researchers, such as Tulving (1983), disagree with this position and would claim that cue/memory contact is simply better in the case of pictures than in the case of words. It is not clear, however, why this would be the case under conditions in which no biasing context is provided with the words. It may be that pictures are simply easier to associate with the needed context information. That is, once the picture is accessed, it may be easier to determine that it was seen during the original learning session. Pictures are usually more distinctive than words, such that it would relatively easy to discriminate, for instance, a picture of a garden from the general concept *garden* stored in LTM, whereas a discrimination between the word *garden*, coded semantically, and the general concept garden stored in LTM, would presumably be difficult to make. It might be easier to activate the context information in cases where the stimulus is unique, as against cases where it is not unique.

Pictures of objects that can be identified are recalled considerably better than pictures of objects that cannot be identified. In the illustration offered in Figure 12.3, patterns of nonobjects (unidentifiable pictures) were sometimes remembered so poorly after a period of just 20 seconds that they could not be matched with the original drawings.

There is general agreement that part of this effect depends on inference (Glass & Holyoak, 1986, chap. 4). If an individual is drawing a horse, he may not have formed a strong code for the presence of legs or neck but could infer that these must have been present. Clearly, no such filling-in can occur in the case of unidentifiable objects.

Some researchers believe that factors in addition to inference are also at work, however (Kosslyn, 1980, 1996; Paivio, 1991). Again, according to Paivio's dual coding hypothesis, there would be more than one path of access in the case of an identifiable image (the path to the image and the path to the meaning code). Piaget and Inhelder (1973) adopted a different view, according to which semantic and perceptual content in LTM interact, in the particular sense that when both types of structure are available, they support one another, increasing overall memory strength. In particular, the semantic information supports the visual. Here it is assumed that the superior recall of identifiable images is due to this factor, and to inference, but not to differences in access.

The issue of propositional versus analog codes in visual imagery appears to have been resolved in favor of the analog position, this having been supported by both neuroimaging and experimental findings. It has also been found that symbolic AI programs represent visual information poorly. One major difficulty is that such programs depend on symbolic descriptions, and if even one object moves in a given scene, its relations to all other objects, and to boundaries, change and must be described again. If many objects move and interact, the needed description becomes so large as to overwhelm the capacity of any current digital computer (Boden, 1977). In contrast, analog representations can code for all such movements directly and perception, in living things, appears to be an easy task. That we do possess analog perceptual codes is also clearly evident, since we experience them in perception. The functionalist (symbol-based functionalist) view concerning consciousness has been that consciousness is an epiphenomenon, not part of the real work of human cognitive functioning. But this is a difficult position to defend when it emerges that perception is handled more efficiently in the medium of awareness than can be achieved through symbol-based computation.

CHAPTER 13

Implicit Memory

Overview

1. Implicit or nondeclarative memory involves the processing of information that does not enter awareness.

2. Priming involves a change in response to a stimulus that occurs because the same or a similar stimulus has been presented in the past. For instance, if a word such as SPARROW is presented, the same word will be identified faster on its second presentation.

3. Some researchers believe that implicit memory involves a separate system from explicit memory.

4. Theories concerning priming divide primarily between those that assume a processing structure has been activated by the first stimulus, and remains activated across time, and those that assume the effect is due to the relationship between the test cues and earlier memory content.

5. Implicit learning involves unconscious learning. The individual is not aware of having learned anything, but shows the learning through correct responses. Such learning typically involves patterns or sequences of stimuli. The frequency of occurrence of stimuli can also be learned on an implicit basis.

6. Emotional responses to stimuli can also be learned unconsciously. There is no evidence, however, to support sleep learning of actual information.

Learning Objectives

1. Understanding the concepts of implicit and explicit memory, and the nature of perceptual and semantic priming.

2. Understanding structural/activity models and episodic models of priming.

3. Understanding the nature of implicit learning: the kind of information that can be acquired and the effectiveness of this kind of learning.

mplicit memory involves changes that occur in long-term memory (LTM) but do not result in conscious recall. This contrasts with explicit memory, in which material is actually recalled (Schacter & Graf, 1985). Squire (1992c, 2004) has suggested the terms *nondeclarative* and *declarative* for the same distinction, while Jacoby and Witherspoon (1982) designated the two kinds of function as "memory without awareness" and "memory with awareness."

Explicit memory is widely believed to include two subsystems—namely, the episodic, dealing with life events, and the semantic, dealing with general information. Implicit memory appears to divide into a larger number of subgroups. There is procedural memory, which involves knowledge of how to perform actions (either motoric or cognitive-processing activities), classical conditioning, priming, and implicit learning.

Individuals suffering from the amnesic syndrome show impairment in explicit memory, but they often demonstrate normal implicit memory. For instance, the French doctor Claparède reported that he had shaken hands with an amnesic patient while concealing a pin, which pricked her. When they met again, the patient had no recollection of having encountered the doctor before, but she refused to shake hands with him (Claparède, 1911).

There has not been a great deal of research into procedural memory, but it has been established that most amnesics can perform as well as controls on motor-learning tasks, and there is also evidence that procedural-motoric learning operates independently of priming (Schacter, 1994b). That is, one such function can be impaired although the other is not.

PART I: PRIMING

1. Perceptual and Semantic Priming

It is possible to learn a list of words and, later, fail to recall some of them on the ensuing test. For instance, a given individual, John, may fail to remember the item GARMENT, among others. This is a failure of explicit memory. But if John is later engaged in another task in which the stem GAR_____ is presented, and he is asked to complete the stem in the form of a word, John is likely to reply with "garment." This is the case even though an item such as "garden" is more commonly encountered. The generation of "garment" is here an example of implicit memory. Something changed in John's LTM due to the earlier presentation of this word, even though he could not explicitly recall it.

This outcome is known as *priming*. The response "garment" was primed, due to the earlier presentation of the word. The particular example used here is known as a *stem completion test*. Many researchers believe that there are two kinds of priming: perceptual and semantic, as described below.

1.1. Perceptual Priming

Perceptual priming involves a priming effect based on the surface appearance of the stimulus: how it looks or how it sounds.

Stem completion is believed to reflect perceptual priming. A second test believed to involve perceptual priming is *fragment completion*. Here the task involves making a word out of a series of letters, such as CH – – – – NK or – L – M – T –.

Participants are more successful at completing the words if they are items that were presented earlier, in the list-learning session, even when the words involved items that the participants had failed to recall during the memory test. Successful completions here would be CHIPMUNK and CLIMATE. Clearly something in LTM has changed due to the earlier presentation of the items.

Another form of implicit memory comes into play when a word is presented twice, with the requirement that it be identified. Identification will be faster on the second exposure. This is known as *repetition priming*.

A word is said to be primed when it appears to be processed more quickly than usual, or when it appears more ready to come into play, within a given context, than other words (Schacter, 1994a).

The theory that the three forms of priming named above involve perceptual structures is supported by the following data. Priming of this kind is often sensitive to the fine-grained physical properties of the stimulus. For instance, if a word is presented in uppercase letters, followed later by the same word in lowercase letters, the repetition-priming effect is diminished. The same outcome obtains when the font type is changed (Jacoby & Witherspoon, 1982) Perhaps even more striking, when subjects have been trained to read letters that have been inverted, they will perform less well on a subsequent task with inverted letters if these are presented in a different size or font, as compared to identical, inverted letters (Kolers, 1973, 1974, 1975a, 1975b). This effect can last as long as a year.

These forms of priming also appear to be modality specific. Jacoby and Dallas (1981) found, for instance, that if a word is presented auditorily, followed by the same word presented visually, there is little or no priming effect. However, an auditory word item can produce priming effects for a later-presented auditory word item (Church & Schacter, 1994; Schacter, Church, & Treadwell, 1994; Schacter, McGlynn, Milberg, & Church, 1993). In general, there is a greater priming effect for unusual surface forms (unusual type, etc.) than for standard forms.

As described above, changes in the surface form of words often produces priming effects. This is not always the case, however. Graf and Ryan (1990), for instance, found that when words were presented in backward order at study, and again at test, there was a priming effect; but when words were presented upside down at study and a test, there was none.

One of the reasons that researchers posit two different memory systems (the explicit and the implicit) is the existence of variables that affect tests of implicit and explicit memory differently. For instance, when words are memorized, for an explicit memory test, certain manipulations generally improve performance. One of these is performing a task that requires "deep" semantic analysis. If the participants are asked, for each item, "Is this a pleasant, neutral, or unpleasant word?" they are likely to perform better on a subsequent explicit memory test. But performance on many implicit tests, including all those described above, does not improve.

1.2. Semantic Priming

There are other forms of priming that appear to involve meaning codes, as against physical format information. These involve *semantic priming.*

Priming was first identified within the context of semantic effects (Meyer & Schvaneveldt, 1975; Neely, 1977). Meyer and Schvaneveldt (1975), for instance, found that if two semantically related words are presented together on a screen, the second word is identified significantly faster than words in a control condition. A control condition involves two unrelated words. An example of the stimuli materials is shown below.

NURSE   DOCTOR (*doctor* is identified faster in this context than in the control condition)

BREAD   BUTTER (*butter* is identified faster than in the control condition)

BREAD   DOCTOR (the control)

Another form of semantic priming occurs when a series of items are presented from a given conceptual category. For instance, if SPARROW, FINCH, CROW are presented, all from the bird concept, and participants are then asked to generate a bird name from memory, they are likely to retrieve an item from among those that were presented earlier, rather than recalling a new bird name (Shimamura, 1986). Thus, the response CROW is more likely than the response ROBIN, which is in general a more familiar bird name.

Unlike perceptual priming, semantic priming *is* influenced by conceptual manipulations, such as depth of coding tasks but not by perceptual manipulations (Blaxton, 1989; Schacter et al., 1993; Srinivas & Roediger, 1990).

Many types of priming have now been identified. They are shown in Box 13.1.

In summary, there are forms of priming that appear to center on physical codes reflecting the appearance of the target item. These involve a test stimulus that is perceptually identical to the priming item or to part of that item. The second form of priming involves a relationship between the priming item and the primed item, in which the two items are semantically related, as in NURSE DOCTOR. This effect is believed to center on the meaning codes of the words.

A semantic association between words or concepts involves the two being connected in meaning. NURSE and DOCTOR are both health professionals. Other forms of association of course exist in LTM. Contiguity is a well-known example.

Box 13.1 Types Of Priming

1. Stem Completion.

Subjects are exposed to a list of words. In a later task, the beginning letters of a word are presented. This is the stem. The task is to complete the word. Any appropriate word can be used. Subjects tends to respond with one of the earlier-presented words, if it is appropriate. E.g., ANT_____ will be completed as ANTEATER, if ANTEATER had been present on the earlier list of words.

2. Fragment Completion.

The same procedure as in stem completion, except that in the task of word completion, several separated letters of the target item are presented. E.g: C—I—ATE. A correct completion would be CLIMATE. If subjects were earlier exposed to this word, they are more likely to succeed in the completion task.

3. Repetition Priming.

A word is identified more quickly if the same word was presented earlier.

4. Lexical Decision.

Subjects are presented with a verbal item. The task is to determine whether it is a word or a nonword (e.g., BREAD v. PLAME). Response times are measured. Prior exposure to the word item will lead to speeded identification of it as a word.

5. Speeded/Degraded Identification.

Stimuli are presented at very brief exposures. The earlier presentation of a word or a picture will facilitate subjects' ability to identify the speeded stimulus. The same is true of a degraded stimulus.

6. Direct Semantic Priming.

When two semantically related words, such as DOCTOR NURSE, are presented together or in close succession, the second is primed. (In fact, the first word also shows a small priming effect.)

7. Category-Exemplar Generation.

Items are presented with words that are examples of a conceptual category. Subjects are later asked to generate exemplars of that category. Subjects who have been exposed to appropriate items perform better than subjects who have not. Subjects are also likely to respond with an earlier-presented item. For instance, if the items ROSE, BLUEJAY, and WILLOW were among those presented in the original list, and in the later task subjects are asked to provide an example of the BIRD concept, they are likely to respond with BLUEJAY.

8. Associative Priming.

If words are exposed in pairs, such as APRICOT-SUN, the second word can subsequently be identified faster if it is presented within the context of the first word (APRICOT SUN), as against being presented alone (SUN).

BAKER and BREAD would be an example; the two words do not share similar meanings (a baker is not at all like a loaf of bread) but are routinely associated on the basis of contiguity. Researchers have therefore investigated whether other forms of association, besides the semantic, might provide priming effects. The data on this point have been mixed. In some studies, no nonsemantic priming has been reported, while in others, it has been reported (Thompson-Schill, 1995).

1.3. The Time Course of Priming Effects

Semantic priming is not generally long-lived, but a markedly different pattern has emerged in the case of perceptual priming. The mere exposure to a stimulus can produce (perceptual) priming effects that continue for weeks or months (Moscovitch, Vriesent, & Gottstein, 1993; Schacter, Chiu, & Ochsner, 1993; Wiggs & Martin, 1998). Sloman, Hayman, Ohta, Law, and Tulving (1988) reported priming extending to sixteen months in normal subjects, while Tulving, Hayman, and MacDonald (1991) reported effects enduring for 12 months in amnesics. When subjects were trained to read inverted letters, there was a facilitation effect when subsequent letters were shown in exactly the same size or font, with a diminishment in the priming effect if either of these factors was changed. The priming based on size and font endured for a year (Kolers, 1976).

Note the striking contrast between this kind of persistence and the explicit memory function that typically follows brief exposure to random items or to visual shape.

1.4. Priming Across Altered States of Consciousness

When good hypnotic subjects are hypnotized and instructed not to remember some given event, they do not explicitly recall the event. However, implicit memory is not affected by the instructions (Bower, 1990; Kihlstrom & Hoyt, 1990). Priming effects also extend across the varying states involved in a dissociative disorder. For instance, if an individual claims to possess two or more personalities, the second personality will show priming for items encountered by the first personality and vice versa (Nissen, Ross, Willingham, Mackenzie, & Schacter, 1994). An example of this form of priming is shown in Figure 13.1.

1.5. Priming by a Nonpresented Stimulus * * * * *

As described in Chapter 7, when many words on a to-be-learned list are associated with a particular "lure" word, not on the list, participants often recall that word as having in fact been on the list. Since the lure word is recalled, the question arises as to whether it could produce priming effects, just like words that actually are on the list. McDermott (1997) demonstrated that lure words will in fact produce both semantic priming (on a free-association test) and perceptual priming (on a fragment-completion test).

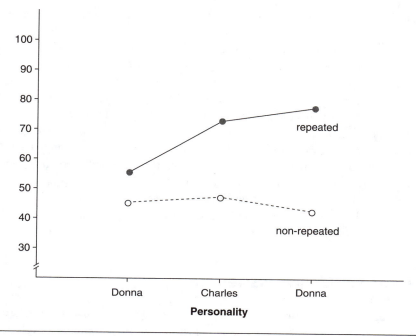

Figure 13.1   An Example of Priming Effects Across Different Personalities Expressed in the Same Individual

SOURCE: From Nissen, M. J., Ross, J. L., Willingham, D. B., Mackenzie, T. B., & Schacter, D. L. "Memory and awareness in a patient with multiple personality disorder," in *Brain and Cognition 8,* copyright © 1988. Reprinted with permission of Elsevier.

There exist data indicating that perceptual priming does not occur when the priming word (1) is established in the form of a semantic code alone (not a perceptual code) and (2) is not experienced consciously. The lure word in these experiments is assumed to be established only as a semantic representation, since it is not seen or heard. McDermott concluded that the data support the view that the lure word occurs to the participants consciously as they are learning the list.

1.6. Explicit and Implicit Memory Tests: Demonstration of a Double Dissociation

Jacoby (1978) provided a striking example of the way in which processing activities influence tests of explicit and implicit memory differently. Here a target item, COLD, was presented in one of three forms, as shown below.

XXX COLD   (Condition 1: No context)

HOT——COLD   (Condition 2: Opposites)

HOT——?   (Condition 3: Generation)

In Condition 3, participants were asked to report the opposite of the word shown.

An explicit memory test was given, in which participants were asked to recall the target word. They performed best under Condition 3, second best under Condition 2, and worst under Condition 1. Performance under Condition 3 involves the generation effect. Individuals tend to recall word items better if they have generated the items themselves, rather than simply read them.

A second test involved implicit memory. Here items were presented at high speed, and the task was to identify them. The critical question centered on the degree of priming for the item COLD, given that this item had been encountered in the previous study phase. Here, identification was most successful under Condition 1, second best under Condition 2, and weakest under Condition 3.

What had been involved was a double dissociation: Variables that aided the explicit memory test most were of least help to the implicit memory test and vice versa.

2. Implicit Memory: Major Issues

According to one view, implicit memory, as measured in particular by tasks involving perceptual codes, reflects a different memory system from that involved in explicit memory (see Chapter 6, Section 6). The separate memory system hypothesis was developed in part due to the fact, described above, that amnesic individuals, who cannot form new explicit memories, generally show intact or close to intact implicit memory functions for perceptual content. Implicit memory also shows certain properties that appear to distinguish it from explicit memory. For instance, it tends to be rigid. Once a pattern is begun, the rest of the pattern will play through, while changes in an established pattern either cannot be achieved or are extremely difficult to achieve. As described below, interference effects also differ between the two kinds of memory function. Some researchers believe that implicit memory may be a phylogenetically older function, emphasizing perceptual content and inflexible associations (Schacter, 1993, 1995). Others take the position that explicit and implicit recall involve the same system (Roediger, Weldon, & Challis, 1989).

A second critical distinction between models of implicit memory reflects either the belief that interpretive structures play the critical role in providing phenomena such as priming, on the one hand (Bower, 1996; Meyer & Schvaneveldt, 1971) and the opposing belief that it is the relationship between the cues operating at test and the memory codes established during study (or prior experience) that determine priming effects (Jacoby, 1983; Kolers, 1979). A range of titles have been applied to these positions (each of which has many variants). They include the terms *structural* or *activation* theory for the former view and *processing* or *episodic* theory for the latter.

3. Structural/Activation Theory

Among researchers who believe that meaning codes are qualitatively different from perceptual codes, the following reasoning has been explored since at least the 1950s.

When we see a stimulus, the corresponding concept is activated. Given that a typical individual holds many tens of thousands (at least) of concepts in LTM, the question emerges as to how the right concept—the one corresponding to the stimulus—is found. This must be achieved through the perceptual information available to the senses, since there would be no other way to "reach" the target concept. Jerome Bruner (1956) provided an example of these issues within the context of the idea of a poisonous mushroom. Suppose I know that at least one kind of poisonous mushroom is large, mottled, and white. This involves perceptual information, stored in LTM, relevant to the concept. If I do in fact see a large, mottled, white object of the correct shape, this information will activate the corresponding meaning code in memory. The meaning code in my case might be something like "a fungus that can make you sick if you eat it." Note that the semantic/meaning code (fungus, make you sick) is qualitatively different from the associated perceptual information (large, white, mottled). Note also that the meaning or nature of an encountered external stimulus is reached via the perceptual information.

Based on the ideas outlined above, a range of models have been developed concerning the events that occur between the moment when a stimulus is encountered and the moment when its representation appears in awareness. The relevant sequence of events is known as the *perceptual cycle*. Models of the cycle differ considerably, since there are many ways in which sensory information might make contact with conceptual meaning information (Biederman & Cooper, 1991; Marr, 1982; Palmer & Rock, 1994).

3.1. Activation Models of Priming

A simple model of the perceptual cycle involves the view that sensory input is first analyzed. If the stimulus were a table, its size and shape would be established, among many other perceptual properties. This stage of the relevant processing is known as *stimulus encoding*. The system attempts to match this body of information with a *perceptual structure* or *perceptual schema* (two terms for the same thing). Suppose the individual observing the table is called Jane. Jane will have known what tables look like for many years. This knowledge is coded in her table perceptual schema. In order to identify the stimulus, the system matches incoming perceptual information (the size and shape of the object) with the relevant perceptual schema. Once this structure has been activated, it triggers the activation of an associated *identification structure* (the concept). In this fashion, it is possible to "find" the correct concept among the many millions of representations stored in LTM. The first three steps described above occur at an unconscious level. At some point, the name of the object is also established. Many researchers believe that this occurs late in the various stages of processing (Tenpenny, 1995). Once identification has occurred, the percept of the table (its organized image) and the relevant meaning code enter simultaneously into awareness. This is why we know what "something is" at the same moment that we see it. The series of hypothesized events are shown in Figure 13.2.

When priming was first discovered, researchers interpreted the phenomenon in terms of a (structural) *activation theory*. According to this approach, if you

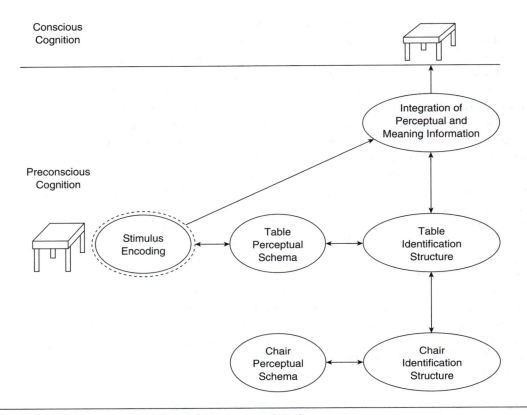

Figure 13.2 A Hypothetical Model of the Perceptual Cycle

NOTE: Stimulus encoding establishes the information concerning the shape and size of the external object. This information accesses the table perceptual schema in LTM on a matching basis. (The table perceptual schema may also feed back information into the level of stimulus encoding, directing the relevant processing.) The table perceptual schema activates the associated identification structure (the concept). The identification structure provides the identity or meaning of the stimulus. The perceptual and meaning codes are then unified, and the identified percept is entered into awareness.

encounter and identify a word, such as *bread,* the bread-perceptual structure will increase in activation, above its background level, when it is contacted by the word stimulus. A residue of this activation will continue across an extended period of time, such that if the word *bread* is encountered again, the bread-perceptual structure, which remains activated somewhat above baseline, will be able to come into play (achieve threshold activation) more quickly than usual. As a result, the word will be identified more quickly than would ordinarily be the case (repetition priming).

Semantic priming can also be explained in terms of the perceptual cycle. When the word *bread* is encountered, the bread *identification structure* will also be activated above its normal or background level. This activation will spread from the bread concept (the bread semantic identification structure) to other, semantically related, concepts in LTM. For instance, the BUTTER semantic identification structure will receive some of the spreading activation. This structure will therefore be primed. As a result, if the word *butter* is then presented, the BUTTER structure will be able to come into play more quickly than usual, in the same fashion as occurs in perceptual priming (Bower, 1996; Collins & Loftus, 1975; Corcoran, 1971; Diamond & Rozin, 1984; Meyer & Schvaneveldt, 1971; Morton, 1969, 1970).

Meyer and Schvaneveldt (1976) provided some of the first research into priming effects. Their seminal model of priming is shown in Figure 13.3.

Current activation models attempt to deal with the particular variables known to be associated with priming. Bower (1996), for instance, developed a neural net type activation model based on the concept of *logogens*, originally introduced by Morton (1969, 1970). A logogen is a focus or node for all the information relevant to a word item. That is, for any given word, information concerning how it is written, its sound properties, its meaning, and possibly a perceptual image of the word's referent, are all associated with the relevant logogen.

Bower used the word *hare* to illustrate his theory of priming. The logogen model provides a hierarchy of representations. The visual features of letter stimuli are associated with certain letters. Thus, the features (I), (–), and (I), when (and only when) they occur together, and in the correct order, are associated with the letter H. When they occur together, they will therefore contact the letter H constituent in LTM and increase its activation. Order plays a critical role here. If the letters H, A, R, and E occur, and occur in the right order, they will provide increased activation to the yet

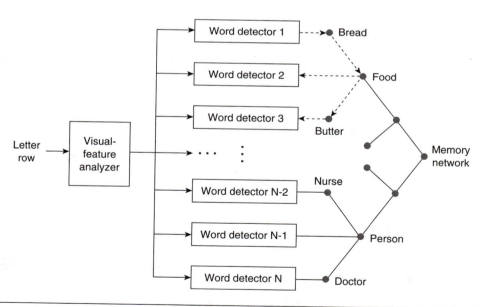

Figure 13.3   Meyer and Schvaneveldt's Model of Priming

SOURCE: From *Structure of Human Memory*, edited by Charles N. Cofer © 1976 by W. H. Freeman and Company. Used with permission.

NOTE: If the stimuli *bread* and *butter* are presented in sequence, activation will spread from the bread item in long-term memory to the butter item. This occurs because the two concepts are semantically related. The activation then feeds into the *butter* word detector, increasing its level of activation. The bread and butter items may also be strongly associated on the basis of their frequent co-occurrence.

higher-level HARE logogen. (Note that the same letters, in a different order, will not provide the same activation: REAH will not activate HARE.) Finally, the perceptual aspect of the logogen (HARE) will activate the meaning code for the concept.

Any given input feature will provide activation to (all) words possessing that feature. For instance, a short horizontal line, — , will contact the letter H and also the letters A and E. However, these letters will not become highly activated because their other features are not present in the stimulus.

Once the logogen has been activated to threshold, it will maintain a residual activation across time. As a result, if *hare* is presented again, the HARE logogen will reach a threshold level of activation more quickly than usual (repetition priming). Since the meaning component of "hare" is associated in LTM with the meaning component of "rabbit," if the word *rabbit* is presented, it too will be identified faster than usual (semantic priming). Negative priming can also be explained by the model. If HARM is presented as a priming word, followed by HARE, the identification of HARE will be slowed. (This outcome has been empirically demonstrated.)

This occurs because the HARM logogen will maintain activation across time, such that when HARE is presented, and three of the letters in HARE match with HARM, the HARM logogen will become yet further activated and provide serious competition with the correct HARE constituent. This will reduce the speed at which the system can settle into a dominant activation for HARE. This model is shown in Figure 13.4.

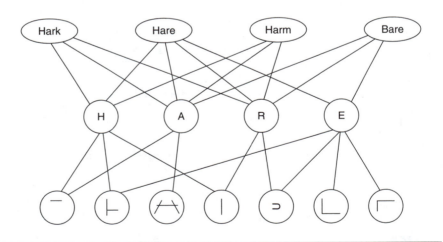

Figure 13.4   Bower's Activity Model of Priming

SOURCE: From Bower, G. H., "Reactivating a reactivation theory of implicit memory," in *Consciousness and Cognition, 5,* copyright © 1996. Reprinted with permission of Elsevier.

NOTE: Feature stimuli make contact with the letters that contain those features, in the correct spatial organization. Any letter containing a feature present in the stimulus will increase its level of activation, but the letters containing all the input features (of a single input letter) will become most highly activated. In the same way, a word containing all the most highly activated letter elements in the correct order will also become most highly activated and reach the threshold at which identification occurs.

4. Processing/Episodic Models of Priming

Kolers (1979) and Kolers and Ostry (1974) suggested that when material is studied, analyzing operations occur. These may be either perceptual or conceptual. The effect of the analyzing operations is to increase the ease or efficiency with which the same operations could occur again. For instance, if you read and identify the word GARDEN, this will make it easier to read and identify GARDEN if the item occurs for a second time (a standard priming effect). This view is the foundation of *processing models* of priming. Note that the present model (unlike the activation model) remains neutral as to the exact mechanism that results in increased efficiency during the second occurrence of processing.

Jacoby and Brooks (1984) developed a theory of priming based on the ideas outlined above. According to this view, if Stimulus X is processed and then an identical or similar stimulus is encountered, the processing of the second stimulus will occur more easily (more "fluently") than the processing of a new, nonsimilar stimulus.

When structural/activation approaches were developed during the 1960s through the 1980s, it was assumed that a perceptual structure must operate at a highly generalized or abstract level. The DOG perceptual structure, for instance, should apply equally to all dogs and thus should include only properties shared in common by all dogs. Thus, the dog-perceptual structure would probably include a generally canine outline, and four legs and a hairy coat, but it would not include properties such as "red coat," even though some dogs do have red coats. If this model were correct, nonuniversal properties should not influence perceptual identification. The same argument held for the perceptual identification of words. Effective computer models of letter recognition had been developed by the 1970s, in which the idiosyncratic properties of a word (its size, the height of the letter, the width of the letters, etc.) played no role in identification.

Priming studies have clearly shown, however, that the particular surface properties of word items can indeed influence their perceptual identification. A word presented twice in the same unusual font type will be identified faster on the second presentation, and the same is true of capital or lowercase letters and so on. Sometimes surface form makes a difference and sometimes it does not, but the fact that it frequently and predictably can make a difference means that perceptual identification is not achieved on the basis of a highly general analysis only (analysis of the properties that all exemplars share in common). Unique, changing, surface forms also play a role.

Jacoby and Brooks urged that this means that stable, ongoing processing structures, such as perceptual schemas, cannot be involved in perceptual identification. By *stable* is meant a single structure, brought into play again and again to identify stimuli.

If an individual sees a coffee mug and then another coffee mug, the second will be identified significantly faster than a nonrepeated stimulus. This is standard repetition priming. It could be explained by the assumption that the mug-perceptual schema had been activated by the first stimulus. But Jacoby and Dallas (1981) showed that a yellow mug with a lion on it primed (speeded) identification of a blue mug with a dog on it faster again that would occur for a simple mug-mug rep-etition! How could this occur? It would clearly be implausible to suggest that human cognition possesses a particular structure for "mug with an animal on it," that could be primed by the mug with a dog. By the same logic, it might appear highly unlikely that we would possess separate, stable perceptual structures for all the different types of stimuli that have now been shown to influence identification. That would have to include large letters, small letters, inverted letters, red letters, blue letters, and so on. The number of "stable structures" would be too large.

Jacoby suggested an alternative, "episodic" explanation of both priming and identification (and also conceptual classification). According to this view, we iden-tify stimuli on the basis of their similarity to other stimuli, stored in LTM. If I encounter and process Stimulus Xi and then encounter an identical Stimulus Xi, I will identify the second because it matches with the first. If I see a dog, the stim-ulus is matched with other dog representations in LTM and so identified as a dog. The more similar the stimuli, the faster and easier the match. Also, if there are a large number of similar representations in LTM, the faster and easier the match. I will identify a dog faster than a newel, having stored more representations of dogs than of newels across my life. This explains why a lion mug will strongly prime a dog mug (over and above the mug-mug priming). The two images are markedly similar, and so the second finds a speedy match with the first. In the same way, a word in unusual font will find a quick, close match with the same word presented earlier in the same font.

According to the present model, universal features, described as products of *ana-lytic processing*, are involved in identification. But so are unusual or idiosyncratic features, described as involving *nonanalytic processing*. The argument is essentially that identification involves matches with earlier memory representations, and that priming involves a quick, close match, usually with the codes produced by a recently encountered stimulus. What is rejected in the present model is the structural view—that there exist specific, stable perceptual identification structures for words or other stimuli.

4.1. Episodic/Compound Cue Models of Semantic Priming

The direct matching between new stimuli and memory representations posited by episodic models can be readily conceptualized in the case of perceptual priming. There is an obvious match. But in the case of semantic priming, the two represen-tations may not closely resemble one another in appearance. How then does semantic priming operate under an episodic model?

In response to this issue, Dosher and Rosedale (1989), McKoon and Ratcliff (1988), and Ratcliff and McKoon (1988, 1994) offered a *compound cue theory* of priming.

According to the compound cue assumption, items in short-term memory (STM) operate as cues. The cues are associated with content in LTM. The higher the association value, the more likely the cue is to activate some specific LTM content.

Typically, a set of cues will be held in STM at any given time, and will work together (as a compound cue) to access memory. Also, the stronger the overall association value between cues and memory content, the faster access will occur.

If the items "nurse" and "bread" are presented, each will be strongly associated with the corresponding representation in memory (nurse with nurse, bread with bread, etc.), but there will be only a weak association between the cue "bread" and the memory constituent NURSE. Thus, the presence of "bread" will not facilitate the identification of "nurse." If, on the other hand, "nurse" and "doctor" are presented together, the "nurse" item, being semantically related to "doctor," has a fairly strong association with the DOCTOR constituent in memory, while the "doctor" item will have the usual strong association with itself (that is, with DOCTOR coded in LTM). The stimuli "nurse" and "doctor" operating together as a compound cue will thus strongly activate the DOCTOR memory element, enabling "doctor" to be identified more quickly than usual. This is the compound cue explanation of semantic priming effects. Thus, the present model differs from the activation assumption described earlier in that the probability and/or speed of identification depends wholly on relations between cues and memory content, while in the activation models, a critical factor is the associations among items in LTM.

A schematic representation of the compound cue model of priming is shown in Figure 13.5.

4.2. Negative Priming

Ratcliff and McKoon (1996) presented their experimental participants with pictures that reflected pairs of visually similar items. The stimuli are shown in Figure 13.6.

When the participants were later shown an identical picture, with the requirement that they name the object in the picture, performance was speeded in comparison to a control condition. This was a standard priming effect. When they were shown a second picture that was merely *similar* to the first, however, responses were slowed compared with the control. A slowed response of this kind is characterized as *negative priming*. There were also intrusion errors, in which the object in the first picture was named instead of actually being shown. The authors reported the same pattern of inhibition in the case of similar stimuli across a wide range of materials and testing conditions (Ratcliff & McKoon, 1997; Rouder, Ratcliff, & McKoon, 2000).

The negative priming found above was clearly due to a similarity factor making it relatively difficult to provide a correct response.

4.3. The Bias Model * * * * *

The explanations of priming described above all assume that a prime works to improve the processing of a related target. Having seen "garden" results in a

RETRIEVAL STRUCTURE	
DOCTOR-DOCTOR	1.0
NURSE-NURSE	1.0
BREAD-BREAD	1.0
NURSE-DOCTOR	0.5
NURSE-BREAD	0.1
BREAD-DOCTOR	0.1

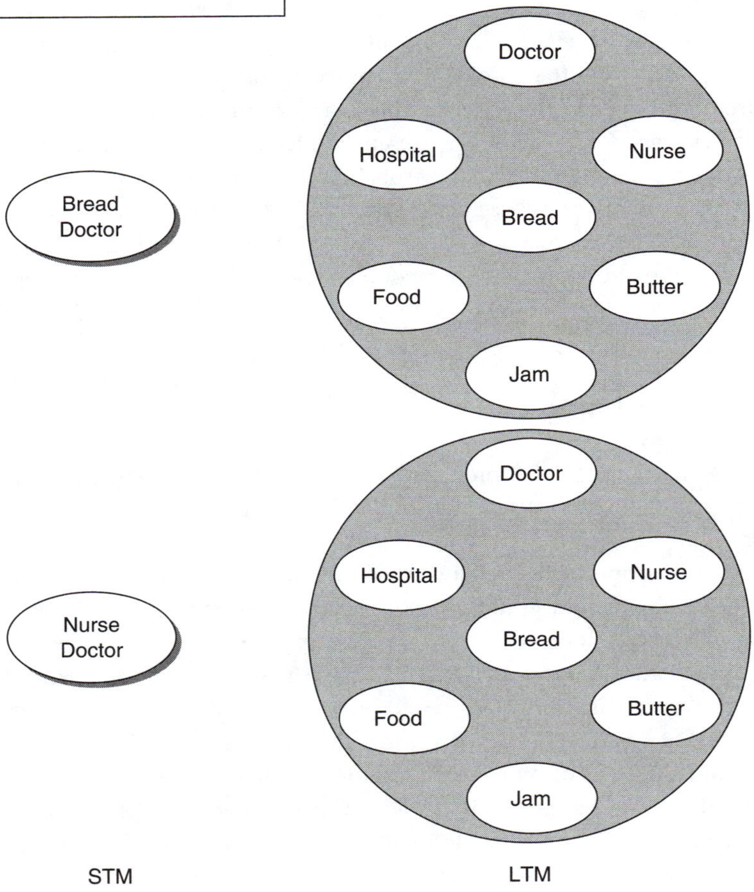

Figure 13.5 A Compound Cue Model of Priming

NOTE: Stimuli enter short-term memory (STM). Each item in STM has an association value with items in long-term memory (LTM). An item in STM has a strong association value with the representation of the same item in LTM (that is, with itself). Semantically related items have an association that is weaker than that of an identity relation, but stronger than that of unrelated items. If NURSE and DOCTOR are presented in sequence, DOCTOR will be strongly associated with itself in LTM, and NURSE will have a medium association with doctor in LTM. As a result, the match with doctor in LTM is made more quickly than usual (a priming effect).

Figure 13.6   Examples of the Stimuli Used in the Ratcliff and McKoon (1996)
Experiment

SOURCE: From Ratcliff, R. & McKoon, G., "Bias effects implicit memory tasks," in *Journal of Experimental Psychology: General, 125*(4), copyright © 1996, American Psychological Association. Reprinted with permission.

NOTE: The presentation of a second stimulus that was similar in appearance to the first (a lightbulb following the image of a hot-air balloon, etc.) produced negative priming.

second "garden" stimulus being processed more efficiently than the first. Ratcliff and McKoon (1995, 1996) suggested that in fact a prime does not provide better or more accurate processing of the target, but instead establishes a *bias* toward the selection of the target items, as against other items stored in LTM.

The authors reasoned that if the presentation of a stimulus, A, makes later processing of an identical stimulus, A_1, easier, then it would not make sense that A should *impair* the processing of a similar stimulus, A_2. Facilitation should not turn into worse processing. They therefore suggested that the negative priming found in their studies was due to a bias factor. When a stimulus is identified, its features are analyzed. In the case of similar stimuli, A and A_1, some features will be unique to A, and some will be shared with A_1. If a prime, A, is presented, the system then shows a bias toward attributing a shared feature to the prime. Thus the "count" toward identification of the prime is increased. This will lead to a slowing of responses (negative priming) if the target is in fact A_1, not A. In summary, the prime does not facilitate the processing of a later identical stimulus; it simply introduces a bias toward its own selection (as against the selection of a similar candidate) when a test stimulus is identified.

Bowers (1999) and Wagenmakers, Zeelenberg, and Raaijmakers (2000), using words, examined what occurs when primes are presented corresponding to both of the alternative test stimuli. Under a bias model, this should eliminate the tendency to choose one stimulus over the other at the time of test, and so there should be no priming effect at all. Under a model positing improved processing due to the prime, there should be a priming effect. The researchers found that there was in fact a priming effect in the case of low-frequency (but not of high-frequency) words. Zeelenberg, Wagenmakers, and Raaijmakers (2002) devised a methodology through which the effects of bias and improved processing could be examined separately. Their data supported the view that both factors operate.

5. Unconscious Perception and Priming

There is evidence that stimuli can enter implicit memory even when they have not been seen consciously (Merikle, Smilek, & Eastwood, 2001).

When two lines of equal length are viewed, with wings at the end of the lines that bend either inward or outward, the line with the outward wings is perceived as being longer than the other (the Muller Lyer illusion). Moore and Egeth (1997) presented two equal lines to their participants, against a background of dots. The dots suggested inward wings in the case of one line, and outward wings in the case of the other. This was a subtle aspect of background context, and none of the participants noticed it. The participants nonetheless showed the Muller Lyer illusion when asked to judge the length of the lines.

The data implied that the wings had been processed, and produced the usual effect on perception, even though the participants had not "seen" them consciously.

Further support for the (fully) unconscious processing of complex information has been provided by neuroimaging studies. Morris, Öhman, and Dolan (1998), using positron emission tomography (PET) found that participants showed a selective neural response to the presence of angry faces, although they remained consciously unaware of the representation of anger. The response involved activation in the right amygdala. Danziger, Kingstone, and Rafal (1998) found that clients who demonstrated visual neglect (the inability to see stimuli in one half of the visual field) nonetheless showed a facilitation effect when a cue indicated the location of a to-be-presented target, the cue being received only in the blind area of their visual field.

Probably the most famous studies of unconscious identification, however, involve the similar *blindsight* effect reported by Weiskrantz (1986). Some individuals who have suffered damage to one half of the visual cortex are blind in the opposite half of the visual field, in both eyes. Weiskrantz found that when stimuli were projected to these blind areas, his participants reported that they saw nothing. But a subset of the participants, when asked to guess whether a cross or circle had been shown, were able to identify the stimulus at a significantly higher rate than could have occurred by chance. Information was being processed through the first three stages of the perceptual cycle described above and failing only at the last stage (the entry of the identified percept into awareness). Correct responses could only be given, however, to large and simple stimuli.

It has been found that when stimuli are presented too quickly for them to be seen in awareness or under degraded conditions such that again they cannot be seen, individuals with normal vision may show a response similar to blindsight. If they are required to guess the nature of the stimulus, such guessed responses are often better than chance (Fernandez-Duque & Thornton, 2000; Merikle & Daneman, 1998). The implication is of course that some processing of the stimuli has occurred at an unconscious level.

5.1. Unconscious Registration of Change

Pictures of scenes can be presented in such a way that the scenes are difficult to see. One such approach is a paradigm in which the images are presented quickly, producing a sense of flickering. When individuals view a repeated picture under these unusual conditions, it is not generally possible to see even large changes within the picture, from one frame to the next (Rensink, O'Regan, & Clark, 2000). The effect is termed *change blindness*.

Rensink (2004) presented scenes using the flicker paradigm (240 milliseconds [ms] presentation, followed by 80 ms of a blank gray area). There were changes from one frame to the next that included the presence or absence of an object, the location of an object, and color. Participants were told to press a key when they "sensed" that a change had occurred, although they had not seen a change, and to press another key when (or if) they actually saw a change.

Thirty percent of the participants correctly sensed a change. When a "sense" response was given, the hit rate (correct response) was 88%. The false alarm rate, when an individual thought they had sensed a change but no change had occurred, was 16.7%. Based on the absence of a correlation between the "sensing" responses and the "seeing" responses, Rensink concluded that the two events involved different mechanisms within the brain.

5.2. Rejection of the View of Fully Unconscious Semantic Priming * * * * *

It is known that perceptual priming can occur when the individual is not conscious of the stimulus that produces the priming effect. Some researchers believe, however, that *semantic* priming cannot occur without conscious awareness (Block, 2001; Holender, 1986; Kouider & Dupoux, 2001, 2004). In contrast, Heil and Rolke (2004) reported data that supported the hypothesis of automatic semantic priming. The issue has not as yet been resolved.

6. Interference in Implicit Memory

Several studies have reported that no interference effects operate in implicit memory under conditions that produce (standard) interference in explicit memory (Graf & Schacter, 1987; Jacoby, 1983; Sloman et al., 1988).

The lack of interference effects involves the following. If participants learn two lists in succession and are then presented with a fragment-completion test, which involves items present on List 1, there is as great a priming effect as occurs when only one list has been learned. In other words, the second list did not diminish the priming effect.

Recent studies, however, have indicated that interference effects can occur in tests of implicit memory, under certain conditions (Martens & Wolters, 2002; Nelson, Keelean, & Negrao, 1989). If items on the interpolated list have components, such as stems, that correspond to the target items, then interference in priming does occur.

7. Implicit Memory as a Separate Memory System

A straightforward interpretation of implicit memory would be that it involves weak codes, while explicit memory requires stronger codes. There are several difficulties with this view, however. One such difficulty is that perceptual priming effects often operate at the same level in normal and amnesic individuals. If the former can handle explicit recall because the codes they establish are stronger, then it might be expected that implicit memory would also be superior within this group, as compared with amnesics. The data also indicate a marked difference between the perceptual and semantic priming. Amnesics appear to be able to handle the former but are generally impaired in the latter area (Fleischman & Gabrieli, 1998).

Given these and similar data, a number of researchers have suggested that two separate memory systems may be involved (Moscovitch, 1992; Schacter, 1985, 1994a, 1994b; Squire & Kandel, 1999; Tulving & Schacter, 1990; Weiskrantz, 1989).

Schacter has developed a model of priming effects, labeled PRS, for *perceptual representation system*. According to this view, explicit memory involves both perceptual and semantic information. However, there exists a separate and independent memory system that operates wholly at an unconscious level, and is involved only with perceptual content. This system does not find direct expression in awareness.

A critical point here is precisely that PRS is independent of the memory system that handles semantic information. It comes into play in perceptual priming. It is because of its strictly perceptual nature that levels of processing tasks that engage semantic memory, and enhance explicit recall, have no influence on stem completion and fragment completion tasks. Also, a modality shift (from visual to auditory stimulus presentation or vice versa) erases almost all of the priming effects found with these tasks.

Schacter (1994b) has noted that there exist several clinical syndromes in which individuals can read words (can process their shape and relate this to word names) but are unable to identify the meaning of the words, or they are aware of the structural properties of words but, again, cannot retrieve their meaning. In short, a large range of data point to a major dissociation between visual/structural word knowledge and knowledge of word meanings.

Schacter posits that implicit memory involves a function in which perceptual information is acquired in unitized form. That is, the memory function involves the establishing of sequences of material that, once started, "run off" as a unit. These sequences are rigid; they cannot be broken into components and rearranged. This situation contrasts with that of explicit memory, in which constituents can be placed together and then separated and reorganized. In other words, new associations can be formed with relative ease among the constituents. Explicit memory is thus dissociable and flexible.

8. Priming as Transfer of Processing * * * * *

Other researchers reject the view that implicit and explicit memories involve separate systems (Roediger et al., 1989). These researchers operate within the processing tradition, described in Section 4. According to this view, if two similar stimuli are encountered, the analysis of the first facilitates or enhances the analysis of the second. This assumption is further related, within the present theory, to the transfer of processing (TAP) model, introduced in Chapter 6, Section 3.2. TAP involves the view that successful memory performance depends on a match between the material processed during the learning phase of an experiment and the material later tested. If the learning and the test involve the same kind of material, there will be facilitation at the time of test, which is then identified as a priming effect. If you have been exposed to GARDEN and are later given a word completion test beginning with GAR——, the "garden" response will emerge because it matches the earlier-studied item (such that the response has been facilitated).

According to the present view, implicit and explicit memories do not involve separate systems. Instead, implicit tests tend to involve perceptual information and so "prime" responses also based on perceptual information. Explicit tests usually involve semantic information and so "prime" semantic responses. It is a question of a match between studied and tested material. The Jacoby and Whitehouse (1989) double-dissociation study (Section 1.5) can be explained in this way. Indeed, Jacoby and Whitehouse themselves believed that the effects they had identified were due to TAP.

PART II: IMPLICIT LEARNING

1. Associative Learning

Associative learning involves the linking or association of two or more items. For instance, in paired-associate learning, words are presented in pairs, such as

APRICOT-SUN. The test involves the presentation of the first word, with the requirement that the second word be recalled. Or, in language learning, words need to be associated in memory with their meanings and vice versa. Associative relations also come into play in daily life. Here such relations need to be established, and then changed, on an ongoing basis. I may see Jane in blue jeans on Monday, raking leaves, and these constituents will be appropriately related together in the ensuing memory. And I may see Jane on Friday in an office, using a computer, in a white dress. Thus Jane, location, activity, color of clothes, and so on, must all be interrelated in a new fashion on Friday.

1.1. Implicit Learning of Visual-Verbal Associations

Clark Hull (1920) presented his experimental participants with a series of Chinese letters. Each letter had been give a nonsense name, such as "flub" or "zop," and each letter contained a radical, a particular visual feature (such as ✓:) that determined the letter's name. Participants did not know that a critical feature of this kind was present in the letters.

After repeated trials in which the letters were presented with their names, participants in the experiment were able to correctly name new letters, although they were not aware of how they made this determination. They had unconsciously associated the presence of the critical feature with the name of the letter.

2. Monitoring of Frequency and Temporal Information

Hasher and Zacks (1979, 1984) reported data indicating that information concerning stimulus or event frequency is routinely acquired on an implicit basis.

If the same stimulus occurs repeatedly, across a given time interval, we learn its pattern: that is, how frequently it is likely to occur. This is often noticed only when the pattern changes. If a number of people were in a room where a clock was ticking loudly, they would be likely not to "hear" it (due to habituation) unless the pattern of ticking abruptly altered. If this did occur, they would be likely to direct attention to the clock. This could not occur unless the original frequency of the sound had been established. A similar unconscious process appears to keep track of time, even when we sleep. In some individuals, this monitoring activity is precise enough to enable them to wake at a particular hour, of their choosing.

The ability to unconsciously monitor certain repeating patterns, such as frequency information, may be shared across the higher animal kingdom. Pigeons can be trained to respond to frequency-based schedules of reinforcement. If a pigeon has been rewarded for every other peck at a given stimulus, the animal will maintain a steady pecking rate across time. In contrast, a pigeon that has been rewarded only once for every 30 responses will peck slowly until it nears the 30-response mark and then speed up.

3. Complex Associative Learning

3.1. Implicit Learning of Complex Patterns and Sequences

Reber and his colleagues have examined the issue of implicit learning of complex, novel structure across an extended program of research (Reber, 1965, 1967; Reber & Allen, 1978; Reber & Lewis, 1977; Reber, Walkenfeld, & Hernstadt, 1991). One approach within this context involved strings of letters that had been produced by an artificial grammar (AG). An AG is a series of arbitrary rules for how letter strings can be generated. For any given letter, only certain other letters are permitted to follow.

Figure 13.7 shows a simple Markovian (left to right) model of this kind. The links show the letters. Here, the first state (shown in the circles) can be followed by either T or P. If T is followed, this leads to S. A loop indicates that a given letter can be repeated. Thus, the string could begin TSS. The letter following the last S will be X, which can be followed either by X or by S. If it is followed by S, the series will terminate.

Reber and Allen (1978) required their participants to memorize a series of letter strings that were correct in terms of the grammar. As the participants continued to memorize new (but correct) strings, they acquired them faster than before. They had not been told that any rules were involved in generating the strings. A control group was shown the strings for an equivalent period of time and told that they

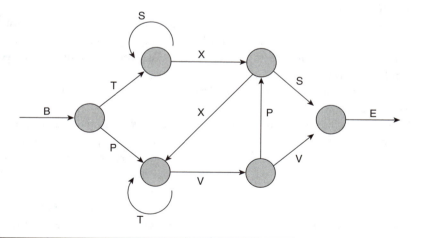

Figure 13.7   Example of an artificial grammar

SOURCE: Reprinted with permission of Arthur Reber.

NOTE: State 1 can lead to T or P. If T is selected, T leads to S, which can lead either to S again or to X. X leads to either S or X again. If S, the sequence ends. If X, the system leads to T or V. T can lead to T again or to V. If V, V goes to V or to P. If P, P leads to S and exits. If V, the system exits.

If the system moves first to T, possible sequences include (1) TSXS, (2) TSSXXVV, and (3) TSXXTVPS. If the system moves first to P, possible sequences include (1) PTTVPS, (2) PTVPXVPS, and (3) PTVPXVPS.

were generated by rules. The task of the control group was to figure out the rules. In a final test, both experimental groups were presented with new strings of letters and asked to determine whether they were "correct" strings or not. The participants in the experimental group were now told that the strings they had memorized were examples of correct sequences. (The test strings were new combinations generated by the grammar, which none of the participants had seen before.)

The experimental (memorization) group, who had not been aware that any rules were operating to generate the strings, was generally successful in identifying the correct instances among the test strings. Certain forms just "looked right." The control group, who knew there were rules and had been trying to identify them, performed less well. The experimental group did not know why they thought some strings were correct: That is, they had no conscious awareness of the information they were using to make this decision.

Here implicit learning had been more effective than conscious learning. It appears that we have a marked ability to acquire patterns or sequences implicitly, without awareness either of the learning or of the basis for the learning. Our ability to learn this information unconsciously is considerably stronger than our ability to learn it consciously.

The same findings emerged when participants were asked to predict certain event outcomes on the basis of probability. A series of lights were shown in specific locations, and whether a light would appear or not appear was determined by a pattern. After considerable exposure to this pattern, participants were able to predict whether a light would or would not appear with a high degree of accuracy. They had no conscious awareness of why they thought a light would or would not appear. Even very complex and extended sequences could be learned in this manner (although an enormous amount of exposure was required).

Berry and Broadbent (1984, 1988) demonstrated similar results in more natural contexts. In one study, participants were asked to change variables that might influence sugar production in a factory. They were shown the results of the changes. A complex arbitrary pattern of change led to better production. The participants learned the right choices unconsciously. Again, they were not aware of why a given choice seemed right.

Reber (1993) interpreted this large body of data as meaning that we possess marked capacities to acquire information unconsciously. Our performance in such areas is stronger than can be achieved through conscious effort. However, it is only certain kinds of learning that can be handled in this fashion. The capacity appears to center on frequency, covariance, and sequential order.

Reber believes that we can in fact acquire both specific and abstract representations on the basis of implicit learning but that unless there is a definite goal involving the specific (memorizing an individual item, an individual image, etc.), the system will code abstract, "deep" information. That is its default mode. Reber also makes the plausible argument that almost all of our daily cognition is a mixture of implicit and conscious processes. The notion that we are (almost) fully rational beings who make decisions or solve problems on the basis of conscious, logical rules is incorrect. Much of our thinking is directed by implicit processes, such as those involved when individuals have a feeling that changing a certain variable in the production of sugar will lead to a better outcome. A critical point is that Reber is not suggesting that we are irrational (that our reasoning goes against logic). It is simply to a great extent not related to what is generally identified as logical thought. It is arational. The author suggests that there is a great deal of structure in the world around us, and we have evolved extremely strong capacities to identify that structure (unconsciously). This function is probably old, in evolutionary terms, antedating conscious thought.

Several claims have been advanced concerning cognitive functions that are phylogenetically old. One is that they are likely to show little individual variation. The other is that they will tend to show minimal or no correlation with thought processes that have evolved more recently (Hasher & Zacks, 1984; Reber, Walkenfeld, & Hernstadt, 1991). In the present case, it would be predicted that implicit knowledge would function at about the same level from one person to the next and not be related to capacities involved in conscious thought or to the functions measured by tests of intelligence. In support of this general position, Reber et al. (1991) demonstrated that participants engaged in an implicit, artificial-grammar, task, showed significantly less variability in scores than emerged in the performance of an explicit task. It was also shown that the explicit task showed a significant correlation with IQ scores, while the implicit task did not.

A further claim is that implicit memory, being phylogenetically old, should be less vulnerable to brain damage than the arguably more complex and recent functions involved in explicit memory (Abrams & Reber, 1988). There is abundant evidence that this is the case. Chapter 16 describes a range of explicit learning and memory functions that are impaired following injury to the brain, while those involved in implicit learning and memory remain largely intact.

3.2. Implicit Learning and Natural Language

Children acquire their first language by means of listening and talking activities. They do not study grammar. Yet they nonetheless master an intricate and demanding set of grammatical constructions, of a kind that can be described by rules. They achieve this, although individuals less than 7 years of age cannot learn grammatical rules *consciously* at all. It's a hard subject. The great linguist Noam Chomsky believes that we must possess innate knowledge of syntactic structure (Chomsky, 1986, 2000). This would be the only way, he reasons, that a preschooler could master such a difficult skill.

There is no question that children's acquisition of language involves implicit learning. Reber (1993) has urged, however, that it is not the learning of rules but, rather, the learning of patterns. According to this view, the child picks up the regularities in grammatical construction that he hears around him after what is in fact extended practice (several years of exposure to language models). This is certainly an intriguing idea, and one that makes research into implicit learning an area of particular importance.

4. Implicit Processing and Emotion

It has been found that when individuals are exposed very briefly to a drawing, they tend to like it when they encounter it for a second time, and they choose it in preference to other drawings. They are not aware that they have seen the item before (Kunst-Wilson, & Zajonc, 1980). This pattern appears to underlie the success of some advertising techniques. Items to which individuals pay only very brief attention, in an advertisement, have been found to be reliably preferred over novel items. Again, the individuals involved do not recall the preferred item as having been seen earlier (Perfect & Askew, 1994).

It has also been shown that exposing experimental participants to biasing words at high speeds, such that the words were difficult to identify consciously and difficult to remember, influenced the participant's judgment of the nature of a fictional character. The briefly encountered items apparently set up a negative emotional context of which the individual was not aware. It appears that a good deal of social biasing and stereotyping is achieved in the same fashion, in the form of ideas that may influence behavior, although the individual has no conscious awareness of holding such ideas and, thus, has no means of examining them critically (Greenwald & Banaji, 1995).

The preceding material may raise questions concerning the unconscious learning of bodies of general information and perhaps also questions about subliminal perception. Could we learn, for instance, about history, while asleep? This idea has been examined and found to produce no positive results. It appears that general/semantic information is of a different kind from that involved in pattern or association learning and in specialized functions such as linguistic grammar.

Subliminal perception involves being exposed to a stimulus so briefly that the information does not enter awareness. An individual called James Vicary claimed to have flashed the words "Buy Popcorn!" on the screen of a movie house, with the result that there was an increase in popcorn buying in the part of the audience. But the claim proved untrue. There is little support for the belief that subliminal messages can influence complex behaviors (Merikle, 1988). As described above, however, they may influence emotional responses, and they can achieve both perceptual and semantic priming.

Summary

Implicit/nondeclarative memory involves information, or changes in LTM, that does not enter awareness. One of these is known as priming. In priming, the presentation of a stimulus alters the response made to a second, identical or related, stimulus.

Perceptual priming is based on similarity between the physical appearance (or sound) of the prime and the primed stimulus. Semantic priming is based on a semantic relation between the two. Perceptual priming can endure over extremely long periods. Semantic priming does not. Negative priming also exists. Cognitive tasks such as levels of processing influence semantic but not perceptual priming. Amnesics generally show intact perceptual, but not intact semantic, priming.

The perceptual cycle involves the processing events that occur when a word is encountered and attended. Perceptual priming is believed within some traditions to depend on specific perceptual structures, while semantic priming depends on identification structures (concepts).

According to activation theories, priming occurs when the priming stimulus increases the level of activation of the structures that process the primed stimulus, in LTM. These may be either the perceptual schemas or the identification structures.

Another kind of processing model, related to the phenomenon of priming, involves the view that when a stimulus is analyzed, this simply facilitates the analysis of a second, similar stimulus. One version of this view, the episodic model, posits that identification occurs when a stimulus is matched with earlier memories of a stimulus of the same kind. If the two stimuli are similar, there is facilitation in identification (that is, priming). This view contrasts with the assumption of specific perceptual structures as the vehicle that provides perceptual priming.

Priming can occur even when the individual is not aware of the priming stimulus. It is possible to pick up information about the world unconsciously and experience this as a "sense"; we appear to pick up some environmental changes in this fashion.

Schacter has urged that the system involved in priming, the perceptual recognition system, and implicit memory in general, is a separate and distinct memory from that involved in explicit recall.

In implicit learning, individuals acquire information about the passage of time and the frequency of stimuli. Other forms of implicit learning include sequences or patterns of stimuli, and thus probability information (how likely it is that a stimulus or event will occur), and covariance of stimuli. Learning of this kind requires massive repetition, but it is highly effective. Sequences can be acquired more efficiently based on implicit learning than on an attempt to consciously discover the rules governing the sequences.

It appears that implicit learning of emotional responses does occur. However, it is not possible to provide subliminal directives and have people act on them. Unconscious learning of "regular" information (the kind handled by explicit memory) also does not seem to occur.

Discussion

One of the more intriguing ideas emerging from research into priming is Jacoby's theory that we identify objects by matching them with actual, similar memories. According to this view, there are no perceptual identification structures as such. This conclusion was reached based on such findings as the discovery that a yellow mug with a lion on it will provide stronger priming of a blue mug with a dog on it than with will occur if two mugs (without pictures) are presented. We cannot possess an individual perceptual structure for mugs with animals on them.

Historically, it happened to be the case that models of perceptual and identification structures both involved the view that only universal features would be included in the structure. In other words, the dog perceptual structure would code only for properties possessed by all dogs and so on. Research into priming has clearly shown, however, that individual perceptual properties are used when we identify stimuli. Roughly, if we see a white dog with black spots, this animal should significantly enhance the priming found if we next see another white dog with black spots.

Models of identification structures, however, have a long history, usually in traditions sympathetic to the constructivist view. These models did not endorse the "universal feature only" assumption. For instance, in the Piagetian approach, a perceptual schema involved all information known to the individual concerning the relevant class of objects (Piaget, 1952). For example, if I had seen only white swans across my life, my swan schema would include white sensory information.

But if I then encountered a black swan, black sensory information would be entered into the schema. Here, a perceptual structure involves a large body of diverse information, rather than separate structures for each type of information (a separate structure for large swans, small swans, etc.). The subproperties of the schema could be individually primed. This is, if I just saw a white swan, both the general swan perceptual imagery and the white sensory component could be activated and primed. The black subcomponent would not be primed. In short, this approach overcomes the theoretical difficulty of multitudes of perceptual structures to encompass all the different, nonuniversal properties of exemplars of a given concept.

The discovery of unconscious pattern learning, and the fact that it appears to operate in daily life, has led to a new way of understanding human cognition. Its difference from explicit learning is also instructive. You may have been puzzled as to why a task that at first seemed so difficult becomes increasingly easy, although no change in comprehension or skill is obvious. This probably involves implicit learning.

The area of implicit memory in general has opened some important questions that remain, however, unanswered at present. One involves the issue of whether implicit processing does involve a separate system from that engaged in explicit representation or memory. Although attempts have been made to resolve this question empirically, this has not been possible up to the present time. The factors involved are complex. The same is true of priming effects. The two models outlined above imply markedly different ways of viewing cognition and memory, and as yet it has not been possible to resolve which of them is essentially on the right track.

CHAPTER 14

Traumatic Memory and False Memory

Overview

1. Trauma was historically identified as providing a spotty, incomplete memory of the traumatizing event, and flashbacks, which are extremely vivid and long-lasting memories of some aspect of the traumatic event. Recent research has suggested that memory is not always negatively influenced in traumatized individuals.

2. Freud suggested that traumatic events are repressed: that is, actively held out of consciousness as a whole. P. Janet believed that trauma produced a different form of cognition from the usual and that aspects of the traumatic memory could be walled away from consciousness.

3. The 1990s saw a very large number of individuals who believed they had recovered memories of childhood abuse, during therapy. Techniques used to recover memories, however, are at risk for producing false recollections, and many of the recovered memories are probably false.

4. Groups known to have experienced trauma do not usually show a loss of memory of the traumatic event, although this may occur in some individual cases.

5. Researchers have demonstrated that false memories of autobiographical events can be produced, through suggestion, in about 20% of experimental participants.

Learning Objectives

1. Knowledge of the characteristics of memory in traumatized individuals, both as established historically and as described in recent research.

2. Knowledge of the issues involved in the repressed-memory controversy.

3. Knowledge of the memory function among groups of individuals who have experienced severe trauma.

4. Knowledge of experimental findings concerning the generation of false memories through suggestion.

This chapter covers memories based on traumatic events, memories that are false, and recovered memories, which may or may not be based on episodes that actually occurred.

Bessel A. Van der Kolk (1996), a well-known clinician, defines trauma as an "inescapably stressful event that overwhelms the person's existing coping mechanisms" (p. 279).

Data concerning the effects of trauma on memory have been gathered primarily within the clinical and medical communities. According to these findings, individuals who have suffered severe trauma show heightened recall of certain aspects of the event, with other aspects being either poorly recalled or forgotten. There is partial amnesia in that sense. Traumatized individuals also show a pattern in which learning in general (of, for instance, new information) is difficult. They may also fail to notice and remember events in the world around them that most people would retain (Goldstein, van Kammen, Shelly, Miller, & van Kammen, 1987; Sutker, Winstead, Gallina, & Allain, 1991; Thygesen, Heermann, & Willanger, 1970).

Probably the most typical symptom of trauma, however, is the experience of a flashback. Here, extremely vivid images of the traumatic event intrude into awareness. The images are so powerful that a memory of this kind often appears to be unfolding in the present. The individual has no control over the appearance of the traumatic content, which can emerge even when an active effort is being made to avoid or block it.

As described within the present tradition, memories related to trauma have particular characteristics. They tend to be perceived in fragments, as hyper-vivid images, and are accompanied by strong emotion. There is overall a large sensory basis (as compared to abstract material), and there is also diminished narrative content (as compared with ordinary memories).

Flashbacks can intrude into awareness for no obvious reason, but they are particularly likely to appear in response to cues. Anything that might remind the individual of the original event appears capable of acting powerfully as a cue. A common response on the part of persons suffering from trauma is therefore to go to considerable lengths to try to avoid anything that might remind them of the traumatic episode or episodes. The cues can be either internal or external (Van der Kolk, 1996).

The intrusive memories have been described as "indelible," given that they persist over long periods of time (Krystal, Southwick, & Charney, 1995, chap. 5). An accompanying symptom is often the experience of repeated nightmares.

Victims of trauma often show decreased responsiveness to the general world or a numbing (Litz, 1993) At the same time, in spite of attempts to avoid reminders of the trauma, the affected individuals appear to be sensitive to any stimuli that might relate to the source of their anxiety. Both victims of rape (Foa, Rothbaum, Riggs, & Murdock, 1991) and traumatized combat veterans (McNally, Kaspi, Riemann, & Zeitlin, 1990) are more easily distracted by trauma-related words than by other emotionally charged stimuli.

1. Memory and Posttraumatic Stress Disorder

For the majority of individuals who live through a traumatizing experience, the effects weaken with time (Lee, Vaillant, Torrey, & Elder, 1995). But a small number of victims of trauma do not recover, or they recover only after very long periods. Instead, the original symptoms persist, with a range of severe behavioral difficulties. The condition is labeled today as posttraumatic stress disorder (PTSD).

Individuals suffering either from immediate trauma or from PTSD show symptoms of hyperarousal and excessive vigilance, in that they respond in an extreme manner to unexpected stimuli, and most particularly to any stimulus that might be associated with the trauma. Also, memories relating to the trauma, although they may be fragmented, endure over extremely long periods of time. In the case of childhood sexual abuse, the degree of trauma appears to be positively related to the length of life of the memory (Alexander et al., 2005). Krystal et al. (1995) suggested that what is involved is a kind of profound fear conditioning. They cite parallels with animal studies in which animals acquire conditioned emotional responses (CERs) either to individual stimuli, associated with a frightening experience, or with the entire context relevant to that experience. In support of this general view, CERs are extremely resistant to extinction (Hoffman, Selekman, & Fleshler, 1966).

1.1. Trauma Following Combat

When episodes involving combat are recalled, the details are not always accurate. McCurdy (1918), pursuing an extended study of flashbacks experienced by veterans, found that some of the content did not reflect the original event but, rather, the men's worst fears. Frankel (1994) described the same phenomenon. For example, one combat veteran experienced a repeated flashback in which he killed a villager, who kept getting up to be killed again.

From the time of World War I, it has been reported that traumatized soldiers frequently show "spotty" recollections of their combat experiences. The following is an official account of traumatized soldiers in World War II. Here, the men displayed a very acute . . . disturbance combined with a state of exhaustion resembling physical illness . . . (many) wore a blank or confused expression and some degree of disorientation and objective confusion were seen . . . (including, in some cases) loss of voice, paralysis, or gross tremors. Physical exhaustion, as shown by a weight far below normal for the individuals in question, was often present. (Sargent & Slater, 1941, p. 760)

In 1941, the doctors had assumed that men in this condition had nonetheless formed ordinary memories, and that the memories had been lost through dissociation. The amnesic soldiers were subjected to hypnosis, often mixed with drugs such as sodium amytal, to regain their lost memories. The memories returned. The 1941 article notes, however, that they were "a mixture of reality and fantasy."

1.2. Worst Fears Unrelated to Combat

The concept of the projection of worst fears may be relevant to a range of situations involving apparent traumatic memories. Frankel (1994) described a patient who was troubled by a memory of having her clitoris removed at the age of 5 years. She suffered from nightmares concerning the trauma. However, when she was later examined by a doctor it was found that her clitoris was intact.

2. Controlled Observational Research

Byrne, Hyman, and Scott (2001) identified 77 students who had experienced a traumatic episode, such as violence, sexual abuse, and so on. The students' memories for a pleasant, unpleasant, and traumatic episode were measured. It was found that recall was roughly the same across these conditions, with traumatic memories not being more fragmented than nontraumatic memories. Porter and Birt (2001) and Gray and Lombardo (2001) reported similar findings.

A second unexpected outcome of the Byrne et al. (2001) study was that the participants rated all three types of recollections (pleasant, unpleasant, and traumatic) as being equal in emotional intensity.

Rubin, Feldman, and Beckham (2004) examined veterans diagnosed with PTSD for their memories of the instigating traumatic events. They found that traumatic memories were characterized by higher levels of sensory content, a sense of reliving, and emotion, as compared with nontraumatic memories: But the traumatic memories did not show diminished organization and coherence. If anything, the trend was in the opposite direction.

With regard to the finding that participants reported traumatic memories to be equal in emotional intensity to simply unpleasant or pleasant memories, there is a growing body of evidence to the effect that subjective reports of emotional intensity can be fallible, particularly in the case of fear (Lambie & Marcel, 2002; LeDoux, 1989).

The repeated findings of nonfragmented traumatic memory across these studies are more difficult to explain. Reports of spotty and incomplete recollections of trauma have been gathered across at least four wars. A diagnosis of PTSD is provided, however, on the basis of a cluster of symptoms, but not of every symptom associated with the condition. It is possible that disorders of memory occur in some cases of PTSD, but not in others.

3. Repression, Dissociation, and Consolidation Failure

3.1. The Construct of Repression

There has been a long-standing belief in Western culture that traumatic memories may undergo repression. The concept of repression originated with Freud, who believed that unacceptable drives and ideas, and possibly episodic memories, are held out of awareness by an active psychological function (Freud, 1916/1963).

In a paper read to the Viennese Society for Psychiatry and Neurology in 1896, Freud suggested that hysterical symptoms (called *conversion reactions* today) may be caused by sexual trauma, which has been repressed. The symptoms include inability to move an arm or leg, deafness, or inability to speak (with no physical cause). Freud did not believe that any other clinical presentations, such as, for instance, depression, were reliable indications of repressed sexual trauma. He did claim, however, that the unconscious material could exert a harmful influence on the mind and that healing would occur in most cases only when that material was brought back into awareness.

Along with J. Breuer, Freud at first used hypnosis as a means of recovering the lost memories. He found that hypnosis did indeed result in recollections of abuse, with the memories being accompanied by violent emotion, and at first took this as an indication that the memories were real. A year later, however, he had rejected these aspects of the theory, having concluded that memories of abuse recovered under hypnosis were not generally memories of actual events. They appeared instead to be unconsciously generated fictions.

According to a repression interpretation of weak traumatic recall, certain aspects of the inciting episode or episodes have been repressed, in an attempt to protect the individual from the content of the memories.

3.2. The Dissociative Hypothesis

Pierre Janet (1904) offered a somewhat different interpretation of the fragmented quality of trauma-based memories. His model centered on the concept of *dissociation*. According to the dissociative hypothesis, at the time of the trauma the individual enters a state of arousal so extreme that it disrupts ordinary cognitive processing. This state might be understood as one of overwhelming anxiety or panic. The trauma dissociates certain forms of ordinary cognitive organization, such as the use of higher-order structures that supply an understanding of time, location, and causality (among other abstract properties), from the memory that is experienced in awareness. What remains is a body of sensory or perceptual impressions and a record of the emotion itself. There may also be obsessional ruminations and codes that could provide behavioral reenactments of the critical event.

Janet posited that the intense emotional force of the trauma resulted in the event being imprinted very strongly into memory, possibly in the form of a perfect, filmlike record. As described above, some of this record would become dissociated and not available to awareness. It would continue to exist, however, in long-term memory (LTM). Also, those aspects of the experience that had not been lost would remain as extremely powerful elements, available to awareness. These would reflect the "hypervivid images," which appear to persist for years, associated with severe trauma.

In support of this general view, Janet (1904) cited several cases involving amnesia that he believed were trauma related. In one, a client had reenacted a traumatic experience, while having no memory of the original episode.

There is a good deal of evidence that trauma produces dissociated states of various kinds. A mild form is a feeling of depersonalization and an absence of emotion. Such reactions have been repeatedly recorded following disasters, such as the collapse of the Hyatt Regency Skywalk and the Loma Prieta earthquake (Cardena & Spiegel, 1993). Associated symptoms are intrusive images, accompanied by problems with memory for ongoing events or information in the period of time following the disaster.

3.3. Consolidation Failure

A third interpretation of the impoverished memory function traditionally associated with trauma involves the view that extreme anxiety can disrupt the consolidation process, preventing the establishment of detailed LTMs. McGaugh (1989, 2000) and Pittman (1989), for instance, have suggested that certain neuromodulatory mechanisms come into play during and probably following traumatic experiences, such that the altered brain biochemistry leads to abnormalities in the memory function. Higher-order cognitive processes appear to be disrupted, while perceptual, emotional, and perhaps response factors are coded at unusual strength.

3.4. Trauma and Neuroimaging Data

Rauch, Savage, Alpert, Fischman, and Jenike (1997) examined brain responses when traumatized patients were reminded of the relevant threatening events (through reading an account written earlier). Regions in the right hemisphere implicated in visual and affective codes showed increased activity, while there was decreased activation in Broca's area, the area associated with speech production. Van der Kolk (1996, chap. 12) in reporting these data, noted that there may be some physiological basis for the folk saying "scared speechless."

4. An Epidemic of Recovered Memories

During the 1980s and 1990s a very large number of people in the United States, the United Kingdom, Australia, New Zealand, and other countries, reported having recovered memories of sexual abuse dating from childhood. These individuals had entered therapy with no recollection of such abuse and emerged from therapy with the "recovered" memories. Many had been leading productive lives but had sought counseling due to a variety of problems, such as depression or eating disorders.

Across the countries involved in these events, there had historically been a permissive attitude with regard to the use of (some) children in sexual activities. Until Queen Victoria in England passed a reform bill, it had been legal for 9-year-old girls to be sent out as prostitutes. The queen's effort changed this, making prostitution of a child legal only when the individual had achieved her 13th birthday. Another documented practice, dating from the same era, had been to chloroform children under the age of 5 years, as a means of preparing them to be sexually molested by men who paid for the opportunity (Pendergrast, 1996, chap. 1). These were of course the children of the very poor. Added to the widespread tolerance of sexual abuse, however, there had developed a social tendency to deny or belittle claims of such abuse, and notably of incest, even in cases where middle-class girls or women were involved. This pattern appears to have persisted well into the 20th century.

Sexual abuse became a target of the feminist movement in the 1960s, however, and an increasingly effective campaign was waged to make society aware of the problem. A number of books were written during this and later periods in which individual case histories of rape, molestation, and incest were documented (Bass, 1983; Brownmiller, 1975; Butler, 1978; Finkelhof, 1994; Herman, 1981). Almost all the published histories involved individuals who had been abused and had consistently remembered the abuse. Following this trend toward badly needed reform, a new idea emerged, dating from perhaps the mid-1970s. This was the notion that it would be possible to have been abused and not to recall the abuse. The absence of recollection was assumed to be due to repression. This view appears to have disseminated quickly among clinicians, many of whom began to use coercive techniques, such as hypnosis, to enable their clients to "recover" the memories.

From the beginning of this extended episode, other members of the clinical community warned against the use of aggressive techniques as a means of recovering content from long-term store. To put the case at its simplest, there was a danger that material retrieved in this fashion could involve unconsciously generated false memories (Ganaway, 1991).

The 1980s and 1990s saw the publication of a spate of "self-help" books, intended to help people who had been victims of incest. Unfortunately, these books also targeted women who had no memories of sexual abuse but who were assured that they too had been victims. They offered lists of symptoms that were claimed to be indicators of repressed sexual abuse. These included "wearing a lot of clothes, even in summer; baggy clothes; failure to remove clothes even when appropriate to do so (swimming, bathing, sleeping); and extreme requirement for privacy when using the bathroom" (Blume, 1990). "I often have nightmares; I have difficulty falling or staying asleep; basements terrify me; I startle easily; I space out or daydream; I do some things to excess and don't know when to quit" (Fredrickson, 1992). The lists further included depression, eating disorders, phobias, risk taking, and unwillingness to take risks!

Perhaps the most dangerous suggestion proposed by the self-help books, however, was that simply the idea or feeling that something might be wrong or that some form of abuse might have occurred was a probable sign that it had occurred. Bass and Davis's (1988) *The Courage to Heal*, for instance, noted confidently, "If you think you were abused and your life shows the symptoms, then you were" (pp. 21, 22). Note the symptoms listed above.

Clients who retrieved the suggested memories often showed intense distress. This was taken as confirmation of the reality of the recalled episodes. (As described above, Freud had at first drawn the same conclusion.) It was also widely claimed by clinicians who believed that the retrieved memories were real and that it would not be possible for so many people to remember events that had never happened.

There is now some hard evidence concerning the question of whether intense emotional response to a memory means that the memory is based on fact. McNally et al. (2004) examined individuals who recalled being abducted by aliens. The researchers tested physiological measures related to emotion while their participants listened to tape-recorded accounts of their encounters with the abductors. It was found that they were experiencing intense emotion.

4.1. Techniques Used to Recover Memories

Techniques used to recover the hypothesized repressed memories included hypnosis, guided imagery (also called guided recollection), trance writing, relaxation training, and the writing of journals in which clients were instructed to make up memories if they could not recall them, narcosynthesis, dream interpretation, and the examination of "body memories." Narcosynthesis involves the use of barbiturates, such as sodium amytal, which have the effect of making people less guarded than usual, such that they will disclose thoughts or feelings that they would not otherwise disclose or perhaps not otherwise remember.

The concept of journal writing centered on the belief that the recollections would emerge unconsciously in this fashion. The same view was taken of dreams, such that dream content was examined as if it reflected or suggested actual events.

A critical aspect of the techniques listed above, in terms of memory, is that the nonhypnotic or nondrug approaches usually involve massively repeated attempts to activate a memory that is assumed to exist at an unconscious level. Guided imagery can take many forms. The client may be asked to try to imagine a situation in which abuse might have occurred, and be directed to go back again and again to this context, and visualize any possible images. The therapist may also repeatedly ask questions concerning what is being experienced in the memory, trying to uncover information related to abuse.

The dangers involved in guided imagery have become more clear following the use of neuroimaging research techniques. Gonsalves, Reber, and Gitelman (2004), for instance, found that when participants were asked to imagine visual content, the greater the degree of activity in the visual areas of the brain following these instructions, the more likely the imagined content would later be mistaken for an actual memory.

Laboratory data have led to the same conclusion. It has been found that when experimental participants are led to imagine a given event, such as breaking a window, even a minute of such imagery generation can lead some individuals to recall the event as a memory (Garry & Polaschek, 2000; Loftus, 2004).

Yet another danger involves the authoritative status of the therapist. In many cases, therapists informed a client that the reported symptoms (for example, depression) indicated that she had in fact been abused. What remained was simply the task of recovering the memories that were clearly present at some level. It was also widely believed that any form of bulimia indicated the past occurrence of sexual abuse. (There is no evidence for this connection.)

The use of hypnosis as a means of recovering memories is not supported by the official psychiatric and clinical communities. This is the case because it has been established that hypnosis can generate false memories that are not distinguishable, on any currently known basis, from real memories. It is also the case that hypnotized subjects may become highly vulnerable to suggestion and lose their ability to reject implausible "memories" or other information (Kihlstrom, 1998, chap. 1; Kihlstrom & Eich, 1994). With regard to narcosynthesis, it appears to have effects similar to hypnosis. Apparently lost memories can be recovered through this technique, but it has not been established whether the content is reliable (Piper, 1993).

Krystal et al. (1995) noted that the Freudian belief in the desirability of retrieving (repressed or dissociated) memories and allowing the client to vent or express the accompanying ideas and violent emotions (an event known as *abreaction*) has not been well supported by the clinical evidence. There is a general belief that if traumatic memories can be reintegrated with ongoing conscious cognition, their pathological impact will be reduced. While this is probably true (in the case of traumatic episodes that really have occurred), there are difficulties with the process aimed at such reintegration. When traumatic recollections are stirred up, they tend to feed back into the intense emotional state of the individual (a process known as *kindling*) and make the condition worse. The authors conclude that there are better strategies available for helping individuals suffering from PTSD.

Stuss (1992) urged the critical point that there is a property held in common by techniques used in therapy to recover unconscious memories. Addressing in particular the use of guided recollection, narcosynthesis, relaxation training, and dream interpretation Stuss noted,

Each of these . . . takes advantage of an altered state of consciousness associated with increased suggestibility in which there is a reduction in functions usually associated with the frontal cortex, such as reflection, monitoring and editing of thought. (p. 17)

In other words, these approaches, just as obtains with hypnosis, undermine ordinary reality testing.

Ganaway (1991) warned with some force that content recalled in therapy is in many cases the unconscious projection of fears and anxieties. Such content is like the material in a dream (or, more exactly, a nightmare). It should never be assumed that material of this kind necessarily reflects an actual memory. "Only recently," Ganaway noted, "when some therapists . . . began to completely ignore the psycho-dynamic influence of unconscious fantasy on their patients' memories did this current epidemic of abuse memories take root."

4.2. Therapeutic Intervention and Recovered Memories: The Effects on Society

Loftus and Ketcham (1994, chaps. 3, 4) investigated a number of cases involving individuals who had recovered memories of sexual abuse. The women studied had had no recollection of abuse prior to entering therapy, but under the impact of one or more of the techniques described above, they came to believe that abuse had occurred. A parent was frequently believed to be the abuser. In one particularly troubling case, an individual who had sought help due to eating disorders was told that her symptoms indicated sexual molestation, that the abusers were indeed her parents, and that she was attempting to "vomit up a memory." Other cases involved attempted suicide or full mental breakdown. A common outcome was severe depression, leading to considerably worse emotional difficulties than had been experienced prior to therapy.

4.3. False Confessions

There are individuals accused of child molestation, on the basis of recovered memories, who have admitted to the crime, although in some cases they appear to have been innocent. A particularly notorious example is that of Paul Ingram, who was accused of child molestation by his daughters and, following extended questioning by the police, admitted to the abuse.

At first Ingram did not recall any acts of abuse but was told that he had repressed the memories. He came to believe that this was true and later began, as he thought, to remember the abusive episodes.

Ofshe, a social psychologist called in to examine the case, suspected that Ingram was entering states of self-induced trance in order to "remember," on cue, the events of which he was being accused (Ofshe, 1992). They included participation in satanic rituals. Ofshe fabricated an episode and described this as an event reported by Ingram's children. At first Ingram could not recall the event (which of course had never happened), but later he did recall it. In spite of the obvious unreality of some of the accusations made, and in spite of Ofshe's demonstration, Ingram was convicted of child molestation, based on the fact that he had confessed.

4.4. Recovered Memories of Sexual Abuse

McNally, Clancy, Barrett and Parker (2005) examined groups of individuals who had always remembered childhood sexual abuse, those who had recovered such memories in adulthood, and controls who reported that they had never been abused, concerning their ability to respond to directed-forgetting instructions: the instruction not to recall certain words that had been presented. If the recovered group had once lost actual memories through dissociation, they might be expected to be better at forgetting content than the other participants. The recovered-memory group, however, did not show superior performance in the directed-forgetting task.

5. Satanic Rituals

When recovered memories first appear in a therapeutic setting, they may involve relatively mild forms of abuse. In some cases, however, the recollections become increasingly bizarre.

There have been claims of involvement in satanic cults. These are typically reported to be intergenerational groups, which practice an array of horrors, including torture, the sexual abuse of children, and murder, with particular emphasis on the killing of babies. The babies have been bred for this purpose. Individuals may recall events in which dozens of the victims were buried, perhaps in a cult member's backyard, or in which they themselves were tortured (for instance, being doused in oil and set on fire), although there are no physical marks or scars. It is important to understand that individuals who "recover" such episodes experience them as actual memories (not simply a belief that these things have happened). The risk of later severe depression is not hard to understand.

In spite of the highly implausible nature of recollections of this kind, they have been repeatedly investigated. In 1994, a massive federal probe was carried out by the FBI. There proved to be no basis to the satanic allegations (Goodman, 1988). There was an occasional case of an individual who imagined himself possessed of satanic powers, but no massive conspiracy or secret coven inside the main society. A number of private investigators have also researched the satanic cult issue and found it to be a curious modern—although also ancient—myth (Ellis, 1992; Nathan & Snedecker, 1995; Wright, 1994).

6. Individuals Accused of Child Abuse

A second class of victims in this long cultural episode comprises the parents of individuals who recover abuse memories, and who are innocent. Goldstein (1992) in her sobering book, *Confabulations: Creating False Memories, Destroying Families*, chronicled some of their stories. Pendergrast (1996, chap. 7) has done the same.

In 1992, the False Memory Foundation was created with the goal of helping individuals who had been unjustly accused. Its membership quickly numbered in the thousands. Some important concerns have also been raised, however, with regard to the influence of the rejection of claims of recovered memories of sexual abuse. Such rejection is now widespread; it appears clear that many such memories are indeed false. But this leads to the probability that valid claims may now be treated lightly or with suspicion. There is also concern that institutions such as the False Memory Foundation may attract not only innocent parents but also individuals disposed to being critical of any claims of childhood abuse, leading back to the distorted social beliefs that prevailed before the 1960s.

7. Recovered Memories: Empirical Findings

A large population of individuals were abused by (some) Catholic priests prior to the 1990s, when the issue was made public. One victim, Frank Fitzpatrick, was instrumental in exposing this long history of child molestation. When in his 40s, Fitzpatrick spontaneously remembered being sexually abused by a particular priest, then Father James Porter, while attending St. Mary's Elementary School in Massachusetts. He succeeded in tracking Porter down and elicited a confession. After the case was made public, scores of individuals who had also been assaulted came forward, and Porter was accused, and convicted, of child molestation (Bruni & Burkett, 2002).

The people who had been molested by Porter offered similar accounts concerning their memories. Some always remembered. Some made a deliberate attempt to forget, with partial success. A little surprisingly, the passage of years seemed to obscure the recollections. However, it took only a reminder of the case for the details to be recovered.

The term *conscious suppression* has been used to describe the volitional effort to keep troubling content out of awareness. The reports described above appear to conform either to ordinary forgetting or to conscious suppression.

Williams (1995) interviewed 129 women who had been admitted to hospital as children following an episode or episodes involving molestation. These ranged from inappropriate touching to sexual intercourse. Thus the fact of abuse was documented. The hospital admission had occurred when the individuals were from 10 months to 12 years of age.

Twelve percent of the women reported no memory of abuse. This could have provided a strong case for repression or dissociation, except that the ages of these individuals at the time of the abuse were not reported. For those who were 5 years or younger, ordinary childhood amnesia could explain the finding. Another critical factor involved the number of occasions on which abuse occurred. As described earlier, abuse that occurs only once or on a few occasions can be forgotten with the passage of time (just as other events may be forgotten).

Of considerable interest, 16% of the women reported that there had been a time when they had forgotten about the abuse, only to encounter something that triggered the memory at a later date. Most began to forget some years after the incident.

A typical example involved a woman who reported that she had been molested at the age of 7, forgot about the event at roughly age 12, and remembered it again at 22. The memory came back when someone asked her whether she had ever been abused. Others claimed that they blocked the recollection off immediately after it had occurred.

Schooler, Bendiksen, and Ambadar (1997) and Shobe and Schooler (2001) described seven cases in which a memory of abuse occurring many years earlier had been abruptly recovered due to an event that cued the memory. There was evidence that the abusive event or events had occurred. The people involved reacted with extreme surprise, since they could not understand how such an episode could have been forgotten, and strong emotion. There was evidence that some of these individuals had in fact remembered the event at an earlier date and then apparently wholly forgotten it again. These cases provide support for the view that content may be lost from memory under conditions in which such loss might not normally be expected. If this is a correct interpretation, it remains unclear precisely what mechanisms of forgetting are involved.

Finally, there is evidence that an adult may become amnesic directly following a violent, traumatic episode, such as rape. Here, memory for the event and for the entire period of time surrounding the event is lost and later spontaneously recovered.

7.1. Claims of Documented Repression

There are studies that have been widely cited as documenting the loss of traumatic memories through repression or dissociation and their later recovery.

Herman and Schatzow (1987) examined 53 women who had entered therapy. In 21 of these cases, there was corroborating evidence of sexual abuse, and 14 individuals had suffered from amnesia for the later-recovered memories. The study did not report, however, whether any of the amnesic individuals fell into the category of those with confirmed abuse.

Briere and Conte (1993) examined 450 women currently in therapy to determine whether there had ever been a time in their lives, prior to the age of 18, when they had forgotten that they had been abused. The women had current memories of abuse. Fifty-nine percent answered that there had been such a period. No attempt was made, however, to provide any confirmation of the claim that abuse had actually occurred. Nor did the authors describe the techniques that had been used to recover the memories. The client's self-report was considered evidence of abuse, even though the respondents had all been in therapy.

8. Trauma Associated With Incarceration: Memories of Concentration Camp Survivors

A concentration camp known as Camp Erica was established in the Netherlands during the German occupation. The Germans abandoned the camp in 1943, and from 1943 to 1948 the Dutch authorities interviewed individuals who had been interned there. A second investigation was begun in the 1980s. There was thus a report of the relevant memories made at or close to the time of the event, followed by a second report 40 years later.

Wagenaar and Groeneweg (1990) examined these records, with the intention of discovering whether there were data to support the view, endorsed by Pierre Janet, of "imprinted," permanent, and wholly accurate memories of trauma. Their study was equally relevant to the question of whether traumatic memories may be repressed.

The authors' findings were of "remarkable" and detailed recall of the experience of the camp. The witnesses were able to confirm one another's memories. They recalled the details of camp life. Seventeen of 30 remembered the date of their arrival; 16 of 30 recalled their registration number.

There was also evidence of forgetting. In the original interview, two individuals recalled their date of entry with an error of more than 1 but less than 6 months. Forty years later, 11 individuals erred by this amount, and 3 recalled the wrong season.

Martinus de Rilke had been a particularly brutal kapo at the camp. Yet six individuals had forgotten his name by the 1980s, even though three had been beaten by him. Most recalled his hair correctly as dark, but a few misrecalled it as light. The names of other internees had been largely forgotten (an average of 1.3 names recalled). Twelve witnesses spontaneously recalled, again in the 1980s, that the Jewish prisoners had been housed in tents and the others in barracks. Only one act of spontaneous recall was mistaken on this point. But when direct questions were asked of other individuals (who had not simply recalled this information), 14 remembered correctly, and 11 misrecalled the Jews as being housed in barracks.

All the men remembered the brutalities of the camp. However, by the 1980s, most had forgotten some individual episodes (including cases of extreme violence).

Thus, there was no support for the view of imprinted and unchanging memory of traumatic events within this context. Forgetting and memory distortion were clearly documented. That at least some of the forgetting was of the ordinary (unmotivated) kind is indicated by the loss of nontraumatic material, such as the names of other prisoners. Similar findings have been reported in other studies of concentration camp victims (Chodoff, 1963; Langer, 1991).

9. Memories of Crimes and Disasters

Studies examining the memory function of victims and bystanders of violent crimes have provided mixed results. Yuille and Tollestrup (1991) found that witnesses of a murder showed excellent recall of the event, including the recall of details. Other studies have shown impaired memory for events involved in a crime or emergency situation (Baddeley, 1972).

It appears likely that studies involving crimes do not invariably include traumatic memories, however. It may be that many individuals who see violent events, or are engaged in such events, nonetheless remain relatively calm.

Other cases approximate more closely to the conditions associated with trauma. In 1981, the skywalk of the Hyatt Regency Hotel in Kansas City collapsed, killing a large number of people.

Wilkinson (1983) interviewed 102 witnesses to the event. Roughly 90% of them reported that they kept remembering what had happened; they could not put the episode out of their minds. They also showed weak memories for the details of the event. Here, the classic pattern of traumatic memory was clearly illustrated.

Terr (1979, 1983) studied the recollections of 23 children who had been kidnapped on a school bus in Chowchilla, California, and held for 16 hours underground before they escaped. The children possessed vivid and detailed memories of the event. But there were also distortions of recall in about half of the group. Terr believes that a component of these were due to the stress of the moment disrupting accurate encoding. But some were memory errors. There were children who remembered details accurately directly after the episode but whose memory had changed 4 years later. For instance, one recalled two female kidnappers, when there had been none, or a kidnapper with pillows stuffed into his pants.

Other studies of children involved in violence also found continuing memory of the event. Malmquist (1986) examined 16 children who had witnessed the murder of a parent. All recalled the murder.

Thus, the findings concerning trauma due to criminal violence or dangerous accidents show no pattern of repression or dissociation, fairly strong recall of detail, and good recall over time, but they also show change and distortion in the original memory.

It should be noted, however, that repeated trauma across childhood could be expected to produce a different outcome from the experience of a single, even if devastating, episode. There is evidence that abused children tend to develop dissociative disorders, such that the pattern of recall in these cases might be different (Terr, 1994).

10. False Memories in Natural Contexts

It had been demonstrated by the 1980s that components of a memory can be changed, in particular by misleading postevent information (see Chapter 9). These cases involved emotionally neutral material, however, such as stop signs, bottles of Coke, and cans of peanuts.

Some individuals who believed in the reliability of the recovered-memory evidence urged that while it would be possible to change memories for trivial and unimportant details, and in a laboratory setting, it would not be possible to change, or to create false, "real-life" content that was of some importance to the individual. In response to this issue, Loftus and Pickrell (1995) and Loftus, Coan, and Pickrell (1996) conducted studies in which the parents of the participants were contacted and asked to provide information concerning events that had occurred when the (student) participants were very young. Some false, although plausible, episodes that involved the individual getting lost in a shopping mall or store, were then included among the "true" memories. When the false events were described to them, 25% of the participants began to hazily recall these target episodes and (critically) often began to remember additional details that had not been described by the experimenters. The usual pattern was that the false event would not be remembered on the first test, but it might be recalled under repeated testing.

Hyman and Billings (1998) and Hyman, Husband, and Billings (1995) conducted similar studies involving both very pedestrian and slightly unusual false events (spilling punch on an adult at a wedding). No participant recalled any of the false events during the first testing session, but false recall began in a second session and continued to the third and last test, with, in one study, 13 participants (25% of the present sample of 58) then remembering and describing an event that had never happened.

Critics of the view implied above (that recovered memories need not be real memories) further urged that although it had now proved possible to create false, real-life memories, these involved ordinary or everyday events. But people could not be brought to generate false memories for well out-of-the-ordinary, or for particularly horrible, episodes. In response to these further objections, Heaps and Nash (2001) led a minority of their participants to "remember" that they had nearly drowned as children: that is, to remember the incident itself. The incident had never in fact occurred. And Porter, Yuille, and Lehman (1999) were able to produce false memories in their participants of various horrible events, such as being the victim of a vicious animal attack, that were supposed to have occurred when they were small.

It had also been suggested that when researchers produce apparently false memories, the event may actually have occurred. (Given the number of individuals within a single study led to believe they had almost drowned, this appears quite unlikely, but the argument was perhaps within the bounds of possibility.) Braun, Ellis, and Loftus (2002) responded to the issue by convincing some of their experimental participants that they recalled shaking hands with Bugs Bunny at Disneyland by the magic castle. Bugs is not a Disneyland character. Mazzoni and Memon (2003) brought their participants to recall that, during childhood, a nurse had removed a skin sample from their finger. This was achieved through asking the participants to imagine the event, until it "triggered" their memory. Removal of skin from a finger is not a procedure used within the medical community here. And perhaps even more striking, Lindsay, Hagen, Read, Wade, and Garry (2004) persuaded many of their subjects that they had put "slime" (a goo marketed for children's play) in their teacher's desk when they were in first or second grade. This belief was inculcated through the medium of a parent "reminding" them that this had happened and the provision of a photograph of the relevant first- or second-grade class. The study was very effective; many participants found it hard to believe that they had not slimed the desk when they were debriefed. The study is of particular interest because of the role of the photograph. As described in Chapter 12, when a false memory is supported by a background of plausible, known-to-be-true information, the likelihood of its being accepted as a real event is significantly increased. Here, seeing the faces of children who really had been in the relevant class appears to have increased the plausibility count on which such decisions, involving weak memories, appear to depend (at least in part).

In summary, there is clear evidence that false memories can be created by certain techniques, including precisely many traditionally used within a clinical setting to recover repressed memories. Notably, these include repetition of the suggestion of the target event and also the use of repeatedly imagining the event.

11. False Memories in Young Children

During the 1990s, numerous cases were brought to the courts in which an adult or adults were accused of molesting a child. The evidence for the abuse depended on the testimony of the purported victims, generally children of preschool age.

Research in the 1980s had indicated that children's memories are reliable. More recent studies have shown, however, that this is true only when certain conditions hold. The child must be questioned in an unbiased fashion and must genuinely understand the nature of the content about which he or she is being questioned. It is also important that the individual not be exposed to misleading ideas (prior to an interview). If these conditions are maintained, even preschoolers can resist the influence of a misleading question. If such conditions are not maintained, however, a child's memory can be quite easily changed (Leightman & Ceci, 1995; Peterson & Bell, 1996; Saywitz, Goodman, Nicholas, & Moan, 1991).

Developmental psychologists began to suspect that the testimony provided by children (in the spate of abuse trials that occurred during the 1980s and the 1990s) was the result of coaching. A particularly effective strategy is to present a kind of background context of ideas to the witness, prior to any public questions being asked. The child may then come to believe that the suggested ideas are real.

Ceci and Bruck (1995) found that preschoolers' recollections of an actual event (a medical visit involving an inoculation) were generally accurate if no misleading information was suggested, but their memory of the event could be changed when such suggestions were made. An interesting additional finding was that once the children began to accept the inaccurate, experimenter-provided ideas, they then tended to add more incorrect details spontaneously.

Researchers also found that the more often misinformation was suggested, the more likely the child was to recall it, believing it to be true. The tendency to misremember also increased with increased interviewing, even if no further incorrect details had been supplied (Bruck, Ceci, & Melnyk, 1997; Leightman & Ceci, 1995; Salmon & Pipe, 1997). Also, the longer the delay between the original event and the interview, the easier it was to implant a false memory.

The children tended to think that they knew the answers to questions that they did not know. Thus when asked of an earlier event, "What did the man do for a living?" they typically generated an answer, although they had no way of knowing this. When asked, "Is milk bigger than water?" 5- to 7-year-old subjects were found to give an answer in almost all cases.

A number of researchers duplicated the suggestive interviewing techniques that had been used during the earlier criminal investigations, such as the McMartin case in California, in which extremely bizarre and implausible events were reported by the children. The interviewing techniques (performed prior to the trial) included the use of repeated sessions in which an event implying abuse was described to the children, who could be asked to pretend that the suggested event had happened and then asked to describe the event happening, again and again, until they began to "remember" it. This approach was combined with a failure to explore any possible alternatives to the belief (that the accused were guilty) held by the examiner or to check on the sources of information that was provided spontaneously by the child (for example, "Did your mommy say this, or did you think of it for yourself?"), and no attempt was made to urge authenticity ("Did this really happen?"). Finally, inconsistent and bizarre evidence was ignored (Bruck & Ceci, 1999).

Goodman and Aman (1990) presented preschool children with anatomically correct dolls, following a medical checkup, and asked the children to show what had happened during the checkup. Many touched the doll's genitals, presumably because these were an unusual feature of a doll. (No such touching had occurred during the actual examination.) The same behavior had been used as evidence for abuse in a range of court cases. Also, and critically, Leightman and Ceci (1995), having induced false memories in their participants, later debriefed them, explaining that the suggested events had not really happened. A significant number of the children refused to believe this.

The bizarre events reported in the trials involving current child abuse were often very bizarre indeed. They included child testimony to the effect that they had been forced to eat live babies or (in one case) that a subject had been handcuffed but had freed himself by karate-chopping the handcuffs.

Piaget (1926), researching young children's cognitive grasp of reality, had found that his subjects were prone to confusing ideas suggested from the outside (by the experimenters) with their own ideas. There was also a tendency to reinterpret material that had not been understood. Piaget noted that the individual is not lying in such cases. The boundary between internal and external information, in young children, is simply fragile.

In summary, the evidence to date indicates that under some conditions child memory can be detailed and accurate. If content is suggested to the child, however, recollection can be quite easily changed. Young children are also prone to fantasy.

12. Hypnosis and Memory

Individuals vary in their capacity to be hypnotized. Some, estimated at about 25%, are good hypnotic subjects, some (50%), fall into the middle range, and some, the remaining 25%, may not be capable of being hypnotized or may achieve this state only with difficulty. Individuals who are suggestible tend to be better hypnotic subjects (Lynn & Sivec, 1992).

In the case of good subjects, both positive and negative hallucinations can be suggested. Thus, an individual may on demand hallucinate the presence of a buzzing insect or a voice or, if told that an object (such as the hand on a watch) is not present, will fail to see it (Hilgard, 1965, chap. 1).

An important characteristic of the hypnotic state involves a marked reduction in reality testing. Information will be found acceptable that would be rejected in the waking state. Orne (1962), for instance, reported the case of a subject who, when asked to describe the individual sitting to his right, correctly identified Mr. X. But when he was told that Mr. X was sitting on his left, he then "saw" Mr. X simultaneously in both places. When asked if he found this odd, he said that he did. But there was no serious questioning of the reality of the experience.

Stalnaker and Riddle (1932) tested their participants' recall of the Longfellow poem "The Village Blacksmith" and found enhanced recall under hypnosis. There was also a heightened count of errors in recall. This outcome (of increases in both accurate and inaccurate memory) is typical of information recovered under hypnosis.

Memories recalled under hypnosis tend to appear valid to the individual when he or she returns to the waking state, even when they are false. Otani (1992) reported the case of a young woman who had difficulty with dental sessions because of a gag reflex. She was hypnotized in an attempt to discover the reason for this. Under hypnosis she remembered that the gagging began soon after she had undergone a tonsillectomy at the age of 7. The hypnotist told her that now that she understood the source of the problem, it would no longer bother her; and this proved to be the case. However, her family doctor later informed her that her tonsils had never been removed.

Perry, Laurence, D'Eon, and Tallant (1988) and Nash (1987) reported that when subjects are age-regressed under hypnosis, their experience of their earlier life tends to be a mixture of fact and fantasy.

It has been established for some years that memory will often improve when repeated efforts are made at retrieval (Payne, 1987). Nogrady, McConkey, and Perry (1985) tested their participants' memories either under hypnosis or under a waking condition in which repeated efforts were made to retrieve the material. Recall increased significantly in both groups, and the level of increase was the same.

Whitehouse, Dinges, Orne, and Orne (1988) conducted a study in which half of the participants were hypnotized during the critical recall test and half were not hypnotized (the waking condition). However, the requirement at test was that every question be answered.

Given these instructions, participants in the waking condition were compelled to guess or infer some of the answers. The result was that the hypnotized and waking condition participants recalled at an equal level. The only difference was that the hypnotized subjects were confident of their answers, while the waking subjects were not.

It has also been found that meaningless material (random words, etc.) is less subject to improved or changed recall under hypnosis than meaningful material (McConkey, 1992, chap. 15).

Many studies have found that participants are more likely to develop a false memory when they are hypnotized, as compared with being in the waking condition (Sheehan, Statham, & Jamieson, 1991a, 1991b; Sheehan, Statham, Jamieson, & Ferguson, 1991). Intriguingly, however, Barnier and McConkey (1993) and McConkey, Labelle, Bibb, and Bryant (1990) reported that high-hypnotizable subjects, when repeatedly exposed to the plausible suggestion of a false memory, were likely to develop the memory, even when not hypnotized.

In summary, the data on hypnosis do not appear to support the view of improved access to stored memory content but, rather, a function in which both weakly coded and inferred, not-always-accurate, material will be generated and accepted as valid.

Summary

Traumatic memories as studied historically were described as involving high sensory content, low-abstract, structuring content, high emotion, incomplete, fragmented memories, and flashbacks. Recent research has questioned the claims of incomplete memories, however.

Freud believed that traumatic memories were repressed: held out of awareness by an active psychological force. P. Janet believed that trauma causes changes in cognition, reducing the normal level of organized abstract thought, and that aspects of the trauma can become walled off from awareness.

During the 1980s and 1990s many individuals came to believe that they had recovered repressed memories of childhood abuse. The memories were recovered during therapy. Techniques used to recover memories are now known to be at risk for generating false memories that appear real to the individual. Combat veterans, survivors of concentration camps, and individuals who have experienced disasters or violent crimes typically recall the event.

Young children can be manipulated to produce false memories quite easily.

Researchers have demonstrated that false autobiographical memories can be produced in about 20% of a typical, healthy experimental adult population. Repeated suggestions of false information are needed to achieve this outcome. Hypnotic techniques can also lead to false memories, particularly when good hypnotic subjects are involved.

Discussion

With regard to memories based on trauma, the current data fail to support the long-held belief in "imprinted," perfect memory content. The memories can include distortion. The alternative claim of trauma being associated with memory loss appears better supported, although that too has been questioned.

Cues appear to play a powerful role in the retrieval of memories that have simply been forgotten or that may reflect some form of dissociative process.

It appears that people can forget a traumatic incident, or series of incidents, with the passing of long periods of time, in the ordinary sense of the term *forget*. Current research has led to a wide range of questions, however, concerning what it means to forget and the various kinds of forgetting that may exist. It is certain that there are many thousands of episodes within my autobiography memory that I have not thought about for years. But if I were to recall such an episode, I would not normally say that I had previously forgotten it. I had simply not thought about it for a long time. Yet there are occasions when people report that they "forgot" and seem to mean more than just the happenstance fact that the memory had not been retrieved over many years.

Data supporting the Freudian notion of repression appear to be very scant, if there are any such data at all. There is clear evidence that among the huge number of recovered abuse memories of the 1980s and 1990s, many were false. It has also been established that techniques traditionally used within the therapeutic context to recover "lost" episodes are at risk for producing memories that are indeed false.

The recovered memories that are considered most suspect, with regard to their veracity, involve reasonably well-adjusted individuals who claim to have forgotten abuse at an age when a strong memory function could be expected and who yet retain a normal episodic memory for their lives in general. It should be noted that the absence of evidence does not mean that such recovered episodes do not exist. They could reflect rare occurrences. However, the absence of evidence should imply, at the least, caution within this context.

Abused children appear likely to develop dissociative disorders, either in childhood or in later life. These are serious disorders, in which memory content does appear capable of being divorced from awareness. A person suffering from this kind of illness might indeed fail to recall episodes of abuse dating from after the normal period of childhood amnesia. However, such individuals typically show other disorders of memory as well as severe emotional disturbance; they could not be described as reasonably well-adjusted.

The notion of childhood sexual abuse has been widely disseminated by the media. Everyone has heard the story. It appears that many individuals now enter therapy thinking that they may have been abused. This leads to the risk of recovered, false memories of abuse even if the therapist does not suggest or encourage any such notion. The extent to which clinicians have "implanted" memories in their clients is thus probably overrated, and many clinicians now feel that they are walking on eggshells even in standard, nonintrusive efforts to help the people who come to them. It has become dangerous to deal with memory at all.

A particular problem within this context is that people will not always accept the information that a weak, "recovered" memory may not be true.

A therapist friend of mine has been approached by individuals who wish her to hypnotize them so that they may search for memories of abuse that they think they harbor or may harbor. They are disappointed when they learn that she will not use hypnosis.

It is clear, nonetheless, that many innocent people have become victims of what are simply false memories. There are men and women who have spent years in prison on the basis of the recovered, unconfirmed memory of an adult or the forced recollection of a child. As described above, evidence of this kind is no more reliable than if the accused had been thrown in water and convicted if they float, as in the more traditional witch trials. And the pain suffered by others, not sent to prison but accused of heinous acts by their children, would be hard to measure. It could be said today that there exist two major groups of victims: those who have been abused and innocent adults accused of perpetrating abuse. But we understand more about memory today than 20 years ago, and perhaps this can help us.

CHAPTER 15

Disorders of Memory

Overview

1. In the amnesic syndrome, individuals are unable to form new episodic memories and, typically, forget much of the past. Established semantic memory is generally not impaired in the amnesic syndrome. The acquiring of new semantic knowledge may or may not be impaired. Short-term, procedural, and implicit memory generally functions at a normal or close to normal level.

2. Damage to the frontal lobes typically results in confabulation: a confusion of imagined information with real memories. The imagined information can be quite unrealistic. Ability to recall order and temporal information is also impaired.

3. Amnesia can involve the selective loss of certain kinds of information. Some individuals may lose concepts of living but not of nonliving things, or vice versa, and others may recall public but not personal events and vice versa. Even more selective amnesias also exist.

4. Dementia is a condition in which memory deteriorates, and there is also loss of rational thought. It is caused by a range of diseases and can also occur due to aging. Alzheimer's disease is a severe form of dementia in which memory, conceptual representation, language, and reasoning are progressively lost.

Learning Objectives

1. Knowledge of the amnesic syndrome. Knowledge of amnesia caused by medial temporal lobe (MTL) and by diencephalic damage. Knowledge of the functions that are spared. Knowledge of the fact that different classes of concept can be lost selectively from memory.

2. Knowledge of the effects of damage to the frontal lobes.

3. Knowledge of the symptoms and causes of dementia, including Alzheimer's disease.

T he present chapter deals with various forms of abnormal functioning in memory.

The field of research into cognitive disorders is known as *neuropsychology*. This is generally defined as the relation between damage to the brain and psychological functioning.

Disorders of memory are classified as being either or *organic* or *psychogenic* in origin. Psychogenic disorders, which have a psychological origin, were covered in Chapter 14. Organic disorders, which have a physical cause, form the subject of the present chapter.

Familiarity with Chapter 13, on implicit memory, will be helpful in understanding the following material.

1. The Amnesic Syndrome

The *amnesic syndrome*, sometimes simply called *amnesia*, results when certain structures of the brain are damaged. An individual suffering from this condition will not be able to form new long-term memories. That is, she may eat dinner but will then be unable to remember that she has eaten. Or she might be introduced to a new person and will not remember that this has occurred. Difficulty in learning new semantic information is also present.

The amnesic person will generally have trouble remembering the past, involving the period before the trauma, as well as difficulty in forming new memories. Memory for the most recent pretraumatic events shows the greatest impairment, with remote episodes often spared.

The syndrome is caused by damage to certain structures deep within the brain, particularly the *diencephalon* or the *medial temporal lobes* (MTLs), structures that form part of the limbic system. The damage can result from viral infections, neurosurgery, injury originating inside the head, external head injury, brain tumors, strokes, or anoxia.

The inability to form new memories is called *anterograde amnesia*. Here events are experienced and understood, but forgotten after a few minutes. Inability to remember the past is called *retrograde amnesia*. Retrograde amnesia may extend back in time for only a short period or for years. In either case, a *temporal gradient* is involved, in that the most remote memories are usually retained, while episodes dating from just before the trauma are forgotten. If recovery from the retrograde component occurs, the individual begins to regain the oldest memories first, with recovery moving progressively to include more recent events.

The terms *semantic* and *episodic* memory are helpful in understanding the patterns of normal and impaired functioning in the amnesic syndrome. Semantic memory involves memory for general information (the name of the president, the location of Alaska on a map, etc.), including knowledge of language and word meanings. Episodic memory involves recollection for the events of one's life.

Semantic memory, as established before the trauma, generally remains intact. As a result, individuals suffering from the amnesic syndrome are likely to score as well as ever on tests of intelligence. The quality of episodic memory concerning events dating from before the onset of the amnesic condition varies. Some individuals recall this period quite clearly. Others recall the premorbid period, but without normal clarity. And in some cases there is a gradient of recall, with clarity increasing, the more remote in time the memory. The most common pattern, however, is one of retrograde amnesia, lasting for varying periods.

Figure 15.1 shows patterns of autobiographical recall on the part of amnesics, dating from childhood to recent events.

1.1. Damage to the Diencephalon: Korsakoff Syndrome

In 1881, the neurologist Carl Wernicke described a condition involving abnormalities of vision and gross confusion. It was labeled as Wernicke's encephalopathy. About the same period, Sergei Korsakoff identified the properties associated with the amnesic syndrome, as described above, in a particular group of patients. It emerged that the symptoms described by Wernicke were precursors of the full-blown amnesia, such that the latter condition became known as the Wernicke-Korsakoff syndrome. It is often characterized, however, simply as Korsakoff syndrome. The syndrome is caused by prolonged and severe drinking. This pattern is associated with a poor diet, which leads to thiamine deficiency. Some researchers believe that thiamine deficiency as such causes the illness, while others attribute it to some interaction between thiamine deficiency and the effects of alcohol on the brain. In the Korsakoff syndrome, the damage is to a group of subcortical structures called the *diencephalon*. The diencephalon includes the *thalamus* and the *mamillary bodies*. In some cases, there is also damage to the *hippocampus* and other MTL areas, and it is increasingly believed that some deterioration of the frontal cortex is involved.

The structures that mediate memory are for the most part lodged deep within the brain. And since the brain is a three-dimensional object, imaging the relevant areas can be effected in several ways. For instance, it is possible to show the image that would be seen when a division is made between the right and left sides of the brain, and the half-section is viewed from inside. This is known as a *saggital section*. Or it is possible to divide the front half from the back half, an approach that produces a *coronal section*. A third division involves separating the top half of the brain from the bottom. This is a *horizontal section*. The three ways of examining brain structures are shown in Figure 15.2.

Figure 15.3 shows sites of the brain involved in memory formation and retrieval, as shown in saggital section.

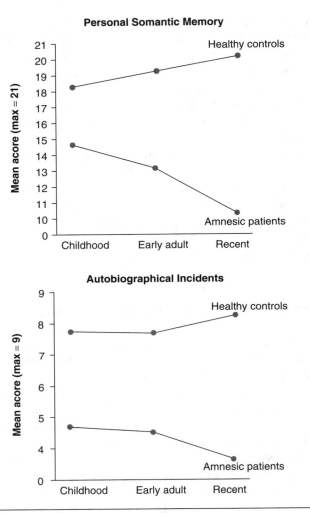

Figure 15.1 Recall of Autobiographical Information on the Part of Amnesics and Healthy Controls

SOURCE: From Baddeley, A., *Human Memory: Theory and Practice.* Published by Allyn and Bacon, Boston, MA. Copyright © 1990 by Pearson Education. Reprinted by permission of the publisher.

NOTE: The upper panel shows recall of facts relating to one's life, such as the names of friends or that one held a job of a certain kind. The lower panel shows recollection of episodes.

Individuals suffering from Korsakoff syndrome often pass through an initial period of confusion, in which they may *confabulate* (generate memories that are not real), followed by a state of severe amnesia. They are then unable to form new episodic memories and have difficulty, varying in severity across individuals, with new semantic memory content (learning new words or concepts). There is also in most cases an acute retrograde amnesia, involving episodic memory, which can extend back for as long as 30 years (Albert, Butters, & Levin, 1979). In contrast, patients with Korsakoff syndrome function normally, or close to normally, in the

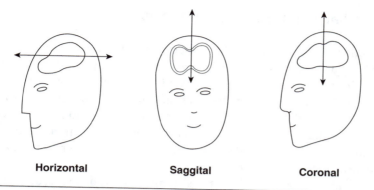

Horizontal   **Saggital**   **Coronal**

Figure 15.2   Horizontal, Saggital, and Coronal Cross Sections of the Brain

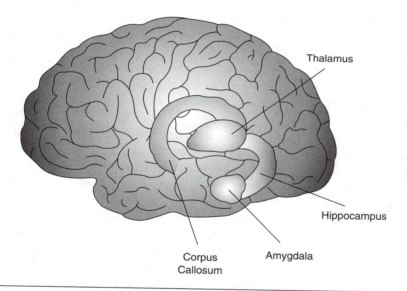

Thalamus

Hippocampus

Corpus   Amygdala
Callosum

Figure 15.3   Structures Within the Brain Involved in Memory

NOTE: The structures shown are part of the limbic system.

recall of remote episodes (beyond the period of the amnesia), in intelligence, linguistic competence, short-term recall, and procedural memory. However, they appear to lose motivation and pay little attention to events or input that would normally be attended (Parkin, 1987, chap. 3).

Patients with Korsakoff syndrome respond to classical conditioning, and most forms of implicit memory are undamaged. They can also master certain recognition tasks, although they learn very slowly.

Once learning has occurred, however, the information is then retained for an extended period, comparable with normal functioning. In contrast, few tasks involving recall can be mastered.

1.2. Medial Temporal Lobe Amnesia

A second form of amnesia involves temporal lobe damage. The condition can be caused by a variety of factors, including viral infection. This produces a condition known as *herpes simplex encephalitis*. The resulting amnesias differ in kind, depending on the sites penetrated by the virus, although the diencephalon (the area involved in Korsakoff disease) is not usually affected. Damage to the temporal lobes can also occur due to accidents or surgical intervention. The most common form of the latter involves *closed head injury*, in which the skull remains intact but damage is nonetheless inflicted on the brain.

An individual known as HM suffered from epilepsy, dating from his teenage years. The damage may have occurred when he was knocked down by a bike. The condition meant that he could not pursue his earlier plans for a career, and apparently his father was intolerant concerning it. Perhaps for all these reasons, HM agreed at the age of 25 to undergo surgery, involving removal of structures within his temporal lobes. This approach had been successful with regard to epilepsy in the past, although the standard procedure was to remove tissue from one temporal lobe only. HM's physician was less conservative and removed the structures in both temporal lobes, including the hippocampus and the amygdala. This was done even though physicians at that time (the 1950s) did not know the functions served by these areas of the brain.

Following the surgery, HM showed a severe amnesic syndrome, with complete anterograde amnesia and retrograde amnesia extending back for several years. It was also very difficult for him to establish any new semantic memory content. His intelligence, language skills, short-term memory, working memory, and procedural memory were not affected.

Deliberate attempts to teach HM the meaning of new words failed. However, he did acquire the phrase "rock and roll." He also ultimately learned his way about the hospital, an achievement indicating that certain forms of episodic memory could function, although very weakly. Again, however, spatial recognition may involve codes that are more primitive than those involved in most forms of episodic recognition and recall.

In contrast to patients with Korsakoff syndrome, individuals suffering from MTL amnesia cannot in general learn to recognize new stimuli. They also tend, when they have acquired some information, to forget very quickly (Lhermitte & Signoret, 1972; Squire, 1981). Note that this also differs from the Korsakoff syndrome, where recognition learning is very slow but is well retained once it has been established. MTL amnesia patients do not generally show retrograde amnesia stretching as far back into the past as occurs with patients with Korsakoff syndrome, however. Anterograde amnesia, which is severe in MTL patients, leaves the individual with no sense of an immediate past. It appears to be somewhat like perpetually waking up, but with no memory of having slept or of any recent event.

Figure 15.4 shows sites of the brain that are damaged in individuals suffering from the amnesic syndrome.

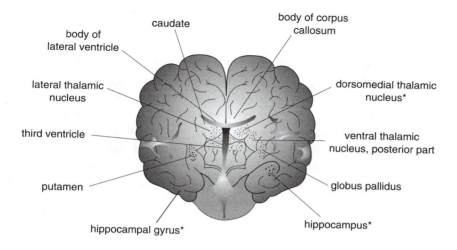

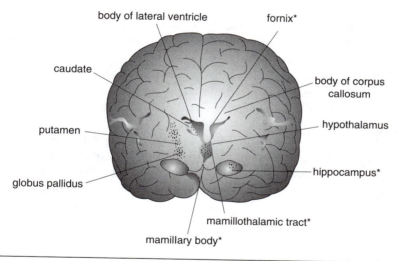

Figure 15.4   Structures in the Brain That Are Damaged in the Amnesic Syndrome

SOURCE: From Butters, N. & Cermak, L. S., *Alcoholic Korsakoff's syndrome: An information processing approach to amnesia,* copyright © 1980. Reprinted with permission from Elsevier.

NOTE: Damaged structures are marked with an asterisk. Coronal section.

1.3. Specific Capacities That Are Impaired in the Amnesic Syndrome

In addition to anterograde and retrograde amnesia within the present syndrome, certain specific areas of impaired function can be identified. Amnesics have difficulty coding for the order in which events occur or stimuli are seen.

A second area in which amnesics function poorly involves *relational informa-tion*. Relational properties are needed in all forms of verbal learning and in auto-biographical recall. For instance, if a series of word items are learned, it is necessary to relate them to the target list: to identify the fact that these particular words were on that list. In paired-associate learning, associative relations must be established between the stimulus-response pairs. And in general episodic recall, to retain an event in memory it is necessary to recall a wide series of relations obtain-ing among the objects or people involved in the event. For instance, the individual might live through an episode in which a coat was thrown over the back of a sofa (but not of a chair), and in which two individuals spoke to one another, while a third did not speak to either of them, and in which the third individual left the room while the others stayed, and so on. These are all relational properties. It also appears to be the case that when some form of relational connection has been learned by individuals suffering from the amnesic syndrome, it is then difficult for them to unlearn it and substitute a different relationship for the first one. Yet in the everyday world, the relations between objects, people, and abstractions change constantly.

It should be noted that the relative weakness in handling relations reflects *new* content: that is, the entry of new information into LTM. Amnesics do retain the complex relational information present in their remote, intact memories, and in already-established semantic memory.

Unlike MTL patients, individuals suffering from Korsakoff syndrome can learn to recognize stimuli, and can generally form new if weak episodic memories, but are markedly vulnerable to interference effects, particularly proactive interference (Winocur & Kinsbourne, 1978).

This group also has difficulty with temporal codes. They do not distinguish when an event happened, or where stimuli were encountered, as well as control subjects do. There is some evidence that when there is a need to judge the recency of encoun-tered stimuli, patients with Korsakoff syndrome depend on a sense of familiarity, rather than precise contextual coding information (Huppert & Piercy, 1978).

1.4. Functions That Are Spared in the Amnesic Syndrome

1.4.1. Short-Term Memory

Amnesics typically show a normal short-term memory function. This is gener-ally tested by a memory span procedure, in which random verbal items are pre-sented for immediate recall.

It is believed that verbal short-term recall is not mediated within the hippocam-pus but involves an area of the brain known as the *parietotemporal-occipital (PTO) cortex*.

Certain regions of the brain are involved in sensory processing, and others are involved in motor response. Two major additional areas are known as *association cortex*. These involve the prefrontal association neocortex and the PTO cortex described above. The location of the PTO cortex is shown in Figure 15.5.

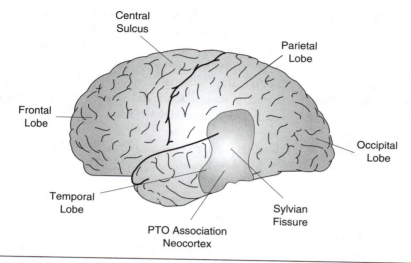

Figure 15.5   The Parietotemporal-Occipital (PTO) Cortex

NOTE: Damage in the parietotemporal-occipital cortex can result in impaired short-term recall.

1.4.2. Priming

Individuals suffering from amnesia generally show normal perceptual priming.
Priming involves a function in which the presentation of a stimulus can influence the processing of a later, similar, identical, or related stimulus. For instance, if the same word is presented twice, across two different testing periods, amnesics recognize the word faster on its second presentation. This occurs even when they cannot recall having seen the word earlier.

It is widely believed that priming phenomena of the kind described above involve perceptual structures. Perceptual structures are the structures in LTM that provide information concerning the sensory properties of stimuli. For instance, the perceptual structure for the word *chair* specifies the size and shape of the word. According to this view, when the word *chair* is encountered, it is matched with the LTM chair-perceptual structure. An alternative form of priming, known as *semantic priming*, involves a meaning relationship between two stimuli. For instance, a word might be primed because it is similar in meaning to an earlier-presented word. Amnesics generally do not show semantic priming, or they show it weakly.

Perceptual priming effects are usually the same for amnesic and normal individuals, although there are some forms of perceptual priming in which amnesics are again weaker than nonamnesics (Mayes & Montaldi, 1999; Richardson-Klavehn & Bjork, 1988).

1.4.3. Perceptual and Motor Learning

Amnesics show repetition priming for objects as well as for words. More strikingly, if a picture of a completely *novel* object is shown twice, amnesic individuals can identify the object more quickly on the second exposure, even when they cannot recall having seen the picture before. The findings are of some theoretical interest, because it is believed that this group has difficulty dealing with novel semantic and semantic-associative information. Thus, it appears likely that the processing of new visual-perceptual material is spared in the amnesic syndrome. This conclusion fits what is known about the location of processing of visual information, which centers on the occipital region and the striate and prestriate cortex.

When amnesic individuals are exposed to new pseudowords (FLANG, etc.), or random letter strings (XXPG), they show a priming effect here too (Keane, Gabrieli, Noland, & McNealy, 1995).

Amnesics also exhibit a phenomenon known as *perceptual learning,* in which a perceptual task is performed more quickly on the second or third exposure. For instance, there is a test of such learning that involves showing participants a picture with incomplete lines, such that it is difficult to identify the object or scene. If the participant cannot identify it, more lines are added to the picture, until identification does occur. With repeated exposure to the same original (incomplete) picture, both normally functioning individuals and amnesics show improvement in the speed with which they can identify the relevant stimuli. An example of this kind of picture stimulus is shown in Figure 15.6. The amnesics, however, show no recollection of having seen the picture before (Crovitz, Harvey, & McClanahan, 1981).

Another capacity that is spared in amnesia involves motor learning. Improvement is shown on repeated motor tasks, similar to improvement shown by control subjects. HM, for instance, learned to trace the outline of a star while looking at it in a mirror, his performance getting better with practice (Corkin, 1968). Amnesic individuals can also generalize their newly learned motor skills to other, similar activities.

1.4.4. Associative and Probabilistic Priming and Learning

As described above, amnesics do not generally learn relational information well. However, this statement does not hold in the case of relations that never change. For instance, if Stimulus A and Stimulus G always occurred together, in the same order, this pattern can be learned by some amnesic individuals and, once learned, tends to be well retained. The difficulty for amnesic people appears to be that such associations are rigid. Once A-G has been linked, they appear to be strongly or permanently linked, such that alternative relations to A become difficult to acquire.

Associative priming involves a priming effect in which two items are first presented together, such that the subsequent presentation of the first item primes the second. For instance, if BELL-CRAYON is presented to nonamnesic individuals, and later they are presented with a stem completion task, such as CRA————, they are more likely to respond with the word *crayon* if they are tested with BELL-CRA, than with CRA—— alone. Amnesics do not show this form of priming (Shimamura, Salmon, Squire, & Butters, 1987).

Figure 15.6   Examples of Pictures First Shown in Degraded Form and Then Gradually Clarified

NOTE: Previous exposure improves the ability to identify the degraded pictures.

In contrast, amnesics show no impairment in implicit learning involving *probabilities*. For instance, if a certain representation, or state of affairs, is generally followed by another representation, or state of affairs, amnesic individuals can often anticipate the "correct" outcome. Amnesic participants have shown the ability to learn artificial language sequences, in which a given symbol, such as B, may be followed by other, specific symbols, such as H or M, but not by yet other symbols, such as R or A. Here the individual is not aware of the patterns being learned, but simply learns them, such that an H looks "right" following a B, while an R looks "wrong" (see Chapter 14, Part II, Section 4).

In striking contrast to memory functions, people suffering from the amnesic syndrome show completely normal *understanding* of events or new material. They do not appear to differ from others until some form of actual memory function is involved. They interpret ongoing events in a standard, intelligent fashion and can solve problems, again so long as no memory function need come into play in the course of the problem solving. New episodic information is retained for roughly a few minutes. Thus, the information appears to be competently encoded and to enter long-term store briefly, but then it either fails to be adequately consolidated, or otherwise become unavailable, almost at once. Following that time, even the most dramatic, or striking, or repeated events are not remembered. For instance, an individual who had been told that she had just inherited a million dollars would not recall this information a few minutes later.

2. The Amnesic Syndrome: Theoretical Models * * * * *

Milner (1966) suggested that the failure of amnesics to form new episodic memories is due to an inability of the system to consolidate the relevant information. As described above, events are understood, but cannot later be "fixed" into long-term memory.

A different approach to the issue of amnesia was suggested by Teyler and DiScenna (1986). According to this view, an episodic memory is stored in many modules across the neocortex. This approach conforms to the finding that information is routinely processed in separate areas across the brain, and later recombined for entry into awareness. The authors hypothesized that the hippocampus plays a critical role in recombining the memory content. Basically, this structure holds the indices specifying how such recombining should occur. If it is damaged, the memory function can no longer integrate the dissociated content into a coherent memory. An implication of this view is that the memory function will not enter inchoate material into awareness.

In contrast, Schacter (1985) reasoned that there are two different kinds of memory codes. The one, which provides implicit memory, is "unitized." It involves a perceptual-type unit, which is not interactive with more generalized content. The basis of explicit memory, on the other hand, involves nested structures: that is, information that is accessed through higher-order content, identified here as a global context. For instance, items on a list would be accessed via the information "List X" or "list learned this morning." Note that even a recognition test requires this kind of information: The individual must recognize that an item, such as BIRDCAGE, was present on the target list. In contrast, if the cue BIR————— is given, the system need only play through the remaining content on a recently activated item. The fact that it was on List X may not be available. According to this view, amnesia is the result of damage to those structures that provide global context and associative connections between such context and more specific memory content.

Mayes (1988, chap. 6) further developed the notion of context as being critical to explicit memory. Mayes suggested that amnesia may be the result of deficiencies in the processing of the context relevant to events (context deficit theory). Such contextual processing could be handled in the temporal lobes of the brain, at least in the case of recent and intermediate memories. According to this view, it is also possible that the weakness is not in processing extrinsic context information as such, concerning the place, general nature, and time of an event, but rather in the integration of this material with the lower-level, target material. Both might be stored in memory but disconnected from one another. For instance, it would be impossible to recall the items on a given list, say, List X, if no link could be maintained between the representation of List X (or the time when it was learned) and the items. By the same logic, if the system could not connect general context information such as "Holiday taken in Maine last year," with any specific happenings, then the holiday could not be recalled.

3. Deficits in Short-Term Recall

A disorder exists in which individuals can recall only one or two items in a memory-span test, although their long-term memory is normal or close to normal. The condition is believed to be associated with damage to the PTO association cortex.

Other forms of impaired short-term recall have also been tentatively identified. These include the inability to retain visual patterns across very short periods of time and the inability to hold spatial information, also across very short periods of time (Mayes, 1988, chap. 3). Such individuals show relatively normal long-term visual memory. The impairment in short-term memory (STM) tasks is modular: That is, when impairment occurs in one of these domains (auditory, visual, or spatial), it does not necessarily extend to the others.

There is also a case on record of short-term deficiency in the ability to recall colors. The individual appeared to be able to see the different colors, but could not retain them across a period of seconds (Davidoff & Ostergard, 1984). The individual appeared nonetheless to have a concept of color stored in LTM and could point to colors correctly when they were named. He could not, however, name colors himself, when he saw them.

There is debate as to whether these selective deficiencies in short- and long-term recall reflect different memory systems or one system in which certain kinds of information can be retrieved, while other kinds cannot.

4. Frontal Lobe Damage

It has become increasingly clear that many aspects of memory loss involve the frontal lobes of the brain. In most cases of severe amnesia, the diencephalon or the temporal lobes are implicated, but with damage also present in the frontal lobes.

The most striking symptom of frontal lobe damage involves *confabulation*. This is essentially the generation of false memory content that is taken by the individual as an actual memory. As described in Chapters 9 and 12, when questions are asked of individuals whose memory function is normal, or other pressure to recall applied, there is a tendency on the part of the subject to infer more broadly than would otherwise be the case. This tendency appears in extreme form among individuals suffering from frontal lobe damage (FLD).

In some cases, the recollections may be inaccurate, but reasonable, in that they reflect the kind of events that might normally occur. A more striking pattern involves the generation of wild, implausible, or impossible "memories." Due to these differences, some researchers believe that the two forms involve qualitatively different functions. In both cases, the false content is accepted by the individual and appears to present itself as a clear and genuine memory.

Dalla Barba (1995) described two people, both suffering from FLD, one of whom showed reasonable confabulations, and the other, fantastic confabulation. The first, MB, described having seen his wife the day before and also an event in which he visited her in his mother's company. Both women were in fact dead. In contrast, the second patient, SD, told his physician that he had won a race and that his prize had been a slab of meat that he had placed on his knee.

Individuals suffering from FLD display a cluster of symptoms that are also shown in the amnesic syndrome. They display poor capacity to code for temporal order, including the inability to place autobiographical events in the correct sequence in time. Order information is equally impaired (Shimamura, Janowsky, & Squire, 1990). There is also a tendency to perseverate: that is, to repeat the same action or statement, with small variations, over and over. Baddeley and Wilson (1986, chap. 13) described an individual identified as RJ, who had suffered frontal lobe damage in a car accident. When asked about the accident, he claimed to have first escaped injury from one lorry (truck), only to be directly hit by a second vehicle of the same kind. Still confabulating, he went on to describe the scene as follows:

> [S]o there was I in the middle of the road with no car. He stopped and I stopped and he said, "I'm sorry, mate," and I said, "Don't worry about it, it was as much my fault as yours," and he said, "Well, it was really." So I said, "Well, there's nothing much I can do about it," so he said, "Well, there isn't, is there really" and I said, "No, not really" so he said, "Well, what's going to happen now?" I said, "Well, as far as I am concerned nothing will happen at all because it was my fault, or most of it was my fault.

. . . and so on, at great length.

RJ at one time asked his wife why she "kept telling people" that they were married. She said that they were and that they had children. He replied that children do not necessarily imply marriage. She showed him their wedding photographs. He then noted that the person in the photographs looked like him, but claimed that this was in fact some other individual.

FLD patients also show marked *source amnesia*. This means that they can enter new information into semantic memory (they can learn new facts), but they do not recall when and where the learning took place (Janowksy, Shimamura, & Squire, 1989). A pattern of confabulation is quite frequently seen when the individual is asked to tell where he or she acquired some piece of knowledge.

Recognition memory is not impaired. That is, in a recognition test for words presented in an earlier session, FLD patients tend to recognize true, "old" items at about a normal level. However, they make many false alarms (false recognition) errors, accepting as "old" items that they had not seen before during the learning session (Delbecq-Derousne, Beauvois, & Shallice, 1990). False alarm rates can be as high as 40% (Parkin, Bindschaedler, Harsent, & Metzler, 1996). This pattern appears related to the tendency to accept false episodic memory content as true memories. In both cases, the individual shows a high degree of confidence in the accuracy of his or her memory.

Many researchers believe that patients with FLD are susceptible to false alarm errors on recognition tests, and also to confabulation, because the frontal lobes mediate an evaluation function with regard to memory. This process may include the rejection of impossible content and some form of assessment of all content with regard to the likelihood of its being, or not being, a target memory.

A capacity not directly related to recall that is impaired in FLD patients involves the ability to plan. This may reflect problems with order information, since planning typically involves a sequence of actions or events that must be maintained in a certain order. It has been urged that the frontal lobes in fact involve an executive function within the context of memory, in that here the nature of the information used at retrieval (cueing "descriptions") will be generated, and here too that generated potential memory content will be evaluated, and in some cases rejected (Norman & Shallice, 1986; Shallice, 1988). FLD patients also show difficulty in initiating actions.

Finally, damage to the frontal lobes can result in a destabilization of emotional functioning, as well as changes in personality that, when they do occur, appear to be generally negative.

5. Loss of Memory for Selective Information

Damage to different areas of the brain produces different forms of memory loss (Parkin, 1998, chap. 6). At a fairly general level, injury to the left temporal lobe leads to a deficiency in recalling verbal material, and injury to the right temporal lobe leads to difficulties in recalling spatial information. It appears that the processes involved in memory are modular, in the sense that there are distinct types of function that are mediated by separate domains, such that they can be selectively impaired.

It is not the case, however, that there is typically just one area of the brain dedicated to a given function. For instance, it has been found that the retrieval of memory content, of the same kind, is handled by nonidentical sites, depending on whether it has been encoded recently or at a more remote period in time. In other words, anterograde and retrograde amnesia appear to involve damage to separate areas of the brain. This conclusion has been reached on the basis of clinical cases in which one form only of the amnesic condition was present (Butters, 1984).

Unlike Korsakoff syndrome, herpes viral encephalitis tends to strike different, random sites within the cortex, such that impairments in memory differ from one individual to the next.

In the case of the patient known as LD, for instance, there was extended damage to the right temporal lobe, with some extension into the frontal cortex. LD, a 17-year-old girl, suffered from dense retrograde amnesia. Following the viral attack, she could not recognize friends or family. But there was no anterograde amnesia, although she learned new information slowly. She was able to recognize most stimuli, but showed *agnosia* (inability to recognize objects or sounds) for historic monuments, birds, and insects. The second major impairment in LD's functioning involved visual memory, in that she could perceive visual objects coherently, but could not subsequently recall how they looked. Associated with this difficulty, she could not generate images from memory (Butters, O'Connor, & Verfaellie, 1995). Figure 15.7 shows an example of LD's attempt to first copy, and then recall and draw from memory, the picture of an elephant. She could copy the picture well enough, but not recall it at a later time.

Figure 15.7   LD's Drawing of an Elephant From a Physically Present Picture, and Her Attempt to Draw the Elephant From Memory

SOURCE: From Butters, N., O'Connor, M. G., & Verfaellie, M., "My Own Remembered Past: Insights Into the Structure and Processes of Retrograde Amnesia From a Patient With Visual Access Problems Subsequent to Encephalitis," in R. Campbell & M. A. Conway (Eds.), *Broken Memories: Case Studies in Memory Impairment,* copyright © 1995. Reprinted with permission of Blackwell.

NOTE: Original picture is top left, the copy drawing is bottom left, and the memory drawing is shown at right.

There is a large body of evidence indicating selective impairment within retrograde amnesias. Some individuals, for instance, can recall personal episodic information well but show amnesia for public events, while others display the opposite pattern and recall public events relatively well but are unable to remember episodes from their own lives (Baddeley, 1990, chap. 16).

5.1. Selective Impairments of Memory Within a Single Domain

It has become increasingly clear not only that general functions, such as visual memory, can be selectively impaired but also that impairment can occur at a more detailed level within a particular domain. For instance, there are numerous cases on record of individuals who could in general recall visual information, but were wholly amnesic for faces, even those of individuals who had been well known to them before the trauma.

A widely documented form of selective amnesia involves the inability to recognize objects from specific conceptual categories. The most common of these involves living as against nonliving things. Some individuals cannot identify animals, although they can identify objects (Hillis & Caramazza, 2001; Sacchett & Humphreys, 1992; Sheridan & Humphreys, 1993; Warrington & Shallice, 1984). For instance, when asked to explain what an ostrich was, one patient's description was simply "unusual." In the same way, a patient studied by Hart, Berndt, and Caramazza (1985) showed a deficiency in naming fruits and vegetables, being unable to find the name "peach," although he knew such uncommon object names as "abacus."

The most direct interpretation of these data is that the domains or structures involved in representing a specific conceptual category (living thing vs. nonliving thing) have been selectively damaged. This view has been criticized, however, on the basis of the possibility that it is not the concept itself (or rather its neural substrate) that has been damaged, but that some associated variable may account for the selective memory loss. For instance, it is possible that animal stimuli are encountered less frequently than object stimuli, such that it might be a frequency or familiarity factor that accounts for the selective memory loss. Also, since the testing is done with pictures, it is possible that the two categories might differ from one another, on average, in the complexity of the pictures.

In response to the issue raised above, Barry and McHattie (1995) conducted a multivariate study in which the relation of each of these variables to the ability to recognize a stimulus was tracked separately. The patients were individuals who could not recognize animals at a normal level. Animal and object stimuli were presented. The findings were that familiarity with the stimulus did influence the likelihood of recognition. That is, individuals suffering from difficulty with identifying animals might in some cases recognize a picture of a dog or cat, but could not recognize a picture of a donkey or an elephant. However, these patients nonetheless showed more difficulty in recognizing animals than nonanimal stimuli, even when complexity of stimuli, and familiarity and frequency, were matched. In other words, there was a specific weakness present in the recognition of animals.

Related to the finding that familiarity played a role in the present syndrome, it has been established that individuals suffering from this form of inability often show a pattern in which they cannot recognize specific animal names, but they can recognize names reflecting higher-order categories. For instance, the item "robin" might not be identified, although the item "bird" can be identified (Warrington & Shallice, 1984).

Even more specific forms of conceptual-category amnesia have been identified. Goodglass, Klein, and Carey (1966) found that some patients had difficulty with specific conceptual categories only, such as foods or kitchen implements, while Damasio (1990) reported the case of an individual who could recognize human-made objects, with the exception of musical instruments!

An intriguing discovery within the present context has been that infants acquire higher-order concepts, such as animal versus nonliving thing, first, and subclasses, such as rabbit versus fish, only later in development (Mandler, 1988, chap.7). The high-level distinction emerges as early as 7 months of age; the sublevel, not until the child is 24 months or older. In other words, the concepts that are retained longest in an adult with impaired conceptual function are those that are acquired earliest in life.

5.2. The Source of Impaired Functioning

There are several processing structures involved in identifying a stimulus. Damage to any one of them could produce the observed impairment.

In the case of a visual stimulus, its physical properties, such as its shape and size, must be coded. Here perceptual structures are involved. If this cannot be achieved, then the system will not be able to access the meaning codes related to the stimulus. Then there are the meaning codes themselves (the relevant concept). This structure or structures could also be selectively damaged. And finally, there are the name codes, which again involve distinct information as compared to appearance and meaning.

There is evidence that the inability to recognize a stimulus can result from selective damage to just one of these structures. Beauvois, Saillant, Meininger, and Lhermitte (1978) described a patient who could not recognize a stimulus if it was presented visually, although he could recognize it by touch. The concept was present, but the ability to access this information through a visual medium was impaired. It is likely that the damage here was to the visual perceptual structure. The evidence suggests that different sensory modalities provide separate access to identification structures (the concept). In other cases, the concept itself appears to have been the source of the impaired functioning. Data supporting this view involve patients who can partially describe the properties of a given object, but who fail at describing other properties. For instance, a patient known as LP was able to say, of an elephant, that it was an animal and had four legs, but the patient thought it was a small animal and "had no idea" if it possessed tusks (De Renzi, Liotti, & Nichelli, 1987). This individual could name only 5 of 60 objects, but showed some knowledge of their use, an ability that clearly reflected conceptual functioning. When asked to define a lemon, however, she said that it "is used by people who study."

Some amnesic patients also show what might be described as a crude level of semantic coding only. Howard and Orchard-Lisle (1984), for instance, showed their patients pictures of various objects. If a tiger was shown, the question, "Is this a house?" could be answered correctly, but the patient would respond to, "Is this a lion?" by affirming that it was indeed a lion. This appears to reflect the difficulty outlined above, that within-subclass concepts can be lost even though higher-order concepts remain. Here, the within-subclass distinction between lion and tiger has been lost, but that between animal and inanimate object (tiger vs. house) is still functional.

5.3. Discussion

The data concerning familiarity and higher-order-category recall, described above, indicate that damage within a conceptual domain may not result in total loss of the relevant memory content. Variables that are known to influence memory strength under normal functioning also appear to help within the context of severe impairment.

Researchers often assume that if there is memory loss for one form of information, A, but not for another, B, then this phenomenon implies that A and B are stored in different locations within the brain. But it would seem strange that the meaning codes for living thing and nonliving thing should indeed be handled at different physical sites. In response to this issue, a number of researchers have suggested that the critical distinction may be that between *perceptual information* and *function information* (Damasio, 1990; Farah & McClelland, 1991; Warrington & Shallice, 1984). Here it is posited that animal concepts may be based primarily on perceptual information, while concepts involving objects, such as tools, may be based primarily on function information.

It should be noted, however, that there are other ways of conceptualizing function, in addition to the direct function of a thing that we use, like a hammer. For instance, we think of animals as things that breathe and move and generally possess the functions of life. Thus, the argument can be made that function codes are as important to the understanding of living things as of tools. This view, of course, does not imply that function information and perceptual information are not coded at different sites within the brain, only that one is not likely to be more fundamental to an object representation than to a living-thing representation.

An even simpler hypothesis is that there are different neural structures, operating within one domain, that handle the two forms of information (living vs. nonliving), and that these structures can be selectively impaired by physical damage to the brain. Presumably this could occur even if both draw on certain bodies of perceptual and of functional information.

6. Reduplicative Paramnesia and Capgras Syndrome

There is an experience with which we are all familiar, known as *déjà vu* ("already seen"). Here, we may walk into a place that we have not visited in the past, and yet it feels as though we have in fact seen it before. Or a person, when first introduced, may give rise to the same feeling. Déjà vu can also occur for particular moments in time or for particular objects seen. I recall as a child looking at a bread box across a large kitchen and having an extremely strong sense of having lived through that exact moment—exactly the same, down to sights and thoughts—before.

The opposite experience is known as *jamais vu* ("never seen"). Here, you may encounter a place or person that you know to be familiar, even highly familiar, and yet it feels as if you had in fact never seen that place, person, or object before.

The cause of these momentary experiences is not understood. They may be linked to states of fatigue or illness, although they do not appear to be limited to such conditions. A more serious form of disorder in the judgment of familiarity occurs following damage to the brain, probably associated with the right hemisphere (Rohrenbach & Landis, 1995). Here, individuals believe across an extended period of time that places or people have been duplicated. The experience is known as *reduplicative paramnesia* (Pick, 1903). For instance, an individual may see that a hospital ward in which he is a patient is entirely familiar, but he believes it is an exact duplicate of some other hospital ward, in another place.

Eerily, the same experience can occur in the case of people. Here it is labeled as *Capgras syndrome* (Capgras & Reboul-Lachaux, 1923). In this case, the patient may feel that certain individuals, highly familiar to him, are in fact duplicates of the individuals he knew in the past. The effect may also extend to the patient: That is, he may feel that people exist who are duplicates of himself. This sense usually centers on familiar places, often the relevant hospital ward, or well-known people, such as family members and close friends.

The syndrome involving a sense of duplication has also been established in the case of individual body parts, objects, and events (Christodoulou, 1986; Cutting, 1991).

The condition tends to vanish with time. Its cause remains unknown. It is clear, however, that we normally maintain information concerning the identity of objects and persons through time. If I walk into my living room and see a small table, I understand that it is the same table that was present when I was last in the living room. This continuity of identity could not be achieved simply by establishing that the two objects look exactly alike, since in some cases different physical objects also look exactly alike (such as two identical small tables). There must be some cognitive function in addition to that of establishing sameness of appearance that maintains identity across time. Clearly, that function has been damaged in the syndromes described above.

7. Remediation * * * * *

Individuals suffering from anterograde, or retrograde, amnesia can be classically conditioned, and can demonstrate associative learning.

Schacter (1996, chap. 2) reported the case of a woman who had contracted meningitis. Although she recovered her health, she was left with a dense amnesia that made it almost impossible for her to learn new general information. The company where she had worked before her illness was willing to open a new position for her, but it required the ability to master technical terms and to perform various skilled tasks with a computer.

Schacter reasoned that the subject's implicit associative memory might have been spared by the illness. He developed a computer program based on the method of *vanishing cues*. One task, for instance, involved learning the correct name for a certain procedure or definition, such as the word *loop* to describe a repeated portion of a program. If the correct answer was not known, the participant was given the first letter of the word. If this was not sufficient, the second letter (*lo—*) was given, and the number of cueing letters was increased until the participant gave a correct response.

When the answer had been given, on the next trial the cue letters were presented again but with one letter fewer than had been required in the successful trial. Thus, if the participant had been able to reply correctly when cued with *loo—*, on the next trial she would be presented with *lo—*. Once a correct answer had been given to *lo—*, the cue on the following trial would be simply *l*.

The participant was able to learn the key terms in this fashion. By using the same method, the researchers were able to teach her 250 rules, symbols, and codes, until she was skilled at entering data into a computer from a variety of company records. Other individuals suffering from problems with memory were later trained in the same fashion. Strikingly, the skills remained at their original high level a year after training (Glisky & Schacter, 1987, 1989). The approach was later extended to word processing, computer entry, and database management (Butters & Glisky, 1993; Leng, Copello, & Sayegh, 1991).

A limitation of the present approach, however, is that the knowledge remains inflexible. A response can be learned to a complex stimulus, but if the stimulus is changed, even if its meaning is preserved under the change, the response will no longer be available. For instance, if a definition is reworded, the learned response to it will be lost.

Elaborative techniques were found to work better for the retention of names, among individuals suffering from memory impairment, than the vanishing-cues approach (Glisky, 1995). Equally, however, elaborative techniques are not generally appropriate for learning more complex information, such as definitions.

Hunkin and Parkin (1995) and Aldrich (1995) found the vanishing-cue approach was not in fact more effective than rote learning. In rote learning of the kind of computer skills described above, for instance, the definition would be provided, and then the entire answer, repeatedly, until the material was mastered. However, the method of vanishing cues was preferred by the participants, given that it is less boring than passive rote repetition.

Baddeley and Wilson (1994) noted that if an amnesic individual makes an error while learning, he or she tends to retain the error across future trials, and that this can be a particular problem within the context of implicit learning. They devised an *errorless learning* procedure, in which the question and the correct answer were first given, with the requirement that the participant then write down the answer. The alternative condition involved the question, following which the participants attempted to give an answer. If they failed to do so on several trials, the correct answer was given. A cued test then followed. A significant advantage was found for the errorless learning approach.

8. Memory and Aging

It is well known that memory functions tend to weaken in the elderly. The most serious impairment is found in *prospective memory*: the ability to remember actions that need to be performed, such as a trip to the dentist (Henry, MacLeod, Phillips, & Crawford, 2004). According to one view, prospective memory depends on the ability to maintain ongoing awareness that some action must be performed, a monitoring requirement (Smith, 2003). This involves a heavy drain on processing capacity, which is believed to diminish in old age. An alternative view is that other factors, in addition to monitoring, may operate. For instance, Einstein and McDaniel (2005) suggested that individuals may simply form an association between the cue to perform the task ("Monday morning," if that is when you have a dental appointment) and the task. This would require a much smaller drain on processing capacity, such that elderly individuals using the present associative approach should handle prospective memory tasks quite well. The authors found support for this "multiprocess" view.

Episodic recall of the recent and intermediate past, and recall of isolated constituents, such as names, may also be impaired in the elderly. By "isolated" within this context is meant information that does not relate to other bodies of information. In contrast, episodic recall of the remote past, dating to the individual's youth, does not appear to weaken. Nor does short-term recall as measured by memory span tasks (Botwinick & Storandt, 1974). However, the elderly do show impaired function, as compared with young subjects, in more complex tasks of immediate recall, such as the *loaded word span task*. Here the participant is asked to determine whether a presented sentence makes sense, and then to recall the final word in the sentence.

The elderly are also less competent than younger individuals at generating strategies to aid in the work of encoding and retrieval (Parkin, 1987, chap. 8).

In general, recognition memory shows no decrement due to age, although complex recognition tests, in which distractors play a prominent role, have revealed some underlying weaknesses. In the multiple item recognition memory (MIRM) test, participants are shown a target word in the company of one, or three, other nontarget words. On a later recognition test, elderly participants are more likely to confuse the nontargets with the target (Kausler & Kleim, 1978).

The findings outlined above have been interpreted as meaning that older individuals rely more on familiarity judgments in recognition, and less on context (time and place) information, than do younger individuals. In the Kausler and Kleim study, both targets and distractors had been presented in the past and so had equal familiarity judgment. However, it should be noted that the information needed here for a correct response was more fine grained than the simple identification of the correct time or place. All items had been encountered at the same time. A correct response required coding the additional information, for each item, that it was or was not a target.

There is no clear evidence that semantic memory declines with age. Older participants perform as well, and often better, in tests of vocabulary as compared to younger participants.

Elderly individuals show the usual range of priming outcomes, although the speed of the effect tends to be reduced (Howard, Shaw, & Heisey, 1986). That is, priming will appear after a very short interval between the prime word and the test word in younger subjects, while a somewhat longer interstimulus interval is needed to produce the same effect in the elderly.

There has been little testing of elderly participants within the context of meaningful semantic memory. The standard tests, as described above, require the ability to recall a series of random words or numbers. This is exactly the type of memory function in which the elderly tend to perform at their weakest. Owens (1966) tested 363 college freshmen on an Army IQ test, involving intellectual functioning and semantic memory, in 1919. He then tested his participants again when they were 50 or 61 years old. Ninety-six members of the original group were available. The participants scored at a higher level on the second test.

According to one currently popular view of memory, success in recall depends on skill in encoding and retrieval processes, mostly under the control of the participant. It is not assumed that background knowledge plays a major role. Under an alternative, structuralist, tradition, it is explicitly posited that background knowledge influences memory strength (Piaget & Inhelder, 1973). According to this latter hypothesis, semantic memory should not decline with age, assuming that the individual remains physically healthy.

9. Dementia

Dementia is a general term used to characterize a loss of rational functioning, of practical competence in everyday tasks, and of memory.

Multi-infarct dementia (MID), also known as *vascular dementia*, is a fairly common form of the illness. It is caused by irregularities in the flow of blood to the brain. A number of other conditions can also lead to dementia. These include multiple sclerosis, progressive supranuclear palsy, Huntington's chorea (HC), Parkinson's disease, and HIV.

Dementia typically involves decline in both episodic and semantic memory. There is an increased probability of dementia with aging, as there is of general physical ailments. The particular forms of memory loss in dementia, however, may differ from those found in the amnesic syndrome. For instance, individuals suffering from MID do not show a tendency toward high levels of false alarms in word recognition tests (as occurs with patients with Korsakoff syndrome and some other forms of dementia). MID patients in fact may make fewer false alarms than controls.

The breakdown of semantic knowledge is common in dementia. Here, as occurs following selective damage to particular sites within the brain, the loss of conceptual representation occurs first within conceptual categories, beginning at the lowest, and works upward through conceptual classes to the highest levels. Graham, Patterson, and Hodges (1995), for instance, reported the case of an individual who lost the ability to distinguish between within-domain, subclass objects, such as RABBIT and FISH, although she could still distinguish between animate and inanimate objects (BIRD and HAMMER), and who in the end lost even the ability to discriminate between animate and inanimate objects.

A particularly terrible form of dementia involves the illness known as Alzheimer's disease, described below.

9.1. Alzheimer's Disease

Alois Alzheimer, a Moravian physician of French descent, was the first to describe the illness now named after him. His patient was a 51-year-old woman. She showed impairment in recall and recognition, which was particularly severe in the area of recent memory. Her language skills had deteriorated. She was unable to express herself verbally, or understand speech, at a normal level (a condition known as *aphasia*). She could not understand how to use ordinary objects around her (*apraxia*), nor could she identify them (*agnosia*). The woman's condition reflected an advanced form of the illness. She died soon after.

An autopsy revealed a high level of neuronal death within her brain. There was also what Alzheimer described as an unusual substance present, and changes in the neurofibrils normally found inside neurons.

The condition was the form of Alzheimer's now known as early onset, which strikes its victims typically between their mid-forties and mid-fifties. The late-onset form of the disease is more common. This form develops at 60 years or older, with the chance of an individual developing the illness increasing markedly with age. Victims of Alzheimer's usually die within 4 to 8 years following the appearance of symptoms. These can include irritability, character change, paranoia and psychotic behaviors, and in some cases debilitating stiffness in the limbs. One of the first signs is the loss of normal memory function.

Early-onset Alzheimer's is caused by a mutation in a single gene (although there are several different genes that can produce the disease). The locus of the gene in one, relatively rare, early-onset form, has been identified as occurring on the 21st chromosome; the location of the gene causing the more common early-onset form has been identified as involving the 11th chromosome. Both discoveries date to the 1990s.

Once a gene has been located, the proteins for which it codes can be identified. In the present case, involving early-onset Alzheimer's, it appears that the problem is caused by the incorrect "cutting" of a long protein, which results in a shorter form known as the *beta-amyloid peptide*. The latter substance sets in motion a chain of events that leads to the death of neurons in the hippocampus and other areas of the cortex. The source of the more common late-onset Alzheimer's has not been found with certainty, although some leads exist. Since the form taken by the neural damage is the same in both early and late onset, however, any successful therapy should be effective for both.

Alzheimer's is characterized by the accumulation in the brain of substances called *beta-amyloid plaques* (senile plaques). They accumulate between cells and form distinctive clumps. Plaques occur in normal aging too, but not at the same density. A second typical symptom involves *neurofibrillary tangles*. These are formed from structures that normally give physical support to the cell and provide conduits for nutrient and other critical substances, but that begin in this context to form abnormal proteins. The result is that the structures collapse, killing the cell. The tangles continue in the brain after the neuron has died and the resulting detritus has been cleared away. St. George Hyslop (2000) has suggested that it is the tangles, rather than the plaques, that provide the fundamental damage to the cells.

Because Alzheimer's becomes progressively worse with time, it is difficult to make exact comparisons with other forms of memory disturbance. By the time the condition has taken hold, however, its symptoms are more severe than those involved in the amnesic syndrome. The victims suffer both retrograde and antero-grade amnesia, and (unlike the typical case with amnesia) show impaired memory span. If a list of items is learned, however, to the extent possible, victims of Alzheimer's do show a recency effect.

Individuals suffering from this illness demonstrate impairment both in attended, conscious activities and in automatized activities, but with greater impairment in the former. Both episodic and semantic memory are severely impaired, with increasing difficulties in speech, language comprehension, reasoning, and functional responses (dealing with the requirements of daily life), as described above. Spatial disorienta-tion is common: That is, afflicted individuals may not be able to remember routes that were once familiar or may have difficulty finding their way around their own homes. Finally, in the area of implicit memory, victims of Alzheimer's generally per-form more poorly than individuals suffering from the amnesic syndrome (Shimamura et al., 1987).

Beauregard, Chertkow, Gold, and Bergman (2001) conducted a stem completion study in which individuals suffering from Alzheimer's were compared with normal controls. A depth-of-processing task was used. As with amnesic-syndrome patients, the deep-processing condition did not improve performance over the shallow-processing condition in the Alzheimer's group. The controls did show improve-ment. Of particular interest, however, the Alzheimer's patients' knowledge of the relevant concepts had been measured before the study. For most individuals, the meaning code for a concept had deteriorated, and it was among these participants that the deep-encoding measures failed to improve performance. Although it is widely believed that stem completion tasks reflect perceptual priming only, these findings suggest that a semantic component also may be involved.

9.1.1. Treatment of Alzheimer's

Recent studies have indicated that individuals who have been more cognitively active prior to the onset of Alzheimer's, and continue so, are less impaired by the illness than others (Scarmeas, Levy, Tang, Manly, & Stern, 2001; Wilson & Bennett, 2003). The mental exercise does not seem to delay the progression of the illness, however; it appears rather that more effective ways are found to compensate for the various forms of impairment.

The source of Alzheimer's was identified only a little more than a decade ago. Research continues today in the attempt to find a cure—or, at least, remediation.

The neurotransmitter acetylcholine is broken down by an enzyme, acetylcholinesterase. The introduction of drugs that can inhibit this process (since there is not enough acetylcholine in the brains of Alzheimer's patients) has been one approach taken. Unfortunately, it is effective only in the early stages of the disease, because it does not counteract the processes causing neuron death. Other hopes of therapy include compounds that may block the enzymes that lead to the forming of the beta-amyloid peptide. Another avenue of attack would be to find substances capable of breaking down the plaques once they have formed.

At present, five drugs have been approved for the treatment Alzheimer's, and researchers associated with the Alzheimer's Association report that means of preventing the illness may be found within the next decade.

Summary

The amnesic syndrome is an organic disease associated with anterograde amnesia (loss of ability to form new memories) and varying degrees of retrograde amnesia (loss of old memories). Semantic knowledge is usually spared, as is short-term memory, understanding of information, implicit memory, and perceptual and procedural learning.

Damage to the medial temporal lobes leads to anterograde amnesia and some varying degree of retrograde amnesia. Damage to the diencephalon results in anterograde and usually more severe retrograde amnesia, although amnesics in this class can learn to recognize some stimuli. They are, however, highly subject to interference effects. Korsakoff syndrome is a type of diencephalic amnesia that results from prolonged abuse of alcohol.

In identifying sites within the brain, a saggital section involves dividing the left from the right hemispheres. A coronal section involves dividing the front of the brain from the back. A horizontal section divides the top from the bottom.

Frontal lobe damage results in confabulation and impairment in order and temporal recall. Selective loss of memory for conceptual information can occur. Individuals may be able to identify living things, but not inanimate objects or vice versa, or may be able to recall public events but not personal memories or vice versa. In some cases highly fine-grained conceptual losses may occur.

Dementia is a disturbance of memory and rational thought that can result from a range of diseases, including multiple sclerosis, Parkinson's disease, Huntington's chorea, and HIV. It sometimes occurs as an aspect of the aging process.

Alzheimer's disease is a severe form of dementia in which memory first declines, followed by a loss of conceptual representation, language, and reasoning. Short-term memory is also impaired. Other symptoms can include stiffness, loss of spatial orientation, changes in character, and psychosis. In Alzheimer's, senile plaques form between neurons and neurofibrillary tangles appear within the neurons. The tangles are due to the breaking down of structures that normally support the cell and also provide conduits for nourishment.

CHAPTER 16

Neuroscience
and Memory

Overview

1. Neurons form the physical basis for the coding of information in the human brain. Electrical impulses cause the release of neurotransmitters into the gaps (synapses) between neurons. The patterns of neural firing form the basis of memories.

2. Various neuroimaging techniques have been developed. These show structures within the brain and also blood flow within the brain.

3. Neuroimaging techniques have shown left-hemisphere activation during the encoding of words and right-hemisphere activation during retrieval of words. Autobiographical memories show an opposite pattern. Areas of the brain activated at retrieval depend on the type of content retrieved and the depth of processing of the content, among other variables.

4. The hippocampus plays a critical role in the formation of new long-term memories. Its role may be that of integrating different bodies of memory content.

5. Perceptual memory content appears to be stored in the areas of the brain that operate to process perceptual information.

6. The amygdala mediates the influence of emotion on memory. Mood-related chemicals can either enhance or impair recall or recognition. They may influence a consolidation process within the brain.

7. Long-term memory is not a single function, in terms of the retention of content across extended periods of time. Some researchers believe that the label "long-term memory" should be subdivided to reflect this fact, with "intermediate memory" being used for the first period of long-term retention.

Learning Objectives

1. Knowledge of the functioning of neurons.

2. Knowledge of neuroimaging techniques.

3. Knowledge of findings concerning the location of function for the encoding and retrieval of word items and of autobiographical information.

4. Knowledge of the role of the hippocampus and frontal lobes in memory.

5. Knowledge of the role of the amygdala and mood-influencing chemicals.

T he present chapter deals with the physical basis of human memory and research reflecting neuroimaging techniques. Although it can be read by itself, it will be understood in greater depth if Chapters 13 (on implicit memory) and 15 (on disorders of memory) have been covered.

Neuroscience is concerned with the role of neurons in cognitive activity. The field can probably be divided into two components, old and new, reflecting ideas that were developed before the advent of current neuroimaging and ideas developed after, respectively. This division is also reflected here.

1. The Neuron

Neurons are nerve cells involved in the coding of information. There are roughly 100 billion neurons in the human brain, supported by additional *glial cells*. The glial cells provide nutrient and other forms of support for neurons. They also influence communication among the neurons by changing the chemical environment, and they remove dead neural cell bodies. A further role for glial cells is that they guide newly formed neurons to their correct position within the brain. Glial cells outnumber neurons by about 10 to 1.

Typically, a major portion of the neurons are active (firing) at any given time. Neurons interconnect with one another, and information, including memory content, appears to be represented in patterns of activation among sets of neurons or among combinations of neural nets. The exact computing power of the neurons in a human brain has not been identified, but according to some estimates it is something in the order of 100 billion interacting computers, this involving greater capacity than the combined operation of all computers in the world (Anderson, 1990, p. 20).

Each individual neuron has a cell body, numerous dendrites, and an axon. The cell body contains a nucleus and manufactures the proteins and enzymes that the cell needs to function. The dendrites are branching extensions that receive electrical impulses from other cells (via chemical events). Axons normally connect to the dendrites of other cells, but can also connect with cell bodies, and other axons. An axon is a single, long extension, varying greatly in length among different types of cells, which begins at the cell body and extends into small branches at the end. There are different types of neurons in the brain, possessing different shapes, with particular variation in the nature of the dendrites and axons. Figure 16.1 shows a schematized picture of a typical neuron.

Impulses coming from other neurons are picked up by the dendrites, which convey such impulses to the cell body. (A neuron can receive information from up to 100,000 different sources.) If there is sufficient stimulation, an electrical/chemical event known as an *action potential* begins at the point where the axon is attached to the cell body. The action potential will then move down the axon and influence structures on the final branches of the axon. These are called *terminal boutons* and contain other structures called *synaptic vesicles*. These are bags of chemical neurotransmitters.

When the neuron is at rest, its entire membrane is electrically charged (polarized). This is because there is a preponderance of positively charged ions (charged particles) in the fluid outside the cell and a preponderance of negatively charged ions in the fluid inside the cell. This difference creates an electrical charge, usually of −70 mV (1 mV, or millivolt, is 1/1000 of a volt), which is known as the cell's *resting potential*.

Ions involved in the cellular environment include sodium (Na), which carries a positive charge, chlorine (Cl), which carries a negative charge, and potassium (K), which carries a positive charge. In the cell's resting state, there are more Na^+ and Cl^- ions outside the membrane and more K^+ inside. There is also, however, a large protein molecule, A^-, inside the cell.

Ions can enter and leave the cell body through specialized ion channels, but the cell membrane is generally less porous to Na^+, keeping the majority of these positively charged ions out. A balance is kept between the other ions by means of

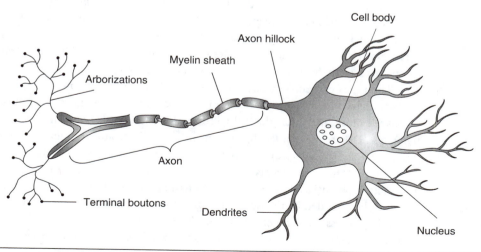

Figure 16.1   A Typical Neuron

electrostatic pressure and *diffusion.* Electrostatic pressure refers to the tendency of similar charges to repel one another and of unlike charges to attract. Diffusion means the tendency of substances to move from areas of higher concentration to areas of lower concentration.

A third force involved in maintaining the cell's resting potential is the sodium-potassium pump. Some Na^+ ions do move through ion channels into the cell. When this occurs, the pump forces them out again. The pump also transports K^+ ions into the cell. It pumps about three Na^+ ions out, however, for each K^+ ion pumped in.

When a neuron is stimulated, the Na^+ ion channels open. Na^+ flows into the cell, leading to a reduction of the negative charge within the cell. When the negative charge goes down to about -60 mV, the cell reaches threshold and fires. That is, it is activated. At this point the cell membrane undergoes a greater change in polarization. The Na^+ channels open further and Na^+ pours into the cell. As this occurs, the inside of the cell develops a positive charge, which increases to $+30$ mV. At $+30$ mV the Na^+ channels close and the K^+ channels open. K^+ exits the cell, leading to a progress that will restore the negative internal charge. This stage is called the *absolute refractory period*, and during it the cell cannot fire again. The tendency to negative charge within the cell continues, until the interior shifts further than the usual resting potential level, to a condition known as *hyperpolarization.* This is known as the *relative refractory period*, during which the neuron can only be stimulated (made to fire) by stimulation that is more intense than usual. Finally the distribution of ions returns to normal, that is, to the original resting-potential state. This is known as *repolarization.* This entire sequence of events is known as an *action potential.*

When the action potential reaches the farthest portion of the axon, the synaptic vesicles migrate to the membrane at the end of the axon, and release their chemicals (the neurotransmitters) into a small gap that is present between the end of the axon, and the dendrites of other cells. This gap is called the *synapse.* A synapse is about 100 to 200 angstroms in size (an angstrom is 1 ten-millionth of a millimeter). The membrane at the end of the axon is thus called the *presynaptic membrane.*

The released neurotransmitters bind onto specific receptor cells on the corresponding membrane of the receiving neuron, the *postsynaptic membrane.* The receptor cells are complex molecules that can only be activated by neurotransmitters that exactly fit them, much as a key fits into a lock.

The types of neurotransmitters that are picked up by the postsynaptic membrane determine what will occur in the receiving cell. Some neurotransmitters make it more likely that the cell will fire, this situation being called an *excitatory synapse.* Others make it less likely that the cell will fire and are therefore described as an *inhibitory synapse.* Often both forms of synapse are in play simultaneously. Figure 16.2 shows the events that occur at the synapse when a cell fires.

Action potentials do not differ in strength; they are all or none. The intensity of a stimulus is coded by the rate of firing of the cell: that is, by how many times the cell fires across a given period of time. The greater the intensity of the input, the faster the neuron fires. This is known as the *rate law.* In the central nervous system (CNS), neurons are active—firing—all the time. It is an increase (or decrease) in

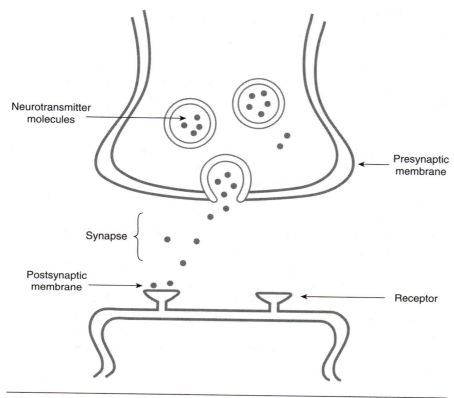

Figure 16.2   The Events That Occur at the Synapse When a Cell Fires

NOTE: Synaptic vesicles in the presynaptic neuron contain neurotransmitters. When an action potential occurs, these are released into the synapse. The neurotransmitters bind with receptors on the postsynaptic membrane. This causes a local change in electrical voltage.

the background rate of firing that codes for information. An increase in stimulation will result in the cell firing during its relative refractory period. Also, the absolute refractory period of different neurons varies, so that some are capable of faster recovery, and so faster rates of firing, than others.

Memory codes are believed to reflect changes in the likelihood of sets of neurons firing, given that previous neural sets have fired. A highly complex pattern of such activation, probably in most cases involving many neural complexes working together, is believed to provide the code for memory content.

1.1. Long-Term Potentiation

When short bursts of stimulation are applied to certain (afferent, that is, inward leading) neural pathways in the hippocampus of animals, there is an increase in the excitatory potential of the cells, both pre- and postsynaptic, that can endure for months (Bliss & Lomo, 1973; Lynch, 1986; Zalutsky & Nicoll, 1990). This effect is known as *long-term potentiation* (LTP).

If LTP has occurred, the result is that an action potential, affecting one neuron or a neural complex, is more likely than before to trigger action potentials in an associated neuron or neural complex: That is, the relevant pattern of activation is more likely to be maintained.

The research described above involved artificial stimulation of neurons in the hippocampus. There is increasing evidence, however, that the effect also occurs naturally, as a component of learning (Berger, 1984; Roman, Staubli, & Lynch, 1987). Several different kinds of LTP are known to exist, and it is likely that more will be discovered (Lynch, Granger, & Staubli, 1991).

Many researchers believe that either LTP or events similar to LTP must be involved in the formation of enduring memories, and work in this area continues to be pursued vigorously (Bliss & Collingridge, 1993; Silva, Stevens, & Tonegawa, 1992).

As noted above, it is generally believed that LTP is the best candidate at the present time for the vehicle that provides long-term memory coding, in part because no other plausible mechanism has been identified. Nonetheless, a few voices have been raised in dissent. Martinez and Derrick (1996) noted that the actual link between LTP and memory is tenuous, although those authors believe LTP must play at least some role in retention. Shors and Matzel (1997) have urged that LTP is possibly not involved in the actual formation of memories but, rather, in increases in arousal or attention that facilitate the development of memory codes.

The majority of researchers, however, appear to believe that LTP is involved nonetheless in long-term memory formation. Although conditions that increase arousal show a profile similar to that of LTP, it is difficult to separate the two variables: Arousal is known, under certain conditions, to facilitate the processes that provide memory consolidation, and LTP could be involved in the arousal component, but it could equally reflect the enhanced memory consolidation component (and not arousal).

1.2. Chemical Agents and Memory

Many of the events described above are controlled by chemical processes. For instance, the action potential passing along the axon further changes the permeability of the cell membrane and so influences the continuing movement of ions between the cell and the surrounding chemical environment. An increase in calcium ions causes presynaptic vesicles to move to the end of the presynaptic membrane. The rate of release of the neurotransmitters thus appears to be a function of the quantity of calcium ions that enter the presynaptic membrane. These ions may stimulate other events that lead to the increasing release of specific neurotransmitters.

An extensive body of research has now shown that certain ingested or introjected chemicals can either enhance or weaken memory. The effects occur in most cases in the period immediately following learning. There is a class of chemicals that appear to be secreted under conditions of emotional arousal and conditions of stress. These include the adrenocorticotrophic hormone (ACTH), epinephrine, vasopressin, and the amphetamines.

In small doses, these chemicals enhance memory. Epinephrine influences the release of the neurotransmitter norepinephrine within the amygdala (Liang, Juler, & McGaugh, 1986; McGaugh, 1990, 1991). If the dosage of these chemicals is increased, however, memory is impaired. The findings correspond to behavioral data suggesting that strong emotion heightens recall and recognition, while severe stress diminishes both.

In contrast, there are chemicals that specifically impair recall. Scopolamine, which interferes with the normal use of acetylcholine, weakens memory formation (Sherman, Atri, & Hasselmo, 2003). Gamma amino butyric acid (GABA) also impairs memory; and drugs that block its receptors enhance memory (Brioni & McGaugh, 1988; McGaugh, 1961). Opiates, such as B-endorphin, inhibit the release of norepinephrine and so weaken memory. Opiates of this kind are released in times of severe stress or pain (and may explain the weak human recall function for notably painful experiences).

The release of epinephrines appears to increase the amount of glucose in the bloodstream. Glucose enhances memory in general and has been found to alleviate some of the problems in recall exhibited by aged rats and mice (Gold & Stone, 1988).

2. The Human Brain

The human brain is divided into two major hemispheres, each of which possesses four specific regions. The outermost areas of the brain are known as the cortex, while structures deeper within are identified as subcortical structures. The brain shows a pattern of convolutions, raised areas, known as *gyri* (sing. gyrus); the bumpy quality is due to the fact that neurons are packed tightly together in these areas. The valleys between them are known as *sulci* (sing. sulcus). If these are very deep, they are known as fissures. The fissures separate distinct areas of the brain from one another.

The central fissure (the Rolandic fissure) separates the front (anterior) and back (posterior) regions of the brain, in each hemisphere. The sylvian (lateral) fissure separates or distinguishes top (dorsal) and bottom (ventral) regions of the brain, in each hemisphere. In general, motor areas are situated in front of the central fissure, and sensory areas are found at the back of the central fissure.

Figure 16.3 shows the major areas of the brain, with associated fissures, gyri, and sulci.

More detailed areas of the brain are identified by means of a Brodman map, in which each area is numbered. Figure 16.4 shows a Brodman map.

Since the brain is a three-dimensional object, terms are needed to describe three constituents: the front and back, the top and bottom, and regions in the outer regions and internal regions. The frontal areas are referred to as *anterior* regions, and the back as *posterior* regions. Equivalent terms are *rostral* and *caudal* (referring to head and tail, respectively, as on an animal). The top portions are referred to as

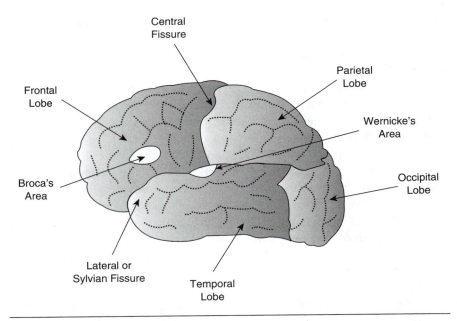

Figure 16.3   Major Areas of the Brain

NOTE: Broca's area controls speech. If this area is damaged, the individual cannot speak, although speech is understood. Wernicke's area controls the organization found in speech. If it is damaged, the individual cannot understand language, and although he may talk, the speech is garbled and incoherent. It is believed that the sensory memory content is stored in the areas of the brain where the sensory information was originally processed, with visual memories in the visual-processing regions, and so on.

superior regions, and the bottom ones are *inferior* regions. Equivalent terms are *dorsal* and *ventral* (referring to back and stomach, respectively, as on an animal.) The inner areas of the brain are referred to as *medial*, while areas toward the outer surfaces are referred to as *lateral*.

Slices through the brain, to reveal the various internal structures, are named according to the fashion in which the brain has been divided. The three major divisions were shown in Figure 15.2 on page 227.

3. Neuroimaging Techniques

A number of techniques have been developed that are capable of providing information concerning neural activity within the brain. One of the first of these was electroencephalography (EEG), in which electrodes attached to the scalp measure the electrical responses that occur when neurons fire. The amplitudes of these responses are recorded. Electrodes can be placed in various locations on the scalp, making it possible to trace activity occurring across the brain.

An *event-related potential* (ERP) is a pattern of brain activity recorded by averaging EEG waves across trials. The waves consist of a series of positive and negative

(a)

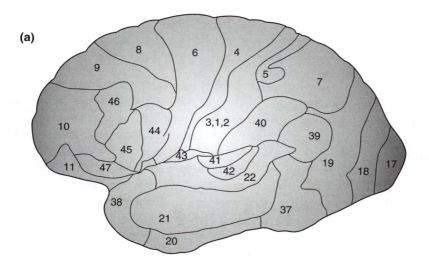

(b)

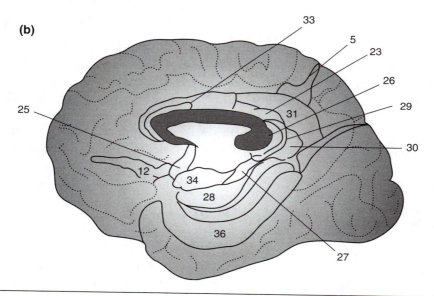

Figure 16.4   A Brodman Map

NOTE: The different areas reflect different types of neural structure, believed to involve different functions. Figure (a) shows areas that extend to the surface of the brain. Figure (b) shows a saggital representation within the brain. Regions 44 and 45 are Broca's area. Region 22 is Wernicke's area.

voltage peaks, called *components*. They change in latency, amplitude, and polarity as cognitive tasks are performed.

ERPs can track brain activity in milliseconds. They can thus record the precise flow of temporal activity within the brain. They are less effective at identifying the location of the structures in the brain whose activity they measure.

Magnetoencephalography (MEG) is a technique that also picks up signals generated by neural firing, here by the use of the small magnetic pulse that neurons generate when active. The signals from MEG also operate quickly, but tend to be weak, and therefore cannot always be read.

An ERF (event-related magnetic field) is the equivalent of an ERP, except that the measurement involves magnetic changes, Both ERFs and ERPs are derived from electrical (ionic) currents passing through the membranes of the neurons.

A third approach, magnetic resonance imaging (MRI), involves the use of magnetism to align the atomic particles in living tissue. The particles are then bombarded with radio waves, which causes them to give off radio signals. The signals differ as a function of the type of tissue involved. A computer software system (computerized tomography, or CT) then converts this information into a three-dimensional picture. Structures within the brain can be clearly shown in this fashion.

A more important tool for psychological purposes, however, is a technique known as *functional magnetic resonance imaging* (fMRI), which is capable of measuring the flow of blood to any given area of the brain. When neurons become active above base level, blood flows into the region of the activity. The blood carries oxygen and glucose, believed to provide the energy required in the course of neural activity. Thus, fMRI can show those regions of the brain that have become highly activated in response to some situation or cognitive task. It can provide four images per second, which enables it to show the movement of activity within the brain as processing occurs. fMRI is thus highly efficient but, unfortunately, also very expensive.

Positron emission tomography (PET) is an older and cheaper technique. PET also measures the flow of blood and so the fuel intake within the brain. The pictures are clear, but an injection of a radioactive marker into the bloodstream is required. This limits the use of PET, which also does not provide the resolution available with fMRI.

4. Memory Content and Distributed Processing

When information is coded in the brain, it is generally broken up into components that are processed in different regions, a phenomenon known as *distributed processing*. The brain appears to be able to move information from site to site at great speed and also to recombine the elements that have been separated, for processing, at great speed.

Ungerleider and Mishkin (1982), working with monkeys, found that visual processing involves two distinct, specialized paths. One of these, the ventral path, carries information to the temporal lobe, where the authors posited that shape, texture, and color information were coded. The second, dorsal, path carries information to the parietal lobe, where size and location information were assumed to be established. The hypothesized pathways for visual information are shown in Figure 16.5.

For the animal to respond to the visual stimulus as a whole, this separated information must then be recombined into a unity.

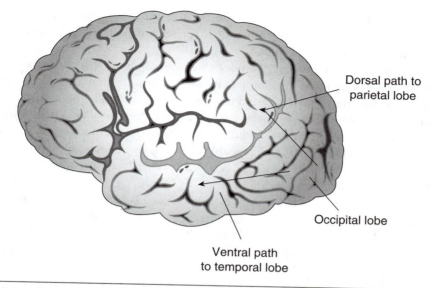

Dorsal path to
parietal lobe

Occipital lobe

Ventral path
to temporal lobe

Figure 16.5 Hypothesized Pathways for the Processing of Visual Information

NOTE: Shape and color information are coded in the ventral region; size and location are coded in the dorsal region.

Kohler, Shitij, Moscovitch, Winocur, and Houle (1995), using PET imaging, reported a similar outcome with human participants. There was increased activity in the temporal lobes (specifically, an increase in activation in both hemispheres in the occipitotemporal cortex) when the shape of an object in a picture was identified, while processing that established the location of the object increased parietal lobe activity (the right hemisphere occipitotemporal region).

It is the shape of an object that makes identification possible: That is, we know that a certain stimulus is a table not because of its size or location but because of its shape. The ventral path in humans is therefore sometimes characterized as providing information about "what" (what the thing is), and the dorsal path as providing information about "where." (The situation may not be as simple as suggested here, however. Section 6 explores the issue further.)

Tulving's research, described in Chapter 6, has shown that when we learn word items the principal code entered into long-term memory (LTM) is not the shape of the word or its sound. It is possible to code the stimulus BIRD, and yet not recognize BIRD when the same item is presented again. This would not occur if the item had been primarily represented as a copy of the word (either visual or auditory). Instead, the code that plays the major role in determining retrieval involves the *meaning* of the item. It is not clear at present where this form of processing occurs, relevant to the two pathways described above. The individual known as HM, who had suffered the loss of the anterior temporal lobes of his brain, was able to identify objects. However, he was unable to form new memories of objects. It is possible that the site that codes for the newly formed memory of a stimulus is located in the temporal lobes, close to the structures that interpret information concerning shape, but that the permanent conceptual representations (the knowledge of the meaning of the stimulus) are not.

The general implication of the research described above, that the brain may break down bodies of information that we would normally think of as being unified, or as reflecting "one thing," and process them separately, has been supported across many varying forms of content. For instance, in the case of associative learning, neuroimaging studies have indicated that the association-forming activity is handled by specific cortical loci, probably involving the hippocampus, while the information that becomes associated is coded in other locations, possibly within the neocortex (Mayes & Montaldi, 1999).

The picture emerging from neuroimaging research became less clear, however, when researchers found that shape information is not always coded at the same site within the brain. Several studies, for instance, have reported increased parietal activity, without increased temporal activity, in rotation tasks (Alivisatos & Petrides, 1997; Just, Carpenter, & Maguire, 2001; Peronnet & Farah, 1989). In a rotation task, participants imagine an object of a particular shape rotating. The task involves imagining changes not only in its location but also its shape, as the object moves.

It may be that specific regions of the brain are dedicated to coding certain kinds of information but that these regions may be in a sense shared. Thus, temporal and parietal areas may be involved in processing shape and size information, with the region used differing, depending on the specific requirements of the task.

5. Structures That Mediate Memory

When there is damage to the temporal lobes, the result is a loss of the ability to form new long-term memories, although short-term recall is not impaired, and long-established memories, although perhaps weakened, remain available. Thus there may be at least three different stages of content maintenance and consolidation, in which the relevant processing occurs at different regions within the brain (Squire, 2004; Squire & Zola Morgan, 1991).

The system that retains general content and episodic information is known as *declarative memory*. Declarative memory includes both one's general knowledge, such as knowledge of the fact that the brain has two hemispheres, and also personal, episodic memories, such as the fact that you ate cereal for breakfast this morning. It is believed that declarative memories are stored in a distributed fashion that includes many brain regions. However, areas critical for the storing of new declarative memories are the two temporal lobes, specifically the medial temporal regions, including the hippocampus and the amygdala. A second area involves the diencephalon. This involves the midline diencephalic area, including the dorsomedial nucleus of the thalamus and the mammillary bodies of the hypothalamus. If either of the two major regions (the temporal lobes or the diencephalon) is damaged, the result is an inability to form new declarative memories and, also, in most cases, the loss of some past memories.

It is also widely believed that components of a given memory, or set of information, are stored in the same region as the processing structures used to encode the memory. For instance, visual aspects of a memory may be stored in visual-processing areas. The hippocampus may then play a critical role in integrating this information with other information. It is for this reason that declarative memory is often considered to be distributed in nature. The hippocampus plays a less critical role with the passage of time. This conclusion has been reached because well-established memories are not lost when the hippocampus is damaged or even removed. The site of these long-term memories has not been clearly established, but it is believed to involve the neocortex. Various models have been developed in the attempt to capture the relations between regions involved in new long-term memory formation, and the storage of long-term memories across time.

Procedural memory is defined, within neuroscience and neuropsychology, as the memory function involved in perceptual and motor skills. It is the memory developed when we learn how to track a stimulus faster, how to catch a ball, to ride a bike, or to identify a visual object more quickly when it has been presented on many occasions. There is evidence that procedural memory also includes aspects of *probabilistic learning*: that is, the ability to code for repeated sequences of stimuli or patterns of stimuli that recur across time. For instance, if a certain kind of light were always to precede rain, an individual might begin to anticipate rain when he or she experienced that particular light. Critically, this could occur without conscious awareness of the relationship between the two. This form of probabilistic learning does not appear to be associative or relational. That is, it may not establish two separate elements and a dissociable relation between them. Instead, it codes for the two elements together as an indissociable unit.

It is believed that procedural memory is not distributed memory. In the case of motor skills, the neural changes appear to be centered in the areas of the motor cortex activated during learning. Also, the hippocampus is not involved.

The *basal ganglia* are also critical in the formation of many forms of procedural memory. These are a collection of subcortical nuclei, including the *caudate nucleus, putamen,* and *nucleus accumbens.* These together are called the *striatum.* Also included in the basal ganglia are the *globus pallidus,* the *substantia nigra,* and the *subthalamic nucleus.* These structures form several loops with cortical regions and can be seen as the crossroads of the neural circuits involved in motor control.

Cortical areas are also involved in procedural learning and memory. For instance, the acquisition of specific finger movements was found to engage areas of the motor cortex and the cerebellum (Seitz, Roland, & Bohm, 1990). In the same way, it is assumed that visual and auditory cortices are involved in procedural memory for skills that include visual and auditory components.

6. Memory Functions and Brain Structures: Neuroimaging Data

6.1. Declarative Memory Formation and Retrieval

The hippocampus shows increased activity during encoding. This has been demonstrated with faces, scene, and word stimuli, although it is not clear whether the hippocampal response is to encoding as such or to the functions involved in consolidating the memory. *Consolidating* is used here to refer to the processes that operate to retain memory content over time. Individuals with damage to the hippocampus, or, as in HM's case, who have suffered removal of the hippocampus, can encode information effectively but cannot retain it.

In further support of the hippocampus as being critical to new memory formation, fMRI studies have indicated that there is an increase in hippocampal activity when individuals try to memorize content, as against simply looking at a fixation point. It is also the case that the higher the degree of hippocampal activity at learning, the better the target information is recalled at a later test (Friedman & Trott, 2000; Wagner, Desmond, Glover, & Gabrieli, 1998). This is known as the *subsequent memory effect.*

There are indications of specialized functions (a lateralization effect) between the right and left hippocampal structures. The left shows more activity when verbal material is learned, and the right, when nonverbal content is learned.

The hippocampus is also activated during retrieval (Nyberg, McIntosh, Houle, & Nilsson, 1996a; Schacter & Wagner, 1999). Given that the relevant memories are in some cases stored in neocortical sites, the hippocampus may be interacting with those sites. Since recall of remote memories can occur without hippocampal involvement, however, there may be more than one method, or more than one activation, of brain regions, by which such recall can be achieved.

Frontal regions of the brain also show increased activity when material is entered into LTM. In the early 1990s, it was thought that there might be particular areas of the cortex devoted to encoding memory content and other areas devoted to retrieving memory content. Tulving, Kapur, Craik, Moscovitch, and Houle (1994), using fMRI, found that the left prefrontal hemisphere was differentially activated during encoding across all the forms of declarative content examined in the study, while the right prefrontal hemisphere was differentially activated at the time of retrieval. (Other sites also showed activity at both encoding and retrieval, but these latter sites varied.) The authors summarized their findings in a model called *HERA* (hemispheric encoding/retrieval asymmetry in episodic memory). Cabeza and Nyberg (1997) and McIntosh, Nyberg, Bookstein, and Tulving (1997), using PET, also reported increased response in the right prefrontal cortex during retrieval.

The data described above involved tasks such as list learning and other semantic learning, and appeared to show a consistent pattern for both encoding, performed in the left hemisphere, and retrieval, performed in the right. When memory for autobiographical content was tested, however, the pattern changed.

Conway, Pleydell, Pearce, and Whitecross (1999) used EEG to monitor increases in neural firing when a cue word, such as RESTAURANT or BEACH, was presented to their participants, with the requirement that the participants retrieve a personal memory based on these cues. Participants were also required to hold the memory in their thoughts for several minutes and then drop it from awareness. Note that studies of this kind do not involve memory formation, since the target memory is already established in LTM.

As the memory was recalled (that is, at the period of retrieval), at first activation increased in the *left* frontal hemisphere, with some weaker activation at the right frontal hemisphere. The activation then flowed to the right temporal and occipital regions, with some weaker left-hemisphere activation continuing in the temporal and occipital areas as the memory was maintained.

Yet another pattern was found by Fink et al. (1996), in the case of strongly emotional memories. In this study participants read sentences concerning events either from their own lives or from the lives of other people, and were told to imagine the event. These were emotional memories for the individuals involved. Very extensive *right* hemisphere activity followed in the case of the participants' personal memories. The areas involved were the right prefrontal cortex and the right temporal lobe, especially the right temporopolar cortex and the right hippocampal structure. There was no left frontal activation. Similar findings for emotional memories were described by Craik et al. (1998) and by Maguire and Mummey (1999).

Conway et al. (1999) reported data that appeared to fit with the findings outlined above. The researchers used PET to examine brain activity in the case of word learning (paired-associate recall) and also autobiographical memories. Retrieval of word items led to strongest activity in the right frontal hemisphere, although with some activity in the left, and engagement of both right and left temporal and occipital regions. Of the latter two regions, the most marked activity was in the right hemisphere. In contrast, the focus of activity for the recall of autobiographical memories was the left hemisphere, particularly the left frontal areas, with only minor activity in the right.

In conclusion, it is clear that frontal regions of the brain are engaged in both memory formation and retrieval. However, the areas of the frontal cortex that are activated appear to differ, depending on the type of material being encoded or recalled. There is no one location, for instance, for either memory formation or memory retrieval. The findings suggest that the right hemisphere is most frequently engaged in retrieval of random word items, whereas the left is more engaged in the case of autobiographical memories.

However, even the modest conclusion outlined above is too simple to accommodate the data. If autobiographical memories are markedly emotional, then recall appears to switch to primary activity in the right hemisphere. A general conclusion that can be reached is that the particular sites of the brain that are employed in memory depend on quite fine-grained differences in the type of material being processed. Also—and critically—there may be an interaction between one set of information, perhaps a personal memory, and whatever other functioning (not related to that memory) the brain is handling at the time. The location of processing may alter, depending on the latter variable (Carpenter, 2001).

As in the hippocampus, there is lateralization of activity in the prefrontal regions depending on whether the material is verbal or nonverbal, with increased activity for verbal content, such as words, in the left hemisphere during learning and increased activity for nonverbal/spatial content, such as faces, in the right. When *objects* are presented for subsequent recall, there is increased activation in both hemispheres (Kelley et al., 1998), The findings on lateralization may relate to the data indicating left-hemisphere retrieval for many autobiographical memories, if it is assumed that there may be a pattern of encoding in one hemisphere (here, primarily the right) and retrieval in the opposite hemisphere (here, the left). As described above, this pattern has been found in the case of word learning.

6.1.1. The Frontal Cortex and Memory

The greater the prefrontal activity during learning, the more likely the target information is to be recalled (Kirchoff, Wagner, & Maril, 2000). Some researchers believe that the role of the prefrontal cortex is primarily one of executive function and organization. These regions may, for instance, establish strategies for learning. It could also be that these areas provide the higher-order information into which new memory content will be integrated.

Damage to the frontal regions of the brain results in a behavior known as *confabulation*. This involves the generation of false memories, which can range from simply incorrect or nonfactual information to extremely bizarre content. In the latter case, there may be direct conflict with other evidence. McCarthy and Hodges (1995), for instance, reported the case of an individual who believed in the 1990s that he was still serving in the navy in the 1940s, in spite of massive evidence to the contrary. It is therefore clear that the frontal regions of the brain perform some kind of evaluative function, inhibiting the acceptance of impossible or implausible content as a genuine memory. These findings fit the general theoretical view that, in the course of recall, the brain generates information on an extended basis and that only some of this information is accepted in awareness as an actual memory.

During encoding of words, the ventrolateral areas of the prefrontal cortex (PFC) are strongly activated, along with the hippocampus. There can be activation in other areas. The left posterior PFC also has been reported as active during this time. At retrieval, two areas of the PFC are activated. One is in a posterior area of the PFC, near Brodman Areas 44 and 6, and the other in an anterior frontopolar region, near Brodman Area 10 (Buckner & Wheeler, 2001).

Some studies have found lateralization in the posterior PFC area, with activation in the left hemisphere for verbal materials (both at encoding and retrieval) and in the right for visual/spatial materials (McDermott, Buckner, & Peterson, 1999). These data do not fit well with the view that random-item verbal material is primarily encoded on the basis of left prefrontal hemisphere activation and primarily retrieved on the basis of right prefrontal hemisphere activation. However, as described above, the findings with regard to location of processing show a complex pattern, with variable results depending on the specific situation involved.

The left parietal cortex appears to operate in the retrieval of both verbal and nonverbal content and in reflecting input from any modality. When word items are correctly recognized, there is increased activity in this region (Habib & LePage, 2000; Henson, Rugg, Shallice, Josephs, & Dolan, 1999; Sanders, Wheeler, & Buckner, 2000). There is also increased activity when an individual views an OLD (a target) item, but does not make a report concerning it. Thus, the activity appears to reflect successful retrieval (Donaldson, Peterson, & Buckner, 2001). Figure 16.6 shows the structures involved in declarative memory.

6.2. Changes in Task Requirements * * * * *

Nyberg (1999) examined what occurs within the brain when word items are learned under varying conditions. Participants were required to use either shallow

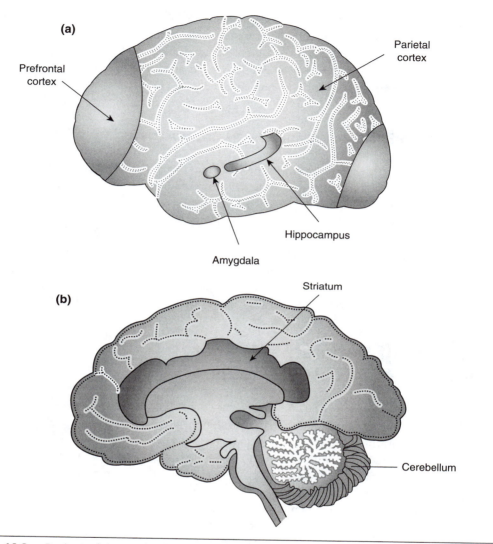

Figure 16.6   Regions of the Brain Involved in Memory

NOTE: Figure (a) shows areas that code for declarative or explicit memory. Figure (b) shows areas that code for implicit memory.

or deep encoding strategies during learning. A shallow task involves, for instance, attending to the sound of the words; a deep encoding task involves making decisions about their pleasantness. Nyberg found that the locus of activity in the brain at the time of retrieval differed, depending on whether the original task had involved shallow or deep encoding.

This finding agrees with the suggestion outlined above, that fine-grained aspects of the type of content entered into LTM influences the regions engaged in both memory formation and memory retrieval. In the present case, however, the data indicate that even the varying properties of a single stimulus, such as a word, can lead to variability in the regions of the brain processing the target information.

Nyberg (1999) also found differences in the activation of brain regions depending on whether retrieval was successful or not successful. There was activation in the right prefrontal cortex when retrieval was attempted. But the site varied within this area, depending on whether retrieval was attempted but did not lead to success or whether retrieval was attempted and did lead to success.

6.3. False Memories and Brain Activity * * * * *

Urbach, Windmann, Payne, and Kutas (2005) examined brain activity when participants were exposed to the DRM procedure, in which false memories for word items are routinely generated (see Chapter 7). They found differences in neural responses when word items would later be falsely recalled, as against when they would not.

Slotnick and Shacter (2006), using fMRI, also found differing brain activity when shape patterns that had been seen earlier were correctly recognized and when foil patterns (not seen earlier) were falsely recognized. Here, the activity centered on very early stages of visual processing, believed to be involved in implicit memory.

7. Storage of Declarative Memory Content: Perceptual Structures

There now exists a body of evidence suggesting that certain forms of memory content are stored (at least in part) within the brain region that originally processed the information. Wheeler, Peterson, and Bruckner (2000) presented words that were paired either with a picture or a sound. At the time of test, when participants correctly recalled that a given word stimulus had been paired with a picture, the areas activated were the same as those activated when the picture had originally been seen, and stored in memory.

It also appears that the work of imagining visual images uses the same areas of the brain as those involved in encoding visual stimuli. Ishai, Ungerleider, and Haxby (2000) presented their participants with pictures of faces, houses, or chairs, and identified the particular regions in the ventral system activated in response to the stimuli. The participants were later asked to imagine stimuli of the same type (a house, etc.). The same areas of the ventral system increased in activity during the task of imagining these objects.

Other studies support a similar state of affairs for audition, language processing, spatial processing, and the planning of actions. Wheeler et al. (2000) presented auditory stimuli to their participants and found that the same areas of the superior temporal gyrus were activated when these sounds were heard and when they were imagined. Similar data have been reported for motor actions.

Researchers do not assume on the basis of these data that exactly the same regions of the brain come into play when something is encoded and when it is remembered, or a similar object is imagined. It is rather assumed that there is significant overlap between the regions used in these activities.

The temporal region involved in "what" processing projects to the hippocampus, the structure known to be involved in the coding of new memories (Mishkin, 1982). In humans, this area involves both the inferotemporal region and the fusiform gyrus. Damage in these areas not only results in the inability to recognize objects but also disrupts the ability to remember new visual stimuli. Both these impairments, however, could be traced to the inability to construct the overall shape of a stimulus. This would make both recognition and identification impossible.

8. Function and Location * * * * *

A consistent finding that has emerged from neuroimaging research is that the same function may be handled at different sites within the brain, from one study to another. Thus, in some cases visual shape information leads to increased activation in temporal areas, and in other cases it leads to increased activation in the parietal cortex.

Some researchers believe that there are no brain sites that are invariably activated during a particular function: in short, that function and location are not related (Craik, Govoni, Naveh-Benjamin, & Anderson, 1997).

Carpenter (2001) has suggested an alternative position, to the effect that each area of the association cortex may be involved in the execution of *related* processes, as against each being involved in a single process. For instance, specific regions of the temporal and parietal lobes may be capable of representing either shape or position information for visual stimuli. According to the present interpretation, although these areas may be specialized for the functions described, one may be more efficient at processing a given type of information, Information X, than the other. This, the primary area, would normally come into play to handle Information X. But if the overall context changed, then it might be adaptive for the secondary area to take on the needed processing.

Elman, Bates, Johnson, and Karmilof-Smith (1996) noted that neural specialization may begin in infancy. For a given task, a number of different cell types might attempt to achieve the needed processing, but those that were best adapted to the function would be likely to handle it faster and better and preempt it. They would become specialized in that form of processing. But the other, early competitors might retain some residual capacity, as in the case of the right brain hemisphere retaining a limited capacity for processing verbal materials.

According to the present view, processing activities cannot be understood in isolation. It might be said that there is no such thing as an isolated function involved with identifying, for instance, the shape of an object. What exists in human cognition is this form of processing for shape, *in interrelationship with other, concurrent forms of processing*. It follows that in one study shape may be handled by the area of the brain most highly specialized to code for shape. In another situation, aspects of the concurrent general functioning may create a situation in which it is more adaptive for another (specialized) region to handle this component.

The researcher would have no means of knowing what the "concurrent general functioning" might be at any given moment in time. The shape of a room, the color of a wall, a just-activated thought—or any one of a range of unidentified variables—could make a difference.

A similar view has been advanced by McIntosh (1999), who suggested that there may exist large neural networks, involving many brain regions, that may be involved in a given type of process. In some studies, one part only of the network's activation may be identified.

9. Emotion and Memory

Damage to the amygdala causes no direct impairment in either semantic or episodic memory. It is believed that one function of the amygdala is to mediate the influence of emotion on recall and also recognition (LeDoux, 2004).

Researchers in physiological psychology and in neuroscience generally assume that emotion plays a major role in memory, operating through the medium of changed chemical states in the extra-cellular and within-cellular neuronal environment. Many emotional conditions are posited as enhancing the memory function. Thus, damage to the amygdala could influence memory in the sense of reducing the beneficial effects of emotion on recall (Phelps et al., 1998).

In support of claims for the role of the amygdala, Cahill et al. (1996), using PET, demonstrated that the level of activation of neurons in the amygdala correlated with the strength of subsequent recall of emotional stimuli, but there was no correlation in the case of neutral stimuli.

Animal studies have lent solid support to the hypothesis that mood-related chemicals may either heighten or impair the memory function. Gold and Van Buskirk (1975) trained rats to avoid a mild foot shock. The training was followed by injections of epinephrine, at low, moderate, or high levels across different conditions. Recall of the avoidance response increased with the injection of epinephrine, up to a certain level (the moderate injection). At high levels, epinephrine impaired retention. Epinephrine is believed to increase arousal, or what might be understood as an emotional state, in either animal or human.

When the animals were trained to avoid an intense, rather than a mild, foot shock, a low dose of epinephrine then impaired recall. That is, the internal (biochemical) state of the animal interacted with the drug. The influence of the drug was also, as is standardly the case, time dependent. If 30 minutes elapsed before the application of the epinephrine, there was no effect on recall, either of enhancement or impairment.

Findings of this pattern, which have been widely replicated, support the Yerkes-Dodson law, positing an inverted U-curve for the memory function under the influence of arousal. In other words, increasing levels of arousal heighten memory until the arousal reaches a point that might imply extreme anxiety or panic; once this stage is reached, the memory function declines.

The animal study data thus support the hypothesis that emotional arousal can significantly enhance recall. But would the same outcome obtain with humans? Cahill, Prins, Weber, and McGaugh (1994) exposed their experimental participants to different versions of a story, accompanied by slides that also differed at a critical point. Condition A involved an emotionally neutral story, with neutral slides. Condition B involved the same story but included a violent traffic accident, with graphic material in the slides. Directly after exposure to these materials, the experimental group was injected with propanolol hydrochloride, a B-adrenergic receptor antagonist. The control group was injected with a placebo. The propanolol hydrochloride would operate to inhibit the adrenergic system. That is, it would inhibit the standard biochemical reaction of that system to a distressing stimulus.

The participants were tested for memory of the story a week later. The control group displayed significantly higher recall for the emotionally arousing than for the neutral material. The experimental group recalled both the emotional and neutral content at the same level, which corresponded to the control group's (lower) recall of the neutral material.

A further critical finding in the Cahill study was that participants in the control and experimental conditions both evaluated their emotional response to the distressing stimuli at the same level. That is, a cognitive judgment of emotion was the same, although the actual biochemical response, influencing memory, was not. These data relate to studies involving flashbulb memory, which have frequently assessed the emotional impact of information on participants on the basis of their introspective reports (see Chapter 12). It appears that such reports may be quite unreliable.

The data suggest that emotional events, of a certain kind, activate a memory modulating system that involves the release of both peripheral adrenergic hormones and brain noradrenaline. The evidence for the effect on memory of these substances when applied exogenously has been clearly documented. Cahill et al. concluded that the same outcome should obtain when internal states, involving the same or similar biochemical natures, are in play. In more subjective terms, certain forms of emotional state will enhance memory.

The authors noted, however, that they had been investigating one system, the a-adrenergic. There exist many other neuromodulatory systems that have not been investigated, and many or all of these may play the same, similar, or quite different, roles in the memory function.

Other data support the view that the amygdala is involved in emotional or "body-level" responses to stimuli. Bechera et al. (1995) presented a tone to their human participants, followed by a loud noise. Some of the participants had suffered damage to the hippocampus, but these participants, like controls, showed a skin conductance response to the loud noise, and subsequent pairing of the two stimuli led to the same skin conductance response to the tone (a form of classical conditioning). Other participants had suffered damage to the amygdala, and these individuals did not show a conditioned skin conductance response to the tone. However, they recalled the experimental sessions clearly. In contrast, the hippocampal-damaged individuals did not recall the experimental sessions. Thus, damage to the amygdala eliminated the "emotion-based" but unconscious reaction to the tone, while damage to the hippocampus eliminated episodic memory for the relevant events (but not the conditioned response to the tone).

Clinical evidence points to yet additional functions for the amygdala. HM, who had suffered bilateral removal of this organ, could not tell when he was hungry or not hungry, and could not feel pain. That is, he could not distinguish a painful stimulus from one that was not painful. It appears that appetite and the monitoring of painful stimuli are both mediated in some fashion through the amygdala.

It has been widely assumed in the literature on memory that elaborative encoding is needed to strongly code material into long-term store. Phelps et al. (1998) have noted, however, that the effect emotion can produce on recall is not due to elaborative encoding. It is rather the result of direct biochemical changes on the process of consolidation. According to this position, variables that operate within the context of word item learning have at times been inappropriately generalized to explain events whose real causes are quite different in kind.

9.1. The Amygdala and Threat

When individuals are exposed to an angry face, there follows regional activation of the amygdala. This also occurs in the case of aversive noise. The effect is automatic, and will occur even if the face is masked, and so not consciously seen (Öhman, 2002). The response may be one to threatening stimuli in general, designed to provide a speeded reaction to such stimuli.

10. Consolidation Theory Revisited

As described in Chapter 2, the notion of a consolidation process in memory was developed as early as the 1900s. According to consolidation theory, information once encoded undergoes an extended period in which biochemical events operate to set the information into long-term store.

The consolidation assumption was largely rejected by mainstream experimental psychology from the 1940s on. McGeoch (1942), the originator of interference theory, was familiar with the concept, but he claimed that it would not be possible for a consolidation process to explain data such as the findings on similarity-based interference. In the case of order recall, for instance, a list of semantically similar items is more difficult to retain accurately than a list of unrelated items. McGeoch believed that a biochemical process could not be as precise as this: that, under a consolidation theory, the capacity of memory to encode content on a list could not vary depending on the subjective nature of the items.

Current understanding of the events involved in neural activity, however, can at least in theory explain the specificity of interference effects. If a complex of neurons is involved in coding for a certain representation, the availability of chemicals needed for synaptic facilitation could be reduced if the complex was activated repeatedly across a set period of time. Thus, if an individual attempts to retain *lion, puma, ocelot, tiger,* and so on, the structure involved in representing "big cat" would come into play repeatedly, with a likely diminishment in the ions relevant to neural firing. This could lead to interference effects (weakness in the consolidation process) based on semantic similarity.

One of the most characteristic findings of research into mood-related chemicals and memory is that the influence of such chemicals shows a temporal gradient (McGaugh, 1990). Both memory-enhancing and memory-impairing drugs tend to produce their strongest effects when administered directly following learning. It is also the case that some drugs will enhance or disrupt memory across a certain period of time following learning, but they will show no effect after that time. According to a consolidation interpretation, this occurs because there is a temporal period during which specific biochemical processes operate to *fix* the relevant content into LTM. These processes are vulnerable to disruption by certain drugs. Once they have run their course, however, the relevant traces are no longer vulnerable. The findings concerning temporal gradients have been replicated across a large number of studies (Coleman-Mesches, Salinas, & McGaugh, 1996; McGaugh, 1983, 1989, 1990, 1992, 2000; McGaugh & Gold, 1989; Roozendaal, Portillo-Marquez, & McGaugh, 1996).

It should be noted that the idea of a period or substage of consolidation running its course, as described above, does not mean that consolidation will be completed at the end of that period. The implication is only that a given kind of biochemical activity, subject to disruption by certain chemical agents, has been completed. Other chemical processes relevant to the retention of the memory content may continue after that period. This view is supported by the finding that different chemical agents produce effects, particularly amnesic effects, across variable time spans following learning.

A consolidation model explains interference effects as involving a limitation on the chemical resources—for instance, neurotransmitters—available to encode material across a set period of time. According to this view, the learning of two word lists in succession exceeds the capacity of LTM to optimally process the material. Consolidation theory can handle the large body of data on interference quite well. It can explain why delay after learning eliminates such effects, why both proactive and retroactive inhibition would operate when lists are learned sequentially, why changes in code release such inhibition, similarity-based interference (for the reasons explained above), and, arguably, why two lists learned in direct sequence show different relative patterns of recovery.

11. Intermediate Memory

Weingartner and Parker (1984) noted that human memory researchers have tended to focus on the events involved in acquisition and retrieval, and not on any possible events that might occur during the period that material is held in store. In contrast, psychologists involved in animal studies have tended to research events both during and—critically—after the period of actual learning, as well as the time of retrieval. The authors blame positivist methodological influence for the bias in the former group toward research focusing exclusively on time of learning and time of retrieval. Both these periods involve environmental events that can be measured directly; the time of storage does not.

Within physiological psychology, however, it is generally believed that once content is entered into LTM (which for meaningful content occurs at encoding) there are many different processing stages that follow. There is, for instance, a stage of very strong retention of content, including detail retention, directly after encoding, followed by other stages in which higher-order information is retained more reliably than detail information (Gold, 1995; Spear & Mueller, 1984; Wickelgren, 1977). The term *dual trace theory* has been used to characterize the view that there exist short-term and long-term memory stores and that once material has entered LTM it undergoes no further critical processing changes, and the term *multitrace theory* to characterize a consolidation/multiple-stage assumption. Under the latter, it is assumed that LTM content is processed differentially across time—and probably across different sites within the brain—and that these events influence the subsequent strength or retrievability of the content (Gold, 1995; McGaugh, 1995; Wickelgren, 1977). Variable terms are also used to characterize the period of long-term consolidation. Some authors prefer to write about different stages of long-term memory; others favor the label *intermediate memory* to characterize the earlier stages of LTM retention, as against very long-term retention. According to this view, sites in the medial temporal lobes are probably involved in intermediate memory, and possibly other, neocortical sites in very long-term memory (McClelland, McNaughton, & O'Reilly, 1994). Intermediate memory here could last for an extended period, however—apparently as long as 10 years.

Conway et al. (1999) used PET neuroimaging to study the patterns of brain activation that occur when either recent or very remote episodic memories are recalled. According to the hypothesis that temporal lobe structures, particularly the hippocampus, consolidate memories that, after consolidation, are stored elsewhere in the brain, recent memories should involve hippocampal activity, while remote memories should not. The researchers found, however, that there was significant hippocampal activity during the retrieval of both recent and very long-term memories. There was also intense activation of the left frontal hemispheres during recall of both recent and remote memories. In general, the pattern of activation differed very little between the two. There was some unique (but small) engagement of the occipital and parietal lobes in the case of the recent memories.

As frequently occurs, the neuroimaging data do not fit easily with the established facts concerning temporal lobe damage. It may be that in the intact brain, hippocampal sites participate in retrieval, but that in the absence of hippocampal sites, some form of retrieval can still be achieved through the prefrontal areas alone. If the prefrontal regions can only be effective, working alone, in the case of long-established (strongly consolidated) memories, then the data may still imply some critical role for intermediate memory that centers on the medial temporal lobes. These structures could be implicated in the early stages of the maintenance or consolidation of memories (such that their damage would result in anterograde amnesia) and in the normal retrieval of all memories.

Summary

Information is coded in the brain on the basis of neural firing. Electrochemical activity causes an impulse, the action potential, to move down the axon of a neuron and cross the gap between that neuron and another neuron, via the synapse. If the receiving neuron is sufficiently stimulated, it too will fire. LTP involves a condition in which facilitation in neural firing is maintained across extended periods of time.

The central fissure separates the anterior and posterior regions of the brain. The sylvian fissure separates the dorsal (top) and ventral (bottom) regions. The inner areas of the brain are referred to as medial and areas toward the outer surface as lateral.

EEG involves attaching electrodes to the scalp, to measure electrical impulses that occur when neurons fire. MRI involves the use of magnetism to align the atomic particles in brain tissue. When bombarded with radio waves, the particles give off radio signals that can be converted to a three-dimensional picture. Functional MRI (fMRI) measures the flow of blood within the brain.

Researchers working with monkeys have found information relating to shape and texture of a visual stimulus is carried to the temporal lobe, while information relating to size and location is carried to the parietal lobe.

New declarative memories are processed in the medial temporal lobes of the brain, where the hippocampus plays a critical role. Another region involved in the processing of new declarative memories is the diencephalon. Damage of either of these areas normally produces amnesia. These structures do not appear to be critical to the recollection of memories that have been stored for a long period of time, however. Perceptual information is stored in the regions of the brain that process the original perceptual input.

Neuroimaging studies have shown that the hippocampus and the prefrontal brain regions become active during memory formation and retrieval. With word stimuli, the left prefrontal region appears to be most highly activated at encoding, and the right prefrontal region, during retrieval. With autobiographical material, the opposite pattern of activation has been found, except in the case of highly emotional content, where the pattern of activation again favored most activity in the right hemisphere during retrieval. The data indicate that neither hemisphere is specialized uniquely for either encoding or retrieval.

The locus of activity of the brain during retrieval of word items also depends on whether a shallow- or a deep-processing task was used during learning. Also, there are differences in areas of activation depending on whether attempted recall is successful or not.

A recurring finding based on neuroimaging studies is that the same task may be handled by different areas of the brain at different times (as measured by different studies).

The amygdala appears to mediate the influence of emotion on memory, rather than be a processing structure involved in the retention of memory content as such.

It has been established that chemicals can affect memory, either by strengthening the memory function or by impairing it. The data can be interpreted within the frame of a consolidation model. Consolidation also provides an alternative to traditional interference theory. Within physiological psychology it is believed that there are many different processing stages that follow the traditional moment of entry into LTM. There is a stage of very strong retention directly following learning or encoding, followed by the retention of certain kinds of information, and the loss of detail, over longer periods of time. It is likely that different regions of the brain are involved in these processes.

CHAPTER 17

Afterword

I tried recently to recall an old memory. There had been a financial crisis at my college and the chair of the department had spoken to me, outside a classroom. I was one of two junior, nontenured people in the department. We were both to lose our jobs. I remembered how serious he had looked—and where he stood physically.

I went on a visit to England that year. But the events of the visit had mushed together. At first, I could not recall an episode that occurred on this particular visit, as against one that was earlier or later. But then I clearly saw myself sitting in a pub with a friend. We were in fact outside the pub, our backs to a wall. As soon as I remembered this, other material returned. I recalled the mood, the conversation, the country setting.

When I returned home a few weeks later, I learned that money had been found, and I would not after all lose my job.

It seems that any example whatever of memory illuminates all the questions about memory. Why could I recall where I was standing when I heard about the expected job loss? The spatial information could hardly be more trivial, and I had certainly stood in or around the same area on hundreds of occasions. Similarity-based interference might have been expected. Yet that little episode had not mushed with the others. And why could I not remember a nice time-ordered sequence of events on my trip to the United Kingdom: Why had *they* mushed? And why did one moment in the pub suddenly come back and lead at once to other content?

The moment in the pub had been a "strong element." Since the episode was remote in time, it was not surprising that much about it had been forgotten. According to activity theory, a memory that receives no activation across a long period will often weaken: The connections between the relevant neurons will lose some degree of facilitation. And according to a cueing, discrimination theory, events that are remote in time will simply lose discriminability. Here, as described earlier, an analogy has been made with events involved in perception. If you look at a series of receding telephone poles, those nearer remain clearly visible, but as they become more and more remote, they blend together. Why then, under either model, did one constituent of a recalcitrant memory come back? Was there some aspect of the sitting-outside event that had produced particularly strong codes, which had endured over time? Or was there something distinctive about that one moment, much as one telephone pole in the distance might be painted red?

1. Why Do We Forget?

At first encounter, it might appear that mainstream theories of forgetting today can be divided into two major classes. There are cue-dependent retrieval models, and there are activity models. But as will be described below, the surface may be a little deceptive.

In older formulations, the critical event involved *reaching* the target. This was how Ebbinghaus saw memory. The event of recall would begin with a conscious representation, and if this led, via associative links, to the target, the target would be remembered. The strength of the links was critical.

The idea of cues changed this picture. A cue will directly contact a corresponding representation in long-term memory (LTM), and so access no longer needs to involve a kind of journey across associated units. From this emerged the belief that a memory could be recalled if "good" cues were deployed and that recall would fail if the cues were not good. Good cues are cues that overlap adequately with the target memory and also contact the memory in a distinctive fashion. That is, if the cues match with many representations in LTM, they will no longer be capable of providing retrieval.

In a model of this kind, the internal nature or state of the memory content does not matter. It does not matter in two senses. First, there are no conditions corresponding to the concept of strong or weak memory content. Memory is quite egalitarian in this respect: All memories are the same. In other words, a memory is not recalled because it is *strong*; it is recalled if and only if the cues match with it adequately and distinctively.

Within the present tradition, researchers differ in the way in which they conceptualize memory content. McGeoch and Tulving thought of such content as continuing across time, in LTM, in the same state as it had been originally encoded. That is, it was not altered following encoding. Forgetting could be due to blocking, under McGeoch's theory, or to the failure of cues to match adequately with the content stored in LTM, a position endorsed by Tulving and also by McGeoch. Other researchers conceptualize the LTM content as being impaired by either interference or decay. Under a cueing theory of memory, these factors weaken any effort at recall, because they diminish the body of material that is available to be contacted by cues. But it is still the case, within the present tradition, that successful recall depends wholly on the relationship between the cues and memory content.

Cueing models of memory, as defined above, have found their way into the public world. Some years ago, the college president of that time placed a hand on my shoulder and told me that memory depended on what we are thinking at the present moment. If our thoughts corresponded with the desired memory, it would come back. And if they didn't, it wouldn't. He did a fair job of describing cue-dependent theory in about two sentences.

I don't believe he was aware that my field was memory.

The second major class of models of forgetting, cited above, involves *activity models*. Here, it is assumed that memory content has different levels of activity. "Activity" can be viewed as strength. For instance, my name would enjoy a high activation level in memory, whereas the details of a holiday I took 15 years ago might have a low activation level. Here, success in recall depends in major part on the activity level of the target.

Associative relations play a critical role in this tradition. Associative processes do not provide entry into LTM, as they did under the Ebbinghausian model. Cues provide such entry.

It is posited, however, that material in LTM is interassociated, with the strength of the associations varying from one body of material to another.

Once contact with content in LTM has occurred, on the basis of cues, two variables will determine whether the target is remembered or not. One involves its background activity level. The other involves associative relations between the information contacted by cues and the target memory. If they are strongly associated, the target's background activity level will be increased.

Associative relations also play a role in determining background activity *within* a target memory. If the internal constituents are strongly interrelated, then the activation of one component will spread to the rest of the set. A recent memory, for instance, tends to show these properties.

Within the present tradition, cues bring additional activation to whatever body of material they contact. Thus, a weak memory may be retrieved if good cues come into play and so increase its level of activity to the point where it can be returned to awareness. An example would be my finding that I could remember a particular conversation, during a visit to England, only after I had recalled a location and a person. These extra cues strengthened the previously weak content of the memory.

In summary, for activity theories, the internal nature of the memory is critical in determining whether a memory can be recalled. Under a cue-dependent theory, on the other hand, the internal nature of the LTM content does not play a role. The critical factor is the relationship between the cues and LTM content.

1.1. When We Don't Forget

Some material in LTM appears highly resistant to forgetting. There is agreement within every school of thought here that rehearsal will strengthen memory content. Many researchers also believe that associating target memories with other material will also, in and of itself, strengthen the memory.

In contrast to the second view outlined above, there is the tradition that emphasizes the role in memory of background structures, often called knowledge structures. Of these, Schank's is probably the best-known model. Here, it is assumed that information that "fits" with such structures will be better retained in LTM than other information. This is why random word lists are hard to retain, while the memory of a half hour spent walking in the country will provide an extended memory, even though none of the events was rehearsed. But knowledge structures do more than this. They provide meaningfulness, the ability to plan, and the ability to anticipate. A very critical implication here is that memories are not formed and entered into LTM "by themselves." Before this occurs, they are matched with content that already exists in the system. For instance, if you were told of John's activities on Monday, and all were consistent with what people do when they want to buy a house, the account would appear meaningful, and the facts would all relate to one another. It is the case, however, that the operation of structures specifying "what can occur" would not be obvious, unless one of their predictions were violated. For instance, if you learned that John carried away the house owner's wool coat as a means of coming to own the house, there would be a violation of the relevant knowledge structures. You would be confused by the information. This clearly indicates that we do not simply encounter facts and enter them into memory, in a kind of vacuum.

It might at first appear that an event or statement that did *not* fit the background structures would stand out and therefore be well recalled. This is the case, since the odd element would receive a great deal of attention. However, if an entire body of content consisted of similar "facts," the result would be a significant impairment of the memory function. Each bizarre statement could not be deeply attended, and the usual strengthening provided by the (rarely violated) background structures would not be present.

Recent theory has focused on the claim that higher-order structures make it possible for us to anticipate events, as mentioned above. This is the case because they code for what is likely to happen, in any given situation. If I see a bicycle being ridden down a street, I know where it is going to be in the immediate future; I can establish its trajectory and also know about its weight and the properties of a moving object of that weight. This is useful knowledge, because if the wheel turns to the left, and I am standing to the left, I will get out of the way.

The point is that we exist in a world where we must function. Within the context of our understanding of the world, it is not enough to know that objects have certain features: a blue color or a steering wheel or four legs and so on. We need to know how to interact with objects. The higher-order structures are conceptualized in the present tradition as providing this form of anticipatory knowledge. The knowledge must be anticipatory because we need to know what to do with a fork or a sandwich before we touch these things—or that there is danger from a bicycle before it touches us. A similar line of reasoning has emerged within the field of robotics, where it is claimed that the critical question not only for a robot but for all animal life must be, "What do I do now?" (Franklin, 1995, chap. 11).

Models such as Schank's and Kolodner's extend the ideas outlined above to include psychological and social knowledge. We learn how events are likely to unfold based not only on physical law but also on human goals and motivations.

Also related to the concept of higher-order structures, research into episodic/autobiographical memory has consistently led to the conclusion that our recollections involve hierarchical structure. In general, material that conforms to the higher-level structures is retained more strongly than material that is more basic, or "lower level" in the hierarchy. In the case of models that posit a critical role for higher-order structures, there are implications for the issue of memory strength that differ to some extent from traditions in which higher-order structures do not play a fundamental role. For instance, in the latter, a memory is strengthened if it is rehearsed and also if it is elaborated with other material. Both of these activities involve consciously directed, or what might be called executive, functions. The third major variable here involves the operation of cues. Individuals who can develop better cues (often based on good organization of the material) will show a superior memory function.

Where higher-order structures are seen as critical to memory, rehearsal also plays a major role. However, when material fits or is assimilated to higher-order structures, this is an unconscious, automatic form of processing. The implication here is that strategies play a fairly minor role in determining how well (meaningful) material is likely to be retained.

1.2. The Genevan View

Piaget's model of memory lies at the far end of the continuum between theories that posit no variability in memory strength, and theories that posit great variability, largely due to the operation of higher-order structures. In the Genevan tradition, it is not only certain kinds of content that are affected by knowledge structures, because they "fit" the knowledge structures. Instead, the strength of all memory content depends on the nature of the schemas that construct that content when it is first coded (and also when it is retrieved). Highly integrated schemas, of any kind, provide strong memories, and weakly integrated schemas do not. An approach of this kind is compatible with Schankian-type knowledge structures, but makes stronger or more extreme claims that emphasize the role of the preexisting organization of LTM in determining memory strength.

2. The Status of Information Coded in LTM

Prior to McGeoch's time, it was generally believed that forgetting was due to decay. Content would simply fade from memory across time. McGeoch famously noted that decay theory could not be correct, because time itself changes nothing. Only events occurring in time bring changes. Time does not rust iron; rust is achieved through a chemical reaction.

His point was that memories are lost only because new material is entered into LTM, causing interference effects. Note that, as McGeoch viewed things, interference does not alter the condition or state of content in LTM. The interfering material simply blocks other material, so that the latter cannot be recalled.

The opposing tradition involves consolidation theory. Here, it is assumed that the establishment of information in LTM requires biochemical activities within the brain and also—critically—that such activities continue across time to fix (some of) the information into memory.

Here the following sequence of events is posited. When information has just been encountered, the memory function is able to hold it at a high level of strength. It can be recalled, even in detail. For instance, if you try to remember the events of the last hour or so, you will be able to identify even trivial components of that period. Following this, the system begins further work, designed to consolidate or hold the memory over time. The capacity to do this is limited. As a result, certain material will be strongly consolidated, while other material will not. The former reflects strong memory content, capable of being recalled across time. The latter will be forgotten.

Consolidation theorists agree with McGeoch that the entry of new material into LTM causes forgetting (in some cases). But they do not see this as a blocking event; or as an event that diminishes the effectiveness of cues. Instead, individuals within the present tradition posit that the additional content places too much demand on the limited capacity of the system to consolidate material across time. In other words, interference involves an actual weakening of the memory codes as such.

This view does not correspond to the traditional notion of decay. Material is not simply established, such that it will then fade across time. It will either be maintained or not maintained, depending on the processing capacity devoted to it, both during and after the period when the material is actively learned.

Researchers within the present tradition reject McGeoch's argument that content once entered into LTM does not experience change. Here, it is assumed that the "time causes nothing" view reifies memory content. To reify is to treat something as if it were a thing or object, when it is not. For instance, if you place a milk jug in a cupboard, it will remain in the cupboard until some other event—such as the movement of another hand—occurs. By this analogy, the passage of time would certainly not change the jug. But according to consolidation theory, the formation of memory content involves a *process*. Such formation is generally believed to involve a change in the capacity of impulses to cross the synapse between neurons. An electrochemical event can facilitate such passage, but this does not mean that the facilitation will then automatically be maintained. Other processes must follow for this to be achieved. In short, when you enter information into memory, it cannot be seen as a piece of iron or a milk jug, which would indeed not spontaneously change over time. The event needs to be understood as literally an event, which achieves a change that may or may not endure.

3. Memory Change

It is known today that memory content can change. Within the empiricist tradition the historical view had been that such change does not occur. Memory was understood as involving a copy of perception, and perception is generally accurate.

The assumption here was that the original perceptual experience was held in LTM and that it might fade. Thus, a recollection could be incomplete. But it could not transmute into different imagery. In the present tradition, perception and memory have been seen as receiving and maintaining events, respectively—not as episodes that involve interpretation.

It is perhaps ironic that in fact memory images tend to be highly inaccurate in detail, unless they have been studied over extended periods of time (Chapter 13).

The argument is sometimes made that human memory would be improved if it *did* operate like a camera. At least it would then be accurate. The trouble with this view is that celluloid can only represent shapes, and the motions of shapes. The whole vast body of abstract information that informs our real memories would be absent if we did indeed work as cameras.

The debate over memory change has shifted today from the question of whether experienced memories change (since it is clear that this is the case), to the question of whether the memory content stored in LTM does or does not alter too.

As described in Chapter 9, two general models have emerged within this context. According to the first, a retrieval model, the memory content stored in LTM has not changed when experienced memories emerge as changed. What has happened is that some preexisting, nontarget content has been retrieved and mistaken for the target. The actual target remains in its original condition within long-term memory.

The second model holds that LTM traces do change and that this is the reason for the experience of changed memory content. According the memory change view, an event is interpreted as it occurs, and this interpretation is stored. At the time of attempted recall, the system draws on this body of information to regenerate the memory. However, some of the original codes may be too weak for the relevant content to be retrieved, and background knowledge may be used to reconstruct it.

A related idea, central to neural net models of memory, is that the state of the system may be somewhat different at the time of retrieval, not only for the reasons outlined above but also for more happenstance reasons. For instance, when recalling Memory X, I may just have seen a brown dog. This may trigger the previously forgotten information that an individual in target Memory X had actually mentioned a dog.

According to the present model, the system actively reconstructs memory content at the time of recall, and the LTM codes that generate this content may have changed, for the reasons described above, from the set of codes that were in play when the memory was originally established.

Two theories of the events involved in such alteration of LTM codes have been developed. According to one, a replacement model, the new complex of information in LTM, established at the time of retrieval, replaces the original complex. For instance, if I saw a woman in a brown coat and later remembered the coat as black, the black information would replace the brown information in the original complex of codes representing that episode.

The alternative, multiple-trace model, posits that such replacement does not occur. Instead, the new complex of codes established at the time of recall coexists with the old complex established at the time of encoding. That is, one complex would contain (inferred, incorrect) black-coat information, and one would contain brown-coat information. Since the capacity of LTM to maintain content across time is limited, however, there is no guarantee that both sets will remain permanently (or even for highly extended periods) in the system. And it is the older complex that is more likely not to be adequately maintained, simply because it is older, and does not enjoy the advantage of recent reactivation.

There appears to be universal agreement that an experienced memory can change on the basis of source misattribution. Here, a nontarget memory, or some constituent of a memory, is recalled, and is mistaken for the target.

Under a retrieval model, all changed memories are of this kind. Under a constructivist model, as the system attempts to regenerate a memory the operating cues may indeed make contact with the wrong material in LTM and include that material in the recalled memory. The difference between the two theories centers here on the issue of "what is recalled." According to the former model, a memory is moved from LTM to awareness, with no events involving the activation of a newly established body of information at the time of recall. According to the latter, a newly established complex of information *is* generated at this time. The nontarget content is simply inserted into this complex.

3.1. What About Remembering Old, Rejected Information? * * * * *

An argument can be made that the replacement view cannot be valid, based on what we know about everyday memory. But this argument against the replacement view is flawed.

The reasoning can be described as follows. We often encounter some news that contradicts earlier information, and we may believe that the second input is correct, and the first wrong. But we have no difficulty in remembering both sets of content. The second does not erase the first.

If I believe that I saw an oak tree on Monday and am informed on Wednesday (by a most reliable source) that the tree was really a maple, I can of course recall those two episodes. And on Wednesday, I can also remember what I thought, and remembered, on Monday.

But the critical point is how I actually recall the tree now.

Suppose, in the attempt to recall, my memory function has selected the maple alternative. It is early fall. I might begin to remember some edges of red about the leaves. What I am experiencing now is a tree that looks more like a maple. The two psychological events—recalling what I once thought, or once remembered, and actually remembering something in the present—are not the same.

It is only in the act of current remembering that the replaced (oak tree) content would play no role.

4. Memories

When I began writing this section, I tried to recall some remote events. I was looking for difficult, but clearly specified, memories. I simply wanted to describe what such recollections could be like. One of the events that I selected was my 5th birthday.

I could remember nothing about it. The problem was not due to childhood amnesia, because I could recall many events that dated to roughly that period of time and to an earlier time. The cues had specified the target most precisely. Under a retrieval model, it seemed that I should have been able to recall it. The specification was of a unique event (so cue overload should not have been a problem), placed in a quite distinctive context.

One possibility, under a retrieval model, was that other material was blocking this memory. Or under an activity model, the codes may have been too weak for retrieval. In either case, additional cues might be helpful.

I began a search. My birthday falls on December 29th. I knew that when I turned 5 my family had stayed for some months at my grandparents' house. We had celebrated Christmas there. And I could recall a number of little scenes from that time, including the Christmas! Specifically, I remembered being in a room, alone, with the very large Christmas tree. I had seen what I thought was a forgotten present, under the tree. It was a big red book. I crawled in, and took possession of the object, and then I watched the tree—massive, ceiling-high—fall over.

The memory ended at that point. I could not move on in time to my birthday, just 4 days later.

I e-mailed my sister, 2 years older than I, in a search for additional cues.

She told me that she had no recollection of my fifth birthday, but that we had been staying at our grandparents' house when I turned 5. She luckily added that the first thing she remembered, when she thought of that time, was the Christmas day. She had seen a block of wood under the tree. The wood had been red. She pulled the block out, for some reason, and the tree fell over. She commented finally that red was an odd color for a block of wood and that perhaps it had been a book!

This memory cannot involve source misattribution—unless one assumes that both my sister and I knocked over separate Christmas trees on different occasions, showing a remarkably poor capacity for learning. One of us has reconstructed the original event, making herself the agent.

A similar form of memory change had occurred in my student who recalled herself, as a 3-year-old, inside a car whose brakes had given way, when in fact it had been her brother who was inside the car.

There is a tendency today for altered memory content to be generally attributed to source misattribution. As described above, there is universal agreement that source misattribution does occur, and it accounts for many changes in recalled content. The previous examples have been included here, however, to make the point that a good deal of memory change is due to a kind of inference, or active reworking of the content of the *target* memory itself.

In the Prologue to the present book, I described an episode in which I remembered a clock tower but had placed it in memory on the wrong side of the street. Again, I do not think that I possess some recollection of a different clock tower, located among buildings indistinguishable from the town of my childhood. In other words, this was the right memory, but it is also a case of inferred elements—here, spatial in nature—that were not correct.

In conclusion, human memory remains a domain of mysteries yet to be solved, and complexity that could not be overestimated. The present book has provided an introduction to the subject. But the path goes much further, and even if it does seem to turn and change, is worth following.

A good place to begin is to examine your own memories, *especially the weak ones.*

References

Abrams, M., & Reber, A. S. (1988). Implicit learning: Robustness in the face of psychiatric disorders. *Journal of Psycholinguistic Research, 17*, 425–439.

Abramson, L. Y., Metalsku, G. I., & Alloy, L. B. (1989). Hopelessness depression: A theory-based subtype. *Psychological Review, 96*, 358–372.

Ackil, J. K., & Zaragoza, M. S. (1995). Developmental differences in eyewitness suggestibility and memory for source. *Journal of Experimental Child Psychology, 60*(1), 57–83.

Ainsworth, P. B. (1981). Incident perception by British police officers. *Law and Human Behavior, 5*, 231–326.

Alba, J. W., & Hasher, L. (1983). Is memory schematic? *Psychological Bulletin, 93*(2), 203–231.

Albert, M. S., Butters, N., & Levin, J. (1979). Temporal gradients in the retrograde amnesia of patients with alcoholic Korsakoff's disease. *Archives of Neurology, 36*(4), 211–216.

Albrecht, J. E., & O'Brien, E. J. (1993). Updating a mental model: Maintaining both local and global coherence. *Journal of Experimental Psychology: Learning, Memory, and Cognition, 19*, 1061–1070.

Aldrich, F. K. (1995). *Can implicit memory be exploited to facilitate the learning of novel associations?* Unpublished D.Phil. thesis, University of Sussex, UK.

Alexander, K. W., Quas, J. A., Goodman, G. S., Ghetti, S., Edelstein, R. S., Redlich, A. P., et al. (2005). Traumatic impact predicts long-term memory for documented child sexual abuse. *Psychological Science, 16*(1), 33–43.

Alvisatos, B., & Petrides, M. (1997). Functional activation of the human brain during mental rotation. *Neuropsychologia, 35*(2), 111–118.

Allen, B. P., & Lindsay, D. S. (1998). Amalgamations of memories: Intrusion of information from one event into reports of another. *Applied Cognitive Psychology, 12*(3), 277–285.

Ammons, H., & Irion, A. I. (1954). A note on the Ballard reminiscence phenomenon. *Journal of Experimental Psychology, 48*, 184–186.

Anderson, A., Garrod, S. C., & Sanford, A. J. (1983). The accessibility of pronominal antecedents as a function of episodic shifts in narrative texts. *Quarterly Journal of Experimental Psychology, 35*, 427–440.

Anderson, J. A. (1973). A theory for the recognition of items from short memorized lists. *Psychological Review, 80*(6), 417–438.

Anderson, J. R. (1974). Retrieval of propositional information from long-term memory. *Cognitive Psychology, 6*(4), 451–474.

Anderson, J. R. (1976). *Language, memory, and thought.* Oxford, UK: Lawrence Erlbaum.

Anderson, J. R. (1978). Arguments concerning representation for mental imagery. *Psychological Review, 85*, 249–277.

Anderson, J. R. (1981). Effects of prior knowledge on memory for new information. *Memory & Cognition, 9*(3), 237–246.

Anderson, J. R. (1983a). *The architecture of cognition.* Cambridge, MA: Harvard University Press.

Anderson, J. R. (1983b). A spreading activation theory of memory. *Journal of Verbal Learning and Verbal Behavior, 22,* 261–295.

Anderson, J. R. (1990). *Cognitive psychology and its implications.* New York: W. H. Freeman.

Anderson, J. R. (1993). *Rules of the mind.* Hillsdale, NJ: Lawrence Erlbaum.

Anderson, J. R. (2005). Human symbol manipulation within an integrated cognitive architecture. *Cognitive Science, 29*(3), 313–341.

Anderson, J. R., & Bower, G. H. (1972). Recognition and retrieval processes in free-recall. *Psychological Review, 79*(2), 97–123.

Anderson, J. R., & Bower, G. H. (1973). *Human associative memory.* Washington, DC: Winston.

Anderson, J. R., & Bower, G. H. (1974). Interference in memory for multiple contexts. *Memory & Cognition, 2*(3), 509–514.

Anderson, J. R., Budiu, R., & Reder, C. M. (2001). A theory of sentence memory as part of a general theory of memory. *Journal of Memory and Language, 45,* 337–367.

Anderson, J. R., & Pitchert, R. D. (1978). Recall of previously unrecallable information following a shift in perspective. *Journal of Verbal Learning and Verbal Behavior, 17,* 1–12.

Anderson, J. R., & Reder, L. M. (1999). The fan effect: New results and new theories. *Journal of Experimental Psychology: General, 128*(2), 186–197.

Anderson, M. C., & Green, C. (2001). Suppressing unwanted memories by executive control. *Nature, 410,* 366–369.

Anderson, M. C., & Neely, J. H. (1996). Interference and inhibition in memory retrieval. In E. L. Bjork & R. A. Bjork (Eds.), *Memory: Handbook of perception and cognition* (2nd ed., pp. 237–313). San Diego, CA: Academic Press.

Anderson, M. C., & Spellman, D. A. (1995). On the status of inhibitory mechanisms in cognition: Memory retrieval as a model case. *Psychological Review, 102*(1), 68–100.

Anderson, S. J., & Conway, M. A. (1993). Investigating the structure of specific autobiographical memories. *Journal of Experimental Psychology: Learning, Memory, and Cognition, 19,* 1–19.

Aristotle. (1941). De memoria et reminiscentia. In R. McKeon (Ed.), *Parva naturalia: The short physical treatises. The basic works of Aristotle.* New York: Random House.

Aristotle. (1961). *De anima (On the soul).* W. D. Ross (Ed.). Oxford, UK: Clarendon Press.

Arndt, J., & Reder, L. M. (2003). The effect of distinctive information in false recognition. *Journal of Memory and Language, 48*(1), 1–15.

Atkinson, R. C., & Juola, J. F. (1973). Factors influencing speed and accuracy of word recognition. In S. Kornblum (Ed.), *Attention and performance* (Vol. 4, pp. 583–612). New York: Academic Press.

Atkinson, R. C., & Juola, J. F. (1974). Search and decision processes in recognition memory. In D. H. Krantz (Ed.), *Learning, memory and thinking* (Vol. 1, pp. 242–293). San Francisco: W. H. Freeman.

Atkinson, R. C., & Shiffrin, R. M. (1968). Human memory: A proposed system and its control processes. In K. W. Spence & J. T. Spence (Eds.), *The psychology of learning and motivation: Advances in research and theory* (Vol. 2, pp. 89–195). New York: Academic Press.

Averbach, E., & Coriell, A. S. (1961). Short-term memory in vision. *Bell System Technical Journal, 40,* 309–328.

Avon, S. E., Wright, K. L., & Pammer, K. (1994). The word length effect in probed and serial recall. *Quarterly Journal of Experimental Psychology, 20,* 249–264.

Awh, E., Jonides, J., Smith, E. E., Schumacher, E. H., Koeppe, R. A., & Katz, S. (1996). Dissociation or storage and rehearsal in verbal working memory: Evidence from PET. *Psychological Science, 7,* 25–31.

Ayres, T. J., Jonides, J., Reitman, J. S., Egan, J. C., & Howard, D. A. (1979). Differing suffix effects for the same physical suffix. *Journal of Experimental Psychology: Human Learning and Memory, 5,* 315–321.

Baddeley, A. D. (1966). Short-term memory for word sequences as a function of acoustic, semantic and formal similarity. *Quarterly Journal of Experimental Psychology, 18,* 362–365.

Baddeley, A. D. (1972). Selective attention and performance in dangerous environments. *British Journal of Psychology, 63*(4), 537–546.

Baddeley, A. D. (1976). *The psychology of memory.* New York: Basic Books.

Baddeley, A. D. (1986). *Working memory.* New York: Oxford University Press.

Baddeley, A. D. (1990). *Human memory: Theory and practice.* Needham Heights, MA: Allyn & Bacon.

Baddeley, A. D. (1992a). Is working memory working? The fifteenth Bartlett lecture. *Quarterly Journal of Experimental Psychology, 44A,* 1–31.

Baddeley, A. D. (1992b). Working memory: The interface between memory and cognition. *Journal of Cognitive Neuroscience, 4*(3), 281–288.

Baddeley, A. D. (1994). Working memory: The interface between memory and cognition. In D. L. Schacter & E. Tulving (Eds.), *Memory systems 1994* (pp. 351–367). Cambridge: MIT Press.

Baddeley, A. D. (2002). The concept of episodic memory. In A. Baddeley, J. P. Aggleton, & M. A. Conway (Eds.), *Episodic memory: New directions in research* (pp. 1–10). London: Oxford University Press.

Baddeley, A. D., & Andrade, J. (1994). Reversing the word-length effect: A comment on Caplan, Rochon and Waters. *Quarterly Journal of Experimental Psychology: Human Experimental Psychology, 47A*(4), 1047–1054.

Baddeley, A. D., & Andrade, J. (2000). Working memory and the vividness of imagery. *Journal of Experimental Psychology: General, 29*(1), 126–145.

Baddeley, A. D., & Dale, H. C. (1966). The effect of semantic similarity on retroactive interference in long- and short-term memory. *Journal of Verbal Learning and Verbal Behavior, 5*(5), 417–420.

Baddeley, A. D., & Hitch, G. J. (1974). Working memory. In G. A. Bower (Ed.), *Recent advances in learning and motivation* (p. 8). New York: Academic Press.

Baddeley, A. D., & Hitch, G. J. (1976). Verbal reasoning and working memory. *Quarterly Journal of Experimental Psychology, 28*(4), 603–621.

Baddeley, A. D., Lewis, V. J., & Vallar, G. (1984). Exploring the articulatory loop. *Quarterly Journal of Experimental Psychology, 36,* 233–252.

Baddeley, A. D., & Logie, R. (1999). Working memory: The multiple component model. In A. Miyake & P. Shah (Eds.), *Models of working memory: Mechanisms of active maintenance and executive control.* New York: Cambridge University Press.

Baddeley, A. D., Thomson, N., & Buchanan, M. (1975). Word length and the structure of short-term memory. *Journal of Verbal Learning and Verbal Behavior, 14*(6), 575–589.

Baddeley, A. D., & Wilson, B. A. (1986). Amnesia, autobiographical memory and confabulation. In D. Rubin (Ed.), *Autobiographical memory* (pp. 225–252). New York: Cambridge University Press.

Baddeley, A. D., & Wilson, B. A. (1994). When implicit learning fails: Amnesia and the problem of error elimination. *Neuropsychologia, 32,* 53–68.

Bahrick, H. P. (1970). Discriminative and associative aspects of retroactive inhibition. *Quarterly Journal of Experimental Psychology, 22*(4), 565–573.

Bahrick, H. P. (1979). Broader methods and narrower theories for memory research: Comments on the papers by Eysenck and Cermak. In L. S. Cermak & F. I. M. Craik (Eds.), *Levels of processing in human memory* (pp. 141–156). Hillsdale, NJ: Lawrence Erlbaum.

Baker, L. E. (1937). The influence of subliminal stimuli on verbal behavior. *Journal of Exerimental Psychology, 20,* 84–100.

Ballard, B. P. (1913). Oblivescence and reminiscence. *British Journal of Psychological Monograph,* 1–82 (Suppl. 1, No. 2).

Balota, D. A., & Duchek, J. M. (1989). Spreading activation in episodic memory: Further evidence for age independence. *Quarterly Journal of Experimental Psychology, 41,* 849–876.

Balota, D. A., & Lorch, R. F. (1986). Depth of automatic spreading activation: Mediated priming effects in pronunciation but not in lexical decision. *Journal of Experimental Psychology: Learning, Memory, and Cognition, 12*(3), 336–345.

Banks, W. P., & Barber, G. (1977). Color information in iconic memory. *Psychological Review, 84,* 536–546.

Barnier, A. J., & McConkey, K. M. (1992). Reports of real and false memories: The relevance of hypnosis, hypnotizability and context of memory test. *Journal of Abnormal Psychology, 42*(4), 197–205.

Barrouillet, P., & Camos, V. (2001). Developmental increase in working memory span: Resource sharing or temporal decay? *Journal of Memory and Language, 45,* 1–20.

Barrouillet, P., Bernardin, S., & Camos, V. (2004). Time constraints and resource sharing in adults' working memory span. *Journal of Experimental Psychology: General, 133*(3), 83–100.

Barry, C., & McHattie, J. V. (1995). Problems naming animals: A category-specific anomie or misnomer? In R. Campbell & M. A. Conway (Eds.), *Broken memories: Case studies in memory impairment.* Cambridge, UK: Blackwell.

Barsalou, L. W. (1988). The content and organization of autobiographical memories. In U. Neisser & E. Winograd (Eds.), *Remembering reconsidered: Ecological and traditional approaches to the study of memory* (pp. 193–243). Cambridge, UK: Cambridge University Press.

Barshi, I. (1997). *Message length and misunderstandings in aviation communication: Linguistic properties and cognitive constraints.* Doctoral dissertation, University of Colorado, Boulder.

Bartlett, F. C. (1932). *Remembering: A study in experimental and social psychology.* Cambridge, UK: Cambridge University Press.

Bass, E., & Davis, L. (1988). *The courage to heal.* New York: Harper & Row.

Bass, H. (1983). The development of an adults' imaginary companion. *Psychological Review, 70*(4), 519–533.

Bates, E., Bretherton, I., & Snyder, L. (1988). *From first words to grammar: Individual differences in dissociable mechanisms.* Cambridge, UK: Cambridge University Press.

Battig, W. F., & Montague, W. E. (1969). Category norms for verbal items in 56 categories: A replication and extension of the Connecticut norms. *Journal of Experimental Psychology, 80*(2), 1–46.

Bauer, P. J. (1995). *Recalling past events: From infancy to early childhood.* Philadelphia: Jessica Kingsley.

Bauer, P. J. (2002). Long-term recall memory: Behavioral and neuro-developmental changes in the first 2 years of life. *Current Directions in Psychological Science, 11,* 137–141.

Bauer, P. J., van Abbema, D. L., Wiebe, S. A., Cay, M. S., Phill, C., & Burch, M. M. (2004). Props not pictures are worth 1,000 words: Verbal accessibility of early memories under different conditions of contextual support. *Applied Cognitive Psychology, 18,* 373–392.

Bauer, P. J., Wenner, J. A., Dropik, P. L., & Wewerka, S. S. (2000). Parameters of remembering and forgetting the transition from infancy to early childhood. *Monographs of the Society for Research in Child Development, 65*(4), 205–213.

Baxt, N. (1871). Uber die Zeit Welche notig ist, damit ein Gesichtseindruck zum Bewusstsein Kommt. *Pfluger's Archive für die gesamte Physiologie des Menschen und der Tiere, 4,* 325–336.

Bayliss, D., Jarrold, C., Gunn, D., & Baddeley, A. (2003). The complexities of complex span: Explaining individual differences in working memory in children and adults. *Journal of Experimental Psychology: General, 132*(1), 71–92.

Beauregard, M., Chertkow, H., Gold, P., & Bergman, S. (2001). The impact of semantic impairment on word stem completion in Alzheimer's disease. *Neuropsychologia, 39*(3), 302–314.

Beauvois, M. F., & Saillant, B. (1985). Optic aphasia for colours and colour agnosia: A distinction between visual and visual-verbal impairment in the processing of colors. *Cognitive Neuropsychology, 2,* 1–48.

Beauvois, M. F., Saillant, B., Meininger, V., & Lhermitte, F. (1978). Bilateral tactile aphasia: A tacto-verbal dysfunction. *Brain, 101,* 381–400.

Bechera, A., Tranel, D., Damasio, H. Adolphs, R., Rockland, C., & Damasio, N. (1995). Double dissociation of conditioning and declarative knowledge relative to the amygdala and hippocampus in humans. *Science, 269*(5227), 1115–1118.

Bekerian, D. A., & Bowers, J. N. (1983). Eyewitness testimony: Were we misled? *Journal of Experimental Psychology: Learning, Memory, and Cognition, 9*(1), 139–145.

Bellezza, F. S., Cheesman, F. L., & Reddy, B. G. (1977). Organization and semantic elaboration in free recall. *Journal of Experimental Psychology: Human Learning and Memory, 3*(5), 539–550.

Belli, R. F. (1989). Influence of misleading postevent information: Misinformation interference and acceptance. *Journal of Experimental Psychology: General, 118*(1), 72–85.

Belli, R. F., Lindsay, D. F., Gales, M. S., & McCarthy, T. T. (1994). Memory impairment and source misattribution in postevent misinformation experiments with short retention intervals. *Memory & Cognition, 22*(1), 40–54.

Bennett, D. J., & McEvoy, C. L. (1999). Mediated priming in younger and older adults. *Experimental Aging Research, 25*(2), 141–159.

Berger, T. W. (1984). Long-term potentiation of hippocampal synaptic transmission affects rate of behavioral learning. *Science, 224*(4649), 627–630.

Bernstein, R. J. (1983). *Beyond objectivism and relativism: Science, hermeneutics, and praxis.* Philadelphia: University of Pennsylvania Press.

Berntsen, D., & Rubin, D. C. (2002). Emotionally charged memories across the lifespan: The recall of happy, sad, traumatic and involuntary memories. *Psychology of Aging, 17,* 636–652.

Berntsen, D., & Rubin, D. C. (2004). Cultural life scripts structure recall from autoibiographical memory. *Memory & Cognition, 32*(3), 427–442.

Berry, D. C., & Broadbent, D. E. (1984). On the relationship between task performance and associated verbalizable knowledge. *Quarterly Journal of Experimental Psychology, 36,* 209–231.

Berry, D. C., & Broadbent, D. E. (1988). Interactive tasks and the implicit-explicit distinction. *British Journal of Psychology, 79,* 251–272.

Bestgen, Y., & Vonk, W. (1995). The role of temporal segmentation markers in discourse processing. *Discourse Processes, 19*(3), 385–406.

Biederman, I., & Cooper, E. E. (1991). Primary contour-deleted images: Evidence for complete translational and reflectional invariance in visual object priming. *Cognitive Psychology, 23*(3), 393–419.

Bjork, R. A., & Whitten, W. B. (1974). Recency-sensitive retrieval processes in long term free recall. *Cognitive Psychology, 6*(2), 173–189.

Black, J. B., & Bower, G. H. (1979). Episodes as chunks in narrative memory. *Journal of Verbal Learning and Verbal Behavior, 18,* 187–198.

Black, J. B., & Bower, G. H. (1980). Story understanding as problem solving. *Poetics, 9,* 223–250.

Blaney, P. H. (1986). Affect and memory: A review. *Psychology Bulletin, 99*(2), 229–246.

Blaxton, T. A. (1989). Investigating dissociations among memory measures: Support for a transfer-appropriate framework. *Journal of Experimental Psychology, 15*(4), 657–668.

Bliss, T. V., & Collingridge, G. L. (1993). A synaptic model of memory: Long-term potentiation in the hippocampus. *Nature, 361*(6407), 31–39.

Bliss, T. V. P., & Lomo, T. (1973). Long-lasting potentiation pf synaptic transmission in the dentate area of the anesthetized rabbit following simulation of the perforant path. *Journal of Physiology, 232,* 331–356.

Block, N. (2001). Paradox and cross purposes in recent work on consciousness. *Cognition, 79*(1–2), 197–219.

Bloom, C. P., Fletcher, C. R., van den Broek, P., Reitz, L., & Shapiro, B. P. (1990). An on-line assessment of causal reasoning during comprehension. *Memory & Cognition, 18,* 65–71.

Blume, S. E. (1990). *Secret survivors: Uncovering incest and its aftereffects on women.* Oxford, UK: Wiley.

Boden, M. (1977). *Artificial intelligence and natural man.* New York: Basic Books.

Bobrow, D. G., & Norman, D. A. (1975). Some principles of memory schemata. In D. G. Bobrow & A. Collins (Eds.), *Representation and understanding: Studies in cognitive science.* New York: Academic Press.

Bohannon, J. N., III. (1988). Flashbulb memories for the space shuttle disaster: A tale of two theories. *Cognition, 29,* 179–196.

Bohannon, J. N., & Symons, V. L. (1992). Flashbulb memories: Confidence, consistency, and quantity. In E. Winograd & U. Neisser (Eds.), *Affect and accuracy in recall: Studies of "flashbulb" memories.* New York: Cambridge University Press.

Boller, K., Grabelle, M., & Rovee-Collier, C. (1995). Effects of post-event information on infants' memory for a central target. *Journal of Experimental Child Psychology, 59*(3), 372–396.

Bonner, L., & Burton, A. M. (2003). Getting to know you: How we learn new faces. *Visual Cognition, 10*(5), 527–536.

Botwinick, J., & Storandt, M. (1974). *Memory, related functions, and age.* Springfield, IL: Charles C. Thomas.

Bousfield, W. A. (1951, September). *Frequency and availability measures in language behavior.* Paper presented at the annual meeting of the American Psychological Association, Chicago.

Bousfield, W. A. (1953). The occurrence of clustering in the recall of randomly arranged associates. *Journal of General Psychology, 49,* 229–240.

Bower, G. H. (1981). Mood and memory. *American Psychologist, 36*(2), 129–148.

Bower, G. H. (1990). Awareness, the unconscious, and repression: An experimental psychologist's perspective. In J. L. Singer (Ed.), *Repression and dissociation implications for personality: Theory, psychopathology and health* (pp. 209–222). Chicago: University of Chicago Press.

Bower, G. H. (1996). Reactivating a reactivation theory of implicit memory. *Consciousness and Cognition, 5,* 27–72.

Bower, G. H., Black, J. B., & Turner, T. J. (1979). Scripts in memory for text. *Cognitive Psychology, 11,* 117–220.

Bower, G. H., & Mayer, J. D. (1985). Failure to replicate mood-dependent retrieval. *Bulletin of the Psychonomic Society, 23*(1), 39–42.

Bowers, J. S. (1999). Priming is not all bias: Commentary on Ratcliff and McKoon (1997). *Psychological Review, 106,* 582–596.

Brainerd, C. J., & Reyna, V. F. (1988). Memory loci of suggestibility development: Comment on Ceci, Ross, and Toglia (1987). *Journal of Experimental Psychology: General, 117*(2), 197–200.

Brainerd, C. J., & Reyna, V. F. (1998). Fuzzy-trace theory and children's false memories. *Journal of Experimental Child Psychology, 71*(2), 81–129.

Brainerd, C. J., Wright, R., Reyna, V. F., & Mojardin, A. H. (2001). Conjoint recognition and phantom recollection. *Journal of Experimental Psychology: Learning, Memory, & Cognition, 27*(2), 307–327.

Bransford, J. D., Barclay, J. R., & Franks, J. J. (1972). Sentence memory: A constructive versus interpretive approach. *Cognitive Psychology, 3*(2), 193–209.

Bransford, J. D., & Johnson, M. K. (1972). Contextual prerequisites for understanding: Some investigations of comprehension and recall. *Journal of Verbal Learning and Verbal Behavior, 11,* 717–726.

Bransford, J. D., & Johnson, M. K. (1973). Considerations of some problems of comprehension. In W. G. Chase (Ed.), *Visual information processing* (Vol. 14, pp. 383–438). Oxford, UK: Academic Press.

Bransford, J. D., & McCarrell, N. S. (1974). A sketch of a cognitive approach to comprehension: Some thoughts about understanding what it means to comprehend. In W. B. Weimer & D. S. Palmero (Eds.), *Cognition and the symbolic processes.* Hillsdale, NJ: Lawrence Erlbaum.

Braun, K. A., Ellis, R., & Loftus, E. F. (2002). Make my memory: How advertising can change our memories of the past. *Current Directions in Psychological Science, 9,* 6–10.

Brewer, W. F. (1988). Memory for randomly sampled autobiographical events. In U. Neisser and E. Winograd (Eds.), *Remembering reconsidered: Ecological and traditional approaches to the study of memory* (pp. 21–90). Cambridge, UK: Cambridge University Press.

Brewer, W. F. (1999). What is recollective memory? In D. C. Rubin (Ed.), *Remembering our past* (pp. 19–66). New York: Cambridge University Press.

Briere, J., & Conte, J. R. (1993). Self-reported amnesia for abuse in adults molested as children. *Journal of Traumatic Stress, 6*(1), 21–31.

Brioni, J. D., & McGaugh, J. L. (1988). Post-training administration of GABAergic antagonists enhances retention of aversively motivated tasks. *Psychopharmacology, 96*(4), 505–510.

Britton, B. K., & Graesser, A. C. (1996). *Models of understanding text.* Hillsdale, NJ: Lawrence Erlbaum.

Brockelman, P. (1975). Of memory and things past. *International Philosophical Quarterly, 15,* 309–325.

Brooks, L. R. (1968). Spatial and verbal components of the act of recall. *Canadian Journal of Psychology, 22,* 349–368.

Brown, G. D. A., & Chader, N. (2001). The chronological organization of memory: Common psychological foundations for remembering and timing. In C. Hoerl & T. McCormack (Eds.), *Time and memory: Issues in philosophy and psychology* (pp. 77–110). Oxford, UK: Oxford University Press.

Brown, G. D. A., & Hulme, C. (1995). Modeling item length effects in memory span: No rehearsal needed? *Journal of Memory and Language, 34*(5), 594–621.

Brown, J. M. (1958). Some tests of the decay theory of immediate memory. *Quarterly Journal of Experimental Psychology, 10,* 12–21.

Brown, J. M. (2003). Eyewitness memory for arousing events. *Applied Cognitive Psychology, 17*(1), 93–106.

Brown, J. M., Lewis, V. J., & Monk, A. F. (1977). Memorability word frequency, and negative recognition. *Quarterly Journal of Experimental Psychology, 29*(3), 461–473.

Brown, N. R., Shevell, S. K., & Rips, L. J. (1986). Public memories and their personal context. In D. C. Rubin (Ed.), *Autobiographical memory* (pp. 137–158). Cambridge, UK: Cambridge University Press.

Brown, R., & Kulik, J. (1977). Flashbulb memories. *Cognition, 5,* 73–99.

Brownmiller, S. (1975). *Against our will: Men, women and rape.* New York: Simon & Schuster.

Bruck, M., & Ceci, S. J. (1999). The suggestibility of children's memory. *Annual Review of Psychology, 50*(4), 419–439.

Bruck, M., Ceci, S. J., & Melnyk, L. (1997). External and internal sources of variation in the creation of false reports in children. *Learning and Individual Differences, 9*(4), 289–316.

Bruner, J., Goodnow, J. J., & Austin, G. A. (1956). *A study of thinking.* New York: Wiley.

Bruni, F., & Burkett, E. (2002). *A gospel of shame.* New York: Norton.

Buckhout, R. (1974). Eyewitness testimony. *Scientific American, 231*(6), 23–31.

Buckner, R. L., & Wheeler, M. E. (2001). The cognitive neuroscience of remembering. *NatureReviews Neuroscience, 2*(9), 624–634.

Burgess, N., & Hitch, G. J. (1999). Memory for serial order: A network model of the phonological loop and its timing. *Psychological Review, 106*(3), 551–581.

Burke, A., Heuer, F., & Reisberg, D. (1992). Remembering emotional events. *Memory & Cognition, 20*(3), 277–290.

Butler, S. (1978). *The conspiracy of silence: The trauma of incest.* San Francisco: New Glide.

Butters, M. A., & Glisky, E. L. (1993). Transfer of new learning in memory-impaired patients. *Journal of Clinical and Experimental Neuropsychology, 15,* 219–230.

Butters, N. (1984). The clinical aspects of memory disorders: Contributions from experimental studies of amnesia and dementia. *Journal of Clinical Neuropsychology, 6*(1), 17–36.

Butters, N., & Cermak, L. S. (1980). *Alcoholic Korsakoff's syndrome: An information processing approach to amnesia.* New York: Academic Press.

Butters, N., O'Connor, M. G., & Verfaellie, M. (1995). My own remembered past: Insights into the structure and processes of retrograde amnesia from a patient with visual access problems subsequent to encephalitis. In R. Campbell & M. A. Conway (Eds.), *Broken memories: Case studies in memory impairment.* Cambridge, UK: Blackwell.

Byrne, C. A., Hyman, I. E., & Scott, K. L. (2001). Comparisons of memories for traumatic events and other experiences. *Journal of Applied Cognitive Psychology, 15,* 119–134.

Cabeza, R., Mangels, J., Nyberg, L., Habib, R., Houle, S., McIntosh, R. A., et al. (1997). Brain regions differentially involved in remembering what and when: A PET study. *Neuron, 19,* 863–870.

Cabeza, R., & Nyberg, L. (1997). Imaging cognition: an empirical review of PET studies with normal subjects. *Journal of Cognitive Neuroscience, 9*(1), 1–16.

Cahill, L., Haier, R. J., Fallon, J., Alkire, M. T., Tang, C., Keator, D., et al. (1996). Amygdala activity at encoding correlated with long term free recall of emotional information. *Proceedings of the National Academy of Sciences, USA, 93,* 8016–8021.

Cahill, L., Prins, B., Weber, M., & McGaugh, J. L. (1994). B-adrenergic activation and memory for emotional events. *Nature, 371*(6499), 702–704.

Campbell, R., & Dodd, B. (1980). Hearing by eye. *Quarterly Journal of Experimental Psychology, 32,* 85–99.

Capgras, J., & Reboul-Lachaux, J. (1923). L'illusion des sosies dans un delir systemaise chronique. *Societe Clinique de Medicine Mentale, 2,* 6–16.

Caplan, D., Rochon, E., & Waters, G. S. (1992). Articulatory and phonological determinants of word length effects in span tasks. *Quarterly Journal of Experimental Psychology: Human Experimental Psychology, 45A*(2), 177–192.

Cardena, E., & Spiegel, D. (1993). Dissociative reactions to the San Francisco Bay area earthquake of 1989. *American Journal of Psychiatry, 150,* 474–478.

Carmichael, L., Hogan, H. P., & Walter, A. A. (1932). An experimental study on the effect of language on visually perceived forms. *Journal of Experimental Psychology, 15,* 73–86.

Carpenter, P. A. (2001). Neural network models of learning and memory: Leading questions and an emerging framework. *Trends in Cognitive Science, 5*(3), 114–118.

Carpenter, P. A., Just, M. A., Keller, T. A., Eddy, W., & Thulborn, K. R. (1999). Graded functional activation in the visuospatial system with the amount of task demand. *Journal of Cognitive Neuroscience, 11,* 9–24.

Carver, L. J., & Bauer, P. J. (1999). When the event is more than the sum of its parts: Nine-month-olds' long-term ordered recall. *Memory, 7,* 147–174.

Cason, H. (1932). The learning and retention and pleasant and unpleasant activities. *Archives of Psychology, 134,* 1–96.

Ceci, S. J., & Bruck, M. (1995). *Jeopardy in the courtroom: A scientific analysis of children's testimony.* Washington, DC: American Psychological Association.

Ceci, S. J., Ross, D. F., & Toglia, M. P. (1987a). Age differences in suggestibility: Narrowing the uncertainties. In S. J. Ceci, M. P. Toglia, & D. F. Ross (Eds.), *Children's eyewitness testimony* (pp. 79–91). New York: Springer.

Ceci, S. J., Ross, D. F., & Toglia, M. P. (1987b). Suggestibility of children's memory: Psycholegal implications. *Journal of Experimental Psychology: General, 116*(1), 38–49.

Chafe, W. L. (1994). *Discourse, consciousness and time: The flow and displacement of conscious experience in speaking and writing.* Chicago: University of Chicago Press.

Chandler, C. C. (1991). How memory for an event is influenced by related events: Interference in modified recognition tests. *Journal of Experimental Psychology: Learning, Memory, and Cognition, 17*(1), 115–125.

Chandler, C. C. (1992). Accessing related events increases retroactive interference in a matching recognition test. *Journal of Experimental Psychology: Learning, Memory, and Cognition, 17,* 115–125.

Chase, W. G., & Ericsson, K. A. (1981). Skilled memory. In J. R. Anderson (Ed.), *Cognitive skills and their acquisition* (pp. 141–189). Hillsdale, NJ: Lawrence Erlbaum.

Chase, W. G., & Ericsson, K. A. (1982). Exceptional memory. *American Scientist, 70*(6), 607–615.

Chase, W. G., & Simon, H. A. (1973). Perception in chess. *Cognitive Psychology, 4*(1), 55–81.

Cheesman, J., & Merikle, P. M. (1986). Distinguishing conscious from unconscious perceptual processes. *Canadian Journal of Psychology, 40,* 343–367.

Chi, M. T. H., de Leeuw, N., Chiu, M.-H., & LaVancher, C. (1994). Eliciting self-explanations improves understanding. *Cognitive Science, 18*(3), 439–477.

Chiappe, P., Hasher, L., & Siegel, L. S. (2000). Working memory, inhibitory control, and reading disability. *Memory Cognition, 28*(1), 8–17.

Chodoff, P. (1963). Late effects on the concentration camp syndrome. *Archives of General Psychiatry, 8*(4), 323–333.

Chomsky, N. (1986). *Knowledge of language: Its nature, origin, and use.* New York: Praeger.

Chomsky, N. (2000). *New horizons in the study of language and mind.* New York: Cambridge University Press.

Christiansen, D. R. (1989). The influence of choice and elimination attributes on the process of tourist evoked set formation. *Dissertation Abstracts International, 50*(5A), 1435.

Christianson, S. A., & Engelberg, E. (1999). Memory and emotional consistency: The MS Estonia ferry disaster. *Memory, 7,* 471–482.

Christianson, S. A., & Hubinette, B. (1993). Hands up! A study of witnesses' emotional reactions and memories associated with bank robberies. *Applied Cognitive Psychology, 7*(5), 365–379.

Christodoulou, G. B. (1986). The syndrome of Capgras. *British Journal of Psychiatry, 130,* 556–564.

Church, B. A., & Schacter, D. L. (1994). Perceptual specificity of auditory priming: Implicit memory for voice intonation and fundamental frequency. *Journal of Experimental Psychology: Learning, Memory, and Cognition, 20*(3), 521–533.

Churchland, P. (1986). *Neurophilosophy: Toward a unified science of the mind/brain.* Cambridge: MIT Press.

Claparède, E. (1911). Recognition et moite. *Archives de Psychologie. Geneva, 11,* 79–90.

Cohen, B. H., & Saslona, M. (1990). The advantage of being a habitual visualizer. *Journal of Mental Imagery, 14*(3–4), 101–112.

Cohen, M. S., Kosslyn, S. M., & Breiter, H. (1996). Changes in cortical activity during mental rotation: A mapping study using functional MRI. *Journal of Neurology, 119*(Pt. 1), 89–100.

Cohen, N. J. (1996). Functional retrograde amnesia as a model of amnesia for childhood sexual abuse. In K. Pezdek & W. P. Banks (Eds.), *The recovered memory/false memory debate* (pp. 81–95). San Diego, CA: Academic Press.

Cole, W. G. (1980). Access and judgment in semantic memory. *Dissertation Abstracts International, 41*(5B), 1949–1950.

Coleman-Mesches, K., Salinas, J. A., & McGaugh, J. L. (1996). Unilateral amygdala inactivation after training attenuates memory for reduced reward. *Behavioural Brain Research, 77*(1–2), 175–180.

Colgrove, F. W. (1899). Individual memories. *American Journal of Psychology, 10,* 228–255.

Colle, H. A., & Welch, A. (1976). Acoustic masking in primary memory. *Journal of Verbal Learning and Verbal Behavior, 15,* 17–32.

Collins, A. M., & Loftus, E. F. (1975). A spreading-activation theory of semantic processing. *Psychological Review, 82*(6), 407–428.

Collins, A. M., & Quillian, M. R. (1969). Retrieval time from semantic memory. *Journal of Verbal Learning and Verbal Behavior, 8*(2), 240–247.

Collins, A. M., & Quillian, M. R. (1972). Experiments on semantic memory and language comprehension. In L. W. Gregg (Ed.), *Cognition in learning and memory* (pp. 117–147). Oxford, UK: Wiley.

Coltheart, M. (1983). Iconic memory. *Philosophical Transactions of the Royal Society, London, 302,* 283–294.

Coltheart, M., & Glick, M. J. (1974). Visual imagery: A case study. *Quarterly Journal of Experimental Psychology, 26,* 438–453.

Coltheart, V. (1977). Recognition errors after incidental learning as a function of different levels of processing. *Journal of Experimental Psychology: Human Learning & Memory, 3*(4), 437–444.

Conrad, R. (1964). Acoustic confusions in immediate memory. *British Journal of Psychology, 55,* 75–84.

Conrad, R. (1967). Interference or decay over short-term intervals? *Journal of Verbal Learning and Verbal Behavior, 6,* 49–54.

Conrad, R., & Hull, A. J. (1968). Input modality and the serial position curve in short term memory. *Psychonomic Science, 10*(4), 135.

Conway, A. R., & Engle, R. (1994). Working memory and retrieval: A resource-dependent inhibition model. *Journal of Experimental Psychology: Learning, Memory, and Cognition, 20*(5), 1088–1098.

Conway, A. R., Kane, M. J., & Engle, R. W. (2003). Working memory capacity and its relation to general intelligence. *Trends in Cognitive Science, 7*(12), 447–552.

Conway, M. A. (1992). A structural model of autobiographical memory. In M. A. Conway, D. C. Rubin, H. Spinnler, & W. A. Wagenaar (Eds.), *Theoretical perspectives on autobiographical memory* (Vol. 65, pp. 167–193). Dordrecht, The Netherlands: Kluwer Academic.

Conway, M. A. (1995). Autobiographical knowledge and autobiographical memories. In D. C. Rubin (Ed.), *Remembering our past: Studies in autobiographical memory.* New York: Cambridge University Press.

Conway, M. A. (1996). Autobiographical memory. In E. L. Bjork & R. A. Bjork (Eds.), *Memory.* San Diego, CA: Academic Press.

Conway, M. A. (1997). Past and present: Recovered memories and false memories. In M. A. Conway (Ed.), *Recovered memories and false memories.* Oxford, UK: Oxford University Press.

Conway, M. A., & Bekerian, D. A. (1987). Organization in autobiographical memory. *Memory & Cognition, 15,* 119–132.

Conway, M. A., Collins, A. F., Gathercole, S. E., & Anderson, S. J. (1996). Recollections of true and false autobiographical memories. *Journal of Experimental Psychology: General, 125,* 69–95.

Conway, M. A., & Haque, S. (1999). Overshadowing the reminiscence bump: Memories of a struggle for independence. *Journal of Adult Development, 6,* 35–44.

Conway, M. A., Pleydell-Pearce, C. W., & Whitecross, S. E. (2001). The neuroanatomy of autobiographical memory: A slow cortical potentials (SPCs) study of autobiographical memory retrieval. *Journal of Memory and Language, 45,* 493–524.

Conway, M. A., Turk, D. J., Miller, S. L., Logan, J., Nebes, R. D., Meltzer, C. C., & Becker, J. T. (1999). A positron emission tomography (PET) study of autobiographical memory material. In J. K. Foster (Ed.), *Neuroimaging and memory: A special issue of the journal Memory* (pp. 679–702). Hove, UK: Psychology Press.

Cooper, L. A., & Lang, J. M. (1996). Imagery and visual-spatial representations. In E. L. Bjork & R. A. Bjork (Eds.), *Handbook of perception and cognition: Vol. 10. Memory* (pp. 129–164). San Diego, CA: Academic Press.

Cooper, L. A., & Shepard, R. N. (1973). Chronometric studies of the rotation of mental images. In W. G. Chase (Ed.), *Visual information processing* (pp. 75–176). New York: Academic Press.

Cooper, L. A., & Shepard, R. N. (1975). Mental transformation in the identification of left and right hands. *Journal of Experimental Psychology: Human Perception and Performance, 1,* 48–56.

Corballis, M. C. (1966). Rehearsal and decay in immediate recall of visually and aurally presented items. *Canadian Journal of Psychology, 20,* 43–51.

Corcoran, D. W. (1971). *Pattern recognition.* Oxford, UK: Penguin.

Corkin, S. (1968). Acquisition of motor skill after bilateral medial temporal lobe excision. *Neuropsychologia, 6,* 255–265.

Cowan, N. (1988). Evolving conceptions of memory storage, selective attention, and their mutual constraints within the human information-processing system. *Psychological Bulletin, 104*(2), 163–191.

Cowan, N. (1993). Activation, attention, and short-term memory. *Memory & Cognition, 21*(2), 162–167.

Cowan, N. (1995). *Attention and memory: An integrated framework*. New York: Oxford University Press.

Cowan, N. (1997). The development of working memory. In N. Cowan (Ed.), *The development of memory in childhood* (pp. 163–199). Hove, UK: Psychology Press.

Cowan, N. (1999). An embedded-processes model of working memory. In A. Miyake & P. Shah (Eds.), *Models of working memory: Mechanisms of active maintenance and executive control* (pp. 62–101). New York: Cambridge University Press.

Cowan, N. (2001). Processing limits of selective attention and working memory: Potential implications for interpreting. *Interpreting, 5*(2), 117–146.

Cowan, N., Lichty, W., & Groove, T. (1988). Memory for unattended speech during silent reading. In M. M. Gruneberg, P. E. Morris, & R. N. Sykes (Eds.), *Practical aspects of memory: Current research and issues* (Vol. 2, pp. 327–330). Chichester, UK: Wiley.

Craik, F. I. M., Govoni, R., Naveh-Benjamin, M., & Anderson, N. D. (1997). The effects of divided attention on encoding and retrieval processes in human memory. *Journal of Experimental Psychology: General, 125,* 159–180.

Craik, F. I. M., & Jacoby, L. L. (1975). A process view of short-term retention. In F. Restle, R. M. Shiffin, J. J. Castellan, M. R. Lindman, & D. B. Pisoni (Eds.), *Cognitive theory* (Vol. 1, pp. 173–192). Hillsdale, NJ: Lawrence Erlbaum.

Craik, F. I. M., & Lockheart, R. S. (1972). Levels of processing: A framework for memory research. *Journal of Verbal Learning and Verbal Behavior, 11*(6), 671–684.

Craik, F. I. M., Moroz, T. M., Moscovitch, M., Stuss, D. T., Winocur, G., Tulving, E., et al. (1998). In search of self: A PET investigation of self-referential information. *Psychological Science, 10*(1), 26–34.

Craik, F. I. M., & Tulving, E. (1975). Depth of processing and the retention of words in episodic memory. *Journal of Experimental Psychology: General, 104*(3), 268–294.

Crombag, H. F., Wagenaar, W. A., & von Koppen, P. J. (1996). Crashing memories and the problem of "source monitoring." *Applied Cognitive Psychology, 10*(2), 95–104.

Crovitz, H. F., Harvey, M. T., & McClanahan, S. (1981). Hidden memory: A rapid method for the study of amnesia using perceptual learning. *Cortex, 17,* 273–278.

Crovitz, H. F., & Schiffman, H. (1974). Frequency of episodic memories as a function of their age. *Bulletin of the Psychonomic Society, 4,* 517–518.

Crowder, R. G. (1972). Visual and auditory memory. In J. F. Kavanagh & I. G. Mattingley (Eds.), *Language by ear and eye: The relation between speech and learning to read* (pp. 251–275). Cambridge: MIT Press.

Crowder, R. G. (1976). *Principles of learning and memory*. Hillsdale, NJ: Lawrence Erlbaum.

Crowder, R. G. (1992). Eidetic imagery. In L. R. Squiure (Ed.), *Encyclopedia of learning and memory*. New York: Macmillan.

Crowder, R. G., & Morton, J. (1969). Precategorical acoustic storage (PAS). *Perception & Psychophysics, 5,* 365–373.

Curran, T. (2000). Brain potentials of recollection and familiarity. *Memory & Cognition, 28,* 923–938.

Curran, T., & Hintzman, D. L. (1997). Consequences and causes of correlation in process dissociation. *Journal of Experimental Psychology: Learning, Memory, and Cognition, 23,* 496–504.

Cutler, B. L., Penrod, S. D., & Stuve, T. E. (1988). Juror decision making in eyewitness identification cases. *Law and Human Behavior, 12*(1), 41–55.

Cutting, J. (1991). Delusional identification and the role of the right hemisphere in appreciation of identity. *British Journal of Psychiatry, 159*, 70–75.

Daffenbacher, K. A. (1980). Eyewitness accuracy and confidence: Can we infer anything about their relationship? *Law and Human Behavior, 4*(4), 243–260.

Daffenbacher, K. A. (1991). A maturing of research on the behavior of eyewitnesses. *Applied Cognitive Psychology, 5*(5), 377–402.

Da Fontoura, H. A., & Siegel, L. S. (1995). Reading, syntactic, and working memory skills of bi-lingual Portuguese and English Canadian children. *Reading & Writing, 7*, 139–153.

Dalla Barba, G. (1995). Consciousness and confabulation: Remembering "another" past. In R. Campbell & M. P. Conway (Eds.), *Broken memories: Case studies in memory impairment* (pp. 101–114). Cambridge, MA: Blackwell.

Damasio, A. R. (1990). Catergory-related recognition defects as a clue to the neural substrates of knowledge. *Trends in Neuroscience, 13*, 95–98.

Daneman, M., & Carpenter, P. A. (1980). Individual differences in working memory and reading. *Journal of Verbal Learning and Verbal Behavior, 19*(4), 450–466.

Daneman, M., & Merikle, P. (1997). Working memory and language comprehension: A meta analysis. *Psychological Bulletin and Review, 3*, 422–433.

Danziger, H., Kingstone, A., & Rafal, R. (1998). *Psychological Science, 9*(2), 119–123.

Darwin, C. J., & Baddeley, A. D. (1974). Acoustic memory and the perception of speech. *Cognitive Psychology, 6*, 41–60.

Darwin, C. J., Turvey, M. T., & Crowder, R. G. (1972). An auditory analogue of the Sperling partial report procedure: Evidence for brief auditory storage. *Cognitive Psychology, 3*, 255–267.

Davidoff, J. B., & Ostergard, A. L. (1984). Colour anomia resulting from weakened short-term color memory. *Brain, 107*, 415–430.

Deatherage, B. H., & Evans, T. R. (1969). Binaural masking: Backward, forward, and simultaneous effects. *Journal of the Acoustical Society of America, 46*, 362–371.

DeBeni, R., Palladino, P., Pazzaglia, F., & Cornoldi, C. (1998). Increases in intrusion errors and working memory deficit of poor comprehenders. *Quarterly Journal of Experimental Psychology: Human Experimental Psychology, 51A*(2), 305–320.

Debner, J. A., & Jacoby, L. L. (1994). Unconscious perception: Attention, awareness, and control. *Journal of Experimental Psychology: Learning, Memory and Cognition, 20*, 304–317.

Descartes, R. (1901). *Meditations* (J. Veitsch, Trans.). New York: Tudor.

Deese, J. (1959). On the prediction of occurrence of particular verbal intrusions in immediate recall. *Journal of Experimental Psychology, 58*, 17–22.

Deese, J. (1961). From the isolated verbal unit to connected discourse. In C. N. Cofer (Ed.), *Verbal learning and verbal behavior*. New York: McGraw-Hill.

Delbecq-Derousne, J., Beauvois, M. F., & Shallice, T. (1990). Preserved recall versus impaired recognition. *Brain, 113*, 1045–1074.

Dell, G. S. (1986). A spreading activation theory of retrieval in sentence production. *Journal of Experimental Psychology: Learning, Memory, and Cognition, 12*, 207–208.

Dempster, F. N. (1985). Proactive interference in sentence recall: Topic-similarity effects and individual differences. *Memory & Cognition, 13*(1), 81–89.

Dempster, F. N., & Cooney, J. (1982). Individual differences in digit span, susceptibility to proactive inference, and aptitude/achievement test scores. *Intelligence, 6*(4), 399–416.

Dennett, D. (1991). *Consciousness explained*. Boston: Little, Brown.

Dennett, D. C. (1969). *Content and consciousness*. London: Routledge & Kegan Paul.

Dennis, S., & Humphreys, M. (2001). A context noise model of episodic word recognition. *Psychological Review, 108,* 452–478.

De Renzi, E., Liotti, M., & Nichelli, P. (1987). Semantic amnesia with preservation of auto-biographic memory: A case report. *Cartox, 23*(4), 575–597.

De Vega, M. (1995). Backward updating of mental models during continuous reading of narratives. *Journal of Experimental Psychology: Learning, Memory, and Cognition, 21,* 373–385.

Diamond, R. J., & Rozin, P. (1984). Activation of existing memories in anterograde amnesia. *Journal of Abnormal Psychology, 93*(1), 98–105.

Dick, A. O. (1971). On the problem of selection in short-term visual (iconic) memory. *Canadian Journal of Psychology, 25,* 250–263.

Diener, E., & Diener, C. (1996). Most people are happy. *Psychological Science, 7,* 181–185.

Diwadkar, U. A., Carpenter, P. A., & Just, M. A. (2000). Collaborative activity between parietal and dorso-lateral prefrontal cortex in dynamic spatial working memory revealed by fMRI. *Neuroimage, 12,* 85–99.

Dixon, P., Harrison, K., & Taylor, D. (1993). Effects of sentence form on the construction of mental plans from procedural discourse. *Canadian Journal of Experimental Psychology, 47*(2), 375–400.

Dodd, D. H., & Bradshaw, J. M. (1980). Leading questions and memory: Pragmatic constraints. *Journal of Verbal Learning and Verbal Behavior, 21,* 695–704.

Donaldson, D. I., Peterson, S. E., & Buckner, R. L. (2001). Dissociating memory retrieval processes using fMRI: Evidence that priming does not support recognition memory. *Neuron, 31*(6), 1047–1059.

Dong, T. (1972). Probe versus free recall. *Journal of Verbal Learning and Verbal Behavior, 11*(5), 654–661.

Dosher, B. A., & Rosedale, G. (1989). Integrated retrieval cues as a mechanism for priming in retrieval from memory. *Journal of Experimental Psychology: General, 118*(2), 191–211.

Dosher, B. A., McElree, B., & Hood, R. M. (1989). Retrieval dynamics of priming in recognition memory. *Journal of Experimental Psychology: Learning, Memory, and Cognition, 15*(5), 868–886.

Doyle, J. (2001). Discounting the error cost: Cross-racial false alarms in the culture of contemporary criminal justice. *Psychology of Public Policy and Law, 7,* 253–262.

Dudycha, G. J., & Dudycha, M. M. (1933). Some factors and characteristics of childhood memories. *Child Development, 4,* 265–278.

Duff, S. C., & Logie, R. H. (2001). Processing and storage in working memory span. *Quarterly Journal of Experimental Psychology, 54,* 31–48.

Dunning, D., & Perretta, S. (2002). Automaticity and eyewitness accuracy: A 10- to 12-second rule for distinguishing accurate from inaccurate positive identifications. *Journal of Applied Psychology, 87*(5), 951–962.

Eakin, D. K., Schreiber, T. A., & Sergeant-Marshall, S. (2003). Misinformation effects in eyewitness memory: The presence and absence of memory impairment as a function of warning and misinformation. *Journal of Experimental Psychology: Learning, Memory, and Cognition, 29*(5), 813–825.

Ebbinghaus, H. (1964). *Memory: A contribution to experimental psychology* (H. A. Ruger, Trans.). Toronto, Ontario, Canada: Dover. (Original work published 1885)

Efron, R. (1970a). Effect of stimulus duration on perceptual onset and offset latencies. *Perception & Psychophysics, 8,* 231–234.

Efron, R. (1970b). The minimum duration of a perception. *Neuropsychologia, 8,* 57–63.

Eimas, P. D., & Quinn, D. C. (1994). Studies on the formation of perceptually based basic-level categories in young infants. *Child Development, 65*(3), 903–917.

Einstein, G. O., & McDaniel, M. A. (2005). Prospective memory: Multiple retrieval processes. *Current Directions in Psychological Science, 14*(6), 286–290.

Eisen, M. L., & Carlson, E. B. (1998). Individual differences in suggestibility: Examining the influence of dissociation, absorption, and a history of childhood abuse. *Applied Cognitive Psychology, 12,* S47–S61.

Ellis, H. C., & Ashbrook, P. W. (1991). The "state" of mood and memory research: A selective review. In D. Kuiken (Ed.), *Mood and memory.* (Special Issue) *Journal of Social Behavior and Personality, 4,* 1–21.

Ellis, N. C., & Hennely, R. A. (1980). A bilingual word-length effect: Implications for intelligence testing and the relative ease of mental calculation in Welsh and English. *British Journal of Psychology, 71,* 43–52.

Ellis, W. (1992). Satanic ritual abuse and legend ostension. *Journal of Psychology and Theology, 20*(3), 274–277.

Elman, J. L., Bates, E. A., Johnson, M. H., & Karmiloff-Smith, A. (1996). *Rethinking innateness: A connectionist perspective on development.* Cambridge: MIT Press.

Engle, R. W., Cantor, I., & Carullo, J. J. (1992). Individual differences in working memory and comprehension: A test for hypotheses. *Journal of Experimental Psychology: Learning, Memory and Cognition, 18*(5), 972–992.

Engle, R. W., Carullo, J. J., & Collins, K. W. (1991). Individual differences in working memory for comprehension and following directions. *Journal of Educational Research, 84*(5), 253–262.

Engle, R. W., Kane, M. J., & Tuholski, S. W. (1999). Individual differences in working memory capacity and what they tell us about controlled attention, general fluid intelligence, and functions of the prefrontal cortex. In A. Miyake & P. Shah (Eds.), *Models of working memory: Mechanisms of active maintenance and executive control* (pp. 102–134). New York: Cambridge University Press.

Engle, R. W., Nations, J. K., & Cantor, J. (1990). Is "working memory capacity" just another name for word knowledge? *Journal of Education Psychology, 82*(4), 799–804.

Er, N. (2003). A new flashbulb memory model applied to the Marmara earthquake. *Applied Cognitive Psychology, 17*(5), 503–517.

Erdelyi, M. H., & Becker, J. (1974). Hypermnesia for pictures but not words in multiple recall trials. *Cognitive Psychology, 6,* 159–171.

Ericsson, K. A. (1985). Memory skill. *Canadian Journal of Psychology, 39*(2), 188–231.

Ericsson, K. A., & Chase, W. G. (1982). Exceptional memory. *American Scientist, 70*(6), 607–615.

Ericsson, K. A., & Delaney, P. F. (1999). Long-term working memory as an alternative to capacity models of working memory in everyday skilled performance. In A. Miyake & P. Shah (Eds.), *Models of working memory: Mechanisms of active maintenance and executive control* (pp. 257–297). New York: Cambridge University Press.

Ericsson, K. A., & Kintsch, W. (1995). Long-term working memory. *Psychological Review, 102*(2), 211–245.

Estes, W. K. (1972). An associative basis for coding and organization in memory. In A. W. Melton & E. Martin (Eds.), *Coding processes in human memory* (pp. 161–190). Washington, DC: Winston.

Estes, W. K. (1974). Redundancy of noise elements and signals in visual detection of letters. *Perception & Psychophysics, 16*(1), 53–60.

Estes, W. K. (1986). Memory storage and retrieval processes in category learning. *Journal of Experimental Psychology: General, 115*(2), 155–174.

Esteves, F., Dimberg, U., & Öhman, A. (1994). Automatically elicited fear: Conditioned skin conductance responses to masked facial expressions. *Cognition & Emotion, 8,* 393–413.

Eysenck, M. W., & Calvo, M. G. (1992). Anxiety and performance: The processing efficiency theory. *Cognition & Emotion, 6*(6), 409–434.

Farah, M. J., & McClelland, J. L. (1991). A computational model of semantic memory impairment: Modality specificity and emergent category specificity. *Journal of Experimental Psychology: General, 120*(4), 339–357.

Farah, M. J., Peronnet, F., Gonon, M., & Girard, M. (1988). Electrophysiological evidence for a shared representational medium for visual images and visual perception. *Journal of Experimental Psychology: General, 117*(3), 248–257.

Fernandez-Duque, D., & Thornton, I. M. (2000). Change detection without awareness. Do explicit reports underestimate the representation of change in the visual system? *Visual Cognition, 7,* 323–344.

Ferreira, F., & Clifton, C. (1986). The independence of syntactic processing. *Journal of Memory and Language, 25*(3), 348–368.

Fink, G., Markowitsch, H., Reinkmeier, M., Bruckbauer, T., Kessler, J., & Heiss, W. (1996). Cerebral representation of one's own past: Neural networks involved in autobiographical memory. *Journal of Neuroscience, 16*(13), 4275–4282.

Finke, R. A., & Pinker, S. (1982). Spontaneous imagery scanning in mental extrapolation. *Journal of Experimental Psychology, Learning, Memory, and Cognition, 8,* 142–147.

Finke, R. A., & Schmidt, M. J. (1977). Orientation specific color aftereffect following imagination. *Journal of Experimental Psychology: Human Perception and Performance, 3*(4), 599–206

Finkelhof, D. (1994). Current information on the scope and nature of child sexual abuse. *Future of Children, 4*(2), 31–35.

Fisher, R. P., & Craik, F. I. (1977). Interaction between encoding and retrieval operations in cued recall. *Journal of Experimental Psychology: Human Learning and Memory, 3*(6), 701–711.

Fisk, A. D., & Schneider, W. (1984). Memory as a function of attention, level of processing, and automatization. *Journal of Experimental Psychology: Learning, Memory and Cognition, 10*(2), 181–197.

Fivush, R., & Haden, C. A. (2003). *Autobiographical memory and construction of a narrative self.* Mahwah, NJ: Lawrence Erlbaum.

Fleischman, D. A., & Gabrieli, J. D. E. (1998). Repetition priming in normal aging and Alzheimer's disease: A review of findings and theories. *Psychology and Aging, 13*(1), 88–119.

Fletcher, C. R. (1994). Levels of representation in memory for discourse. In M. A. Gernsbacher (Ed.), *Handbook of psycholinguistics* (pp. 589–607). San Diego, CA: Academic Press.

Foa, E. B., Rothbaum, E. O., Riggs, D., & Murdock, T. (1991). Treatment of posttraumatic stress disorder in rape victims: A comparison between cognitive behavioral procedures and counseling. *Journal of Consulting and Clinical Psychology, 59*(5), 715–723.

Fodor, J. A. (1975). *The language of thought.* New York: Thomas Y. Crowell.

Fodor, J. A. (1983). *Modularity of mind: An essay in faculty psychology.* Cambridge: MIT Press.

Frankel, F. H. (1994). The concept of flashbacks in historical perspective. *International Journal of Clinical and Experimental Hypnosis, 42*(2), 321–336.

Frankish, C. (1985). Modality-specific grouping effects in short-term memory. *Journal of Memory and Language, 24*(2), 200–209.

Franklin, S. P. (1995). *Artificial minds.* Cambridge: MIT Press.

Fredrickson, B. L., & Branigan, C. (2005). Positive emotions broaden and scope of attention and thought-action repertoires. *Cognition & Emotion, 19,* 313–332.

Frederickson, R. (1992). *Repressed memories: A journey to recovery from sexual abuse.* New York: Simon & Schuster.

Freud, S. (1963). Introductory lectures on psycho-analysis. In J. Strachey (Ed. & Trans.), *The standard edition of the complete psychological works of Sigmund Freud* (Vol. 15–16, pp. 243–496). London: Hogarth Press. (Original work published 1916–1917)

Friedman, A. (1979). Framing pictures: the role of knowledge in automatized encoding and memory for gist. *Journal of Experimental Psychology: General, 108*, 316–355.

Friedman, D., & Trott, C. (2000). An event-related study of encoding in young and older adults. *Neuropsychologia, 38*(5), 542–557.

Gallo, D. A., & Roediger, H. L., III. (2002). Variability among word lists in evoking associative memory illusions. *Journal of Memory and Language, 47*, 469–497.

Galton, F. (1879). Psychometric experiments. *Brain, 2*, 149–162.

Ganaway, G. K. (1991, August). *Alternative hypotheses regarding satanic ritual abuse memories.* Paper presented at the annual meeting of the American Psychological Association, San Francisco.

Ganis, G., Thompson, W. L., & Kosslyn, S. M. (2005). Brain areas underlying visual mental imagery and visual perception: An fMRI study. *Cognitive Brain Research, 22* (2), 226–241.

Garrod, S., Freudenthal, D., & Boyle, E. A. (1994). The role of different types of anaphor in the on-line resolution of sentences in a discourse. *Journal of Memory and Language, 33*(1), 39–68.

Garry, M., & Polashcek, D. L. L. (2000). Imagination and memory. *Current Directions in Psychological Science, 9*, 6–10.

Geiselman, R. E., Fisher, R. P., MacKinnon, D. P., & Holland, H. L. (1985). Eyewitness memory enhancement in the police interview: Cognitive retrieval mnemonics versus hypnosis. *Journal of Applied Psychology, 70*, 401–412.

Geiselman, R. E., Fisher, R. P., MacKinnon, D. P., & Holland, D. L. (1986). Enhancement of eyewitness memory with the cognitive interview. *American Journal of Psychology, 99*, 385–401.

Geiselman, R. E., Schroppel, T., Tubridy, A., Kinishi, T., & Rodriguez, V. (2000). Objectivity bias in eyewitness performance. *Applied Cognitive Psychology, 14*(4), 323–332.

Gergen, K. J. (2000). *Technology, self, and the moral project.* New Brunswick, NJ: Transaction.

Gernsbacher, M. A., Goldsmith, H. H., & Robertson, R. R., (1992). Do readers mentally represent characters' emotional states? *Cognition & Emotion, 6*, 89–111.

Gernsbacher, M. A., & Robertson, R. R. (1992). Knowledge activation versus sentence mapping when representing fictional characters' emotional states. *Language and Cognitive Processes, 7*(3–4), 353–371.

Gick, M. L., Craik, F. I., & Morris, R. G. (1988). Processing resources and age differences in working memory. *Memory & Cognition, 16*(4), 362–366.

Gillund, G., & Shiffrin, R. (1981). Free recall of complex pictures and abstract words. *Journal of Verbal Learning and Verbal Behavior, 20*(5), 575–592.

Gillund, G., & Shiffrin, R. M. (1984). A retrieval model for both recognition and recall. *Psychological Review, 91*, 1–65.

Glanzer, M., & Cunitz, A. R. (1966). Two storage mechanisms in free recall. *Journal of Verbal Learning and Verbal Behavior, 5*, 351–360.

Glanzer, M., Fischer, B., & Dorfman, D. (1984). Short-term storage in reading. *Journal of Verbal Learning and Verbal Behavior, 23*(4), 467–486.

Glass, A. L., & Holyoak, K. G. (1986). *Cognition.* New York: Random House.

Glenberg, A. M., & Langston, W. E. (1992). Comprehension of illustrated text: Pictures help to build mental models. *Journal of Memory and Language, 31*(2), 129–151.

Glenberg, A. M., Meyer, M., & Lindem, K. (1987). Mental models contribute to foregrounding during text comprehension. *Journal of Memory and Language, 26*(1), 69–83.

Glenn, C. G. (1978). The role of episodic structure ansd of story length in children's recall of simple stories. *Journal of Verbal Learning and Verbal Behavior, 17*(2), 229–247.

Glisky, E. L. (1995). Acquisition and transfer of word processing skill by an amnesic patient. *Neuropsychological Rehabilitation, 5*(4), 299–318.

Glisky, E. L., & Schacter, D. L. (1987). Acquisition of domain-specific knowledge in organic amnesia: Training for computer related work. *Neuropsychologia, 25*(6), 893–906.

Glisky, E. L., & Schacter, D. L. (1989). Extending the limits of complex learning in organic amnesia: Computer training in a vocational domain. *Neuropsychologia, 27*(1), 107–120.

Glucksberg, S., & Cowan, G. N., Jr. (1970). Memory for non-attended auditory material. *Cognitive Psychology, 1,* 149–156.

Godden, D. R., & Baddeley, A. D. (1975). Context-dependent memory in two natural environments: On land and underwater. *British Journal of Psychology, 66*(3), 325–331.

Goff, L. M., & Roediger, H. L. (1998, November). *Imagination inflation: Multiple imaginings can lead to false recollection of one's actions.* Paper presented at the 37th annual meeting of the Psychonomic Society, Chicago.

Golby, A. J., Gabrieli, J. D., Chiao, J. Y., & Eberhardt, J. L. (2001). Different responses in the fusiform region to same races and other races. *Nature Neuroscience, 4,* 845–850.

Gold, P. E. (1995). Modulation of emotional and nonemotional memories: Same pharmacological systems, different neuroanatomical systems. In J. L. McGaugh, N. M. Weinberger, & G. Lunch (Eds.), *Brain and memory* (pp. 41–74). New York: Oxford University Press.

Gold, P. E., & Stone, W. S. (1988). Neuroendocrine effects on memory in aged rodents and humans. *Neurobiology of Aging, 9*(5–6), 709–717.

Gold, P. E., & Van Buskirk, R. B. (1975). Facilitation of time-dependent memory processes with posttrial epinephrine injections. *Behavioral Biology, 13*(2), 145–153.

Golden, R. M., & Rumelhart, D. E. (1993). A parallel distributed processing model of story comprehension and recall. *Discourse Processes, 16*(3), 203–207.

Goldstein, E. C. (1992). *Confabulations: Creating false memories, destroying families.* Boca Raton, FL: SirS.

Goldstein, G., van Kammen, W., Shelly, C., Miller, D. J., & van Kammen, D. P. (1987). Survivors of imprisonment in the Pacific theater during World War II. *American Journal of Psychiatry, 144,* 1210–1213.

Gonsalves, B., Reber, P., & Gitelman, D. R. (2004). *Psychological Science, 15*(10), 655–660.

Goodglass, H., Klein, B., & Carey, P. (1966). Specific semantic work categories in aphasia. *Cortex, 2*(1), 74–87.

Goodman, F. D. (1988). *How about demons? Possession and exorcism in the modern world.* Bloomington: Indiana University Press.

Goodman, G. S., & Aman, C. (1990). Children's use of anatomically detailed dolls to recount an event. *Child Development, 61*(6), 1859–1871.

Goodman, G. S., Rudy, L., Bottoms, B. L., & Aman, C. (1990). Children's concerns and memory: Issues of ecological validity in the study of children's eyewitness testimony. In R. Fivush & J. A. Hudson (Eds.), *Knowing and remembering in young children. Emory symposia in cognition* (Vol. 3, pp. 249–284). New York: Cambridge University Press.

Goodwin, D. W., Powell, B., Bremer, D., Hoine, H., & Stern, J. (1969). Alcohol and recall: State dependent effects in man. *Science, 163,* 1358.

Graesser, A. C., Baggett, W., & Williams, K. (1996). Question-driven explanatory reasoning. *Applied Cognitive Psychology, 10,* 517–531.

Graesser, A. C., Gordon, S. E., & Sawyer, J. D. (1979). Recognition memory for typical and atypical actions in scripted activities: Tests of a script pointer and tag hypothesis. *Journal of Verbal Learning and Verbal Behavior, 18*(3), 319–332.

Graesser, A. C., Millis, K. K., & Zwaan, R. A. (1997). Discourse comprehension. *Annual Review of Psychology, 48,* 163–189.

Graesser, A. C., Singer, M., & Trabasso, T. (1994). Constructing inferences during narrative text comprehension. *Psychological Review, 101*(3), 371–395.

Graf, P., & Ryan, L. (1990). Transfer appropriate processing for explicit and implicit memory. *Journal of Experimental Psychology: Learning, Memory, and Cognition, 16*(6), 978–992.

Graf, P., & Schacter, D. L. (1985). Implicit and explicit memory for new associations in normal and amnesic subjects. *Journal of Experimental Psychology: Learning, Memory, and Cognition, 11,* 501–518.

Graf, P., & Schacter, D. L. (1987). Selective effects of interference on implicit and explicit memory for new associations. *Journal of Experimental Psychology: Learning, Memory, and Cognition, 13*(1), 45–53.

Graham, K., Patterson, K., & Hodges, J. R. (1995). Progressive pure anomia: Insufficient activation of phonology by meaning. *Neurocase 1*(1), 25–38.

Gray, C. R., & Gummerman, K. (1975). The enigmatic eidetic image: Methods, data and theory. *Psychological Bulletin, 82,* 383–407.

Gray, M. J., & Lombardo, T. W. (2001). Complexity of trauma narratives as an index of fragmented memory in PTSD. *Journal of Applied Cognitive Psychology, 15,* 171–185.

Greene, E., Flynn, M. S., & Loftus, E. F. (1982). Inducing resistance to misleading information. *Journal of Verbal Learning and Verbal Behavior, 21*(2), 207–219.

Gregg, V. (1976). Word frequency, recognition and recall. In J. Brown (Ed.), *Recall and recognition* (Vol. 10, pp. 183–216). Oxford, UK: Wiley.

Greenwald, A. G., & Banaji, M. R. (1995). Implicit social cognition: Attitudes, self-esteem, and stereotypes. *Psychological Review, 102,* 4–27.

Grossberg, S., & Stone, G. (1986). Neural dynamics of word recognition and recall: Attentional priming, learning and resonance. *Psychological Review, 93,* 46–74.

Gruneberg, M. M. (1992). The practical application of memory aids: Knowing how, knowing when, and knowing when not. In M. M. Gruneberg & P. E. Morris (Eds.), *Aspects of memory: Vol. 1. The practical aspects* (2nd ed., pp. 168–195). Florence, KY: Taylor & Francis/Routledge.

Gudjonsson, G. H. (1988). Interrogative suggestibility: Its relationship with assertiveness, social-evaluative anxiety, state anxiety and method of coping. *British Journal of Clinical Psychology, 27*(2), 159–166.

Gunter, B., Berry, C., & Clifford, B. R. (1981). Proactive interference effects with television news items: Further evidence. *Journal of Experimental Psychology: Human Learning and Memory, 7,* 480–487.

Gunzelmann, G., & Anderson, J. R. (2001). *An ACT-R model of the evolution of strategy use and problem difficulty.* Mahwah, NJ: Lawrence Erlbaum.

Haber, R. N. (1979). 20 years of haunting eidetic imagery: Where's the ghost? *Behavioral and Brain Sciences, 2*(4), 583–629.

Haber, R. N., & Erdelyi, M. H. (1967). Emergence and recovery of initially unavailable perceptual material. *Journal of Verbal Learning and Verbal Behavior, 6,* 618–628.

Haber, R. N., & Haber, R. B. (1964). Eidetic imagery. I: Frequency. *Perceptual and Motor Skills, 19,* 131–138.

Habib, R., & LePage, M. (2000). Novelty assessment in the brain. In E. Tulving (Ed.), *Memory, consciousness, and the Brain: The Tallinn conference* (pp. 265–277). Philadelphia: Psychology Press/Taylor & Francis.

Haenggi, D., Kintsch, W., & Gernsbacher, M. A. (1995). Spatial situation models and text comprehension. *Discourse Processes, 19*(2), 173–199.

Hamilton, W. (1859). *Lectures on metaphysic and logic* (Vol. 1). Edinburgh: Blackwood.

Hart, J., Berndt, R. S., & Caramazza, A. (1985). Category-specific naming deficit following cerebral infraction. *Nature, 316*(6027), 439–440.

Hartshorn, K., Rovee-Collier, C., Gerhardstein, P., Bhatt, R. S., Wondoloski, T. L., Klein, P., et al. (1998). The ontogeny of long-term memory over the first year-and-a-half of life. *Developmental Psychobiology, 32,* 1–31.

Hasher, L., & Zacks, R. T. (1979). Automatic and effortful processes in memory. *Journal of Experimental Psychology: General, 108,* 356–388.

Hasher, L., & Zacks, R. T. (1984). Automatic processing of fundamental information. *American Psychologist, 39,* 1372–1388.

Hasher, L., & Zacks, R. T. (1988). Working memory, comprehension, and aging: A review and a new view. In G. H. Bower (Ed.), *The psychology of learning and motivation: Advances in research and theory* (Vol. 22, pp. 193–225). San Diego, CA: Academic Press.

Hasher, L., Zacks, R. T., & May, C. P. (1999). Inhibitory control, circadian arousal, and age. In D. Gopher & A. Koriat (Ed.), *Attention and performance XVII: Cognitive regulation of performance: Interaction of theory and application: Vol. 13. Attention and performance* (pp. 653–675). Cambridge: MIT Press.

Hashtroudi, S., Johnson, M. K., & Chrosniak, L. D. (1989). Aging and source monitoring. *Psychology and Aging, 4*(1), 106–112.

Haviland, S. E., & Clark, H. H. (1974). What's new? Acquiring new information as a process in comprehension. *Journal of Verbal Learning and Verbal Behaviour, 13*(5), 512–521.

Healy, A. F. (1974). Separating item from order information in short-term memory. *Journal of Verbal Learning and Verbal Behavior, 13,* 644–655.

Heaps, C. M., & Nash, M. (2001). Comparing recollective experience in true and false autobiographical memories. *Journal of Experimental Psychology: Learning, Memory, and Cognition, 27,* 920–930.

Hebb, D. O. (1961). Sensory deprivation: Facts in search of a theory. Discussion. *Journal of Nervous and Mental Disease, 132,* 40–43.

Heil, M., & Rolke, B. (2004). Automatic semantic activation is no myth. *Psychological Science, 15*(12), 852–857.

Henderson, Z., Bruce, V., & Burton, A. M. (2001). Matching the faces of robbers captured on video. *Applied Cognitive Psychology, 15,* 445–464.

Henri, V., & Henri, C. (1898). Earliest recollections. *Popular Science Monthly, 53,* 108–115.

Henry, J. D., MacLeod, M. S., Phillips, L. H., & Crawford, J. R. (2004). A meta-analytic review of prospective memory and aging. *Psychology and Aging, 19,* 27–39.

Henry, L. A. (1991). Development of auditory memory span: The role of rehearsal. *British Journal of Developmental Psychology, 9,* 493–511.

Henson, R. N. A. (1998). Short-term memory for serial order: The start-end model. *Cognitive Psychology, 36*(2), 73–137.

Henson, R. N. A. (1999). Positional information in short-term memory: Relative or absolute? *Memory & Cognition, 27,* 915–927.

Henson, R. N. A., Rugg, M. D., Shallice, T., Josephs, O., & Dolan, R. J. (1999). Recollection and familiarity in recognition memory: An event-related functional magnetic resonance imaging. *Journal of Neuroscience, 19*(19), 3962–3972.

Herman, J. (1981). Father-daughter incest. *Professional Psychology: Research and Practice, 12*(1), 76–80.

Herman, J. L., & Schatzow, E. (1987). Recovery and verification of memories of childhood sexual trauma. *Psychoanalytic Psychology, 4*(1), 1–14.

Hilgard, E. R. (1965). *Hypnotic susceptibility.* Oxford, UK: Harcourt, Brace & World.

Hillis, A. E., & Caramazza, F. A. (2001). Mechanisms for accessing lexical representations for output: Evidence for a category-specific semantic deficit. *Brain and Language, 40*(1), 106–144.

Hinton, G. E. (1981). Implementing semantic networks in parallel hardware. In G. E. Hinton & J. A. Anderson (Eds.), *Parallel models of associative memory* (pp. 161–187). Hillsdale, NJ: Lawrence Erlbaum.

Hinton, G. E. (1989). Learning distributed representations of concepts. In R. G. M. Morris (Ed.), *Parallel distributed processing: Implications for psychology and neurobiology* (pp. 46–61). Oxford, UK: Clarendon Press.

Hintzman, D. L. (1972). On testing the independence of associations. *Psychological Review, 79*(6), 261–264.

Hintzman, D. L. (1984). MINERVA 2: A simulation model of human memory. *Behavior Research Methods, Instruments and Computers, 16*(2), 96–101.

Hintzman, D. L. (1986). "Schema abstraction" in a multiple-trace memory model. *Psychological Review, 93*(4), 411–428.

Hintzman, D. L. (1988). Judgments of frequency and recognition memory in a multiple trace memory model. *Psychological Review, 95*(4), 528–551.

Hitch, G. J. (1978). The role of short-term memory in mental arithmetic. *Cognitive Psychology, 10*(3), 302–323.

Hitch, G. J. (1990). Developmental fractionation of working memory. In G. Vaar & T. Shallice (Eds.), *Neuropsychological impairments of short-term memory* (pp. 221–246). New York: Cambridge University Press.

Hitch, G. J., Towse, J., & Hutton, U. (2001). What limits children's working memory span? Theoretical accounts and applications for scholastic development. *Journal of Experimental Psychology: General, 130*(2), 713–722.

Hoffman, H. G. (1997). Role of memory strength in reality monitoring decisions: Evidence from source misattribution biases. *Journal of Experimental Psychology: Learning, Memory and Cognition, 23*(2), 371–383.

Hoffman, H. S., Selekman, W. L., & Fleshler, M. (1966). Stimulus aspects of aversive controls: Long-term effects of suppression procedures. *Journal of Experimental Analysis of Behavior, 9*(6), 659–662.

Holender, D. (1986). Semantic activation without conscious identification in dichotic listening, parafoveal vision, and visual masking: A survey and appraisal. *Behavioral and Brain Sciences, 9*, 1–23.

Holmberg, D., & Holmes, J. G. (2001). Reconstruction of relationship memories: A mental models approach. In N. Schwartz & S. Sudman (Eds.), *Autobiographical memory and the validity of retrospective reports*. New York: Springer Verlag.

Holmes, D. S. (1970). Differential change in affective intensity in the forgetting of pleasant and unpleasant experiences. *Journal of Personality and Social Psychology, 3*, 234–239.

Holmes, J. B., Waters, H. S., & Rajaram, S. (1998). The phenomenology of false memories: Episodic content and confidence. *Journal of Experimental Psychology: Learning, Memory, and Cognition, 24*(4), 1026–1040.

Hosch, H. M., & Bothwell, R. K. (1990). Arousal, description and identification accuracy of victims and bystanders. *Journal of Social Behavior and Personality, 5*(5), 481–488.

Hosch, H. M., & Platz, S. J. (1984). Self monitoring and eyewitness accuracy. *Personality and Social Psychology Bulletin, 10*(2), 289–292.

Howard, M. W. (2004). Scaling behavior in the temporal context model. *Journal of Mathematical Psychology, 48*, 230–238.

Howard, M. W., & Kahana, M. J. (2002). A distributed representation of temporal context. *Journal of Mathematical Psychology, 46,* 269–299.

Howard, D., & Orchard-Lisle, V. M. (1984). On the origin of semantic errors in naming: Evidence from the case of a global dysphasic. *Cognitive Neuropsychology, 1,* 163–190.

Howard, D. V., Shaw, R. J., & Heisey, J. G. (1986). Aging and the time course of semantic activation. *Journal of Gerontology, 41,* 195–203.

Howes, M. L. (1994). Dynamics of cognitive development: A unifying approach to universal trends and individual differences. *Learning and Individual Differences, 6*(3), 365–377.

Howes, M. L., & Courage, M. L. (1997). The emergence and early development of autobiographical memory. *Psychological Review, 104*(3), 499–523.

Howes, M. B., Siegel, M., & Brown, F. (1993). Early childhood memories: Accuracy and affect. *Cognition, 47,* 95–119.

Hudson, J. A. (1990). The emergence of autobiographical memory in mother-child conversation. In R. Fivush & J. A. Hudson (Eds.), *Knowing and remembering in young children* (pp. 166–196). New York: Cambridge University Press.

Huitema, J. S., Dopkins, S., Klin, C. M., & Myers, J. L. (1993). Connecting goals and actions during reading. *Journal of Experimental Psychology: Learning, Memory, and Cognition, 19*(5), 1053–1060.

Hull, C. L. (1920). Quantitative aspects of the evolution of concepts. *Psychological Monographs, 123,* 1–86.

Hulme, C., Maughan, S., & Brown, G. D. (1991). Memory for familiar and unfamiliar words: Evidence for a long-term memory contribution to short-term memory span. *Journal of Memory and Language, 30*(6), 685–701.

Hulme, C., Roodenrys, S., Brown, G., & Mercer, R. (1995). The role of long-term memory mechanisms in memory span. *British Journal of Psychology, 86*(4), 527–536.

Hulme, C., Surprenant, A., Bireta, T. J., Stuart, G., & Neath, I. (2004). Abolishing the word length effect. *Journal of Experimental Psychology: Learning, Memory, and Cognition, 30*(1), 98–196.

Hulme, C., Thomson, N., Muir, C., & Lawrence, A. (1984). Speech rate and the development of short-term memory span. *Journal of Experimental Child Psychology, 38,* 241–253.

Hume, D. (1965). *Essential works of David Hum,* R. Cohen (Ed.) New York: Bantam. (Original work published 1739)

Hunkin, N. M., & Parkin, A. J. (1995). The method of vanishing cues: An evaluation of its effectiveness in teaching memory-impaired individuals. *Neuropsychologia, 33,* 1255–1279.

Hunter, I. M. L. (1957). The solving of three-term series problems. *British Journal of Psychology, 48,* 286–298.

Huppert, F. A., & Piercy, M. (1978). Dissociation between learning and remembering in organic amnesia. *Nature, 275*(5678), 317–318.

Hyde, T. S., & Jenkins, J. J. (1969). Differential effects of incidental tasks on the organization of recall of a list of highly associated words. *Journal of Experimental Psychology, 82*(3), 472–481.

Hyman, I. E., Jr., Husband, T. H., & Billings, F. J. (1995). False memories of childhood experiences. *Applied Cognitive Psychology, 9*(3), 181–197.

Ikier, S., Tekcan, A. I., Guelguez, S., & Kuentay, A. (2003). Whose life is it anyway? Adoption of each others autobiographical memories by twins. *Applied Cognitive Psychology, 17*(2), 237–247.

Intons-Peterson, M. J. (1983). Imaginary paradigms: how vulnerable are they to experimenters' expectations? *Journal of Experimental Psychology: Human Perception and Performance, 8*(2), 142–147.

Ishai, A., Ungerleider, L. G., & Haxby, J. V. (2000). Distributed neural systems for the generation of visual images. *Neuron, 28*(3), 979–990.

Ito, T. A., & Urland, G. R. (2003). Race and gender on the brain: Electrocortical measures of attention to the race and gender of multiply categorizable individuals. *Journal of Personality and Social Psychology, 4,* 616–626.

Jacoby, L. L. (1978). On interpreting the effects of repetition: Solving a problem versus remembeting a solution. *Journal of Verbal Learning and Verbal Behavior, 17,* 649–667.

Jacoby, L. L. (1983). Perceptual enhancement: Persistent effects of an experience. *Journal of Experimental Psychology: Learning, Memory, and Cognition, 9*(1), 21–38.

Jacoby, L. L., Begg, I. M., & Toth, J. P. (1997). In defense of functional independence: Violations of assumptions underlying the process dissociation procedure? *Journal of Experimental Psychology: Learning, Memory, and Cognition, 23,* 484–495.

Jacoby, L. L., Bishara, A. J., Hessels, S., & Toth, J. P. (2005). Aging, subjective experience and cognitive control: Dramatic false remembering by older adults. *Journal of Experimental Psychology: General, 134*(2), 131–148.

Jacoby, L. L., & Brooks, (1984). Nonanalytic cognition: Memory, perception and concept learning. In G. H. Bower (Ed.), *The psychology of learning and motivation: Advances in research and theory* (Vol. 18, pp. 1–47). New York: Academic Press.

Jacoby, L. L., & Dallas, M. (1981). On the relationship between autobiographical memory and perceptual learning. *Journal of Experimental Psychology: General, 110,* 306–340.

Jacoby, L. L., & Whitehouse, K. (1989). An illusion of memory: false recognition influenced by unconscious perception. *Journal of Experimental Psychology: General, 118*(2), 126–135.

Jacoby, L. L., & Witherspoon, D. (1982). Remembering without awareness. *Canadian Journal of Psychology, 36,* 300–324.

James, W. (1890). *The principles of psychology.* Oxford, UK: Holt.

Janet, P. (1904). L'amnesie et la dissociation de souvenirs par l'emotion. *Journal de Psychologie, 1,* 417–453.

Janowsky, J. S., Shimamura, A. P., & Squire, L. R. (1989). Source memory impairment in patients with frontal lobe lesions. *Neuropsychologia, 27,* 1043–1056.

Jansari, A., & Parkin, A. J. (1996). Things that go bump in your life: Explaining the reminiscence bump in autobiographical memory. *Psychology and Aging, 11*(1), 85–91.

Jaschinski, U., & Wentura, D. (2002). Misleading postevent information and working memory capacity: An individual differences approach to eyewitness memory. *Applied Cognitive Psychology, 16*(2), 223–231.

Jenkins, J. J., & Russell, W. A. (1952). Associative clustering during recall. *Journal of Abnormal and Social Psychology, 47,* 818–821.

Johnson, M. (1987). *The body in the mind: The bodily basis of meaning, imagination and reasoning.* Chicago: University of Chicago Press.

Johnson, M. K., & Foley, M. A. (1984). Differentiating fact from fantasy: The reliability of children's memory. *Journal of Social Issues, 40*(2), 33–50.

Johnson, M. K., Hashtroudi, S., & Lindsay, D. S. (1993). Source monitoring. *Psychological Bulletin, 114*(1), 3–28.

Johnson, M. K., & Raye, C. L. (1981). Reality monitoring. *Psychological Review, 88,* 67–85.

Johnson, M. K., Raye, C. L., Foley, H. J., & Foley, M. A. (1981). Cognitive operations and decision bias in reality monitoring. *American Journal of Psychology, 94*(1), 37–64.

Johnson, K. J., & Fredrickson, B. L. (2005). We all look the same to me. *Psychological Science, 16*(11), 875–881.

Johnson-Laird, P. N. (1980). Mental models in cognitive science. *Cognitive Science, 4*(1), 71–115.

Jolicoeur, P., & Kosslym, S. M. (1985). Is time to scan visual images due to demand characteristics? *Memory & Cognition, 13*(4), 320–332.

Jones, D. M., & Macken, W. J. (1995). Auditory babble and cognitive efficiency. *Journal of Experimental Psychology: Applied, 1*(3), 216–226.

Jonides, J., Smith, E. E., Koeppe, R. A., Awh, E., Minoshima, S., & Mintun, M. A. (1993). Spatial working memory in humans as revealed by PET. *Nature, 363,* 623–625.

Juola, J. F., Fischler, I., & Wood, C. T. (1971). Recognition time for information stored in long-term memory. *Perception & Psychophysics, 10*(1), 8–14.

Just, M. A., & Carpenter, P. A. (1992). A capacity theory of comprehension: Individual differences in working memory. *Psychological Review, 99*(1), 122–149.

Just, M. A., Carpenter, P. A., Keller, T. A., Eddy, W. F., & Thulborn, R. (1996). Brain activation modified by sentence comprehension. *Science, 274,* 114–116.

Just, M. A., Carpenter, P. A., & Maguire, M. (2001). *Journal of Experimental Psychology: General, 130*(2), 493–504.

Just, M. A., Carpenter, P. A., Maguire, M., Diwadkar, V., & McMains, S. (2001). Mental rotation of objects retrieved from memory: A functional MRI study of spatial processing. *Journal of Experimental Psychology: General, 130*(3), 493–504.

Just, M. A., Carpenter, P. A., & Varma, S. (1999). Computational modeling of high level cognition and brain function. *Human Brain Mapping, 8,* 128–136.

Just, M. A., & Varma, S. (2002). A hybrid architecture for working memory. *Psychological Review, 109*(1), 55–65.

Kahana, M. J. (1996). Associative retrieval processes in free recall. *Memory & Cognition, 24,* 103–109.

Kane, K. A. (2001). Electrophysiological indices of conscious and automatic memory processes. *Dissertation Abstracts International, 61*(11B), 6179.

Kane, M. J., & Engle, R. W. (2003). Working memory capacity and the control of attention: The contribution of goal neglect, response competition, and task set to stroop interference. *Journal of Experimental Psychology: General, 132*(1), 47–70.

Kant, I. (1781/1965). *Critique of pure reason.* (N. K. Smith, Trans.). New York: St. Martin's.

Kaufman, L., & Richards, W. (1969). Spontaneous fixation tendencies for visual forms. *Perception & Psychophysics, 5*(2), 85–88.

Kausler, D. H., & Kleim, D. M. (1978). Age differences in processing relevant versus irrelevant stimuli in multiple item recognition memory. *Journal of Gerontology, 33,* 87–93.

Keane, M. M., Gabrieli, J. D. E., Noland, J. S., & McNealy, S. I. (1995). Normal perceptual priming of orthographically illegal words in amnesia. *Journal of the International Neuropsychological Society, 1,* 425–433.

Kelley, W. M., Miezin, F. M., McDermott, K. B., Buckner, R. L., Raichle, M. E., Cohen, A. J., Ollinger, J. M., Akbudak, E., Conturo, T. E., Snyder, A. Z., & Peterson, S. E. (1998). Hemispheric specialization in human dorsal frontal cortex and medial-temporal lobe for verbal and non-verbal memory encoding. *Neuron, 20,* 927–936.

Kemp, R., Towell, N., & Pike, G. (1997). When seeing should not be believing: Photographs and credit cards. *Cognitive Psychology, 11,* 211–222.

Keppel, G., & Underwood, B. J. (1962). Proactive inhibition in short-term retention of single items. *Journal of Verbal Learning and Verbal Behavior, 1*(3), 153–161.

Keysar, B. (1994). Discourse context effects: Metaphysical and literal interpretations. *Discourse Processes, 18*(3), 247–269.

Keysar, B. (1996). Language users as problem solvers: Just what ambiguity problem do they solve? In S. R. Fussell & R. J. Kreuz (Eds.), *Social and cognitive psychological approaches to interpersonal communication.* Mahwah, NJ: Lawrence Erlbaum.

Kihlstrom, J. F. (1998). Exhumed memory. In S. J. Lynn & K. M. McConkey (Eds.), *Truth in memory* (pp. 3–31). New York: Guilford.

Kihlstrom, J. F., & Eich, E. (1994). Altering states of consciousness. In D. Druckman & R. A. Bjork (Eds.), *Learning, remembering and believing: Enhancing performance* (pp. 207–248). Washington, DC: National Academy Press.

Kihlstrom, J. F., & Hoyt, I. P. (1990). Repression, dissociation, and hypnosis. In J. L. Singer (Ed.), *Repression and dissociation: Implications for personality theory, psychopathology, and health* (pp. 181–208). Chicago: University of Chicago Press.

Kintsch, W. (1970). *Learning, memory, and conceptual processes.* Oxford, UK: Wiley.

Kintsch, W. (1974). *The representation of meaning in memory.* Hillsdale, NJ: Lawrence Erlbaum.

Kintsch, W. (1988). The role of knowledge in discourse comprehension: A construction integration model. *Psychological Review, 95*(2), 163–182.

Kintsch, W. (1992a). *A cognitive architecture for comprehension.* Washington, DC: American Psychological Association.

Kintsch, W. (1992b). *How readers construct situation models for stories: The role of syntactic cues and casual inferences.* Hillsdale, NJ: Lawrence Erlbaum.

Kintsch, W. (1994). Text comprehension, memory and learning. *American Psychologist, 49*(4), 294–303.

Kintsch, W. (1998). *Comprehension: A paradigm for cognition.* New York: Cambridge University Press.

Kintsch, W., & Buschke, H. (1969). Homophones and synonyms in short-term memory. *Journal of Experimental Psychology, 80*(3, Pt. 1), 403–407.

Kintsch, W., & Mross, E. F. (1985). Context effects in word identification. *Journal of Memory and Language, 24*(3), 336–349.

Kintsch, W., & Van Dijk, T. A. (1978). Toward a model of text comprehension and production. *Psychological Review, 85*(5), 363–394.

Kintsch, W., & Welsch, D. M. (1991). *The construction-integration model: A framework for studying memory for text.* Hillsdale, NJ: Lawrence Erlbaum.

Kintsch, W., Welsch, D., Schmalhofer, F., & Zimny, S. (1990). Sentence memory: A theoretical analysis. *Journal of Memory and Language, 29*(2), 133–159.

Kirchoff, B. A., Wagner, A. D., & Maril, A. (2000). Prefrontal circuitry for episodic encoding and subsequent memory. *Journal of Neuroscience, 20*(16), 6173–6180.

Kleinsmith, L. J., & Kaplan, S. (1963). Paired-associated learning as a function of arousal and interpolated interval. *Journal of Experimental Psychology, 65*(2), 190–193.

Kleinsmith, L. J., & Kaplan, S. (1964). Interaction of arousal and recall interval in nonsense syllable paired-associate learning. *Journal of Experimental Psychology, 67*(2), 124–126.

Koehnken, G., Milne, R., Memon, A., & Bull, R. (1994, March). *A meta-analysis on the effects of the cognitive interview.* Paper presented at the biennial conference of the American Psychology and Law Society, Santa Fe, NM.

Kohler, S., Shitij, K., Moscovitch, M., Winocur, G., & Houle, S. (1995). Dissociation of pathways for object and spatial vision: A PET study in humans. *Cognitive Neuroscience and Neuropsychology, 6,* 1865–1868.

Kolers, P. A. (1973). Remembering operations. *Memory & Cognition, 1*(3), 347–336.

Kolers, P. A. (1974). Remembering trivia. *Language and Speech, 17*(4), 324–336.

Kolers, P. A. (1975a). Memorial consequences of automatized encoding. *Journal of Experimental Psychology: Human Learning and Memory, 1*(6), 689–701.

Kolers, P. A. (1975b). Specificity of operations in sentence recognition. *Cognitive Psychology, 7*(3), 289–306.

Kolers, P. A. (1976). Reading a year later. *Journal of Experimental Psychology: Human Learning and Memory, 2*(5), 554–565.

Kolers, P. A. (1978). A pattern analyzing basis of recognition. In L. S. Cermark & F. I. M. Craik (Eds.), *Levels of processing and human memory* (pp. 363–384). Hillsdale, NJ: Lawrence Erlbaum.

Kolers, P. A., & Ostry, D. J. (1974). Time course of loss of information regarding pattern analyzing operations. *Journal of Verbal Language and Verbal Behavior, 13*, 599–612.

Koppenaal, R. J. (1963). Time changes in the strengths of A-B, A-C lists: Spontaneous recovery? *Journal of Verbal Learning and Verbal Behavior, 2*, 310–319.

Kosslyn, S. M. (1980). *Image and mind*. Cambridge, MA: Harvard University Press.

Kosslyn, S. M. (1994). *Image and brain: The resolution of the imagery debate*. Cambridge: MIT Press.

Kosslyn, S. M. (2005). Mental images and the brain. *Cognitive Neuropsychology, 22*(3–4), 333–345.

Kosslyn, S. M. (2006). You can play 20 questions with nature and win: Categorical versus co-ordinate spatial relations as a case study. *Neuropsychologia, 44*(9), 1519–1523.

Kosslyn, S. M., Ball, T. M., & Reiser, B. J. (1978). Visual images preserve metric spatial information: Evidence from studies of image scanning. *Journal of Experimental Psychology: Human Perception and Performance, 4*, 47–60.

Kosslyn, S. M., & Pomeranz, J. R. (1977). Imagery, propositions and the form of internal representations. *Cognitive Psychology, 9*, 52–76.

Kosslyn, S. M., Thompson, W. L., & Sukel, K. E. (2005). Two types of image generation: Evidence from PET. *Cognitive, Affective and Behavioral Neuroscience, 5*(1), 41–53.

Kouider, S., & Dupoux, E. (2001). A functional disconnection between spoken and visual work recognition: Evidence from unconscious priming. *Cognition, 82*, 35–49.

Kouider, S., & Dupoux, E. (2004). Partial awareness creates the illusion of subliminal semantic priming. *Psychological Science, 15*, 75–81.

Kounios, J., & Holcomb, P. J. (1994). Concreteness effects in semantic processing. *Journal of Experimental Psychology: Learning, Memory, and Cognition, 20*(4), 804–823.

Kramer, T. H., Buckhout, R., Fox, D., & Widman, E. (1991). Effects of stress on recall. *Applied Cognitive Psychology, 5*(6), 483–488.

Krystal, J., Southwick, S., & Charney, D. (1995). Traumatic stress disorder: Psychobiological mechanism of traumatic remembrance. In D. Schacter (Ed.), *Memory distortions: How minds, brains, and societies reconstruct the past* (pp. 150–172). Cambridge, MA: Harvard University Press.

Kucera, H., & Francis, W. N. (1967). *Computational analysis of present-day American English*. Providence, RI: Brown University Press.

Kuehn, L. L. (1974). Looking down a gun barrel: Person perception and violent crime. *Perceptual and Motor Skills, 39*(3), 1159–1164.

Kunst-Wilson, W. R., & Zajonc, R. B. (1989). Affective discrimination of stimuli that cannot be recognized. *Science, 207*, 557–558.

Kyllonen. P., & Christal, R. (1990). Reasoning ability is (little more than) working-memory capacity? *Intelligence, 14*(4), 389–433.

Laird, D. (1991). Will the field ultimately need a more detailed analysis of mood/memory? In D. Kuiken (Ed.), *Mood and memory*. Newbury Park, CA: Sage.

Lambie, J. A., & Marcel, A. J. (2002). Consciousness and the varieties of emotional experience: A theoretical framework. *Psychological Review, 109*, 219–259.

Lampinen, J. M., Faries, J. H., Neuschatz, J. S., & Toglia, M. P. (2000). Recollections of things schematic: the influence of scripts on recollective experience. *Applied Cognitive Psychology, 14*(6), 543–555.

Lampinen, J. M., & Smith, V. L. (1995). The incredible (and sometimes incredulous) child witness: Child eyewitnesses' sensitivity to source credibility cues. *Journal of Applied Psychology, 80*(5), 621–627.

Landauer, T. K., & Dumais, S. T. (1997). A solution to Plato's problem: The latent semantic analysis theory of acquisition, induction, and representation of knowledge. *Psychological Review, 104*(2), 211–240.

Langacke, R. (1987). *Foundations of cognitive grammar* (Vol. 1). Stanford, CA: Stanford University Press.

Langer, L. (1991). *Holocaust testimonies: The ruins of memory.* New Haven, CT: Yale University Press.

Larson, S. F. (1992). Personal context in autobiographical and narrative memories. In M. A. Conway, D. C. Rubin, H. Spinnler, & W. A. Wagenaar (Eds.), *Behavioral and Social Sciences: Vol. 65. Theoretical perspectives on autobiographical memory* (pp. 53–74). Dordrecht, The Netherlands: Kluwer Academic.

LeCompte, D. C. (1992). In search of a strong visual recency effect. *Memory & Cognition, 20,* 563–572.

LeDoux, J. E. (1989). Indelibility of subcortical emotional memories. *Journal of Cognitive Neuroscience, 1,* 238–242.

LeDoux, J. (2004). Emotion and the amygdala. In J. P. Aggleton (Ed.), *The amygdala: Neurological aspects of emotion, memory and mental dysfunction* (pp. 339–351). New York: Wiley Liss.

Lee, P. J., & Brown, N. R. (2003). Delay related changes in personal memories for September 11, 2001. *Applied Cognitive Psychology, 17*(9), 1007–1015.

Lee, V. A., Valliant, G. E., Torrey, W. C., & Elder, G. H. (1995). A 5-year prospective study of the psychological sequelae of World War II combat. *American Journal of Psychiatry, 132*(4), 516–522.

Leightman, M. D., & Ceci, S. J. (1995). The effects of stereotypes and suggestions on preschoolers' reports. *Developmental Psychology, 31*(4), 568–578.

Leng, N. R., Copello, A. G., & Sayegh, A. (1991). Learning after brain injury by the method of vanishing cues: A case study. *Behavioral Psychology, 19,* 173–181.

Levin, D. T. (2000). Race as a visual feature: Using visual search and perceptual discrimination tasks to understand face categories and the cross-race recognition deficit. *Journal of Experimental Psychology: General, 129,* 559–574.

Levy, B. A. (1971). Role of articulation in auditory and visual short-term memory. *Journal of Verbal Learning and Verbal Behavior, 10*(2), 123–132.

Lewandowski, S. (1992). Gradual unlearning and catastrophic interference: A compound of distributed architectures. In W. E. Hockley & S. Lewandowski (Eds.), *Relating theory and data: Essays in human memory and learning in honor of B. B. Murdock* (pp. 445–476). Hillsdale, NJ: Lawrence Erlbaum.

Lhermitte, F., & Signoret, J. L. (1972). Analyse neuropsychologique et differenciation des syndromes amnesiques. *Revue Neurologiques, 126,* 86–94.

Liang, K. C., Juler, R. G., & McGaugh, J. L. (1986). Modulating effects of post training epinephrine on memory: Involvement of the amygdala noradrenergic system. *Brain Research, 368*(1), 125–133.

Lindsay, D. S. (1990). Misleading suggestions can impair eyewitnesses' ability to remember event details. *Journal of Experimental Psychology: Learning, Memory, and Cognition, 16*(6), 1077–1083.

Lindsay, D. S., Hagen, L., Read, J. D., Wade, K. A., & Garry, M. (2004). True photographs and false memories. *Psychological Science, 9,* 6–10.

Lindsay, D. S., & Johnson, M. K. (1989). The eyewitness suggestibility effect and memory for source. *Memory & Cognition, 17*(3), 349–358.

Lindsay, D. S., & Johnson, M. K. (1991). Recognition memory and source monitoring. *Bulletin of the Psychonomic Society, 29,* 203–205.

Linton, M. (1975). Memory for real-world events. In D. A. Norman & D. E. Rumelhart (Eds.), *Explorations in cognition* (pp. 376–404). San Francisco: W. H. Freeman.

Linton, M. (1979). Real-world memory after six years: An in vivo study of very long-term memory. In M. M. Gruneberg, P. E. Morris, & R. N. Sykes (Eds.), *Practical aspects of Memory* (pp. 67–76). London: Academic Press.

Linton, M. (1986). Ways of searching and the contents of memory. In D. C. Rubin (Ed.), *Autobiographical memory* (pp. 50–67). New York: Cambridge University Press.

Litz, B. T., (1993). Emotional numbing in combat related post traumatic stress disorder: A critical review and reformulation. *Clinical Psychology Review, 12,* 417–432.

Locke, J. (1690/1956). *An essay concerning human understanding.* Chicago: Henry Regnery.

Loess, H. (1968). Short-term memory and term similarity. *Journal of Verbal Learning and Verbal Behavior, 1,* 87–92.

Loftus, E. F. (1977). Shifting human color memory. *Memory & Cognition, 5,* 696–699.

Loftus, E. F. (1979a). *Eyewitness testimony.* Cambridge, MA: Harvard University Press.

Loftus, E. F. (1979b). Reactions to blatantly contradictory information. *Memory & Cognition, 7,* 368–374.

Loftus, E. F. (1997). Creating false memories. *Scientific American, 277*(3), 70–75.

Loftus, E. F. (2004). Memories of things unseen. *Current Directions in Psychological Science, 13*(4), 145–147.

Loftus, E. F., Altman, D., & Geballe, R. (1975). Effects of questioning upon a witness' later recollections. *Journal of Police Science and Administration, 3*(2), 162–165.

Loftus, E .F., & Burns, T.E. (1982). Mental shock can produce retrograde amnesia. *Memory & Cognition, 10*(4), 318–323.

Loftus, E. F., Coan, J. A., & Pickrell, J. E. (1996). Manufacturing false memories using bits of reality. In L. M. Reder (Ed.), *Implicit memory and metacognition* (pp. 195–220). Hillsdale, NJ: Lawrence Erlbaum.

Loftus, E. F., Feldman, J., & Dashiell, R. (1995). The reality of illusory memories. In D. Schacter (Ed.), *Memory distortion* (pp. 47–68). Cambridge, MA: Harvard University Press.

Loftus, E. F., & Hoffman, H. G. (1989). Misinformation and memory: The creation of new memories. *Journal of Experimental Psychology: General, 118,* 100–104.

Loftus, E. F., & Ketcham, K. (1994). *The myth of repressed memory: False memories and allegations of sexual abuse.* New York: St. Martin's.

Loftus, E. F., & Loftus, G. R. (1980). On the permanence of stored information in the human brain. *American Psychologist, 35,* 409–420.

Loftus, E. F., Loftus, G. R., & Messo, J. (1987). Some facts about "weapon focus." *Law and Human Behavior, 11*(1), 55–62.

Loftus, E. F., Miller, D. G., & Burns, H. J. (1978). Semantic integration of verbal information into a visual memory. *Journal of Experimental Psychology: Human Learning and Memory, 4*(1), 19–31.

Loftus E. F., & Palmer, J. C. (1974). Reconstruction of automobile destruction: An example of the interaction between language and memory. *Journal of Verbal Learning and Verbal Behavior, 13*(5), 585–589.

Loftus, E. F., & Pickrell, J. E. (1995). The formation of false memories. *Psychiatric Annals, 25*(12), 720–725.

Loftus, G. R., & Irwin, D. E. (1998). On the relations among different measures of visible and informational persistence. *Cognitive Psychology, 35*(2), 135–199.

Logie, R. H. (1995). *Visuo-spatial working memory*. Hillsdale, NJ: Lawrence Erlbaum.

Logie, R. H., Gilhooly, K. J., & Wynn, V. (1994). Counting on working memory in arithmetic problem solving. *Memory & Cognition, 22*(4), 395–410.

Longoni, A. M., Richardson, J. T., & Aeillo, A. (1993). Articulatory rehearsal and phonological storage in working memory. *Memory & Cognition, 21*(1), 11–22.

Lovatt, P., & Avons, S. (2001). Re-evaluating the word-length effect. In J. Andrade (Ed.), *Working memory in perspective* (pp. 199–218). Philadelphia: Psychology Press.

Lovatt, P., Avons, S. E., & Masterson, J. (2000). The word-length effect and disyllabic words. *Quarterly Journal of Experimental Psychology: Human Experimental Psychology, 53A*(1), 1–22.

Lovett, M. C., Reder, L. M., & Lebiere, C. (1999). Modeling working memory in a unified architecture: An ACT-R perspective. In A. Miyake & P. Shah (Eds.), *Models of working memory: Mechanisms of active maintenance and executive control* (pp. 135–182). New York: Cambridge University Press.

Lustig, C., Hasher, L., & May, C. (2001). Working memory span and the protective inference. *Journal of Experimental Psychology: General, 130*(2), 199–207.

Lykken, D., & Tellegen, A. (1996). Happiness is a stochastic phenomenon. *Psychological Science, 7,* 193–189.

Lynch, G., Granger, R., & Staubli, U. (1991). Long-term potentiation and the structure of memory. In W. C. Abraham, M. Corballis, & K. G. White (Eds.), *Memory mechanisms: A tribute to G. V. Goddard*. Hillsdale, NJ: Lawrence Erlbaum.

Lynn, S. J., & Sivec, H. (1992). Hypnotizable subject as creative problem-solving agent. In E. Fromm & M. R. Nash (Eds.), *Contemporary perspectives in hypnosis research* (pp. 292–333). New York: Guilford.

Maass, A., & Kohnken, G. (1989). Eyewitness identification: Simulating the "weapon effect." *Law and Human Behavior, 13*(4), 397–408.

MacDonald, M. C., Just, M. A., & Carpenter, P. A. (1992). Working memory constraints on the processing of syntactic ambiguity. *Cognitive Psychology, 24*(1), 56–98.

Mack, A., & Rock, I. (1998). *Inattentional blindness*. Cambridge: MIT Press.

Maclin, O. H., & Malpass, R. S. (2003). The ambiguous face illusion. *Perception, 32,* 445–464.

Magliano, J. P., Baggett, W. B., Johnson, B. K., & Graesser, A. C. (1993). The time course of generating casual antecedent and causal consequence inferences. *Discourse Processes, 16*(1–2), 35–55.

Maguire, E. A., & Mummey, C. J. (1999). Differential modulation of a common memory retrieval network revealed by PET. *Hippocampus, 9,* 54–61.

Malmquist, C. P. (1986). Children who witness parential murder: posttraumatic aspects. *Journal of the American Academy of Child Psychiatry, 25*(3), 320–325.

Mandler, G. (1972). Organization and recognition. In E. Tulving & W. Donaldson (Eds.), *Organization of memory* (pp. 139–166). New York: Academic Press.

Mandler, G. (1980). Recognizing: The judgment of previous occurrence. *Psychological Review, 87*(3), 252–271.

Mandler, G. (1984). Consciousness, imagery and emotion with special reference to autonomic imagery. *Journal of Mental Imagery, 8*(4), 87–94.

Mandler, G. (1992). *Memory, arousal, and mood: A theoretical integration*. Hillsdale, NJ: Laurence Erlbaum.

Mandler, G., Pearlstone, Z., & Koopmans, H. S. (1969). Effects of organization and semantic similarity on recall and recognition. *Journal of Verbal Learning and Verbal Behavior, 8*(3), 410–423.

Mandler, J. M. (1979). Categorical and schematic organization in memory. In C. R. Puff (Ed.), *Memory organization and structure* (pp. 259–299). New York: Academic Press.

Mandler, J. M. (1982). Recent research on story grammars. In J. F. Le Ny & W. Kintsch (Eds.), *Language and comprehension* (pp. 207–218). Amsterdam: North-Holland.

Mandler, J. M. (1984). *Stories, scripts and scenes: Aspects of schema theory.* Hillsdale, NJ: Lawrence Erlbaum.

Mandler, J. M. (1988). How to build a baby: On the development of an accessible representational system. *Cognitive Development, 3,* 113–136.

Mandler, J. M. (1992). How to build a baby II: Conceptual primitives. *Psychological Review, 99*(4), 587–604.

Mandler, J. M., & De Forest, M. (1979). Is there more than one way to recall a story? *Child Development, 50,* 886–889.

Mandler, J. M., & Goodman, M. S. (1982). On the psychological validity of story structure. *Journal of Verbal Learning and Verbal Behavior, 21,* 507–523.

Mandler, J. M., & Johnson, N. S. (1977). Remembrance of things parsed: Story structure and recall. *Cognitive Psychology, 9*(1), 111–151.

Mandler, J. M., & McDonough, L. (1993). Concept formation in infancy. *Cognitive Development, 8*(3), 291–318.

Maurer, D., Le Grand, R., & Mondloch, C. (2002). The many faces of configural processing. *Trends in Cognitive Science, 6,* 255–260.

Marcel, A. J. (1983). Conscious and unconscious perception: Experiments on visual masking and word recognition. *Cognitive Psychology, 15,* 197–237.

Marr, D. 1982. *Vision: A computational investigation into the human representation and processing of visual information.* New York: W. H. Freeman.

Martens, D. S., & Wolters, G. (2002). Interference in implicit memory caused by processing of interpolated material. *American Journal of Psychology, 115*(2), 169–185.

Martinez, J. L., & Derrick, B. E. (1996). Long term potentiation and learning. *Psychology, 47,* 173–203.

May, C. P., Hasher, L., & Kane, M. J. (1999). The role of interference in memory span. *Memory & Cognition, 27*(5), 759–767.

Mayes, A. R. (1988). *Human organic memory disorders.* Cambridge, UK: Cambridge University Press.

Mayes, A. R., & Montaldi, D. (1999). The neuroimaging of long-term memory encoding processes. *Memory, 7*(5–6), 613–659.

Mazzoni, G., & Memon, A. (2003). Imagination can create false autobiographical memories. *Psychological Science, 14,* 186–188.

McCarthy, R. A., & Hodges, J. R. (1995). Trapped in time: Profound autobiographical memory loss following a thalamic stroke. In R. Campbell & M. A. Conway (Eds.), *Broken memories: Case studies in memory impairment* (pp. 31–44). Cambridge, MA: Blackwell.

McClelland, J. L. (1981). Retrieving general and a specific information from stored knowledge of specifics. In *Proceedings of the Third Annual Conference of the Cognitive Science Society* (pp. 170–172), Berkeley, CA.

McClelland, J. L. (1995). Constructive memory and memory distortions. In D. L. Schacter (Ed.), *Memory distortion* (pp. 69–90). Cambridge, MA: Harvard University Press.

McClelland, J. L., McNaughton, B. L., & O'Reilly, R. C. (1994). Why there are complementary learning systems in the hippocampus and neocortex: Insights from the successes and failures of connectionist models of learning and memory. *Psychological Review, 102*(3), 419–457.

McClelland, J. L., & Rumelhart, D. E. (1986). *Parallel distributed processing: Vol 1.* Cambridge: MIT Press.

McClelland, J. L., & Rumelhart, D. E. (1988). *Explorations in parallel distributed processing: Vol 2.* Cambridge: MIT Press.

McCloskey, M., & Cohen, N. J. (1989). Catastrophic interference in connectionist networks: The sequential learning problem. In G. H. Bower (Ed.), *The psychology of learning and motivation* (pp. 109–165). New York: Academic Press.

McCloskey, M., & Zaragoza, M. Z. (1985). Misleading postevent information and memory for events: Arguments and evidence against memory impairment hypotheses. *Journal of Experimental Psychology: General, 114*(1), 1–16.

McConkey, K. M. (1991). Complexities of hypnotic mood and memory. In D. Kuiken (Ed.), *Mood and memory.* Newbury Park, CA: Sage.

McConkey, K. M. (1992). The effects of hypnotic procedures on remembering: The experimental findings and their implications for forensic hypnosis. In E. Fromme & M. R. Nash (Eds.), *Contemporary hypnosis research* (pp. 405–426). New York: Guilford.

McConkey, K. M., Labelle, L., Bibb, B. C., & Bryant, R. A. (1990). Hypnosis and suggested pseudomemory: The relevance of test context. *Australian Journal of Psychology, 42,* 197–205.

McCulloch W. S., & Pitts, W. (1943). A logical calculus of the ideas immanent in neural activity. *Bulletin of Mathematical Biophysics, 5,* 115–133.

McCurdy, J. T. (1918). *War neuroses.* Cambridge, UK: Cambridge University Press.

McDermott, K. B. (1997). Priming on perceptual implicit memory tests can be achieved through presentation of associates. *Psychonomic Bulletin & Review, 4*(4), 582–586.

McDermott, K. B., Buckner, R. L., & Peterson, S. E. (1999). Set- and code-specific activation in the frontal cortex. An fMRI study of encoding and retrieval of faces and words. *Journal of Cognitive Neuroscience, 11*(6), 631–640.

McElree, B. (2001). Working memory and focal attention. *Journal of Experimental Psychology: Learning, Memory, and Cognition, 27*(3), 817–835.

McGaugh, J. L. (1961). Facilitative and disruptive effects of strychnine sulphate on maze learning. *Psychological Reports, 8,* 99–104.

McGaugh, J. L. (1983). Preserving the presence of the past: Hormonal influences on memory storage. *American Psychologist, 38*(2), 161–174.

McGaugh, J. L. (1989). Involvement of hormonal and neuromodulatory systems in the regulation of memory storage. *Annual Review of Neuroscience, 12,* 255–287.

McGaugh, J. L. (1990). Significance and remembrance: The role of neuromodulatory systems. *Psychological Science, 1*(1), 15–25.

McGaugh, J. L. (1991). Neuromodulation and the storage of information: Involvement of the amygdaloid complex. In R. G. Lister & H. J. Weingartner (Eds.), *Perspectives on cognitive neuroscience* (pp. 279–299). London: Oxford University Press.

McGaugh, J. L. (1992). Neuromodulatory systems and the regulation of memory storage. In L. R. Squire & N. Butters (Eds.), *Neuropsychology of memory* (2nd ed., pp. 386–401). New York: Guilford.

McGaugh, J. L. (1995). Emotional activation, neuromodulatory systems, and memory. In D. L. Schacter (Ed.), *Memory distortion* (pp. 255–273). Cambridge, MA: Harvard University Press.

McGaugh, J. L. (2000). Memory: A century of consolidation. *Science, 287,* 248–251.

McGaugh, J. L., & Gold, P. E. (1989). Hormonal modulation of memory. In R. Brush & S. Levine (Eds.), *Psychoendrocrinology* (pp. 305–339). New York: Academic Press.

McGeoch, J. A. (1932). Forgetting and the law of disuse. *Psychological Review, 39,* 352–370.

McGeoch, J. R. (1942). *The psychology of human learning.* Oxford, UK: Longmans.

McIntosh, A. R. (1999). Mapping cognition to the brain through neural interactions. In J. K. Foster (Ed.), *Neuroimaging and memory* (pp. 523–548). Hove, UK: Psychology Press.

McIntosh, A. R., Nyberg, L., Bookstein, F., & Tulving, E. (1997). Differential functional connectivity of prefrontal and medial temporal cortices during episodic memory retrieval. *Human Brain Mapping, 5*(4), 323–327.

McKoon, G., & Ratcliff, R. (1988). Contextually relevant aspects of meaning. *Journal of Experimental Psychology: Learning, Memory, and Cognition, 14,* 331–343.

McKoon, G., & Ratcliff, R. (1992a). Spreading activation versus compound cue accounts of priming: Mediated priming revisited. *Journal of Experimental Psychology: Learning, Memory, and Cognition, 18*(6), 1155–1172.

McKoon, G., & Ratcliff, R. (1992b). Inference during reading. *Psychological Review, 99*(3), 440–466.

McNally, R. J., Clancy, S. A., Barrett, H. M., & Parker, H. A. (2005). Reality monitoring in adults reporting repressed, recovered or continuous memories of childhood sexual abuse. *Journal of Abnormal Psychology, 114*(1), 147–152.

McNally, R. J., Kaspi, S. P., Riemann, B. C., & Zeitlin, S. B. (1990). Selective processing of threat cues in posttraumatic stress disorder. *Journal of Abnormal Psychology, 99*(4), 398–402.

McNally, R. J., Lasko, N. B., Clancy, S. A., Macklin, M. L., Pitman, R. K., & Orr, S. P. (2004). Psycholophysiological responding during script-driven imagery in people reporting abduction by space aliens. *Psychological Science, 15,* 493–497.

McNamara, P. (1992). A transpersonal approach to memory. *Journal of Transpersonal Psychology, 24*(1), 61–78.

McNamara, P. (1994). Memory, double, shadow, and evil. *Journal of Analytical Psychology, 39*(2), 233–251.

McNamara, T. P. (1992). Priming and constraints it places on theories of memory and retrieval. *Psychological Review, 99*(4), 650–662.

Meissner, C. A., & Brigham, J. C. (2001). Thirty years of investigating the own-race bias in memory for faces: A meta-analytic review. *Psychology, Public Policy, and Law, 7*(1), 3–35.

Melton, A. W. (1963). Implications of short-term memory for a general theory of memory. *Journal of Verbal Learning and Verbal Behavior, 2,* 1–21.

Melton, A. W., & Irwin, J. M. (1940). The influence of degree of interpolated learning on retroactive inhibition and the overt transfer of specific response. *American Journal of Psychology, 53,* 173–203.

Merikle, P. M. (1980). Selection from visual persistence by perceptual groups and category membership. *Journal of Experimental Psychology: General, 109,* 279–295.

Merikle, P. M. (1988). Subliminal auditory messages: An evaluation. *Psychology and Marketing, 5*(4), 355–372.

Merikle, P. M., & Daneman, M. (1998). Psychological investigations of unconscious processing. *Journal of Consciousness Studies, 5,* 5–18.

Merikle, P. M., & Daneman, M. (2000). Conscious vs. unconscious perception. In M. S. Gazzaniga (Ed.), *The new cognitive neurosciences* (2nd ed., pp. 1295–1303). Cambridge: MIT Press.

Merikle, P. M., & Joordens, S. (1997). Measuring unconscious influences. In J. D. Cohen & J. W. Schooler (Eds.), *Scientific approaches to consciousness* (pp. 109–123). Mahwah, NJ: Lawrence Erlbaum.

Merikle, P. M., Smilek, D., & Eastwood, J. D. (2001). Perception without awareness: Perspectives from cognitive psychology. *Cognition, 79,* 115–134.

Metzler, J., & Shepard, R. N. (1971, April). *Mental correlates of the rotation of three dimensional objects.* Paper presented at the annual meetiung of the Western Psychological Association, San Francisco.

Metzler, J., & Shepard, R. N. (1974). Transformational studies of the representation of three-dimensional objects. In R. L. Solso (Ed.), *Theories of cognitive psychology: The Loyola symposium.* Potomac, MD: Lawrence Erlbaum.

Mewhort, D. J. K., & Leppman, K. P. (1985). Information persistence: Testing spatial and identity information with a voice probe. *Psychological Research, 47,* 51–58.

Meyer, D. E., & Kieras, D. E. (1997). A computational theory of executive cognitive processes and multiple-task performance: Part 1. Basic mechanisms. *Psychological Review, 104,* 749–791.

Meyer, D. E., & Schvaneveldt, R. W. (1971). Facilitation in recognizing pairs of words: Evidence of a dependence between retrieval operations. *Journal of Experimental Psychology, 90*(2), 227–234.

Meyer, D. E., & Schvaneveldt R. W. (1975). Meaning, memory structure and mental processes. In C. N. Cofer (Ed.), *The structure of human memory* (pp. 54–89). San Francisco: W. H. Freeman.

Meyer, D. E., & Schvaneveldt, R. W. (1976). Meaning, memory structures, and mental processes. *Science, 192,* 27–33.

Miller, G. A. (1956). The magical number seven, plus or minus two: Some limits on our capacity for processing information. *Psychological Review, 63,* 81–97.

Millis, K. K., & Graesser, A. C. (1994). The time-course of constructing knowledge-based inferences for scientific tests, *Journal of Memory and Language, 33*(5), 583–599.

Milner, B. (1971). Interhemispheric differences in the localization of psychological processes in man. *British Medical Bulletin, 27*(3), 272–277.

Milner, G. (1966). The absconder. *Comprehensive Psychiatry, 7*(3), 147–151.

Minsky, M. (1975). A framework for representing knowledge. In P. H. Winston (Ed.), *The psychology of computer vision* (pp. 211–277). New York: McGraw Hill.

Mishkin, M. (1982). A memory system in the monkey. *Philosophical Transactions of the Royal Society of London B, 298,* 85–95.

Miyake, A. (2001). Individual differences in working memory: Introduction to the special section. *Journal of Experimental Psychology: General, 130*(2), 163–168.

Moore, C. M., & Egeth, H. (1997). Perception without attention: Evidence of grouping under conditions of inattention. *Journal of Experimental Psychology: Human Perception and Performance, 23*(2), 339–352.

Moray, N. (1959). Attention in dichotic listening: Affective cues and the influence of instructions. *Quarterly Journal of Experimental Psychology, 11,* 56–60.

Morris, C. D., Bransford, J. D., & Franks, J. J. (1977). Levels of processing versus transfer-appropriate processing. *Journal of Verbal Learning and Verbal Behavior, 16,* 519–533.

Morris, J. S., Öhman, A., & Dolan, R. J. (1998). Conscious and unconscious emotional learning in the human amygdala. *Nature, 393*(6684), 467–470.

Morrow, D. G. (1994). Spatial models created from text. In H. van Oostendorp & R. A. Zwaan (Eds.), *Naturalistic text comprehension* (pp. 57–78). Norwood, NJ: Ablex.

Morton, J. (1969). The modality of post-stimulus cueing of recall order in the memory span. *Psychonomic Science, 17*(4), 224.

Moscovitch, M. (1992). Memory and working with memory: A component process model based on modules and central systems. *Journal of Cognitive Neuroscience, 4*(3), 257–267.

Moscovitch, M., Vriesent, E., & Gottstein, Y. (1993). Implicit tests of memory in patients with focal lesions or degenerative brain disorders. In F. Boller & J. Grafman (Eds.), *Handbook of neuropsychology* (Vol. 8, pp. 133–173). New York: Elsevier Science.

Mowbray, G. H. (1953). Simultaneous vision and audition: The comprehension of prose passages with varying levels of difficulty. *Journal of Experimental Psychology, 46,* 365–372.

Muller, G. E., & Pilzecker, A. (1900). Experimentelle beitrage zur Lehr vom Gedachtniss. *Zeitschrift fur Psychologie und Physiologie der Sinesorgane, 1,* 1–288.

Murdock, B. B., Jr. (1960). The distinctiveness of stimuli. *Psychological Review, 67*(1), 16–31.

Murdock, B. B., Jr. (1961). The retention of individual items. *Journal of Experimental Psychology, 62*, 618–625.

Murdock, B. B., Jr. (1962). The serial position effect in free recall. *Journal of Experimental Psychology, 64*, 482–488.

Murdock, B. B., Jr. (1974). *Human memory: Theory and practice.* Potomac, MD: Lawrence Erlbaum.

Murdock, B. B., Jr. (1982). A theory for the storage and retrieval of item and associative information. *Psychological Review, 89*, 609–626.

Murray, D. J. (1967). The role of speech responses in short-term memory. *Canadian Journal of Psychology, 21*(3), 263–276.

Murray, D. J. (1968). Articulation and acoustic confusability in short-term memory. *Journal of Experimental Psychology, 78*(4, Pt 1), 679–684.

Myers, J. L., O'Brien, E. J., Albrecht, J. E., & Mason, R. A. (1994). Maintaining global coherence during reading. *Journal of Experimental Psychology: Learning, Memory, and Cognition, 20*(4), 876–886.

Nadel, L. (1992). Multiple memory systems: What and why. *Journal of Cognitive Neuroscience, 4*, 179–188.

Nadel, L. (1994). Multiple memory systems: What and why, an update. In D. Schacter and E. Tulving (Eds.), *Memory systems* (pp. 39–63). Cambridge: MIT Press.

Nairne, J. S. (1988). A framework for interpreting recency effects in immediate serial recall. *Memory & Cognition, 16*(4), 343–352.

Nairne, J. S. (1990a). A feature model of immediate memory. *Memory & Cognition, 18*, 251–269.

Nairne, J. S. (1990b). Similarity and long-term memory for order. *Journal of Memory and Language, 29*(6), 733–746.

Nairne, J. S. (1991). Positional uncertainty in long-term memory. *Memory & Cognition, 19*, 332–340.

Nairne, J. S. (1996). Short-term/working memory. In E. L. Bjork & R. A. Bjork (Eds.), *Memory: Handbook of perception and cognition* (2nd ed., pp. 101–126). San Diego, CA: Academic Press.

Nairne, J. S. (2001). A functional analysis of primary memory. In H. L. Roediger, J. S. Nairne, I. Neath, & A. Surprenant (Eds.), *The nature of remembering: Essays in honor of Robert G. Crowder* (pp. 283–296). Washington, DC: American Psychological Association.

Nairne, J. S. (2002a). Remembering over the short-term: The case against the standard model. *Annual Review of Psychology, 53*, 53–81.

Nairne, J. S. (2002b). The myth of the encoding-retrieval match. *Memory, 10*, 389–395.

Nairne, J. S. (2003). Sensory and working memory. In A. F. Healy & R. W. Proctor (Eds.), *Handbook of psychology: Vol. 4. Experimental psychology* (pp. 423–444). New York: Wiley.

Nairne, J. S., & Kelley, M. R. (1999). Reversing the phonological similarity effect. *Memory & Cognition, 27*, 45–53.

Nairne, J. S., & Walters, V. L. (1983). Silent mouthing produces modality and suffix-like effects. *Journal of Verbal Learning and Verbal Behavior, 22*, 475–483.

Nasby, W., & Yando, R. (1982). Selective encoding and retrieval of affectively valent information: Two cognitive consequences of children's mood states. *Journal of Personality and Social Psychology, 43*(6), 1244–1253.

Nash, M. (1987). What, if anything, is regressed about hypnotic age regression: A review of the empirical literature. *Psychological Bulletin, 102*(4), 42–52.

Nathan, D., & Snedecker, M. (1995). *Satan's silence: Ritual abuses and the making of a modern American witch hunt.* New York: Basic Books.

Neath, I. (1993a). Contextual and distinctive processes and the serial position function. *Journal of Memory and Language, 32,* 820–840.

Neath, I. (1997). Modality, concreteness, and set-size effects in a free reconstruction of order task. *Memory & Cognition, 25*(2), 256–263.

Neath, I. (1998). *Human memory: An introduction to research, data, and theory.* Pacific Grove, CA: Brooks Cole.

Neath, I., & Crowder, R. G. (1996). Distinctiveness and very short-term serial position effects. *Memory, 4,* 225–242.

Neath, I., & Nairne, J. S. (1995). Word-length effects in immediate memory: Overwriting trace decay theory. *Psychonomic Bulletin & Review, 2*(4), 429–441.

Neath, I., Surprenant, A. M., & Crowder, R. G. (1993). The context-dependent stimulus suffix effect. *Journal of Experimental Psychology: Learning, Memory, and Cognition, 19*(3), 698–703.

Neely, J. H. (1977). Semantic priming and retrieval from lexical memory: Roles of inhibition-less spreading activation and limited-capacity attention. *Journal of Experimental Psychology: General, 106,* 226–254.

Neisser, U. (1962). Cultural and cognitive discontinuity. In W. Sturtevant (Ed.), *Anthropology and human behavior* (pp. 54–71). Washington, DC: Anthropological Society of Washington.

Neisser, U. (1967). *Cognitive psychology.* New York: Appleton Century Crofts.

Neisser, U. (1982). Snapshots or benchmarks. In U. Neisser (Ed.), *Memory observed* (pp. 43–48). San Francisco: W. H. Freeman.

Neisser, U. (1986). Nested structure in autobiographical memory. In D. C. Rubin (Ed.), *Autobiographical memory* (pp. 71–81). New York: Cambridge University Press.

Neisser, U. (1988). Five kinds of self knowledge. *Philosophical Psychology, 1,* 35–59.

Neisser, U., & Harsch, N. (1992). Phantom flashbulbs: False recollections of hearing the news about *Challenger.* In E. Winograd & U. Neisser (Eds.), *Affect and accuracy in recall: Studies of "flashbulb" memories* (pp. 9–31). Cambridge, UK: Cambridge University Press.

Nelson, C. A. (1995). *Basic and applied perspectives on learning, cognition, and development.* Hillsdale, NJ: Lawrence Erlbaum.

Nelson, D. L. (1989). *Implicitly activated knowledge and memory.* Hillsdale, NJ: Lawrence Erlbaum.

Nelson, D. L., Keelean, P. D., & Negrao, M. (1989). Word-fragment cueing: The lexical search hypothesis. *Journal of Experimental Psychology: Learning, Memory, and Cognition, 15,* 388–397.

Nelson, D. L., & McEvoy, C. L. (2002). How can the same type of prior knowledge both help and hinder recall? *Journal of Memory and Language, 46*(3), 652–663.

Nelson, D. L., McEvoy, C. L., & Pointer, L. (2003). Spreading activation or spooky action at a distance? *Journal of Experimental Psychology: Learning, Memory, and Cognition, 29*(1), 42–51.

Nelson, D. L., McKinney, V. M., & McEvoy, C. L. (2003). Are implicitly activated associates selectively activated? *Psychonomic Bulletin & Review, 10*(1), 118–123.

Nelson, D. L., Zhang, N., & McKinney, V. (2001). The ties that bind what is known to the recognition of what is new. *Journal of Experimental Psychology: Learning, Memory, and Cognition, 27*(5), 1147–1159.

Nelson, K. (1978). *How children represent knowledge of their world in and out of language: A preliminary report.* Hillsdale, NJ: Lawrence Erlbaum.

Nelson, K. (1993). *Explaining the emergence of autobiographical memory in early childhood.* Hillsdale, NJ: Lawrence Erlbaum.

Nelson, K. (1995). *Stories in memory: Developmental issues.* Hillsdale, NJ: Lawrence Erlbaum.

Nelson, K., & Fivush, R. (2000). Socialization of memory. In E. Tulving & F. I. M. Craik (Eds.), *Oxford handbook of memory* (pp. 283–295). New York: Oxford University Press.

Nelson, K., & Gruendel, J. (1981). Generalized event representations: Basic building blocks of cognitive development. In M. Lamb & A. L. Brown (Eds.), *Advances in developmental psychology* (Vol. 1, pp. 131–158). New York: Academic Press.

Newell, A., & Simon, H. A. (1972). *Human problem solving.* Englewood Cliffs, NJ: Prentice Hall.

Nickerson, R. A., & Adams, M. J. (1979). Long-term memory for a common object. *Cognitive Psychology, 11,* 287–307.

Nicolson, R. (1981). The relationship between memory span and processing speed. In M. Friedman, J. P. P. Das, & N. O'Connor (Eds.), *Intelligence and learning* (pp. 179–183). New York: Plenum Press.

Niedzwienska, A. (2003). Misleading postevent information and flashbulb memories. *Memory, 11*(6), 549–558.

Nigro, G., & Neisser, U. (1983). Point of view in personal memories. *Cognitive Psychology, 15,* 467–482.

Nissen, M. J., Ross, J. L., Willingham, D. B., Mackenzie, T. B., & Schacter, D. L. (1994). Evaluating amnesia in multiple personality disorder. In R. M. Klein & B. J. Doane (Eds.), *Psychological concepts and dissociative disorders* (pp. 259–282). Hillsdale, NJ: Lawrence Erlbaum.

Noble, C. E. (1952). An analysis of meaning. *Psychological Review, 59,* 421–430.

Nogrady, H., McConkey, K., & Perry, C. (1985). Enhancing visual memory: Trying hypnosis, trying imagination, and trying again. *Journal of Abnormal Psychology, 94*(2), 195–204.

Noordman, L. G. M., & Vonk, W. (1998). Memory-based processing in understanding causal information. *Discourse Processes, 26*(203), 191–212.

Norman, D. A., & Bobrow, D. G. (1979). Descriptions: An intermediate state in memory retrieval. *Cognitive Psychology, 11,* 107–127.

Norman, D. A., & Shallice, T. (1986). Attention to action: Willed and automatic control of behavior. In R. J. Davidson, G. E. Schwartz, & D. E. Shapiro (Eds.), *Consciousness and self-regulation* (Vol. 4, pp. 1–18). New York: Plenum Press.

Nyberg, L. (1999). Imaging episodic memory: Implications for cognitive theories and phenomena. In J. K. Foster (Ed.), *Neuroimaging and memory* (pp. 585–598). Hove, UK: Psychology Press.

Nyberg, L., McIntosh, A. R., Cabeza, R., Nilsson, L. G., Houle, R., & Tulving, E. (1996). Network analysis of positron emission tomography regional cerebral blood flow data: Ensemble inhibition during episodic memory retrieval. *Journal of Neuroscience, 16,* 3753–3759.

Nyberg, L., McIntosh, A. R., Houle, S., & Nilsson, G. L. (1996). Activation of medial temporal structures during episodic memory retrieval. *Nature, 380*(6576), 715–717.

Nystrom, L. E., Leigh, E., & McClelland, J. L. (1992). Trace synthesis in cued recall. *Journal of Memory and Language, 31*(5), 591–614.

O'Brien, E. J., & Albrecht, J. E. (1992). Comprehension strategies in the development of a mental model. *Journal of Experimental Psychology: Learning, Memory, and Cognition, 18*(4), 777–784.

O'Brien, E. J., Albrecht, J. E., Hakala, C. M., & Rizzella, M. L. (1995). Activation and suppression of antecedent during reinstatement. *Journal of Experimental Psychology: Learning, Memory, and Cognition, 21*(3), 626–634.

O'Reilly, R. C., & McClelland, J. L. (1994). Hippocampal conjunctive encoding, storage and recall: Avoiding a trade-off. *Hippocampus, 4,* 661–682.

Ofshe, R. I. (1992). Inadvertent hypnosis during interrogation: False confessions due to dissociative state, misidentified multiple personality and the satanic cult hypothesis. *International Journal of Clinical and Experimental Hypnosis, 40*(3), 125–156.

Öhman, A. (2002). Automaticity and the amygdale: Nonconscious responses to emotional fces. *Current Directions in Psychological Science, 11*(2), 62–66.

Ohtsuka, K., & Brewer, W. F. (1992). Discourse organization in the comprehension of temporal order in narrative texts. *Discourse Processes, 15*(3), 317–336.

Omanson, R. C. (1982). An analysis of narrative: Identifying central supportive and distracting content. *Discourse Processes, 5,* 195–224.

Orne, M. T. (1962). Hypnotically induced hallucinations. In J. L. West (Ed.), *Hallucinations.* (pp. 211–219). Oxford, UK: Crane and Stratton.

Orne, M. T. (1973). Communication by the total experimental situation: Why it is important, how it is evaluated and its significance for the ecological validity of findings. In P. Pliner, L. Krames, & T. Alloway (Eds.), *Communication and affect: Language and thought* (pp. 157–191). New York: Academic Press.

Otani, A. (1992). Memory in hypnosis. *The Advocate, 16*(1), 111–121.

Owens, W. A. (1966). Age and mental ability: A second follow-up. *Journal of Educational Psychology, 57,* 311–325.

Paivio, A. (1969). Mental imagery in associative learning and memory. *Psychological Review, 76*(3), 241–263.

Paivio, A. (1991). Dual coding theory: Retrospect and current status. *Canadian Journal of Psychology, 45*(3), 255–287.

Palmer, S., & Rock, I. (1994). Rethinking perceptual organization: The role of uniform connectedness. *Psychonomic Bulletin & Review, 1*(1), 29–55.

Parkin, A. J. (1987). *Memory and amnesia: An introduction.* Cambridge, MA: Basil Blackwell.

Parkin, A. J. (1998). *Memory and amnesia.* Cambridge, MA: Blackwell.

Parkin, A. J., Bindschaedler, C., Harsent, L., & Metzler, C. (1996). Pathological false alarm rates following damage to the left frontal cortex. *Brain and Cognition, 32,* 14–27.

Pavlov, I. P. (1927/1960). *Conditioned reflexes.* London: Oxford University Press.

Payne, D. G. (1987). Hypermnesia and reminiscence in recall: A historical and empirical review. *Psychological Bulletin, 101,* 5–27.

Payne, D. G., Elie, C. J., Blackwell, J. M., & Neuschatz, J. S. (1996). Memory illusions: Recalling, recognizing, and recollecting events that never occurred. *Journal of Memory and Language, 35,* 261–285.

Payne, D. G., Neuschatz, J. S., Lampinen, J. M., & Lynn, S. J. (1997). Compelling memory illusions: The qualitative characteristics of false memories. *Current Directions in Psychological Science, 6*(3), 56–60.

Pendergrast, M. (1996). *Victims of memory: Incest accusations and shattered lives.* London: Harper Collins.

Perfect, T. J., & Askew, C. (1994). Print adverts: Not remembered but memorable. *Applied Cognitive Psychology, 8*(9), 693–703.

Perfetti, C. A., & Britt, M. A. (1995). Where do propositions come from? In C. A. Weaver III & S. Mannes (Eds.), *Discourse comprehension: Essays in honor of Walter Kintsch* (pp. 11–34). Hillsdale, NJ: Lawrecne Erlbaum.

Perfetti, C. A., Britt, M. A., & Georgi, M. C. (1995). Text based learning and reasoning: Studies in history. Hillsdale, NJ: Lawrence Erlbaum.

Perky, C. W. (1910). An experimental study in imagination. *American Journal of Psychology, 21*(3), 422–452.

Peronnet, F., & Farah, M. J. (1989). Mental rotation: An event-related potential study with a validated mental rotation task. *Brain and Cognition, 9*(2), 279–288.

Perry, C. W., Laurence, J. R., D'Eon, J. L., & Tallant, B. (1988). Hypnotic age regression techniques in the elicitation of memories: Applied uses and abuses. In H. M. Pettinati (Ed.), *Hypnosis and memory: The Guilford clinical and experimental hyopnosis series* (pp. 128–154). New York: Guilford.

Peterson, C., & Bell, M. (1996). Children's memory for traumatic injury. *Child Development, 76*(6), 3045–3070.

Peterson, L. R., & Johnson, S. T. (1971). Some effects of minimizing articulation on short-term retention. *Journal of Verbal Learning and Verbal Behavior, 10*(4), 346–354.

Peterson, L. R., & Peterson, M. J. (1959). Short-term retention of individual verbal items. *Journal of Experimental Psychology, 58,* 193–198.

Phelps, E. A., LaBar, K. S., Anderson, A. K., O'Conner, K. J., Fulbright, R. K., & Spencer, D. D. (1998). Specifying the contributions of the human amygdala to emotional memory: A case study. *Neuroscience, 4*(6), 527–540.

Piaget, J. (1926a). *Judgment and reasoning in the child* (M. Warden, Trans.). New York: Harcourt, Brace & World.

Piaget, J. (1926b). *The language and thought of the child.* Oxford, UK: Harcourt Brace.

Piaget, J. (1950). *The psychology of intelligence* (M. Percy & D. E. Berlyne, Trans.). London: Routledge & Kegan Paul.

Piaget, J. (1951). *Play, dreams and imitation in childhood* (C. Gategno & F. M. Hodgson, Trans.). New York: Norton.

Piaget, J. (1952). *The origins of intelligence in children* (M. Cook, Trans). New York: Basic Books.

Piaget, J. (1954). The construction of reality in the child. (M. Cook, Trans)., New York: Basic Books.

Piaget, J. (1969). *Collected psychological works.* Oxford, UK: Prosveshchenie.

Piaget, J. (1972). *Principles of genetic epistemology* (W. Mays, Trans.). New York: Basic Books.

Piaget, J. (1976). *The child &and reality* (A. Rosin, Trans.). Oxford, UK: Penguin.

Piaget, J. (1977). *The development of thought: Equilibration of cognitive structures* (A. Rosin, Trans.). Oxford, UK: Viking.

Piaget, J., & Inhelder, B. (1971). *Mental imagery in the child.* New York: Basic Books.

Piaget, J., & Inhelder, B. (1973). *Memory and intelligence* (A. J. Pomerans, Trans.). London: Routledge & Kegan Paul.

Pick, A. (1903). Clinical studies III: On reduplicative paramnesia. *Brain, 26,* 260–267.

Pillemer, D. B. (1984). Flashbulb memories of the assassination attempts on President Reagan. *Cognition, 16,* 63–80.

Pillemer, D. B. (1992). Preschool children's memories of personal experiences: The fire alarm study. In E. Winograd & U. Neisser (Eds.), *Affect and accuracy in recall: Studies of "flashbulb" memories* (pp. 121–137). Cambridge, UK: Cambridge University Press.

Pillemer, D. B., & White, S. H. (1989). Childhood events recalled by children and adults. In H. E. Reese (Ed.), *Advances in child development and behavior* (Vol. 21, pp. 297–340). Orlando, FL: Academic Press.

Piper, A. (1993). Truth serum and recovered memories of sexual abuse: A review of the evidence. *Journal of Psychiatry and the Law, 21,* 447–471.

Porter, S., & Birt, A. R. (2001). Is traumatic memory special? A comparison of traumatic memory characteristics with memory for other emotional life experiences. *Journal of Applied Cognitive Psychology, 15,* 101–118.

Porter, S., Yuille, J. C., & Lehman, D. R. (1999). The nature of real, implanted and fabricated memories for emotional childhood events: Implications for the recovered memory debate. *Law and Human Behavior, 23,* 517–537.

Posner, M. I., & Keele, S. W. (1968). On the genesis of abstract ideas. *Journal of Experimental Psychology, 77,* 353–363.

Postman, L., & Phillips, L. W. (1965). Short-term temporal changes in free recall. *Quarterly Journal of Experimental Psychology, 17,* 132–138.

Postman, L., & Underwood, B. J. (1973). Critical issues in interference theory. *Memory & Cognition, 1*(1), 19–40.

Potter, M. C. (1993). Very short-term conceptual memory. *Memory & Cognition, 21*(2), 156–161.

Poynor, D. V., & Morris R. K. (2003). Inferred goals in narratives: Evidence from self-paced reading, recall and eye movements. *Journal of Experimental Psychology: Learning, Memory, and Cognition, 29*(1), 3–9.

Pozzulo, J. D., & Lindsay, R. C. L. (1998). Identification accuracy of children versus adults: A meta-analysis. *Law and Human Behavior, 22*(5), 549–570.

Putnam, H. (1975a). The meaning of meaning. In K. Gunderson (Ed.), *Language, mind and knowledge* (pp. 131–193). Minneapolis: University of Minnesota Press.

Putnam, H. (1975b). Minds and machines. In H. Putnam (Ed.), *Mind, language, and reality* (pp. 362–385). Cambridge, UK: Cambridge University Press.

Pylyshyn, Z. (1973). What the mind's eye tells the mind's brain: A critique of mental imagery. *Psychological Bulletin, 80,* 1–24.

Pylyshyn, Z. (1981). The imagery debate: Analog media versus tacit knowledge. *Psychological Review, 88,* 16–45.

Pylyshyn, Z. (1984). *Computation and cognition.* Cambridge: MIT Press.

Raaijmakers, J. G., & Shiffrin, R. M. (1981). Search of associative memory. *Psychological Review, 88*(2), 93–134.

Raaijmakers, J. G., & Shiffrin, R. M. (1992). Models for recall and recognition. *Annual Review of Psychology, 43,* 205–234.

Radvansky, G. A. (1993). Recognition, recall, and mental models. *Dissertation Abstracts International, 53,* 9–13.

Radvansky, G. A., Spieler, D. H., & Zacks, R. T. (1993). Mental model organization. *Journal of Experimental Psychology: Learning, Memory, and Cognition, 19*(1), 95–114.

Randall, J. H. (1960). *Aristotle.* New York: Columbia University Press.

Rao, K. V., & Proctor, R. W. (1984). Study-phase processing and the word frequency effect in recognition memory. *Journal of Experimental Psychology: Learning, Memory, and Cognition, 10*(3), 386–394.

Ratcliff, R., & McKoon, G. (1981). Automatic and strategic priming in recognition. *Journal of Verbal Learning and Verbal Behavior, 20*(2), 204–215.

Ratcliff, R., & McKoon, G. (1988). A retrieval theory of priming in memory. *Psychological Review, 95*(3), 385–408.

Ratcliff, R., & McKoon, G. (1992). Inference during reading. *Psychological Review, 99*(3), 440–446.

Ratcliff, R., & McKoon, G. (1994). Retrieving information from memory: Spreading-activation theories versus compound-cue theories. *Psychological Review, 101*(1), 177–184.

Ratcliff, R., & McKoon, G. (1995). Bias in the priming of object decisions. *Journal of Experimental Psychology: Learning, Memory, and Cognition, 21*(3), 754–767.

Ratcliff, R., & McKoon, G. (1996). Bias effects in implicit memory tasks. *Journal of Experimental Psychology: General, 125*(4), 403–421.

Ratcliff, R., & McKoon, G. (1997). A counter model for implicit priming in perceptual word identification. *Psychological Review, 104,* 319–343.

Ratcliff, R., Sheu, C., & Gronlund, S. D. (1992). Testing global memory models using ROC curves. *Psychological Review, 99*(3), 518–535.

Rauch, S. L., Savage, C. R., Alpert, N. M., Fischman, A. J., & Jenike, M. A. (1997). The functional neuroanatomy of anxiety: A study of three disorders using positron emission tomography and symptom provocation. *Biological Psychiatry, 42*(6), 446–452.

Rayner, K., Pacht, J. M., & Duffy, S. A. (1994). Effects of prior encounter and global discourse bias on the processing of lexically ambiguous words: Evidence from eye fixations. *Journal of Memory and Language, 33*(4), 527–544.

Read, J. D. (1996). From a passing thought to a false memory in 2 minutes: Confusing real and illusory events. *Psychonomic Bulletin & Review, 3*(1), 105–111.

Ready, D. J., Bothwell, R. K., & Brigham, J. C. (1997). The effects of hypnosis, context reinstatement, and anxiety on eyewitness memory. *International Journal of Clinical and Experimental Hypnosis, 45*(1), 55–68.

Reber, A. S. (1965). *Implicit learning of artificial grammars.* Unpublished master's thesis, Brown University.

Reber, A. S. (1967). Implicit learning of artificial grammars. *Journal of Verbal Learning and Verbal Behavior, 6,* 317–327.

Reber, A. S. (1993). *Implicit learning and tacit knowledge.* New York: Oxford University Press.

Reber, A. S., & Allen, R. (1978). Analogy and abstraction strategies in synthetic grammar learning: A functionalist interpretation. *Cognition, 6,* 189–221.

Reber, A. S., & Lewis (1977). Toward a theory of implicit learning: The analysis of the form and structure of a body of tacit knowledge. *Cognition, 5,* 333–361.

Reber, A. S., Walkenfeld, F. F., & Hernstadt, R. (1991). Implicit and explicit learning: Individual differences and IQ. *Journal of Experimental Psychology: Learning, Memory, and Cognition, 17,* 888–896.

Reed, S. K. (1996). *Cognition.* Pacific Grove, CA: Brooks Cole.

Reed, S. K., Hock, H. S., & Lockhead, G. R. (1983). Tacit knowledge and the effect of pattern configuration in mental scanning. *Memory & Cognition, 11*(2), 137–143.

Reid, L. S. (1974). Toward a grammar of the image. *Psychological Bulletin, 81,* 319–334.

Reiser, B. J. (1986). The encoding and retrieval of memories of real world experiences. In J. A. Galambo, R. P. Abelson, & J. B. Black (Eds.), *Knowledge structures* (pp. 71–99). New York: Lawrence Erlbaum.

Reiser, B. J., Black, J. B., & Kalamarides, P. (1986). Strategic memory search processes. In D. C. Rubin (Ed.), *Autobiographical memory* (pp. 100–121). New York: Cambridge University Press.

Reitman, J. (1971). Mechanisms of forgetting in short-term memory. *Cognitive Psychology, 1*(2), 185–195.

Reitman, J. (1974). Without surreptitious rehearsal, information in short-term memory decays. *Journal of Verbal Learning and Verbal Behavior, 13*(4), 365–377.

Rensink, R. A. (2004). Visual sensing without seeing. *Psychological Science, 15*(1), 27–32.

Rensink, R. A., O'Regan, J. K., & Clark, J. J. (2000). On the failure to detect changes in scenes across brief interruptions. *Visual Cognition, 7,* 127–145.

Reyna, V. F., & Brainerd, C. J. (1995a). Fuzzy-trace theory: Some foundational issues. *Learning and Individual Differences, 7*(2), 145–162.

Reyna, V. F., & Brainerd, C. J. (1995b). Fuzzy-trace theory: An interim synthesis. *Learning and Individual Differences, 7*(1), 1–75.

Rhodes, C., Brake, S., Tan, S., & Taylor, K. (1989). Expertise and configural coding in face recognition. *British Journal of Psychology, 80,* 313–331.

Richardson-Klavehn, A., & Bjork, R. A. (1988). Measures of memory. *Annual Review of Psychology, 39,* 475–543.

Richardson, R., Riccio, D., & Axiotis, R. (1986). *Developmental Psychobiology, 19*(5), 453–462.

Ridley, A. M., & Clifford. B. R. (2004). The effects of anxious mood induction on suggestibility to misleading post-event information. *Applied Cognitive Psychology, 18*(2), 233–244.

Rinck, M., Haehnel, A., & Becker, G. (2001). Using temporal information to construct, update and retrieve situation models of narratives. *Journal of Experimental Psychology: Learning, Memory, and Cognition, 27*, 67–80.

Rinck, M., Williams, P., Bower, G. H., & Becker, E. S. (1996). Spatial situation models and narrative understanding: Some generalizations and extensions. *Discourse Processes, 21*(1), 23–55.

Roberts, R. J., Hager, L. D., & Heron, C. (1994). Prefrontal cognitive processes: Working memory and inhibition in the antisaccade task. *Journal of Experimental Psychology: General, 123*, 374–393.

Robinson, J. A. (1977). Autobiographical memory. In M. Gruneberg & P. Morris, (Eds.), *Aspects of memory: Vol 1. Practical aspects.* London: Methuen.

Robinson, J. A. (1999). Perspective, meaning, and remembering. In D. C. Rubin (Ed.), *Remembering our past: Studies in autobiographical memory* (pp. 199–217). New York: Cambridge University Press.

Robinson, J. A., & Swanson, K. L. (1993). Field and observer modes of remembering. *Memory, 1*(3), 169–184.

Robinson, K. J., & Roediger, H. L., III, (1997). Associative processes in false recall and false recognition. *Psychological Science, 8*, 231–237.

Roediger, H. L., III. (1974). Inhibition in recall from cuing with recall targets. *Journal of Verbal Learning and Verbal Behavior, 12*, 644–657.

Roediger, H. L., III. (1978). Recall as a self-limiting process. *Memory & Cognition, 6*, 54–63.

Roediger, H. L., III, & Adelson, B. (1980). *Memory & Cognition, 8*, 65–74.

Roediger, H. L., III, Balota, D. A., & Robinson, K. J. (2000). *Automatic mechanisms in the arousal of false memories.* Manuscript in preparation, Washington University, St. Louis, MO.

Roediger, H. L., III, Balota, D. A., & Watson, J. M. (2001). Spreading activation and the arousal of false memories. In H. L. Roediger III, J. S. Nairne, I. Neath, & A. M. Surprenant (Eds.), *The nature of remembering: Essays in Honor of Robert G. Crowder* (pp. 95–115). Washington, DC: American Psychological Association.

Roediger, H. L., III, & McDermott, K. B. (1995). Creating false memories: Remembering words not presented in lists. *Journal of Experimental Psychology: Learning, Memory, and Cognition, 21*(4), 803–814.

Roediger, H. L., III, & Payne, D. G. (1982). Hypermnesia: The role of repeated testing. *Journal of Experimental Psychology: Learning, Memory, and Cognition, 8*, 66–72.

Roediger, H. L., III, & Thorpe, L. A. (1978). The role of recall in producing hypermnesia. *Memory & Cognition, 6*, 296–305.

Roediger, H. L., III, Weldon, M. S., & Challis, B. H. (1989). Explaining dissociations between implicit and explicit measures of retention: A processing account. In H. L. Roediger III & F. I. M. Craik (Eds.), *Varieties of memory and consciousness: Essays in honour of Endel Tulving* (pp. 3–41). Hillsdale, NJ: Lawrence Erlbaum.

Rohrenbach, C., & Landis, T. (1995). Dreamjourneys: Living in woven realities, the syndrome of reduplicative paramnesia. In R. Campbell & M. Conway (Eds.), *Broken memories: Case studies in memory impairment* (pp. 93–102), Cambridge, UK: Blackwell.

Roland, P. E., & Frieberg, L. (1985). Localization of cortical areas activated by thinking. *Journal of Neurophysiology, 53*, 1219–1243.

Roman, F., Staubli, U., & Lynch, G. (1987). Evidence for synaptic potentiation in a cortical network during learning. *Brain Research, 418*, 221–226.

Roodenrys, S., & Quinlan, P. T. (2000). The effects of stimulus set size and word frequency on verbal serial recall. *Memory, 8,* 71–78.

Roozendaal, B., Portillo-Marquez, G., & McGaugh, J. L. (1996). Basolateral amygdala lesions block glucocorticoid-induced modulation of memory for spatial learning. *Behavioral Neuroscience, 110*(5), 1074–1083.

Rouder, J. N., Ratcliff, R., & McKoon, G. (2000). A neural network model of implicit memory for object recognition. *Psychological Science, 11,* 13–19.

Rovee-Collier, C. (1999). The development of infant memory. *Current Directions in Psychological Science, 8*(3), 80–85.

Rovee-Collier, C. (2000). *Shifting the focus from what to why.* Malden, MA: Blackwell.

Rovee-Collier, C., & Boller, K. (1995). *Interference or facilitation in infant memory?* San Diego, CA: Academic Press.

Rovee-Collier, C., Griesler, P. C., & Early, L. A. (1985). Contextual determinants of retrieval in three-month-old infants. *Learning and Motivation, 16,* 139–157.

Rovee-Collier, C., & Gulya, M. (2000). Infant memory: Cues, context, categories and lists. In D. L. Medin (Ed.), *Psychology of learning and motivation* (pp. 1–46). San Diego, CA: Academic Press.

Rovee-Collier, C., Hartshorn, K., & DiRubbo, M. (1999). Long-term maintenance of infant memory. *Developmental Psychobiology, 35*(2), 91–102.

Rubin, D. C., & Berntsen, D. (2003). Life scripts help to maintain autobiographical memories of highly positive, but not highly negative, events. *Memory & Cognition, 31*(1), 1–14.

Rubin, D. C., Feldman, M. E., & Beckham, J. C. (2004). Reliving, emotions, and fragmentation in PTSD. *Journal of Applied Cognitive Psychology, 18*(1), 17–35.

Rubin, D. C., & Kozin, M. (1984). Vivid memories. *Cognition, 16,* 81–95.

Rubin, D. C., Wetzler, S. E., & Nebes, R. D. (1986). Autobiographical memory across the adult lifespan. In D. C Rubin (Ed.), *Autobiographical memory* (pp. 202–221). New York: Cambridge University Press.

Rugg, M. D., Fletcher, P. C., Frith, C. D., Frackowiak, R. S. J., & Dolan, R. J. (1997). Brain regions supporting intentional and incidental memory: A PET study. *NeuroReport, 8,* 1283–1285.

Rugg, M. D., & Yonelinas, A. P. (2003). Human recognition memory: A cognitive neuroscience perspective. *Trends in Cognitive Sciences, 7,* 313–319.

Rumelhart, D. E. (1975). Notes on a scheme for stories. In D. G. Bobrow & R. M. Collins (Eds.), *Representation and understanding* (pp. 211–236). New York: Academic Press.

Rumelhart, D. E. (1977). Understanding and summarizing brief stories. In D. Laberge & S. J. Samuels (Eds.), *Basic processes in reading comprehension* (pp. 265–303). Hillsdale, NJ: Lawrence Erlbaum.

Rumelhart, D. E. (1980). Schemata: The building blocks of cognition. In R. Spiro, B. Bruce, & B. Brewer (Eds.), *Theoretical issues in reading comprehension* (pp. 33–58). Hillsdale, NJ: Lawrence Erlbaum.

Rumelhart, D. E. (1990). Brain style computation: Learning and generalization. In S. F. Zornetzer, J. L. David, & C. Lau (Eds.), *An introduction to neural and electronic networks* (pp. 405–420). San Diego, CA: Academic Press.

Rumelhart, D. E., & McClelland, J. L. (1986). *Parallel distributed processing: Explorations in the microstructure of cognition* (Vol. 2). Cambridge: MIT Press.

Rumelhart, D. E., & Todd, P. M. (1993). Learning and representations. In D. E. Meyer & S. Korblu (Eds.), *Attention and Performance XIV* (pp. 3–30). Cambridge: MIT Press.

Rundus, D. (1980). Maintenance rehearsal and long-term memory. *Memory & Cognition, 8*(3), 226–230.

Ryan, J. (1969). Grouping and short-term memory: Different means and patterns of grouping. *Quarterly Journal of Experimental Psychology, 21*(2), 137–147.

Sacchett, C., & Humphreys, G. W. (1992). Calling a squirrel a squirrel but a canoe a wigwam: A category-specific deficit for artefactual objects and body parts. *Cognitive Neuropsychology, 9*(1), 73–86.

Sachs, J. (1983). Talking about the there and then: The emergence of displaced reference in parent-child discourse. In K. Nelson (Ed.), *Children's language* (Vol. 4, pp. 1–18). New York: Gardner Place.

Sakitt, B. (1976). Iconic memory. *Psychological Review, 83,* 257–276.

Sakitt, B., & Long, G. M. (1979). Spare the rod and spoil the icon. *Journal of Experimental Psychology: Human Perception and Performance, 5,* 19–30.

Salaman, E. (1970). *A collection of moments: A study of involuntary memories.* London: Longman.

Salame, P., & Baddeley, A. (1987). Noise, unattended speech and short-term memory. *Ergonomics, 30*(8), 1185–1194.

Salmon, K., & Pipe, M. E. (1997). Props and children's event reports: The impact of a 1-year delay. *Journal of Experimental Child Psychology, 65*(3), 261–292.

Sanders, A. L., Wheeler, M. E., & Buckner, R. L. (2000). Episodic recognition modulates frontal and parietal cortex activity. *Journal of Cognitive Neuroscience* (Suppl.), 50A.

Sanford, A. J., & Garrod, S. C. (1998). The role of scenario mapping in text comprehension. *Discourse Processes, 26,* 159–190.

Saufley, W. H., Otaka, S. R., & Baversco, J. L. (1985). Context effects: Classroom tests and context independence. *Memory & Cognition, 13*(6), 522–528.

Sargent, W., & Slater, E. (1941). Amnesic syndromes in war. *Proceedings of the Royal Society of Medicine, 34,* 757–764.

Saywitz, K. J., Goodman, G. S., Nicholas, E., & Moan, S. F. (1991). Children's memories of a physical examination involving genital touch: Implications for reports of child sexual abuse. *Journal of Consulting and Clinical Psychology, 59*(5), 682–691.

Scarmeas, N., Levy, G., Tang, M. S., Manly, J., & Stern, Y. (2001). Influences of leisure activity on the incidence of Alzheimer's disease. *Neurology, 57*(12), 2236–2242.

Schactel, E. G. (1947). On memory and childhood amnesia. *Psychiatry, 10,* 1–26.

Schacter, D. L. (1985). Priming of old and new knowledge in amnesic patients and normal subjects. *Annals of the New York Academy of Sciences, 444,* 41–53.

Schacter, D. L. (1990a). Introduction to implicit memory: Multiple perspectives. *Bulletin of the Psychonomic Society, 28*(4), 338–340.

Schacter, D. L. (1990b). Perceptual representation systems and implicit memory: Toward a resolution of the multiple memory systems debate. *Annals of the New York Academy of Science, 608,* 543–571.

Schacter, D. L. (1992). Understanding implicit memory: A cognitive neuroscience approach. *American Psychologist, 47,* 559–569.

Schacter, D. L. (1993). Spared priming despite impaired comprehension: Implicit memory in a case of word memory deafness. *Neuropsychology, 7*(2), 107–118.

Schacter, D. L. (1994a). Implicit knowledge: new perspectives on unconscious processes. *In* O. Sporns & G. Tononi (Eds.), *Selection and the brain: International review of neurobiology* (Vol. 37, pp. 271–284). San Diego CA: Academic Press.

Schachter, D. L. (1994b). Priming and multiple memory systems: Perceptual mechanisms of implicit memory. In D. L. Schacter & E. Tulving (Eds.), *Memory systems* (pp. 233–268). Cambridge: MIT Press.

Schacter, D. L. (1995). Implicit memory: A new frontier for cognitive neuroscience. In M. S. Gazzaniga (Ed.), *The cognitive neurosciences* (Vol. 14, pp. 815–824). Cambridge: MIT Press.

Schacter, D. L. (1996). *Searching for memory: The brain, the mind and the past.* New York: Basic Books.

Schacter, D. L., Chiu, C. Y. P., & Ochsner, K. N. (1993). Implicit memory: A selective review. *Annual Review of Neuroscience, 16,* 159–182.

Schacter, D. L., Church, B., & Treadwell, J. (1994). Implicit memory in amnesic patients: Evidence for spared auditory priming. *Psychological Science, 5*(1), 20–25.

Schacter, D. L., & Graf, P. (1985). Implicit and explicit memory for new associations in normal and amnesic subjects. *Journal of Experimental Psychology: Learning, Memory, and Cognition, 11*(3), 501–518.

Schacter, D. L., McGlynn, S. M., Milberg, W. P., & Church, B. A. (1993). Spared priming despite impaired comprehension: Implicit memory in a case of word meaning deafness. *Neuropsychology, 7*(2), 107–118.

Schacter, D. L., & Tulving, E. (1994). What are the memory systems of 1994? In D. L. Schacter & E. Tulving (Eds.), *Memory systems* (pp. 1–38). Cambridge: MIT Press.

Schacter, D. L., & Wagner, A. D. (1999). Medial temporal lobe activations in FMRI and PET studies of episodic encoding and retrieval. *Hippocampus, 9,* 7–24.

Schank, R. C. (1982). *Dynamic memory: A theory of learning in computers and people.* New York: Cambridge University Press.

Schank, R. C. (1999). *Dynamic memory revisited.* New York: Cambridge University Press.

Schank, R. C., & Abelson, R. D. (1977). *Scripts, plans, goals and understanding: An inquiry into human knowledge structures.* Hillsdale, NJ: Lawrence Erlbaum.

Scheck, C. L., & Kinicki, A. J. (2000). Identifying the antecedents of coping with an organizational acquisition: A structural assessment. *Journal of Organizational Behavior, 21*(6), 627–648.

Schmolck, H., Buffalo, A. E., & Squire, L. R. (2000). Memory distortions develop over time: Recollections of the O.J. Simpson verdict after 15 and 32 months. *Psychological Science, 11*(1), 39–45.

Schneider, W., & Detweiler, M. A. (1987). A connectionist/control architecture for working memory. In G. Bower (Ed.), *The psychology of learning and motivation: Advances in research and theory* (Vol. 21, pp. 53–119). San Diego, CA: Academic Press.

Schneider, W., & Shiffrin, R. M. (1977). Controlled and automatic information processing I: Detection, search and attention. *Psychological Review, 84,* 1–66.

Schooler, J. W., Bendiksen, M., & Ambadar, Z. (1997). Taking the middle line: Can we accommodate both fabricated and recovered memories of sexual abuse? In M. A. Conway (Ed.), *False and recovered memories* (pp. 251–292). Oxford, UK: Oxford University Press.

Schooler, J. W., Clark, C. A., & Loftus, E. F. (1988). Knowing when memory is real. In M. Gruneberg, P. Morris, & R. Sykes (Eds). *Practical aspects of memory: Current research and issues* (pp. 83–88). New York: Wiley.

Schooler, J. W., Gerhard, D., & Loftus, E. F. (1986). Qualities of the unreal. *Journal of Experimental Psychology: Learning, Memory, and Cognition, 12*(2), 171–181.

Schooler, J. W., & Hermann, D. J. (1992). There is more to episodic memory than just episodes. In M. A. Conway, D. C. Rubin, H. Spinnler, & W. A. Wagenaar (Eds.), *Theoretical perspectives on autobiographical memory* (pp. 241–262). Dordrecht, The Netherlands: Kluwer Academic.

Schwartz, G., Howard, M. W., Jing, B., & Kahana, M. J. (2005). Shadows of the past: Temporal retrieval effects in recognition memory. *Psychological Science, 16*(11), 898–904.

Schweikert, R., & Boruff, B. (1986). Short-term memory capacity: Magic number or magic spell? *Journal of Experimental Psychology: Learning, Memory, and Cognition, 12,* 419–425.

Schweikert, R., Guentert, L., & Hersberger, L. (1990). Phonological similarity, pronunciation rate, and memory span. *Psychological Science, 1*(1), 74–77.

Searle, J. (1984). *Minds, brains and science.* Cambridge, MA: Harvard University Press.

Segal, S. J., & Fusella, V. (1970). Influence of imagined pictures and sounds on detection of visual and auditory signals. *Journal of Experimental Psychology, 83,* 458–464.

Seidlitz, L. K., Wyer, R. S., & Diener, E. (1997). Cognitive correlates of subjective well-being: The processing of valenced life events by happy and unhappy persons. *Journal of Research in Personality, 31,* 240–256.

Seifert, C. M., Robertson, S. P., & Black, J. B. (1985). Types of inferences generated during reading. *Journal of Memory and Language, 24,* 405–422.

Seitz, R. J., Roland, P. E., & Bohm, C. (1990). Motor learning in man: A positron emission tomographic study. *Neuroreport: An International Journal for the Rapid Communication of Research in Neuroscience, 1*(1), 57–60.

Service, E. (1998). The effect of word length on immediate serial recall depends on phonological complexity, not articulatory duration. *Quarterly Journal of Experimental Psychology: Human Experimental Psychology, 51A*(2), 283–304.

Shah, P., & Miyake, A. (1996). The separability of working memory resources for spatial thinking and language processing: An individual differences approach. *Journal of Experimental Psychology: General, 125*(1), 4–27.

Shallice, T. (1988). *From neuropsychology to mental structure.* Cambridge, UK: Cambridge University Press.

Shapiro, P. N., & Penrod, S. (1986). Meta-analysis of facial identification studies. *Psychological Bulletin, 100*(2), 139–156.

Sheehan, P. W., Statham, D., & Jamieson, G. A. (1991a). Pseudomemory effects over time in the hypnotic setting. *Journal of Abnormal Psychology, 100*(1), 39–44.

Sheehan, P. W., Statham, D., & Jamieson, G. A. (1991b). Pseudomemory effects and their relationship to level of susceptibility to hypnosis and state instruction. *Journal of Personality and Social Psychology, 60*(1), 130–137.

Sheehan, P. W., Statham, D., Jamieson, G. A., Ferguson, S. R. (1991). Ambiguity in suggestion and the occurrence of pseudomemory in the hypnotic setting. *Australian Journal of Clinical and Experimental Hypnosis, 19*(1), 1–18.

Sheen, M., Kemp, S., & Rubin, D. (2001). Twins dispute memory ownership: A new false memory phenomenon. *Memory & Cognition, 29*(6), 779–788.

Sheingold, K., & Tenney, Y. J. (1982). Memory for a salient childhood event. In U. Neisser (Ed.), *Memory observed* (pp. 201–212). New York: W. H. Freeman.

Shepard, R. N. (1967). Recognition memory for words, sentences, and pictures. *Journal of Verbal Learning and Verbal Behavior, 6*(1), 156–163.

Shepard, R. N. (1986). Spatial factors in visual attention: A reply to Cassini. *Journal of Experimental Psychology: Human Perception and Performance, 12*(3), 383–387.

Shepard, R. N., & Cooper, L. A. (1986). *Mental images and their transformations.* Cambridge: MIT Press.

Shepard, R. N., & Metzler, J. (1971). Mental rotation of three-dimensional objects. *Science, 171,* 701–703.

Sheridan, J., & Humphreys, G. W. (1993). A verbal-semantic category-specific recognition impairment. *Cognitive Neuropsychology, 10*(2), 143–184.

Sherman, S. J., Atri, A., & Hasselmo, M. E. (2003). Scopolamine impairs human recognition memory: Data and modeling. *Behavioral Neuroscience, 117*(3), 526–539.

Shiffrin, R. M., & Cook, J. R. (1978). Short-term forgetting of item and order information. *Journal of Verbal Learning and Verbal Behavior, 17,* 189–218.

Shiffrin, R. M., & Schneider, W. (1997). Controlled and automatic human information processing II: Perceptual lerarning, automatic attending, and a general theory. *Psychological Review, 84*, 127–190.

Shimamura, A. P. (1986). Priming effects in amnesia: Evidence for a dissociable memory function. *Quarterly Journal of Experimental Psychology: Human Experimental Psychology, 38*(4A), 619–644.

Shimamura, A. P., Janowsky, J., & Squire, L. R. (1990). Memory for temporal order events in patients with frontal lobe lesions and amnesiac patients. *Neuropsychologia, 28*, 803–813.

Shimamura, A. P., Salmon, D. P., Squire, L. R., & Butters, N. (1987). Memory dysfunction and word priming in dementia and amnesia. *Behavioral Neuroscience, 101*(3), 347–351.

Shobe, K. K., & Schooler, J. W. (2001). Discovering fact and fiction: Case-based analyses of authentic and fabricated discovered memories of abuse. In G. M. Davies & T. Dalgleish (Eds.), *Recovered memories* (pp. 95–151). New York: Wiley.

Shors, T. J., & Matzel, L. D. (1997). Long term potentiation: What's learning got to do with it? *Behavioral Brain Sciences, 20*(4), 597–655.

Shulman, H. G. (1972). Semantic confusion errors in short-term memory. *Journal of Verbal Learning and Verbal Behavior, 11*(2), 221–227.

Sidis, B. (1898). *The psychology of suggestion.* New York: Appleton.

Siegel, L. S. (1994). Working memory and reading: A life-span perspective. *International Journal of Behavioral Development, 17*(1), 109–124.

Silva, A. J., Stevens, C. F., & Tonegawa, S. (1992). Deficient hippocampal long-term potentiation in a-calcium-calmodulin kinase II mutant mice. *Science, 257*(5067), 201–206.

Simcock, G., & Hayne, H. (2002). Breaking the barrier: Children fail to translate their preverbal memories into language. *Psychological Science, 13*, 225–231.

Singer, M., (1993). Causal bridging inferences validating consistent and inconsistent sequences, *Canadian Journal of Experimental Psychology, 47*(2), 340–359.

Singer, J. A., & Salovey, P. (1988). Mood and memory: Evaluating the network theory of affect. *Clinical Psychology Review, 8*(2), 211–251.

Slamecka, N. J. (1968). An examination of trace storage in free recall. *Journal of Experimental Psychology, 76*, 504–513.

Slamecka, N. J. (1969). Testing for associative storage in multitrial free recall. *Journal of Experimental Psychology, 81*, 557–560.

Slamecka, N. J., & Graf, P. (1978). The generation effect: Delineation of a phenomenon. *Journal of Experimental Psychology: Human Learning and Memory, 4*(6), 592–604.

Sloman, S. A., Hayman, A. G., Ohta, N., Law, L., & Tulving, E. (1988). Forgetting in primed fragment completion. *Journal of Experimental Psychology: Learning, Memory, and Cognition, 14*(2), 223–239.

Slotnick, S., & Schacter, D. L. (2004). A sensory signal that distinguishes true from false memories. *Nature Neuroscience, 7*(6), 664–672.

Smith, E. E., & Jonides, J. (1994). Working memory in humans: Neuropsychological evidence. In M. S. Gazzaniga (Ed.), *The cognitive neurosciences* (pp. 1009–1020). Cambridge: MIT Press.

Smith, E. E., & Jonides, J. (1997). Working memory: A view from neuro-imaging. *Cognitive Psychology, 33*(1), 5–42.

Smith, M. E. (1952). Childhood memories compared with those of adult life. *Journal of Genetic Psychology, 80*, 151–182.

Smith, M. L., & Taylor, M. J. (1995). Age related ERP changes in verbal and nonverbal memory tasks. *Journal of Physiology, 9*(4), 283–297.

Smith, R. E. (2003). The cost of remembering to remember in event-based prospective memory: Investigating the capacity demands of delayed intention performance. *Journal of Experimental Psychology: Learning, Memory, and Cognition, 29*, 347–361.

Smith, S. M. (1979). Remembering in and out of context. *Journal of Experimental Psychology: Human Learning and Memory, 5*(5), 460–471.

Smith, S. M., Gleaves, B. H., Pierce, T. L., Williams, T. R., Gilliland, R., & Gerkens, D. R. (2003). Eliciting and comparing false and recovered memories: An experimental approach. *Applied Cognitive Psychology, 17*, 251–279.

Smith, S. M., Glenberg, A., & Bjork, R. A. (1978). Environmental context and human memory. *Memory & Cognition, 6*(4), 342–353.

Smith, S. M., & Vela, E. (1991). Incubated reminiscence effects. *Memory & Cognition, 19*, 168–176.

Smith, S. M., & Vela, E. (1992). Environmental context-dependent eyewitness recognition. *Applied Cognitive Psychology, 6*(2), 125–139.

Smith, S. M., Vela, E., & Williamson, J. E. (1988). Shallow input processing does not induce environmental context-dependent recognition. *Bulletin of the Psychonomic Society, 26*(6), 537–540.

Smolensky, P. (1988). On the proper treatment of connectionism. *Behavioral and Brain Sciences, 11*(1), 1–74.

So, D., & Siegel, L. S. (1997). Learning to read Chinese: Semantic, syntactic, phonological and working memory skills in normally achieving and poor Chinese readers. *Reading and Writing, 9*(1), 1–21.

Spear, N. E., & Mueller, C. W. (1984). Consolidation as a function of retrieval. In H. Weingartner & E. S. Parker (Eds.), *Memory consolidation* (pp. 111–147). Hillsdale, NJ: Lawrence Erlbaum.

Spearman, C. (1927). *The nature of intelligence and the principles of cognition* (2nd ed.). Oxford, UK: Macmillan.

Spence, I., Wong, P., Rusan, M., & Rastegar, N. (2006). How color enhances visual memory for natural scenes. *Psychological Science, 17*(1), 1–6.

Sperling, G. (1960). The information available in brief visual presentations. *Psychological Monographs, 74*(498), 1–29.

Sperling, G. (1963). A model for visual memory tasks. *Human Factors, 5*, 19–31.

Sperling, G. (1967). Successive approximations to a model for short-term memory. *Acta Psychologia, 27*, 285–292.

Spoehr, K. T., & Corin, W. J. (1978). The stimulus suffix effect as a memory coding phenomenon. *Memory and Cognition, 6*, 583–589.

Sporer, S. L., Penrod, S., Read, D., & Cutler, B. (1995). Choosing, confidence and accuracy: A meta-analysis of the confidence-accuracy relation in eyewitness identification studies. *Psychological Bulletin, 118*(3), 315–327.

Squire, L. R. (1981). Two forms of human amnesia: An analysis of forgetting. *Journal of Neuroscience, 1*, 635–640.

Squire, L. R. (1992a). Mechanisms of memory. In S. M. Kosslyn & R. A. Andersen (Eds.), *Frontiers of cognitive neuroscience.* Cambridge: MIT Press.

Squire, L. R. (1992b). Memory and the hippocampus: A synthesis from findings with rats, monkeys and humans. *Psychological Review, 99*, 195–231.

Squire, L. R. (2004). Memory systems of the brain: A brief history and current perspective. *Neurobiology of Learning and Memory, 82*, 171–177.

Squire, L. R., & Kandel, E. E. (1999). *Memory: From minds to molecules.* New York: Scientific American Library/Scientific American Books.

Squire, L. R., Knowlton, B., & Musen, G. (1993). The structure and organization of memory. *Annual Review of Psychology, 44,* 453–495.

Squire, L. R., & Zola Morgan, S. (1991). The medial temporal lobe memory system. *Science, 253,* 1380–1386.

Srinivas, K., & Roediger, H. L., III. (1990). Classifying implicit memory tests: Category association and anagram solution. *Journal of Memory and Language, 29*(4), 389–412.

St. George-Hyslop, P. H. (2000a). Piecing together Alzheimer's. *Scientific American, 283,* 76–83.

Stalnaker, J. M., & Riddle, E. E. (1932). The effect of hypnosis on long delayed recall. *Journal of General Psychology, 6,* 429–440.

Standing, L. (1973). Learning 10,000 pictures. *Quarterly Journal of Experimental Psychology, 25*(2), 207–222.

Steblay, N., Dysart, J., Fulero, S., & Lindsay, R. C. L. (2001). Eyewitness accuracy rates in sequential and simultaneous lineup presentations: A meta-analytic comparison. *Law and Human Behavior, 25*(5), 549–473.

Stein, B. S. (1978). Depth of processing re-examined: The effect of precision encoding and test appropriateness. *Journal of Verbal Learning and Verbal Behavior, 17,* 165–174.

Stern, W. (1904/1982). Realistic experiments. In U. Neisser (Ed.), *Memory observed* (pp. 199–213). San Francisco: W. H. Freeman.

Stiglerr, S. W., Lee, S. Y., & Stevenson, H. W. (1986). Digit memory in Chinese and English: Evidence for temporally limited store. *Cognition, 23,* 1–20.

Stromeyer, C. F., & Psotka, J. (1970). The detailed structure of eidetic images. *Nature, 225,* 346–349.

Stuss, D. T. (1992). Biological and psychological developments of executive functions. *Brain and Cognition, 20*(1), 8–23.

Suedfeld, P., & Eich, E. (1995). Autobiographical memory and affect under conditions of reduced environmental stimulation. *Journal of Environmental Psychology, 15,* 321–326.

Sulin, R. A., & Dooling, D. J. (1974). Intrusions of a thematic idea in retention of prose, *Journal of Experimental Psychology, 103,* 255–262.

Sutker, P. B., Winstead, D. K., Galina, Z. H., & Allain, A. N. (1991). Cognitive deficits and psychopathology among former prisoners of war and combat veterans of the Korean conflict. *American Journal of Psychiatry, 148,* 67–72.

Swanson, H. L. (1994). The role of working memory and dynamic assessment in the classification of children with learning disabilities. *Learning Disabilities Research and Practice, 9*(4), 190–202.

Talmy, L. (1985). Force dynamics in language and thought. In W. H. Eilfort, P. D. Kroeber, & K. L. Peterson (Eds.), *Papers from the parasession on causatives and agentivity at the twenty first regional meetings* (pp. 293–337). Chicago: Chicago Linguistic Society.

Tanaka, J., & Farah, M. (1993). Parts and wholes in face recognition. *Quarterly Journal of Experimental Psychology A, 46,* 225–245.

Tanaka, J., Kiefer, M., & Bukach, C. M. (2004). A holistic account of the same-race effect in face recogntion: Evidence from a cross-cultural study. *Cognition, 93,* B1–B9.

Teyler, T. J., & DiScenna, P. (1986). The hippocampal memory indexing theory. *Behavioral Neuroscience, 100,* 147–154.

Tehan, G., & Humphreys, M. S. (1996). Cuing effects in short-term recall. *Memory & Cognition, 24,* 719–732.

Tehan, G., & Humphreys, M. S. (1998). Creating proactive interference in immediate recall: Building a dog from a dart, a mop and a fig. *Memory and Cognition, 26,* 477–489.

Tekcan, A. I., Ece, B., Gulgoz, S., & Er, N. (2003). Autobiographical and event memory for 9/11: Changes across one year. *Applied Cognitive Psychology, 17*(9), 1057–1066.

Tekcan, A. I., & Peynircioglu, Z. F. (2002). Effects of age on flashbulb memories. *Psychology and Aging, 17*(3), 416–422.

Tenpenny, P. A. (1995). Abstractionist versus episodic theories of repetition priming and word identification. *Psychnomic Bulletin and Review, 2*(3), 339–363.

Terr, L. C. (1979). Children of Chowchilla: A study in psychic trauma. *Psychoanalytic Study of the Child, 34*, 547–623.

Terr, L. C. (1983). Chowchilla revisited: The effects of psychic trauma four years after a school-bus kidnapping. *American Journal of Psychiatry, 140*(12), 1543–1550.

Terr, L. C. (1994). Unchained memories: *True stories of traumatic memories, lost and found.* New York: Basic Books.

Thompson, C. P., & Cowan, T. (1986). A nicer interpretation of a Neisser recollection. *Cognition, 22*(2), 199–200.

Thompson, C. P., Skowronski, J. J., Larsen, S., & Betz, A. (1996). *Autobiographical memory: Remembering what and remembering when.* New York: Lawrence Erlbaum.

Thompson-Schill, S. L. (1995). *Context effects on word recognition: Implications for models of lexical representation.* Unpublished doctoral dissertation proposal, Department of Psychology, Stanford University, Stanford, CA.

Thorndike, E. L., & Lorge, I. (1944). *The teacher's work book of 30,000 words.* New York: Columbia University Press.

Thorndyke, P. (1977). Cognitive structures in comprehension and memory of narrative discourse. *Cognitive Psychology, 99*(1), 77–110.

Thygesen, P., Heermann, K., & Willanger, R. (1970). Concentration camp survivors in Denmark: Persecution, disease, compensation. *Danish Medical Bulletin, 17*, 65–108.

Toglia, M. P., Neuschatz, J. S., & Goodwin, K. A. (1999). Recall accuracy and illusory memories: When more is less. *Memory, 7*, 233–256.

Tong, F., Nakayama, K., Moscovitch, W., Weinrib, O., & Kanwisher, N. (2000). Response properties of the human fusiform face area. *Cognitive Neuropsychology, 17*, 257–279.

Towse, J. N., & Hitch, G. J. (1995). Is there a relationship between task demand and storage space in tests of working memory capacity? *Quarterly Journal of Experimental Psychology, 48A*, 108–124.

Towse, J. N., Hitch, G. J., & Hutton, U. (1998). A reevaluation of working memory capacity in children. *Journal of Memory and Language, 39*, 195–217.

Towse, J. N., Hitch, G. J., & Hutton, U. (2000). On the interpretation of working memory span in adults. *Memory & Cognition, 28*(3), 341–348.

Trabasso, T., & Magliano, J. P. (1996). Conscious understanding during comprehension. *Discourse Processes, 31*(3), 255–287.

Trabasso, T., & Sperry, L. L. (1985). Causal relatedness and importance of story events. *Journal of Memory and Language, 5*, 595–611.

Treisman, A. M. (1998). The perception of features and objects. In R. D. Wright (Ed.), *Visual attention* (pp. 26–54). New York: Oxford University Press.

Treisman, A. M., & Schmidt, H. (1982). Illusory conjunctions of objects. *Cognitive Psychology, 14*(1), 107–141.

Tulving, E. (1966). Subjective organization and effects of repetition in multi-trial free-recall learning. *Journal of Verbal Learning and Verbal Behavior, 5*, 193–197.

Tulving, E. (1972). Episodic and semantic memory. In E. Tulving & W. Donaldson (Eds.), *Organization of memory* (pp. 381–403). New York: Academic Press.

Tulving, E. (1974). Cue-dependent forgetting. *American Scientist, 62*, 74–82.

Tulving, E. (1983). *Elements of episodic memory.* New York: Oxford University Press.

Tulving, E. (1985a). How many memory systems are there? *American Psychologist, 40*, 385–398.

Tulving, E. (1985b). Memory and consciousness. *Canadian Psychologist, 26,* 1–12.

Tulving, E., Hayman, C. A. G., & MacDonald, C. A. (1991). Long-lasting perceptual priming and semantic learning in amnesia: A case experiment. *Journal of Experimental Psychology: Learning, Memory, and Cognition, 17,* 595–617.

Tulving, E., Kapur, S., Craik, F. I. M., Moscovitch, M., & Houle, S. (1994). Hemispheric encoding/retrieval asymmetry in episodic memory: Positron emission tomography findings. *Proceedings of the National Academy of Sciences, USA, 91*(6), 2016–2020.

Tulving, E., & Madigan, S. (1970). Memory and verbal learning. *Annual Review of Psychology, 21,* 437–484.

Tulving, E., & Psotka, J. (1971). Reproductive inhibition in free recall: Inaccessibility of information present in memory store. *Journal of Experimental Psychology, 87,* 1–8.

Tulving, E., & Schacter, D. L. (1990). Priming and human memory systems. *Science, 247,* 301–306.

Tulving, E., & Thomson, D. M. (1973). Encoding specificity and retrieval processes in episodic memory. *Psychological Review, 80,* 352–375.

Turner, J. E., Henry, L. A., & Smith, P. T. (2000). The development of and the use of long-term knowledge to assist short-term recall. *Quarterly Journal of Experimental Psychology: Human Experimental Psychology, 53A*(2), 457–478.

Turvey, M. T. (1973). On peripheral and central processes in vision: Inferences from an information-processing analysis of masking with patterned stimuli. *Psychological Review, 80*(1), 1–52.

Turvey, M. T., Brick, P., & Osborn, J. (1970). Temporal course of proactive interference in short-term memory. *British Journal of Psychology, 61*(4), 467–472.

Tversky, B., & Tuchin, M. (1989). A reconciliation of the evidence of eyewitness testimony: Comments on McCloskey and Zaragoza. *Journal of Experimental Psychology: General, 118*(1), 86–91.

Underwood, B. J. (1945). The effect of successive interpolations on retroactive and proactive inhibition. *Psychological Monographs, 59*(3), 1–33.

Underwood, B. J. (1948). "Spontaneous" recovery of verbal associations. *Journal of Experimental Psychology, 38,* 429–439.

Underwood, B. J. (1965). False recognition produced by implicit verbal responses. *Journal of Experimental Psychology, 70*(1), 122–129.

Underwood, B. J. (1983). *Attributes of memory.* Glenview, IL: Scott Foresman.

Underwood, B. J., & Ekstrand, B. R. (1967). Response term integration. *Journal of Verbal Learning and Verbal Behavior, 6*(3), 432–438.

Underwood, B. J., & Postman, L. (1960). Extraexperimental sources of interference in forgetting. *Psychological Review, 67,* 73–95.

Ungerleider, L. G., & Mishkin, M. (1982). Two cortical visual systems. In D. J. Ingle, M. A. Goodale & R. J. W. Mansfield (Eds.), *Analysis of visual behavior* (pp. 549–586). Cambridge: MIT Press.

Urbach, T. P., Windmann, S. S., Payne, D. G., & Kutas, M. (2005). Mismaking memories: Neural precursors of memory illusions in electrical brain activity. *Psychological Science, 16*(1), 19–24.

Usher, J. A., & Neisser, U. (1993). Childhood amnesia and the beginnings of memory for four early life events. *Journal of Experimental Psychology: General, 122,* 155–165.

Van den Broek, O., Linzie, B., Fletcher, C., & Marsolek, C. J. (2000). The role of causal discourse structure in narrative writing. *Memory & Cognition, 28,* 711–721.

Van der Kolk, B. A. (1996). Trauma and memory. In B. A. van der Kolk, A. McFarlane, & L. Weisaeth (Eds.), *Traumatic stress: The effects of overwhelming experience on mind, body and society.* New York: Guilford.

Van Dijk, T. A., & Kintsch, W. (1983). *Strategies of discourse comprehension*. New York: Academic Press.

Van Essen, D. C., & Maunsell, J. H. (1983). Hierarchical organization and functional streams in the visual cortex. *Trends in Neuroscience, 6*(9), 370–375.

Voss, J. F., & Silfies, L. N. (1996). Learning from history text: The interaction of knowledge and comprehension skill with text structure. *Cognition and Instruction, 14*(1), 45–68.

Wagenaar, W. A. (1986). My memory: A study of autobiographical memory over 6 years. *Cognitive Psychology, 18*, 225–252.

Wagenaar, W. A., & Groeneweg, J. (1990). The memory of concentration camp survivors. *Applied Cognitive Psychology, 4*(2), 77–87.

Wagenmakers, E. M., Zeelenberg, R., & Raaijmakers, J. G. W. (2000). Testing the counter model for perceptual identification: Effects of repetition priming and word frequency. *Psychonomic Bulletin and Review, 7*, 662–667.

Wagenmakers, E. M., Zeelenberg, R., Schooler, L. J., & Raaijmakers, J. G. W. (2000). A criterion-shift model for enhanced discriminability in perceptual identification: A note on the counter model. *Psychonomic Bulletin and Review, 7*, 718–726.

Wagner, A. D., Desmond, J. E., Glover, G. H., & Gabrieli, J. D. (1998). Prefrontal cortex and recognition memory: Functional MRI evidence for context-dependent retrieval processes. *Brain, 121*(10), 1985–2002.

Waldfogel, S. (1948). The frequency and affective character of childhood memories. *Psychological Monographs, 62*(4), 1–39.

Walker, I., & Hulme, C. (1999). Concrete words are easier to recall than abstract: Evidence for a semantic contribution to short-term serial recall. *Journal of Experimental Psychology: Learning, Memory, and Cognition, 25*, 1256–1271.

Walker, W. R., Skowronski, J. J., & Thompson, C. P. (2003). Life is pleasant and memory helps keep it that way! *Review of General Psychology, 7*(2), 203–210.

Walker, W. R., Vogl, R. J., & Thompson, C. P. (1997). Autobiographical memory: Unpleasantness fades faster than pleasantness over time. *Applied Cognitive Psychology, 11*, 399–413.

Wanner, E. (1975). *On remembering, forgetting and understanding sentences*. The Hague: Mouton.

Warrington, E. K., & Shallice, T. (1984). Category specific semantic impairments. *Brain, 107*, 829–854.

Waters, G. S., & Caplan, D. (1996). The capacity theory of sentence comprehension: Critique of Just and Carpenter (1992). *Psychological Review, 103*(4), 761–772.

Watkins, M. J., & Tulving, E. (1975). Episodic memory: When recognition fails. *Journal of Experimental Psychology, General, 104*, 5–29.

Watkins, O. C., & Watkins, M. J. (1975). Buildup of proactive inhibition as a cue-overload effect. *Journal of Experimental Psychology: Human Learning and Memory, 104*, 442–452.

Waugh, N. C., & Norman, D. A. (1965). Primary memory. *Psychological Review, 72*(2), 89–104.

Weaver, P. A., & Dickinson, D. K., (1982). Scratching below the surface structure: Expanding the usefulness of story grammars. *Discourse Processes, 5*, 225–243.

Weingartner, H., & Parker, E. S. (1984). Memory consolidation: A cognitive perspective. In H. Weingaartner and E. S. Parker (Eds.), *Memory consolidation* (pp. 1–14). Hillsdale, NJ: Lawrence Erlbaum.

Weiskrantz, L. (1986). Blindsight: A case study of the amnesic syndrome. In N. M. Weinberger, J. L. McGaugh, & G. Lunch (Eds.), *Memory systems of the brain*. New York: Guildford Press.

Weiskrantz, L. (1989). Remembering dissociations. In H. L. Roediger III & F. I. M. Craik (Eds.), *Varieties of memory and consciousness: Essays in honour of Endel Tulving* (pp. 101–120). Hillsdale, NJ: Lawrence Erlbaum.

Wells, G. L. (1985). Verbal descriptions of faces from memory: Are they diagnostic of identification accuracy? *Journal of Applied Psychology, 70*(4), 619–626.

Wells, G. L. (1993). What do we know about eyewitness identification? *American Psychologist, 48,* 553–571.

Wells, G. L., Lindsay, R. C., & Ferguson, T. J. (1979). Accuracy, confidence, and juror perceptions in eyewitness identification. *Journal of Applied Psychology, 64*(4), 440–448.

Wells, G. L., & Olson, E. A. (2003). Eyewitness testimony. *Annual Review of Psychology, 54,* 277–295.

Wetzler, S. (1985). Mood state-dependent retrieval: A failure to replicate. *Psychological Reports, 56*(3), 759–765.

Whaley, J. F. (1981). Readers' expectations for story structures. *Reading Research Quarterly, 17,* 90–114.

Wheeler, M. E., Peterson, S. E., & Buckner, R. L. (2000). Memory's echo: Vivid remembering reactivates sensory specific cortex. *Proceedings of the National Academy of Sciences, USA, 97*(20), 11125–11129.

Wheeler, M. E., & Treisman, A. (2002). Binding in visual short-term memory. *Journal of Experimental Psychology: General, 131*(1), 48–64.

White, R.T. (1982). Memory for personal events. *Human Learning, 1,* 171–183.

White, S. H., & Pillemer, D. B. (1979). Childhood amnesia and the development of a socially acceptable memory system. In J. F. Kihlstrom & F. J. Evans (Eds.), *Functional disorders of memory* (pp. 29–73). Hillsdale, NJ: Lawrence Erlbaum.

Whitehouse, W. G., Dinges, D. F., Orne, E., & Orne, M. (1988). Hypnotic hyperamnesia: Enhanced memory accessibility or report bias? *Journal of Abnormal Psychology, 98,* 289–295

Wickelgren, W. A. (1964). Size of rehearsal group and short-term memory. *Journal of Experimental Psychology, 68,* 413–419.

Wickelgren, W. A. (1965a). Short term memory for phonemically similar lists. *American Journal of Psychology, 78,* 567–574.

Wickelgren, W. A. (1965b). Acoustic similarity and retroactive interference in short-term memory. *Journal of Verbal Learning and Verbal Behavior, 4*(1), 53–61.

Wickelgren, W. A. (1966). Phonemic similarity and interference in short-term memory for single letters. *Journal of Experimental Psychology, 71*(3), 396–404.

Wickelgren, W. A. (1976). Network strength theory of storage and retrieval dynamics. *Psychological Review, 86*(6), 466–478.

Wickelgren, W. A. (1977). *Learning and memory.* Oxford, UK: Prentice-Hall.

Wickens, D. D., Born, D. G., & Allen, C. K. (1963). Proactive inhibition and item similarity in short-term memory. *Journal of Verbal Learning and Verbal Behavior, 2*(5–6), 440–445.

Wiggs, C. L., & Martin, A. (1998). Properties and mechanisms of perceptual priming. *Current Opinion in Neurobiology, 8*(2), 227–233.

Wilkinson, C. B. (1983). Aftermath of a disaster: The collapse of the Hyatt Regency Hotel skywalks. *American Journal of Psychiatry, 140,* 1134–1139.

Williams, J. M. G. (1992). Autobiographical memory and emotional disorders. In S. Christianson (Ed.), *The handbook of emotion and memory: Research and theory* (pp. 451–477). Hillsdale, NJ: Lawrence Erlbaum.

Williams, L. M. (1995). Recovered memories of abuse in women with documented child sexual victimization histories. *Journal of Traumatic Stress, 8*(4), 649–673.

Wilson, R. S., & Bennett, D. A. (2003). Cognitive activity and risk of Alzheimer's disease. *Current Directions in Psychological Science, 12*(3), 87–91.

Winocur, G., & Kinsbourne, M. (1978). Contextual cueing as an aid to Korsakoff amnesiacs. *Neuropsychologia, 16,* 671–682.

Wixted, J. T. (2004). The psychology and neuroscience of forgetting. *Annual Review of Psychology, 55,* 235–269.

Wolfradt, U., & Meyer, T. (1998). Interrogative suggestibility, anxiety and dissociation among anxious patients and normal controls. *Personality and Individual Differences, 25*(3), 425–432.

Woodworth, R. S. (1938). *Experimental psychology.* New York: Holt, Rinehart & Winston.

Wright, D. B. (1993). Recall of the Hillsborough disaster over time. *Applied Cognitive Psychology, 7,* 129–138.

Wright, D. B. (1994). *Remembering Satan: A vase of recovered memory and the shattering of an American Family.* New York: Knopf.

Wright, D. B., & Gaskell, G.D. (1995). Flashbulb memories: Conceptual and methodological issues. *Memory, 3,* 67–80.

Wright, D. B., Self, G., & Justice, C. (2000). Memory conformity: Exploring misinformation effects when presented by another person. *British Journal of Psychology, 91*(2), 189–202.

Yeomans, J. M., & Irwin, D. E. (1985). Stimulus duration and partial report performance. *Perception & Psychophysics 37*(2), 163–169.

Yerkes, R. M., & Dodson, J. D. (1908). The relation of strength of stimulus to rapidity of habit formation. *Journal of Comparative Neurology and Psychology, 18,* 459–482.

Yonelinas, A. P. (2002). The nature of recollection and familiarity: A review of 30 years of research. *Journal of Memory and Language, 46,* 441–517.

Yuille, J. C., & Tollestrup, P. A. (1992). A model of the diverse effects of emotion on eyewitness memory. In S. A. Christianson (Ed.), *The handbook of emotion and memory: Research and theory* (pp. 201–215). Hillsdale, NJ: Lawrence Erlbaum.

Zacks, R. T., & Hasher, L. (1994). Directed ignoring: Inhibitory regulation of working memory. In D. Dagenbach & T. H. Carr (Eds.), *Inhibitory processes in attention, memory, and language* (pp. 241–264). San Diego, CA: Academic Press.

Zalutsky, R. A., & Nicoll, R. A. (1990). Comparison of two forms of long-term potentiation in single hippocampal neurons. *Science, 248,* 1619–1624.

Zaragoza, M. S., & Koshmider, J. W. (1989). Misled subjects may know more than their performance implies. *Journal of Experimental Psychology: Learning, Memory, and Cognition, 15*(2), 246–255.

Zaragoza, M. S., & Lane, S. M. (1994). Source misattributions and the suggestibility of eyewitness memory. *Journal of Experimental Psychology: Learning, Memory, and Cognition, 20*(4), 934–945.

Zaragoza, M. S., & McCloskey, M. (1989). Misleading postevent information and the memory impairment hypothesis: Comment on Belli and reply to Tversky and Tuchin. *Journal of Experimental Psychology: General, 118*(1), 92–99.

Zaragoza, M. S., McCloskey, M., & Jamis, M. (1987). Misleading postevent information and recall of the original event: Further evidence against the memory impairment hypothesis. *Journal of Experimental Psychology: Learning, Memory, and Cognition, 13,* 36–44.

Zeelenberg, R., Wagenmakers, E. J. M., & Raaijmakers, J. G. W. (2002). Priming in implicit memory tasks: Prior study causes enhanced discriminability, not only bias. *Journal of Experimental Psychology: General, 131*(1), 38–47.

Zwaan, R. A. (1996). Processing narrative time shifts. *Journal of Experimental Psychology: Learning, Memory, and Cognition, 22*(5), 1196–1207.

Zwaan, R. A. (1999). Situation models: The mental leap into imagined worlds. *Current Directions in Psychological Science, 8*(1), 15–18.

Zwaan, R. A., & Radvansky, G. A. (1998). Situation models in language comprehension and memory. *Psychological Bulletin, 123*(2), 162–185.

Zwaan, R. A., Radvansky, G. A., & Witten, S. (2002). *Situation models and themes.* Amsterdam: John Benjamins.

Index

About the Author

Mary B. Howes is professor of psychology at SUNY, Oneonta. She specializes in cognition and memory, with particular interest in the first memories of life and in the phenomenon of changed memories. She is the author of *The Psychology of Human Cognition: Mainstream and Genevan Traditions.*